THE
COOPERSTOWN
CASEBOOK

THE
COOPERSTOWN
CASEBOOK

WHO'S IN THE BASEBALL HALL OF FAME,
WHO SHOULD BE IN, AND WHO SHOULD PACK THEIR PLAQUES

JAY JAFFE
Foreword by Peter Gammons

THOMAS DUNNE BOOKS ❧ ST. MARTIN'S PRESS NEW YORK

THOMAS DUNNE BOOKS.
An imprint of St. Martin's Press.

THE COOPERSTOWN CASEBOOK. Copyright © 2017 by Jay Jaffe. Foreword copyright © 2017 by
Peter Gammons. All rights reserved. Printed in the United States of America. For information,
address St. Martin's Press, 175 Fifth Avenue, New York, N.Y. 10010.

www.thomasdunnebooks.com
www.stmartins.com

Designed by Steven Seighman

The profiles of Edgar Martinez, Mike Mussina, Tim Raines, Curt Schilling, Alan Trammell, and
Larry Walker are adapted from works originally published on SI.com. Reprinted by permission
of the Sports Illustrated Group. Copyright © 2012–2016 Time Inc. All rights reserved.

The Library of Congress Cataloging-in-Publication Data is available upon request.

ISBN 978-1-250-07121-7 (hardcover)
ISBN 978-1-4668-8218-8 (ebook)

Our books may be purchased in bulk for promotional, educational, or business use. Please
contact your local bookseller or the Macmillan Corporate and Premium Sales Department at
1-800-221-7945, extension 5442, or by email at MacmillanSpecialMarkets@macmillan.com.

First Edition: July 2017

10   9   8   7   6   5   4   3

To Emma and Robin, my inner circle Hall of Famers

CONTENTS

FOREWORD

by Peter Gammons

The envelope usually arrives in the last week of November, a special annual day. There are names who will never be checked, which is no slight; they all played ten years in the major leagues, a remarkable athletic achievement.

There are names who have been on ballots for anywhere from two years to close to a decade, names that are there for the first time.

But they are names that matter, because the Baseball Hall of Fame in Cooperstown, New York, matters, more than any other sports Hall of Fame or museum. Anyone who doesn't understand should attend the July induction ceremony and try to find his way into the Otesaga Hotel, watch Hall of Famers from Henry Aaron to Ken Griffey, Jr., Phil Niekro to George Brett to Whitey Herzog wandering the lobby or sitting on the porch of the hotel looking out at Lake Otesaga.

"I cannot fully express how much it means to be here as a Hall of Famer," Tom Seaver once said. "It is the most exclusive club or at least one of *the* most exclusive clubs in our country. You cannot buy your way in. You cannot be born into it. The Baseball Hall of Fame is all about achievement, about earning your way into membership."

"We come back each July to laugh together, eat together, swap stories and rejoice in the reunion with exceptional peers," Johnny Bench said. "When I'm here, just standing in the hotel lobby reminds me what it means to all of us. If you could sit in on any of our private dinners, you would have access to something that reminds us 'this is really special.'"

Sometime between three and five weeks after the ballot arrives in the mail, I return it. I draw up a faux ballot thirty or fifty times, agonize over the tenth and thirteenth names on my drafted list. It is the first sports museum, a national treasure of a museum, and the responsibility for helping decide who is in and who is not, who sits on the porch of the Otesaga and who stays home in Bakersfield sits in the tip of my pen. So when that ballot gets left at the post office some day between Christmas and New Year's, it deserves its due diligence and respect.

And as you read *The Cooperstown Casebook*, understand what Jay Jaffe means to each and every ballot I mail these days. He is, as the preeminent Hall of Fame scholar, my research library, my conscience, my research assistant and ballast.

When I first received ballots, boxes were often checked based on traditional criteria: boldfaced numbers in *The Baseball Encyclopedia*; wins, with 300 as an automatic standard; home runs, with 500 as an automatic standard; hits, with 3,000 an automatic qualifier; postseason history.

Several writers seemed to relish in returning blank ballots, as if they were an undercooked meal at Gallagher's. Some based their ballots on personal interactions. Players worthy of serious examination and analysis like Ted Simmons, Luis Tiant, Bobby Grich, and Lou Whitaker slid off of the ballot in a year or two, which today would not happen. In time, as baseball analytics grew and the Hall of Fame election became an emotional and academic study, Bert Blyleven made it on his second-to-last year on the ballot, Jack Morris fell short. In 2016, Tim Raines was elected his last year.

No one weighs all the factors in determining a player's place in history better than Jaffe. Many of us understand JAWS as well as we did advanced calculus in the eleventh grade, but then, many of us who have covered and treasured baseball since Carlton Fisk was a rookie are in the eleventh grade in terms of analytics, not graduate school, much less the Sloan School at the Massachusetts Institute of Technology.

We now have defensive, baserunning, catcher framing, and dozens of other metrics. We measure Wins Above Replacement, OPS+, wOBA. Jaffe measures them all, with comparative historic perspective that can let us understand Simmons v. Rick Ferrell, Whitaker v. Nellie Fox, Mike Mussina v. Don Drysdale.

The Cooperstown Casebook takes one from the essentials of the Hall through a course in advanced statistics, positions that have historically been undervalued, the struggle so many of us have lived with weighing the impact and morality of the Steroids Era and its suspicions. He details the work, led by Joe Sheehan, done to examine the credentials of Jack Morris, which leads to the change in the way we vote for MVP and Cy Young Awards; for instance, where once Bob Welch easily won the Cy Young Award because he won 27 games for the Bash Brothers Oakland Athletics, 20 years later campaigns for Zack Greinke and Felix Hernandez were based not on wins but on a combination of analytical evaluations.

This is an evolving process when it comes to Hall of Fame ballots. Mussina presently is a classic example. Many voters and commentators point to his lack of a Cy Young Award, or the fact that he did not win 20 games in a season until his last, while advocates point to the fact that he pitched his entire career in the American League East in the peak of that division's power, that he made 274 starts in hitter-friendly Camden Yards, Yankee Stadium, and Toronto's Skydome, that his player value numbers on Baseball Reference put him in the best 25–30 best starters in history, and that taking a closer look at his postseasons—one-hit and 15-strikeout games in which he did not get a decision, as well as two wins over Randy Johnson, all in October 1997—put him in a place only a notch or two below Curt Schilling.

Who does and does not make the Hall of Fame matters, whether you are Tom Seaver, Johnny Bench, Henry Aaron, or Joe Morgan, a career voter or a passionate lover of the game or analytical scholar who believes in justice.

No one has examined this justice better than Jaffe. *The Cooperstown Casebook* will permanently have a place on my essentials desk right through the last week of December when my ballot is mailed, long after the joyous initial reads.

WHY CARE ABOUT THE HALL OF FAME?

I t's easy not to care about the Baseball Hall of Fame. Founded upon a long-debunked myth regarding the sport's creation by a future Civil War general in a cow pasture, the museum—the National Baseball Hall of Fame and Museum, to use its full name—is tucked away in central New York, roughly 200 miles from the nearest big league ballpark, Yankee Stadium. You could live your whole life without stumbling upon it.

From its origin in 1936, the Hall's selection processes have been arcane, resulting in confusion among voters as well as mistakes in who has been recognized and who has been bypassed. Via the myopia of the Baseball Writers Association of America and the cronyism of the Veterans Committee—the two primary voting bodies—numerous so-called "greats" have been inducted despite having not been so great, many of them hailing from the shameful period when baseball excluded black players.

More recently, the process has become cloaked in sanctimony. A sizable faction of writers who failed to recognize and report the infiltration of performance-enhancing drugs into the game has attempted to negate the accomplishments of some of its top players from the last quarter-century, players whose desire to gain a competitive edge by any means wouldn't have been out of place 50 or 100 years ago. Suddenly, these voters are biochemistry experts, able to extrapolate from scant scientific studies the impact of those drugs on player performance, and its connections to the changes the game saw in the 1990s and 2000s.

Meanwhile, a culture war that has raged within the game for more than a decade has spilled over onto this front, as an army of stat nerds who have changed the way baseball is managed, viewed, and consumed attempt to revise history, and to bury the authority of expert voters in an avalanche of spreadsheets and formulas that even some proponents don't fully understand. Thanks to the 24/7 coverage on the Internet that gives everybody with an opinion a megaphone, the annual election cycle has become inescapable, if not unbearable, at least for the six or seven weeks between the ballot's unveiling in November and the announcement of the voting results in January.

A stuffy private institution that predominantly honors dead white males, some of them virulent racists from over a century ago? That lacks intellectual consistency with regards to whom it honors? That's cloaked in a morality seemingly lifted from the 1950s, and has found ways to exclude both the all-time hits leader (Pete Rose) and the all-time home run leader (Barry Bonds)? That congratulates itself for memorializing a sport that long ago lost its hold on the American public? It might be easier to root for somebody to bulldoze the Hall of Fame out of existence, or at least to acknowledge its irrelevance, and move on.

Indeed, whether you're a traditionalist or a revisionist, it's tempting to walk away from this train wreck—or sprint at Rickey Henderson–like speed. You have no need of crusty old men telling you things were better back in their day. You know greatness when you see it, and you have the power to define it on your own terms, in your own personal pantheon. You don't need a clunky bronze plaque hanging in a remote museum to validate what you hold dear.

I can't say I blame you if you feel that way. Having spent 15 years studying the Hall's contradictions and byzantine ways, I've thrown my hands up in despair more often than the average Cubs fan (pre-2016, at least), sworn at those who have held power over the institution and its voting processes, driven the people around me crazy while railing against the wrongheadedness that seems to predominate, and empathized with players crushed by the cruelty of the proceedings.

Yet in spite of the litany above, I do care. Well beyond the 350,000 people who annually visit the seven buildings and 50,000 square feet of the museum in Cooperstown, the Hall is a place that millions of fans flock to in their mind's eye every time they take stock of excellence or steep themselves in history—to a degree that's unparalleled in other sports. Would Babe Ruth or Ty Cobb succeed in today's game? Does Roger Clemens belong there given the allegations regarding the chemicals he may have ingested? Will Alan Trammell ever get in? Has Mike Trout already sealed the deal? Seemingly every fan and media member has an opinion on such questions, one that they'll happily advance via barstool, blog, broadcast, or ballot. No sports hall of fame's membership is so hallowed, nor its qualifications so debated, or its voting process so dissected. When has anyone cared to connect a particular voter to a candidate for the Pro Football or Basketball Halls of Fame?

The universality of that passion is why I believe that the Hall still matters, and so long as enough of us who love baseball believe that it does, it can remain relevant. Don't get me wrong; the tens of thousands of fans who flock to Cooperstown for induction weekend each year may feel that the place suits their needs just fine, oblivious to the aforementioned complaints. Even so, the vast majority of fans and media has *some* beef with the Hall of Fame, some wrong that they would right if given a chance. You think two-time MVP Dale Murphy belongs, I swear Edgar Martinez's greatness transcends the limitations of the designated hitter role, and the guy at the end of the bar still thinks Pete Rose got a raw deal.

Like ghastly insects trapped in amber, the mistakes preserved within the Hall of Fame aren't going away. As convenient as it may be to wish that we could pack the plaques of some of the least-deserving honorees in the Hall's dusty basement, however, I prefer to focus on improving the institution, primarily by ensuring that the right players are recognized, both from the recent past and from further back. To do that requires acknowledging that many of the Hall's mistakes owed to the primitive quality of information available at the time.

In the decades before television, baseball carved its spot in the sport's fan's psyche thanks to the attraction of those daily parcels of numbers, the box scores. Fans might not get more than a static glimpse of their favorite player via the occasional newspaper photograph, but they could follow along with their exploits on a daily basis, and compare their tallied achievements to those of others in the Sunday papers. Beyond that, even the supposedly well-informed voter found detailed statistical information harder to come by. Annual publications such as the Spalding and Reach guides, *Who's Who in Baseball* (est. 1912), *The Little Red Book of Baseball* (est. 1926), and *The Sporting News Baseball Register* (est. 1940) contained year-by-year stats of active players as well as key major league records, but they were subject to errors, and far from comprehensive. The cover of the 1920 issue of *Who's Who* featured Ruth, whose record-setting, paradigm-shifting 29 homers in 1919 went completely unmentioned in its pages, which did report his unremarkable total of seven stolen bases. Even the 1935 edition, on the eve of the Bambino's last lap around the majors, lacked a column for home runs.

The sport's first attempt at an encyclopedia, George Moreland's *Balldom: The Britannica of Baseball*, was published in 1914; it covered rosters and records for teams from 1871 through 1913, seasonal leaders, and lifetime statistics for the game's greats, but wasn't updated again until 1927. In 1922, BBWAA founding member Ernest Lanigan—who played a role in in popularizing the RBI and other statistics, and who became the Hall's historian in 1948—broke new ground with his *The Baseball Cyclopedia*, which alphabetically listed the name, position, teams, and years played for over 3,500 major leaguers as well as annual league leaders, World Series records, and so on; it was updated annually for 12 years. *The Official Baseball Encyclopedia*, first published in 1951, expanded upon Lanigan's work by including birth and death dates of players, but still contained only games played and batting average for hitters, and won-loss records for pitchers. Not until 1969 did the *Macmillan Baseball Encyclopedia*, encompassing every player in major league history, arrive with a fuller body of pitching and hitting statistics.

Thus, early Hall of Fame voters did not have it easy in comparing players to their predecessors on statistical grounds; they didn't even have home/road splits in order to take full measure of which players were helped or hurt by their surroundings, nor could they quickly compare the scoring context of two players separated by history.

Thanks to the wonders of the Internet and the diligence of many people, today we can do all of that with a few clicks. But even then, as comfortably familiar as batting average, runs batted in, won-loss records, and earned run averages may be, they're not descriptive enough to be very useful for the cross-era comparisons that are the stuff of Hall debates. After all, it makes no more sense to compare hitters and pitchers from 1930 (when teams scored 5.55 runs per game and collectively hit .296) directly against those from 1968 (when teams scored 3.42 runs per game and collectively hit .237) than to compare mile times for a Model T Ford and a Ferrari Testarossa. While those two years constitute the twentieth century's extremes, dramatic fluctuations in scoring levels—driven by changing rules and conditions—have been the norm throughout baseball history, not the exception.

To keep the Hall of Fame relevant in the twenty-first century, we need to pull it out of the twentieth. The election process needs reconsideration and reform, expansions of the ballot beyond the current 10-slot maximum, which has been in place since 1936, when the majors were roughly half their current size, and of the voting body beyond the BBWAA writers and assorted codgers who sit on the smaller committees (the Veterans Committee has evolved into four era-based committees as of 2016). As I'll show in Chapter 7, when measured against the level of player representation from the nineteenth century and the first half of the twentieth, the various voting bodies have been particularly stingy in honoring players not only from the 1990s, but from the 1980s and 1970s as well. Much of the Hall's foot traffic and revenue depends on the patronage of fans who visit to see their favorites celebrated. Ruth, Willie Mays, and Mickey Mantle won't drive attendance forever; failure to keep pace by equitably representing recent eras will doom the Hall to obsolescence.

One key part of a twenty-first-century approach means employing twenty-first-century tools to take the measure of candidates. Tools such as on-base percentage, Adjusted ERA (ERA+), Defensive Runs Saved (DRS), or Wins Above Replacement (WAR) may not have existed during the careers in question, but at this point, they permeate the game. Via WAR and other tools, we can better estimate the impact of every player both current and past—not only on offense, but on defense as well. To do so means embracing a statistical lexicon that goes beyond the numbers traditionally found on the back of baseball cards, and often involves strange new acronyms. That lexicon and the information it conveys may fuel the old school's derision amid debates over the annual Most Valuable Player and Cy Young awards—call it "The War on WAR," a subject I'll take up in Chapter 6. But to one degree or another, such concepts are now in every major league front office, deployed when teams build their rosters or place dollar values on player performance. Hell, as of 2014, WAR *is* on the back of Topps baseball cards.

The foundation of my approach to comparing players for their suitability as Hall of Fame candidates is my JAWS system, a self-consciously christened acronym for the **J**affe **WAR S**core, which I introduced at Baseball Prospectus during the 2004 election cycle and have refined over the years. JAWS uses WAR to estimate a player's total hitting, pitching, and defensive contribution while accounting for the wide variations in scoring levels from era to era and ballpark to ballpark. Via JAWS, each candidate can be objectively compared on the basis of career or peak value to the players at his position who are already in the Hall.

In addition to getting people to scream at the first hint of its approach—wait, that's *Jaws*—the stated goal of my system is to improve or at least maintain the institution's standards by identifying and endorsing for election those players who are at least as good as the average Hall of Famer at the position. That applies not just to recently retired players hailing from a particularly offense-friendly era, but to long-retired players slighted by the process and in danger of slipping through the cracks of history. More than anything, the idea is to bring intellectual consistency to an often disorganized debate. Because of its utility, JAWS has gained mainstream exposure in recent years, cited by actual voters—some as an aid in filling out their ballots, others as a target to rail against, like those teenagers doing donuts on their lawn—and included within the coverage at MLB Network's *MLB Now* show.

The idea of deploying WAR and other advanced statistics for use in Hall of Fame debates owes much to Bill James, who in the late 1970s defined the search for objective knowledge about baseball as "sabermetrics," a neologism arising out of the acronym for the Society for American Baseball Research, SABR. While James's annual *Baseball Abstracts* made bestseller lists as he reached for a mass audience, his ideas struggled to get mainstream acceptance in the last quarter of the twentieth century, particularly inside the game. His work did find enough of an audience to fuel a whole lot of the statistical advances of the twenty-first, and eventually the game found room for him. That the Boston Red Sox hired James to join their front office in the winter of 2002–03 and went on to end their 86-year championship drought and win three World Series during his tenure was hardly a coincidence. In fact, it has helped to validate the application of sabermetrics, though such triumphs remain a sore subject among Luddite baseball scribes and fans.

In his 1985 and 2001 editions of *The Bill James Historical Baseball Abstracts* as well as his 1994 book *The Politics of Glory* (reissued in paperback the following year as *Whatever Happened to the Hall of Fame?*), James turned his attention to Cooperstown using tools that provided objective measurements, such as Similarity Scores, the Hall of Fame Monitor, the Hall of Fame Standards, and Win Shares to advance his arguments. While those tools may not have had much impact on actual voters, they helped build an audience increasingly attuned to the annual election cycle. The aging of those tools and the influx of new knowledge into the field—starting with better all-encompassing value metrics than Win Shares—spurred my own efforts to analyze the annual BBWAA and Veterans Committee ballots, first for Baseball Prospectus, and then for *Sports Illustrated*.

I'll explain more about the basics of the Hall of Fame, JAWS, and other sabermetrics concepts relevant to this book in the next few chapters, but before we leave this one, I should lay something out.

This book covers players inside and outside the Hall whose careers generally exist on the spectrum between very good and truly great. I couldn't stand in the box against the worst of them, and as I was born in 1969, I wasn't fortunate enough to witness most of them, but that doesn't mean that I can't appreciate their abilities or their accomplishments any more than a student of American history can't appreciate those of Abraham Lincoln or Franklin Roosevelt. Baseball players and presidents both leave mountains of data in their wake, data that we can sift through to help make sense of their careers—data that informs stories, and can even tell them.

My focus on that data should not be taken to mean that I don't appreciate the more visceral thrills of watching a game: the awe of seeing the bottom drop out of a perfect curveball, the grace of an acrobatic defensive play, the pent-up excitement unleashed by a towering home run, the day-to-day tension of a great playoff race. I love all of those things, but my waxing poetic to differentiate those thrills will be only so helpful in making sense of the continuum along which the players in this book sit.

Whether you're a stathead already at home with JAWS, WAR, DRS, and so on, or a newcomer to this strange land of acronyms and decimal points, I'm hopeful that *The Cooperstown Casebook* will help you gain a new appreciation for the Hall of Fame even amid its more frustrating aspects. I'm optimistic that as you read these essays and survey the landscape at each position in Chapters 9 through 18, you'll find new reasons to care about who's in, who's out, and how that happened. For many fans and even voters, the numbers crunched herein have already helped to illuminate the greatness not only of familiar icons but also crucially underappreciated players who deserve their days in the sun. Sometimes those numbers jibe with what we think we know, and sometimes they challenge long-standing beliefs (spoiler alert: I love Sandy Koufax, but JAWS does not; if you destroy the binding of this book while tossing it across the room, please consider buying a new copy).

Beyond those numbers is a story of an institution and its gatekeepers, both of which are far from perfect. But rather than give up on this unholy mess, I'm a firm believer that there's more value in appreciating what's there, with an eye toward ensuring the Hall's continued relevance in the twenty-first century.

So away we go . . .

PART I

BATTLES

AND

WARS

CHAPTER 1

THE INS AND OUTS OF
THE HALL OF FAME

The National Baseball Hall of Fame and Museum is an independent, non-profit educational institution dedicated to fostering an appreciation of the historical development of baseball and its impact on our culture by collecting, preserving, exhibiting and interpreting its collections for a global audience as well as honoring those who have made outstanding contributions to our national pastime. The Hall of Fame's mission is to preserve the sport's history, honor excellence within the game and make a connection between the generations of people who enjoy baseball.

—HALL OF FAME MISSION STATEMENT[1]

Including the three players and two executives honored during the 2017 cycle—Jeff Bagwell, Tim Raines, Ivan Rodriguez, John Schuerholz, and Bud Selig—a total of 317 individuals have been elected to the National Baseball Hall of Fame, starting with the inaugural five-man class of 1936. Not all of them have been elected for their playing contributions in the major leagues; some were pioneers, executives, managers, and even umpires. In terms of the primary contributions for which they have been honored, the breakdown is as follows:

Primary Contribution	# in
Major league players	220
Pioneers or executives	30
Managers	22
Umpires	10
Negro Leagues players, managers, or executives	35
Total	**317**

A good number of those elected for their nonplaying contributions did play in the majors at some point; some even starred, often for shorter time spans than those honored primarily for their playing careers. The same is true for Negro Leaguers Satchel Paige, Monte Irvin, and Willard Brown, who spent less than the 10 seasons in the majors required for election; those with Negro Leagues experience who did reach the 10-year mark—Hank Aaron, Ernie Banks, Roy Campanella, Larry Doby, Willie Mays, and Jackie Robinson—are enshrined as major leaguers. Additionally, some players elected as major leaguers did manage as well. Entire books have been written on those aforementioned subjects as they relate to the Hall of Fame, but those topics are tangential to this book, which is founded in the analysis of major league player performance.

"The major leagues" means more than just the currently existing National and American Leagues. Players and other figures from five bygone leagues, four whose lifespans were entirely contained in the nineteenth century, are part of the Hall, though all 220 of the enshrined major league players passed through either the NL (founded in 1876) or AL (founded in 1901) at some point. The lifespans of the National Association (1871–75), American Association (1882–91), Union Association (1884), Players League (1890), and Federal League (1914–15) weren't long enough to contain entire Hall of Fame careers.

Historically, election to the Hall has primarily consisted of two processes. The Baseball Writers Association of America (BBWAA) conducts annual balloting by mail among writers who have at least 10 consecutive years of service with affiliated publications (originally print publications, expanded to include Internet publications in 2007). Their electorate has more than doubled during the Hall's lifespan; for the 1936 election 226 ballots were cast, while the 2011 election saw an all-time high of 581, though a 2016 rule change to eliminate voters more than 10 years removed from covering the game whittled that year's total to 440 ballots. Charged with voting exclusively for major league players through a series of rules that has changed over time, they have elected 124 members through the 2017 ballot.

Beyond the writers is the Veterans Committee (VC), a term whose most common usage refers to a 10-to-20-member committee in service from 1953–2001 but is often used as a shorthand to cover a variety of small committees that have come and gone (detailed at greater legnth in Chapter 5):

Committee Name	Years Active	Player Coverage
Old-Timers Committee	1936, '39, '45, '46, '49	Long-retired players
Centennial Committee	1937–38	Pioneers
Veterans Committee	1953–2001 2002–2010 (expanded)	Long-retired players
Committee on Negro League Veterans	1971–77	Negro leagues and pre–Negro leagues
Special Committee on Negro Leagues	2006	Negro leagues and pre–Negro leagues
Era Committees (I)	2011–16	
Pre-Integration Era Committee	2013, '16	1871–1946
Golden Era Committee	2012, '15	1947–72
Expansion Era Committee	2011, '14	1973–
Era Committees (II)	2017–26	
Early Baseball Era Committee	2021	1871–1949
Golden Days Era Committee	2021, '26	1950–69
Modern Baseball Era Committee	2018, '20, '23, '25	1970–87
Today's Game Era Committee	2017, '19, '22, '24	1988–

Except for a short-lived expansion of the VC in the early 2000s, those various electorates have generally consisted of former executives, managers, players and media members, only some of whom were actual historians. Those bodies have elected 167 members, a breakdown that includes 96 long-retired payers, all of the major league managers, pioneers, executives, and umpires noted above, and nine Negro Leaguers. Additionally, the Committee on Negro League Veterans elected nine members from 1971–77, while the Special Committee on Negro Leagues elected 17 members in 2006.

Via the BBWAA, eligibility for election to the Hall of Fame as a player currently requires the following:

- **Activity as a major league player at some time during a period beginning 15 years before and ending five years prior to election.** Thus a player has 10 years of eligibility on the BBWAA ballot. From 1962–2014, players had 15 years of eligibility instead of 10; they could not be on the ballot once they were 20 years from retirement. A rule introduced by the Hall's board of directors in the summer of 2014, independent of the BBWAA, truncated the eligibility period of all holdover candidates save for three already in their 13th to 15th years, who were grandfathered. In one fell swoop, a candidate such as Tim Raines, who was presumed to have eight years of eligibility remaining following the 2014 ballot, suddenly had only three—a severe blow, given the slow but steady buildup of his support.

- **Activity in a minimum of 10 major league seasons, some part of which must have been within the aforementioned period.** One game is sufficient to count as activity in a season, as established in the precedents of Ross Youngs (elected in 1972) and Amos Rusie (elected in 1977). The 10 "seasons" of Youngs, a 1920s outfielder whose career was cut short by a fatal illness, included seven games in 1917, the year he debuted. Rusie, an 1890s pitcher, outdid that with a three-appearance stint in 1901, after having sat out two years over a salary dispute and then a trade from the Giants to the Reds for Christy Mathewson.

  Aside from the aforementioned Negro Leaguers and those elected as pioneers while falling short of the 10-year mark—Candy Cummings, Al Spalding, and Harry Wright among them—only once has the Hall's board of directors deviated from this rule. A 1977 special resolution made Addie Joss, a pitcher who died of tubercular meningitis in early 1911 after a career that spanned from 1902–10, eligible for consideration. The VC elected him the following January.

- **Retirement from playing for a minimum of five calendar years preceding the election.** Participation as a coach, manager, or even minor league player is allowed in the interim. BBWAA ballots are generally released in late November with the results announced in early January, so the handy rule of thumb for eligibility means adding six to a player's last year in the majors. Thus 2013 retiree Mariano Rivera will be eligible on the 2019 ballot, released in late 2018.

It wasn't always this way. Babe Ruth was elected in 1936, a year after his final season. Lou Gehrig gained entry via a special election in December 1939, just months after the medical condition that would claim his life (and eventually bear his name) forced his retirement. Through 1945, no rule existed to prevent voting for active players, though none was elected as such. In the 1945 election, Joe DiMaggio—who had last played in 1942, prior to entering the military, though he was still understood to be active—received a vote. A rule enacted in 1946 required candidates to have been retired one year; in 1954, the now standard five-year waiting period was enacted, though any candidate who had previously received 100 or more votes in a single election (a caveat that only applied to DiMaggio) was grandfathered. He was elected in 1955, after a career that ended in '51.

The BBWAA has waived the five-year period in the case of an active player's death, albeit in uneven fashion. On March 30, 1973, three months after Roberto Clemente died in a plane crash, the writers voted to waive the five-year period and then held a special election via which he received 92%. Thurman Munson (died in 1979, included on 1981–95 ballots) and Darryl Kile (died in 2002, included on the 2003 ballot) received accelerated consideration but were not elected.

- **A candidate may not be on baseball's ineligible list.** Thus a player under a lifetime ban for gambling (such as Pete Rose or Shoeless Joe Jackson) or three violations of the drug policy (hypothetical at this point; thrice-caught Jenrry Mejia didn't reach 10 years) is ineligible. This rule was enacted by the Hall's board of directors in February 1991, nearly 18 months after Rose was banned for life by Commissioner Bart Giamatti for gambling on baseball games. The move came amid a power struggle, as many in the BBWAA felt the decision to include Rose on the ballot should have been left to them, and the Hall feared he would be elected despite the ban.

- **Eligible candidates meeting the above requirements require nomination from any two members of the six-man BBWAA screening committee.** While usually a formality, for players with no realistic shot at election, for whom just making the ballot is the honor, it can be a coin toss. Though generally of minimal consequence, omissions such as those of All-Stars Chan Ho Park, the majors' first Korean-born player, and Javier Vazquez, ranked 30th all-time in strikeouts and first among Puerto Rico natives in wins, paint the BBWAA in a less than flattering light.

- **Upon reaching the ballot, a candidate must receive at least 5% of the vote in an election to retain eligibility for the following year.** First introduced in 1979, and often referred to as the Five Percent Rule, this is the leading cause of Hall heartbreak. Among those who failed to reach that threshold are many players covered at length or in brief throughout this book, including Dick Allen, Ken Boyer, Dwight Evans, Bobby Grich, Kenny Lofton, Ron Santo, Ted Simmons, and Lou Whitaker. Allen, Boyer, and Santo were among those whose eligibility was restored in a 1985 amnesty, though none was elected by the writers; Santo's 2011 election came via the VC (see Chapter 4).

- **To be elected, a candidate must receive at least 75% of the vote.** For this requirement and the one above, voting percentages are not rounded upward, so 4.9% and 74.9% won't cut it. Nellie Fox (74.7% in 1985, two votes short) and Craig Biggio (74.8% in 2014, also two votes short) are examples of the "close, but no cigar" policy.

- **Voters may list a maximum of 10 candidates per annual ballot.** This is often referred to as the Rule of Ten. In 2015, I was part of a BBWAA committee that recommended that the Hall of Fame revise the election process by expanding to 12 slots, both to help ameliorate a backlog of qualified candidates in the near-term and to help prevent underrepresenting current and future eras. The Hall's board of directors tabled the motion. More on this in Chapter 7.

If a candidate isn't elected during his window of BBWAA eligibility, he may be considered as part of the Today's Game Era Committee, a successor to the VC that focuses on candidates whose greatest contribution came from 1988 onward. That's one of four Era Committees created by a 2016 rule change, along with Early Baseball (1871–1949), Golden Days (1950–69), and Modern Baseball (1970–87). In the Hall's 10-year plan, the recent eras will be voted upon with greater frequency than the earlier ones, but given how often the institution has revamped the process since the turn of the millennium, don't be surprised if this changes again. For more, see Chapter 5.

Candidates who fall off the BBWAA ballot via the Five Percent Rule must wait until the end of their 10-year eligibility window to be considered by the Today's Game Era Committee. A lengthy screening process determines which candidates are considered for election on those committees' ballots, which may also include pioneers, executives, managers, and umpires. The voting for those committees takes place in person at the annual Winter Meetings in December.

As for the electorate itself, the BBWAA restricts voting to writers and editors of affiliated publications who have been active members of the organization for 10 consecutive years. Those who have reached the 10-year mark are eligible to continue voting for 10 years even if they retire or move on to *Cat Fancy* or *Golf Flogger*. In theory, that's because they are voting on players they once covered. Yours truly has been a member of the BBWAA since December 2010, which means that barring any rule change, I will get to vote in December 2020, for the players on the 2021 ballot, including those whose swan songs were in 2015.

CHAPTER 2

STAT SCHOOL

For many a fan—particularly those born after World War II and thus positioned to take advantage of the Topps company's reboot of the genre—our connection to major leaguers as discrete personalities began with a pack of baseball cards. Those little slabs of cardboard not only gave us names, faces, and colorful uniforms to identify with our favorite teams, they sketched out biographical and statistical portraits of each player. "A chart of numbers that would put an actuary to sleep can be made to dance if you put it on one side of a card and Bombo Rivera's picture on the other,"[1] wrote Bill James in 1982.

Whether via cards, box scores, or the seemingly cryptic numbers on the television beneath a slugger's name, batting statistics often proved the most accessible. Batting average was the gateway drug, a bit of simple math magically imbued with the means to measure skill. We learned that stars hit .300 and sepia-toned legends .400. Home run totals measured a player's strength, with numbers like 60 and 61, 714 and 755 telling stories of unprecedented dominance and persistence. Runs batted in measured a player's ability to help his team by driving in other baserunners, and if not his moral fiber then at least his grace under pressure, his so-called "clutchness."

If you arrived in the last two decades clinging to those standards, you were in for a bumpy ride. While nobody hit .400, scoring levels skyrocketed, aided by expansion into better hitting environments such as high-altitude Colorado. In 1996, teams scored just over 5.0 runs per game for the first time since 1936. Every year from 1993–2009 featured teams scoring at least 4.5 runs per game, a level that had been reached just once since 1961, when MLB expanded beyond 16 teams. During the high-scoring 1990s and 2000s, balls flew out of the yard at record paces, and hulking sluggers toppled Roger Maris's single-season home run record and the career home run marks of Babe Ruth and Hank Aaron. Meanwhile, complete games nearly became extinct, but pitchers struck out more hitters, as the stigma against the whiff receded, and careful study by sabermetricians showed that for hitters, strikeouts weren't as costly as previously believed.

Indeed, via both increasingly savvy front offices and the rapidly expanded media covering the game, sabermetrics has left a stamp both on play and team building. Over the past two decades, teams have placed increasing emphasis on everything from on-base percentage and optimal use of one-run strategies to defensive shifting and pitch framing, not to mention prospect and free agent valuations. At its base, sabermetrics provides a toolkit for grappling with the game's eternal questions. When is the right time to bunt or to steal a base? What is the best way to make out a batting order, or run a bullpen? How do baseball skills vary as players age? What do we know about the effects of performance-enhancing drugs on player performance? Entire books have been written about such questions, and Web sites such as Baseball Prospectus, FanGraphs, Beyond the Box Score, Hardball Times, and others continue to explore such matters.

That sabermetrics toolkit is helpful in comparing baseball from different eras, allowing us to place the recent offensive boom in better perspective, and to understand the game's evolution. What follows here is a quick tour through the tools I employ in this book, including Wins Above Replacement; I'll detail the Jaffe WAR Score—JAWS—system in the next chapter. There's more to be said on these topics than space allows—particularly in evaluating contemporary players in an age where we know the velocity of every pitch and batted ball—but for the sake of understanding Hall of Fame arguments, this should get you through the coming pages.

OFFENSE

Going back to those numbers on the baseball card, the oft-cited Triple Crown stats and their benchmark plateaus (a .300 batting average, 30 home runs, 100 RBI) aren't especially good at telling even the most basic stories. Counting stats like runs and RBI are highly context-dependent and don't account for how many outs—how much of baseball's clock, so to speak—a player used.

Consider for a moment a pair of similar seasons by Hall of Fame outfielders Andre Dawson (.272, 31 HR, 104 RBI for the 1991 Cubs) and Larry Doby (.276, 32 HR, 104 RBI for the 1952 Indians). On the surface, not much would appear to separate them, but not shown is that Dawson drew just 22 walks and added 21 doubles and four triples, while Doby walked 91 times and added 26 doubles and eight triples. Dawson's **on-base percentage**, the frequency with which he *didn't* make an out (abbreviated **OBP**), was just .302, which ranked 47th out of the 52 players who qualified for the batting title that year, while Doby's OBP was .383, which placed seventh out of 37 qualifiers. Dawson's **slugging percentage**, his rate of total bases per at-bat (abbreviated **SLG**), was .488, 12th among those 52 players, while Doby's .541 led his league, beating Mickey Mantle by a solid 11 points.

OBP (which measures how well a player gets on base) and SLG (which measures how well a player moves others around the bases) are more demonstrative of skill than Triple Crown stats, and not subject to the influence of a player's teammates or his lineup slot. Those measures correlate much better with scoring runs than batting average does, and scoring runs is the name of the game. A metric such as **On-base Plus Slugging (OPS)** correlates better with scoring than either component does, though math purists blanch at the notion of adding the two, since they have different denominators (plate appearances for the former, at-bats for the latter). In the case of our two outfielders above, Dawson's .790 OPS was dwarfed by Doby's .924.

Throughout this book, I'll refer to a player's batting performance in **"slash stat"** form with batting average (AVG) first, followed by OBP and SLG: .272/.302/.488 for Dawson and .276/.383/.541 for Doby from our example above, or .313/.400/.565 for a current Hall of Fame candidate, Larry Walker. The first number may be the least important of the three, but it does help paint a fuller picture. A .283/.400/.565 line describes a player who walks more often (accounting for the wider gap between AVG and OBP) and hits for more power (accounting for the wider gap between AVG and SLG, a stat called **isolated power, ISO**) than Walker, while a .343/.400/.565 line describes a player who hits a bunch more singles (accounting for the smaller gaps between AVG and the other two stats) instead.

Even those raw rate stats carry distortions. When offensive levels rise as they did in the 1990s or 2000s, the value of each individual run diminishes slightly. The impact of eye-popping stats or even comfortable benchmarks becomes diluted amid inflated offensive levels, whether that means in ballparks such as Boston's Fenway Park and Denver's Coors Field (where Walker spent more than half his career), or a league's, such as the 1930 NL or the 2000 AL. That's why it's useful to call upon **Adjusted OPS (OPS+),** which is park- and league-adjusted to express the combination of OBP and SLG such that 100 is the league average, and any number above that (or below it) is the percentage relative to league average; a 120 OPS+ means that a hitter produced runs at a rate 20% better than average, while an 80 OPS+ means that he produced at a rate 20% below average.

Thus OPS+ is useful for cross-era comparisons in a way that OPS is not. Walker's .313/.400/.565 line produced a .965 OPS, while Reggie Jackson's career .262/.356/.490 line produced an .846 OPS. Both are very good, but they arrive without context. On the other hand, Walker's 141 OPS+ and Jackson's 139 OPS+

tell us that their rate of production was nearly equivalent, with Walker about 2% more productive (141 to 139) than Jackson after we adjust for their environments.

However, rate-based metrics don't convey the number of opportunities involved, and thus the volume of that production. After all, a 120 OPS+ tells us more about a player with 650 plate appearances than one with 60; the first player put together a star-caliber season, while the second had a couple good weeks. Thus it's useful to estimate how many runs above or below average a player's batting performance is using **linear weights**, which assigns fractional run values for each batting event that vary slightly from year to year as scoring levels change. Here they are for the 2012 American League, via Baseball-Reference.com:

Event	Run Value
Walk (BB)	0.301
Hit-by-pitch (HBP)	0.326
Single (1B)	0.456
Infield single (1B_inf)	0.389
Outfield single (1B_of)	0.469
Double (2B)	0.756
Triple (3B)	1.026
Home run (HR)	1.400
Stolen base (SB)	0.200
Caught stealing (CS)	−0.398

Each additional walk adds another three-tenths of a run to a team's expected scoring total, while each triple tends to add slightly more than one run; after all, it clears the bases of all runners while leaving a new one in prime scoring position. Adjustments for other factors can be applied to a player's offensive performance depending upon the depth of data; some statistics didn't become official until the mid-twentieth century, so they can be either included in the sauce or worked around. The end result is a runs above average figure; at B-Ref, it's called **batting runs** (abbreviated on its pages as Rbat). With or without play-by-play data, a player's other offensive contributions can be estimated. **Baserunning runs** (Rbase) accounts not only for stolen base success rate but also advancement on fly balls, ground balls, hits, outs, wild pitches, and passed balls. **Double play runs** (Rdp) accounts for how well a player avoids grounding into double plays; that stuff adds up.

PITCHING

The first thing to know about pitching statistics is that wins and losses don't tell you all that much, particularly the later in baseball history you go. Pitchers were once expected to throw all nine innings—or more, if the game went into extras—

but those days have long passed, thanks to higher scoring levels and strikeout rates, longer at-bats, deeper lineups, pitch counts, and increased reliever specialization, all of which have cut into complete game rates. In 1918, pitchers completed 63% of their starts, but by 1958, that rate was down to 30%; it hit 10% in 1990, and was just 1.7% in 2016. Likewise, the completion rates of the outliers atop the leaderboard have fallen sharply. In 1918, the Red Sox's Carl Mays completed 91% of his starts, while in 1958 the Braves' Warren Spahn completed 64%. In 1990 it was the Dodgers' Ramon Martinez at 36%, while in 2016 the White Sox's Chris Sale completed 19%.

Even when the complete game was still common, a pitcher's won-loss record had plenty to do with the support he received from his offense (which had to score in order for him to get that win) and his defense (which, unless he was striking out every hitter, needed to make the plays behind him). When Bob Gibson set the modern major league record with a 1.12 ERA in 1968 and completed 28 of 34 starts, he still lost nine games (against 22 wins) because his run support was a subpar 3.0 per game in a league where 3.4 was average. His ERA in those losses was 2.14, but his teams scored a total of 12 runs in those nine starts.

The same is even truer today, as that pitcher's record now owes an additional debt to the bullpen support he receives. He might leave in the seventh inning with the tying run on base, and that bullpen can cost him the win. So to reiterate: Wins aren't the ultimate barometer of pitcher success, because so much of what goes into them is utterly beyond a pitcher's control. With all of the factors above plus the impact of moving from four-man rotations to five-man ones, even the best pitchers don't stick around to rack up wins the way they used to. In 1973, the year the designated hitter was introduced into the AL, 13 pitchers won 20 games —the same number as from 2012–16 combined.

The sabermetrics revolution has shifted the focus on pitcher quality from won-loss records to run prevention, putting it into context in a few different ways. **Earned run average (ERA)** is the oldest and most familiar of those, the rate of earned runs allowed per nine innings. **Adjusted ERA (ERA+)** is an index that, like OPS+, measures the extent to which a player is better or worse than average at preventing runs after adjusting for scoring environment. A 120 ERA+ means that a player is 20% better than average at preventing earned runs, an 80 ERA+ means he's 20% worse than average.

ERA and ERA+ have their problems, however. The distinction between earned and unearned runs is archaic because the percentage of the latter has dwindled over time. In 1893, the year that the 60'6″ pitching distance was introduced, 30% of all runs were unearned, but that was down to 18% by 1923, 11% by 1953, and 7.5% by 2016. Generally speaking, good pitchers allow fewer unearned runs as well as fewer earned runs than bad pitchers. **Runs allowed per 9 innings (RA9)** uses both earned and unearned runs in the same manner as ERA. If Baseball-Reference.com offered an Adjusted RA9 (RA+), it would be worth making the jump, at least for the purposes of comparing a pitcher to his league, but for polite conversation, ERA+ will do.

Whether we're talking about earned runs or all runs in general, it's important to note that a pitcher has more control over some aspects of run prevention than others. One key sabermetrics finding of the early 2000s, first advanced by Voros McCracken, is that major league pitchers don't differ greatly on their ability to prevent hits on balls in play. Pitchers have far more control over the frequency with which they strike batters out, issue walks, and yield home runs—outcomes that are defense-independent—than the frequency with which they allow hits on balls in play. That is to say, at the level of the individual pitcher, his strikeout, walk, and home run rates—expressed either as their **frequency per nine innings (K/9, BB/9, HR/9)** or as a **percentage of plate appearances (K/PA or K%, BB/PA or BB%, HR/PA or HR%)**—correlate well from year to year; a pitcher who strikes out hitters at a high rate one year will tend to do so the next year, and likewise for walks and homers. On the other hand, a pitcher who gives up hits on balls in play with a high frequency in one year—a high **batting average on balls in play (BABIP)**—will not necessarily surrender hits with a similar frequency the next.

When a pitcher isn't striking out or walking a player, damn near anything can happen once the ball is put into play. The year-to-year variance in those BABIPs is often attributed to luck, but it's more accurate to say that randomness is involved, because it's only over large sample sizes that such things tend to even out toward a league average of around .300.

DEFENSE

"There is nothing on earth anybody can do with fielding,"[2] wrote Branch Rickey in a 1954 *Life* magazine article that was otherwise decades ahead of its time in extolling the virtues of on-base percentage and isolated power. Sixty-some years later, smart people have found ways to do *something* with fielding, and while it's far less easily measured than offense or pitching, it's still worth doing. Not only does it help us demystify a critical portion of the game and appreciate the impact of fielding wizards such as Ozzie Smith or Andruw Jones, it facilitates a fuller grasp of each player's total contribution.

The mainstream numbers generally associated with defense, error totals and fielding percentage, tell only bits and pieces of the story, namely how many mistakes a player made and what percentage of the time he avoided making them. What they don't reveal is how many plays per game he made successfully. In his *Base-*

ball Abstract annuals, Bill James introduced **range factor (RF)** as the number of putouts plus assists per game; as detailed by John Thorn and Pete Palmer in *The Hidden Game of Baseball*, that stat was around as far back as 1875 under the guise of "fielding average." By any name, it's far more useful than fielding percentage, for if one shortstop makes eight more errors while getting to 201 more balls than another—as was the case for Smith versus Davey Concepcion in 1980, a changing-of-the-guard year among NL shortstops—it's clear that the first one has the greater range and is the better fielder, because the plays that the second one isn't making often turn into hits. Of course, it's even more helpful to know how often the pitching staffs of each shortstop put the ball in play, either to generate a ground ball or an "air ball" (an infield popup, outfield fly, or a line drive to either).

The further back we go, the less information we have when it comes to fielding, though even with the most rudimentary team-level data, we can calculate how often each team converted a ball in play into an out, its **defensive efficiency**, the starting point for any defensive valuation metric. With that same data, we can also calculate the average number of plays made at each position in a given league. Throw in some data about opposition hitting, and pitcher and batter handedness, and we have the basis for rough estimates of each player's defensive value—his range, his arm (particularly for outfielders and catchers), his ability on the double play (for infielders)—dating back to the nineteenth century via the **Total Zone** system invented by Sean Smith, and used at Baseball-Reference.com. Our ability to estimate defensive value (**fielding runs** above or below average, abbreviated on B-Ref both as Rfield or Rtot) via Total Zone benefits with the introduction play-by-play data, which is largely (if not entirely uniformly) available back to 1950.

Where Total Zone is a nonobservational system, the new millennium has brought observational systems involving types of batted ball data (ground balls, popups, fly balls, and line drives) and their locations. Those types are distinguished from one another by a trained scorer; they can carry subjective biases—balls that becomes hits are more likely to be scored line drives than balls that become outs, for example—but they also offer some advantages. The two most popular ones are **Ultimate Zone Rating (UZR)** and **Defensive Runs Saved (DRS)**, introduced in 2002 and 2003, respectively.

UZR is based upon the frequency with which a ball hit into a given slice of the field—one of 64 zones—is converted into an out, and the average run value of a hit in that zone. Each player's body of work at a given position is compared against a three-year baseline average of all fielders at the position. UZR ignores certain types of batted balls—infield flys and line drives, outfield fouls—from its data because the differences between players on those balls is negligible.

UZR doesn't handle catcher defense, which is one reason to prefer DRS, which has its basis in a plus/minus system that compares each play made with the average fielder at his position that year, awarding increasing credit for plays of greater difficulty. DRS incorporates fielding range, batted ball timing, outfield arm ratings based on exact counts of baserunner advancements, infielder double play ratings based on the exact number of opportunities, bunt fielding, pitcher and catcher stolen base prevention, pitch framing for catchers (a hot area of development at this writing), and good play/bad play values for things such as robbing a home run, missing a cutoff man, or pulling a foot off a base. Baseball-Reference's fielding runs from 2003 onward are based on DRS.

While estimates of defensive value improve with the availability of more data, it must be said that even today, competing methodologies (which also include the play-by-play-based **Defensive Regression Analysis**, Baseball Prospectus's batted-ball-based **Fielding Runs Above Average**, and others) using detailed data can yield divergent measurements of the same player's defensive value, and are still surrounded in controversy. Things like batted ball distribution (which isn't guaranteed to be uniform from year to year, particularly as the members of a pitching staff change) and the influence of one's neighbors in the field (a particularly rangy one can "steal" chances) can contribute to year-to-year fluctuations that have very little to do with skill. More so than batting or pitching statistics, truly accurate measures of defensive skill require larger sample sizes, i.e., multiple years of data, an inconvenient truth when attempting to quantify single-season performance.

THE DEFENSIVE SPECTRUM

Not all defensive positions are created equally. It's much easier to be an average first baseman, who doesn't have to cover very much ground, than an average shortstop, who covers a whole lot. In his *Baseball Abstract* series, James introduced a useful and enduring concept called the **Defensive Spectrum**:

DH - 1B - LF - RF - 3B - CF - 2B - SS - C

The spectrum arranges the positions according to raw abilities—speed, agility, reaction time, and throwing—needed to play each, with the hardest ones on the right. James actually didn't include catchers, but when one lets go of speed as a consideration and observes positional drift over time, it's clear that catchers are to the right even of shortstops. Offensive ability increases the further to the left a position sits on the spectrum, due to the selective pressure applied to the talent pool; it's easier to find a good-hitting DH (who doesn't even play defense) than a good-hitting catcher or shortstop. This explains the seemingly endless supply of big galoots who can mash but wear iron gloves, as well as the flyweight middle infielders who can pick it but can't hit their weights.

The spectrum has evolved over time; for one thing, third base used to require more defensive skill than second due to prominence of bunting during the dead-ball era. The spectrum also explains why players drift leftward as they age and develop, sometimes long before they reach the majors. A high percentage of major leaguers played shortstop, catcher, or center field as amateurs and were drafted as such, but gravitated to easier positions while rising through the professional ranks and proving themselves as stronger hitters than fielders. Hank Aaron played shortstop and third base in high school and then second base in the minors before settling in as a rightfielder in the majors. Mickey Mantle began his professional career as a shortstop. Mike Schmidt and George Brett were drafted as shortstops via consecutive second-round picks in the 1971 amateur draft but moved to third base by the time they reached the majors. Bryce Harper was predominantly a catcher as an amateur, and so on.

REPLACEMENT LEVEL AND POSITION PLAYER VALUE

The payoff from turning to the context-adjusted measures outlined above for offensive and defensive performance is that they can be combined for the purposes of answering the question, "Which player is more valuable?" However, it's not as easy as it sounds.

It isn't too difficult to compare a player to the average one in his league, at his position, in terms of offense and defense, but the measure alone doesn't convey the scale of the number of opportunities. If Player A is five runs above average when you combine his offense and defense, but Player B is five below average via the same combination, it is natural to assume that Player A is more valuable, but that comparison may not tell us that Player A played in 50 games while Player B played in 162 games. It's no given that Player A could have maintained his performance over a longer time span, and finding a fill-in for the other 112 games is a nontrivial concern; we might have had one (or a combination of several) who was 20 runs below average in that span.

The solution is to measure not against average but against **replacement level**, an approximation of what a minor league call-up or waiver-wire pickup—a garden-variety replacement—could provide. Replacement level is a fairly low bar; by definition, Baseball-Reference and FanGraphs peg it at an identical .294 winning percentage, meaning that a team full of replacement-level players would win about 48 games over the course of a 162-game season. What replacement level does is reward slightly below-average play, which may not seem worth rewarding, except that average play actually has tremendous value due to the true rarity of even average players—that's how competitive the major leagues are. Teams can survive even if they get below-average-but-above-replacement-level play from a few spots on the roster.

From an offensive standpoint, the replacement level centers at 20.5 **replacement level runs** below average per 600 plate appearances, a number that can change in either direction based upon the quality of a league (older leagues, particularly the bygone major leagues from the nineteenth century, were of lower quality). From a defensive standpoint, things are slightly more complex, because defensive skill is distributed differently than offensive skill. A player whose defensive work at shortstop is as bad relative to his peers as a replacement level hitter is to his is almost invariably moved off of shortstop long before he reaches the majors. If he can hit, he might become a second baseman or an outfielder; if he can't, he won't get anywhere near a big league job.

For the purposes of valuing defensive performance in a similar manner to offensive performance, the bar for replacement level is considered to be league average at the position plus a **positional adjustment** (in runs) that is in accordance with the aforementioned Defensive Spectrum. These values change over time, particularly as both scoring and strikeout levels change, since the rate at which balls in play have been converted into outs changes. During the dead-ball era, first basemen needed to be more adept defensively than they are today, because they had to make many more plays, and third base, as previously noted, was a more demanding defensive position than second base due to far more bunts.

Here are the current positional adjustments based upon 1,350 innings per year (approximately 150 games):

Position	DH	1B	RF	LF	3B	CF	2B	SS	C
Adj. Value (Runs)	-15.0	-10.0	-7.5	-7.5	2.0	2.5	3.0	7.5	10

Those values tell us that the defense of the average catcher is more valuable than that of the average second baseman by 7.0 runs per year (10 -3) thanks to the scarcity of talent at the two positions, and that of the average catcher is more valuable than the average first baseman by 20 runs per year (+10 minus -10). A catcher who is 10 runs above average over a full season is thus 20 runs above replacement level on the defensive side. A first baseman who is five runs below average is thus 15 runs below replacement, at which point he might as well be a DH.

Given the measures discussed above—batting runs, baserunning runs, double play runs, fielding runs, positional adjustment runs, and replacement level runs (based on playing time)—we can calculate how many runs above or below replacement level a position player is, and then convert those runs into wins; roughly speaking, 10 runs equals one win, but that changes over time, as scoring levels vary. Those wins are the Wins Above Replacement over which I'll spill so much ink. For a single player, WAR figures generally range between −1.0 and 10.0 for a given season. It takes truly terrible play and a commitment to that terrible-ness from a team for a player to persist in the lineup such that he's more than a full win below replacement-level —a long-term contract, or possession of photographs of the GM in a compromising position—because theoretically, one should be able to find that replacement level player with little trouble. If he's not stashed at Albuquerque or Des Moines, then he's sitting by the phone waiting for the call.

Over the course of a full season, a role player or a below-average regular will generally be between 0 and 2.0 WAR, with an average full-timer at any position around 2.0, an All-Star generally around 5.0, an MVP candidate around 8.0, and a season for the ages in the double digits. Via Baseball-Reference, position players have produced just 56 seasons of at least 10.0 WAR, with Babe Ruth (14.0 in 1923 and 12.9 in 1921) occupying the top two spots and six of the top 12. Among non-Ruthians, Carl Yastrzemski's Triple Crown 1967 season (12.4 WAR) is tied with the Bambino's 1927 for third, with Rogers Hornsby's 1924 (12.1) fifth, and Barry Bonds's 73-homer 2001 season sixth (11.9). Mike Trout's 2012 rookie campaign (10.9), which is tied for 21st, is the best season since Bonds's 2002 (11.8). As to what a great career total for WAR looks like, we'll get to that.

Before we do, it's worth noting: Throughout this book, I will discuss seasonal WAR figures for position players and hitters in a manner that suggests they were as readily available in 1916 or 1986 as in 2016. Obviously, that wasn't the case—at various points, the same was true about more traditional stats including ERA, RBI and saves—so MVP voters had no exact way of knowing that Andre Dawson's 49-homer season in 1987 was worth a run-of-the-mill 4.0 WAR, less than 13 other individuals who received votes in the NL that year alone—was. Nor could Hall of Fame voters fully appreciate just how inferior Lloyd Waner (24.1 career WAR, despite a .316 average and 2,459 hits) was to brother Paul (72.8 WAR, with a .333 average and 3,152 hits) when they honored the former with a plaque of his own. That's not to excuse those bad choices, which could have been avoided with a bit of deeper thinking, but it's worth remembering that not every award that went to the player with the lower WAR is worth deeming a mistake or that voters should be faulted for not recognizing that candidate X had more top 10 WAR finishes than candidates Y and Z combined.

REPLACEMENT LEVEL AND PITCHER VALUE

Calculating replacement level for pitchers starts with determining how many runs (earned and unearned) the average pitcher in a given league would have given up in the same number of innings, adjusting for ballpark, level of opposition, team defense (and, via a pitcher's strikeout rate, his own reliance upon that defense), role (starter or reliever; the latter tend to have lower ERAs than starters), and **leverage**, the multiplier by which a situation can have an impact on the expectation of winning. A starter in the top of the first inning of a scoreless game is working in a situation with a 1.0 leverage, a closer working in the ninth inning of a one-run game is around 2.0, while a mop-up man in the late innings of a blowout might be down around 0.2.

One of Bill James's most fundamental inventions called the **Pythagorean Theorem of Baseball**—swiped from basic geometry because every variable in it is squared—holds that a team's winning percentage can be predicted from their runs scored (RS) and runs allowed (RA) totals in the formula $WPCT = RS^2 / (RS^2 + RA^2)$. If we know the rate at which player X prevents runs relative to the average after making these adjustments above, and the winning percentage of a replacement level team (.294), we can calculate the **Runs Above Replacement** (RAR) and convert those runs to Wins Above Replacement, again using the rough exchange rate of 10 to 1 but customizing based upon league scoring level.

For starting pitchers, the WAR scale is similar to that for position players; 2.0 is around average for a full-season starter, 5.0 for an All-Star, 8.0 for a Cy Young–caliber season, 10.0 for the ages, at least in modern times. From 1871 through 1900, when pitchers threw upward of 400, 500, or even 600 innings under rules very different from today, there were 66 10.0 WAR seasons. In more than a century since, there have been only 51 such seasons, with Walter Johnson's 1913 (14.6) and 1912 (13.5) the two highest, followed by Cy Young's 1901 (12.6). The fourth-highest modern season is a tie between Dwight Gooden's 1985, Steve Carlton's 1972, and Grover Cleveland's 1920, all at 12.1. Roger Clemens's 1997 (11.9) is the highest since Gooden.

Since they tend to have lower ERAs—in part because the runners they inherit are charged to the previous pitcher if they wind up scoring—replacement level for relievers is higher, and because they throw far fewer innings than starters, reliever WAR totals tend to be much lower. From 2014–16, relievers had just six seasons with at least 3.0 WAR, while 54 were between 2.0 and 3.0. The highest single-season WAR for a reliever is Rich Gossage's 1975 (8.2) followed by John Hiller's 1973 (8.1). Gossage threw 141⅔ innings, Hiller 125⅓—workloads roughly double those of twenty-first-century closers. The highest WAR of a pitcher throwing fewer than 100 innings was Jonathan Papelbon's 5.0 in 2006. Mariano

Rivera's best total (5.0) came in 1996, when he threw 107⅔ innings in setup duty; his top mark as a closer was 4.3 in 2008, when he threw 70⅔ innings.

It bears mentioning that unlike the counting stats on the back of the baseball card, WAR figures can change slightly over time as the underlying methodology evolves. Smart people putting their heads together will inevitably create better estimates of offense, pitching, and especially defense given enough time. More play-by-play information from half-century-old games will be unearthed, coded, and processed, new whiz-bang defensive metrics will replace older ones, somebody's breakthrough in one metric will be applied to somebody else's conception of WAR, and what was once a career WAR of 65.0 will become 67.5 or something.

If that happens, most likely our conclusions about the player in question won't change much, because similarly, the WARs of all the players to whom he's compared will change as well. That these numbers aren't static makes some people uncomfortable with them to the point of dismissal; they want numbers like 61 and 755 that they can etch into their brains for eternity. The chance that WAR totals may change underscores the fact that these newfangled numbers are *estimates* of player values, built on complex models that can be refined. Outside of the world of baseball statistics, the notion that we should stop trying to improve those models because somebody can't cope with the inevitable change is laughable. We strive for accuracy in our measurements, and when better tools come along to improve that accuracy, we adopt them.

Having offered you enough sabermetrics to stay afloat, it's time to plunge into the shark-infested waters where JAWS lurks.

CHAPTER 3

SWIMMING WITH *JAWS*

S uppose that you are one of the roughly 450 BBWAA members eligible to vote in the annual Hall of Fame election. Having spent your 10 consecutive years with an affiliated baseball outlet, long enough to have covered at least part of the careers of most of the 30-odd players up for election, you've received that long-awaited ballot in late November and have just over a month to decide for whom to vote. Within the rules for election that you've received are a couple of key guidelines:

> Voting shall be based upon the player's record, playing ability, integrity, sportsmanship, character, and contributions to the team(s) on which the player played.
>
> No automatic elections based on performances such as a batting average of .400 or more for one (1) year, pitching a perfect game or similar outstanding achievement shall be permitted.[1]

Beyond knowing that those players met the eligibility criteria outlined in Chapter 1—a minimum of 10 years of service in the majors, activity between five and 15 years ago, absence from baseball's ineligible list, nomination via the BBWAA screening committee, and receipt of at least 5% of the vote if they've been on the ballot before—the only information you receive with the ballot is the number of years each player has been on it and the previous year's voting totals and percentage. A cover letter from Hall president Jeff Idelson invites you to the institution's Web site for candidate bios that amount to thumbnail sketches of the players' careers. Atop the ballot is this paragraph:

> *Players listed are eligible for election to the National Baseball Hal of Fame in 2017. They are the only players eligible. Please check the candidate(s) of your*

choice. You may vote for up to 10 players. You are not required to vote for 10 but you may not vote for more than 10. Ballots must be submitted by mail only by December 31, 2016.[2]

How to proceed? Some choices may appear obvious. Historical precedent suggests that the guys with 300 wins or 3,000 hits will gain entry whether or not you follow along, and the ones far short of either of those numbers don't have much chance. The ones with 500 homers may seem less clear-cut because of rumors or even proof that they used performance-enhancing drugs, about which you may have deeply seated beliefs ranging anywhere on the spectrum from "who cares?" to "hang 'em high!"

All of that may narrow your choices down to a more manageable number, but how will you pare them down to a maximum of 10? For those players in the middle ground, the ones who aren't no-brainers, odds are that you can find somebody at his position with lesser numbers—hits, batting average, homers, wins, All-Star appearances, Gold Gloves, MVP or Cy Young awards—who's already enshrined . . . and somebody with better numbers who's not.

Take Larry Walker, a candidate I've stumped for since his ballot debut in 2011. In comparing him to other rightfielders, his 2,160 hits and 383 homers are fewer than those of non–Hall of Famer Joe Carter (2,184 and 396) but more than Hall of Famer Chuck Klein (2,076 and 300). His 1,311 RBI are just ahead of the enshrined Paul Waner, Roberto Clemente, Sam Thompson, and Enos Slaughter (who at 1,304 trails this closely packed bunch), but fewer than outsiders like Harold Baines (1,628), Dave Parker (1,493), and Juan Gonzalez (1,404). His seven Gold Gloves are the equal of Hall of Famer Dave Winfield, but fewer than non–Hall of Famer Dwight Evans, who has nine. He's got three batting titles, but so does Tony Oliva, who's outside, too. He won an MVP award, but so did Jeff Burroughs, and Gonzalez even won two—yet they're not in this particular country club, either.

You could spend all day searching for direction amid thickets of such numbers when it comes to the 10 or 20 candidates in the middle of your ballot. Certainly, you're bringing your own opinions to this exercise based on your experience covering the players in question, and probably a few conversations with your peers as well, but navigating the ballot isn't easy.

Enter JAWS, which I created for such a purpose, whether you're casting a vote or following along at home. As outlined before, JAWS (**J**affe **WAR S**core) is a tool for objectively measuring a candidate's Hall of Fame worthiness by comparing him to the players at his position who are already enshrined. The basis for that measurement is WAR—Wins Above Replacement—a metric that estimates a player's total hitting, pitching, and defensive value while accounting for the wide variations in scoring levels that have occurred throughout the game's history and from ballpark to ballpark. Instead of simply using a player's career WAR total as a yardstick and calling it a day, JAWS encompasses both career value and peak value, with the last defined as a player's best seven seasons.

For each candidate, those three figures (often expressed as **Career WAR/Peak WAR/JAWS**) can easily be compared to the average Hall of Famer at his position, the idea being that those who meet or exceed that average (the **JAWS standard** for the given position) are identified and thereby endorsed by the system as worthy Hall of Famers. Why the *average* Hall of Famer at the position? From the start, the stated goal of my system has been to improve or at least maintain the institution's standards (such as they are), rather than erode them. We have to pick a reference point for comparison, and the average (mean) is a good place to start, both objective and intuitive. If we're comparing every centerfielder to Willie Mays (156.2 career WAR/73.7 peak WAR/110.2 JAWS, making him number one at the position), nobody else will ever get in, while if we're comparing them to Hugh Duffy (43.0/30.8/36.9, 46th among all centerfielders and 18th out of 18 Hall of Famers), we'd need to more than double the rolls at the position.

If you're a so-called "small Hall" type who believes that the voters should be more strict about who gets in, you can mentally nudge that average up a few points to meet your own personal threshold of worthiness, though—as I'll show throughout this book—time and again that will mean not recognizing some players who are as good or even significantly better than current Hall of Famers. If the average Hall shortstop is at 54.8 JAWS, what's the justification for keeping Derek Jeter (57.0), Alan Trammell (57.5), and Bill Dahlen (57.7) out, and won't it look silly when held up against the fact that Luis Aparicio (44.2) and Travis Jackson (39.5) are in?

If you're a "large Hall" type who believes the voters should be more lenient, likewise you can mentally nudge that average down a bit. However, the reality is that if you go much lower—say, to the median, which is lower at six of the nine positions (not counting relievers), often by several points—then the system winds up flagging far more candidates as worthy than can fit into the 10 slots of an individual ballot, a problem that I identified years before BBWAA voters created such a backlog anyway.

In using both an individual player's career and peak WARs, JAWS effectively double-counts his best seasons, an appropriate strategy given research into the premium value of star talent, which shows that individual greatness can have a nonlinear effect on a team's results both in the standings and on the bottom line. Add an eight-win player—roughly the equivalent of 1964 Dick Allen, '75 Fred Lynn, or 2001 Ichiro Suzuki—to a contending team and you will increase their chances of reaching the postseason crapshoot by a greater degree than you would by adding two four-win players.

The idea for JAWS developed out of my coverage of the 2002 and '03 Hall of Fame ballots for my own Futility Infielder blog, which was written in light of *The New Bill James Historical Abstract*'s introduction of Win Shares as well as older Jamesian tools such as Similarity Scores and the Hall of Fame Monitor. The series generated an invitation from the folks at Baseball Prospectus, the leading sabermetrics Web site, to write about the 2004 ballot, for which I turned to BP's relatively new Wins Above Replacement Player (WARP) metric, a WAR predecessor that used BP's own batting, fielding, and pitching framework as well as a significantly lower replacement level. Initially, I defined peak as a player's best run of five *consecutive* seasons, making allowances for injuries and years lost to military service. That and the career score were (and still are) averaged into one number to allow any user—including progressively minded voters—to compare each candidate along any of its three axes.

The metric evolved, gaining its catchy acronym a year later and a redefinition of peak the year after that. For the latter, I judged a player's best seven years at large to be the sweet spot, as it did a reasonable job of accounting for the enshrinement of short-career/high-peak players such as Hank Greenberg, Ralph Kiner, Sandy Koufax, and Jackie Robinson, not that other factors—historical importance, postseason heroics, time lost to military service, or the color line—didn't come into play. After leaving BP, for the 2013 ballot I switched to the Baseball-Reference version of WAR upon striking a partnership with B-Ref creator Sean Forman, who agreed to add the stat to every player page, and to build leaderboards at each position, exponentially expanding the metric's reach while reducing the system's labor-intensive nature.

For the purposes of the system, every player is assigned a primary position based upon where he accrued the most value during his career, which may be different from where the Hall itself classifies him, or where he played the most games—particularly as players tend to shift to positions of less defensive responsibility (and thus less overall value) as they age. This is yet another place that the Defensive Spectrum and its associated positional adjustments (introduced in Chapter 2) come into play.

Consider Ernie Banks. From 1953–61, he was primarily a shortstop, and a great one, accumulating 54.7 WAR on offense and defense. From 1962–71, he was primarily a first baseman, declining as a hitter while playing a much less valuable position in the field, adding just 12.7 WAR. He played more games at first (1,259) than at short (1,125), but he's not enshrined for his work there, which was nothing special; he's in because he was a groundbreaker as a power-hitting shortstop. Such is true for many other enshrined players, though not every one of them works out so tidily.

Once the Hall of Famers are grouped by primary position, the **Career/Peak/ JAWS standards** at each position are calculated. Here is the breakdown by positions through the 2017 election cycle (including the trio elected):

Position	#	Career	Peak	JAWS (unadjusted)	JAWS (adjusted)	Closest Match HOFer
SP	62	73.9	50.3	62.1	62.1	Nolan Ryan
RP	5	40.6	28.2	34.4	34.4	Goose Gossage
C	15	53.4	34.4	43.5	43.9	Mickey Cochrane
1B	20	66.4	42.7	54.3	54.6	Willie McCovey
2B	20	69.4	44.5	57.2	56.9	Jackie Robinson
3B	13	67.5	42.8	54.7	55.2	Home Run Baker
SS	21	66.7	42.8	54.6	54.8	Joe Cronin
LF	20	65.2	41.5	52.8	53.3	Billy Williams
CF	19	71.2	44.6	58.4	57.9	Duke Snider
RF	24	73.2	43.0	58.1	58.1	Paul Waner
CI (1B + 3B)	33	66.8	42.7		54.8	
MI (2B + SS)	41	68.0	43.7		55.9	
OF (LF, CF, RF)	63	70.0	43.0		56.5	
CO (1B, 3B, LF, RF)	77	68.4	42.5		55.4	
MID (C, 2B, SS, CF)	75	65.8	42.0		53.9	
All Hitters	152	67.1	42.2		54.7	

Because of the discrepancy between the number of players at the least populated positions (catcher and third base) and the most populated positions (right field), I apply a slight adjustment for the positions, recalculating the position's JAWS after adding (24 -n) generic Hall of Fame position players. So the adjusted JAWS for first basemen is 20 times the average unadjusted JAWS (really, just the sum of those 20 individual JAWS) plus four generic position players (54.7 JAWS) divided by 24. This decreases the spread from position to position slightly. I don't do this for pitchers.

The last six lines in the table show the aggregates for common position combos—corner infield, middle infield, outfield, four-corner, and up-the-middle—useful for measuring candidates who spend significant time at multiple positions. For example, one can argue that it's not appropriate to measure Craig Biggio strictly against second basemen because he spent 13% of his career as a catcher (where his playing time was constricted by the need for extra days off) and another 9.5% as a centerfielder. Thus, comparing him to the up-the-middle players (C, 2B, SS, and CF above) may be more appropriate.

Note that in calculating the standards, Hall of Famers inducted as pioneers, managers, or executives are excluded. Because he split his career between pitching and playing the infield while also managing and founding the short-lived Players League, I've classified Monte Ward as a pioneer and kept him out of the sauce as well (though a capsule on his career is included with the pitchers). Likewise, Negro Leagues players with less than 10 years in the majors—namely Satchel Paige, Monte Irvin, and Willard Brown—aren't included in JAWS, and the paucity of consistent data from the Negro Leagues makes it unlikely that we'll ever be able to fill in the blanks to the point that we can make direct comparisons to major leaguers. On the other hand, Jackie Robinson, Roy Campanella, and Larry Doby are among the former Negro Leaguers who had short but substantial major league careers, with solid enough peak scores to merit their inclusion in the metric.

For all that is included, JAWS can't incorporate everything that goes into a player's case for Cooperstown. I can't stress this enough: **JAWS is not intended to be used in a binary YES/NO fashion in which a player falling short by a narrow margin should be barred from election.** JAWS makes no attempt to account for postseason play, awards won, leagues led in important categories, career milestones, military service, and historical importance. It does not wade into the murky waters of performance-enhancing drug allegations, though it's worth noting that WAR's built-in adjustments for scoring environment take some of the shine off the inflated offensive numbers of the 1990s and 2000s. All of that information is germane to a discussion of a candidate's merits, and can tilt the balance for or against a player whose WAR-based credentials may otherwise be borderline.

Aside from military service, some of those aforementioned credentials that are external to JAWS—the awards, milestones, black ink (league leads in key categories, often boldfaced in print and Web stat resources), and regular play for teams that made the postseason—are handled reasonably well via the aforementioned Bill James Hall of Fame Monitor and Hall of Fame Standards metrics, which have since been revived by Baseball-Reference. I will reference those from time to time; a full breakdown of the point system is available at http://www.baseball -reference.com/about/leader_glossary.shtml#hof_monitor. But whether we're talking about a candidate's WAR or JAWS or Monitor score, sooner or later, our arguments are better served by going beyond the numbers and appreciating the details, nuances, and contexts of their careers.

With that, it's time not only to see JAWS in action, but to see the Hall of Fame in all of its inaction and dysfunction.

CHAPTER 4

HOW VOTERS PUT
THIRD BASE IN A CORNER

On December 5, 2011, around 10 a.m. Central Time, Jane Forbes Clark ascended to the podium in the media room of the Hilton Anatole Hotel in Dallas, Texas. As the chairwoman of the board of directors for the National Baseball Hall of Fame and Museum—an institution founded by her grandfather back in 1936—the honor of announcing the results of the previous day's Golden Era Committee vote fell to her.

Comprised of Hall of Famers, major league executives, and media members, the 16-member committee was charged with reconsidering the credentials of eight former players and two executives whose greatest contributions to the game took place during the 1947–72 period. Each candidate had been bypassed for election multiple times; some had endured the annual cycle of hope and disappointment 15 years in a row via the BBWAA ballot, exhausting their eligibility on that front before their cases were taken up by the Veterans Committee. The Golden Era Committee had been created as one of three VC successors, along with the Pre-Integration Era (1871–1946) and Expansion Era (1973–89) Committees, to be voted on triennially (the process was overhauled again in 2016).

Hundreds of reporters, on hand for MLB's annual Winter Meetings, settled into their chairs as Clark rattled off the names of committee members, then announced that just one of the 10 candidates had received the 75% of the vote necessary for election: Ron Santo. Delivered on an upbeat note, her words were meant to confer baseball's highest honor, but they hit the floor of the Hilton Anatole with a resounding thud. The room fell silent for four seconds, a pause that felt like an eternity, before the polite applause began, as those gathered struggled to digest the sad irony of what had transpired. "You could feel the weight of it," said one media member.

Santo, a Chicago Cubs great, had died almost precisely a year before the Hall corrected one of its most glaring oversights. He had spent 15 years in the majors (1960–74), mostly as a star third baseman for the Cubs, then 15 years on the BBWAA ballot (1980, then '85–98, after a rule change restored his eligibility), and nearly a decade being bypassed by various forms of the Veterans Committee (2003, '05, '07, and '09) before finally gaining election. Unfortunately, the beloved Chicago icon had passed away at the age of 70 due to complications from bladder cancer and a body worn out from battling diabetes, which had shortened his career and eventually cost him both legs from the knees down. Rarely had claims of baseball immortality collided with the reality of human mortality so violently.

Alas, the BBWAA and VC voters have rarely gotten it right when it comes to third basemen. Through the 2017 election cycle, fewer major league third basemen are enshrined (13) than at any other position except relievers. Through eight decades of Hall history, at no other position have voters' inconsistent standards and the messy, inefficient process been so readily apparent. Few players have borne the brunt of their missteps as directly as the late great Cub.

The idea for the National Baseball Hall of Fame and Museum hatched in 1934, when local businessmen who wanted to give tourists a reason to flock to Cooperstown crossed paths with league officials who wanted to honor the greatest players in baseball history. A resort village on the shore of Otsego Lake in central New York state, Cooperstown had been hit hard by the one-two punch of the Great Depression and Prohibition, since the region's economy was built on growing the hops needed to produce beer. And since 1905, the town had held a special significance in baseball lore, as the site where future Civil War General Abner Doubleday had (allegedly) invented baseball in a local cow pasture.

That the location for baseball's origin is by legend a cow pasture is fitting, for the reality is pure bullshit. Doubleday was at West Point in 1839, and the only documentation connecting him to baseball is an 1871 letter in which he requested that his superiors supply baseball equipment for a regiment of African American soldiers in Texas. His status as the game's recognized inventor was conferred upon him posthumously by the Mills Commission, a group of early baseball movers and shakers who convened in 1905 for the purpose of putting in the fix by claiming that the sport was a uniquely American invention, not evolved from the British game of rounders.

The commission's conclusion in favor of Doubleday rested on the otherwise unsubstantiated report of a 71-year-old mining engineer named Abner Graves, who via a newspaper article in the *Akron Beacon Journal* claimed to have been present when Doubleday drew up diagrams of the field and revised the rules of a variant called Town Ball. It was a difficult proposition to swallow given that Graves had been born in 1834—and thus would have been five years old at the time.

Ultimately, that baseball's supposed origins stem from a pile of bullshit matters little. Bullshit makes great fertilizer, and out of this particular mound grew the National Pastime. So, back to 1934: Representing the forces of Cooperstown was Stephen Carlton Clark, whose grandfather Edward Clark was the brains behind the Singer Sewing Machine Company, and whose granddaughter Jane Forbes Clark we've already met. As the chairman of the Clark Foundation, Stephen Clark had seized upon the idea of a baseball museum, fueled by his $5 purchase of an old baseball from a nearby attic—said to have belonged to Graves, and thusly dubbed "the Doubleday Baseball"—and by the enthusiasm of employee Alexander Cleland. Having drawn considerable interest with the display of their artifact, the two men took their idea to Ford C. Frick, president of the National League, in search of further donations to display in the nascent National Baseball Museum, to which Clark had appointed Cleland as secretary.

As it turned out, organized baseball had for years wanted to do something to recognize the game's all-time greats and to celebrate its alleged origins in Cooperstown, particularly as the 100th anniversary of its alleged founding approached in 1939. Frick convinced American League president Will Harridge and commissioner Kenesaw Mountain Landis to get on board, and in mid-1935 plans for the Baseball Hall of Fame were announced, with the newly formed institution appointing the BBWAA (founded in 1908, and at that point still spelling Base Ball as two words, undoubtedly as a warning that they were in no rush to embrace new ideas) with electing the best players from the twentieth century up to that point. An Old-Timers Committee (OTC), consisting of former players, writers, managers, and officials who had firsthand familiarity with nineteenth-century baseball, was charged with electing players from that century. The intent was to elect 10 players from the twentieth century and five from the nineteenth by the time the Hall of Fame building opened in 1939.

In December 1935, the wizened scribes of the BBWAA announced a field of 33 candidates, and soon afterward, 226 members cast ballots under Cleland's guidelines: "those worthy of Hall of Fame election should be selected from the ranks for ability, character, and their general contribution to base ball [sic] in all respects."[1] Each voter was allowed to list as many as 10 names on his ballot, and 75% of the vote was necessary for a candidate to be elected. At that point in time, no rules were in place regarding a player's career length or retirement status. Even players banned for life such as Hal Chase and Shoeless Joe Jackson weren't excluded; it would take until 1991 before that prohibition was formally established.

In February 1936, the first five inductees were announced: Ty Cobb, Babe Ruth, Honus Wagner, Christy Mathewson, and Walter Johnson. Alas, the 78 grizzled (and somewhat addled) men on the OTC pitched a shutout—a harbinger of all-too-frequent things to come—with nobody getting more than 50.6% of the vote. In part, that was because it wasn't clear whether write-in candidates were allowed, or how to handle players such as Cy Young whose careers straddled the two centuries; he received 49.1% from the BBWAA and 41.7% from the OTC. Some voters labored under the impression that they were charged with selecting an All-Star team with one player at each position. Their ballots were returned, but some of those voters declared that they wanted them accepted as-is. The institution was off to a flying start.

Young was elected by the BBWAA the following year, along with Tris Speaker and Nap Lajoie. The OTC was put on hiatus for retooling, while a six-member Centennial Committee (CC) that included Landis, Harridge, and Frick elected five nonplayers, most notably managers John McGraw and Connie Mack, standout nineteenth-century players before becoming their respective leagues' most successful skippers. Over the next three years, the BBWAA, CC, and a revived three-man OTC (just Landis, Frick, and Harridge), stocked the Hall with eight more players and five pioneers. Just 11 of the 25 individuals honored were actually alive and on hand for the festivities when the doors to the National Baseball Hall of Fame and Museum were formally opened on June 12, 1939. The pioneers had all passed away, as had Mathewson and Willie Keeler. The lofty notion of baseball immortality had already crossed paths with the reality of human mortality, but the sport's seven-decade head start on a mechanism for honoring its greats at least afforded it an excuse.

That intersection would be further highlighted at the Winter Meetings in Cincinnati in December 1939, when the writers called a special election on behalf of Lou Gehrig. The Iron Horse's remarkable career and 2,130-game streak had come to an end on April 30, 1939, due to an illness that was soon diagnosed as amyotrophic lateral sclerosis, a degenerative disease attacking the brain and spinal cord. Doctors had given him less than three years to live; on July 4, the Yankees held their appreciation day in which he gave his famous "luckiest man on the face of the earth" speech. The writers elected Gehrig unanimously but the institution's switch to a triennial election cycle, with the next election not until 1942—a decision made in part to shift the focus to the neglected nineteenth-century stars—meant that no formal induction ceremony took place before his death on June 2, 1941.

The 1942 BBWAA election produced just one honoree (Rogers Hornsby), while the OTC's planned consideration of nineteenth-century candidates was delayed endlessly. When they finally convened in early December 1944, it was to elect Landis, who had died on November 25.

The next four years brought progress in fits and starts. The BBWAA failed to elect anyone in January 1945, with Frank Chance (72.5%) falling seven votes shy, "a draw that stirred up the biggest sports rumpus since the Dempsey-Tenney long count,"[2] as Hall director Ken Smith later wrote. In April of that year, the OTC delivered their 10 honorees: one twentieth-century manager (Wilbert Robertson) and a mixed bag of nine good and great position players, mostly from the nineteenth century, though some had crossed into the twentieth: Roger Bresnahan, Dan Brouthers, Fred Clarke, Jimmy Collins, Ed Delahanty, Hugh Duffy, Hughie Jennings, Mike "King" Kelly, and Jim O'Rourke.

At a subsequent meeting in September 1945, instead of considering pitchers from the nineteenth century, the OTC (which by now included Stephen Clark himself as chairman, and had the power to set the rules of the process) decided that an overhaul was necessary. It ordered the BBWAA—which had elected just one player in the previous six years—to return to voting annually to work through the logjam of highly qualified candidates. Also coming out of this reorganization were new rules: candidates now had to have been retired for at least one year; could not be on the ballot more than 25 years after retirement; and should be chosen "on the basis of playing ability, integrity, sportsmanship, character, their contribution to the teams on which they played and to baseball in general,"[3] the so-called "character clause" whose ramifications I'll revisit in Chapter 8.

Still, the BBWAA failed to elect anyone in 1946, when the process was split into two stages, a nominating stage in which voters could choose 10 of 76 candidates, and a final ballot in which they could vote for five of the top 20 from the first stage. While Chance again topped all candidates, neither he nor anyone else reached 75%. The format was abandoned (but later revisited in 1949, '64, and '67 in the form of a run-off ballot involving the top 20 or 30 finishers from the original balloting), but Chance was among the 11 candidates elected when the OTC met in April, along with his fabled Cubs teammates and partners of verse, shortstop Joe Tinker and second baseman Johnny Evers ("*These are the saddest of possible words: 'Tinker to Evers to Chance'...*"[4]). Also selected were Jesse Burkett, Jack Chesbro, Tommy McCarthy, Joe McGinnity, Eddie Plank, Rube Waddell, Ed Walsh, and executive Clark Griffith. As with the OTC honorees from the year before, while the group had a few standouts, several of the new additions had statistics and other credentials indistinguishable from a number of their contemporaries.

In 1947, with the two-tiered process scrapped, the BBWAA logjam broke, as Mickey Cochrane, Frankie Frisch, Lefty Grove, and Carl Hubbell all crossed the 75% barrier. The next year, Herb Pennock and Pie Traynor were elected. Exhausted from all that heavy lifting, the writers failed to elect anyone in 1949 or '50, though from '51–56 they added a total of 15 players. When this proved to be too much of a good thing, they backed off and returned to voting in even-numbered years, a state of affairs that held through 1966. A rule requiring a player to have been retired for at least five years was enacted in 1954, though candidates who had received at least 100 votes in a previous election were grandfathered in. Two years later the length of time between a player's retirement and the end of his eligibility was increased from 25 to 30 years.

By the time Ron Santo became eligible in 1980, just five third basemen had been elected to the Hall, three of whom now look like strong choices and the other two . . . not so much. None of them had an easy time getting in, and taken together they illustrate some of the voting bodies' most maddening tendencies.

The five, with some key stats:

Player	PA	H	HR	AVG/OBP/SLG	OPS+	Rbat	Rfield	WAR
Jimmy Collins	7452	1999	65	.294/.343/.409	113	118	121	53.2
Pie Traynor	8297	2416	58	.320/.362/.435	107	93	-32	36.2
Home Run Baker	6663	1838	96	.307/.363/.442	135	255	35	62.8
Fred Lindstrom	6108	1747	103	.311/.351/.449	110	81	21	28.3
Eddie Mathews	10100	2315	512	.271/.376/.509	143	505	33	96.4

Collins, elected by the OTC in 1945, was the Hall's first third baseman, a solid inaugural choice. His career with the Boston Beaneaters, Louisville Colonels, Boston Americans, and Philadelphia A's spanned 1895–1908. Agile and cerebral, he had for decades served as the yardstick by which third basemen were measured, thanks in part to his pioneering work in handling bunts—in his 1895 debut at the position, he moved closer to the plate, to the edge of the grass, to play them—and to offense that stood out far more in the nascent AL than it had in the NL. In 1902, *The Sporting Life's* Jacob C. Morse called him "the greatest third baseman ever built,"[5] while in 1933, *The Sporting News* called him an undisputed choice for that honor, "just about last word in third basing."[6] His defensive reputation holds up via Total Zone; his 121 runs above average leads all third basemen prior to World War II.

The Sporting News agitated for his election in January 1943 ("There isn't a single reason why Jimmy Collins should not be chosen"[7]), but by the time the BBWAA and OTC next voted in '45, his candidacy had an additional facet: He was dead, having passed away on March 6, 1943, at age 73. While he'd received at least 25% in every BBWAA election cycle up to that point, he couldn't get over the hump without shuffling off this mortal coil.

Traynor, elected by the BBWAA in 1948, was a less inspired choice. He spent his entire career (1920–35 plus five games in '37) with the Pirates, becoming player-manager in mid-1934, his age-35 season, and guiding the team through '39. An exceptional contact hitter who never struck out more than 28 times in a season, he had put up some impressive batting averages during his career—.342 in 1927, then .337, .356, and .366 in each of the next three years—but those gaudy numbers came when offense was at its twentieth-century apex. The entire NL had half a dozen seasons where the league batting average (excluding pitchers) exceeded .300; those leagues hit .294 during Traynor's career, a mark he outdid by 26 points, but he rarely walked and lacked power, particularly relative to his time. Once you incorporate the Pie-man's OBP and SLG—which weren't in common circulation then, but which have a greater impact on scoring than batting average does—for the offensive context via OPS+, he was the least productive hitter of the quintet.

Traynor's other big selling point was his defense, which both rivals and teammates lauded. Former Pirate Charlie Grimm said, "He had the quickest hands and the quickest arms of any third baseman I ever saw."[8] Variants on "A hitter doubled down the line and Pie Traynor threw him out"[9] weren't uncommon. Legendary columnist Red Smith wrote of Traynor in 1971, "Watching this broad-shouldered six-footer charge a slow bounder to the left of the mound and throw from the grass tops was like looking over Da Vinci's shoulder."[10]

Despite such praise, Total Zone estimates Traynor to be 32 runs *below* average for his career, making for a serious gap between the metrics and his reputation, or at least one part of it. It turns out he had a tendency to throw wildly even on routine plays; he led the league in throwing errors three times from 1930–33, the earliest years for which we have error-type breakdowns. Hall of Fame second baseman Billy Herman, who praised Traynor's hands as the "most marvelous pair . . . you'd ever want to see,"[11] was less laudatory regarding his throwing. "You'd hit a shot at him, a play that he could take his time on, and he'd catch it and throw it right quick, so that if his peg was wild, the first baseman had time to get off the bag, take the throw, and get back on again. It was the only way Traynor could throw; if he took his time, he was *really* wild."[12]

Nonetheless, Traynor rode his strong defensive reputation and his shiny batting average into Cooperstown, rocketing from 32.8% in 1945 to 73.9% in '47 (two votes short), aided by his higher profile as a sportscaster on Pittsburgh's KQV radio station, and then to 76.9% the next year. He was the vanguard of a wave of hitters whose superficially shiny numbers from the high-scoring 1920s and '30s would lead to an era disproportionately represented within Cooperstown (see Chapter 7).

The elections of Collins and Traynor meant that it took way too long to give Baker, who'd been a plausible candidate to be the Hall's first third baseman and a BBWAA elected one, his due. His career with the A's and Yankees spanned 1908–22—he succeeded Collins in Philadelphia—though he lost 1915 to a salary dispute and '20 to the aftermath of his wife's death. He'd been part of Connie Mack's powerhouse A's teams that won four pennants and three championships from

1910–14; he not only led the league in homers in the last four of those years, he hit two in the 1911 World Series, which yielded his famous nickname.

While famed for his offense, the bowlegged and awkward-looking third baseman's fielding drew mixed reviews, even as he led the league in putouts seven times and in double plays four times, and via Total Zone grades out as above-average. In 1913, F. C. Lane—the Bill James of his day—compared Baker to the bowlegged Honus Wagner, writing, "The Athletic star is not a finished fielder. . . . Where Baker's awkwardness militates against him more than anywhere else is in his covering of the bag."[13] In a World Series preview that same year, though, Hugh Fullerton lavished praise on Baker's glovework, which in his eyes had improved: "He fields bunts well, gets as many foul flies as any third baseman in the game and can now handle thrown balls splendidly."[14]

Taken together, Baker's offense (including his considerable power) and defense made him significantly more valuable than either Collins or Traynor; the latter would still be true even if you swapped their defensive numbers, for Baker's advantage on offense is more than twice as great. Yet he struggled for support from the writers, maxing out at 30.4% in 1947, having never broken 20% before. Finally elected by the VC in 1955, when he was 69 years old, he had one advantage on Collins. "I heard a fellow say once he'd rather have a rose bud when he's alive than a whole rose garden after he's gone," Baker said. "It looks like they've thrown the roses my way while I'm still here."[15]

It took another 21 years for either the BBWAA or the VC to elect another third baseman. During that time, the writers passed up two noteworthy players who produced value similar to Collins in Stan Hack and Bob Elliot. Hack, a four-time All-Star and staple of four pennant winners for the Cubs from 1932–47, was primarily a leadoff hitter who hit .301/.394/.397 for his career, with 2,193 hits, a 119 OPS+, and 52.5 WAR, third behind Baker and Collins at the time he retired. Neither as popular nor as well regarded defensively as Traynor, he never even received 5% of the vote. Elliot, a career .289/.375/.440 hitter from 1939–53 for the Pirates, Braves, and three other teams, collected 2,061 hits including 170 homers, made seven All-Star teams and won NL MVP honors in '47. His 50.4 WAR placed him just behind Hack, but he topped out at 2% in 1964. Tough crowd.

Neither was a great candidate, but viewed in context with the tools at our disposal, they were better than Traynor in every department save for one: fame. While, yes, it is the Hall of *Fame*, there's nothing about popularity contests in the voting rules.

When the hot corner drought ended, it was with the VC making a particularly questionable choice in 1976: Lindstrom, who played for the Giants, Pirates, Cubs, and Dodgers from 1924–36. A phenom who debuted at 18 due to Giants injuries, he became the goat of the 1924 World Series via a couple of bad hops that allowed the Senators to score the tying and winning runs in Game 7. He overcame that to spend nine years as a regular, hitting as high as .358 in 1928 and .379 in '30, while being hailed for his defense as well.

Lindstrom broke his leg during his age-25 season (1931), and while he was on the mend some hurt feelings over whether he was in line to succeed the ailing McGraw as Giants manager led the team to realize that they could live without him. He was traded to Pittsburgh—where Traynor was entrenched at third base— in December '32, and upon moving to the outfield was simply less special. He bounced around for a few years, but injuries led him to retire after his age-30 season, in 1936, making for a particularly short career by Hall standards.

Lindstrom never cracked 5% on BBWAA ballots spanning 1949–62. His election was one of several particularly questionable VC choices during the 1967–76 span, when Hall of Famers Frankie Frisch, Bill Terry (McGraw's eventual successor), and Waite Hoyt collectively elected eight former teammates from the Cardinals, Giants, Red Sox, and Yankees. The whiff of cronyism there is a phenomenon I'll examine in Chapter 5.

While Lindstrom became the fourth enshrined third baseman, Eddie Mathews couldn't get arrested. A nine-time All-Star who teamed with Hank Aaron to help the Braves to two pennants and a world championship during a career that ran from 1952–68, Mathews was a fearsome slugger who led the NL in homers twice, ranked in the top five nine times, and retired with 512 long balls, the sixth-highest total at the time and second in NL history behind Willie Mays. Despite his modest .271 batting average, his power made him the best-hitting third baseman in history up to that point, and even today his 96.2 WAR ranks second at the position behind only Mike Schmidt.

Mathews's career wasn't without ups and downs. After hitting an NL-high 47 homers as a 21-year-old in 1953, he was described as "the home run king and the boy given the best chance to knock off Babe Ruth's record of 60 homers in one year"[16] by one unnamed sportswriter that winter. Many echoed that sentiment, including teammate Warren Spahn: "His power is terrific and he's the one most likely to break Ruth's record."[17] Amid such pressure, Mathews never topped 47 homers, but he remained ahead of Ruth's career pace through his age-33 season (477), owing to the Bambino's late start. Unfortunately, back and shoulder woes cut into Mathews's production and forced his retirement at age 36. He managed the Braves when Aaron, two years younger, surpassed his pace and broke Ruth's career record in 1974.

For all of his accomplishments, Mathews needed five ballots to get elected. Although *The Sporting News*'s Bob Broeg touted him as a potential first-ballot honoree in 1974 alongside Mickey Mantle, he received just 32.3% while Mantle and Whitey Ford went in together. Two years later, he was still below 50%. He finally got 79.4% in 1978, his fifth try. To date, no 500-homer slugger who wasn't linked to performance-enhancing drugs has waited longer (see Chapter 8).

Born in Seattle on February 25, 1940, Ron Santo grew up in the shadow of Sicks Stadium, home of the Pacific Coast League's Seattle Rainiers, and was caught in the ballpark's pull. He worked at Sicks as a batboy, a groundskeeper, and a clubhouse attendant during his summers, and played three sports in high school, emerging as a baseball star during his senior year. He signed with the Cubs for a $20,000 bonus out of high school in 1959, spurning higher offers—the Reds were said to have offered $80,000—because he had his eye on playing in Wrigley Field alongside Ernie Banks, their slugging shortstop.

During a routine physical before reporting to spring training in 1959, Santo was diagnosed with type 1 diabetes, which he kept secret, out of fear that the team would drop him, particularly after he learned that no one with the disease had ever played in the majors. The Cubs recalled him from the minors in late June of 1960, amid a nine-game losing streak that had sunk them to the bottom of the NL standings. Replacing the Don Zimmer/Frank Thomas combination at the hot corner, he collected three hits and five RBI in a June 26 doubleheader against the Pirates. Manager Lou Boudreau started Santo in 94 of the team's final 96 games, and he made a respectable showing for a 20-year-old, hitting .251/.311/.409 with nine homers. While the Cubs finished 60–94, they had found a cornerstone.

Santo improved to .284/.362/.479 with 23 homers in 1961, his first full season in the majors, but he struggled in '62 (.227/.302/.358), in part because he was still learning how to juggle his insulin injections with the odd hours of a baseball career, all while trying to conceal his condition from his teammates. He finally got the hang of it (though not until 1971 would he reveal it publicly), and rebounded to .297/.339/.481 with 25 homers in '63, making his first All-Star team.

That 1963 season kicked off a stellar 11-year run that encompassed his All-Star appearances and included five straight Gold Gloves (1964–68). He clouted at least 25 homers a year for eight straight years—ranking in the top 10 in the first seven—while generally batting cleanup. Pitchers accorded Santo a healthy respect, pitching around him when they could, and he was disciplined enough to draw at least 80 walks in seven straight seasons, leading the league four times. Twice he led in on-base percentage, and seven times he was in the top 10. He was durable, too, averaging 159 games a year over that 11-year stretch despite playing his home games at lights-free Wrigley Field during the day, often under stifling heat. His 364 consecutive games from April 19, 1964, through May 31, '66, set a record at the position; his 164 games in '65, when the Cubs played two extra games due to ties, remains a record.

From 1964–67, Santo ranked among the best hitters in baseball. In a low-offense era, his .302/.395/.531 line translated to a 156 OPS+, tied with Aaron for fifth in the majors among batters with 2,000 plate appearances. Based on batting average alone he stood out, for only 10 players maintained a .300 mark over that four-year span, and only Frank Robinson had a higher OBP. From 1963–69, his 53.8 WAR was surpassed only by Mays (55.4) and Aaron (54.9).

As good as Santo was, he couldn't elevate the Cubs to the postseason, not even with three future Hall of Famers as teammates, namely Banks (bound for first base and the downslope of his career as of 1962), leftfielder Billy Williams, and staff ace Fergie Jenkins, who didn't find his footing until 1967. The team hadn't won a pennant since 1945, or a World Series since '08. From 1947–66, they finished at or above .500 just twice, and bottomed out to 59–103 in '66 under future Hall of Fame manager Leo Durocher before things began to turn, with an 87-74 record in '67, and 84-78 in '68.

With two new expansion teams and the split of each league into East and West divisions in 1969, the Cubs' odds at making the playoffs almost doubled. They led the newly formed NL East by 4½ games as September dawned, but skidded to 9–18 the rest of the way. The Mets blew past them on a 24–8 tear, winning the division by eight games. Though the Cubs would finish above .500 in each of the next three years, twice in second place, that was as close to the postseason as Santo ever got.

The Cubs tried to deal Santo to the Angels in December 1973, but he became the first player to exercise his 10-and-5 rights. Secured via the Collective Bargaining Agreement between the Marvin Miller–led players union and the owners, the clause allowed a player with 10 years of major league service, including the last five with his current team, to refuse a trade. At 33 and coming off an All-Star season, Santo didn't want to move to the West Coast, so the Cubs arranged a trade to the crosstown White Sox. The hitch was that the Sox already had a solid third baseman in Bill Melton, so Santo shifted to second base, where he had minimal experience. The move was disastrous; he hit .221/.293/.299 in 1974, played the new position poorly enough that he spent more time as a designated hitter, and retired at season's end, despite being just 34, with one more year under contract. "You're going to give me back $130,000 for not playing?" asked White Sox owner John Allyn. "No player has ever walked away from that kind of money."[18]

Santo finished his career with a .277/.362/.464 line (125 OPS+) and 342 homers in his 15 years, with nine All-Star appearances (four as a starter). At the time he reached the ballot, he ranked sixth in hits (2,254) among players who spent most of their careers at third base, as well as second to Mathews in homers, third in total bases (3,779), and fourth in RBI (1,331). His five Gold Gloves were tied with Ken Boyer and Doug Rader for second all-time behind Brooks Robinson, who had retired in 1977 with 16; though hardly the be-all and end-all of fielding prowess, those awards do provide a record of how players' defense is perceived, and for Santo, that should have been a plus.

Sure, Santo lacked the longevity of Robinson, who rapped out 2,848 hits in 23 seasons, albeit with a far less imposing .267/.322/.401 line. Santo also lacked the postseason experience of Robinson, who had played in six postseasons and four World Series with the powerhouse Orioles, winning MVP honors in 1970. Robinson had the 1964 AL MVP on his mantel, too, while Santo topped out at fourth in the MVP voting in 1967. This wasn't a head-to-head election, however; Robinson wasn't eligible yet, which should only have helped Santo's cause.

That said, the marquee newcomer on the 1980 ballot was 3,000-hit-club member Al Kaline, who shared headline billing with Duke Snider (who had missed by 16 votes the previous year) in the Associated Press report trumpeting the ballot's release. Santo, former NL MVP Orlando Cepeda, and Kaline's longtime teammate Norm Cash were relegated to the next tier of players mentioned from among the 62-candidate slate, a poorly vetted mess that made for the largest ballot since 1962.

With Kaline a lock and Snider receiving a vigorous endorsement from Mays, who had been elected the year before, the odds of the BBWAA electing a third candidate that year were low, having happened just once since 1955 (1972, with Sandy Koufax, Yogi Berra, and Early Wynn). While Kaline and Snider breezed in, and holdovers Don Drysdale, Gil Hodges, and Hoyt Wilhelm topped 50%, 18 other candidates received more votes than Santo, whose 15 votes made for a 3.9% share. Under a rule put in place in 1979, that meant he was ineligible for future elections.

At the Hall of Fame board of directors' request, the rule was revised after the 1980 election such that a player had to receive 5% in one of the previous two elections, though that was too late to save Santo. The 1982 death of Boyer, a Santo contemporary who had starred with the Cardinals, spurred St. Louis–based writer Bob Broeg to challenge the rule; Boyer had fallen off after receiving just under 5% in both 1978 and '79. In a compromise, the rule was changed back to its '79 form—one year with less than 5% meant done—but 150 players who had received less than 5% in the previous five elections were reviewed again by the BBWAA screening committee, with Boyer, Santo, and nine others restored for eligibility on the 1985 ballot.

It helped, in that Santo's 13.4% that year kept his candidacy alive, and his support slowly grew. Joining the Cubs as a broadcaster in 1990 increased his visibility; he rose to 31.6% in 1992, and topped out at 43.1% in '98, his final year of eligibility.

By this point, the BBWAA had elected both Robinson and Schmidt, a three-time MVP who clubbed 548 homers from 1972–89 with the Phillies, leading the NL eight times. Both were elected in their first year of eligibility, in 1983 and '95, respectively. In 1999, they granted first-ballot entry to George Brett, a former AL MVP who won three batting titles and tallied 3,154 hits and 317 homers for the Royals from 1973–93. Meanwhile, in 1983 the VC voted in George Kell, a 10-time All-Star in 15 years (1943–1957) with five AL teams; an outstanding contact hitter who won a batting title in 1949, and finished above .300 in eight straight years, his superficially snazzy .306/.367/.414 boiled down to a modest 112 OPS+. The election of those men brought the number of Hall of Fame third basemen to nine.

Though the writers bypassed Santo, by then they had elected his high-profile teammates. Banks, with 512 homers and a pair of MVP awards, went in on the first try in 1977. Williams, with 2,711 hits and 426 homers, needed six years; he debuted on the ballot in 1982, surpassed 50% percent in '84, and went over the top in '87. Jenkins, with 284 career wins and a Cy Young Award, was elected in his third year in 1991.

All three had greater longevity than Santo, but Banks aside, it's not as though their credentials were particularly stronger. Why had the voters passed up a player whose basic "Triple Crown" numbers—the ones that writers and fans referred to with the most frequency—were perennially solid? Cut off the first and last years of Santo's career, the only ones where he played in fewer than 133 games, and he had hit .281 with an average of 25 homers and 96 RBI over a 13-year period. When he couldn't live up to that, when he had been humiliated by a forced change to an unfamiliar position, he walked away from a six-figure salary, though admittedly it was to take a lucrative job as a VP and sales manager of a Chicago oil company.

One theory regarding third basemen's struggles with respect to Hall of Fame voting is the dual nature of the position. They're at the center of the Defensive Spectrum: expected to provide offense along the lines of corner outfielders and first basemen, which is to say preferably with a bit of thump, and also defense that, if not quite at the level of centerfielders and middle infielders, is still quite vital. Finding a player very good at both is harder than finding a mashing first baseman who's merely an adequate fielder or a slick-fielding shortstop who at best can hold his own with the bat.

Recognizing that a player is very good at both things is even harder. Today, offense is relatively easily measured and can be done at a distance, with cold hard numbers, much more easily than defense. Contemporary opinions of hitters can be revealing, but they're window dressing once we break out tools like OPS+ and batting runs. As for defense, for all of the weight placed on it via WAR in this book, it bears repeating that we're still working with estimates whose accuracy may decrease with our volume of data; we can be off-base with our assessments, particularly the further back we go. Contemporary eyewitnesses and their opinions—"this guy had the strongest arm in the league"—can buttress the numbers, but introduce subjectivity and bias into the mix.

Often those opinions spring from unequal sample sizes. To use an example, if John McGraw thought his own third baseman, Freddie Lindstrom, was the greatest he'd ever seen (as he said in a 1930 article that his son Andy sent to the VC), he certainly had more opportunity to observe him than he did the Pirates' Traynor, the AL's Baker, or almost anyone else. Additionally, McGraw never saw Robinson, Santo, Adrian Beltre, or anybody after his 1934 death.

Of course, we're still talking about this from our privileged perch in the twenty-first century. Absent advanced metrics, one can see how third basemen might get short shrift when it comes to valuing their offense. Consider the frequency with which they've led the league in the two most visible offensive categories, batting average and home runs, relative to other positions since 1901. This table includes ties, and position is determined on a season-by-season basis:

Pos	Led AVG	Led HR	Total
RF	48	62	110
1B	36	66	102
LF	36	46	82
CF	29	38	67
3B	24	32	56
2B	29	5	34
SS	18	6	24
C	7	2	9
DH	1	3	4

Forget the newfangled DH position and note that only shortstops and catchers have won batting titles less frequently than third basemen; even second basemen have won more often, in part because in the dead-ball era, that was the heavier-hitting position given the hot corner men's necessary aptitude for handling bunts. Third basemen have far more homer titles than middle infielders or catchers but still fewer than outfielders or first basemen. They lead rarely enough that if you're rewarding Hall of Fame candidates for doing so, there's not a ton of credit to dole out.

One can get a sense of the twisted logic Santo was up against in looking at a few votes from one of *The Sporting News*'s most visible Hall of Fame voters from the late '80s and early '90s, Moss Klein. A longtime Yankees beat writer for the *Newark Star-Ledger*, Klein would devote a whole column in *The Sporting News* explaining his ballot, not unlike many of today's voters, albeit as a "small Hall" voter who generally tabbed only a few candidates. In 1990, he wrote, "One strange aspect of the voting each year is the lack of support for Ron Santo . . . an out- standing third baseman who rarely missed a game."[19] Klein didn't supply any support himself, voting only for Jim Palmer and Joe Morgan that year while by- passing Santo, Jenkins, Cepeda, and 314-game winner Gaylord Perry because "a Hall of Famer should jump out from the list, as Palmer and Morgan clearly did. If you have to spend time trying to build a case for a candidate, then he doesn't belong."[20] In 1991, when he voted only for Rod Carew, Rollie Fingers, and Bill Mazeroski, Klein wrote, "Santo almost made this ballot. . . . As is the case with second basemen and shortstops, third basemen haven't received proper recogni- tion."[21] Jeez, if only somebody could do something about that, right? In 1992, when he tabbed newcomer Tom Seaver, plus Fingers and Mazeroski again, he wrote, "Santo probably retired too early to enjoy a buildup of Hall of Fame–type numbers."[22] Of course, in the previous sentence, Klein had lauded Santo's num- ber four ranking among those at the position in homers and RBIs: "Only Mike Schmidt and Eddie Mathews are ahead of him in both categories."[23] So . . . there aren't enough third basemen in the Hall, but the guy who's fourth in two big stats somehow didn't play long enough. Good grief, Charlie Brown.

At least Klein was attempting to compare apples to apples. The *Los Angeles Times*'s Mike Downey got lost in the fruit salad in 1993:

Santo played 15 seasons ([first baseman Tony] Perez, for example, played 23), had 2,254 hits ([centerfielder] Vada Pinson, for example, had 2,757) and batted .277 lifetime ([third baseman] Bill Madlock, for example, bat- ted .305). If I vote for Santo, what about Perez, Pinson and Madlock?

Look at those four batting championships Madlock won. Yet, be hon- est, was Bill Madlock a Hall of Famer? If he was, what of Ken Boyer, who also hasn't made it to the Hall? Or how about Ron Cey, who got only eight votes, despite a better average than Santo, more homers than Boyer and more hits than Madlock? Ah, but what of Santo's making 10 All-Star teams? See? This isn't easy.[24]

Downey at least got around to comparing Santo to a few third basemen in there, but failed to note that Madlock, despite playing 15 seasons and finishing with a higher average than Santo, collected 246 fewer hits and 179 fewer homers, made just three All-Star teams, and never won a Gold Glove (the metrics suggest he was a terrible defender).

It's not just that Santo couldn't measure up, it's that voters didn't know what to make of him. Jerome Holtzman, the longtime writer for both the *Chicago Sun-*

Times and the *Chicago Tribune*—and later the official historian of Major League Baseball—wrote of Santo in 1988:

> Ordinarily I don't pump for Chicago players. It doesn't seem proper. I have preferred to assume it should not be necessary to bang the drum, that the 400-plus voters . . . constitute an educated electorate. Then I think of Ron Santo and realize some campaigning is necessary. . . . Probably because he was such a strong hitter, Santo, who for many years was the Cub captain, never received much acclaim for his defensive ability. Through hard work and nothing else . . . he made himself an acceptable third baseman and soon thereafter was the best defensive third baseman in the National League.[25]

Holtzman's campaigning barely moved the needle. "I think the baseball writers have been very negligent in regards to Ron Santo,"[26] he said in 1992.

Santo's candidacy wasn't unblemished. In particular, he was saddled with his connection to the Cubs' 1969 collapse. In the ninth inning of a July 8 game against the Mets at Shea Stadium, rookie centerfielder Don Young ignored instructions from Santo and Jenkins (who was pitching at the time) to reposition himself, then misplayed two fly balls, leading to a game-winning rally. Durocher told reporters after the game, "My 2-year-old could have caught those two f—ing balls."[27] Santo piled on, adding, "He's worrying about his batting average, not the team."[28] When Young violated the clubhouse code by leaving without speaking to reporters, Santo added, "He can keep going out of sight, for all I care."[29]

Realizing his own violation of the code, Santo made a point to apologize to Young personally, then called a press conference the next day to make a public apology, and told reporters he would apologize in the clubhouse as well. The damage was done, however, and it divided the team. "I had never seen something so hurtful,"[30] said Banks—rarely one for a discouraging word—to *Sports Illustrated* in 2014.

During that season, Santo developed a postgame ritual of sprinting from Wrigley's third base side toward the entrance to the clubhouse in leftfield, leaping in the air and clicking his heels together three times. Fans and Durocher loved the display, but it rubbed opponents the wrong way. "We didn't think much of that," Nolan Ryan said in 2009. "In those days, people just didn't do those kind of things."[31] Mets ace Tom Seaver mocked Santo by clicking his heels after a key win over the Cubs at Wrigley on July 16. Santo ceased the practice in early September, just before the Cubs sank from first place, but the memory lingered.

It would take a petty voter to hang his hat on such excuses for withholding Hall of Fame recognition over such matters. While none came forward to volunteer such reasons for doing so, it's not outside the realm of possibility. *Chicago Tribune* writer Phil Rogers felt that Santo's antics "alienated New York–based BBWAA voters and his fellow players (who would comprise the new Veterans Committee)."[32]

More likely, the big issue was simply Santo's career length, and the fact that he had his last good season at age 33. Obviously, a player retiring in his mid-30s has forgone the opportunity to pad those all-important counting stats, an issue given that none of the voting bodies has selected a player from the post-1960 expansion era who finished his career with fewer than 2,000 hits, and that only three starting pitchers with fewer than 300 wins have been elected by the writers since 1990. Even a modern player like Santo, with well over 2,000 hits, has the deck stacked against him.

Of the 40 Hall of Fame players who were done in the majors by the end of their age-35 seasons, only nine finished their careers after 1960, including four pitchers done in by the inevitable arm trouble: Sandy Koufax, Don Drysdale, Catfish Hunter (incidentally, also diagnosed with diabetes in late career), and Bruce Sutter. Four of the five remaining players left immediately following their age-35 seasons: Richie Ashburn, Bill Mazeroski, Johnny Bench, and Kirby Puckett. The only one who hung up his spikes at a younger age was Santo. That probably worked against him, even given his unprecedented daily battle with diabetes.

By aging off the BBWAA ballot, Santo had to wait five years before being considered by the VC. In the interim, the Hall undertook a drastic change, expanding the 15-member committee to include every living Hall of Famer as well as every living recipient of the Frick and Spink Awards, the lifetime achievement awards for broadcasters and writers, respectively. Those "Old VC" members whose terms had not yet expired were also included. The plan was for the group to vote by mail every two years, starting in 2003, with managers, umpires, and executives considered every four years.

The number of third basemen in the Hall of Fame still stood at nine when the 2003 VC election came around, fewer than at any other position, but enough to use for the purposes of sketching out a general standard for election. The Baseball Prospectus version of Wins Above Replacement Player had been introduced mere months before the election, in October 2002, though the JAWS system was still just a twinkle in its inventor's eye. Both WAR and JAWS have taken advantage of more than a decade's worth of refinement since, but either their primitive form or their more modern one would have reflected the strength of Santo's candidacy relative to the enshrined third basemen:

Player	Avg HOF 3B c. 2003	Santo
PA	8847	9397
H	2289	2254
HR	227	342
AVG/OBP/SLG	.292/.359/.455	.277/.362/.464
OPS+	124	125
TZ Def	73	20
Career WAR	65.3	70.6
Peak WAR	41.8	53.8
JAWS	53.6	62.2

Via the traditional numbers, Santo measured up on the offensive side despite a relatively low batting average; his outstanding plate discipline and power kept his OPS+ right around the group average, and while he ranked eighth among the 10 players in fielding, he had spent far less time at easier positions (mainly first base, designated hitter, and the outfield) than others. In terms of Defensive WAR (dWAR), which incorporates the player's value relative to average at each position plus the positional adjustment, converted from runs to wins, Santo (8.8) ranks fifth behind Robinson (35.0), Schmidt (17.6), Collins (16.7), and Baker (9.8). All of that—as well as his extra playing time relative to the group average—is reflected in Santo's career WAR, peak WAR, and JAWS. Among the group, he ranks fifth, third, and fourth in those three categories, strong enough to support the conclusion that to that point, he was one of the top five third basemen in history.

The new voting body didn't see things that way. After surviving a nominating process involving 200 candidates, Santo was included on the 2003 VC ballot as part of a 25-player slate. From among the 81 ballots received, nobody attained that threshold; Gil Hodges led with 61.7%, followed by Tony Oliva (59.3%) and Santo (56.8%). The story was similar in 2005 as Santo shared the lead with 65.0% and in '07 when he led the pack with 69.5% but still came up short.

"I thought it was going to be harder to deal with, but it wasn't," Santo told reporters when the 2007 results were announced. "I'm just kind of fed up with it. I figure, 'Hey, it's not in the cards.' But I don't want to go through this every two years. It's ridiculous."[33]

By that point, the number of enshrined third basemen had increased, as Paul Molitor and Wade Boggs, both with over 3,000 hits, had been first-ballot honorees in 2004 and '05. Their addition raised the JAWS standard—hardly uncommon as new players are elected—from 53.6 to 55.7, but Santo was still a healthy 6.5 points above.

With the new VC having struck out on three pitches, the Hall changed things again. For 2009, they took the vote away from those frickin' Spinkers and the spinkin' Frickers, trimming the electorate to the living Hall of Famers and limiting the ballot to 10 players from the 1943–87 period. Santo again topped the voting, but his 60.9% wasn't enough. In a separate election covering pre-1943 players, voted on by 12 Hall members and members of the media, second baseman Joe Gordon was elected, the only major league player honored by the VC from 2002–11.

"Everybody felt this was my year," said Santo after the 2009 announcement. "I thought it was gonna happen, and when it didn't. . . . What really upset me was nobody got in again." He spoke of his chances at enshrinement in the past tense, and said he didn't want to go in posthumously. "[Induction] wasn't going to change my life," he said. "I'm OK. But I know I've earned it."[34]

In the summer of 2010, the Hall of Fame announced *another* change, splitting candidates into three historical eras of unequal size, the Expansion Era (1973–89), Golden Era (1947–72), and Pre-Integration Era (1871–1946) Committees, to be considered in that order. Santo didn't live to see his name come up again. He lapsed into a coma on December 1, 2010, and died the next day.

When his election was announced a year later, emotions were particularly raw among Cubs fans, with some suggesting that his family boycott the ceremony. The news was bittersweet even to peers such as Brooks Robinson, who was on the committee. "I always thought he was a terrific player, both offensively and defensively and deserved to be in," he said. "It's just sad that he wasn't alive to see it." [35] Even so, Santo's family found a measure of closure, with his widow, Vicki, calling the election "a thrilling, thrilling day for us."[36]

If election to the Hall of Fame is an honor, it is one that holds far less value to the dead than the living. We'd all like to believe our best work will outlive us, that our accomplishments will be recognized after we're gone. Even if that's the case, wouldn't it be nice if we could stick around for the celebration? To echo Frank Baker, better to have a rose bud when alive than a rose garden after you're gone.

The three decades that the voters spent kicking Santo's candidacy around denied him his moment of validation, the phone call from the Hall. He was deprived of being introduced to a crowd as "Hall of Famer Ron Santo" and then basking in the cheers on his behalf, whether at Wrigley Field or at Cooperstown.

Santo should have heard those cheers. Even without breaking out the advanced metrics, he clearly had the numbers for Cooperstown all along. His JAWS ranking, now seventh with the completion of Chipper Jones's career and a late push by Adrian Beltre, only underscores that. With some homework by the writers, and some consistency in the voting rules, he might have lived to see his election. An unintended effect of the restoration of his eligibility in 1985 was that it prevented him from reaching the VC when it was still a small committee; he'd have been eligible in 1999 instead of 2003, when the living Hall of Famers who suddenly had the right to vote could use their resentment of his heel-clicking to drag their own heels on recognizing him.

On the subject of timing, it's also worth considering that had Santo played for the Cubs a decade or so later, he would have benefited from the additional exposure that came with Chicago superstation WGN carrying their games nationwide on cable TV, starring on the field instead of in the booth. Banks, Williams, and Jenkins may have not needed such exposure to get elected, but it couldn't have hurt 2005 enshrinee Ryne Sandberg, a 10-time All-Star and nine-time Gold Glove winner who spent 15 years with the team (1982–94 and 1996–97), put together very Santo-like numbers (.285/.344/.452 with 2,386 hits, 282 homers, a 114 OPS+ and 57.2 JAWS) at a key defensive position, and retired (for the second time) at age 38.

Even with the closure of a plaque in Cooperstown, the tragedy is that the timing was never right for Santo, who like any player with an obviously Hall-caliber résumé deserved to be honored in his lifetime. While it's too late for him, let's hope that's not the case for the similarly worthy players whom I'll discuss over the course of this book.

CHAPTER 5

THE HALL OF CRONYISM

As a practicing schizophrenic, the Baseball Hall of Fame makes Jekyll and Hyde look like a model of consistency. . . . To get into the Baseball Writers' wing of the Hall of Fame, you better be Babe Ruth. Or better. To get in the veterans' wing, all you have to be is a crony. Be able to sing 'Mother Machree' over the bar after midnight or be able to tell locker-room jokes with the boys at Old-Timers Day.[1]

—JIM MURRAY

No element of the Hall of Fame has opened it up to more complaint and ridicule over the years than the Veterans Committee, which served as the side door for membership from 1953–2010, flanked on either end by committees serving a similar purpose: electing those outside the purview of the Baseball Writers Association of America. Comprised of between 10 and 20 executives, writers, and Hall of Fame players, the VC fleetingly rescued the Hall from great embarrassment, functioning as a righter of historical wrongs by electing players overlooked by the writers. But all too often, the group scraped the bottom of the barrel by electing substandard candidates, many with clearly traceable connections to committee members, opening it up to charges of cronyism.

While the BBWAA has been charged with electing recently retired players since the institution's beginnings in 1936, their 124 selections through the 2016 cycle account for less than half of the 317 total members of the Hall of Fame. The rest—long-retired players, managers, umpires, executives, pioneers, and Negro Leaguers—were elected not only by the VC but by other entities known as the

Old-Timers Committee, the Centennial Committee, the Committee on Negro League Veterans, the Special Committee on Negro Leagues . . . and that only takes us to 2011. At that point, the VC process split into a triennial cycle featuring the Pre-Integration Era, Golden Era, and Expansion Era Committees. In 2016, that gave way to the Early Baseball Era, Golden Days Era, Modern Baseball Era, and Today's Game Era Committees, which vote within a more complicated cycle.

These committees have generally done their business in secret, meeting behind closed doors with very little public discussion of the proceedings or results aside from who was elected and who came close. The Hall is said to have hundreds of bankers' boxes and other documents in remote storage, some of which may pertain to the VC but aren't available for public perusal. A couple folders from the 1960s and '70s can be found in the Hall library, with lists of potential nominees, actual candidates, voting bylaws, letters from the public to the committee promoting a particular candidate, and statistical one-sheets with a few bullet points for each player regarding records and character descriptions. A particularly vivid one for 1979 honoree Hack Wilson—likely written a few years earlier, as he was a perennial candidate in the mid-'70s—notes his single-season MLB record of 190 RBI and NL record 56 homers, both from 1930, while noting that "Wilson had exceptional power to all fields. Struck out a lot. Was a very colorful player, short of stature, roly-poly. Excited controversy. Had an extremely florid face that enraged enemy crowds."[2]

With the exception of the VC, the committees have been short-lived, and with the exception of the one-shot Special Committee on Negro Leagues, which elected 16 men and one woman in 2006, the distinctions between them have blurred at times. The Old Timers and Centennial Committees, which we met in Chapter 4, were basically forerunners of the VC, while the era-based committees are its successors, voting cyclically since 2011. The responsibilities of the Committee on Negro League Veterans, which from 1971 to 1977 elected Satchel Paige, Josh Gibson, and seven other players, were absorbed into the VC, which elected nine more Negro Leaguers from 1978–2001. From among those various committees, 96 players have been elected primarily for their major league playing careers.

Via JAWS, the gap between the groups of players elected by the BBWAA and those elected by committees is roughly equivalent to that between Rod Carew (65.5 JAWS) and Bobby Doerr (43.9), though it varies considerably from position to position:

Pos	BBWAA-elected	JAWS	Committee-elected	JAWS	Gap
SP	36	67.0	26	55.4	11.6
C	10	49.1	5	32.2	16.9
1B	11	58.6	9	49.1	9.6
2B	11	69.8	9	41.7	28.1
3B	7	64.6	6	43.1	21.6
SS	11	60.2	10	48.5	11.7
LF	11	58.5	9	45.9	12.6
CF	9	77.7	10	41.1	36.7
RF	13	73.5	11	39.9	33.6
Non-P/C	74	65.7	64	43.6	22.1

Here I've lumped the OTC and CC choices in with the VC ones; without them, the sample sizes only get smaller and less meaningful. Excluded from this table are the relievers, none of whom was elected by a committee, and the VC-elected Monte Ward, who split his career between pitcher and shortstop.

The Carew/Doerr comparison works on a deeper level. In Carew, we've got a seven-time batting champion who surpassed 3,000 hits, a first-ballot choice so obvious that 90.5% of the voters got it right in 1991. Not every BBWAA choice is so clear, but with first dibs, they've gotten most of the top players. Among enshrined position players, the top 39 in WAR since 1901, and 55 of the top 60, were elected by the BBWAA. Among enshrined pitchers, 29 of the top 33 in WAR since 1901 were elected by the writers.

In Doerr, we've got a good player with a short career that was interrupted by World War II, one who peaked at 25.0% on the writers' ballot, temporarily became ineligible while vying for attention from the VC thanks to a short-lived rule change, had his eligibility restored, and was finally elected when close pal and former teammate Ted Williams joined the committee and told 17 other guys just what he thought. There might be very good reasons to enshrine such a player who's several points off the JAWS standard, reasons that go beyond his numbers due to his niche in baseball history and/or circumstances beyond his control. Then again, there might not be.

As outlined in Chapter 4, the Old-Timers Committee, which was given the responsibility of focusing on nineteenth-century honorees, voted in 1936, '39, '44, '45, '46, and '49, with the Centennial voting in '37 and '38. The shifts in responsibility and designation occurred after the first OTC, a 78-member panel of retired players, writers, managers, and other officials with familiarity with nineteenth-century baseball, pitched a shutout in 1936. The inability of the CC, a group of half a dozen old men led by Commissioner Kenesaw Landis and including NL president Ford Frick and AL president Will Harridge, to meet in 1939 resulted in the second, smaller OTC, which was just Landis and the two league presidents. Landis then appointed a four-man Hall of Fame Committee, consisting of A's owner/manager Connie Mack, Yankees president Ed Barrow, Braves president Bob Quinn, and sportswriter Sid Mercer, but the panel never officially convened.

In August 1944, Landis beefed up that panel with the additions of founder Stephen Clark and sportswriter Mel Webb and made the group trustees of the institution, with the power not only to elect pre-1900 honorees (under the OTC designation) but to set the rules for the whole selection process, as the Permanent Committee. At their first meeting, they elected museum treasurer Paul S. Kerr as committee secretary. Landis died on November 25, 1944, was the OTC's lone honoree that year, and was followed by a glut of 21 honorees in 1945 and '46. This outsized reaction to the BBWAA's back-to-back shutouts included some players who had been considered by the writers just months earlier, including Tinker-Evers-Chance, Ed Walsh, and Eddie Plank. Amid that group, the OTC threw in dubious choices such as Roger Bresnahan and Hughie Jennings, good-not-great players, to make sure that several decades later, we'd have something to kvetch about. "From that moment on, the argument that the Hall of Fame should be only for the greatest of the great was irretrievably lost," wrote Bill James in *The Politics of Glory*.[3]

As a further reaction to the BBWAA's 1945–46 blankety-blank, the Permanent Committee made two big changes in December 1946, limiting the writers' voting pool to those with 10 years of membership (a requirement that still holds today), and their purview to players who had been active in the past 25 years; the buffer would change to 30 years for 1956–61 elections, 20 years for 1962–2014 elections, and 15 years for elections from 2015 onward. The belief was that the young whippersnappers didn't know enough about old-timey baseball to make informed voting decisions, but the upshot was that modern-day candidacies suddenly had expiration dates. Even with 10 spaces on each ballot, the backlog of qualified candidates was too heavy for the BBWAA to work through efficiently. The decision to add a time limit created a need for a permanent process to sweep up the leftovers.

The OTC/Permanent Committee, whose membership was growing increasingly long in the tooth, voted just once more, by mail, in 1949, electing pitchers Three-Finger Brown and Kid Nichols. In August 1953, as part of the same set of changes that formalized the five-year waiting rule for the BBWAA ballot, the Committee on Baseball Veterans was established, with 11 members, including *Sporting News* publisher J. G. Taylor Spink (chairman), Kerr, Harridge, NL president Warren Giles, NL secretary-treasurer Charles Segar, Pirates general manager Branch Rickey, International League president Frank Shaughnessy, writers Warren Brown, Frank Graham, and John Malaney, and Hall of Fame second baseman Charlie Gehringer. The plan was for the group to vote in odd-numbered years, electing a maximum of two candidates save for in its first meeting in September of that year, where it could elect two players, two managers, and two umpires.

That situation held until 1959, when the committee could agree upon only leftfielder Zach Wheat. Frustrated by the slow pace of honoring the older players, Spink resigned from the VC on July 28, 1959, eight days after Wheat's induction. In his letter of resignation, he expressed dismay over the slow pace of election and stressed a need for a revised system "in order that more of these outstanding players might gain rightful recognition."[4]

Spink's letter cited five nineteenth- and early-twentieth-century candidates he had in mind: Billy Hamilton, Tim Keefe. and Amos Rusie, who were eventually elected, and Bob Caruthers and Jack Coombs, who never were. Two weeks after his letter ran in *The Sporting News*, the publication mounted a campaign for reform, with a front-page article focusing on Sam Rice, Eppa Rixey, and Edd Roush ("The Three Rs of Shrine Campaign"), all active from the 1910s to the '30s and still alive at the time. Heavyweights such as Ty Cobb, Joe Cronin, Frank Baker, and Rogers Hornsby weighed in on their behalf, with Cobb and Hornsby both referring to "lost generations" of players whose firsthand eyewitnesses were dwindling in number. Writer Joe King pointed to the VC's two-pick limit as a serious bottleneck, "an injustice working to the detriment of men who may be deemed qualified by electors."[5] He noted that while Hall officials understandably didn't want to cheapen selections, the risk of waiting until after these potential honorees passed away was increasing, and cited Cobb's vigorous campaign on behalf of former teammate Harry Heilmann, who died of cancer in 1951 and was elected by the BBWAA the following year.

In July 1960, after a Hall of Fame weekend that featured zero inductions—with just one in the past three years—and a mere four returning Hall of Famers, the Permanent Committee shifted the VC to an annual schedule, enlarging the committee from 11 members to 12 (thereby returning the threshold for election to 75%; with 11, it had effectively been 81.8%), naming Brown as the new chairman, and adding Cronin and writers Dan Daniel and Roy Stockton to the committee to replace departed members. The Permanent Committee would loosen the restrictions to allow for more than two picks after the 1961 election.

In the July 6, 1960, issue of *The Sporting News* trumpeting these changes, the venerable Fred Lieb, who had been covering baseball since 1911, sketched out short bios of 12 overlooked old-timers as potential honorees, including Spink's aforementioned quintet plus Max Carey, John Clarkson, Pud Galvin, Addie Joss, Joe Kelley, Harry Stovey, and umpire Billy Evans. The issue's editorial took the Hall to task for not naming Lieb to the committee, calling it "a real boner and we hope it will be corrected."[6] It was, eventually; Lieb served on the VC from 1966–80.

By this time, Hall of Fame historian Lee Allen, who had joined the institution in 1959, had emerged as a key figure in VC elections. Allen, who had begun building the Hall's library into a first-class research facility that made a flood of great baseball books possible, supplied the committee with stats and relevant information on nineteenth-century candidates such as Hamilton (elected in 1961), Clarkson ('63), Keefe ('64), Ward ('64), and Galvin ('65). James termed that group "the Lee Allen picks," though Spink and Lieb had chimed in on behalf of most of those players previously. Still, Allen played a key role, extolling the accomplishments and fleshing out the backstories of many of these players in his "Cooperstown Corner" column in *The Sporting News* from 1962 to until his May 1969 death from a heart attack.

The Allen picks were hardly the VC's only ones in this span. From 1961–66, they elected 16 men, including the aforementioned "three Rs" as well as three managers. They did this in uneven fashion, electing four in 1963, six in 1964, and then just Galvin the following year, a result that led to the decision to shift the BBWAA voting back to annually. Most of the VC's choices during that span weren't unreasonable. Those in the stretch from 1967–76, however, represent the nadir of the entire process.

Hall of Fame second baseman Frankie Frisch joined the VC in 1967. A graduate of Fordham, where he had majored in chemistry, Frisch wasn't just the rare college boy from his day, he was a particularly outspoken and respected figure within the game. "*Opinionated*, like *volatile*, is too weak a term for his firmly held, and loudly articulated, opinions on anything and everything," wrote Leonard Koppett. "And behind it all was a quick and well-educated mind."[7]

Several writers who had covered Frisch's career in New York (1919–26) and St. Louis (1927–38, the last year solely as a manager) were already on the committee. Two from his days in New York, Lieb and Daniel (on the VC 1961–76), were, in James's words, "highly susceptible to Frisch's arguments about the greatness of that team."[8] Lieb and the St. Louis–based Stockton (a VC member from 1961–71) had both written books about the Cardinals of that era. Cronin and Gehringer were the only other players on the committee at the time besides Frisch. The Fordham Flash "very quickly became the dominant personality on the committee. Frisch thought modern players paled in comparison with the studs he had played with and against,"[9] wrote Zev Chafets.

From 1967–71, the Frisch-dominated group elected 13 players, plus three nonplayers (Rickey in '67, Frick in '70, and George Weiss in '71). Via a one-year relaxation of the rules—to encourage the committee "to reach back into the stone-age years of baseball for four selections"[10]—they were allowed to choose six players in 1971, the year that Frisch's Giants teammate Bill Terry and '69 honoree Waite Hoyt joined the committee. Frisch left after 1972, and died of injuries sustained in a car accident the following year, while Hoyt and Terry stuck around through '76 as the committee added the maximum of two more players and one nonplayer per year.

It would be tough to understate the damage done to the Hall by this wave of 23 players, or at least the 18 twentieth-century players from within that group. It was far worse than the 1945–46 group that represented the institution's initial fall from grace. Apart from the caliber of the honorees in terms of performance—which I'll get to below—was the unmistakable whiff of cronyism, likely accompanied by vote trading. Four of Frisch's former teammates were elected during his tenure: short-stop Dave Bancroft (1971) and rightfielder Ross Youngs ('72) from the Giants, and pitcher Jesse Haines ('70) and leftfielder Chick Hafey ('71) from the Cardinals. He had managed a fifth, centerfielder Lloyd Waner ('67) in 1940–41 with the Pirates. Terry, whose career ran from 1923–36 with the Giants, and Hoyt, whose career spanned 1918–38 with the Yankees, Pirates, and five other teams, each had four teammates from among this group elected, with some crossover between the two.

Charges of cronyism specific to this cluster surfaced in 1973, in the wake of the election of former Giants first baseman George "High Pockets" Kelly, a team-mate of Terry and Frisch, the latter no longer on the committee and not long for the world. A 1973 column by Bob Burnes in *The Sporting News*, titled "Does Vet Panel Vote Pals into Shrine?" wrote of Kelly, "At best his qualifications are mar-ginal. Without question, he was a popular figure on a convivial team, well liked by teammates, opponents and the media. The thought has to be there that crony-ism had to exist among some members of the committee who knew him, played with him or against him or wrote stories of his day. This does not add to the stat-ure of the Hall of Fame, which wants only the very best."[11] In 1975, Jack Brum-mell called the Hall "a House of Cronies. Objective standards certainly can't be a guide when players like [1971 choice Harry] Hooper (who played with Babe Ruth but battered [*sic*] a lifetime .281 with 75 career homers) are enshrined."[12] Hooper had been a teammate of Hoyt's in Boston.

"The Veterans Committee should put in a turnstile. It has become a Hall of Cronyism," quipped Jim Murray in 1977. "Sometimes, the problem is, it's not pos-sible to gauge the relative excellence of a player until a generation after his retire-ment. Based strictly on numbers, [1976 choice Fred] Lindstrom's lifetime average (.311) or Kelly's (.297) would seem impressive alongside the .270s that today's can-didates post. But, for the era in which they played, Lindstrom's and Kelly's marks would put them somewhere in the bottom third of the league. The Veterans' Com-mittee must have just wanted a fourth for bridge."[13]

A January 22, 1977, editorial by *Sporting News* editor-publisher C. C. Johnson Spink (son of J. G. Taylor Spink, who had died in '62) wrote about the growing rift between the BBWAA and the VC over the latter's choices, quoting BBWAA secretary-treasurer Jack Lang as noting that Kelly and Lindstrom had both fared poorly in the writers' vote during their eligibility. Updating Lang's math to jibe with Hall records, Kelly received just 14 votes from 1947–62, never reaching 2%, while Lindstrom received 22 votes from 1949–b62, with a high of 4.4%. Spink also noted the high concentration of recent honorees from the 1920s and '30s; indeed, the careers of all 18 of the twentieth-century players honored in this period overlapping with those of Frisch, Terry, and Hoyt. He wrote, "Some critics have charged that the committee has been governed in its selections by sentimentality, nostalgia and 'cronyism.' The 'youthful' period of most committee members covers the years from 1920 to 1935. That now is the most heavily represented period in the Hall of Fame. About 40 players in the shrine (out of 121) were active during all or part of that time."[14]

"The Veterans Committee has always been prone to favoritism," wrote James in 1995. "It has, from 1953 on, often selected Player A while Player B, who had credentials just as good, was asked to wait outside—and when you look at the makeup of the committee, you can almost always see bloodlines which help to explain the decision."[15] In perhaps his harshest words for the proceedings, he added, "Selecting eight marginally qualified or frankly unqualified Hall of Famers from the same narrow well of talent, clearly defined by its proximity to members of the committee, is favoritism of the ripest, rottenest and most obvious nature."[16]

The "bloodlines" of which James wrote aren't hard to spot. Moving past the 1967–76 period to incorporate the 1953–2001 span of the VC's run, here's a revised version of a table originally done by James Vail for *The Road to Cooperstown: A Critical History of Baseball's Hall of Fame Selection Process*.[17] It shows VC members whose former teammates (or employees, in the case of executives and managers) were elected while they were on the committee:

Committee Member	VC Tenure	Former Teammates Elected (Year)
Branch Rickey	1953–1965	Bobby Wallace (1953)
Charlie Gehringer	1953–1990	Heinie Manush (1964), Goose Goslin (1968)
Joe Cronin	1961–1984	Manush (1964), Goslin (1968)
Frankie Frisch	1967–1972	Lloyd Waner (1967), Jesse Haines (1970), Dave Bancroft (1971), Chick Hafey (1971), Ross Youngs (1972)
Bill Terry	1971–1976	Bancroft (1971), Youngs (1972), George Kelly (1973), Fred Lindstrom (1976)
Waite Hoyt	1971–1976	Harry Hooper (1971), Lefty Gomez (1972), Kelly (1973), Lindstrom (1976)
Stan Musial	1973–2001	Johnny Mize (1981), Enos Slaughter (1985), Red Schoendienst (1989)
Burleigh Grimes	1977–1985	Travis Jackson (1982), Arky Vaughan (1985)

(continued)

Committee Member	VC Tenure	Former Teammates Elected (Year)
Roy Campanella	1978–1993	Pee Wee Reese (1984), Vaughan (1985)
Al Lopez	1978–1994	Hack Wilson (1979), Vaughan (1985)
Buzzie Bavasi	1978–1998	Reese (1984)
Birdie Tebbetts	1979–1994	George Kell (1983), Bobby Doerr (1986), Hal Newhouser (1992)
Joe L. Brown	1979–2001	Bill Mazeroski (2001)
Ted Williams	1986–2001	Doerr (1986)
Yogi Berra	1994–2001	Phil Rizzuto (1994)
Bill White	1994–2001	Jim Bunning (1996), Orlando Cepeda (1999)
Juan Marichal	1998–2001	Cepeda (1999)

Not every committee member is represented here. Hank Aaron and Billy Herman had no teammates elected during their tenures, and the same is true for exec Gabe Paul. I haven't included the numerous writers or the handful of broadcasters, either. Admittedly, considering only teammates of honorees in this context is a narrow definition of cronyism, when the truth is that such relationships may have extended beyond shared uniforms. Reese was on the committee that elected his crosstown rival Rizzuto, for example, and had spoken up publicly on behalf of his candidacy.

Correlation doesn't prove causation, but the Frisch/Terry/Hoyt trio stands out for its connections to nine of the 26 players identified as having links to a sitting committee member; four honorees are connected to two trio members. Only two other VC members were connected to more than two elected players, and both served much longer tenures on the committee than the trio in question.

These connections could be brushed aside as coincidence if the players in question were actually worthy of enshrinement, but that was rarely the case. Of the 23 players elected by the VC from 1967–76, 21 are below the JAWS standard at their position, with only first baseman Roger Connor (elected in '76) and left-fielder Goose Goslin ('68) measuring up, though starting pitchers Mickey Welch ('73) and Stan Coveleski ('69) come close. Connor, Welch, Jake Beckley and Joe Kelley (both 1971), and Sam Thompson ('74) all spent the bulk or entirety of their careers in the nineteenth century, playing shorter schedules; all but Thompson are within at least 10 points of the JAWS standard and even including him, they're only an average of 6.0 points off the pace at their respective positions. They're not really the problem.

Among the rest of the players elected during that stretch, five rank *dead last* among the Hall of Famers at their positions according to JAWS, namely Hafey (24.7 points below the standard), the by-now-familiar Lindstrom (27.4 points below), Kelly (29.6 points below), Haines (34.8 points below), and Waner (35.0 points below). For good measure, in this span the VC also elected the Hall's second-lowest-ranking first baseman—another former Frisch teammate, but elected in 1974—Jim Bottomley (25.4 points below), its second-lowest-ranking rightfielder, Youngs (26.8 points below), and both its second- and third-lowest-ranking pitchers, Rube Marquard (31.6 points below) and Lefty Gomez (25.1 points below). Beyond cheapening the honor, every awful choice risks becoming the justification for future awful choices. "He's better than Lindstrom" was no doubt an argument advanced by some committee member on behalf of George Kell, and while true from a JAWS standpoint, the same could be said about dozens of other third basemen outside the Hall.

Beyond those nine bottom-dwelling enshrinees, another seven twentieth-century players added in this period are now at between 11.9 and 18.8 points below their position standards, including Hoyt (18.5 points below). The best of that group in terms of relative rankings is Billy Herman (13th of 20 second basemen, 11.9 points below), who at least has a good excuse, having missed two seasons due to World War II military service.

The players whose careers overlapped with Frisch played in an era when offense was king. Seventeen of the 22 highest-scoring seasons from the 1901–93 period came during Frisch's career, all with at least 4.73 runs per team per game. Even with just 16 major league teams at the time, 18 of the 19 seasons that featured the most batting-title-qualified .300 hitters took place during Frisch's playing days. In those 19 seasons, an average of 21 players per year reached that plateau, roughly one in every six regulars. Without any means of putting their performances into context, the ones that reached the committee as candidates carried the superficial sheen of all-time greats, but Hafey, Youngs, Lindstrom, Coombs, and Kelly had among the shortest careers of any twentieth-century Hall of Famers to go with their inflated batting averages.

Amid this mess, the BBWAA and VC clashed both publicly and privately because the writers resented "what they termed election of their 'rejects' by the older group," wrote Lang in 1973. "The writers sought some method whereby they would not be embarrassed by these veterans' votes."[18] A sitdown between the two sides brokered by Kerr, by that point the Hall of Fame president, resulted in the VC being limited to players who had been retired at least 25 years—in other words, with another five-year waiting period inserted between consideration by the two voting bodies—with lip service paid to considering the level of support a player received during his time on the writers' ballot.

When that didn't take (as noted regarding Lindstrom), a 1977 compromise between the two voting bodies was hammered out: Players retired in 1946 or later had to have received at least 100 votes in one or more BBWAA election to be considered by the VC; those who retired prior had no such restriction. That rule created a bad look by effectively barring players who had returned from World

War II military service to play in the majors but failed to garner much support from the writers, among them current Hall of Famers Doerr, Joe Gordon, Ernie Lombardi, and Arky Vaughan, far stronger candidates than the Frisch/Terry/Hoyt dregs. The rule was adjusted in 1984 such that players whose careers *began* prior to 1946 weren't subject to the 100-vote threshold. Vaughan was elected in 1985, Doerr and Lombardi in 1986.

Not content to leave well enough alone, in 1991, the Hall board changed the 100-vote threshold rule to a 60% threshold for those whose careers began in '46 or later, a much steeper requirement given the growth of the voting body. A hundred votes in 1968, the year that Richie Ashburn (who played from '48–62) became eligible, represented 35.3% of the vote; during his run on the writers' ballot, Ashburn maxed out at 41.7%, with 158 votes in '78. After falling two votes shy of VC election in 1990—with two supporters, Stan Musial and Roy Campanella, absent and unable to vote due to illness—he was suddenly ineligible with this change. That rule was overturned in 1993 thanks to the grassroots efforts of fan Jim Donahue, who was allowed to collect some 200,000 signatures for a petition at Veterans Stadium, and Ashburn, a pretty good candidate as these things go (today eighth among enshrined centerfielders in JAWS, 4.0 points below the standard) was elected in '95.

Even without Frisch, Terry, or Hoyt, the VC continued to mix in dubious choices after 1976. Travis Jackson and the aforementioned Wilson, two more Frisch-era Giants (though the latter's star turn came as a Cub), were elected in 1982 and '83, respectively; the former is the Hall's second-lowest-ranked shortstop according to JAWS, the latter is the third-lowest-ranked centerfielder. Kell, the Hall's third-lowest-ranked third baseman, was also elected in 1983, while Rick Ferrell, its lowest-ranked catcher and a player who received a grand total of three votes in the 1956–60 elections, was added in '84.

The one that brought the system crashing to a halt was the election of light-hitting glove man Bill Mazeroski (the Hall's lowest-ranked second baseman according to JAWS) in 2001, via a committee chaired by Joe L. Brown, the Pirates general manager from 1955–76, which encompassed the entirety of Mazeroski's career. Ted Williams, absent due to open-heart surgery, was reportedly among the Hall of Famers displeased with the selection, as he had long opposed the Pittsburgh second-sacker's candidacy; the previous year, Mazeroski had missed by one vote. The selection stirred resentment among the Hall of Famers:

"At the Hall of Fame dinner (Sunday) night, one of the great players said, 'It's becoming too easy to get into the Hall of Fame,'" said [Joe] Morgan, vice chairman of the hall's board of directors. "This came from the players."

. . . Mazeroski's name was not mentioned Monday by Morgan or other

Hall officials, but some Hall of Famers—including Ted Williams—were unhappy the fielding whiz was elected this year by the former Veterans Committee headed by Joe L. Brown.[19]

Right after Mazeroski's induction, the Hall announced the expansion of the VC to include all of the living Hall of Famers, the Spink and Frick Award winners, and VC members whose terms had not yet expired. As noted in Chapter 4, the expanded group—which voted by mail rather than meeting in person—failed to elect anyone in 2003, '05, '07, or '09, with the only selections in this span coming via small-panel groups. In 2008, a 16-member panel elected three executives while a 12-man panel tabbed two managers, and in '09 a 12-man panel for pre-1943 players elected Gordon.

That led to the 2010 announcement of the split into the era-based committees, the Pre-Integration (1871–1946), Golden (1947–72), and Expansion (1973–onward), voting on a triennial basis starting with the Expansion Era one for 2011. Even including the long-overdue election of Santo for 2012, one year after his death, the results were far from satisfactory, with Deacon White, who collected the first base hit in National Association history in 1871, the only other player honored. Coupled with the BBWAA's shutout that year, the slate of White, Yankees owner Jacob Ruppert, and umpire Hank O'Day made for a lively induction day: All three honorees had been dead for at least 75 years.

The 2011 Expansion Era panel drew a complete blank, while the '14 one froze out all players while electing managers Bobby Cox, Tony La Russa, and Joe Torre. In the 2015 Golden Era panel vote, Dick Allen and Tony Oliva fell one vote shy of election, while Minnie Minoso fell three votes shy; he died two months later, well past his 90th birthday. Much more than the 2013 slate, the '16 Pre-Integration ballot drew pointed criticism for highlighting baseball's segregated era, particularly as Major League Baseball itself came under fire for a lack of diversity among managers and general managers. No candidates of color were included within the slate, not even 2006 Special Committee on Negro Leagues near-miss Buck O'Neill.

Citing the 2006 panel, Hall president Jeff Idelson offered a less-than-satisfactory explanation: "At that time, we indicated that the books were closed on the Negro Leagues pending more information that came forth from the research community. That's something that we addressed 10 years ago, so it's not unusual that they're not part of this slate."[20]

As we've seen, the Hall has a long history of tinkering with its voting processes when it's perceived that either too many or too few candidates are gaining entry, albeit with the law of unintended consequences often throwing a wrench into the works. After three straight years of electing no players and two years of electing nobody at all, the 2016 retooling produced the Early Baseball (1871–1949), Golden

Days (1950–69), Modern Baseball (1970–87), and Today's Game (1988 on) Era Committees and laid out a 10-year cycle that emphasized the more recent two groups from eras less well represented among the enshrined (see Chapter 7).

2017: Today's Game
2018: Modern Baseball
2019: Today's Game
2020: Modern Baseball
2021: Golden Days and Early Baseball
2022: Today's Game
2023: Modern Baseball
2024: Today's Game
2025: Modern Baseball
2026: Golden Days

The boundary years for the various eras raised questions as to which eras the likes of Allen or Jack Morris, with the bulk of value in one period but signature accomplishments in another, belonged; three committees with cutoffs at the 1961 and 1977 expansion junctures might have sufficed, though the skewing toward more modern eras is welcome.

Yet another of the process's imperfections was underscored with the 2017 ballot, which consisted of five players and five executives. The committees' long streak of not electing a living former player continued, as only longtime general manager John Schuerholz and former commissioner Bud Selig were tabbed; Selig's anointment may have paved the way for the eventual election of Barry Bonds and Roger Clemens (see Chapter 8). Aside from Mark McGwire, the player side of the slate was weak, because such candidates' windows of BBWAA eligibility needed to have lapsed before moving on to this process, meaning that Kenny Lofton (one-and-done in 2013) and Larry Walker (going nowhere with the writers since 2011) are years away from eligibility. Of the candidates besides McGwire, only Will Clark was within 10 points of the JAWS standard.

With eight nonplayers and two deceased players the only ones elected by the small-committee processes since the 2011 cycle, and 15 nonplayers and three deceased players all that they've produced since Mazeroski's election in 2001, it seems apparent that the deck is stacked against any player who slips through the cracks of the BBWAA process—and that will continue. Separating the nonplayers, many of them 65 or older and due for immediate recognition, from the players would be more sensible if the Hall actually wanted to give Minoso, Allen, et al. a legitimate shot. We shall see if the institution grasps that before this 10-year cycle is complete.

All told, who are the best VC selections? Excluding the committees before 1953, here's a top 10 based on JAWS points above the standard:

Player	Pos	Year	JAWS	+/–
John Clarkson	SP	1963	79.5	17.3
Tim Keefe	SP	1964	76.6	14.4
Roger Connor	1B	1976	65.6	11.4
George Davis	SS	1998	64.6	9.8
Ron Santo	3B	2012	62.2	7.2
Arky Vaughan	SS	1985	61.8	7.1
Amos Rusie	SP	1977	68.0	5.9
Pud Galvin	SP	1965	67.9	5.8
Johnny Mize	1B	1981	59.8	5.7
Goose Goslin	LF	1968	54.7	1.4

That's a list heavy on nineteenth-century pitchers, all from the Spink/Lieb/Allen names. Via their incredible workloads from a time before the pitching distance was 60′6″, they threaten to break JAWS, which is one reason not to take these rankings too literally. While I wouldn't kick any of these players out, I'd argue that third baseman Home Run Baker (elected 1955, –0.3 points relative to the standard), rightfielder Sam Crawford ('57, –0.7), shortstop Pee Wee Reese ('84, –1.2 in a career missing his age-24–26 seasons due to military service), and centerfielder Larry Doby ('98, –13.4 but constrained by the color line) are all more historically important, and go with second baseman Joe Gordon (2008, –5.4 with ages 29–30 lost to the war) over Goslin, on the strength of a higher peak.

As for the worst selections, you've seen them already: Little Poison Waner, followed by Haines, Marquard, Kelly, Lindsrom, Youngs, Mazeroski, Gomez, Hafey, Kell, and Bottomley, because like Nigel Tufnel's amplifier, this one goes to 11.

CHAPTER 6

BLYLEVEN, MORRIS, AND THE WAR ON *WAR*

In 1998, Bert Blyleven first became eligible for election to the Hall of Fame. Despite impressive totals of wins (287) and strikeouts (3,701, third all-time at that point) from a 22-year career that began in 1970, he was initially greeted with indifference by most BBWAA voters, netting just 17.5% in his first year, less than a quarter of the support he'd need for election.

Two years later, Jack Morris became eligible for the first time. Despite his own hefty win total (254) compiled over 18 seasons (1977–1994), and the still fresh memory of one of the greatest World Series pitching performances, his 10 shut-out innings in the Twins' 1–0 win over the Braves in Game 7 of the 1991 World Series, he received an underwhelming 22.2%.

Over the next decade and a half, without throwing a single additional pitch, the two pitchers—or rather their Hall candidacies—came to symbolize one front of a culture war within the game, and to redefine Hall of Fame debates in the twenty-first century. The candidacy of Blyleven, who spent much of his career toiling for mediocre teams, benefited from sabermetric research and a grassroots campaign in which a new generation of baseball media, many of them independent bloggers, reached out to, and often clashed with, older voters. He was finally elected in 2011, the 14th year of his 15-year eligibility window.

The candidacy of Morris, who spent most of his career on good teams, was initially slowed by sabermetric research (including JAWS) that showed that he wasn't quite up to snuff relative to the enshrined pitchers, and revealed that many claims regarding his prowess, such as his ability to "pitch to the score," were considerably overstated. But as the years passed, he benefited from a backlash against the same forces that helped elevate Blyleven, with an emphasis on old-school grit and things that (supposedly) couldn't be measured by statistics. Morris's old-media supporters lashed out at the statistically savvy critics of his candidacy, "the vigilante sabermetric brigade"[1] as the New York *Daily News*'s Bill Madden called them in 2012.

Despite receiving 66.7% in 2012, his 13th year of eligibility, Morris couldn't get over the top via the writers' ballot. He gained just one point the next year, then got lost in the shuffle as the ballot became flooded with more prominent and controversial candidates. Here's the year-by-year breakdown of both pitchers' shares of the vote:

Year	Blyleven	Morris
1998	17.5%	
1999	14.1%	
2000	17.4%	22.2%
2001	23.5%	19.6%
2002	26.3%	20.6%
2003	29.2%	22.8%
2004	35.4%	26.3%
2005	40.9%	33.3%
2006	53.3%	41.2%
2007	47.7%	37.1%
2008	61.9%	42.9%
2009	62.7%	44.0%
2010	74.2%	52.3%
2011	79.7%	53.5%
2012		66.7%
2013		67.7%
2014		61.5%

BBWAA voters were particularly low on imagination when the two pitchers reached the ballot. The writers had been spoiled by a cohort of acclaimed hurlers who reached the majors in the 1960s, held up under the strain of now unthinkable workloads in the '70s, and pitched well into the '80s. As the job of the starting pitcher evolved over the years, that group's statistics and accomplishments cast an increasingly long shadow across subsequent candidacies.

That Seventies Group	Years	W-L	IP	SO	ERA	HOF
Steve Carlton	1965–1988	329-244	5218	4136	3.22	1994
Nolan Ryan	1966–1993	324-292	5386	5714	3.19	1999
Don Sutton	1966–1988	324-256	5282	3574	3.26	1998
Phil Niekro	1964–1987	318-274	5404	3342	3.35	1997
Gaylord Perry	1962–1983	314-265	5350	3534	3.11	1991
Tom Seaver	1967–1986	311-205	4783	3640	2.86	1992
Fergie Jenkins	1965–1983	284-226	4501	3192	3.34	1991
Jim Palmer	1965–1984	268-152	3948	2212	2.86	1990
Catfish Hunter	1965–1979	224-166	3449	2012	3.26	1987
Average inductee		**300-231**	**4813**	**3484**	**3.16**	

The Overshadowed	Years	W-L	IP	SO	ERA	HOF
Bert Blyleven	1970–1992	287-250	4970	3701	3.31	2011
Jack Morris	1977–1994	254-186	3824	2478	3.90	
Jim Kaat	1959–1983	283-237	4530	2461	3.45	
Tommy John	1963–1989	288-214	4710	2245	3.34	

To say that those nine pitchers constituted an exceptionally skilled and durable bunch would be an understatement, for it's one of the greatest concentrations of talent in major league history. That Seventies Group (as I christened them in *Extra Innings*) accumulated 14 Cy Young awards, tossed 12 no-hitters, made 11 All-Star starts, and appeared in 16 of 18 World Series from 1966–83. The *average* pitcher from that bunch spent 21 years in the majors and won 300 games.

Within a span of 13 election cycles (1987–99), the BBWAA elected those nine starters, equaling the total honored in 26 cycles from 1956–86. It was against that backdrop that Blyleven and Morris became eligible, and their candidacies had to vie for attention with two other pitchers with vaguely similar statistical footprints as well. Lefty Jim Kaat lasted 25 years in the majors, and was the ace of the Twins staff on which a 19-year-old Blyleven broke in back in 1970. He debuted with 19.5% in 1989, and while he never topped 30%, he lingered in the mid-20s for most of his 15-year ballot run. Fellow lefty Tommy John pitched for 26 years in the majors, not including the season he missed for an unprecedented elbow ligament repair surgery that now bears his name. While he had never won a Cy Young or a World Series, he had enjoyed a five-year peak during which he won 20 games three times, finished second in the Cy voting twice, and pitched for three pennant winners. He debuted with 21.3% on the 1995 ballot, and while he wouldn't top 30% until his final year of eligibility, he, too, would linger in the high 20s, ahead of Blyleven and Morris, who both deserve closer looks.

Born in Zeist, Holland, on April 6, 1951, Rik Aalbert Blyleven and his family emigrated to Saskatchewan when he was two, and then to California when he was six. At Santiago High School in Garden Grove, California, he learned a curveball, which would become his signature pitch. Jesse Flores, a legendary scout who signed or drafted over 70 major leaguers, discovered him while scouting another pitcher, and on June 5, 1969, the Twins chose the 6'3", 180-pound righty with the 55th overall pick in the amateur draft. At 18, he made a strong showing during that winter's Florida Instructional League, throwing curveballs "with the same precision as the Curvemaster pitching machine."[2]

A year to the day after being drafted, Byleven made his major league debut. Gushed manager Bill Rigney, "He's the best looking prospect I've seen. I've got to rate him with all the real young players I've ever looked at. He's just beautiful."[3] Relying on a live fastball and the power curve that drew comparisons to Sandy Koufax and former Twins star Camilo Pascual, he went 10-9 with a 3.18 ERA and 135 strikeouts in 164 innings as the 98-win Twins cruised to the AL West flag.

The young Blyleven emerged as a workhorse, averaging 283 innings per year from 1971–77, more than anyone but Perry, Carlton, and Palmer. Excellent innings, too: He racked the AL's top five four times in ERA, with a 2.76 mark for the stretch; his 133 ERA+ trailed only Seaver (142) and Palmer (138). He ranked second, third, or fourth in strikeouts in the first six of those years, and trailed only the record-setting Ryan and Seaver in both strikeout total and rate. Unlike Ryan, he wasn't wild; twice he led the league in strikeout-to-walk ratio.

Alas, his elite performance was camouflaged by middling won-loss records: 16-15, 17-17 (twice), 20-17, 15-10, 13–16, 14-12. Instead of garnering accolades, he made the All-Star team only in 1973, the lone year in that span when he received Cy Young votes; he finished seventh despite 20 wins and AL bests in shut-outs (nine) and ERA+ (156). Despite a lineup that included future Hall of Famers Rod Carew and Harmon Killebrew, the Twins eked out just 3.8 runs per game from 1971–76 when he pitched, compared to a league average of 4.2. While he was getting screwed by baseball's traditional accounting, we now know he ranked as the AL's most valuable pitcher from 1971–77, with 47.6 Wins Above Replacement, including an AL-high 9.9 in 1973 and a second-ranked 7.9 in '74.

A contract clash with tight-fisted Twins owner Calvin Griffith led to a June 1, 1976, trade to the Rangers and a three-year, $500,000 deal. In Texas Blyleven found a mentor in Gaylord Perry, who noticed a mechanical flaw: "He was open-ing up with his body too quickly."[4] Blyleven added a sinker to his repertoire, which so baffled opponents that they accused him of loading up the ball, à la Gaylord.

A groin injury limited Blyleven to 30 starts in 1977, but he returned from a 16-day absence on September 22 to no-hit the Angels in Anaheim. With one year plus an option remaining on his deal, he signed a six-year extension estimated at $200,000 per year—but no no-trade clause. He was soon dealt to the Pirates in a four-team, 11-player deal.

In Pittsburgh Blyleven pitched well but clashed with manager Chuck Tanner over his workload, feeling that he should be pitching every fourth day and working deeper into games. After completing 11 out of 34 starts in 1978, he went the dis-tance just four times in 37 starts in 1979, and finished with a single-season-record 20 no-decisions while going 12-5. "I was always looking over my shoulder waiting for the manager to come get me. He never let me finish,"[5] complained Blyleven. Nonetheless, the Pirates won the NL East, aided by an excellent, deep bullpen.

Pitching in the postseason for the first time since 1970, Blyleven closed out the NL Championship Series with an eight-hit, one-run complete game against the Reds. He worked six solid innings in Game 2 of the World Series against the Orioles, which the Pirates won via a ninth-inning rally, then relieved on two days' rest in Game 5. The Pirates trailed three games to one in the series, and 1–0 in the fifth inning, when Tanner pinch-hit for starter Jim Rooker and gave the ball to Blyleven with the season on the line. He threw four scoreless innings while his teammates kept their championship hopes alive by scoring seven runs. He wasn't needed again, as the Bucs became just the fourth team in World Series history to rally from a three-games-to-one deficit. For the postseason, Blyleven finished with a 1.42 ERA in a staff-high 19 innings.

Continuing to object to Tanner's quick hooks, Blyleven bolted the team in late April 1980, citing "the non-support and lack of confidence from my manager,"[6] and demanding a trade. Though he returned 10 days later, his 8-13 record, 3.82 ERA, and 97 ERA+ made for his worst season to that point. In December the Bucs sent him to the Indians in a six-player trade. Stellar in the strike-shortened 1981 season, with a 2.88 ERA and a league-leading 5.6 WAR, he was limited to four starts in '82 due to elbow surgery, and 24 in '83 due to shoulder tendinitis. He rebounded in 1984, going 19-7 with a 2.87 ERA (third in the league, good for a 144 ERA+), 170 strikeouts (fourth), and 7.2 WAR (fourth) for a 75-win team, placing third in the AL Cy Young balloting.

On August 1, 1985, Blyleven was sent back to Minnesota in a five-player deal. Despite a typically bland 17-16 record, he made his second All-Star team and again placed third in the Cy Young vote after leading the league in innings (293⅔), strikeouts (206), starts (37), complete games (24), and shutouts (five), and placing third in WAR (6.7) and fifth in ERA (3.16). On August 1, 1986, he became the 10th pitcher to reach the 3,000 strikeout milestone. Though he served up 46 homers in 1987 (down from a record 50 the year before), he helped the 85-win Twins win the AL West and then upset the 98-win Tigers in the ALCS. In Game 2, he squared off against Morris, who allowed six runs in eight innings; Blyleven yielded three in 7⅓ as Minnesota took a two-games-to-none lead in the best-of-seven series. Morris didn't get the call for Game 5; Blyleven worked six innings and departed with a 4–3 lead; the Twins sealed their first pennant since 1965. Facing the 95-win Cardinals in the World Series, his seven strong innings in a Game 2 victory pushed the Twins to a two-games-to-none series lead; though he lost Game 5 as the Cardinals went up three games to two, the Twins claimed their first championship by winning the final two games in Minnesota. In his four October turns, the 36-year-old righty went 3-1 with a 3.42 ERA in 26⅓ innings.

After a dreadful, injury-wracked 1988, Blyleven was rejuvenated by a homecoming trade to the Angels. At 38, he went 17-5 with an AL-best five shutouts, a 2.73 ERA (fourth in the league) and 6.0 WAR (third). Shoulder woes in 1990 led to 1991 rotator cuff surgery. Hoping he could milk another 21 wins out of his arm to reach 300, he returned in 1992 at age 41, but after going 8-12 with a 4.74 ERA, he retired upon being cut at the end of camp the following spring.

Blyleven's lost 1982 and '91 seasons cost him membership in the 300-win club, and while he was generally snubbed with regards to All-Star and Cy Young recognition, his résumé was still a full one. Within his leagues, he had 13 top five finishes in strikeouts and strikeout-to-walk ratio, nine in both WAR and shutouts, seven in ERA, and six in innings; he led those categories a total of 11 times. In addition to ranking fifth in career strikeouts, he's ninth in shutouts (60), 11th in WAR (96.5) and starts (685), and 14th in innings (4,970). In the postseason, he pitched to a 2.47 postseason ERA in 47⅓ innings.

Born on May 19, 1955, in St. Paul, Minnesota, Jack Morris grew up watching the Twins. In addition to ski jumping (!) and basketball, he played primarily third base and shortstop, but Brigham Young University recruited him as a pitcher, offering him a scholarship where powerhouses such as Arizona and Florida State would not. At BYU, former major league hurler Vernon Law helped Morris convert to the mound.

The Tigers drafted Morris in the fifth round in 1976, part of a banner draft by general manager Jim Campbell and scouting director Bill Lajoie that also yielded shortstop Alan Trammell in the second round and rotation-mate Dan Petry in the fourth. Fast-tracked, he made just 29 minor league starts before debuting with the Tigers on July 26, 1977. In September, Trammell, Lou Whitaker, and Lance Parrish all made their debuts; that quartet became a fixture by the following season, and would hold together through 1986.

After spending much of 1978 in the bullpen and beginning the '79 season in the minors, Morris returned for good by mid-May and went 17-7 with a 3.28 ERA (fifth in the league, good for a 133 ERA+) and 5.8 WAR—the last a mark he never topped. That began a 12-season run as a Tigers starter during which he averaged 33 starts, 13 complete games, 241 innings, 5.9 strikeouts per nine, a 3.71 ERA (109 ERA+) . . . and just 3.1 WAR. He reached 20 wins in 1983, and topped that with 21 in '86, while he dipped below 30 starts only in '79, '81 (the strike season), and '89, when he spent two months on the disabled list.

Morris made four All-Star teams in Detroit, and topped 250 innings six times. Fueled by a split-fingered fastball learned from pitching coach Roger Craig, he led the league in both innings (293⅔) and strikeouts (232) in '83—both for the only time—and finished third in the AL Cy Young voting. Even so, his 4.0 WAR that year didn't crack the league's top 10.

Morris no-hit the White Sox on April 7, 1984, the signature moment in Detroit's 35-5 start en route to a world championship. Through the end of May he was 10-1 with a 1.88 ERA, but he slumped to finish 19-11 with a 3.60 ERA (109 ERA+), drawing criticism from the media about his level of intensity as the Tigers ran away with the AL East. He went 3-0 with a 1.80 ERA in three postseason starts as the Tigers steamrolled the Royals in the ALCS and the Padres in the World Series.

Morris tried to test free agency after a top-notch 1986 season (21-8, 3.27 ERA, and a league-best six shutouts), but baseball's collusion scandal cooled interest. Instead of the three-year contract he sought, he returned to Detroit on a one-year, $1.85 million deal. With another strong season in 1987 (18-11, 3.38 ERA, 126 ERA+, 5.1 WAR), he helped the Tigers win the AL East, but was rocked by Blyleven's Twins in the ALCS. That winter he signed a two-year, $4 million deal with the Tigers, making him the game's highest-paid pitcher.

Though he averaged 218 innings during his final three years in Detroit (1988–90), Morris's 4.40 ERA (89 ERA+) wasn't pretty. When the collusion grievances were settled, the 35-year-old was allowed to declare free agency. Spurning the Tigers' three-year, $9.3 million offer, he signed a one-year deal with the Twins worth $3.7 million with player options and additional incentives. He rebounded to go 18-12 with a 3.43 ERA (125 ERA+) and 4.1 WAR, earning his fifth and final All-Star appearance.

Knocked out after just 5⅓ innings against the Blue Jays in the 1991 ALCS opener, Morris threw eight strong innings in Game 4, and the Twins prevailed in five. They won the World Series opener against the Braves behind his seven innings of two-run ball, but lost Game 4, in which Morris, working on three days' rest, was pulled after six innings of one-run ball. He started Game 7 on three days' rest as well, and put forth a performance that some consider the greatest in postseason history: a 10-inning shutout in which he scattered seven hits and two walks while striking out eight. No starter since Tom Seaver in 1969 had pitched into extra innings in a World Series game, and none had ever done so in a deciding Game 7. Only one other pitcher had thrown a 1–0 shutout in Game 7, Ralph Terry for the 1962 Yankees, but his was "just" nine innings. Morris's game was truly one for the ages.

Despite the championship and the hometown-boy-makes-good narrative, Morris opted out and signed a two-year $10.85 million deal with the Blue Jays. Though his 4.04 ERA translated to just a 101 ERA+, an AL-high 5.6 runs per game of support tilted his record to 21-6. The Blue Jays won the AL East, the ALCS, and the World Series, but Morris couldn't duplicate his postseason magic; chased before completing five innings in two of his four starts, he managed just 23 innings with 15 walks and a 7.43 ERA. That was the beginning of the end. Dreadful in 1993 (6.19 ERA), he missed the postseason due to a strained elbow ligament, and was lit for a 5.60 ERA with Cleveland in strike-shortened 1994. A 1996 comeback attempt—10 starts for his hometown St. Paul Saints in the independent

Northern League—ended when he declined a deal with the Yankees, who wanted him to make two Triple-A starts instead of one.

Morris finished with 254 wins, ranking in the league's top five eight times in that category, in starts, and in complete games. By comparison, he had four top five finishes in shutouts, three in strikeouts, and just two in ERA and WAR. He made five All-Star teams and received Cy Young votes in seven seasons, but never placed higher than third. Even with his 10-inning shutout, his overall postseason ERA was an unremarkable 3.80 in 92⅓ innings, with a 7-4 record.

In the early years of the new millennium, the view of That Seventies Group—the nine Hall of Famers from the 1960s to '80s—plus Kaat, John, Morris, and Blyleven began to change, increasingly cast in the light of sabermetrics. Though the Bill James *Baseball Abstract* annuals and John Thorn and Pete Palmer's *The Hidden Game of Baseball* had already introduced many to the field, further interest was stoked by the Internet, which offered far more flavors of baseball-related news and analysis than had ever been available before. Those looking beyond traditional media coverage now had access to the daily work of ESPN's Rob Neyer, a former research assistant to James, as well as the *Big Bad Baseball Annual* and *Baseball Prospectus*, two books that arose out of the rec.sport.baseball newsgroup. They also had the baseball blogosphere, an informal network of Web sites largely written by hobbyists wanting to connect with those who shared similar interests, from gripes about the home nine to explorations of the Hall of Fame voting and other deep statistical dives, though not all blogs were of a sabermetric bent. The most popular were aggregated at a site called Baseball Primer (later Baseball Think Factory), as was more mainstream baseball content.

Baseball Primer cofounder Sean Forman also founded the Baseball-Reference.com Web site, which came online in February 2000 and offered comprehensive year-by-year statistics for every player and team, as well as leaderboards and more. Among the stats the site popularized was one from Thorn and Palmer's *Total Baseball* encyclopedia called ERA+, which adjusts for the vast historical and environmental differences in scoring throughout baseball history, normalizing each pitcher's ERA to a scale where 100 equals league average, with 120 translating to 20% better than the league and 80 to 20% worse. In that light, pitchers like Phil Niekro (3.35 ERA, 115 ERA+) and Blyleven (3.31 ERA, 118 ERA+) look superior to Don Sutton (3.26 ERA, 108 ERA+) and Hunter (3.26 ERA, 104 ERA+), the latter of whom bears a strong resemblance to Morris (3.90 ERA, 105 ERA+).

In 2001, *The New Bill James Historical Baseball Abstract* introduced a value metric called Win Shares that not only incorporated the type of adjustments built into ERA+ but also the extent to which a pitcher relied upon his defense. Building upon a distinction he made in the 1985 edition of his *Historical Baseball Abstract* between career value and peak value, James created top 100 rankings at each position using not only total Win Shares but also a player's best three seasons at large, his best run of five consecutive seasons, and a prorated per-season measure. James ranked Blyleven 39th on his pitchers list while lumping Morris in among his unranked "second 100" with a jumble of good non–Hall of Famers such as Chuck Finley, Jerry Koosman, Frank Tanana, and Allie Reynolds.

Win Shares didn't click with the statheads, given a methodology that was difficult to understand (a year later, he delivered a highly technical 700-page tome devoted to it), and some very odd choices, such as each Win Share representing one-third of a win, or a 52-48 split for pitching and defense versus offense. Even so, the notion of comprehensive metrics to estimate a player's contribution on offense, defense, and/or pitching resonated. In late 2002, Baseball Prospectus's Clay Davenport introduced Wins Above Replacement Player (WARP), which estimated each player's total value above that of a theoretical "replacement player," a freely available minor league call-up.

In 2003, sabermetrics was thrust into the spotlight via *Moneyball*, Michael Lewis's bestselling profile of the Oakland A's and their general manager, Billy Beane. As a small-market team that lacked the financial resources of the powerhouse Yankees or the division rival Angels, Beane and his protégés incorporated cutting-edge statistical analysis into their process, discarding a good deal of the received wisdom that passed for baseball knowledge along the way. Those A's won 296 games from 2000–02, making the playoffs in all three seasons despite shoestring budgets.

Lewis's book transcended baseball and particularly resonated with Fortune 500 companies and Wall Street firms, given its portrayal of the A's emphasis on remaining ahead of the curve in exploiting market inefficiencies. Within the game, however, it was both widely misunderstood and extremely polarizing—particularly for the way that Lewis's streamlined narrative portrayed the A's rejection of and contempt for the value of traditional scouting and, by extension, the grizzled, underpaid lifers who beat the bushes in search of raw talent. "Stats versus scouts" became the shorthand for a culture war that hinged upon a false dichotomy pitting the use of objective data and quantification against the subjective expertise of "baseball men" who believed in what their eyes told them, and that immeasurable intangibles played critical parts in individual and team success. As Baseball Prospectus's Dayn Perry wrote, scouts-or-stats was no more an either-or choice than beer or tacos. The proper answer? "Both, you fool."[7]

In his epilogue (first published in *Sports Illustrated* and then included in the paperback edition), Lewis characterized the conflict *Moneyball* created within the baseball industry as a religious war, "or like the endless, fruitless dispute between creationists and evolutionary theorists. On the one side, parrying half-baked questions and insults, was the community of baseball fans who thought hard about the use and abuse of baseball statistics. On the other side, hurling the half-baked questions and insult were the Club members, who felt a deep, inchoate desire to preserve their status."[8] For Lewis, the Club "includes not only the people who manage the team but also, in a kind of Women's Auxiliary, many of the writers and the commentators who follow it and purport to explain it."[9]

While Beane and *Moneyball* received a great deal of heat, elsewhere an even more successful union of sabermetrics and baseball management was unfolding. In November 2002, mere months before the book's publication, Red Sox owner John Henry (who had bought the team a year earlier) hired Bill James as an advisor, and nearly poached Beane from the A's before appointing 28-year-old assistant general manager Theo Epstein to the GM job. By augmenting the application of similar principles with considerably more cash than the A's could muster ("*Moneyball* with money"), the Sox won the World Series in 2004, their first in 86 years, and again in '07 and '13, with James still on board. By that point, nearly every front office had integrated quantitative analysis into its decision making, with small-market teams such as the Tampa Bay Rays and Pittsburgh Pirates using it to turn their fortunes around—and *Moneyball* had been made into a successful movie starring Brad Pitt as Beane.

As sabermetrics found footing in front offices, it also entered into debates over the BBWAA's annual MVP and Cy Young awards. The 2009 AL Cy Young award, which went to Zack Greinke (16-8, 2.16 ERA, 9.5K/9) over Felix Hernandez (19-5, 2.49 ERA, 8.2 K/9) in a landslide, "might have been a watershed moment in baseball's statistical revolution,"[10] wrote the *New York Times*'s Tyler Kepner, for the way that win totals were overlooked in favor of run prevention and, in particular, Fielding Independent Pitching (FIP), an ERA estimate based on strikeout, walk, and home run rates. The next year, it was Hernandez (14-12, 2.27 ERA, 3.04 FIP) beating out David Price (19-6, 2.72 ERA, 3.42 FIP).

The incorporation of sabermetrics into awards discussions hit a speed bump in 2012, when Miguel Cabrera won the Triple Crown via a .330 batting average, 44 home runs, and 139 RBI. Via subpar defense at third base, he totaled 7.2 WAR, very respectable but well below the 10.8 of 20-year-old rookie sensation Mike Trout, who in addition to hitting .326 with 30 homers stole a league-high 49 bases and played outstanding centerfield (+21 runs). No player had won a Triple Crown since 1967, but no rookie position player had ever posted a 10-WAR season. That the old-school numbers won out, with Cabrera receiving 22 out of 28 first-place votes, was less surprising than the schoolyard-level anger vented by his supporters.

"In a battle of computer analysis versus people who still watch baseball as, you know, a *sport*, what we saw with our Detroit vision was what most voters saw as well," gloated Mitch Albom of the *Detroit Free Press,* celebrating Cabrera's award as "a win for fans, defeat for stats geeks," before taking time to parade his ignorance of WAR ("Honestly, who comes up with this stuff?") and deride "nerds" who "want to reduce [baseball] to binary code."[11]

"In basements across America, Mike Trout groupies are crying in their mother's meat loaf,"[12] tweeted the *Washington Times*'s Thom Loverro, echoing a deathless stereotype proffered by high-profile media members—Bob Costas, Tony Kornheiser, Rick Reilly, and Dan Shaughnessy, to pull a few names from a 2009 Deadspin inventory[13]—to denigrate anyone sharing an opinion from outside the mainstream, generally depicted as a blogger in his underwear. By that point, namecalling had become an all-too-familiar feature within the Hall of Fame debates.

As *Moneyball* was making waves, JAWS was born. Built on BP's WARP, which used a lower replacement level than current formulations of WAR, and first deployed for the 2004 ballot (albeit without the catchy, self-conscious acronym), it was an opening salvo in the use of all-encompassing advanced metrics to sketch out the Hall of Fame standards at each position. Its most startling finding—at least to its inventor—was that Blyleven was well above the bar set by the average enshrined starting pitcher, while Morris was significantly below it.

That conclusion remained the same even as JAWS evolved, first from a definition of peak that used a player's best five consecutive seasons (with allowances for injuries and military service) to his best seven at large, and then from a measure whose currency was WARP to one using Baseball-Reference's version of WAR (introduced in 2010). In 2012, after I left Baseball Prospectus for *Sports Illustrated*, Forman agreed to add a WAR-based JAWS to every player page on Baseball-Reference, building position-by-position sortable leaderboards and giving the metric far more reach.

In its current conception, Blyleven's 95.3 career WAR ranks 13th among all starting pitchers, a hefty 21.4 wins above the average Hall of Famer. Of the enshrined pitchers from That Seventies Group, only Seaver (110.5) and Niekro (96.6) are above him—a radical conclusion, given the short shrift Blyleven received with respect to awards. His peak score of 50.7 isn't as robust, ranking 38th, 0.4 WAR above the standard but behind Seaver, Niekro, Carlton, Perry, and Jenkins. Overall, Blyleven's 73.0 JAWS ranks 16th, again behind only Seaver and Niekro. That's a no-doubt Hall of Famer, not a borderline one, particularly when augmented by Blyleven's postseason contributions and his exceptional strikeout and shutout rankings.

As for Morris, he was not tremendously adept at preventing runs relative to his league; his 105 ERA+ is tied for 110th all-time among pitchers with at least 3,000 innings (Blyleven's 118 is tied for 40th). Nor did he strike out batters at a particularly impressive clip, save for a brief stretch in his career (1983–88, when he was in the top 10 five times); his total of 2,478 is 34th all-time, but his rate of 5.8 per nine is 18th among the 35 pitchers who accumulated 3,000 innings from 1961–2000. That means that a relatively larger share of the credit for his workload belongs to his fielders, in particularly the BBWAA-slighted double play combo of Trammell and Whitaker.

Morris's 44.1 career WAR is nearly 30 wins (!) below the standard (73.9), ranking 148th all-time, ahead of just three enshrined starters (Addie Joss, Hunter, Jack Chesbro, and Lefty Gomez), and a few hairs behind non-Hall types such as Vida Blue, Steve Rogers, and Milt Pappas. His 32.8 peak WAR ranks 185th, ahead of only one Hall of Famer, Rube Marquard; it's behind Fernando Valenzuela, Dan Haren, Dennis Martinez, and Jamie Moyer. His 38.4 JAWS ranks 163rd, ahead of only Hunter and Gomez—two out of 62 enshrined starters. That's not a good Hall of Fame choice, at least from a sabermetric point of view. Here's how the two pitchers stack up relative to That Seventies Group by JAWS:

Pitcher	HOFM	Career	Peak	JAWS	JAWS Rk
Tom Seaver	244	110.5	59.6	85.0	6
Phil Niekro	157	96.6	54.6	75.6	15
Bert Blyleven	121	95.4	50.7	73.0	16
Steve Carlton	266	90.4	54.4	72.4	17
Gaylord Perry	177	91.0	52.8	71.9	20
Fergie Jenkins	132	84.9	51.8	68.4	24
Nolan Ryan	257	81.9	43.3	62.6	31
AVG HOF SP		**73.9**	**50.3**	**62.1**	
Jim Palmer	193	69.4	48.0	58.7	37
Don Sutton	149	67.3	34.0	50.7	69
Catfish Hunter	134	41.4	35.2	38.3	165
Tommy John	112	62.0	34.7	48.4	82
Jim Kaat	130	51.4	38.4	44.9	105
Jack Morris	122	44.1	32.8	38.4	163

HOFM is the Bill James Hall of Fame Monitor, which gives credit for awards, league leads, postseason performance, and other things that largely go uncaptured via WAR; Morris and Blyleven both rank near the bottom of the group, albeit for different reasons.

Unlike Blyleven, Morris's case for Cooperstown rests not on a sabermetric reckoning but with an appeal to traditional stats and particularly his win total, which is tied for 43rd all-time. Morris reached 20 wins three times, won at least 18 six times, and compiled more wins in the 1980s (162) than any other pitcher; Dave

Stieb (140) ranks second. The exaltation of Morris's win total owes much to a more recent era in which five-man rotations, concern about pitch counts, and the systematic use of specialized bullpens have turned 20-win seasons and 250-win careers into endangered species. Since Morris's final season in 1994, just seven other pitchers have reached 250 wins, and four have matched his total of three 20-win seasons. The same forces have led to the near-disappearance of the complete game and the 250-inning season. Since Morris retired, pitchers have combined for just 24 250-inning seasons; since 2003, there have been just five, one fewer than Morris in his career. The durable, W-collecting Morris became a symbol for a bygone era.

Of course, even Morris completed just 33% of his starts, and like any other pitcher he needed support from his offense, defense, and bullpens to secure those wins. On the offensive side, we can express a pitcher's run support in normalized form just as we can ERA+, with 100 representing the park-adjusted league average; call it SUP+. Morris's 106 SUP+ is higher than any of That Seventies Group save for Hunter (112) and Palmer (108); Niekro, Perry, Ryan, and Seaver were all below 100, as was Blyleven (96). Via Bill James's Pythagorean Theorem, each extra percentage point difference in run support translates roughly to a .005 gain in winning percentage, or an extra win for every 200 decisions. All else being equal, Morris's 6% advantage (6.4%, before rounding) would translate to a record of 234-206 over the course of his total of 440 decisions, assuming average run prevention ability. Via ERA+, we know he was roughly 5% better than average on that front as well, which would push his expected record to 244-196. In that light, his actual 254-186 record isn't particularly remarkable.

As for defensive support, Morris's career .272 batting average on balls in play was 14 points better than the league average during his career, thanks in large part to Trammell and Whitaker. That .272 mark ranks 31st among the 309 pitchers with at least 1,000 innings during the span of Morris's career, not as good as Stieb (.263, ninth) but better than Blyleven (.285, tied for 118th) and Clemens (.289, tied for 167th). As for bullpen support, the relievers who followed Morris coughed up the leads he relinquished 30 times, far fewer than the relievers behind Sutton (48), Blyleven (47), Niekro (47), or Ryan (45); among That Seventies Group, only Hunter (27), Jenkins (26), and Palmer (23) were victimized fewer times by their bullpens.

Morris's supporters tended to dismiss his high ERA with claims that he "pitched to the score"—that he allowed fewer runs in close games than in games in which he was granted a large lead. Baseball Prospectus's Greg Spira and Joe Sheehan took their swings at examining such claims in 1997 and 2003, respectively. Wrote Spira, who based his analysis on Morris's annual won-loss records and run support, "Jack's records are clearly the result of how many runs are scored when he pitches and how many runs he allows. Thus, his ERA (or RA), along with his innings pitched, are a perfectly accurate measure of how valuable Jack has been to his teams."[14] In other words, that high ERA isn't camouflaging anything.

Wrote Sheehan, who pored over Morris's career inning by inning via Retrosheet and found that he put his team *behind* in 344 of his 527 career starts, either by allowing the game's first run or surrendering a lead, concluded: "I can find no pattern in when Jack Morris allowed runs. If he pitched to the score—and I don't doubt that he changed his approach—the practice didn't show up in his performance record."[15] In 2013, Joe Posnanski, echoing Sheehan, found that while Morris had a better-than-expected record when his teams scored four or more runs, he went 32-87 with a 4.08 ERA when his teams scored one, two, or three runs, and a 4.33 ERA when they went scoreless: "Pitch to the score? No. Not unless the score was high."[16]

While WARP and JAWS gained traction with Baseball Prospectus's readership, a subscription pay wall limited the site's reach. More influential in the early 2000s was Lee Sinins's *Sabermetric Baseball Encyclopedia*, a CD-ROM alternative to Baseball-Reference that found its way into the columns of ESPN's Peter Gammons and Jayson Stark, and the blog entries of a moonlighting investment manager in Long Beach, California, named Rich Lederer.

The son of a former Dodgers beat writer for the *Long Beach Press-Telegram*, Lederer became the most influential proponent of Blyleven's candidacy via his popular *Baseball Analysts* blog. He used the *Encyclopedia*'s ability to create tables in virtually every traditional and advanced statistical category of the time to illustrate the strength of Blyleven's case. He pointed out that Blyleven was the only eligible pitcher with at least 3,000 strikeouts or 50 shutouts outside the Hall, and likewise, the only eligible outsider in the top 20 in the *Encyclopedia* metrics of runs saved above average and ERA relative to league.

Closer in age to the average voter than most of the statheads advancing Blyleven's cause, Lederer wasn't shy about taking his case directly to voters. He published interviews with and/or guest columns from voters such as Bob Klapisch of the *Bergen Record*, Jeff Peek of the *Traverse City* (Michigan) *Record-Eagle*, Posnanski of the *Kansas City Star,* and Tracy Ringolsby—a past BBWAA president and future Spink Award winner—of the *Rocky Mountain News*. Of that quartet, only Posnanski voted for Blyleven at the first opportunity, but the others were gradually won over to Blyleven's side, not just by the data offered by Lederer and others but by their own investigations and reflections.

As Klapisch wrote in a December 2005 piece for *Baseball Analysts,* a flyer from a professional-looking Web site called BertBelongs.com inspired him toward further examination, talking to Mariano Rivera and Goose Gossage as well as reviewing the numbers. "Finally, it dawned on me: Blyleven was a Hall of Famer not just because of his 3701 strikeouts or 287 wins or a 2.47 ERA in the post-season. It was the uniqueness of his best weapon, the curveball, that set him apart. All the great ones manage to put a singular mark on the game."[17]

"Between the information you provided and the constant conversations I have had with Blyleven's contemporaries, I became convinced that I had slighted him in the past," wrote Ringolsby in a December 2006 e-mail to Lederer. "He is the first guy I can remember that I have ever failed to vote for on the first time and then added later."[18]

The public acknowledgments of being swayed by outside sources, from high-profile scribes such as those mentioned above, are why Blyleven's candidacy and eventual election represents a turning point in the Hall process. Once upon a time, a veteran scribe could intuit who was Cooperstown material. As Dick Young told Klapisch, "Choosing a Hall of Famer is like voting for president. You'll just know who the right guy is."[19]

Wrote Leonard Koppett in *The Sporting News* in 1981, "I don't think any home-work, in the sense of research, deep thought or extensive analysis is needed. If you don't know who belongs in the Hall of Fame (in your own opinion) by the time you get to vote, you're a hopeless case, and further study will produce only greater confusion."[20]

Though they both won Spink Awards, Young and Koppett represented oppo-site poles of the baseball coverage spectrum. The self-educated Young was a pioneer of working the clubhouse, known for his street-level reportage, while Koppett was a Columbia University graduate renowned for his analytical approach; columnist Jimmy Cannon once asked him if his attaché case was "full of decimal points."[21] Neither of those old-school writers wanted anybody's help in filling out a ballot, and while the likes of Ringolsby and Klapisch may not have relished it, either, they proved more adaptable. They weren't necessarily convinced by a single source or statistic; it was their openness to reevaluating their own positions and incorporating new information, whether or not that information arrived via the expected route.

With the testimonials of converts such as these under his belt, Blyleven shot to 61.9% in 2008. Two years later, he received 74.2%, missing election by just five votes. At that point, Lederer's partial list of converts included Jim Caple, Bill Conlin, Jerry Crasnick, Gammons, Klapisch, Peek, Ringolsby, Ken Rosenthal, and T. R. Sullivan.[22] Of course, the actual number was far greater; Blyleven's sup-port increased by 380 votes over the life of his candidacy, which ended in 2011, when he was elected with 79.2%.

Not every voter climbed upon the Blyleven bandwagon, and some proved par-ticularly resistant to the influx of new information and the campaigning. In Jan-uary 2009, *Sports Illustrated*'s Jon Heyman said on MLB Network, "I never thought [Blyleven] was a Hall of Famer when he was playing, and I saw him play his entire career. . . . [His popularity] is based on a lot of younger people on the Internet who never saw him play."[23] This was—and remains—an all-too-common tack from many insiders in this context, attempting to discredit those advancing the argument, particularly outsiders, rather than the argument itself.

In a December 2010 column for *Sports Illustrated*'s Web site titled "Why I Didn't Cast a Hall of Fame Vote for Bert Blyleven, Again," Heyman spent nearly 2,000 words detailing his reasoning, referring again to won-loss records, the lack of All-Star appearances and awards, the minimal number of league leads. After supplying a solid laundry list of the counterarguments against the pitcher's candidacy—not just traditional stats but even Bill James's MVP shares—Heyman steered the argument into the subjective realm: "If you put Blyleven's lifetime numbers through a computer, the computer would probably determine that he . . . is a Hall of Famer. But the game is about human beings, not just numbers. It's about impact. The Hall of Fame is about fame, and Blyleven's greatest fame came not while he was pitching well for five teams over 22 seasons but instead through his extended candidacy and the controversy surrounding it after he had retired."[24]

"Impact" and "fame" aren't quantifiable, they're attempts to shift the focus from the stat-based arguments that the Blyleven detractors were by that point losing. Still, Heyman's jabs were less venomous than those of Murray Chass. In 2007, while still at the *New York Times*, he railed against "Statistics mongers promoting VORP and other new-age baseball statistics,"[25] referring to Baseball Prospectus's Value Over Replacement Player (a precursor to WARP). "To me, VORP epitomized the new-age nonsense. For the longest time, I had no idea what VORP meant and didn't care enough to go to any great lengths to find out,"[26] wrote Chass, suddenly unable to summon the reporting skills via which he won a Spink Award.

Leaving the *Times* in 2008, Chass grew more bellicose via his own blog, where in addition to launching unfiltered, unsubstantiated attacks on everything from Mike Piazza's Hall candidacy due to alleged steroid use (a long-standing obsession of his) to Stan Musial's alleged racism (based upon thirdhand anecdotes), he took aim at anyone who criticized his Hall of Fame votes with an appeal to authority. By Chass's logic, his vote for any candidate was justified merely by his status as a voter, therefore immune to criticism from nonvoters. To him, the critics of Morris's candidacy were "stat zealots [who] don't have a formula for intestinal fortitude or determination,"[27] while the election of Blyleven was the result of using "new-age statistics to persuade ignorant voters to vote for a candidate."[28] Alas, nobody ever calculated how many hundreds of converts to Blyleven's candidacy took umbrage at that statement.

Chass was hardly the only high-profile writer reduced to name-calling over the voting. For Bill Madden, critics of Morris's candidacy were "the vigilante sabermetric brigade"; for Dan Shaughnessy, they were "sun-starved stat geeks."[29] Even from award-winning writers, such responses—accompanied by no shortage of anti-sabermetric swipes in other contexts—evinced insecurity and fear of irrelevance in front of a younger generation of baseball fans.

Despite the vigilantism and zeal of the statistically minded, over time Morris's vote total climbed in a manner not dissimilar to that of Blyleven. Comparing their levels of support after seven years on the ballot, Morris actually received a larger share of the vote, 41.2% to 35.4%. But Blyleven pulled ahead late, topping 50% in his ninth year and 60% in his 11th year, while Morris lagged two years behind in reaching both thresholds.

Blyleven's near-miss in 2010 and return to the ballot the following year was presumed to have dealt a significant blow to Morris's candidacy, as he gained just 1.2% from 2010 to '11. Closer study shows that gain exceeded Morris's increases from 2008 to '09 (1.1%) or from 2012–13 (1.0%). The Hall of Fame Ballot Tracker (bbhoftracker.com), which in those days recorded only between 17–30% of the ballots (compared to 70.8% in 2017), offers only limited clues. Of the 31 voters who published ballots that included Blyleven but not Morris in 2011 and then published their ballots again in 2012, only six used the freed space to support Morris. Two of the 36 published voters who included both pitchers in 2011 dropped Morris in 2012, neither with an explanation.

One of the more detailed explanations of a voter withdrawing his support from Morris came from the *Dallas Morning News*'s Tim Cowlishaw, who hadn't supported Blyleven in 2011 but apparently had in the past. Of Morris he wrote, "I think the image of the man and what we remember is a bit different from the career numbers. . . . Morris seldom had the lowest ERA in his own rotation and was over 3.50 11 times in his 18-year career. . . . Facts, not memories. That should be the priority in determining how we vote, and the facts say Morris comes up just short."[30]

Indeed. Morris came up short, and while some of that had to do with voters such as Cowlishaw reevaluating their perceptions and/or taking into account the same types of information that swayed them to vote in favor of Blyleven, the matter isn't closed. He'll likely become a candidate on the 2018 Modern Baseball Era Committee ballot—a successor to the Veterans Committee—for those whose greatest contribution came during the 1970–87 period. There, BBWAA writers will occupy just four seats on a 16-person committee alongside four current executives and eight Hall of Fame players and/or managers, a group likely more sympathetic to arguments centered around the old-school metrics like wins, winning percentage, complete games, and Opening Day starts.

That committee's predecessor, the Expansion Era Committee (1973 onward), never elected anyone as a player, and at this writing, none of the era-based committees has elected a living player. When that streak finally breaks, Morris could be the candidate in light of his previous support. Just five players have fallen off the BBWAA ballot after receiving at least 60% of the vote at some point. Three were elected by the VC:

Player	Final Year BBWAA	%	Elected by VC
Nellie Fox	1985	74.7%	1997
Orlando Cepeda	1994	73.5%	1999
Jim Bunning	1991	63.7%	1996
Gil Hodges	1983	63.4%	
Jack Morris	2014	61.5%	

If and when Morris gets in, it will be another example of a small committee electing a subpar candidate, though hardly the worst. Those committees' processes are opaque, with ballots never seeing the light of day and voters far less accountable than the writers. They're more likely to share Morris's disdain for sabermetrics— "Ninety percent of the general managers are in it. That's why the game is messed up,"[31] he told Chass in 2013—than to reexamine his (or anyone's) career in an objective light.

If Morris does get elected via that route, will it mean the battles of the late 2000s were for naught? I don't think so. Subsequent elections have solidified the incorporation of advanced statistics into Hall of Fame debates, with that of Tim Raines—elected in 2017 after a slow, Blyleven-esque climb (see Chapter 14)—a shining example. WAR may not be a staple of every fan's daily diet or every writer's work, but its appearance on broadcasts, on ballpark scoreboards, in daily game coverage and other reporting, and even on the backs of baseball cards, is no longer uncommon. As the BBWAA electorate evolves, with younger voters having greater exposure to Bill James, Baseball Prospectus, FanGraphs, JAWS, and much more, that trend will continue.

Beyond that, there's no real joy in turning away Morris. Many of us who devoted time and energy to arguing against his case grew up watching his no-hitter, Game 7 shutout, and other highlights from his 18-year career. We know he was a very good pitcher for a long time, an intense competitor and a durable workhorse. It takes a hard heart to avoid acknowledging the man's pain in being close enough to taste his inevitable election, yet falling short due to forces unforeseen at the outset of his candidacy. He didn't ask to become a battlefront in a culture war.

Still, relying upon emotion and sentiment to govern the Hall of Fame processes will inevitably water down the honor of induction. We cannot merely wave through our personal favorites, without regard to how they measure up. For the sake of the institution and the players it honors, we're better off with reason pointing the way.

CHAPTER 7

BOOMS, BUSTS, BOTTLENECKS, AND BALLOT REFORM

"The great sportswriter Red Smith once suggested blowing up the Hall of Fame and starting over."[1]

—Zev Chafets

P op quiz, hotshots: How many future Hall of Famers are currently active? Without a crystal ball, we can't know, but the question is worth pondering if we're going to imagine the future of the Hall, the voting processes that stock it, and ways that the system might reasonably be improved in the coming years.

Given the missteps we've seen from the institution over the years, it's easy to lob a verbal grenade about improving the imperfect shrine by destroying it, but tough luck. If they didn't dynamite it at the suggestion of one of the press box's all-time greats, they ain't doing it for you. Anyway, Smith was all in favor of inducting Fred Lindstrom and Hack Wilson, didn't believe the Veterans Committee was guided by cronyism, and suggested they be allowed to elect more than two men a year. "Failing that, let's throw out everybody except the original five and start over,"[2] he wrote in 1980, making no reference to explosives. You could look it up.

So let's get back to that question, which becomes a bit easier to consider if we think about players in three groups: late-career stars who have clinched a berth or are nearly there; mid-career guys who appear to be on pace; and young superstars who have taken little time to begin beating a path to Cooperstown. As I write this in early 2017, a logical list might include Carlos Beltran, Adrian Beltre, David Ortiz, Albert Pujols, and Ichiro Suzuki—but not Alex Rodriguez, thanks to that PED suspension—from the first group; Miguel Cabrera, Robinson Cano, Zack Greinke, Felix Hernandez, Clayton Kershaw, Joe Mauer, and Buster Posey from the second; and Mike Trout, Bryce Harper, and Manny Machado from the third. You can quibble with some of those, but that's 15 who come to mind easily, and while a few might wind up falling short, a couple dark horses could enter the picture via unusual staying power or late-career renaissances. Maybe Beltran, Posey, and Greinke will fizzle, but Carlos Correa, Dustin Pedroia, and Justin Verlander will pick up the slack.

Fifteen feels about right when we consider the common refrain from Hall chairwoman Jane Forbes Clark and president Jeff Idelson in recent years, recognizing the bottlenecks in the process and the desire to limit the game's highest honor to the truly elite. Said Clark, after nobody from the 2015 Golden Era panel was elected, "Only one percent of the 18,000 players who have played in the Major Leagues [are] in the Hall of Fame."[3]

Thirty teams times 25 roster spots is 750, which would mean only seven or eight Hall of Famers active at a time. But once you include players shuttling between the minors, the majors, and the disabled list, the actual number making at least one appearance in 2016 was 1,353, with an average of 1,322 for the 2012–16 period. One percent of that, 13, is within spitting distance of our initial ballpark estimate.

Hold on to your hats: If the history of the Hall of Fame is any kind of guide, that estimate isn't even halfway there. Using the Hall's own definition of activity, where a single appearance is enough to count as a season, for a span of more than a century, from 1885 to 1993, the average number of Hall of Famers per team per year exceeds 1.0—occasionally doubling or even tripling that rate. Even 1.0 per team would equate to 30 future Hall of Famers currently active, so we've undercounted by half.

Again using that definition of activity, this graph illustrates the number of Hall of Famers per team going back to 1871—major league players only, the ones for whom we have JAWS:

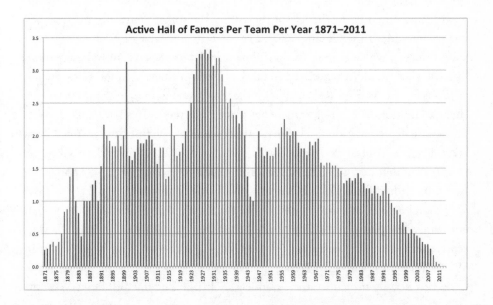

There's much to digest here, but let's continue with our current exercise by starting on the right, where the level tails off pretty considerably over the last 25 years, and falls below 0.5 after 2002. The books on that era aren't closed yet, because the BBWAA voters are still working through the ballot's backlog: The 2017 ballot featured one player active as far back as 1979 (Tim Raines), and 17 active in 1993, the last year that the level was at 1.0. Ten of those 17 are above the JAWS standards at their position. Not all of them will be elected by the writers, with the twice-suspended Manny Ramirez one likely to fall short, but on the other hand, Trevor Hoffman, who's below the reliever standard, is a lock, having reached 74.0% in 2017. We haven't counted sure bets from among upcoming candidates like Chipper Jones and Jim Thome, who both debuted in 1993 and will become eligible for election in 2018, and after the writers are done, the Today's Game Era Committee or its successor might someday elect Jack Morris, Lee Smith, and/or someone else.

In other words, that 1993 number will rise above 1.0 before it's all said and done—but even then it will be below the historical norm, just about any way you define it. For the 1885–1993 period, it's 1.79 Hall of Famers per team per season, the equivalent of 54 Hall of Famers active in 2016. For the period from 1961–97, covering all but the last wave of expansion and edging into a period that's not yet settled as far as representation is concerned, it's 1.36, the equivalent of 41 Hall of Famers active in 2016.

All of which is to say that the Clark/Idelson One Percent figure is too conservative. It already was, going by the total of 220 Hall of Famers in for their work as major league players, out of 18,910 total major leaguers through the 2016 season (including the bygone leagues—you can't get to 18,000 without counting them).

Turning attention to the left of the graph, the spikes aren't all random; they have a lot to do with small sample sizes. The arrivals and departures of various early stars and even whole leagues could dramatically shift the level of representation. The 1880 season, for instance, kicked off the careers of Roger Connor, Buck Ewing, Tim Keefe, and Mickey Welch, all with the Troy Trojans; in an eight-team league, that's a jump of 0.5 Hall of Famers per team right there. The 1892 spike, which pushed the representation level above 2.0 per team for the first time, resulted from consolidation, as both the American Association (1882–91) and Players League (1890) went defunct, with the NL absorbing the best players. The spike above 3.0 in 1900 resulted from the NL's contraction from 12 teams to eight.

From 1901–21, from the birth of the AL into the early part of the live-ball era, with the coming and going of the Federal League (1914–15) along the way, representation is fairly stable at 1.78 per team—but the next era, look out. From 1923–37, teams featured an average of 3.0 Hall of Famers. This, of course, is the period so heavily mined by the Frankie Frisch/Bill Terry/Waite Hoyt Veterans

Committees, with cronyism running rampant, as explored in Chapter 5. The point that *The Sporting News*'s C. C. Johnson Spink made in 1977 holds true: This is the most heavily represented period in the Hall of Fame.

The 1938–68 span, which includes a temporary drop due to World War II—with roughly 40 player-seasons missed among Hall of Famers, not including partial seasons—is closer to that long-term historical level at 1.87, not much affected by the 1961–62 wave of expansion. The point of inflection comes with the addition of the next four teams in 1969, when the level instantly drops to 1.58 and has yet to rebound. To put it another way, there were 39 Hall of Famers active in 1968, the highest total since 1937, but there has never been another point with that many since. From 1969–93, the long-term average dips to 1.33.

As illustrated above, the level goes even lower after that, leaving a hole in the Hall. If you're a "small Hall" advocate, you might reasonably root for the voters in both processes to be selective enough to limit themselves to the One Percent, but as this book illustrates, that's no guarantee that either the writers or the committees have the clear-eyed focus to choose "the right" One Percent, which is what makes the inequities so maddening. Even if you do think that the One Percent approach is the way to go, it's worth considering how out of whack that is relative to what's come before. Breaking it down by birth decades:

Birth Year	HOF	Players	Pct HOF	10-year	Pct HOF	Qual	Pct HOF
<1900	84	5,279	1.59%	620	13.5%	383	21.9%
1900–09	30	1,075	2.79%	186	16.1%	97	30.9%
1910–19	15	1,230	1.22%	169	8.9%	67	22.4%
1920–29	17	1,014	1.68%	200	8.5%	77	22.1%
1930–39	24	976	2.46%	237	10.1%	93	25.8%
1940–49	17	1,277	1.33%	356	4.8%	161	10.6%
1950–59	17	1,479	1.15%	411	4.1%	149	11.4%
1960–69	14	1,740	0.80%	581	2.4%	170	8.2%
1970–79	2	1,996	0.10%	460	0.4%	154	1.3%
Total	**220**	**16,066**	**1.37%**	**3,220**	**6.8%**	**1351**	**16.3%**
Thru 1939	170	9,574	1.78%	1,412	12.0%	717	23.7%
1940–79	50	6,492	0.77%	1,808	2.8%	634	7.9%
Ratio			2.3		4.4		3.0

The first percentage is the number enshrined out of all major leaguers; note that on a percentage basis, the ratio of those born prior to the 1940s to those born in that decade or later is 2.3 to one, and it's still more than 1.7 to one if you cut out the 1970s kids, as voters have barely grazed the surface of that decade thus far, electing Pedro Martinez and Ivan Rodriguez in 2015 and '17, respectively. Even to get to one percent from Pedro's cohort means finding room for 18 other players who are either already retired or nearing the finish line.

What's worth noting about the One Percent guideline is that such a small fraction of players reach even the minimum requirements for enshrinement, both by the letter of the rules (10 years in the majors, the totals and percentage shown in the fifth and sixth columns from left) and by the practical qualifying thresholds of 5,000 plate appearances or 2,000 innings (the column second from right). This is particularly true since the biggest area of growth among players in recent decades is among middle relievers with no chance at building Hall-worthy careers. Even including nineteenth-century players, the only major leaguers in the Hall who don't meet those plate appearances or innings thresholds are Roy Campanella, Dizzy Dean, and three of the five relievers (Rollie Fingers, Rich Gossage, and Bruce Sutter). The color line cut Campy's career short, while voters decided that Ol' Diz's fame trumped the fact that six of his 12 seasons amounted to fewer than 250 total innings.

The 10-year and playing time thresholds illustrate that as things stand, the gap in representation levels between pre-1940 and post-1940 players is massive, with three or four times as many of the older guys in, even if one counts the '40s and '50s babes as the "new" ones—and after Raines (b. 1959), they're all out of the writers' jurisdiction. For the number of threshold-qualified players from the 1940–79 birth years to match the overall percentage (16.1%), you would have to add 52 more to the 50 currently enshrined.

Barring a radical change in the Era Committee process—where no living player has been elected thus far, and some of the most qualified candidates can't even get space on the ballot—that puts equitable levels of representation on the shoulders of the writers. They've generally lagged behind the pace of expansion, but with the recent ballot crunch (more on which momentarily), the total of 12 candidates elected on the 2014–17 ballots matches the dozen from 1936–39 as the largest four-year parade in Hall history. Here's a look at their work since returning to annual voting in 1966, both the actual rate and one adjusted for the number of major league teams:

Period	BBWAA-Elected	Avg	Adj. Avg
1966–1975	13	1.30	2.44
1976–1985	17	1.70	2.58
1986–1995	16	1.60	1.95
1996–2005	16	1.60	1.85
2006–2017	22	1.83	1.95

For the adjustment factor, I've calculated the number of major league teams in the stretch 15 years prior to either end point, representing the Hall minimum of a 10-year career and a five-year waiting period, then projected it to a 30-team level. (For 1966–75, that means multiplying by 30 divided by the average of 16 teams per year from 1951–60, and so on; for the most recent period, that means capturing the 1991–2002 stretch, which began with 26 teams and ended with 30, so even that figure gets a bump upward—just not as big as the others.)

The picture would look even more dire if not for the recent surge, because from 2006–13, the writers elected just 10 players, fewer than in the four years since. The 2013 ballot was more fully stocked than any since 1946, including first-year candidates Craig Biggio, Barry Bonds, Roger Clemens, Mike Piazza, Curt Schilling, and Sammy Sosa, all with hooks that in a previous era would have made them automatic selections based on hits (Biggio's 3,060), homers (Bonds's 762, Sosa's 609, Piazza's 427, the last the record for a catcher), wins (Clemens's 354), and strikeouts (Schilling's 3,116). No ballot in modern history had ever contained as many players who had reached the levels of 2,000 hits (18), 300, 400, 500, or 600 homers (13, 7, 4, and 2, respectively), JAWS above the position standard (10)—all the candidates that could fit on a 10-slot ballot, a total that didn't even include Biggio, or top 10 centerfielder Kenny Lofton—or a JAWS of at least 50.0, a threshold that demarcates a fairly decent candidate (14). The voters' response to this glut was to elect nobody.

Some voters were understandably overwhelmed by the number of statistically qualified candidates, but others withheld their support from those reportedly connected to performance-enhancing drugs—not only Bonds, Clemens, and Sosa, whose names had surfaced via BALCO, the Mitchell Report, and the *New York Times* via a leaked survey test, respectively (more on this topic in Chapter 8), but even Biggio and Piazza based on rumors and speculation. Even so, the 6.6 names per ballot was the highest rate since 2003.

With that ridiculous logjam still in place, the 2014 ballot added a pair of 300-game winners (Greg Maddux and Tom Glavine) and another 500-homer slugger (Frank Thomas), producing a slate that surpassed even its predecessor in the JAWS categories (14 above the standard, 17 above 50.0), the home run and 250-win levels (the 1994 ballot also featured a trio of 300-win pitchers, causing a backlog that took five years to clear up). Even with voters required to conduct ballot triage, the three marquee newcomers were all elected, and Biggio fell two votes short.

Voters set modern records with 8.39 votes per ballot and 50.4% of ballots using all 10 spots. The previous high for votes per ballot had been 8.36, set in 1983, when Brooks Robinson and Juan Marichal were elected, while the high in 10-slot usage was 23%, from 2013. Voters inched past both marks in 2015 with 8.42 votes per ballot and 51% using all 10 slots, electing Biggio and three more first-ballot no-brainers, namely Martinez, Randy Johnson, and John Smoltz—the writers' first four-man class since 1955. According to BBWAA secretary-treasurer Jack O'Connell, only one other time during his tenure as (dating back to the 1995 election) had 20% of voters used all 10 slots: 1999, when Nolan Ryan, George Brett, and Robin Yount were elected.

Both inside and outside the BBWAA, the 2013 shutout sparked discussion of the voting process and the ways it might be tweaked in order to address the growing backlog of candidates. At the 2013 Winter Meetings, the organization drafted an eight-person committee to study the matter with a focus on the 10-slot ballot limit and present a proposal at the next Winter Meetings, to be forwarded to the Hall of Fame if it were approved. Even then, the Hall would be free to reject or ignore the proposal, as it's their ballgame.

Chaired by outgoing BBWAA president Susan Slusser, the ballot study committee was stocked with members who reflected a broad spectrum of viewpoints, ranging from "the system is fine" to "the system is broken." Six of the committee members had the 10 years of service required to vote and a seventh was a couple years away; the eighth was this scribe, the grunt with the spreadsheets.

The "Rule of 10" has been in place since the outset in 1936, and the Hall is quite attached to it, even with the majors nearly doubling in size since its founding. One of the more provocative ideas to be introduced recently is what Slusser's successor as BBWAA president, Derrick Goold, calls "the binary ballot." "With the 10-player limit, the ballot isn't a vote, it's an exercise in game theory," wrote Goold. "When distilled, the Hall is asking the writers to answer one question: Is this player a Hall of Famer? This is a yes or no question."[4]

As sensible as the binary ballot is, effective removal of the limit on the number of players a voter can support is far too radical for Cooperstown. It was too radical even to gain a consensus within the ballot study committee. Ultimately, our proposal was to expand the number of slots on the ballot to 12, an incremental move that figured to be easier for the Hall to stomach. Approved by the BBWAA membership, the proposal was sent to the Hall in February 2015, by which point some of the wind had been taken out of our sails via the election of seven candidates in 2014–15. Shutouts or a continued trickle of honorees might have spurred the board of directors to action, but instead they never formally responded to the proposal, with no clarification coming until November, when the 2016 ballot preserved the status quo. At that point, Hall spokesman Brad Horn said that the board voted not to change the limit in late July, but that it was inaccurate to term it a "rejection" of the proposal, adding, "This was something that was considered, and there will continue to be active dialog with the BBWAA."[5]

As for other ways in which the process might be tweaked, the 75% rule also is going nowhere. It's been in place since the beginning, and deviated from only in a trio of run-off elections (Charlie Gehringer in 1949, Luke Appling in '64, Red Ruffing in '67), when no candidate reached the magic mark in the first round of voting and then the highest vote getter from a second, more limited ballot, was elected. This one makes sense to reconsider, because excluding 2017 candidates with eligibility remaining, only three players have reached 50% on the BBWAA ballot and then failed to gain election eventually either via the BBWAA or committee: Gil Hodges, Jack Morris, and Lee Smith. The last two have yet to reach committee (Morris will likely get his first try on the 2018 Modern Baseball ballot, with Smith on the 2019 Today's Game one). The point is that once a simple majority of the electorate has spoken in a candidate's favor, all that's left is several rounds' worth of bureaucracy—during which the odds increase that a given candidate won't live to experience the honor.

Changing the Five Percent Rule, by which candidates become ineligible if they don't obtain a minimum threshold on the ballot, would probably have a minimal effect on electing more candidates. In place in one form or another since 1979 (see Chapter 4), it's intended to clear the deadwood from the bottom of the ballot, something that a bit of restraint on the part of the six-man BBWAA screening committee that creates that ballot would also solve. Undeniably the rule has given some candidacies a square kick in the crotch, particularly in their first year of eligibility; you can read about Ron Santo, Bobby Grich, and others elsewhere in this book. In most cases their underperformance owes to the perceptions of those candidacies in the days before advanced metrics, as well as the tendency of old-school writers to withhold votes for all but the elite first-year candidates, perhaps with a few personal grudges thrown in. Overcoming such a slow start would appear to be a long shot given that in the modern era of voting (since 1966), the lowest percentage a BBWAA-elected candidate received from the writers at his debut is 17.0% (Duke Snider), and the lowest one has received at any point is 14.1% (Bert Blyleven, second year). While it's harmed individual candidacies, it's tough to make a case that the Five Percent Rule affects the rate at which candidates are elected. The correlation between ballot size and the number of candidates elected in a given year since 1979 is just .02, basically random.

At first glance, the other major rule change in recent years, the Hall's 2014 decision to truncate ballot eligibility from 15 years to 10, seems more likely to slow down the pace of elections than to accelerate them. When the change was announced, Clark claimed that "The steroid era had nothing to do with the decision,"[6] a statement that was difficult to take seriously given that the only candidacies grandfathered into the rule were on their last legs: 15th-year candidate Don Mattingly, 14th-year candidate Alan Trammell, and 13th-year candidate Smith. The rest, including the aforementioned ones linked to PEDs, suddenly had five fewer years for voters to come around, with Mark McGwire the first pushed off the ballot by the change (after the 2016 election) and Bonds and Clemens cut from 13 years remaining to eight. While one can't blame the Hall for wanting fewer annual debates centering around PED issues, not grandfathering all current candidates into the rule was unfair. Non-PED-linked candidates with considerable ground to make up saw their remaining eligibility more or less cut in half, with slow starters Raines (from seven years left on the ballot to two), Edgar Martinez and Fred McGriff (from 10 years to five), and Larry Walker (from 11 years to 6) hit the hardest.

Said Idelson, "In a study of voting over its history, it's become evident, especially over the last 30 years, that the likelihood of election after 10 years is incredibly minimal."[7] It's true that since Snider was elected in his 11th year in 1980, only Bruce Sutter, Jim Rice, and Blyleven were elected in their last five years of eligibility. Given the low JAWS rankings of Sutter and Rice, that may not have flattered the process, but at least the slow starters could retain hope for a Blylevenesque rally. One insider suggested to me that the Hall may have had an eye on putting a fresher slate of candidates in front of Era Committee voters, but those have proven to be a dead end for players thus far. Through 2017, they haven't elected a living one (see Chapter 5).

Eligibility period changes aside, the recent flow of BBWAA-elected candidates suggests that the basic rules of Hall of Fame voting are unlikely to change significantly for the foreseeable future. What's more likely to have an effect is a change in the electorate, a topic I'll address in Chapter 19, as I look to the future.

CHAPTER 8

THIS IS YOUR BALLOT ON DRUGS

You can't discuss the Baseball Hall of Fame in the twenty-first century—let alone write a book about it—without addressing the topic of performance-enhancing drugs, even if doing so presents a prospect only slightly more fun than being spiked by Ty Cobb.

The full extent to which anabolic steroids, human growth hormone, and stimulants altered the on-field performances not only of hitters but of pitchers will never be known, as it's impossible to create a definitive list of who used what and for how long, and no direct studies were ever designed to determine the ways that such drugs could alter baseball-specific actions. What is inarguable is that PEDs altered perceptions of the game among both fans and media, introducing levels of anger and cynicism that inevitably spilled over into Hall of Fame debates. Voters introduced previously unseen levels of moral judgment into the process, as candidates were evaluated not only on the strength of their accomplishments but their authenticity—whether they did it "the right way."

If you've followed baseball at all for the past two decades, no doubt you have strong opinions on the influx of PEDs into the game, though those opinions could fall anywhere on the spectrum of "Those dirty cheaters ruined baseball! Off with their heads!" to "It's their bodies, what business is it of mine?" The only certainty is that no matter where you fall, a sizable segment of fans and media will disagree with you, just as surely as Chance follows Evers and Tinker.

While many voters and fans would just as soon disqualify anybody who so much as looked at a hypodermic needle from consideration for the Hall, to these eyes such an extreme position is untenable. If baseball had no means to punish PED users for what they were doing—the case up until 2004, when testing began— then Hall of Fame voters should not, either. The lack of deterrence in the form of penalties meant that not only could players take the drugs without consequence (except perhaps to their own health) but that they might feel pressured into taking them to keep up in the pharmaceutical arms race. Who among us hasn't gone 65 or 70 miles per hour on a 55 mph speed limit interstate when that's the prevailing speed of traffic and cops aren't handing out tickets?

PED use didn't just spring up overnight, the result of a few bad actors plotting to gain an advantage on their competition. In fact, the first known attempt of a ballplayer using a testosterone-based performance enhancer dates back to 1889, when Pud Galvin, already the first pitcher to reach 300 wins, openly used "Brown-Séquard Elixir" via subcutaneous injection. Created by Dr. Charles Edouard Brown-Séquard, the concoction, which was supposed to impede the aging process and boost strength and virility, contained an extract from monkey testicles. Galvin's dosing was celebrated by the *Washington Post* ("If there still be doubting Thomases who concede no virtue of the elixir, they are respectfully referred to Galvin's record in yesterday's Boston-Pittsburgh game"[1]), but by then his best days on the mound were behind him, and later views on the elixir ranged from snake oil to placebo. None of this was brought up when the Veterans Committee elected Galvin to the Hall in 1965. Similarly, no objection was raised among the inaugural Hall voters in 1936 over Babe Ruth's alleged self-injection of extract from sheep testicles in '25, the year of Ruth's infamous "Bellyache Heard 'Round the World," an ulcer that required surgery and cost him the first 41 games of the season.

Those isolated incidents underscore the fact that PED use by baseball players evolved over decades within a culture of both competitiveness and permissiveness. Amphetamines had been widely available in clubhouses since the late 1950s (as first detailed by pitcher Jim Brosnan in *The Long Season*, then later amplified by Jim Bouton in *Ball Four*) in the form of "greenies," used to fight fatigue and gain physical and mental edges. Hall of Famers from Willie Mays, Mickey Mantle, and Hank Aaron to Mike Schmidt, Johnny Bench, Willie Stargell, and Frank Thomas have been connected to amphetamines, some by their own accounts, and they were hardly alone. We generally don't wring our hands about their usage—which helped keep players in the lineup and closer to the tops of their games—both because the pills were commonplace, and because there were no real deterrents in place, even after these drugs were regulated via the Controlled Substances Act as of 1970.

What's more, disqualifying PED users from Hall consideration makes little sense because no suspended player has had his statistics disavowed or expunged, and with the exception of three-time test-flunker Jenrry Mejia, none has been banned for life for his offenses. Barry Bonds's 762 home runs stand as the all-time record—they are a *record* of what happened, apart from whatever judgment one attaches to them—and he remains a member of baseball in good standing, allowed to work within the game as a batting coach (the possible collusion that forced him into retirement after the 2007 season is another matter). Nobody who otherwise meets the Hall of Fame's basic requirements (10 years of activity and then retirement for at least five seasons) has been deemed ineligible for consideration due to PED usage.

Nor has the Hall given any special instructions to eliminate such players from consideration, placed scarlet letters next to their names on the ballot or shunned the artifacts associated with their achievements. "If Bonds is breaking home run records, we have the responsibility to record it,"[2] said then-Hall president Dale Petroskey in 2007, as the slugger closed in on Aaron's mark. "In the Museum, you'll find artifacts from players who tested positive for performance-enhancing substances or played under that cloud of suspicion. It's up to you to decide how you feel about those players and their feats,"[3] said Petroskey's successor, Jeff Idelson, in 2012.

Yet the Hall seems to want it both ways. Asked about how the voters should handle candidates linked to steroids, in a 2011 interview with *Sports Illustrated*'s Joe Posnanski, Idelson pointed to what's informally referred to as "the character clause." Officially, it's now Rule 5 for BBWAA voters: "Voting shall be based upon the player's record, playing ability, integrity, sportsmanship, character, and contributions to the team(s) on which the player played."[4] The rule was introduced in 1944 by Hall founder Stephen Clark and Commissioner Kenesaw Landis, a man so brimming with integrity, sportsmanship, and character that he spent his 24-year tenure upholding the game's color line.

In Idelson's view, "Baseball has historically been held to a very high standard, right or wrong. There's a certain integrity required when it comes to baseball's highest honor. . . . The character clause exists as it relates to the game on the field. The character clause isn't there to evaluate and judge players socially. . . . The voters should have the freedom to measure that however they see fit."[5]

That would seem to give the voters carte blanche to impose moral judgments upon the on-field accomplishments of the players. But in the same interview, Idelson added, "When you look at the Hall of Fame elections, you see that those who are elected are representative of that era. The Hall of Fame election is a continuum. And the standards have upheld the test of time. . . . When you look at who the writers have voted into the Hall of Fame, you would be hard-pressed to find someone who doesn't belong there."[6]

Leaving aside the parts about standards and who doesn't belong—we've got a whole book ahead of us for that—"representative of that era" suggests that even in a period sullied by pervasive PED use, voters should recognize the best players, and even the Hall is comfortable with that. Again from Idelson, "Only 1% of all players are making it to Cooperstown. Am I worried that this era will be under-represented? No . . . we're happy with the diligence of the voters who have participated, and the chips will fall as they fall."[7]

At the time of Idelson's interview, Bonds had yet to reach the ballot, but the voters were already giving a rough time to Mark McGwire, who had just slipped below 20% of the vote in his fifth year on the ballot, and Rafael Palmeiro, who received just 11.0% in his debut. With 586 homers for the former and 569 for the latter (along with 3,020 hits), historical precedents suggested that their elections should have been a formality.

It was anything but. When the 2007 ballots were released in November '06, the AP's Ronald Blum and Ben Walker polled 125 voters, many of whom provided their rationales with regards to McGwire, pro or con. A sampling of responses:[8]

> **Jayson Stark, ESPN:** "I'm going to vote for him. I can't say I feel good about voting for him. . . . Just as baseball allowed Gaylord Perry to go out and cheat his way to 300 wins—which got him to the Hall of Fame—it allowed McGwire and all of these players to compile their stats and break their records and earn their money and accolades based on those feats. So I think I'm stuck with evaluating what the sport allowed to happen on the field."
>
> **Ron Rappaport, retired:** "I'll vote for him. You can't rewrite the history of the game after the fact."
>
> **Scott Miller, CBS SportsLine:** "No. I will not vote for any admitted or highly suspected steroid user until more time passes and more information is uncovered. I think this era stained the game."
>
> **Dave Newhouse, *Oakland Tribune*:** "I turned in my Baseball Writers' card this year, specifically so I wouldn't have to vote on cheaters after possibly already having voted in cheaters without knowing so, because there was no steroids testing at the time."

Many other voters elaborated on their rationales in their own columns. Wrote Ann Killion of the *San Jose Mercury News*, "I'm not voting for McGwire. What would I tell my kids, who saw my disgust at the congressional hearings in March 2005 and have heard my opinion over the years?"[9] Wrote the *San Francisco Chronicle*'s John Shea, who also kept McGwire off his ballot: "Vote for McGwire, you're endorsing everything for which he stands, including his non-denials and empty promise to help kids and other players to stay off steroids. Don't vote for McGwire, you're portrayed as the morality police even though that's part of the job description."[10]

It's worth remembering that at the time no hard evidence that McGwire had used anything illegal had yet surfaced. The androstenedione that AP reporter Steve

Wilstein found in his locker during the 1998 home run chase was available over the counter, widely used within the game, and legal under both United States law and MLB policy, though as a testosterone precursor it had been banned by the International Olympic Committee in '97. It wasn't barred by baseball until April 2004, when the Food and Drug administration banned its sale and while Congress was in the process of adding it to Schedule III of the Controlled Substances Act, for drugs that have less potential for abuse than narcotics as well as some accepted medical use, but that nonetheless carry the risk of psychological or physical dependence. While the allegations against him via Jose Canseco's book *Juiced*, and his 2005 appearance in front of Congress did not make for good optics, he did not admit to using PEDs until January 2010.

Still, many voters were satisfied to go on rumor, innuendo, and "the eyeball test," and even before suspicions about McGwire proved correct, voters had loosened their inhibitions with regard to using their own assumptions and beliefs as evidence. As New York *Daily News* columnist Bill Madden, a member of the Hall's Historical Overview Committee (responsible for vetting Veterans Committee ballot candidates) and future recipient of the Hall of Fame's Spink Award, told the *Los Angeles Times* in July 2006, "I'm not voting for any of those guys—Bonds, McGwire, Sosa, Palmeiro, any of them. I draw the line at eyeball evidence and what I personally believe. . . . If the Hall of Fame doesn't want me or any other writers to take a stand, then take that clause out of the ballot."[11]

We'll return to the clause, but first, the envelope. McGwire received 23.5% of the 2007 vote, less than one-third of what he needed to be elected. To that point, only one of the 12 players with at least 500 homers to reach the ballot in modern voting history received less than 50% of the vote: Eddie Mathews, whose 32.3% share in 1974 I puzzled over in Chapter 4. He needed five cycles to get elected. Only one other such player failed to gain first-ballot entry: Harmon Killebrew, who debuted with 59.6% in 1980 and needed four cycles. The only real knock on either was their low batting averages (.271 and .258 respectively, the two lowest among 500-homer players though 1975).

Since 1999, the number of players to reach 500 homers has nearly doubled, from 15 to 27. While steroids has been blamed for that surge, it came amid a backdrop of rapid change around the game, including new ballparks (smaller in capacity but actually larger in terms of fence distances), expansion into high-altitude Denver and Phoenix (at 1,059 feet above sea level, Chase Field is second only to Coors), and the composition of the baseballs themselves, topics I explored at length in Baseball Prospectus's 2012 book, *Extra Innings*. From 1993–2009—past the point when random PED testing and suspensions were introduced—teams averaged more than 1.0 homers per game, something that had previously happened only in the strange, offense-happy 1987 season.

At this writing, just two of the 12 newcomers to the 500-homer club have been elected: Frank Thomas and Ken Griffey Jr., both on the first ballot. The same will likely hold true for Jim Thome, eligible in 2018, and Albert Pujols, who won't hit the ballot until '27, assuming that he completes his current contract. The other eight newcomers—McGwire, Bonds, Sosa, Palmeiro, Ramirez, Gary Sheffield, Alex Rodriguez, and David Ortiz—have been linked to PEDs to various degrees, though only Palmeiro, Ramirez, and Rodriguez were ever disciplined by MLB. Not every such slugger is a slam-dunk candidate, but until McGwire came along, the voters had never shunned one to the point that he fell off the ballot. BBWAA voters have judged the six of these players who have already gained eligibility quite harshly, with Bonds the only one to receive even 25%. Not until 2017, his fifth year of eligibility, did the all-time home run leader cross the 50% threshold, with 53.8%.

To date, just two pitchers with PEDs allegations and Hall-caliber numbers have reached the ballot, Kevin Brown and Roger Clemens. Brown, whose 211 wins were low for a Hall of Fame pitcher, served as the ace of the World Series–winning 1997 Marlins and ranks 46th in JAWS, in the vicinity of Juan Marichal and Don Drysdale. Accused via the Mitchell Report of acquiring HGH and steroids, he received just 2.1% in 2011, knocking him off the ballot. Clemens, who after appearing in the Mitchell Report attempted to clear his name via a congressional hearing, only to be indicted for lying to Congress, became eligible in 2013. Like Bonds, he didn't cross the 50% threshold until 2017, when he reached 54.1%, far below expectations for a player with 354 wins, seven Cy Youngs, and the number three ranking in JAWS.

What's remarkable is that, prior to McGwire's appearance on the ballot, the character clause was rarely mentioned by voters. When it was, it was in the context of justifying a vote *in favor* of a candidate, whether or not his election was a foregone conclusion.

In December 1945, syndicated columnist Henry McLemore cited Dizzy Dean's integrity for pitching in a '34 World Series game the day after being hit on the head while pinch-running, and as for character, "He'll be the biggest character in that Hall of Fame before he has been there a night. Just let them set up a bust of ol' Diz in the place, and it'll enliven the building."[12] Perhaps not what Judge Landis had in mind, but definitely in Dean's favor.

In 1948, syndicated columnist Frank Eck touted rightfielder Harry Heilmann, who "easily measures up to all standards"[13] with respect to the clause. That same year, Arthur Daley wrote in *The Sporting News*, "If 'integrity, sportsmanship and character' are to be taken into consideration, as the voting rules prescribe, Pie [Traynor] fits the description as if it were hand-tailored for him."[14] In 1950, Walter L. Johns wrote of Mel Ott, with respect to the clause, "It seems to us that

Master Mel has these recommendations."[15] In 1958, Eck touted Al Lopez, who "fits each of these categories."[16] Eck also mentioned his intent to vote for 1930s slugger Hack Wilson, whose character, integrity, and sportsmanship were apparently above reproach despite his reputation as one of the game's most notorious drunks.

The clause was invoked with respect to several Brooklyn and Los Angeles Dodgers. In 1962, syndicated columnist Joe Reichler cited Jackie Robinson in connection with the clause (as if there could be any doubt), and two years later Eck cast Roy Campanella in the same light. Jimmy Cannon mentioned the clause in connection to Sandy Koufax in 1972. "There are bad men in the Hall of Fame, and ball journalists pretend they didn't know they were wrong-os. But the rules tell the selectors that integrity, sportsmanship and character, as well as contributions to their team and baseball as a whole count as much as playing ability. Sandy Koufax also qualifies big here. This is a beautiful guy. He has more class than a man needs and chivalrous style."[17]

The late Gil Hodges was a particular character clause favorite. Hodges "is high in all departments and his death will result in a big sentimental vote,"[18] wrote Bill Moeller in 1972. In 1976, Dick Young echoed those words, and beseeched his fellow voters to invoke the clause: "I can think of no words more befitting of Gil Hodges, and I respectfully ask that you write his name on the ballot."[19] In 1979, Red Smith wrote, "if the votes are based, as the rules said, on the player's integrity, sportsmanship and character, Gil will ride in."[20] In the same column, Smith also applied those words to Elston Howard and Red Schoendienst.

In the *New York Times* in February 1991, Ira Berkow even suggested that the clause could be applied in favor of the recently banned-for-life Pete Rose:

> It is not spelled out whether [the clause] means on-the-field only, or on-the-field and off-the-field both. If it means both, then of course a number of bad actors who were great pitchers and hitters should be thrown out. And if it means good players who were outstanding citizens, then some like Dr. Bobby Brown, or Saul Rogovin, the pitcher-turned-school teacher, should be in. If it means on-the-field only, then no one played with more character, integrity or sportsmanship than Rose.[21]

Prior to McGwire, the clause was very rarely used against a candidate. One of the first times it was invoked in a negative light was in connection to a player already banned for life: In the January 15, 1947, edition of *The Sporting News*, columnist Dan Daniel noted, "In the past, there was no official regulation by which the Black Sox or other scallywags of record could be kept out of the Hall of Fame. There was no restriction in electing Joe Jackson."[22]

Once in a blue moon, the clause was cast as a means of avoiding voting for disagreeable sorts. Even while citing Hodges et al., Smith wrote of it, "Translated, this means that all my baseball friends are or should be enshrined in Cooperstown and any player who gives me a short answer is obviously deficient in character and must languish in outer darkness."[23] Along those same lines, in 1978, Will Grimsley wrote that Roger Maris and Enos Slaughter were "two men who have been victimized by their own negative personalities. They are snubbed by some voters who use the intangibles of the Hall of Fame's guidelines—'integrity, sportsmanship, character'—as an excuse for omission."[24]

Even before the PED issue arrived, not everybody agreed that sportswriters should be in the business of judging character. In the January 31, 1994, *Sporting News*, William C. Rhoden wrote a column titled "Keep the Vote Between the Lines," expressing disappointment at Orlando Cepeda's narrow miss in his final year of eligibility (he received 73.5%) after slowly rehabilitating his image in the wake of a '75 arrest and prison stint for smuggling 165 pounds of marijuana. "Who interprets character?" Rhoden asked. "Some 400 baseball writers whose characters have never been examined?"[25] Cepeda, elected in 1999, stands as one of many Hall of Famers against whom the character clause could be invoked for things arguably worse than using steroids. Consider:

- Protectors of the color line, including: Cap Anson, who was instrumental in drawing it back in the 1880s; Landis; Red Sox owner Tom Yawkey, whose franchise didn't integrate until 1959; Yankees general manager George Weiss, whose team didn't integrate until 1955.

- Members of the Ku Klux Klan. "Rogers Hornsby and Tris Speaker, fellow stars from the old Confederate states, told me they were members of the Ku Klux Klan," wrote Fred Lieb in his 1977 memoir, *Baseball As I Have Known It*. "I do not know whether [Ty] Cobb was a Klansman, but I suspect he was."[26]

- Illegal drug users, including Cepeda, Ferguson Jenkins (arrested in 1980 when customs agents found cocaine in his suitcase), Paul Molitor (who used cocaine and marijuana early in his career), and Tim Raines (who underwent this treatment for cocaine use after the 1982 season), and not to mention the aforementioned amphetamine users.

- Leo Durocher, manager of the 1951 Giants, whose miraculous pennant race comeback was aided by an elaborate system of illegal sign stealing using a high-powered telescope and a buzzer system running between the

Giants' dugout and right field bullpen. In his previous job as manager of the Dodgers, Durocher was suspended for the entire 1947 season due to his alleged association with known gamblers.

- Domestic violence offenders, such as Roberto Alomar (accused of pushing and threatening his wife with a knife in 2010), Bobby Cox (arrested for punching his wife in 1995), and Kirby Puckett (charged with false imprisonment, criminal sexual conduct, and assault of one woman in 2001; accused of threatening his wife with a gun and attempting to strangle her in '03).

And then there are the spitballers and other ball defacers, such as Gaylord Perry (who confessed to using saliva, mud, sweat, Vaseline, and K-Y Jelly), Don Sutton (nicknamed "Black and Decker" for his use of sandpaper and other items), and Whitey Ford (who used his wedding ring to cut baseballs and also employed a "gunk" mixture of baby oil, turpentine, and resin). Actual rules against such forms of cheating have been on the books since 1920, but enforced at roughly the same frequency with which such players have been celebrated as scalawags.

Some of those people were elected before the character clause was drafted, and others before their misdeeds came to light. Still, is their sportsmanship, integrity, or character demonstrably better than those players alleged to have used PEDs? Six decades of selectively applying or ignoring the character clause makes for a flimsy precedent when it comes to invoking a retroactive morality with respect to McGwire and company—at least with respect to the time before baseball instituted random testing and penalties in 2004.

If the PED users were affecting the competitive integrity of games by trying to get an illegal or extralegal edge, then so were the spitballers and sign stealers, though at least they were all pulling in the same direction: toward winning. The drunks and drug users, showing up to ballparks hungover, still intoxicated, and/ or battling addictions, not so much. Baseball lore has made lovable rogues out of many such players. The same can't be said for the racists and color line preservationists, but even as we view them with disdain from our twenty-first-century vantage point, we also recognize them as products of a time when such views were normalized. The transgressions of PED users also took place in a certain context. On that note, it's worth reviewing how baseball took so long to implement a coherent policy with respect to PEDs.

Anabolic steroids, more accurately called anabolic-androgenic steroids, arose out of 1930s efforts to isolate and synthesize testosterone for use in hormone replacement therapies in both men and women. In the early 1940s, scientists discovered that testosterone could enable the growth of muscle tissue, and West Coast bodybuilders were experimenting with them by the late '40s and early '50s. So were Soviet weightlifters. After learning of the Soviets' use of injectable testosterone at the World Weightlifting Championship in Vienna in 1954, U.S. Weightlifting team physician Dr. John B. Ziegler began experimenting with it on himself and on team members. Concerned with the androgenic side effects (aggressiveness, increased libido, facial hair, enlarged prostate), Ziegler—working at CIBA, a pharmaceutical company—manipulated the molecular structure of testosterone in an effort to decrease those side effects, creating methandrostenolone. That made its way into track and field and football starting in the early 1960s, under the trade name Dianabol.

For both legitimate pharmaceutical companies and illicit underground labs, the subsequent challenge in developing other steroids such as stanozolol (Winstrol) and nandrolone (Deca Durabolin) has been to balance the anabolic effects (building muscle and tissue) with the androgenic ones (the "side effects"). The International Olympic Committee banned anabolic steroids in 1975, and in '90 they were added to the U.S. Controlled Substances Act as Schedule III substances, a label reserved for drugs with currently accepted medical uses but also the potential for physical dependency and abuse, albeit less than for Schedule II drugs such as cocaine and amphetamine. That made possession of anabolic steroids without a prescription a federal crime, and distribution an even greater one.

Via a memo sent to major league teams in 1991, Commissioner Fay Vincent explicitly banned anabolic steroids, but the ban had no means of enforcement under the Collective Bargaining Agreement. Teams could not test for steroids, but players would be subject to treatment and penalties if caught with them, at least in theory. "This memo was never publicized and, seemingly, was largely ignored by both management and the players' union," wrote an *ESPN The Magazine* team in 2005. "Commissioner Bud Selig reissued the same memo in 1997, with minor changes but with the same lack of conviction."[27]

By the time of Vincent's memo, steroids had already been in baseball for decades. In 2005, former reliever Tom House—whose biggest claim to fame during his eight-year major league career was catching Hank Aaron's 715th home run in the Braves' bullpen in 1974—told a reporter that PEDs were widespread in the game in the 1960s and '70s. "We were doing steroids they wouldn't give to horses," he said, estimating that six or seven pitchers per team were experimenting with steroids or HGH. "We didn't get beat, we got out-milligrammed. And when you found out what they were taking, you started taking them."[28]

Even before the 1994–95 players' strike, which wiped out the World Series, owners and team employees were loath to go after stars they suspected of using, such as Canseco, who heard chants of "Steroids! Steroids!" from Boston fans as early as the '88 American League Championship Series. The owners were too busy fighting a seemingly endless labor war to push for enforcement of Vincent's ban, even colluding by not signing each other's free agents in a futile attempt to depress salaries and cripple the players union. In 1990, after a string of losses in front of arbitrators, the owners agreed to pay the union $280 million in damages as a settlement for their 1985–87 collusion. Not satisfied with having been trounced in such fashion, the owners' attempt to eliminate salary arbitration, restrict free agency, and institute revenue sharing tied to a salary cap precipitated the 1994–95 strike, which cost them about $1 billion.

Once baseball returned, the 20% attendance drop from '94 to '95 left owners in dire need of winning back fans by any means necessary. They were only too happy for musclebound sluggers to set turnstiles spinning while chasing home run records. McGwire, Sosa, and Bonds, threatening to burst through their jerseys like the Incredible Hulk, combined to surpass Maris's 1961 record of 61 homers six times from 1998–2001, while six other sluggers hit 50 or more homers in a season at least once from 1995–2001.

As balls flew out of the yard at record rates, pressure to implement a PED policy with teeth arose in the wake of a June 2002 *Sports Illustrated* cover story[29] that included eye-opening estimates of the percentage of players using steroids from Ken Caminiti ("at least half," including himself when he won the 1996 NL MVP award), Chad Curtis (40–50%), and Canseco (85%). That captured the attention of the Senate Commerce Committee, which had legislative jurisdiction over U.S. professional and amateur sports. Headed by senators Byron Dorgan and John McCain, the committee urged baseball to implement mandatory testing. Union executive director Donald Fehr said testing would violate the privacy rights of players, though both he and MLB executive vice president Rob Manfred expressed the belief that Congress should legislate against the usage of androstenedione, the substance found in McGwire's locker in 1998.

In late 2002, as part of negotiations for their next CBA, which nearly resulted in another World Series–threatening strike, the owners and the players union agreed to anonymous survey testing in the spring of 2003 to determine the extent of steroid use within the game. If 5% of players on 40-man rosters tested positive either in 2003 or '04, mandatory testing would be implemented. In November 2003, MLB announced that enough players tested positive in the survey—96 for substances banned by MLB at that point, and 104 in all—to trigger the testing program, though both Selig and MLB Players Association second-in-command Gene Orza downplayed the number of positives as evidence that usage levels were nowhere near the Caminiti or Canseco estimates.

The new regulations called for players to be tested twice during the 2004 season without prior notice, placed on a "clinical track" for treatment and counseling upon first offense and then an "administrative track" for a second failed test, subject to discipline and public identification. Nobody reached that point of public shaming during 2004, but with the Bay Area Laboratory Co-Operative story unfolding—involving Bonds, Gary Sheffield, and Jason Giambi, among others—the Senate Commerce Committee continued to apply public pressure. In January 2005, the league and the union agreed to a new policy that included random testing, offseason testing, and public identification for even one positive test, with unpaid suspensions of 10, 30, and 60 days for first, second, and third offenses, and a one-year ban for the fourth. Two months later, in the wake of Canseco's tell-all memoir *Juiced*—which included his accounts of injecting teammates McGwire, Giambi, Palmeiro, Juan Gonzalez, and Ivan Rodriguez—the House Government Reform Committee grilled half a dozen players (including the tearful McGwire and the finger-wagging Palmeiro), Selig, Fehr, and two general managers in an 11-hour hearing. The committee told Selig and Fehr to strengthen baseball's program—or force Congress to do it for them.

A dozen mostly lesser-known players received 10-day suspensions that season, but Palmeiro was popped just weeks after surpassing the 3,000-hit milestone. Owing to his high-profile denial in front of the House Governemnt Reform Committee, he received such an outpouring of outrage from booing fans that he took to wearing earplugs while batting. After going 2-for-26 over the course of seven games upon being reinstated, he left the Orioles, jeered into retirement.

In November 2005, the league and union agreed to more stringent penalties of 50- and 100-game suspensions for first- and second-timers, and a lifetime banishment for a third offense. They also banned amphetamines—the ubiquitous "greenies" in clubhouses since the late 1950s—for the first time. The next spring, Selig appointed former Senate majority leader George Mitchell to head an independent investigation into the game's steroid usage. Based upon interviews with more than 500 current or former team officials, managers, coaches, team physicians, athletic trainers, and security agents, as well as 68 interviews with former players (out of more than 500 requests) but just two active players, the 409-page Mitchell Report, published in December 2007, outlined the game's history of PED use and the steps that were (and weren't) taken to curb it. The report implicated 89 former and current players, including many already known (Bonds and his fellow BALCO participants), and stars such as Clemens and Andy Pettitte—yes, pitchers—as well as scrubs.

The far-from-comprehensive report had its critics and its flaws, but it took a broad view when it came to spreading the blame around:

> Obviously, the players who illegally used performance enhancing substances are responsible for their actions. But they did not act in a vacuum. Everyone involved in baseball over the past two decades—Commissioners, club officials, the Players Association, and players—shares to some extent

in the responsibility for the steroids era. There was a collective failure to recognize the problem as it emerged and to deal with it early on. As a result, an environment developed in which illegal use became widespread.

. . . The onset of mandatory random drug testing, the single most important step taken so far to combat the problem, was delayed for years by the opposition of the Players Association. However, there is validity to the assertion by the Players Association that, prior to 2002, the owners did not push hard for mandatory random drug testing because they were much more concerned about the serious economic issues facing baseball.[30]

Mitchell recommended amnesty for the players named, to keep the focus on combating future use rather than crying over spilt milk.

Though far from the end of the story of PEDs in baseball, that will suffice for our purposes. My point is that when it comes to Hall of Fame voting, we should view players' drug usage in the context of this complete institutional failure. Yes, the players who used them violated both federal laws and baseball's (laxly enforced) rules. A split within the union, with a lack of consensus regarding testing, concerns about privacy that would prove legitimate when survey test failures were leaked to the press years later, and the absence of a critical mass of nonusers willing to speak out on the issue didn't help matters.

The players got away with it first because the owners were engaged in nefarious schemes every bit as damaging to the game, if not more so, and then because the owners profited as home runs soared. MLB's gross revenue doubled from 1995 ($1.4 billion) to '99 ($2.8 billion) and reached $3.7 billion in 2001.[31]

The media glorifying the new power kings while failing to report the entirety of the story was part of that failure as well. Wilstein, who found the andro in McGwire's locker in 1998, was quickly dubbed a pariah by some of his peers, his professionalism questioned. Wrote the *Boston Globe*'s Dan Shaughnessy, "No wonder ballplayers loathe the media. Mark McGwire is stalking one of baseball's most cherished records . . . and suddenly he's engaged in a tabloid-driven controversy that's painting him as a cheater and a bad role model. It's unfair."[32]

For all of the profits taken as the era unfolded, and all of the blame to spread around in the aftermath, when PED-tainted players have come up for election to the Hall of Fame, they and a small handful of others—some with far more tenuous connections to PEDs—have been left to carry the weight for an entire era. It shouldn't be that way.

From here, the most coherent way to handle the PED question with regards to candidates is to differentiate between what came before random testing and suspensions were implemented in 2004, and what came after. McGwire's andro,

Bonds's BALCO cocktails, Clemens's HGH and steroids, the leaked survey tests implicating Ortiz, Ramirez, Rodriguez, and Sosa, the names from Canseco's book—all of that hails from a time when use was rampant and unchecked. MLB couldn't punish users, the Joint Drug Agreement completed in the wake of the Mitchell Report granted the named players amnesty, and Bonds and Clemens have been acquitted of perjury and/or obstruction of justice charges, though only after tens of millions in taxpayer money was flushed down the toilet in high-profile show trials.

Voters should let go of the drug transgressions from the game's Wild West era. It's not their place to administer frontier justice, or to drag their feet over voting for obviously qualified candidates whose only connections to PEDs amount to rumors and speculation. That doesn't mean they're obligated to vote for every last player connected to PEDs; indeed, via JAWS, McGwire, Sosa, and Sheffield are all below the bar at their positions, albeit not tremendously so. For their candidacies as well as those of Bonds and Clemens, voters would be better off sticking to the proverbial backs of the baseball cards, particularly after the elections of Mike Piazza in 2016 and Jeff Bagwell and Ivan Rodriguez in '17. Piazza and Bagwell both admitted to using andro when it was still legal, while Rodriguez had the Canseco allegation. Many voters believed that those players were further involved with PEDs, but with a lack of hard evidence, the writers reached a consensus on their worthiness—overdue in the cases of Piazza and Bagwell, but in time to elect Rodriguez on the first ballot.

The benefit of electing those players and moving on is that candidates further down-ballot can get a fair shake; voters could slot Edgar Martinez and Larry Walker (or another combo) into the Bonds and Clemens spaces on an overstuffed ballot. Shifting the debate back to non-PED-linked candidates can't help but dial down the inflammatory rhetoric around the voting process.

As for those whose transgressions occurred during the testing era, that's a different ballgame. Withholding votes based on the positive tests and suspensions of Palmeiro, Ramirez, Rodriguez, Ryan Braun, and whoever else flunks a whizz quiz is much easier to justify, as those players knew the rules and the punishments. They fought the law and the law won, so to speak.

I'd love to believe a voting body of roughly 450 people could take such guidelines to heart. In the wake of the 2017 election, I'm even a little optimistic. After a handful of high-profile voters came around on Bonds and Clemens in 2016— and a whole lot of holdouts were culled from the rolls for their inactivity—an even larger contingent did so in 2017. Bonds's and Clemens's shares of the vote climbed to around 54%, making for gains of roughly 17% in two years. Via data from Ryan Thibodaux's Ballot Tracker, which accounted for 70.8% of the 442 votes,

13 of 15 first-time voters included them on their ballots, and they each gained a net of 27 votes from among returning voters.

For some of the latter, the impetus was the December election of Selig by the Today's Game Era Committee, which some, including past BBWAA president Susan Slusser, viewed as a sign that it was time to drop objections to the gruesome twosome. "Senseless to keep steroid guys out when the enablers are in the Hall of Fame," she wrote via Twitter. "I will now hold my nose and vote for players I believe cheated."[33]

Voter Kevin Cooney of the Bucks County (Pennsylvania) *Courier Times* told the *New York Times*, "To me, it would be hypocritical to put the commissioner of the steroid era and a manager who had connections with the steroid era in and leave out the greatest pitcher and the greatest hitter of that time."[34]

Viewing the matter more charitably, it's worth noting that for all of his enabling, Selig stuck around long enough to leave MLB with the strongest drug testing program of the major North American sports. On the other hand, that doesn't erase the damage he caused by exacerbating the game's labor problems (including his involvement in the late 1980s collusion) and by his slow reaction to PED proliferation at a time when he should have been showing real leadership. Nor does it change the fact that he was richly rewarded for what transpired.

If the committee voters could judge Selig's transgressions as not disqualifying him, and not eclipsing his considerable accomplishments, then the writers should do the same regarding Clemens and Bonds. Note that the Today's Game Era Committee included eight Hall of Famer players and managers, a minimum of seven of whom must have voted for Selig (since he received 15 of 16 votes). As a group, they're the ones who grouse the most about the possibility of PED-linked players getting in, but if they could view Selig as having the "integrity, sportsmanship [and] character" to satisfy the voting rules, then either the clause is meaningless or Bonds and Clemens are on the right side of it, too.

Having passed the 50% threshold, and with five years of eligibility remaining, history says it's only a matter of time before Bonds and Clemens gain entry. That won't please everybody, but it might be the road out of the Hall's PED quagmire, which in turn would help alleviate the ballot's bottleneck and shift the focus to more positive stories. We can hope.

PART II

AROUND

THE

DIAMOND

Within this section, for every position, I have included case studies of one or two players—long-lost candidates as well as current or upcoming ones—whose Hall of Fame cases are particularly interesting in light of JAWS and my other research. In many instances, these are the very best players outside the Hall at their positions, but that isn't uniformly true. I've kept Tim Raines, who was elected in 2017, while omitting the case studies of his fellow honorees, Jeff Bagwell and Ivan Rodriguez, due to space considerations. Similarly, I've had to leave out those of several other candidates: Barry Bonds and Roger Clemens, the Hall's two most obvious omissions at this writing, both statistically overqualified but not yet voted in due to their connections to performance-enhancing drugs; 2017 near-misses Vlad Guerrero and Trevor Hoffman, both more qualified via traditional statistical reckoning than by JAWS; and recent BBWAA ballot casualties Jim Edmonds, Kenny Lofton, Mark McGwire, Rafael Palmeiro, and Lee Smith. My profiles of all of those candidates, as well as nearly every other player who has reached the BBWAA ballot since 2013 with a JAWS within 20 points of the standard, are available online at SI.com.

Rest assured that the aforementioned cut-list players are covered in brief within the **Further Consideration** section of **The Roundup** here, as are most of the other frequently asked-about outsiders. Every major league player in the Hall of Fame is covered within The Roundup, which is divided into three tiers: **The Elite** (above the career WAR, peak WAR, and JAWS standards), **The Rank and File** (most everyone else), and **The Basement** (the most dubious honorees). Every attempt has been made to ensure that the WAR figures cited herein are accurate as of February 2017. For a table of abbreviations, see page 409.

CHAPTER 9

CATCHERS

CASE STUDY: TED SIMMONS

> Simmons has a square-jawed, alert face (he looks very much like an Ivy
> League football player from the eighteen-nineties) and he talks baseball as
> articulately as anyone I know.[1]
>
> —ROGER ANGELL

It's an understatement to suggest that the 1970s was a bountiful era for outstanding catchers. Via the JAWS rankings, seven of the top 14 backstops hail from the decade, including three of the top four: Johnny Bench (first), Gary Carter (second), and Carlton Fisk (fourth), all enshrined. On the outside looking in are Ted Simmons (10th), Thurman Munson (12th), Gene Tenace (13th), and Bill Freehan (14th).

With the exception of Tenace, who caught more than half his team's games just four times and was frequently used at first base, all of the aforementioned spent more than a decade behind the plate before being moved elsewhere. All of them could hit, not only better than the average catcher but significantly better than the average major leaguer. The lowest OPS+ from among the group is Freehan's 112; the others are at 115 or above, six of the 20 players in history to spend a majority of their careers at catcher while accumulating at least 5,000 PA at that level of productivity.

With just 15 major league catchers enshrined—a total that includes 2017 honoree Ivan Rodriguez but not, for example, Negro Leagues star Josh Gibson, 2013 honoree Deacon White (who had more value at third base), or 2014 honoree Joe Torre (who was elected primarily for his managerial accomplishments)—it may seem as though we should avoid mining a particular period for more honorees. On the other hand, the position has fewer enshrinees than any besides third base, four fewer than the next-lowest total of 18 (shared by first basemen and centerfielders).

Such a concentration of top-tier players at a single position in a given time period is hardly unprecedented, even among those already enshrined. Using the Hall's own definition of activity—at least one game played in a given season—five enshrined catchers were active in 1929, and every year from 1931–37. In the 1929 group are Mickey Cochrane, Bill Dickey, Rick Ferrell, Gabby Hartnett, and Ray Schalk, the last of those in his final season; in 1931, Ernie Lombardi arrived to replace him. Here's a look at the maximum concentration of Hall of Famers at each position:

Position	Max	Years
Pitcher	16	1965, 1966
Catcher	5	1929, 1931–1937
First base	7	1930
Second base	6	1929, 1937, 1947
Third Base	4	1973, 1974, 1982–1989
Shortstop	6	1930, 1932–1933, 1941–1942
Leftfield	6	1975–1976
Centerfied	7	1927–1928
Rightfield	7	1926, 1928–1931

As you'd expect given the Hall's oversaturation of players from the 1920s and '30s, several positions had their highest concentrations during those decades; with a total of 14 centerfielders and rightfielders in the 1926–31 range, teams averaged nearly one Cooperstown-bound outfielder per year. Of more interest are the concentrations outside those periods—the pitchers, third basemen, and leftfielders—with the quartet of enshrined third basemen from the 1980s (Mike Schmidt, George Brett, Wade Boggs, and Paul Molitor) together for a particularly strong stretch.

Long story short, it shouldn't be unthinkable to deem Hall-worthy a fourth catcher from the 1970s. The switch-hitting Simmons offers a compelling case given his combination of strong offense, longevity, and brutal treatment at the hands of the voters. His 2,472 career hits stood as the record among players who spent the majority of their careers at catcher until Rodriguez surpassed him, and, at the time he retired, ranked fourth among switch-hitters at *any* position, though he's slipped to 11th. Meanwhile, his 1,908 hits as catcher (the strict split) ranks fourth all-time behind Rodriguez (2,749), Jason Kendall (2,160), and Fisk (2,145), one hit ahead of Carter and two ahead of Piazza.

As with Piazza two decades later, Simmons's strong offense made him disproportionately prone to criticism for his defense, particularly because his Cardinals failed to reach the playoffs. Though he made eight All-Star teams, he didn't fit the mold of what was expected, both from a catcher and from a ballplayer in general, and after clashing with manager/general manager Whitey Herzog, he was traded to the Brewers. In Milwaukee he finally tasted the postseason, but struggled upon moving out from behind the plate.

For all of his accomplishments, Simmons received surprisingly little support upon becoming eligible for the Hall of Fame in 1994. His 3.7% knocked him off the BBWAA ballot, and since then he's failed to make headway with Era Committee voters. He deserves a closer look.

The Career

Cardinals 1968–80 • Brewers 1981–85 • Braves 1986–88

Player	Career	Peak	JAWS	H	HR	SB	AVG/OBP/SLG	OPS+
Simmons	50.1	34.6	42.4	2472	248	21	.285/.348/.437	118
Avg HOF C	52.4	33.8	43.1					
C Rank	10th	11th	10th					
(Above HOF)	(12/15)	(11/15)	(12/15)					

Born in 1949 and raised in the Detroit suburb of Southfield, Simmons was the son of a harness horse owner and trainer. He played basketball, hockey, and football as well as baseball as a youth, and was talented enough as a halfback to be offered a scholarship by the University of Michigan. He was even better at baseball, so good that the Cardinals drafted him with the 10th pick of the first round in 1967, nine picks ahead of Bobby Grich (see Chapter 11), and signed him for a $50,000 bonus. Simmons hit very well in the minors, particularly for his age: .331/.415/.570 with 28 homers at A-level Modesto as an 18-year-old in 1968, then .317/.365/.495 with 16 homers at Triple-A Tulsa the following year.

In the offseason, Simmons attended the University of Michigan. Ineligible for intercollegiate athletics, he absorbed the surroundings of campus life amid a hotbed of anti-Vietnam sentiment. He made brief cameos with the Cardinals in both 1968 and '69, and was finally called up for good in late May '70, after finishing his army reserve duty. His arrival forced Torre, the Cardinals' regular catcher, to third base.

Simmons didn't hit much as a rookie, but in his first full season he batted .304/.347/.424 with seven homers, a 3.3 WAR year that earned him down-ballot MVP consideration; meanwhile, Torre survived the transition to the hot corner and won the NL batting title and MVP award. Simmons improved to .303/.336/.465 with 16 homers and 4.5 WAR in 1972, but his season was more notable for something else: He became the first playing holdout in major league history.

After making $17,500 in 1971, Simmons received a raise to $25,000 via the Cardinals' unilateral right to renew his contract under the Reserve Clause —but he wanted $30,000, in part because at the request of management, he had passed up an opportunity to earn extra money by playing winter ball. Instead of sitting out the regular season, he continued to play. As Marvin Miller, the executive director of the Major League Baseball Players Association, later explained, "Simmons refused to be bluffed into signing a new unsatisfactory contract in order to be 'allowed' into uniform. The union advised [him] that once his contract was renewed, he was under contract and could not be barred from spring training or from the regular season, even if he refused to sign that contract."[2]

Simmons suggested that he could take his case to court. His lack of a signed contract raised the question of what would happen if he made it through the entire season without one. Would he be a free agent, since the Reserve Clause, which allowed the team "to renew the contract for the period of one year"[3]—a clause that the owners interpreted as "in perpetuity," with each one-year period rolling over to the next—would no longer be in effect? Wary of allowing him to test the case, which had ramifications for the entire industry, the Cardinals signed him to a two-year, $75,000 deal on July 24.

Simmons went against the grain in other ways. A 1978 *Sports Illustrated* profile by Ron Fimrite introduced him as the St. Louis Art Museum's newest trustee, described his and wife Maryanne's collection of early-eighteenth-century furniture and summarized his early-career rebelliousness:

> He was unyielding even when it became evident that his views did not sit well in a community as conservative as St. Louis. He denounced the Vietnam War and was outspoken in his contempt for the Nixon Administration. He allowed his hair to grow to his shoulders; that gave him a leonine look and earned him the nickname Simba. . . . At that time, he was a lion roaring his defiance.[4]

Despite his iconoclasm, Simmons performed consistently throughout the decade. Even with an off year in 1976 (five homers and a .394 slugging percentage), he hit a combined .301/.367/.466 from 1971–80, averaging 17 homers per year. His 131 OPS+ ranked 16th in the majors for that span. Thanks to occasional appearances at first base or left field, he averaged a hefty 148 games for that stretch, and topped a .300 batting average six times, cracking the league's top 10 in five of those seasons, including a second-place finish in 1975 (.332). Meanwhile, he made the top 10 in on-base and slugging percentages four times apiece.

Defensively, though he led the league in passed balls three times, Simmons was more or less average according to Total Zone (-11 runs for the decade, with some of that owed to lousy work in limited outfield duty), and average or better when it came to throwing out would-be base thieves in seven out of those 10 seasons. When combined with the value of his bat, he ranked among the league's top 10 in WAR five times. His 44.6 WAR for the stretch ranked 11th in the majors, and second among catchers behind Bench (54.7).

Simmons made six All-Star teams across that decade, and in 1978, broke Bench's nine-year stranglehold on the NL starting catcher job. Alas, he remained stuck on a team that hadn't been to the postseason since 1968, in part because they traded away Steve Carlton, heir apparent to Bob Gibson as the staff ace. The Cardinals finished second in the NL East three times with Simmons, winning as many as 90 games, but slipping below .500 three times, including both '78 and '80.

In mid-1980, Herzog joined the Cardinals, first as manager and then adding general manager duties. He and Simmons didn't click, to say the least, but his main beef wasn't the catcher's hair length or taste in antique furniture, it was his defense. In a league where stolen base attempts were about 70% more common than today, and where the 116 steals allowed by Simmons ranked as the second-highest total (albeit with a league-average 31% caught rate), Herzog viewed Simmons's throwing as a liability. In his 1999 memoir, *You're Missing a Great Game*, Herzog expounded:

> Ted Simmons, God bless him, was a fine person who cared about winning. But he had one major weakness as a ballplayer: poor arm strength. Unfortunately for the Cardinals organization, that one flaw was a bigger disaster than anybody around me seemed to realize. Ted's fluttery throws to second were enough to scuttle the Cards and keep the fans away. . . . Because Ted threw poorly to second, every team in the world knew they could swipe that base in the late innings.[5]

To a degree, Herzog may have had a point, in that Simmons's Cardinals were weak in defending the stolen base in the late innings. Via Baseball-Reference.com, from 1971–80 the Cardinals ranked sixth out of 26 teams in terms of both stolen base rate from the seventh to ninth innings (prorated to 0.61 per nine) and success rate (68%). Even so, the cost was minimal. Using a typical era-appropriate linear weights value of 0.2 runs for a successful steal and -0.4 runs for an unsuccessful one, Cardinals' opponents gained a net 4.6 runs via late-inning steals, where the average team's opponents cost themselves 2.8 runs—a difference of 8.4 runs for the decade, or 0.84 runs per year. For 1980, the team allowed the second-highest stolen base total of any NL team in innings 7–9 (46, at a 74% success rate) and the difference via linear weights between the Cardinals and the average team amounts to 2.0 runs, with Simmons catching 76% of the team's innings — so perhaps 1.5 runs, in a year when his offense was 24 runs better than the average hitter (not average catcher). Herzog's suggestion that the combination not only had a significantly deleterious effect on the Cardinals' chances of winning but on their attendance, which rose and fell with their record but was generally in the middle third of the league, is a gross exaggeration.

In any event, after mulling the prospect of moving Simmons to first base and 1979 NL co-MVP Keith Hernandez to left field—a plan that was received lukewarmly at best—Herzog instead signed his former Royals catcher, Darrell Porter, a nominally superior defender, as a free agent. After four days and two other blockbuster trades, he traded Simmons to the Brewers, the only team truly interested in keeping him at catcher, no small consideration for a player who could use 10-and-5 rights (10 years of major league service time, five with the same team) to block any deal. Also heading to Milwaukee were Rollie Fingers (whom Herzog had just acquired from the Padres) and Pete Vuckovich, for the much younger David Green, Dave LaPoint, Sixto Lezcano, and Lary Sorensen.

In the 1983 *Baseball Abstract*—more than two years removed from the trade—Bill James wrote at length about the Herzog-Simmons clash, coming down firmly on the side of authority:

> Look at the situation, as it must have looked to Herzog. You've got a highly talented team that isn't winning. The team doesn't hustle; it doesn't execute fundamentals; it doesn't play very good defense. You've got a player who is universally recognized as the leader of that team. He is a public idol. He is on the board of directors of the art museum. He is, reportedly, good buddies with the owner. He is a .300 hitter with power. But, unfortunately, he is a catcher, and he is not a good one. So you sign another catcher, and you tell [Simmons] that, for the good of the team he is going to have to move. And he says, "No, I won't do it. The hell with what's good for the team." What are you going to do? . . . If I had to trade that man for five cents on the dollar, I'd trade him. . . . If Whitey Herzog didn't have the guts to run Ted Simmons out of St. Louis, he might as well have quit on the spot.[6]

Ouch. As with Herzog's estimate of the cost of Simmons's defense, James's characterization of the catcher as self-centered reeks of hyperbole, particularly when held up against Dan Okrent's more nuanced depiction of him in *Nine Innings*, which caught up with him as a Brewer in 1982. Via Okrent's telling, Simmons's reluctance to move had everything to do with fear that he would embarrass himself attempting to replace Hernandez, the best defensive first baseman in the league (and, sabermetrically speaking, the second-best all-time).

While Herzog's trio of blockbusters laid the groundwork for the Cardinals' 1982 championship, the Simmons deal wound up helping Milwaukee more than St. Louis. In the strike-torn 1981 season, Fingers won both Cy Young and MVP honors while helping the Brewers reach the postseason for the first time via their 31-22 second-half record. Backed by a robust offense, Vuckovich went a combined 32-10 in 1981 and 1982, winning the Cy Young in the latter year. Simmons hit 16 homers but batted a career-worst .216/.262/.376 with 0.3 WAR in 1981, but he rebounded in '82 (.269/.309/.451 with 23 homers and 3.3 WAR) as the Brewers won the pennant. Facing Herzog's Cardinals in the World Series, he received a warm welcome from St. Louis fans and homered in each of the first two games there, but finished just 4-for-23 in a losing cause.

Simmons enjoyed a strong 1983 season, serving as the AL's starting catcher for the All-Star Game and accumulating 4.0 WAR even while spending an increasing amount of time at DH, but his performance crashed through the floor in 1984, his age-34 season. With the much more defensively adept Jim Sundberg joining Milwaukee via a trade, Simmons couldn't find a comfort zone at first base, third base, or DH and wound up hitting a woeful .221/.269/.300 with just four homers in 132 games. His -2.6 WAR was not only the worst in the league, it remains tied for the 14th-lowest in the post-1960 expansion era. While he did rebound slightly the next year, he spent his final three seasons with the Braves as a backup catcher/first baseman/pinch-hitter. He retired following the 1988 season and remained in baseball, working as a coach, scout, and executive (including as general manager of the Pirates from early 1992 to mid-1993) but never landing a managerial job.

The Case

Given Simmons's standing on the hits leaderboards for catchers and switch-hitters as well as his eight All-Star appearances, he figured to have a legitimate shot at election to Cooperstown when he reached the BBWAA ballot in 1994. His score of 124 on James's Hall of Fame Monitor, based on common statistical benchmarks and accomplishments for "old-school" stats, is near "virtual cinch" territory (130), between contemporaries Fisk (120) and Carter (135). Yet for some reason, he got lost in the shuffle, receiving just 3.7% of the vote. Not only was that not enough to return for the 1995 ballot, it eliminated him from consideration in front of the Veterans Committee through 2008, which would have been his 15th year of eligibility. With the Hall of Famer–engorged VC in flux, he didn't get onto another ballot until 2011, by which time the process was back to the "old VC" style as the Expansion Era Committee.

What happened? On the BBWAA front, one has to wonder if Simmons's early-career contract rebellion, long hair, and his not being cut from the typical major league cloth hurt his standing among an older generation of writers who saw him as too radical. That's pure speculation on my part, as I found no mention of such factors in the election coverage. His missing the cut by just four votes (receiving 17, when 21 were needed) took many by surprise, including the *St. Louis Post-Dispatch*'s Bob Broeg, who covered Simmons during his career and voted for him. Calling his shortfall "a shame," Broeg noted that had the Five Percent Rule been in place earlier (it was adopted in 1979), Bob Lemon and Red Ruffing wouldn't be Hall of Famers, yet, "no one seems to begrudge their subsequent election."[7]

It probably didn't help Simmons's cause that three eventual Hall of Famers also became eligible in his first year on the ballot, namely 300-game winners Steve Carlton and Don Sutton as well as pioneering closer Bruce Sutter. That trio joined top holdovers Phil Niekro, Tony Perez, and Steve Garvey, all of whom had received at least 40% the previous years, as well as 15th-year candidate Orlando Cepeda. In the sparse coverage of the upcoming election, Carlton and Cepeda had been the focal points, with Simmons noted merely as one of 18 ballot newcomers, listed alphabetically between Larry Parrish and Mario Soto—that despite his having left his job as the Pirates' GM just six months earlier in the wake of a heart attack. He didn't get any pity votes, to say the least.

His sinking without a trace didn't entirely escape notice. In 1996, the BBWAA petitioned the Hall of Fame's board of directors to reconsider eligibility of Simmons, '91 candidates Larry Bowa and Al Oliver, and '93 candidate Bill Madlock, all of whom had fallen short of 5% in their first year on the ballot. As they did with Dick Allen, Ken Boyer, Ron Santo, and others in 1984, the board approved the petition. But unlike in 1985, those names never made it back to the ballot; a dispute within the BBWAA led to their exclusion.

When the VC was retooled to include all living Hall of Famers within its voting process, initial reports suggested that Simmons and other sub-5% candidates would get a new look, but in fact they were all withheld from consideration through the duration of their 15-year windows. Thus Simmons was not reconsidered until 2011, when he was included on the Expansion Era Committee ballot. As fate would have it, Herzog was among the eight Hall of Famers sitting on the 16-man panel appointed by the Hall's board of directors, which elected executive Pat Gillick and came within one vote of electing Marvin Miller, the former union head. The group gave eight votes to one former player, Davey Concepcion, whose former teammates Johnny Bench and Tony Perez were on the committee. The eight other candidates (including Simmons) all received fewer than eight votes, though the Hall didn't announce their actual totals.

Herzog was still on the committee when Simmons's next turn at bat came in 2014. Bench and Perez were gone, but fellow catcher Fisk and Simmons's former Brewers teammate Paul Molitor were both on the committee. It made no difference. The committee unanimously elected managers Bobby Cox, Tony La Russa, and Torre; none of the six players (including Concepcion and Simmons) or three nonplayers (Miller, Billy Martin, and George Steinbrenner) received more than six votes. While it's not hard to imagine Herzog's view of Simmons carrying considerable weight among those undecided, two other *Post-Dispatch* writers have reported that it's Simmons's short stay on the BBWAA ballot that's hurting him. Said Rick Hummel, who has served on the Historical Overview Committee that puts together the ballot, "The first question these Hall of Famers ask you is, 'How many ballots was he on for the writers' election? One? They must not have liked him very much.' "[8]

Wrote Derrick Goold, "[The voters] have a chance to prove the writers wrong—and they should . . . and instead they choose to use that vote to legitimize theirs. It's maddening."[9]

Looked at today, Simmons's merits are clear. He ranked among his league's top 10 in WAR five times, and in one of the three slash stats (average, on-base percentage, and slugging percentage) a combined 15 times. Among his contemporaries, Bench ranked among the top 10 in WAR eight times, and in a slash stat six times. For Carter the balance is six times and four times, respectively, and for Fisk it's three times and nine times. Simmons's 118 OPS+ ranks "only" 13th among catchers with at least 5,000 plate appearances, but his ranking climbs considerably when playing time is considered: 10th at the 6,000 PA cutoff, seventh at the 7,000 PA cutoff. In terms of batting runs (i.e., runs above average), which accounts for his offensive excellence and playing time in one fell swoop, he's 11th among catchers at 172, just ahead of Fisk (168) and Carter (160).

Simmons's defense, so maligned at times during his playing days, wasn't nearly as costly as it was made out to be. Among catchers in the post-1960 expansion era, his 182 passed balls rank second and his 1,188 stolen bases allowed sixth, but some of that is a by-product of playing time; he's 12th in innings caught with 15,092⅓. On a per-nine-innings basis among catchers with at least 8,000 innings in the post-expansion era, his 0.11 passed ball rate is a close third, but his stolen base rate of 0.71 per nine is 16th, Carter (0.78 per nine) is eighth in that category, and just below Simmons is Tony Pena (0.69), widely considered among the best defenders of his day; Simmons's 34.0% caught stealing rate is less than a point behind Pena's 34.8%.

Given that stolen base rates (per game and per attempt) changed dramatically over the course of these catchers' careers—from 0.49 per team per game in Simmons's rookie season (1970) to 0.79 per game in his last (1988)—it makes more sense to turn to a total defensive metric that attempts to capture such evolution. Via Total Zone, while Simmons was 34 runs below average for all of his defensive work, he was just eight below average for his time behind the plate; he was much worse in small samples at first base, left field, and third base. That's not insignificant, but neither is it grounds for eliminating him from consideration, particularly with Piazza (-63 runs, offset by particularly strong framing), Ernie Lombardi (-21), and Roger Bresnahan (-14) enshrined.

Overall, Simmons's 50.1 career WAR and 42.4 JAWS both rank 10th among all catchers, while his 34.6 peak WAR is 11th. He's 0.2 wins above the peak standard for catchers, 3.3 below for career, and 1.5 below for JAWS. His WAR numbers paint him as borderline (he was closer to the standard before Piazza and Rodriguez were elected), but he still ranks among the top 10 catchers of all time—a perfectly reasonable basis for inclusion on its own—and the best eligible one outside the Hall, ranked below eight enshrined backstops and the still active Joe Mauer. It remains to be seen whether the Modern Baseball Era Committee (due to vote in December 2018) gives him the modern look he deserves.

THE ROUNDUP

The number before each player name refers to his JAWS ranking *among all players at the position*, not necessarily those in the Hall. Average HOF catcher: 53.4 career WAR/34.4 peak WAR/43.9 JAWS.

The Elite (above standard in career, peak, and JAWS)

1. Johnny Bench

Teams:	Reds 1967–83
Stats:	.267/.342/.476 • 126 OPS+ • 2,048 H • 389 HR • 68 SB
Rankings:	14× All-Star • 10× GG • 8× top 10 WAR • 5× top 5 SLG • 4× top 5 HR • 4× top 10 OPS+
Voting/JAWS:	BBWAA 1989 (1st, 96.4%) • 75.2/47.2/61.2

The Big Red Machine's most vital cog, Bench helped Cincinnati to six playoff appearances, four pennants, and two championships while dominating on both sides of the ball from 1968–80. He towers over the field despite just 84 innings behind the plate over his final three seasons (ages 33–35), but then, catchers heavily used in their twenties don't tend to accrue much value in their thirties, and Bench was no exception. While he's 16th all-time in games caught (1,742), only Bob Boone and Jason Kendall had more 120-game seasons than his 11 (three others had as many). What's even more remarkable is Bench's combination of offense and defense. He's the only catcher since Buck Ewing (1883) to lead his league in homers (45 in 1970, and 40 in '72, his two MVP seasons), and his 269 batting runs ranks a close third among players who spent at least half their careers as catcher. Meanwhile, his 97 fielding runs at catcher (excluding his -25 elsewhere) rank seventh. Nobody active is a threat to dethrone him from the top spot.

2. Gary Carter

Teams:	Expos 1974–84, '92 • Mets 1985–89 • Giants 1990 • Dodgers 1991
Stats:	.262/.335/.439 • 115 OPS+ • 2,092 H • 324 HR • 39 SB
Rankings:	11× All-Star • 8× top 5 WAR • 7× top 10 HR • 4× top 10 OPS+ • 3× top 10 SLG • 3× GG
Voting/JAWS:	BBWAA 2003 **(6th, 78.0%)** • **69.9/48.2/59.1**

"The Kid" inherited the mantle of the NL's best catcher from Bench, made 10 straight All-Star teams from 1979–88, helped the Expos to their lone postseason appearance in '81, and was part of the Mets' '86 World Series winners and '88 NL East champs. Outstanding both offensively and defensively, his nine times among the league's top 10 in WAR (1977–85, consecutively) are a record for catchers, and his peak score actually eclipses that of Bench, ranking number one at the position. For all of that, it took Carter a ridiculous six ballots to get elected. He debuted at just 42.3% in 1998, as Don Sutton reached 75%, and had to wait as George Brett, Nolan Ryan and Robin Yount ('99), Tony Perez and Carlton Fisk (2000), Dave Winfield and Kirby Puckett ('01), and Ozzie Smith ('02)—none of whom ranked higher at their positions—cut the line. His tragic 2012 death from a brain tumor at age 57 meant that he had only nine years to enjoy his status; it should have been much longer.

3. Ivan Rodriguez

Teams:	Rangers 1991–2002, '09 • Marlins 2003 • Tigers 2004–08 • Yankees 2008 • Astros 2009 • Nationals 2010–11
Stats:	.296/.334/.464 • 106 OPS+ • 2,844 H • 311 HR • 127 SB
Rankings:	14× All-Star • 13× GG • 4× top 10 WAR • 4× top 10 AVG All time: 1st Games Caught
Voting/JAWS:	BBWAA 2017 **(1st, 76.0%)** • **68.4/39.7/54.0**

The man with the golden arm, Rodriguez set a new standard defensively thanks to his ability to stifle the running game, throwing out 45.7% of would-be base thieves in his career en route to the position's highest total of fielding runs (+146).

That number doesn't reflect his so-so pitch framing (-10 runs via Baseball Prospectus), caused in part by his leaving his crouch early to throw, but Rodriguez shepherded the Rangers to their first three postseason appearances, then guided youngish Marlins and Tigers staffs to the World Series (the former in victory), and for a while he was a force with the bat as well, posting a 127 OPS+ from 1997–2003. The prophetically monikered "Pudge" had enough staying power to secure the all-time records for games caught (2,427) and hits by a catcher (2,749), surpassing his nicknamesake; meanwhile his 304 homers ranks third at the position.

4. Carlton Fisk

Teams:	Red Sox 1969, 1971–80 • White Sox 1981–93
Stats:	.269/.341/.457 • 117 OPS+ • 2,356 H • 376 HR • 128 SB
Rankings:	11× All-Star • 4× top 10 SLG • 3× top 10 OBP • 3× top 5 WAR
Voting/JAWS:	BBWAA 2000 **(2nd, 79.6%)** • **68.3/37.5/52.9**

Despite injuries that limited him to fewer than 80 games behind the plate in three of his Boston seasons, and experiments at DH and left field that similarly cut into his catching time in Chicago, Fisk broke the all-time record for games caught (2,225, set by Bob Boone in 1990) in '93. He never played again: Days later, he was released by the White Sox at age 45, ending his career. The record stood until 2009, when "the other Pudge" surpassed him. Unlike so many burnt-out backstops, Fisk retained his value late; among qualified catchers—those who accrued more WAR at the position than anywhere else—nobody had more WAR from his age-30 season onward (at *any* position, not just catcher) than Fisk, whose 39.3 WAR outdistances second-ranked Gabby Hartnett's 31.8. It's not as though his twenties were a loss, either; when available, he was worked hard, catching at least 130 games in four of his six noninjury seasons, all of them part of his peak score.

5. Mike Piazza

Teams:	Dodgers 1992–98 • Marlins 1998 • Mets 1998–2005 • Padres 2006 • A's 2007
Stats:	.308/.377/.545 • 143 OPS+ • 2,127 H • 427 HR • 17 SB
Rankings:	12× All-Star • 7× top 10 HR • 7× top 10 SLG • 4× top 5 OPS+ • 3× top 10 WAR
Voting/JAWS:	BBWAA 2016 **(4th, 83.0%)** • **59.4/43.1/51.2**

"Mike hits it harder than I did when I was 16. . . . I guarantee you, this kid will hit the ball. I never saw anybody who looked better at his age." [10]

—TED WILLIAMS

Tutored for an afternoon by the Splendid Splinter, who liked what he saw, and drafted in the 62nd round in 1988 as a favor to his father (a childhood friend of Tommy Lasorda's), Piazza spent his entire career in pitchers' parks but nonetheless emerged as the best-hitting catcher of all time whether measured by OPS+, batting runs, or homers. His defense was roundly criticized due to his 23% caught stealing rate, but compelling sabermetric research places him among the best at pitch blocking (via Baseball-Reference's Sean Forman), framing, and staff handling (both via Baseball Prospectus's Max Marchi). Piazza's -63 fielding runs doesn't incorporate Marchi's findings; BP's more modern methodology credits Metal Mike with 87 framing runs, a number that needn't be taken as gospel to illustrate that he held his own behind the plate. As for the PED allegations, Piazza's quiet 2002 admission to having used androstenedione when it was still legal flew beneath the radar amid high-decibel allegations of illegal use, including blogger Murray Chass's endless obsession with his back acne. With Rodriguez and Jeff Bagwell following in 2017, Piazza's election is either the vanguard of voters' more rational treatment of the era's drug users or the downfall of civilization.

6. Yogi Berra

Teams:	Yankees 1946–63 • Mets 1965
Stats:	.285/.348/.482 • 125 OPS+ • 2,150 H • 358 HR • 30 SB
Rankings:	15× All-Star • 9× top 10 SLG • 9× top 10 HR • 7× top 10 WAR • 7× top 10 OPS+
Voting/JAWS:	BBWAA 1972 **(2nd, 85.6%)** • 59.5/37.0/48.2

As funny as all of the quotes attributed to Berra are, the extent to which his career has been reduced to a series of punch lines does him such a disservice that he's among the most underrated Hall of Famers, not to mention a guy who played on 14 pennant winners and 10 champions. While he never led his league in WAR, he ranked in the top 10 for seven straight years (1950–56), a stretch that included his three MVP awards. During that span, his 37.0 WAR was topped by only Mickey Mantle (40.8) and Larry Doby (38.6) among AL players. Any team that can put five-win players at up-the-middle positions for seven straight years is going to win something; the Yankees had two such players and took six pennants. While Berra fell short of first-ballot election, his 85.6% was the high for a modern second-year candidate until Roberto Alomar surpassed him with 90.0% in 2011.

The Rank and File

7. Bill Dickey

Teams:	Yankees 1928–43,'46
Stats:	.313/.382/.486 • 127 OPS+ • 1,969 H • 202 HR • 36 SB
Rankings:	11× All-Star • 5× top 10 OPS+ • 4× top 10 WAR • 4× top 10 SLG. 3× top 10 OBP
Voting/JAWS:	BBWAA 1954 **(7th†, 80.2%)** • **55.9/34.2/45.0**

Dickey can lay claim to the title of best catcher of the pre-integration era in terms of WAR and JAWS, though Mickey Cochrane had the higher peak and probably would have surpassed his career WAR had he not gotten hurt.

Here's a fun one: Which has been more essential to the Yankees' winning, their run of great players (Hall of Famers and near-Hall-of-Famers) at catcher, or in center field? Considering the top four at each position, it's actually a squeaker:

Catcher	Yrs Starter	Span	WS	Pennant
Bill Dickey	15	(1929–1943)	7	8
Yogi Berra	11	(1949–1959)	7	9
Thurman Munson	10	(1970–1979)	2	3
Jorge Posada	11	(1998–2007, 2009)	4	6
Total	**47**		**20**	**26**
Earle Combs	8	(1925–1929, 1931–1933)	3	4
Joe DiMaggio	11	(1937–1941)	8	8
Mickey Mantle	13	(1952–1962, 1964, 1966)	6	10
Bernie Williams	14	(1991, 1993–2005)	4	6
Total	**46**		**21**	**28**

8. Mickey Cochrane

Teams:	A's 1925–33 • Tigers 1934–37
Stats:	.320/.419/.478 • 129 OPS+ • 1,652 H • 119 HR • 64 SB
Rankings:	8× top 10 OBP • 7× top 10 WAR • 5× top 10 OPS+ • 5× top 10 AVG • 2× All-Star
Voting/JAWS:	BBWAA 1947 **(5th†, 79.5%)** • **52.1/36.9/44.5**

Though renowned as a handler of pitchers, Cochrane was nothing special defensively even according to the traditional stats, but he was an elite hitter for the position. Thanks to his keen batting eye and mid-range power, he held the OPS+

† Years receiving votes prior to final year of career not counted.

lead among catchers with at least 6,000 PA until Piazza came along. He helped the A's and Tigers to five total pennants, including back-to-back flags for the latter as player-manager in 1934–35, with an MVP award in '34 as well. From 1927–35, Cochrane was remarkably consistent, averaging 5.0 WAR per year and never falling below 4.0. He played just 71 games after that run, however, suffering a nervous breakdown that limited him to 44 games in 1936 (his age-33 season) and a near-fatal beaning that ended his playing career after just 27 games in '37. Eyeballing what he might have done via a normal decline instead of catastrophe, a conservative guess is perhaps 7–8 WAR en route to around 48.0 JAWS, pushing him past Dickey and alongside Berra.

11. Gabby Hartnett

Teams:	Cubs 1922–40 • Giants 1941
Stats:	.297/.370/.489 • 126 OPS+ • 1,912 H • 236 HR • 28 SB
Rankings:	7× top 10 SLG • 6× top 10 OPS+ • 6× All-Star • 5× top 10 WAR
Voting/JAWS:	BBWAA 1955 **(11th, 77.7%)** • 53.3/30.3/41.8

Before Bench, Hartnett—nicknamed "Old Tomato Face" for his ruddy complexion—was the heavyweight champion among NL catchers, a six-time All-Star, and a starter on three Chicago pennant winners. His offensive numbers are inflated by playing in a hitter-friendly era, but he stands as one of the great-hitting catchers; his 232 batting runs and 126 OPS+ both rank sixth at the position (6,000 PA minimum for the latter). No slouch defensively, he was widely regarded as having the league's best throwing arm and threw out 56% of would-be thieves in his career, leading the league six times. An injury to that arm cost him nearly all of the 1929 season, when he was 28. He had his best year (.337/.404/.630 with 37 homers and 5.4 WAR) upon returning, and much like Fisk he was exceptional in his thirties, notching his second- and third-highest WARs in his age-34 and -36 seasons.

15. Buck Ewing

Teams:	Troy Trojans 1880–82 • Giants 1883–92 • Cleveland Spiders 1893–94 • Reds 1895–97
Stats:	.303/.351/.456 • 129 OPS+ • 1,625 H • 71 HR • 354 SB
Rankings:	9× top 10 SLG • 6× top 10 AVG • 6× top 10 WAR • 6× top 10 OPS+
Voting/JAWS:	OTC 1939 • **47.7/30.5/39.1**

Many writers considered Ewing the best player of the nineteenth century thanks to his numerous skills and an unequaled knowledge of hitters' strengths and weaknesses. However, the stats don't support the notion that he was more valuable than Cap Anson, Roger Connor, Dan Brouthers, and others; his 47.7 WAR through 1900 ranks ninth and is roughly half Anson's total. Ewing does have a case as the best catcher of the nineteenth century, at least to the extent that he was a catcher. He caught 636 games out of a total of 1,315 games played, and dabbled at every other position including pitching. At the start of his career, catchers typically used tight-fitting, unpadded gloves, but Ewing popularized the oversized padded mitt, first using it in 1888. Even so, he was more or less done with the position by the end of 1890, catching just 37 games thereafter. He joined Anson, Wee Willie Keeler, and Old Hoss Radbourn in the first wave of nineteenth-century figures elected for their play rather than their pioneering.

17. Ernie Lombardi

Teams:	Dodgers 1931 • Reds 1932–41 • Braves 1942 • Giants 1943–47
Stats:	.306/.358/.460 • 126 OPS+ • 1,792 H • 190 HR • 8 SB
Rankings:	8× top 10 SLG • 7× All-Star • 7× top 10 AVG • 5× top 10 OPS+
Voting/JAWS:	VC 1986 • 45.9/27.8/36.9

"Ted Williams considers Lombardi the best hitter he ever saw."[11]
—VETERANS COMMITTEE STATISTICAL PACKET,
1968, PAUL S. KERR, SECRETARY

Listed at 230 pounds, Lombardi was one of the heaviest players in the league—and one of its heaviest hitters. Perennially among the league leaders in slugging percentage as well as batting average, he owns two of the eight batting titles won by catchers in all of major league history. So slow that most glaciers could outrun him, he lost hits because infielders played him very deep; among career .300 hitters with at least 6,000 PA, his .297 BABIP is in a virtual tie for the fourth-lowest mark. No great shakes defensively, Lombardi led the league in passed balls nine times, though his whiplike throws to second base engendered the respect of opponents, and he led in caught stealing percentage twice. The Splendid Splinter's high regard for Lombardi's prowess, which dated to the Reds and Red Sox sparring as they traveled north from spring training, culminated in Lombardi's election in Williams's first year on the VC.

20. Roger Bresnahan

Teams:	Senators 1897 • Cubs 1900, '13–15 • Orioles 1901–02 • Giants 1902–08 • Cardinals 1909–12
Stats:	.279/.386/.377 • 126 OPS+ • 1,252 H • 26 HR • 212 SB
Rankings:	7× top 10 OBP • 4× top 10 OPS+ • 3 top 10 WAR
Voting/JAWS:	OTC 1945 • **41.9/28.9/35.4***

In *The Politics of Glory*, Bill James called the 1945 Old Timers Committee selection of Bresnahan and Hughie Jennings as part of a 10-player slate "the Hall of Fame's first clear, unmistakable errors,"[12] citing a combination of Bresnahan's unjustified credit for inventing (instead of merely popularizing) shin guards, his high-profile coaching tenure under John McGraw, and his 1944 death as factors that elevated him on the basis of popularity rather than merit. As true as all of that may be, Bresnahan does have a claim as the best catcher of the dead-ball era, at least via WAR. Of those with at least 50% of their games played at catcher from 1901–19, his 41.0 WAR tops the field. That said, about 30% of his defensive innings came at other positions, mainly the outfield. His slash stats don't look special, but his 126 OPS+ is the equal of Lombardi and Hartnett, albeit in just 5,375 PA to Lombardi's 6,352 and Hartnett's 7,297, and he did have some speed to go with his on-base skills. JAWS doesn't love him due to his shortish career, but the Hall can live with him.

25. Roy Campanella

Teams:	Dodgers 1948–57
Stats:	.276/.360/.500 • 123 OPS+ • 1,161 H • 242 HR • 25 SB
Rankings:	8× All-Star • 5× top 10 HR • 5× top 10 OPS+ • 5× top 10 SLG • 3× NL MVP (1951, '53, '55)
Voting/JAWS:	BBWAA 1969 **(5th, 79.4%)** • **34.2/32.8/33.5**

Campanella spent just 10 years in the majors, constrained on one side by the color barrier and on the other by the car accident that paralyzed him. But in his short stay, he established himself as one of the game's top power hitters and most durable, strong-armed backstops while helping the Dodgers to five pennants. It's the front end of his career where we really missed out. Though he debuted in the Negro Leagues at 15 (!), became a first-stringer at 17, and won MVP honors at the East-West All-Star Game at 19, he didn't make his major league debut until age 26. He averaged 4.6 WAR in his first six major league seasons, and it's not incon-

---

* Pitching WAR included in player's career WAR & JAWS (not used in calculating position standards).

ceivable he'd have approached that in the six prior to his arrival had he been allowed to play. Hampered by hand injuries, he fell short of 1.0 WAR in three of his final four seasons (but not his MVP- and championship-winning 1955) before his crash at age 35. Though he debuted on the 1964 ballot at 57.2%, the voters sure took their time in finishing the job.

The Basement (the most dubious honorees)

42. Ray Schalk

Teams:	White Sox 1912–28 • Giants 1929
Stats:	.253/.340/.316 • 83 OPS+ • 1,345 H • 11 HR • 177 SB
Voting/JAWS:	VC 1955 • **28.6/22.2/25.4**

A zero with the stick save for good foot speed and a willingness to walk from the eighth spot in the lineup, Schalk was an outstanding defender with a top-flight reputation for pitcher handling and a strong arm despite his diminutive size (5'7", 155 pounds). He led the league in caught stealing percentage four times and threw out 51% of would-be thieves against a league average of 44%, while his 46 fielding runs is the highest mark among catchers from 1901–46. Beyond that, and his lack of involvement in the fixing of the 1919 World Series, there isn't a whole lot to recommend him for Cooperstown. The BBWAA didn't give him much support until 1955, his last year of eligibility, when he polled 45%. Five days later, the VC elected him.

46. Rick Ferrell

Teams:	Browns 1929–33, 1941–43 • Red Sox 1933–37 • Senators 1937–41, '44–45, '47
Stats:	.281/.378/.363 • 95 OPS+ • 1,692 H • 28 HR • 29 SB
Rankings:	7× All-Star
Voting/JAWS:	VC 1984 • **29.8/19.9/24.9**

Two explanations exist for Ferrell's election: either the members of the Veterans Committee were confused, thinking they were voting for brother Wes, who for a stretch in the 1930s was one of the AL's best pitchers; or a vote-swapping scheme designed to prevent hurt feelings due to a shutout went awry. Either way, catcher Rick was a typically lousy VC choice, a better hitter than Schalk but not nearly as good a defender via either traditional or advanced stats (including -4 fielding runs). He wasn't half the hitter that his brother was (.280/.351/.446 with 38 homers in just 1,345 PA to Rick's 28 homers in 7,077 PA). Which isn't to say that he was a bad player; he's roughly even in the JAWS rankings with Tim McCarver, Tony Pena, Bob Boone, and Mike Scioscia, guys who stuck around for eons because they could catch and occasionally help out with the stick.

Further Consideration (upcoming or overlooked candidates)

9. Joe Mauer

Teams:	Twins 2004–16
Stats:	.308/.391/.446 • 127 OPS+ • 1,826 H • 130 HR • 50 SB
Rankings:	7× top 3 OBP • 6× All-Star • 6× top 10 OPS+ • 4× top 10 WAR • 3× GG • 3× led AVG
JAWS:	**50.0/38.5/44.3**

Concussions and other injuries led the Twins to end Mauer's career as a catcher following the 2013 season, his age-30 campaign. Moving him to first base was an admirable attempt to preserve his health, and a reasonable bid to keep his bat in the lineup, but he's hit for just a meager .267/.353/.380 with a 103 OPS+ and 5.8 WAR since, a performance short of living up to the second half of an eight-year, $148 million extension that runs through 2018. Before that, Mauer established himself as one of the game's great-hitting backstops; if he wasn't Piazza, then he's still the only one to win three batting titles, and his peak score and JAWS already top the standards for catchers. At this point, the only real obstacles between him and Cooperstown are getting to 2,000 hits, not landing in the midst of some scandal (which would be totally out of character), and not spending a prolonged period as an expensive, light-hitting shadow of his former self, because voters hate long dénouements. The last could prove the biggest challenge.

12. Thurman Munson

Teams:	Yankees 1969–79
Stats:	.292/.346/.410 • 116 OPS+ • 1,558 H • 113 HR • 48 SB
Rankings:	7× All-Star • 5× top 10 AVG • 3× GG
JAWS:	**45.9/36.9/41.4**

Munson accumulated a boatload of Cooperstown-worthy credentials during a career cut short by his tragic 1979 death in a plane crash. Beyond his 1970 AL Rookie of the Year award, '76 AL MVP, and Gold Gloves, he led the Yankees out of their 1965–75 Dark Age and into three straight World Series. What's more, he hit a sizzling .357/.378/.496 in 135 postseason PA. His untimely death leaves him short of the career WAR and JAWS standards, but even so, he's 14th in the former and ranks eighth in peak, surpassing the standard by a full three wins via strong defense (+32 runs) and solid offense (+127 runs including baserunning and double play avoidance). While his bat was in decline over his final two seasons, his on-base skills kept his offense above average for the position. As short-career guys go, that's Hall-worthy, though neither the BBWAA—which introduced him on the 1981 ballot, but only in that year gave him more than 10%—nor the various committees have shown much inclination.

13. Gene Tenace

Teams:	A's 1969–76 • Padres 1977–80 • Cardinals 1981–82 • Pirates 1983
Stats:	.241/.388/.429 • 136 OPS+ • 1,060 H • 201 H • 36 SB
Rankings:	6× top 10 OBP • 4× top 10 HR • 4× top 10 OPS+ • 3× top 10 WAR
JAWS:	46.8/34.9/40.8

A unicorn will be made commissioner of baseball before the man born Fiore Gino Tennaci is elected to the Hall. This stathead favorite was an on-base machine, topping 100 walks in seven seasons, four of them paired with at least 20 homers. Yet with no contemporary appreciation for his stellar OBPs (four times in his league's top five), his low batting average, and the lack of recognition (one All-Star berth, never higher than 18th in MVP voting) went hand in hand. Though overshadowed by the many colorful stars of the A's mid-'70s dynasty, he was part of six playoff teams; he even won 1972 World Series MVP honors via four homers, picking up the slack for the absent Reggie Jackson. His 136 OPS+ trails only Piazza among catchers with at least 5,000 PA, and even with slightly subpar defense (-8 runs overall, -6 at catcher), his peak score clears the bar, and his JAWS is higher than six elected backstops. Just sayin'.

14. Bill Freehan

Teams:	Tigers 1961, '63–76
Stats:	.262/.340/.412 • 112 OPS+ • 1,591 H • 200 HR • 24 SB
Rankings:	11× All-Star • 5× GGs • 3× top 10 SLG • 3× top 10 WAR
JAWS:	44.7/33.7/39.2

In retrospect it's shocking that Freehan never got more Hall of Fame support, but he was one-and-done with 0.5% in 1982. A very good defender (+28 runs) with pop and plate discipline, he had the misfortune of playing in a pitcher-friendly era that suppressed his numbers; his .272/.377/.450 in 1967–68 equals a 144 OPS+, which is to say that it had a Piazza-like impact. An All-Star Game starter every year from 1966–72, he finished third and second in the MVP voting in '67–68, the latter in a championship season. Retirement at age 35, after the Tigers wore him down to the nub, didn't help his cause, nor did the stacked 1982 ballot with Hank Aaron and Frank Robinson debuting and six candidates returning with 58–61% of the vote. Not even venerable Detroit scribe Joe Falls, whose ballot was published in *The Sporting News*, could find room among his 10 spots. Because of his low voting percentage, he's never gotten another sniff, much like a later Tiger, Lou Whitaker.

29. Yadier Molina

Teams:	Cardinals 2004–16
Stats:	.285/.338/.400 • 98 OPS+ • 1,593 H • 108 HR • 47 SB
Rankings:	8× GG • 7× All-Star • 4× top 10 AVG
JAWS:	**33.3/26.9/30.1**

From time to time, Molina is called a Hall of Fame lock, but while there's little doubt that he's the heir apparent to Rodriguez as a defender—he's tied for fourth all-time at 112 fielding runs—the rest is premature, at least if WAR and JAWS are to bolster his case. Through his age-33 season, he's helped the Cardinals to nine postseasons, four pennants, and two championships, and has made great strides with the bat relative to where he began. However, to date Molina has just two seasons worth more than 3.1 WAR, and his quick decline from a 2012–13 peak looks all too typical for a catcher heading into his mid-30s. Long story short, he'll need a bunch of 4-5 win seasons from age 34 onward to reach the JAWS standard, but since 1961, there have been only six seasons of catchers 34 and older with at least 4.0 WAR, three by position player converts Jorge Posada (16th in JAWS, but one-and-done on the 2017 ballot) and Elston Howard, both of whom lacked Molina's mileage. What's more, the six other expansion catchers who caught at least 1,500 games through age 33—Bench, Carter, Freehan, Jason Kendall, Rodriguez, and Simmons—totaled 12.1 WAR for the remainder of their careers, at any position.

Via *Baseball Prospectus*, which estimates that Molina has added 149 run via pitch framing (fifth since 1988), his 46.8 WARP (their metric) ranks 12th among catchers since 1949, compared to 20th with 33.3 WAR in that span. Perhaps further advances in quantifying framing and staff handling will build him a more convincing case than JAWS currently can.

CHAPTER 10

FIRST BASEMEN

DAVID ORTIZ

Papi is even more famous than he is great, occupying his own space in baseball's cultural catalog with the likes of Mickey Mantle, Dizzy Deane, Satchel Paige, and others who layered personality upon skill in outsized measures. October has much to do with that space.[1]

—Tom Verducci

In December 2002, the Twins released David Ortiz, which is to say that they looked at the bulky, oft-injured 27-year-old slugger, who was coming off his first 20-homer season, considered the possibility of doubling or tripling his $950,000 salary in his first year of arbitration eligibility and thought, "Nah." Five weeks later, and two months into his new job, Red Sox general manager Theo Epstein signed Ortiz on the cheap as one of several potential first base and designated hitter options.

The rest is history. Ortiz became one of the most important and beloved players in the history of the Red Sox, homering more times than any Boston player besides Ted Williams and serving as the common thread—and offensive centerpiece—of the franchise's 2004, '07, and '13 World Series winners. In addition to producing some of the most dominant postseason performances of any hitter in any era, "Big Papi" became an icon throughout the sport, a mentor to younger players and an ambassador for the city in the wake of the horrific Boston Marathon bombing.

Such was Ortiz's status throughout the majors that he became the rare player around whom a "retirement tour" was planned—a sendoff akin to those of first-ballot Hall of Famers Tony Gwynn, Cal Ripken Jr., Chipper Jones, Mariano Rivera, and Derek Jeter. Yet a berth in Cooperstown circa 2022 or beyond is hardly guaranteed, as Ortiz will have to overcome a few obstacles. Thus far, the electorate has resisted players who spent most of their careers at DH—rightly so, in most cases—and by the advanced accounting of JAWS, Ortiz appears to be significantly short of the standards at first base (where he played in the rare instances he donned a glove) and with respect to all Hall position players. What's more, he reportedly failed the supposedly anonymous 2003 survey test, the results of which triggered the implementation of a drug testing-and-penalty program.

With regards to the advanced stats, it must be acknowledged that JAWS doesn't capture Ortiz's postseason prowess or his unique spot in baseball history. As for the drugs, that obstacle appears to be shrinking in significance as the electorate evolves, as Mike Piazza, Jeff Bagwell, and Ivan Rodriguez have all been elected despite pre-testing-era PED allegations; Barry Bonds and Roger Clemens likely will be by the time Ortiz becomes eligible. The opposition to his candidacy shouldn't be taken for granted, but neither should his fame.

The Career

Twins 1997–2002 • Red Sox 2003–16

Player	Career	Peak	JAWS	H	HR	SB	AVG/OBP/SLG	OPS+
David Ortiz	55.4	35.0	45.2	2,472	541	17	.286/.380/.552	141
Avg HOF 1B	65.9	42.4	54.2					
1B Rank	24th	34th	28th					
(Above HOF)	(7/19)	(5/19)	(4/19)					

Ortiz was born in 1975 in the baseball hotbed of Santo Domingo, Dominican Republic. The oldest of four children of Enrique—a former semipro player who turned to selling auto parts when he needed to support his family—and Angela Rosa Ortiz, he starred in basketball at Estudia Espallat High School as well as baseball. After his 1992 graduation, the Mariners signed the tall, powerful 17-year-old, who took his mother's maiden name, Arias, upon turning pro.

After spending 1993 in the Dominican Summer League, Arias came stateside and struggled so mightily in the Rookie-level Arizona League that the Mariners had him repeat the level, hardly a sign of future stardom. He got his career back on track, making the All-Star teams of the Arizona League in 1995 and the Midwest League in '96. Just prior to the August 31 trading deadline, the Mariners bolstered their infield, acquiring Twins third baseman Dave Hollins for a player to be named later. Two weeks later, Arias was sent to Minnesota, and by the time he debuted for the organization in 1997, he was David Ortiz again—literally the player to be named later.

The 6'4", 230-pound lefty tore through three minor league stops in 1997, hitting a combined .317/.372/.568 with 31 homers before making a 15-game cameo with the Twins. *Baseball America* rated him as Minnesota's number two prospect heading into 1998, and he opened the season as their starting first baseman. Though he started strongly, a broken right wrist cost him two months and sapped his power. He finished at .277/.371/.446 with nine homers in 86 games, a solid showing for a 22-year-old rookie.

The Twins were not enamored. Manager Tom Kelly, who had a reputation for being particularly hard on younger players, often sat Ortiz against lefties or lifted him late in games for pinch-hitters or defensive replacements. Despite his power potential, his poor conditioning and awkwardness around first base opened the door for slick-fielding, light-hitting Doug Mientkiewicz. Rather than shift Ortiz to the DH spot opened by Paul Molitor's retirement, the Twins sent him back to Triple-A Salt Lake City, where he languished despite mashing. He went 0-for-20 in an overdue September call-up; Mienkiewicz hit a grim .229/.324/.330.

Ortiz regained his roster spot and spent the next three seasons DHing, hitting a combined .265/.344/.473 for a 109 OPS+, showing glimpses of his awesome power but battling injuries. He homered 10 times in 130 games in 2000, and 18 in 89 games in 2001, missing time due to another fracture in his right wrist. His .272/.339/.500 showing with the career-high 20 homers in 2002 came in just 125 games, as he missed over three weeks due to surgery to remove bone chips in his left knee. Still, the Twins remained fixated on his shortcomings. Though his pull-happy approach provided plenty of pop, he drove Kelly crazy by refusing to focus on hitting to the opposite field. As he told the *Boston Globe* in 2004:

> I could never hit for power [in Minnesota]. Whenever I took a big swing, they'd say to me, "Hey, hey, what are you doing?" So I said, "You want me to hit like a little bitch then I will."[2]

By then, Ortiz had enough service time to qualify for arbitration, but the budget-minded Twins, who had ranked 26th out of 30 teams in 2002 payroll—yet still won 94 games and the AL Central—were unwilling to multiply the salary of a player with so many limitations, particularly given a farm system booming with inexpensive alternatives. General manager Terry Ryan spent two months trying to trade Ortiz. "Not one team made an offer,"[3] he said in 2006. Needing a roster spot after picking in the Rule 5 draft, Ryan designated Ortiz for assignment on December 16, 2002, four days ahead of the nontender deadline. "I made a bad baseball decision,"[4] he admitted later.

Forces conspired to bring Ortiz to Boston. For one, fellow Dominican Pedro Martinez, by that point already a three-time Cy Young winner, ran into the sullen, just-released Ortiz in Santo Domingo, and recalled the slugger homering off him. "I threw you a cutter last season, high and inside. I threw it perfect—92 miles an hour, jam-city. And you smashed it into the upper deck. . . . You're the only one who's ever hit a home run off that pitch. You're coming with me to Boston, homie."[5] Martinez put in his good word in a voice mail for Epstein.

Sox scout Dave Jauss, who had managed Ortiz in the Dominican Winter League, also recommended him to Epstein. Jauss had seen Ortiz beat up left-handed pitching and believed that the incentive of taking aim at Fenway Park's 37-foot Green Monster in left field (just 310′ down the line, and 379′ in left-center) could help him thrive as an all-fields hitter, as lefties Mo Vaughn and Trot Nixon had done in Boston. The GM asked Jauss to work him out, hitting him an endless supply of groundballs "like he was a 16-year-old free agent."[6]

The Sox signed Ortiz to a one-year, $1.25 million deal, but he had to fight for playing time until corner infielder Shea Hillenbrand was traded to Arizona in late May. Thanks to tweaks to his swing from hitting coach Ron Johnson, who told him to "load up" (draw his arms back) and wait as long as possible to swing, Ortiz settled into the lineup's fifth spot behind Nomar Garciaparra and Manny Ramirez and bashed 31 homers while hitting .288/.369/.592. The Red Sox, who had missed the playoffs in the previous three seasons, won 95 games and the AL Wild Card. After beating the A's in the Division Series, they pushed the Yankees to extra innings in Game 7 of a thrilling AL Championship Series. Ortiz powered Boston to victory with a two-run homer off Mike Mussina in Game 1, drove in three runs in a Game 6 win, then hit a solo shot that gave the team a 5–2 lead in the top of the eighth in Game 7, just before the Yankees mounted a comeback capped by Aaron Boone's 11th-inning walkoff home run.

Under new manager Terry Francona, Boston did even better in 2004, boosting their win total to 98. "Big Papi" had become a fixture in the lineup and clubhouse; a raise to $4.6 million was soon accompanied by a two-year, $12.5 million extension covering 2005–06. Picking up the slack for the injured-and-then-traded Garciaparra, he made his first All-Star team while hitting .301/.380/.603 with 41 homers and 139 RBIs; the last three numbers all ranked second in the AL, as did his 351 total bases, while his 145 OPS+ ranked fifth. The Wild Card–winning Sox swept the Angels, with Ortiz's 10th-inning walkoff homer off Jarrod Washburn in Game 3 sealing the deal.

In their ALCS rematch against the Yankees, the Red Sox fell behind three games to none, a deficit that had never been surmounted in any postseason series in baseball history. Despite Ortiz's two-run single off Orlando Hernandez, they trailed 4–3 in the ninth inning of Game 4 against Mariano Rivera before scratching out a run thanks in large part to pinch-runner Dave Roberts's steal of second base. Ortiz ended the five-hour epic in the 12th inning with a walkoff solo homer off Paul Quantrill, then summoned even more heroics in Game 5, which began roughly 17 hours after the end of Game 4 and stretched even longer: 14 innings and five hours and 49 minutes. After collecting an RBI single and a solo homer, he delivered the winning hit in the 14th via a bloop single off Esteban Loaiza. While he went hitless in Game 6, his two-run first-inning homer off Kevin Brown keyed a 10–3 rout in Game 7. Ortiz won ALCS MVP honors for his .387/.457.742 performance and record-setting 11 RBIs. He then hit a three-run homer in the first inning of the World Series opener against the Cardinals. Boston swept the series and ended their 86-year championship drought, while Ortiz finished October hitting .400/.515/.764 with five homers and a record-tying 19 RBIs.

Over the next three seasons, Ortiz continued to put up monster numbers, hitting a combined .306/.418/.620 for a 163 OPS+. In 2005, he led the league with 148 RBIs and ranked second with 47 homers, an astonishing 20 of which either tied the game or gave Boston the lead. In gratitude, Sox owner John Henry presented Ortiz with a plaque in September 2005 that proclaimed him "The Greatest Clutch Hitter in the History of the Boston Red Sox." In 2006, he led the AL in homers (a franchise-record 54), RBIs (137), and walks (119), including 23 intentional passes. Shortly after the season opened, the Sox extended him again, this time for four years (through 2010) and $52 million. In 2007, though his homer total dipped to 35, he led the league with a .445 OBP and set a career high with a 171 OPS+ despite playing through a torn meniscus in his right knee. The 96-win Sox won the AL East, and Ortiz continued to blaze a trail through October, hitting a combined 370/.508/.696 with three homers and 10 RBIs in 63 PA as the Sox swept the Angels (who walked him six times when he wasn't going 5-for-7), downed the Indians in a seven-game ALCS, and then swept the Rockies in the World Series.

A partially torn tendon sheath in his left wrist cost Ortiz 45 games in 2008, the start of a three-year dip across which he averaged "only" 28 homers while batting a combined .257/.356/.498 for a 120 OPS+ and struck out with increasing frequency—24% of all plate appearances in 2010. Though hardly a pushover, the 34-year-old slugger looked to have entered the decline phase of his career.

On July 30, 2009, the *New York Times* reported that both Ortiz and Ramirez (by then a Dodger) were among the 104 major leaguers who tested positive for performance-enhancing drugs via the 2003 survey testing that triggered the implementation of a bona fide testing-and-penalty program. Records of the test were supposed to have been destroyed, but before they could be, the government subpoenaed and then seized them as part of a larger investigation into the distribution of PEDs. The list of positives was placed under a court seal, and a month later the U.S. Court of Appeals for the Ninth Circuit ruled that in seizing records and urine samples from testing facilities, federal agents had far exceeded the limits of a search warrant that gave them access to the records of only 10 players linked to BALCO, including Bonds. By that point, several names had been leaked to the media, including those of Alex Rodriguez, Sammy Sosa, Jason Grimsley, and David Segui.

Though he had been notified in 2004 that he was on the 2003 survey, Ortiz described himself as "blindsided"[7] by the news. Soon afterward, he admitted that he had been "careless"[8] in taking over-the-counter nutritional supplements, an explanation that actually left him some wiggle room. More on that below.

A cynic might be tempted to draw a link between Ortiz's survey positive and his post-2010 resurgence, but it's important to note that he did not test positive once MLB began issuing suspensions for PEDs starting in 2004, nor was he named in the 2007 Mitchell Report. Against the odds, he cut his strikeout rate back to a mere 14% in 2011, kicking off a six-year stretch across which he hit .296/.386/.567 for a 154 OPS+, nearly on par with his 2003–07 run (156 OPS+). With four All-Star teams in that span, he ran his career total to 10, and averaged 32 homers despite missing Boston's final 71 games in 2012 due to a right Achilles tendon strain. The injury was part of a deluge that helped turn a near-miss 2011 team— eliminated on the last day of the regular season—into a 93-loss disasterpiece.

Still battling Achilles inflammation, Ortiz would miss the first 15 games of the 2013 season as well. By the time he took the field, his folk-hero status throughout New England had grown. On the afternoon of April 15, two pressure cooker bombs exploded near the finish line of the Boston Marathon, killing three spectators and injuring an estimated 264 others. The Red Sox had just left town for Cleveland; their return to Fenway Park on Friday, April 19, was postponed while the city shut down as police continued a manhunt for the suspects. Dzhokhar Tsarnaev was captured later that night. The following afternoon, Ortiz gave a brief, rousing speech during a pregame ceremony to honor the victims of the attacks and pay tribute to law enforcement officials, first responders, and race participants:

> This jersey that we wear today, it doesn't say Red Sox. It says Boston. We want to thank you Mayor Menino, Governor Patrick the whole police department for the great job they did this past week. This is our fucking city and nobody is going to dictate our freedom. Stay strong.[9]

Ortiz's F-bomb went out live over radio and television, but even the chairman of the Federal Communications Commission, Julius Genachowski—a Brookline, Massachusetts, native, as it turned out—gave him and the networks airing the speech a pass, saying via the FCC's official Twitter account, "David Ortiz spoke from the heart at today's Red Sox game. I stand with Big Papi and the people of Boston—Julius."[10]

The catharsis provided by that speech resonated throughout the Red Sox's 97-win season. Making up for lost time, Ortiz bopped 30 homers in 137 games and finished with a 159 OPS+, his highest since 2007, then went on yet another remarkable postseason run. In 68 PA against the Rays, Tigers, and Cardinals, he hit a combined .353/.500/.706 with five homers and 13 RBIs, not to mention 16 walks. Highlights included a two-homer Game 2 against Tampa Bay in the Division Series, a game-tying grand slam in the eighth inning of Game 2 of the ALCS while Detroit's Torii Hunter tumbled over the wall into the Boston bullpen, and then an 11-for-16 showing with eight walks (four intentional) in the World Series as the Cardinals desperately tried to avoid engaging him. Ortiz reached base multiple times in all six games, led all players in runs (seven) and RBIs (six) as well as hits and walks and even drew credit for helping to turn the series via an impromptu pep talk in the dugout during Game 4, just before the Sox turned a 2–1 deficit into a 4–2 lead.

As the Sox won their third World Series in a decade, Ortiz secured Series MVP honors and kindled talk of Cooperstown. "This month, David Ortiz has probably become the first player in history to get over the hump and into the Hall of Fame by the margin of his spectacular postseason play,"[11] wrote the *Washington Post*'s Thomas Boswell. "At 37, Ortiz remains the game's best designated hitter and has played himself into at least a conversation about his Hall of Fame viability,"[12] wrote the *New York Post*'s Ken Davidoff.

The Sox slipped back to last place in the AL East in both 2014 and '15, though Ortiz continued to defy his age. His 614 PA the latter year represented his highest total since 2009 and vested a $16 million option for 2016, while his 37 homers were his most since 2006. On September 12, he hit the 500th of his career off the Rays' Matt Moore in Tampa Bay, becoming the 27th player to reach that milestone.

On November 18, Ortiz's 40th birthday, he announced via a two-and-a-half-minute video on The Players' Tribune that the 2016 season would be his last. He did more than just show up to the tributes; he put together the greatest farewell season of any hitter by several measures including home runs (38), RBI (an AL-best 127), and WAR (5.1). He hit .315/.401/.620, leading the league in slugging percentage and doubles (48) and helping the Red Sox back into the postseason. Still, he remained firm in his decision to retire given the lengthy pregame preparation to manage the pain associated with his Achilles injury.

The Case

Ortiz ended his career with 10 All-Star appearances, eight Edgar Martinez Awards (prior to 2004, known as the Designated Hitter of the Year Award), and three championship rings. Along those lines, he retired as the career leader among DHs in key categories such as plate appearances (8,861), hits (2,191), homers (485), runs (1,254), and RBI (1,569). Via the Hall of Fame Monitor, his portfolio of accomplishments gives him a 171 score, beyond "a virtual cinch." Indeed, of the 16 other eligible players within 10 points of that score, 14 are enshrined, including Joe Morgan, Reggie Jackson, and Ernie Banks, all within one point of Ortiz. Only the PED-connected Rafael Palmeiro (178) and Mark McGwire (170) are outside.

In any other era, Ortiz's 541 home runs alone—good for 17th all-time—would have made him a lock for Cooperstown, but the near-doubling of that club, from 14 players through Mike Schmidt in 1987 to 27 players through 2016, has lessened that milestone's prestige, not only because of its rapid growth but because eight newcomers including Ortiz have been linked to PEDs (see Chapter 8). Those connections have damaged their cases for Cooperstown to such an extent that just three of the nine players to reach the BBWAA ballot thus far have been elected, namely 3,000-hit-club member Eddie Murray, Frank Thomas, and Ken Griffey Jr. Meanwhile, Palmeiro slipped below 5% after four years, McGwire aged off after 10, Ramirez, Sosa, and Gary Sheffield have fallen far short of induction, and even Bonds has languished. Rodriguez, the first player to miss an entire season for a PED infraction, likely will as well even given his 696 homers.

Like Sosa, Ortiz is linked to PEDs only by the 2003 survey test; he didn't turn up in the 2007 Mitchell Report or any other investigation. "In the eyes of baseball . . . Ortiz is a zero-time offender. He never has failed a test that featured individual discipline, and he never has been charged with a non-analytical positive,"[13] wrote Davidoff in 2013.

Beyond the survey test's intended anonymity—which is to say the violation of players' privacy rights via the leak—there's that wiggle room mentioned above with regards to supplements. "Because neither Major League Baseball nor the Players Association is believed to know the substances for which the players tested positive during that survey testing year—only the government has those results—if a player thinks he tested positive for a supplement, he might have a reasonable case,"[14] wrote the New York *Daily News*'s Christian Red and Teri Thompson shortly after the leak. "The supplement 19-norandrostenedione was legal in 2003 and contained the steroid nandrolone, a hard-core performance-enhancing drug used to build muscle."[15]

As Red and Thompson, MLBPA executive director Michael Weiner, and even the league itself pointed out, there was a discrepancy between MLB's count of positives (96) and the number of samples seized by the government (104). The union planned to contest some of the 96 positive survey tests but never did because the threshold to trigger mandatory testing for 2004 had already been exceeded. Said MLB in a statement, "Given the uncertainties inherent in the list, we urge the press and the public to use caution in reaching conclusions based on leaks of names, particularly from sources whose identities are not revealed."[16]

With an eye toward Ortiz's eventual Hall of Fame eligibility, Commissioner Rob Manfred reiterated that point in late 2016. "If there were test results like that today on a player, and we tried to discipline, there would be a big grievance over it. It would be fully aired, vetted, tried, resolved. . . . Even if Rob Manfred's name was on that list, he might have been one of those 10 or 15 where there was probably, or possibly, a very legitimate explanation that did not involve the use of a banned substance. I think it's really unfortunate that anybody's name was ever released publicly."[17]

None of which entirely clears Ortiz's name, but it does confirm that his explanation was at least plausible. By the time he becomes eligible in 2022, with Piazza, Bagwell, Ivan Rodriguez, and possibly Bonds in Cooperstown, the matter with regards to Big Papi might become a footnote.

Beyond that obstacle is the voters' handling of designated hitters. Molitor's 2004 election made him the first player with a plurality of plate appearances as a DH to gain entry, though his 3,319 hits virtually guaranteed his election. Frank Thomas's 2014 election set another precedent, as he became the first honoree who had taken the majority of his plate appearances (57%) as a DH, but his 521 homers and reputation as one of the era's few players to speak out against PEDs made him a lock as well. Meanwhile, Edgar Martinez, who played a more-than-passable third base for over 500 games but took 72% of his PA at DH, took until 2017, his eighth year of eligibility, to top 50%—likely aided by the head-to-head comparisons with Ortiz as his career wound down.

Ortiz, who took 88% of his PAs at DH, is Martinez's only rival for the title of the position's greatest. Ortiz owns the advantage in counting stats, but his .288/.380/.552 batting line, assembled largely while calling Fenway Park home, is not the equal of Martinez's .314/.428/.532 in the more pitcher-friendly environments of the Kingdome and Safeco Field. Adjusting for park and era and including their offensive performances at other positions, Martinez holds a 147–141 edge in OPS+ and a 531–457 edge in batting runs (the offensive component of WAR).

Martinez (whose case is taken up in Chapter 12) doesn't have Ortiz's lengthy postseason résumé, but he fares far better in terms of WAR and JAWS. Defensive value is built into WAR, both via a comparison of the player's fielding work to that of the average player and via a positional adjustment that rewards those at harder positions on the right of the Defensive Spectrum and penalizes those at the easier ones on the left. A "full-time" DH, playing 150 games a year, is assessed a positional adjustment of -15 runs, 5.5 fewer than the same amount of time at first base, and 17 fewer than the same time at third (which pertains to Martinez's case).

Because of that significant penalty, Ortiz only cracked the league's top 10 in WAR in 2005 (5.3 WAR, eighth), 2006 (5.7 WAR, sixth), and 2007 (6.4 WAR, sixth); meanwhile, he placed second, third, and fourth in the MVP voting in those years, respectively. He had three other seasons worth at least 4.0 WAR, the championship seasons of 2004 (4.2) and '13 (4.4) plus his swan song (5.1).

As with Molitor, Martinez and others who spent substantial time at DH, in my JAWS evaluations I have compared each Hall of Fame candidate to those at the positions where they accrued the most value. The precedent is applicable here as well; Ortiz, who played 278 games at first base and was 15 runs below average while doing so, is most fairly measured against first basemen. He doesn't measure up resoundingly well. His 55.4 career WAR is 24th, his 35.0 peak WAR is 34th, and his 45.2 JAWS is 28th, nine points below the standard; he outranks just four of 19 enshrinees in JAWS.

Those metrics don't capture the value of Ortiz's postseason accomplishments, however, and there's no magically correct answer as to how to weigh them. Even taken at face value, they are impressive, starting with Ortiz's .455/.576/.795 line in 59 World Series plate appearances. One has to drop the threshold to 30 PA—half the playing time—to find players with better rate stats; only Bonds (.471/.700/1.294 in 30 PA) beats him across the board. Having played in "only" three World Series, Ortiz's counting stats are lost in a sea of Yankees, Giants, Dodgers, and A's, but in six ALCS it's his counting stats that have primacy while his slash stats (.255/.357/.490) don't stand out; he's third in RBI (30), fifth in homers (eight), sixth in total bases (71).

Consider the entire body of his postseason work, which also includes nine Division Series. His .289/.404/.543 line is better than his regular season numbers, over the course of 369 PA, roughly two-thirds of a year, against the pitching of top-shelf teams. With the caveat that here he's largely competing with contemporaries from the Wild Card era, he's fourth in doubles (22) and RBIs (61), fifth in total bases (165) and RBIs (60), seventh in walks (59), tied for seventh in homers (17), 10th in hits (88)—an impressive collection, if not quite a dominant one.

There's no WAR to go with postseason stats, but one lens through which to view Ortiz's accomplishments—particularly given his "clutch" reputation—is that of Win Probability Added, a context-sensitive measure that accounts for the incremental increase (or decrease) in a team's chances of winning produced in each plate appearance given the inning, score, and base-out situation. Via data from researcher Dan Szymborski, Ortiz's 3.2 postseason WPA is the highest of any position player, beating out Albert Pujols's 2.9 (in 334 PA) and Carlos Beltran's 2.5 (in 235 PA). In part that's a function of his volume of opportunities within the expanded format, though the 14 other players with at least 300 postseason plate appearances average just 0.4 WPA, with some of them in the red (Jorge Posada -2.3 in 492 PA) and Saint Derek Jeter right at 0.0.

In an attempt to level the playing field for pre–Wild Card era players, Szymborski also crunched an Adjusted WPA by multiplying the raw figure by the ratio of the number of possible playoff games in the 2012–16 period (20 including the Wild Card game) to the number of games possible in the year in question (seven or occasionally nine for 1903 and 1905–68, 12 for 1969–84 except 1981, et cetera). By that measure, Ortiz ranks eighth:

Player	G	PA	WPA	AdjWPA
Lou Gehrig	34	150	2.3	6.9
Charlie Keller	19	79	1.9	5.6
Mickey Mantle	65	273	1.5	4.5
Home Run Baker	25	97	1.4	4.2
Pete Rose	67	301	2.6	3.9
Babe Ruth	40	167	1.2	3.6
Jimmie Foxx	18	73	1.2	3.6
David Ortiz	82	369	3.2	3.5
Duke Snider	36	149	1.1	3.3
Albert Pujols	77	334	2.9	3.2

Six of those 10 players are enshrined, Pujols will be the seventh, Rose certainly has the numbers, and Keller was on a Hall of Fame path before military service and chronic back problems wiped out his chance. In other words, this is a very distinguished group. That said, those players would probably be in Cooperstown anyway based on their regular season accomplishments.

One postseason hero with a similarly low JAWS score comes to mind as an Ortiz comp: Willie Stargell, a powerful and magnetic seven-time All-Star who inherited the Pirates' leadership mantle from the late Roberto Clemente and earned universal respect throughout the game. Said Joe Morgan, "When I played, there were 600 baseball players, and 599 of them loved Willie Stargell. He's the only guy I could have said that about. He never made anybody look bad and he never said anything bad about anybody."[18]

In his 21-year career, the slugging leftfielder/first baseman put up raw numbers that Ortiz eventually outdistanced, though in the lower scoring environment, he created more value:

Player	Career	Peak	JAWS	H	HR	AVG/OBP/SLG	OPS+
Stargell	57.5	38.0	47.7	2,232	475	.282/.360/.529	147
Avg HOF LF	65.1	41.5	53.3				
Ortiz	55.4	35.0	45.2	2,472	541	.286/.380/.552	141
Avg HOF 1B	65.9	42.4	54.2				

Like Ortiz, Stargell starred in the postseason, hitting a combined .278/.359/.511 with seven homers in 153 PA, including .315/.381/.574 with three homers in 63 PA in the Pittsburgh's 1971 and '79 World Series wins over Baltimore. In the latter, he drove in the winning runs in Game 7 and became the first player to run the table with the regular season MVP award as well as those of the LCS and World Series. That came in his age-39 season, though to be fair, the regular season award, shared with Keith Hernandez in a season where Stargell was worth just 2.5 WAR, was weak on paper, relying heavily on his perceived leadership of the colorful cast for whom Sister Sledge's disco hit "We Are Family" became an anthem.

From a sabermetric standpoint, Stargell's value is held back by subpar defense at both left field and first base to the tune of -70 runs. He's short on all three WAR fronts when measured against leftfielders, including 5.6 points short in JAWS—closer to the mark than Ortiz, albeit with lesser Monitor (106) and adjusted postseason WPA (0.5) numbers. Still, both on the field and off—where he won the Roberto Clemente Award, for the player who "best exemplifies the game of baseball, sportsmanship, community involvement and the individual's contribution to his team," in 1974, as Ortiz would do in 2011—Stargell touches the bases in a similar manner to Ortiz, an outsized icon whose collection of accomplishments in the regular and postseason are more than enough to get elected.

We won't know that until at least 2022, however, as Ortiz is just beginning his five-year waiting period. His candidacy has its flaws, but inarguably he rates as one of his era's most transcendent stars. The flags that fly over Fenway Park thanks to his contribution will outlive him, just as those from 1915, '16, and '18 outlive Babe Ruth. The people of Boston won't forget that, and I suspect neither will the BBWAA voters.

THE ROUNDUP

The number before each player name refers to his JAWS ranking *among all players at the position*, not necessarily those in the Hall. Average HOF first baseman: 66.4/42.7/54.6.

The Elite (above standard in career, peak, and JAWS)

1. Lou Gehrig

Teams:	Yankees 1923–39
Stats:	.340/.447/.632 • 179 OPS+ • 2,721 H • 493 HR • 102 SB
Rankings:	12× top 5 SLG • 12× top 5 HR • 11× top 5 OBP • 10× top 3 WAR • 9× top 5 AVG • 9× top 3 OBP • 7× All-Star All-time: 3rd SLG • 3rd OBP • 4th OPS+ • 8th AVG • 13th WAR • 17th TB • 28th HR
Voting/JAWS:	BBWAA 1939 **(special election)** • **112.4 /67.7/90.0**

Nearly eight decades after the onset of amyotrophic lateral sclerosis ended his playing career, the extent to which "The Iron Horse" eclipses the first base field is still startling, particularly given that his final game—and the end of his storied 2,130-game streak—preceded his 36th birthday. Prorated to a 162-game basis, his 8.4 WAR is more than a win and a half above every other first baseman save for Dan Brouthers (7.9). Because he spent the bulk of his career in Babe Ruth's shadow, Gehrig topped the AL in WAR only three times, but in their 10 years together as regulars (1925–34), the Bambino had only a 3.5-WAR edge (85.8 to 82.3). Among all position players, only Ruth, Willie Mays, Rogers Hornsby, Ted Williams, and Ty Cobb have higher peak scores. With his health further deteriorating, the BBWAA made sure to pay tribute to Gehrig while he was still alive, electing him unanimously at the 1939 Winter Meetings. It would be the writers' last vote until '42.

3. Jimmie Foxx

Teams:	A's 1925–35 • Red Sox 1936–42 • Cubs 1942, '44 • Phillies 1945
Stats:	.325/.428/.609 • 163 OPS+ • 2,646 H • 534 HR • 87 SB
Rankings:	9× All-Star • 9× top 3 OBP • 5× led OPS+ • 5× top 3 AVG • 5× led SLG • 4× led HR All-time: 4th SLG • 8th OBP • 8th OPS+ • 18th HR
Voting/JAWS:	BBWAA 1951 **(6th[†], 79.2%)** • **97.4/59.4/78.4***

[†] Years receiving votes prior to final year of career not counted.

[*] Pitching WAR included in player's career WAR & JAWS (not used in calculating position standards).

Remembered primarily for battling Ruth and Gehrig on the home run leaderboards, "Double X" was far from one-dimensional. In his younger days he offered speed and a strong arm as well as power, with the versatility to catch or play third base; late in his career, he even pitched (1.0 WAR in 23⅔ IP). Circa 1933, Joe Cronin called him "the greatest all-around ball player today,"[19] and revisited those sentiments in '40, when Foxx spent six weeks behind the plate for his Red Sox. Offensively, Foxx had far more help from his local bandboxes than Ruth or Gehrig, batting .345/.453/.663 at home and .307/.405/.561 elsewhere, for a gap of 150 points of OPS. From his 1945 retirement until '66, when he was surpassed by Mays, he ranked second only to Ruth in homers; as late as 1940, Ted Williams himself believed his teammate could challenge the Bambino, but Foxx hit just 15 homers after '41, his age-33 season, as chronic sinus problems and blurred vision—traced to a 1934 beaning while barnstorming in Canada—led him to seek relief from the bottle. He received Hall votes as early as 1936, but his percentage didn't reach double digits until '48, after which he inched fitfully toward induction.

5. Roger Connor

Teams:	Troy Trojans 1880–82 • New York Gothams/Giants 1883–89, '91, '93–94 • Giants (PL) 1890 • Phillies 1892 • St. Louis Browns 1894–97
Stats:	.316/.397/.486 • 153 OPS+ • 2,467 H • 138 HR • 244 SB
Rankings:	11× top 3 OPS+ • 11× top 5 SLG • 10× top 5 WAR • 8× top 5 HR • 6× top 5 AVG
Voting/JAWS:	VC 1976 • **84.1/47.0/65.5**

One of baseball's first great sluggers, Connor is among its most underappreciated figures, an early star who was somehow forgotten for decades. An outstanding lefty hitter whose strapping 6'3", 200-pound physique helped turned the New York Gothams into the Giants, he's believed to be the first player to clear the Polo Grounds fences and to hit a fair ball out of that park. Connor led his league in WAR three times while annually ranking among the game's top power hitters, though he hit more triples (233, fifth all-time) than homers, and led the latter category only in 1890, when he bolted to the Players League. He stood as the all-time home run leader from 1895 (upon surpassing Harry Stovey) through 1920, when Babe Ruth hit his 139th, but nobody at the time—including Connor himself—was aware, since career statistics were so poorly maintained. Hank Aaron's chase of Ruth's record illuminated Connor's feats; two years after Aaron claimed it—and 31 years after legendary umpire Bill Klem first took up his cause—Connor was elected by the VC.

6. Jeff Bagwell

Teams:	Astros 1991–2005
Stats:	.297/.408/.540 • 149 OPS+ • 2,314 H • 449 HR • 202 SB
Rankings:	6× top 5 OPS+ • 6× top 10 WAR • 6× top 10 HR • 5× top 5 OBP
	All-time: 23rd OBP • 28th OPS+
Voting/JAWS:	BBWAA 2017 **(7th, 86.2%)** • **79.6/48.2/63.9**

Even with a career shortened by a shoulder injury, Bagwell should have sailed into Cooperstown. A durable slugger with power, patience, and positive value on the basepaths (+31 runs) and in the field (+54 runs), he not only rated among the era's best hitters, he's second in WAR behind Albert Pujols among postwar first basemen. Famously acquired from the Red Sox for reliever Larry Andersen on August 30, 1990, Bagwell moved from third base to first and instantly became a cornerstone, winning Rookie of the Year honors and then MVP in 1994. Remarkably, he hit better in the run-suppressing Astrodome (.303/.421/.546 from 1991–99) than on the road (.305/.412/.544); his 160 OPS+ during that span ranked fourth behind Bonds (180), McGwire (176), and Thomas (169), while his 56.7 WAR was third behind Bonds and Griffey. When he hit the 2011 ballot, voters weren't shy about vocalizing suspicions of PED use, ignoring that in 1998 Bagwell had admitted to using still legal androstenedione. He debuted at 41.7%, and it took some perspective and advanced-stat contextualizing (ahem) to get his due.

7. Dan Brouthers

Teams:	Troy Trojans 1879–80 • Buffalo Bisons 1881–85 • Detroit Wolverines 1886–88 • Boston Beaneaters 1889 • Boston Reds (PL) 1890 • Boston Reds (AA) 1891 • Brooklyn Grooms 1892–93 • Orioles 1894–95 • Louisville Colonels 1895 • Phillies 1896 • Giants 1904
Stats:	.342/.423/.519 • 170 OPS+ • 2,296 H • 106 HR • 256 SB
Rankings:	8× led OPS+ • 6× led SLG • 5× led OBP • 5× led WAR • 4× led AVG • 3× S/S TC
	All-time: 7th OPS+ • 8th AVG • 11th OBP
Voting/JAWS:	OTC 1945 • **79.4/47.2/63.3**

While Connor slipped into obscurity, Brouthers (pronounced BROO-thers) was recognized as baseball's first great slugger. He has a solid claim as the best hitter of the nineteenth century. His 170 OPS+ through 1900 bests Pete Browning (163), Connor (153), and everyone else with at least 5,000 PA. Though he led in homers just twice, he dominated advanced-stat categories; in fact, he was the first three-time winner of the slash stat Triple Crown (1882, '83, '91), and ranked among his league's top five in WAR every year from 1882–92 save '90, when he was sixth. Like Connor—who was very briefly his teammate with Troy in 1880, playing third base left-handed (!)—Brouthers was a strapping fella (6'2", 207 pounds), which certainly gave him physical advantages relative to the competition, and like Connor he hit more triples (205, eighth all-time) than homers. Unlike Connor, he was elected in relatively timely fashion, albeit 13 years after his death.

8. Johnny Mize

Teams:	Cardinals 1936–41 • Giants 1942, '46–49 • Yankees 1949–53
Stats:	.312/.397/.562 • 158 OPS+ • 2,011 H • 359 HR • 28 SB
Rankings:	10× All-Star • 9× top 3 SLG • 9× top 10 SLG • 9× top 3 OPS+ • 8× top 5 WAR • 6× top 5 AVG • 4× led HR All-time 12th SLG • 13th OPS+
Voting/JAWS:	VC 1981 • **71.0/48.8/59.9**

"The Big Cat" would rank even higher if injuries—including a 1934 groin tear that forestalled his major league arrival—and military service hadn't shortened his career. Given his average of 6.5 WAR in the six seasons sandwiching his hitch, he might have lost 18–20 WAR to the service. Regularly among the elite in slash stats, Mize's 171 OPS+ through age 29 ranks 11th among players with at least 3,000 PA; only in his first year in New York, after being nosed out of St. Louis by young Stan Musial, did he fail to reach the .300/.400/.500 "golden ratio." He led in homers twice on either side of the war; his 51 in 1947 made him the oldest player (34 years) to reach 50 to that point. Banged up and chafing under manager Leo Durocher, he was traded to the Yankees in late 1949, and helped them to five straight championships as a part-timer. An undeservedly shaky defensive reputation, belied by both traditional and advanced stats (+18 runs), may have cost him votes, as Mize maxed out at just 43.6%. A VC featuring Musial and longtime St. Louis writer Bob Broeg elected him.

9. Frank Thomas

Teams:	White Sox 1990–2005 • A's 2006, '08 • Blue Jays 2007–08
Stats:	.301/.419/.555 • 156 OPS+ • 2,468 H • 521 HR

Rankings:	7× top 3 OPS+ • 7× top 5 SLG • 6× top 10 WAR • 5× All-Star • 4× led OBP
	All-time: 10th BB • 13th OBP • 15th OPS+ • 18th SLG • T-20th HR
Voting/JAWS:	BBWAA 2014 **(1st, 83.7%)** • **73.7/45.2/59.5**

The brawniest slugger (6′5″, 270 pounds) in an era typified by brawn, "The Big Hurt" was the era's most outspoken major leaguer against PEDs, calling for testing as early as 1995 and voluntarily testifying for the Mitchell Report. Few could match his track record as a hitter, which included a batting title, back-to-back MVP awards, three leads in OPS+ and four in OBP. He's one of seven players to maintain the .300/.400/.500 "golden ratio" over the course of at least 10,000 PA, joining Ruth, Cobb, Musial, Tris Speaker, Mel Ott, and Chipper Jones, and he's tied for 19th in homers with Ted Williams and Willie McCovey, a fitting combo given his power and precision in carving up the strike zone. He stands tall via advanced metrics as well despite subpar defense (-64 runs) and the built-in positional penalty that comes with spending 57% of his career as a DH; he's the first enshrinee who spent the majority of his career at that spot.

The Rank and File

4. Cap Anson

Teams:	Rockford Forest Citys (NA) 1871 • Philadelphia Athletics (NA) 1872–75 • Chicago White Stockings/Colts 1876–97
Stats:	.334/.394/.447 • 142 OPS+ • 3,435 H • 97 HR • 277 SB
Rankings:	10× top 3 AVG • 10× top 3 OBP • 8× top 5 WAR
	All-time: 4th RBI • 7th H • 9th R • 17th AVG
Voting/JAWS:	OTC 1939 • **93.9/41.7/67.8**

One of the game's earliest greats, Anson was considered a high-character man in his day, but he was openly racist, refusing to play exhibitions against black players such as Moses Fleetwood Walker and George Stovey. In 1887, he became a central figure in drawing the game's color line via the "gentleman's agreement," the unwritten rule against signing black players. He managed the White Stockings to five NL pennants, and is credited with ensuring the survival of the nascent league by popularizing the practice of raiding other leagues for top talent. A four-time batting champion, Anson played past his 45th birthday as the game's rules were still evolving, but shorter schedules—he didn't play in 100 games in a season until 1884 and topped 140 only once—cut into his stats, so his peak score falls below the standard. Even today, his hits total is in dispute; MLB, the Elias Bureau, and Hall disregard all National Association stats but count his 1887 walks as hits (a dumb, quickly discarded rule), crediting him with 3,081. Pete Palmer and Baseball-Reference include the NA but not the walks, crediting him with 3,435.

13. Willie McCovey

Teams:	Giants 1959–73, 1977–80 • Padres 1974–76 • A's 1976
Stats:	.270/.374/.515 • 147 OPS+ • 2,211 H • 521 HR • 26 SB
Rankings:	7× top 5 SLG • 7× top 5 HR • 6× All-Star • 6× top 10 WAR • 3× led OPS+
	All-time: T-20th HR • T-30th OPS+
Voting/JAWS:	BBWAA 1986 **(1st, 81.4%)** • **64.4/44.8/54.6**

This hulking 6'4", 200-pound thumper was tied for eighth on the all-time home run list when he retired, but had he not battled knee woes, a pitcher-friendly environment, and competition for time at first base from fellow Hall of Famer Orlando Cepeda, "Stretch" would have clubbed at least 600. Cepeda and McCovey won back-to-back NL Rookie of the Year honors in 1958–59, then spent the next five seasons trying not to trip over each other as the Giants shoehorned both into the lineup; Cepeda's 1965 knee injury and trade to the Cardinals the following year finally solved the problem. McCovey, who had struggled against lefties, found his way and from 1965–70 tied with Hank Aaron for most homers (226) while leading the league twice and winning '69 NL MVP honors. Age and arthritis in his right knee (and eventually damage to his left) took their toll thereafter; McCovey qualified for the batting title (502 PA) just once in his final 10 years but remained a power threat. Even with his limitations (including -80 runs in the field), he sailed into Cooperstown on the first ballot.

15. Eddie Murray

Teams:	Orioles 1977–88, '96 • Dodgers 1989–91, '97 • Mets 1992–93 • Indians 1994–96 • Angels 1997
Stats:	.287/.359/.476 • 129 OPS+ • 3,255 H • 504 HR • 110 SB
Rankings:	8× All-Star • 8× top 10 HR • 7× top 10 SLG • 6× top 5 OPS+ • 5× top 5 OBP • 4× top 10 WAR • 3 Gold Gloves
	All-time: 6th G • 10th TB • 27th HR
Voting/JAWS:	BBWAA 2003 **(1st, 85.3%)** • **68.3/39.0/53.6**

The third of five 3,000-hit/500-homer players after Aaron and Mays, Murray—like 99.9% of all players in history—lacked that pair's high peaks, and rarely cracked the upper reaches of leaderboards. Never an MVP, he had five straight top five finishes in the 1981–85 voting, including back to-back second places to Robin Yount and teammate Cal Ripken in 1982–83. Indeed, the ultimate "Steady Eddie" only once fell short of 25 homers or failed to notch between 171 and 186 hits during his first 12 years, excluding strike-torn 1981 (his only year leading in homers); during that span, only six players with at least 3,000 PA outdid his 141 OPS+. After a strong 1990, he was mostly below-average save for a resurgence as the DH of the 1995 pennant-winning Indians. The milestones carried him into Cooperstown, but the WAR numbers reflect his trajectory: 12th in career, but 21st in peak, 3.7 wins below the standard. Still, it's tough to quibble with his overall résumé.

16. Hank Greenberg

Teams:	Tigers 1930, '33–41, '45–46 • Pirates 1947
Stats:	.313/.412/.605 • 158 OPS+ • 1,628 H • 331 HR • 58 SB
Rankings:	8× top 10 OBP • 7× top 3 SLG • 7× top 5 OPS+ • 6× top 5 WAR • 5× All-Star • 4× top 10 AVG • 4× led HR
Voting/JAWS:	BBWAA 1956 **(8th[†], 85.0%)** • **57.5/47.7/52.6**

Masher and mensch, Greenberg exceeded 100 games just nine times due to a 1936 wrist fracture and a four-year stint in the army; he played a combined 97 games in 1941 and '45. When available, he pulverized AL pitching, placing first or second in homers six times and in the top 10 in three others, including 1945, when his 13 homers in 78 games helped the Tigers win their fourth pennant and second championship on his watch. After a stellar age-35 season (AL-high 44 homers, .604 SLG, 6.5 WAR), he was traded amid a salary dispute and played just one more year before taking over the Indians' farm system and soon becoming general manager. He's fourth in WAR among players who didn't reach 7,000 PA, and tied for 13th in OPS+ at a 6,000-PA cutoff. His peak score is sixth among first basemen; even without adding to that during the lost years—say, with 30 WAR from 1941–45, instead of 3.2 from his fragmentary seasons—he might rank fifth here with 66.0 JAWS. The BBWAA lollygagged in honoring him; after receiving 43.8% in 1949, he didn't surpass that figure until 1955.

---

† Years receiving votes prior to final year of career not counted.

18. George Sisler

Teams:	Browns 1915–22, 1924–27 • Senators 1928 • Braves 1928–30
Stats:	.340/.379/.468 • 125 OPS+ • 2,812 H • 102 HR • 375 SB
Rankings:	7× top 5 AVG • 7× top 10 OPS+ • 6× top 5 WAR • 6× top 5 SLG • 5× top 10 OBP • 4× led SB All-time: 13th AVG
Voting/JAWS:	BBWAA 1939 **(4th, 85.8%)** • **57.0/47.2/52.1***

Sisler dabbled in pitching, outdueling Walter Johnson in one of his six complete games as a rookie southpaw, and creating 2.5 WAR overall (included above) before making his mark as a contact-hitting machine whose career bridged the dead- and live-ball eras. After suggesting in the first *Historical Baseball Abstract* that he might have reached 4,000 hits while batting around .362 had he not gotten sick (a sinus infection affecting his optic nerve cost him all of 1923), Bill James called him "perhaps the most over-rated player in baseball history"[20] in *The New Bill James Historical Abstract*, noting his relatively low OBP and inflated defensive reputation. That smacks of overstatement. Despite modest power and a thin 5.2% walk rate, Sisler did his best work before the offensive upswing of the 1920s, so his big numbers—batting titles with averages over .400 in both 1920 (setting a single-season record for hits with 257) and '22, annual top five finishes in OPS+ every year from 1916–22, and in average and WAR every year from 1917–22—had real value. The longer run constitutes a peak score that's tied for seventh at the position.

20. Harmon Killebrew

Teams:	Senators 1954–60 • Twins 1961–74 • Royals 1975
Stats:	.256/.376/.509 • 143 OPS+ • 2,086 H • 573 HR • 19 SB
Rankings:	11× All-Star • 10× top 5 OPS+ • 8× top 3 SLG • 6× led HR • 6× top 10 WAR All-time: 11th HR
Voting/JAWS:	BBWAA 1984 **(4th, 83.1%)** • **60.3/38.1/49.2**

It's tricky to get a true sense of Killebrew's place because of the gap between his hitting—which produced an MLB-high 504 homers from 1959–71—and his de-

---

* Pitching WAR included in player's career WAR & JAWS (not used in calculating position standards)

fense, which kept his managers bouncing him around the diamond through his age-35 season. A bonus baby who played sparingly in his first five seasons (113 games, -0.6 WAR), "The Killer" broke out with an AL-high 42 homers in 1959, kicking off a 14-year stretch in which he missed the top five in homers just twice while averaging 100 walks and winning the 1969 AL MVP award. Stocky (5'11", 210 pounds) and slow-footed, he at least had good hands and a decent arm. He spent 35% of his innings at third base, where he was brutal (-50 runs), 21% in left field (-9 runs), and 43% at first (-6 runs). While the subpar defense limited his WAR, what hurt him in the eyes of BBWAA voters were his low batting average and high strikeout total (1,699, second when he retired but sixth by the time he hit the ballot). Though he polled 59.6% in his 1981 debut, he needed three more years to gain entry.

22. Bill Terry

Teams:	Giants 1923–36
Stats:	.341/.393/.506 • 136 OPS+ • 2,193 H • 154 HR • 56 SB
Rankings:	6× top 5 AVG • 6× top 10 OBP • 6× top 10 OPS+ • 6× top 10 WAR • 5× top 10 SLG • 3× All-Star
	All-time: 11th AVG
Voting/JAWS:	BBWAA 1954 (12th[†], 77.4%) • 54.2/41.2/47.7

Like Sisler, Terry tends to be overrated thanks to his high batting average. He hit .401 in 1930—the last NL player to reach .400—amid six straight years among the league's top five, but that marked his only title; a season-ending rainout washed away hits that would have given him another in 1931. Beyond that, Terry's decent pop and excellent glove (+73 runs) helped him to the NL's highest WAR from 1927–34 (44.6). The real knock against him is career length, as he spent 1918–21 (ages 19–22) playing semipro ball while working for Standard Oil; was blocked by High Pockets Kelly for two years in New York; and after becoming a regular at age 26, lost a chunk of 1926 to a holdout. He succeeded John McGraw as Giants manager in early 1932, won three pennants in his first five full seasons, and retired as a player after '36 due to a left knee problem. Even with that brevity, his peak is near the standard, and the size of his footprint on the game during the 1920s and '30s mandates his inclusion, though his impact on the Veterans Committee is another matter.

[†] Years receiving votes prior to final year of career not counted.

26. Jake Beckley

Teams:	Pittsburgh Alleghenys 1888–89 • Pittsburgh Burghers 1890 (PL) • Pirates 1891–96 • Giants 1896–97 • Reds 1897–1903 • Cardinals 1904–07
Stats:	.308/.361/.436 • 125 OPS+ • 2,934 H • 87 HR • 315 SB
Rankings:	6× top 10 SLG • 5× top 10 AVG • 4× top 10 OPS+ All-time: 4th 3B
Voting/JAWS:	VC 1971 • **61.5/29.8/45.7**

The Hall's most obscure first baseman, Beckley never played for a pennant winner, and led a league in an offensive category just once; he's forever the triples leader of the one-and-done Players League. Indeed, triples were Beckley's signature skill: He had eight seasons among the top 10, held the all-time lead from 1905–12, and still ranks fourth at 244. He was also renowned for his ability to bunt with the handle of the bat, holding the thicker end. While it likely went unnoticed, his 2,934 hits trailed only Anson when he retired, and he led all first basemen in games played (2,380) until Murray surpassed him. He never really peaked, but was alarmingly consistent, with 11 seasons of between 3.8 and 4.6 WAR from 1889–1904. Reflecting that, he's 16th in career WAR among first basemen, but 47th in peak score. He received virtually no attention from either BBWAA or VC voters until being elected 53 years after his death.

28. Tony Perez

Teams:	Reds 1964–76, 1984–86 • Expos 1977–79 • Red Sox 1980–82 • Phillies 1983
Stats:	.279/.341/.463 • 122 OPS+ • 2,732 H • 379 HR • 49 SB
Rankings:	7× All-Star • 6× top 10 HR • 5× top 10 SLG • 4× top 10 WAR • 3× OPS+
Voting/JAWS:	BBWAA 2000 **(9th, 77.2%)** • **53.9/36.4/45.2**

Perez's claim to fame was as the Big Red Machine's RBI collector. "The Big Dog" plated at least 90 runs 13 times, cracked the top 10 11 times (but never led) and totaled an MLB-high 1,375 ribbies from 1967–80, 116 more than runner-up Bench. Beyond that, Perez doesn't stand out as a great. A free swinger who's 12th all-time in strikeouts (1,867), he didn't walk much for a slugger (7.1% unintentionally), and cost himself a combined 42 runs on the bases via double plays. He's light in the Hall Monitor (81), black ink (league leads in important categories), and WAR; his most valuable work (including three All-Star seasons) came via competent play at third base from 1967–71. Despite being below both traditional and sabermetric standards, Perez debuted at 50.0% and inched upward until his election became a formality.

33. Orlando Cepeda

Teams:	Giants 1958–66 • Cardinals 1966–68 • Braves 1969–72 • A's 1972 • Red Sox 1973 • Royals 1974
Stats:	.297/.350/.499 • 133 OPS+ • 2,351 H • 379 HR • 142 SB
Rankings:	9× top 10 SLG • 9× top 10 HR • 8× top 10 AVG • 7× All-Star
Voting/JAWS:	VC 1999 • **50.3/34.5/42.4**

Though forced to battle with McCovey for playing time at the outset of the two players' careers, "The Baby Bull" quickly began beating a path to Cooperstown, rivaling Foxx, Pujols, and Gehrig in key "through age 26" stats among first basemen. Alas, a 1965 right knee injury, suffered while playing left field, wiped out his age-27 season and spelled his exit from San Francisco. Though some big Triple Crown–stat seasons lay ahead, only two of his seven peak years came after '64, including an MVP- and World Series–winning 1967 campaign for St. Louis with a career-best 6.8 WAR. He played just 277 games after 1970 due to injuries to his left knee, and cracked the league's top 10 in WAR just twice due to subpar defense (-11 runs), baserunning (-11), and double play avoidance (-22). A 10-month jail stint following a 1975 drug bust involving 165 pounds (!) of marijuana compromised his iconic status in his native Puerto Rico as well as his support among writers, but as he restructured his life, he gained votes, topping out at 73.5% (seven votes shy) in his final year, 1995. Four years later, the VC made him the second Puerto Rican player elected, after Clemente.

35. Frank Chance

Teams:	Chicago Orphans/Cubs 1898–1912 • Yankees 1913–14
Stats:	.296/.394/.394 • 135 OPS+ • 1,274 H • 20 HR • 403 SB
Rankings:	6× top 10 SB • 5× top 5 OBP • 5× top 10 WAR • 4× top 5 AVG • 4× top 10 OPS+
Voting/JAWS:	OTC 1946 • **45.6/35.6/40.6**

The first baseman from the most famous double play combination in history was originally a catcher, before transitioning to right field in 1901 and then first base in '02, the same year Joe Tinker took over shortstop; Johnny Evers settled into second in '03. Despite frequent broken fingers from catching, Chance didn't appreciate being moved, but a pay raise and increased success at the plate eased the transition. An excellent defender (+47 runs) and exceptional base stealer, his run as a great player lasted only five years (1903–07), during which only Honus Wagner and Nap Lajoie topped his 29.2 WAR; from 1902–10, his 40.2 WAR ranked fifth. "The Peerless Leader" took over managerial duties from the ailing Frank Selee while still at the height of his game in mid-1905, and led the Cubs to three straight pennants (1906–08) plus another in '10, winning the World Series twice. Injuries caused by his hard-nosed play and propensity for beanings (he was a plate crowder), took their toll, and after 1910 he played in just 46 more games. Even with less fruitful stints with the Yankees and Red Sox, his .593 winning percentage is fifth among those who managed at least 1,500 games, and he's enshrined as much as for his play.

The Basement (the most dubious honorees)

55. Jim Bottomley

Teams:	Cardinals 1922–32 • Reds 1933–35 • Browns 1936–37
Stats:	.310/.369/.500 • 125 OPS+ • 2,313 H • 219 HR • 58 SB
Rankings:	8× top 10 SLG • 5× top 10 OPS+ • 4× top 10 WAR • 4× top 10 OBP • 3× top 3 AVG
Voting/JAWS:	VC 1974 • **35.3/28.8/32.0**

A well-liked slugger who helped the Cardinals to four pennants and two championships from 1926–31, "Sunny Jim" put up superficially eye-opening numbers under favorable offensive conditions. In 1928, he won MVP honors for the NL champs and led the league in triples (20), homers (31), RBI (136), and total bases (362) while ranking second in OPS+ (162) and third in WAR (6.3). He never led in a slash stat but did have 15 top 10 rankings. Total Zone doesn't think much of his defense; his -73 fielding runs rank the fourth worst at the position, which crushes his value, limiting him to just two seasons of more than 4.5 WAR, not to mention a grand total of 2.8 over his age-32–37 seasons (1932–37). He maxed out at 33.1% from the writers in 1960, but nonetheless was elected by the VC; while ex-teammate Frankie Frisch had died by 1974, Bottomley fits in among the Frisch/Terry cronies.

87. George Kelly

Teams:	Giants 1915–17, 1919–26 • Pirates 1917 • Reds 1927–30 • Cubs 1930 • Dodgers 1932
Stats:	.297/.342/.452 • 109 OPS+ • 1,778 H • 148 HR • 65 SB
Rankings:	7× top 10 HR • 3× top 10 SLG • 2× top 10 OPS+ • 2× top 10 WAR
Voting/JAWS:	VC 1973 • **25.2/23.9/24.6**

Standing a gangly 6'4"—hence "High Pockets"—Kelly is simply one of the worst players enshrined, yet another reminder of the importance of "fame" in the equation. During the Giants' four-year run as NL champs (1921–24), he built a reputation as a stellar defender and clutch hitter. While the system values his defense (+52 runs), we lack play-by-play data to support his ostensible "clutchness" via splits like batting average with runners in scoring position or close-and-late, leaving his five top five finishes in RBI as the strongest evidence. For what it's worth, he hit just .248/.283/.297 in 109 World Series PA, for the fourth-lowest OPS in World Series history (100 PA minimum). He rarely cracked the leaderboard in WAR or OPS+ and never broke 2.0% percent on the BBWAA ballot. It took a VC starring ex-teammate/understudy Bill Terry to elect him, hardly the institution's finest hour.

Further Consideration (upcoming or overlooked candidates)

2. Albert Pujols

Teams:	Cardinals 2001–11 • Angels 2012–16 (active)
Stats:	.309/.392/.573 • 157 OPS+ • 2,825 H • 591 HR • 107 SB
Rankings:	10× All-Star • 8× top 3 OPS+ • 7× top 5 SLG • 6× led WAR • 7× top 5 OBP • 6× top 5 AVG • 3× MVP
	All-time: 9th HR • 10th SLG • 13th OPS+
JAWS:	101.1/61.6/81.3

Barring some unforeseen turn of events, Pujols is on his way to Cooperstown, his place in the pantheon secure, if not quite as elevated as it might have appeared a few years ago. Through his first 11 seasons—the run of his career with the Cardinals—he generated more value (86.4 WAR) than any player save for Willie Mays (87.4 WAR) had to that point in his career, and hit more homers (445) than anyone while helping the Cardinals to seven playoff berths, three pennants, and two championships, and dominating leaderboards. Since signing a 10-year, $240 million deal with the Angels, a series of leg and foot injuries has significantly slowed down his pace, but barring an abrupt retirement, big milestones appear to be inevitable, though surpassing Gehrig for the JAWS lead at the position is probably out of the question.

10. Jim Thome

Teams:	Indians 1991–2002, '11 • Phillies 2003–05, '12 • White Sox 2006–09 • Dodgers 2009 • Twins 2010–11 • Orioles 2012
Stats:	.276/.402/.554 • 147 OPS+ • 2,328 H • 612 HR • 19 SB

Rankings:	10x top 10 SLG • 8x top 5 HR • 7x top 5 OBP • 7x top 5 OPS+ • 5x top 10 WAR • 5x All-Star
	All-time: 7th HR • 7th BB • 20th SLG • T-30th OPS+
JAWS:	**72.9/41.5/57.2**

Possessed of prodigious power, Thome led his league in homers just once, but with six seasons of at least 40, another six with at least 30, and four more with at least 20, he piled enough taters on his plate to become the eighth player to reach 600, without ever being connected to PEDs. Because his tater-mashing ability put the fear of God in pitchers, he had ten seasons ranking among the top five in walks; he's seventh all-time at 1,747 (and second in strikeouts with 2,548). Initially a third baseman, he didn't make anyone forget Buddy Bell, but the metrics suggest he was close to average both there and after moving to first base in 1997. He spent the final third of his career DHing due to injuries (particularly lower back troubles) but even with his defensive handicaps, he cracked the league's top 10 in WAR five times from 1995–2003, with a total of 49.0 that trailed only Bonds, Alex Rodriguez, and Bagwell. He'll have no trouble gaining entry in 2018.

11. Miguel Cabrera

Teams:	Marlins 2003–07 • Tigers 2008–16
Stats:	.321/.399/.562 • 155 OPS+ • 2,519 H • 446 HR • 38 SB
Rankings:	12x top 10 SLG • 11x All-Star • 10x top 5 OPS+ • 10x top 10 OBP • 9x top 10 HR • 7x top 10 WAR • 4x led AVG
	All-time: 13th SLG • T-18th OPS+
JAWS:	**69.6/44.6/57.1**

With four batting titles, including a Triple Crown, not to mention a pair of MVP awards and a World Series ring, Cabrera has already punched his ticket to Cooperstown. What remains to be seen is just how high he climbs on the leaderboards by the end of his contract in 2023 (his age-40 season). Three thousand hits and 500 homers is probably selling him short; placing among the top 10 in both (surpassing Paul Molitor's 3,319 hits and Frank Robinson's 586 homers) is possible, Aaron/Mays-flavor country. Even with wretched defense (-83 fielding runs and counting) and an eventual move to DH, he's already above the JAWS standard at first base.

12. Rafael Palmeiro

Teams:	Cubs 1986–88 • Rangers 1989–93, 1999–2003 • Orioles 1994–98, 2004–05
Stats:	.288/.371/.515 • 132 OPS+ • 3,020 H • 569 HR • 97 SB
Rankings:	11× top 10 HR • 7× top 10 SLG • 5× top 10 AVG • 5× top 10 WAR • 4× All-Star • 3× GG
	All-time: 11th TB • 13th HR • 27th H
JAWS:	71.6/38.7/55.2

Palmeiro became the poster boy for an era in 2005, when just 4½ months after wagging his finger at the House Government Reform Committee and declaring, "I have never used steroids. Period," he tested positive for stanozolol. While the 10-game ban—the first for a star—was small potatoes, it cast a shadow not just over his recent 3,000th hit but over a 20-year career, in which he was just the fourth player to accompany that milestone with 500 homers. His bronze plaque slipped away; he fell off the BBWAA ballot after four years, having never received more than 12.6%. Was that fair? An eternity in purgatory due to a mistake in the final lap of an illustrious career seems draconian. Performance-wise, Palmeiro never led his league in a Triple Crown stat, a rate stat one, or a major sabermetric one. His JAWS still suggests he's Hall-worthy, albeit more as a compiler than a superstar; he's 10th in career WAR among first baseman, but 24th in peak. He won't get another shot until the 2022 Today's Game ballot.

14. Todd Helton

Teams:	Rockies 1997–2013
Stats:	.316/.414/.539 • 133 OPS+ • 2,519 H • 369 HR • 37 SB
Rankings:	8× top 5 OBP • 7× top 5 AVG • 6× top 10 SLG • 5× All-Star • 5× top 10 OPS+ • 5× top 10 WAR • 3× GG
JAWS:	61.2/46.4/53.8

Baseball-Reference.com's AIR stat express the offensive conditions under which a player played in the manner of OPS+, with 100 as average, over 100 as favorable to hitters, etc. Via a career spent entirely with the Rockies, Helton's 122 AIR leads all players with at least 6,000 PA, a fancy way of saying that he played under the most favorable offensive conditions of any Hall candidate. Helton posted video-game numbers at Coors Field (.345/.441/.607 with 227 homers) while hitting a respectable .287/.386/.469 with 142 homers elsewhere. His 1.048 home OPS is sixth all-time behind Ruth, Williams, Foxx, Bonds, and Gehrig, while the 193-point gap between that and his road split is fifth. In addition to his altitude-aided power, he drew a ton of walks (1,335), led the league twice in OBP, played stellar defense (+74 fielding runs), and helped the Rox to two postseasons and a pennant. A sharp decline after age 33 left him short in career WAR, but he's well above the standard for peak; he's a borderline case, but the voters' mistreatment of Larry Walker doesn't bode well for him.

17. Mark McGwire

Teams:	A's 1986–97 • Cardinals 1997–2001
Stats:	.263/.394/.588 • 163 OPS+ • 1,626 HR • 583 HR • 12 SB
Rankings:	12x All-Star • 8x top 3 HR • 6x top 10 WAR • 4x led SLG • 4x led OPS+
	All-time: 6th SLG • 10th OPS+ • 11th HR
JAWS:	62.0/41.8/51.9

No modern player has been left to carry the weight of an era like McGwire, whose prodigious home runs helped heal the wounds caused by the 1994 strike, and whose ability to connect to the game's history while surpassing Roger Maris's record during the 1998 chase was lauded. Only after his retirement, when the still legal andro and other PEDs were explicitly banned by MLB, did the meaning of those homers change, as those who exalted him turned against him, piling on when they felt his 2010 admission was less than comprehensive. In some obvious ways, McGwire's numbers are Hall caliber. His 7.6% HR/PA rate is the all-time best; his homer total was in the top 10 until recently; and he's got black ink for days. His hits total is lower than any post-1960 enshrined hitter because he's 42nd all-time in walks (1,317), and while hardly a great defender (-29 runs career), his lone Gold Glove is supported by the metrics and his JAWS is borderline. Amid the hysteria, he barely inched past his 23.5% debut and was heading toward single-digit territory when his truncated eligibility lapsed. Though he's already appeared on the 2017 Today's Game ballot, it could take decades before his case gets a clear-eyed look.

19. Keith Hernandez

Teams:	Cardinals 1974–83 • Mets 1983–89 • Indians 1990
Stats:	.296/.384/.436 • 128 OPS+ • 2,182 H • 162 HR • 98 SB
Rankings:	11x GG • 7x OBP top 3 • 7x AVG top 10 • 6x WAR top 10 • 5x All-Star
JAWS:	60.0/41.0/50.5

Though lacking the power associated with modern first basemen, Hernandez was an on-base machine and an elite defender whose tactic of charging at batters attempting to bunt revolutionized the position; he closed off the right side of the infield, using his range and strong arm to turn sacrifices into forceouts. Not only did he win 11 straight Gold Gloves from 1978–88 (more than any other first baseman), his 117 fielding runs ranks second at the position behind Pujols's 140. His 1979 batting title and shared MVP award (he tripled Willie Stargell's WAR, 7.6 to 2.5) began an eight-year stretch during which only Mike Schmidt, Rickey Henderson, and George Brett topped his 45.2 WAR, and he helped the 1982 Cardinals and '86 Mets win championships. Short-counting stats—injuries that forced him into retirement at age 36—and his nontraditional offensive profile probably hindered his candidacy more than his 1985 Pittsburgh drug admission of "massive" cocaine use. He never exceeded 10.8% in nine ballot turns, and hasn't gotten a deserved second look from the small committees.

28. Fred McGriff

Teams: Blue Jays 1986–90 • Padres 1991–93 • Braves 1993–97 • Devil Rays 1998–2001, '04 • Cubs 2001–02 • Dodgers 2003

Stats: .284/.377/.509 • 134 OPS+ • 2,490 H • 493 HR • 72 SB

Rankings: 7× top 5 HR • 6× top 5 OPS+ • 5× All-Star • 5× top 5 SLG • 4× top 5 OBP • 4× top 10 WAR

JAWS: 52.6/36.0/44.3

The "Crime Dog" nickname, the *Tom Emanski Defensive Drills* commercial, high home run totals in the pre-steroid era—McGriff is remembered for things that seem decidedly square these days. From 1988–94, his 242 homers led all of baseball, and he became the first player to lead each league in homers since the dead-ball era; his 155 OPS+ for that span ranked second. Traded to the Braves amid the Padres' infamous 1993 fire sale, McGriff settled in as a solid supporting cast member on a dynamo, hitting .303/.385/.532 with 10 homers in 218 PA in the postseason. Even so, he struggled to stand out, making just five All-Star teams, finishing among the top five in MVP voting just once, and getting released for the final time while nearing hit and homer milestones. His accomplishments got lost amid the inflated offensive numbers that followed; he peaked at 23.0% in his third year on the ballot. The advanced metrics suggest that's the right call, as subpar defense, baserunning, and double play avoidance (-69 runs combined) limited his value; he's no higher than 28th in career, peak, or JAWS. Maybe his 500th homer would have helped, but only three players with at least 450 have lower WARs: Adam Dunn (16.6), Canseco (42.3), and Carlos Delgado (44.3).

35. Gil Hodges

Teams:	1943, 1947–1961 Dodgers • 1962–1963 Mets
Stats:	.273/.359/.487 • 120 OPS+ • 1,921 H • 370 HR • 63 SB
Rankings:	10× top 10 HR • 8× All-Star • 6× top 10 SLG • 4× top 10 OPS+ • 3× GG • 3× top 10 WAR
JAWS:	45.0/34.3/39.6

More collective emotion has been spent trying to will Hodges into Cooperstown than any other player. The closest miss, he reached 60.1% twice, yet stands as the only player to cross that threshold without getting in via the VC (let's wait and see on Jack Morris). Biographer Danny Peary claims that in 1993, when Ted Williams led the VC, he would not allow ailing committee member Roy Campanella to vote by phone; thus, Hodges missed by one vote. He's never gotten closer. Emotion and popularity aside, it's not clear that he belongs. Yes, he was a three-time Gold Glove winner whose reputation is supported by the metrics (+48 runs), with big homer and RBI totals while playing regularly on six pennant winners and two champions. However, he never led in a major category, and once you adjust for the bandbox of Ebbets Field, his impact on the OPS+ and WAR leaderboards (never higher than sixth in either) is underwhelming. His 40.9 WAR from 1949–57, while ninth in the majors, ranked third on the Dodgers behind Duke Snider (58.2) and Jackie Robinson (53.0), with Pee Wee Reese (39.4) close behind. Despite a few strong World Series performances, his 0-for-21 in 1952 drags his October line to .267/.349/.412 in 151 PA. Both the old-stats-focused Hall of Fame Monitor (82 points) and JAWS suggest he's significantly short. He gets credit for the 1969 Miracle Mets, but that was an aberration in a managerial career that—while cruelly cut short by his sudden death at age 47—was otherwise 131 games below .500. I'll leave it to somebody else to make a stronger case.

CHAPTER 11

SECOND BASEMEN

BOBBY GRICH

> Bobby Grich always wore uniforms that looked like 'before' on a detergent commercial.[1]
>
> —RON LUCIANO

Bobby Grich was a player ahead of his time. Though he didn't go entirely unappreciated during his 17-year major league career, making six All-Star teams, winning four Gold Gloves, and helping his teams to five division titles while gaining a reputation as one of the game's grittiest players, he rarely landed in the spotlight, and didn't receive the level of recognition that his talents deserved. He was overshadowed by more decorated teammates, such as Hall of Famers Brooks Robinson and Jim Palmer in Baltimore, and Rod Carew, Nolan Ryan, and Don Baylor—the last not a Hall of Famer but the 1979 AL MVP, and a longtime teammate at both stops in his career—in Anaheim.

Grich took a backseat due to his relatively modest traditional statistics, which were all media and fans had to go on for most of his career. His batting averages generally landed in the .250–.280 range, topping .300 only in the strike-shortened 1981 season. He hit 20 or more homers and drove in 70 or more runs just twice apiece. Only in 1981 did he lead the league in a key offensive category. The defensive accolades he won owed more to his low error totals and high fielding percentage than to his instincts and range.

It took the arrival of Bill James and his newfangled numbers for Grich to start getting his due. Via formulas that rewarded Grich for his high walk rate, considerable power, and outstanding range within a low-scoring era and a pitcher-friendly environment, James ranked Grich as the game's top second baseman in his 1982 and '83 *Baseball Abstracts*, his first two mass-market books; he ranked him second in '84, ninth in career value in his first *Historical Abstract* in '88, and 12th all-time in his updated one in 2001. "Without exception, the most underrated player in baseball today. He is one of the ten, perhaps one of the five best players in the game. . . . His statistics are badly hurt by playing in Anaheim,"[2] James wrote in 1982, adding a year later, "A lot of AL second basemen are close to him in one respect or another—but as a complete player, nobody else is on the same planet."[3]

Alas, such praise arrived late in Grich's career, and not enough writers were paying attention to James even by the time Grich came up for election to the Hall of Fame in 1992. He received just 2.6%, not enough to maintain eligibility, and in the quarter-century since that slight, he hasn't been included on a committee ballot either, though modern advanced statistics still make a strong case for his inclusion in Cooperstown.

The Career

1970–76 Orioles • 1977–86 Angels

Player	Career	Peak	JAWS	H	HR	SB	AVG/OBP/SLG	OPS+
Bobby Grich	70.9	46.3	58.6	1833	224	104	.266/.371/.424	125
Avg HOF 2B	69.3	44.4	56.9					
2B Rank	8th	11th	7h					
(Above HOF)	(14/20)	(12/20)	(14/20)					

Though he was born in Muskegon, Michigan, in 1949, Bobby Grich was a California boy, spending most of his childhood in Long Beach, where he was a fan of the Los Angeles Angels of the Pacific Coast League, and particularly slugging first baseman Steve Bilko. Grich starred as a shortstop at Woodrow Wilson High School, playing on the same team as future major leaguers Ed Crosby and Jeff Burroughs. He also excelled on the gridiron, and signed a letter of intent to attend UCLA. "We thought he was the best high school quarterback prospect we saw that year,"[4] said UCLA coach Tommy Prothro, who envisioned him not only as a starter but as a Heisman Trophy candidate.

The Orioles thought highly of Grich as well, drafting him in the first round in 1967 with the 19th pick overall. They signed him for a $40,000 bonus and sent him to Bluefield, their Appalachian League affiliate, and then to Stockton, their A-level affiliate in the California League. While Baylor, their second-round 1967 pick, rocketed from Stockton to Double-A Elmira to Triple-A Rochester in the same year, Grich climbed the ladder one step at a time. After struggling at

Stockton, he hit .310/.383/.402 at Double-A Dallas-Fort Worth in 1969, earning Texas League All-Star honors.

While he was doing that, the Orioles were winning the 1969 AL pennant with an impervious infield featuring shortstop Mark Belanger (12 runs above average via Total Zone), second baseman Dave (later Davey) Johnson (+8 runs), and third baseman Brooks Robinson (+23 runs), all Gold Glove winners. With that trio in place in 1970, Grich was sent to Rochester, where he played mostly second base until his hot bat and progress at the new position earned him a promotion. Manager Earl Weaver limited him to spot starts at second and short; Grich hit .211/.279/.284 in 104 plate appearances and was left off the postseason roster, a bystander as the Orioles beat the Reds in the World Series.

At times, the fiery 20-year-old grew frustrated with Weaver's machinations. According to one oft-told (but perhaps apocryphal) story, during a 1970 game Weaver sent up Grich to pinch-hit against a lefty, only to pull him in favor of lefty-swinging Elrod Hendricks when the opposing manager switched to a righty. A livid Grich confronted Weaver, screaming, "How do you expect me to hit when you're up there swinging for me all the time?"[5]

"He was so mad, I thought he might start swinging," said Weaver. Pitcher Dave McNally suggested that Grich might come to blows with general manager Harry Dalton if he was demoted again. "I'd advise him to have someone else in the room. Grich is apt to start firing punches."[6]

Inevitably, Grich returned to Rochester (and shortstop) in 1971. Heeding Weaver's advice to work on pulling the ball for more power, he hit .336/.439/.632 with a league-leading 32 homers en route to the International League MVP and *The Sporting News* Minor League Player of the Year awards. Hall of Famer George Sisler, then serving as IL president, called him "the best minor league player I have ever seen come through our league."[7] Not until Belanger injured his knee in mid-September did Grich get a call-up that Weaver conceded was overdue. He played in just seven games and again was a bystander as the Orioles won the AL pennant but lost to the Pirates in the World Series.

Though the White Sox and Yankees inquired about obtaining Grich in the winter of 1971–72, the Orioles finally found room. Weaver, who compared him to 1950s Yankees handyman Gil McDougald, used Grich at all four infield spots; he made 68 starts at shortstop, spending most of June and July as the regular there, and 43 at second, including most of September. Not only did the versatile 23-year-old hit .278/.358/.415 with 12 homers, 13 steals, and a 127 OPS+, his 6.0 WAR ranked fifth in the league, and he wound up starting the All-Star Game at short. Boston's Luis Aparicio, who had been elected by the fans, and Weaver's first choice for a sub, the Rangers' Toby Harrah, both withdrew due to injuries. Weaver not only started Grich but used him for all 10 innings to the chagrin of Oakland's Bert Campaneris, who complained to the press about how he should have started.

Despite Grich's strong work, the three-time pennant winners slipped to 80-74, third in the AL East. After Belanger (.186/.236/.246) and Johnson (.221/.320/.335) both sputtered offensively, the team shook things up, trading the latter to Atlanta, clearing second base for Grich. He started all 162 of the Orioles' games in 1973, hitting .251/.373/.387 with 12 homers, 17 steals, and 107 walks, the league's second-highest total. His defense drew particular attention as he set a fielding percentage record (.995) with just five errors in 945 chances, breaking Jerry Adair's 1964 mark. Via Total Zone, his work was worth an off-the-charts 29 runs above average, propelling him to a league-best 8.3 WAR, not to mention his first Gold Glove. The 97-65 Orioles won the AL East but fell to Oakland in the ALCS; Grich went just 2-for-20, but his homer off Rollie Fingers was the decisive blow in Game 4.

The O's won 90 games but met the same ALCS fate against the A's in 1974. Grich enjoyed another stellar season, batting .263/.376/.431 for a 135 OPS+ with a career-high 19 homers, 90 walks, and a league-high 20 hit-by-pitches; his 7.3 WAR ranked second in the league. He made the All-Star team as a reserve, and won another Gold Glove, the second of four straight. Even as the Orioles took a back-seat to the Red Sox in 1975 and the Yankees in 1976, he continued to rank among the league's most valuable players thanks to high on-base percentages and strong defense, with 7.3 WAR in the former year and 6.1 in the latter, good for third and sixth in the league, respectively. He edged the Yankees' Willie Randolph in the fan voting to start the 1976 All-Star Game.

After the 1976 season, the 27-year-old Grich was eligible to explore the market as a free agent, a new option open to players with enough service time thanks to the landmark Messersmith-McNally arbitration decision. With four straight Gold Gloves, his reputation for strong defense put him in an enviable position; had WAR existed then, the knowledge that his 34.9 from 1972–76 was the game's second best behind two-time MVP Joe Morgan would have enhanced it further. "In my opinion, Bobby Grich is as good as any and probably the best ballplayer in the American League,"[8] said Weaver, whose Orioles nonetheless made little effort to keep him.

With the 21-year-old Randolph in place, the AL champion Yankees didn't need a second baseman, but owner George Steinbrenner was down on his partner in the middle infield. "We are not going to win a championship with Fred Stanley at shortstop,"[9] he told his front office, still seething about a throwing error that had cost the Yankees a win in Game 2 of the World Series. General manager Gabe Paul eyed Grich as his replacement, and the maximum 12 teams chose him in what was called the reentry draft so as to establish the right to negotiate with him. When Baylor and former A's outfielder Joe Rudi both signed with the Angels (for whom Dalton was now GM), Grich told agent Jerry Kapstein he wanted to join them as well. The Angels, who had been rumored to covet Grich, signed him to a five-year, $1.55 million deal with the intention of returning him to shortstop. A jilted Steinbrenner turned around and signed Reggie Jackson, who had spent 1976 as Grich's teammate in Baltimore, for five years at $3 million.

The preseason hype for the new-look Angels landed Baylor, Grich, and Rudi on the cover of the March 5 edition of *The Sporting News*, but Grich's season got off to a rocky start. On Valentine's Day, shortly after reporting for spring training, he injured his back carrying an air conditioner up a stairway, and spent three weeks in traction due to muscle spasms. Though he got off to a typically productive start while handling the move back to shortstop well, he hit the disabled list amid a 4-for-36 slump; pain overwhelmed him as he rounded the bases following a walkoff homer against the Blue Jays on June 8. Discovered to have a herniated lumbar disc, he underwent season-ending surgery on July 3.

Grich returned to second base in 1978 and played in 144 games, but struggled, hitting .251/.357/.329 with six homers, one fewer than in 52 games in '77. The down season prompted him to hit the weights during the winter. He improved his flexibility as well as his strength, and experimented with his swing during the spring, emulating new teammate Rod Carew's wrist action so as to produce more topspin, and raising his hands. Via *Sports Illustrated*'s Joe Jares, "He stands deep in the batter's box and holds his hands near his right ear, which he feels has eliminated his old uppercut swing that produced far too many strikeouts and fly balls."[10]

The changes paid off in a big way. Grich hit .294/.365/.537, setting career bests in batting average, slugging percentage, home runs (30), RBI (101), and OPS+ (145). He made the AL All-Star team and helped the Angels to their first division championship in franchise history (alas, they lost to the Orioles in the ALCS). Had Baylor not hit 36 homers and driven in an AL-best 139 runs, Grich might have received strong MVP consideration. While he was the more valuable of the two in terms of WAR (5.9 to 3.7), the voters went with the butter-and-egg man, with Grich placing a distant eighth, his highest finish in five years of receiving votes.

After slipping to 14 homers and 4.1 WAR in 1980 while the Angels crashed to a 66-95 record, Grich tapped into his 1979 form the following year, hitting .304/.378/.543 with 22 homers, 10 in the first 17 games after play resumed following the seven-week strike. His slugging percentage, 165 OPS+, and home run total all led the AL (the last tied with three other players), while his 5.4 WAR ranked fourth, but the Angels' 51-59 record left them outside the playoff picture both pre- and post-strike, so he received just token MVP consideration. A free agent that winter, he re-signed with the Angels via a four-year, $4 million deal.

He did help the Halos back to the postseason in 1982, hitting .261/.371/.449 with 19 homers and starting at second base in the All-Star Game, but again, they fell short of the World Series, ousted by the Brewers in the ALCS. A strong 1983 campaign (.292/.414/.460 with 16 homers and 4.3 WAR) ended with a season-ending metacarpal fracture in his left hand via an August 28 hit-by-pitch.

Grich spent three more years with the Angels, shifting into a utility role that included time at third and first as well as second. While still an above-average player, he averaged just 119 games for that stretch. He hit a respectable .268/.354/.412 in 1986 while helping the 92-win Angels to another AL West title, but the ALCS against the Red Sox was a series of extreme peaks and valleys.

In Game 2, he couldn't handle a Dwight Evans popup that fell for an RBI double, and was cut down at the plate trying to score the tying run from second base after third base coach Moose Stubing failed to give him a stop sign; the Angels lost. In Game 4, despite striking out three times previously, he drove in the winning run in the 11th inning to give the Angels a 3–1 series lead. In Game 5, he hit a two-run homer in the sixth inning that put the Angels ahead 4–1, but they wound up losing 7–6 in 11 innings. In Game 6, playing first base for the injured Wally Joyner, he took a cutoff throw and threw to first base, but nobody was there to field it; two runs scored on the play, and the Angels lost. "The stuff that's happened to me in this series has been unbelievable," he said afterward. "I love baseball one day, I hate it another day. Right now, I'm hating it."[11]

In Game 7, Grich went 0-for-2 with a pair of strikeouts before being replaced by a pinch-hitter in the ninth inning of an 8–1 loss. Afterward, he announced his retirement, a decision he had made in August. "It's a bitter ending to an outstanding career. I hate to go out this way."[12]

The Case

Grich was 37 when he played the last of his 2,008 regular season games, both relatively low numbers by the standards of Hall of Fame second basemen. The 20 who are enshrined averaged 2,193 games, and of the seven who played fewer than Grich, two missed time due to military service (Bobby Doerr and Joe Gordon) and one due to the color barrier (Jackie Robinson). Only five walked away at a younger age: Doerr (33), Gordon, Tony Lazzeri, and Bill Mazeroski (all 35), and Roberto Alomar (36), the last two of whom had more games under their belts than Grich.

That early exit is a problem, because it left Grich short of several common milestones, most notably 2,000 hits. No position player whose career crossed into the post-1960 expansion era has gotten in with fewer than that. Regardless of when they played, just 34 out of 148 position players in the Hall finished with fewer than 2,000 hits, most of whom can be classified as nineteenth-century or dead-ball-era players, catchers, servicemen, or ex–Negro Leaguers. Even given that Grich walked a great deal, and that his 3,006 times on base (hits plus walks plus hit-by-pitches) outranks 52 Hall of Famers, he's at a disadvantage. In the eyes of the voters, a low hit total is an easy proxy for a career too short for enshrinement.

Likewise, Grich's .266 batting average isn't much help, as just nine players are enshrined with lower marks: elite sluggers Jackson and Harmon Killebrew, catchers Ray Schalk and Gary Carter, and light-hitting middle infielders Aparicio, Rabbit Maranville, Mazeroski, Ozzie Smith, and Joe Tinker, all in the .253–.262 range.

Indeed, the traditional stats don't do much justice to Grich, who led the league in just one Triple Crown category (homers, 1981), and reached 30 homers, 100 RBI, and a .300 batting average just once apiece. No 200-hit seasons, no 100-run seasons, no 20-steal seasons, even. His collection of honors and awards—six All-Star appearances, four Gold Gloves, and a high-water mark of eighth in the MVP voting—is modest; his .182/.247/.318 postseason line in 98 PA, for five teams that won their divisions but never made the World Series, is meager.

In Grich's favor is power. He's 11th in homers among second basemen, whether you measure that by the 224 he hit relative to players who spent the majority of their careers at the keystone or the 197 he hit specifically while playing second instead of at another position. Alas, Hall voters don't place power from second basemen on a pedestal, as the fates of Jeff Kent (377 homers, with a high of 16.7% in four years on the ballot) and Lou Whitaker (244 homers, 2.9% on the 2001 ballot) suggest.

Given the above, Grich scores particularly poorly on the Bill James Hall of Fame Monitor: 42, where a likely Hall of Famer is 100. It's as though he specifically *avoided* the things that draw voters' attention, or came from the dead-ball era, where there was no All-Star Game, a minimal postseason, and a shortage of awards. Hall of Famers within 10 points in either direction include Johnny Evers (34), Buck Ewing (35), Harry Hooper (38), Monte Ward (42), Jimmy Collins (42), Tommy McCarthy (44), Deacon White (47), and High Pockets Kelly (48), of whom only the last crossed into the 1930s.

The advanced metrics, which reward Grich's patience as well as his punch, are where he stands out. Even with the low batting average and hit total, his 256 batting runs rank ninth at the position, with Kent (297) the only one above him outside the Hall. His 125 OPS+ ranks seventh among those with at least 7,000 plate appearances. On the other side of the ball, his 82 fielding runs rank 19th among players who spent most of their careers at second base, and outdoes 13 of the 20 enshrined, including 10-time Gold Glove winner Alomar (-38), nine-time winner Ryne Sandberg (60), five-time winner Joe Morgan (-48), four-time winner Craig Biggio (-100) as well as Carew (14), the five elected by the BBWAA since 1966. Indeed, given his performance at shortstop in a relatively small but not insubstantial sample (+10 runs in 159 games), it's fair to wonder how his career might have transpired had he spent at least its first half at that position. Perhaps the 1972–76 Orioles would have gone further with him at shortstop instead of Belanger, with Johnson, or (eventually) somebody else at second.

One Oriole from that period who owes a whole lot to Grich, Belanger, and Brooks Robinson—perhaps even his whole bronze plaque—is Palmer, who won the AL Cy Young in 1973, '75, and '76 and was brilliant in '72 as well. For the span, Palmer posted a major-league-best 142 ERA+ despite whiffing a modest 14.0% of batters, the 41st-highest rate among pitchers with at least 600 innings. In other words, his fielders did a great deal of the heavy lifting, with Belanger (113 fielding runs), Robinson (68), Grich (66), and centerfielder Paul Blair (64) four of the game's five most productive defenders.

Studying hitters and anticipating outcomes was Grich's forte. "I didn't have Brooks Robinson's hands, Mark Belanger's range or Joe Morgan's quickness, but I got to more balls than other guys who were 6 feet 2 and 200 pounds because, on every pitch, I got a jump," he said in 2015. "I cheated so much, I caught balls on the outfield grass and threw guys out. . . . Nobody put more effort into defense than I did."[13]

Only 11 retired players outside the Hall have WARs that exceed Grich's 70.9, including two currently on the ballot (Barry Bonds and Larry Walker), three waiting to become eligible (Derek Jeter, Chipper Jones, and Jim Thome), and one permanently ineligible (Pete Rose). Whitaker (74.9) is the only second baseman above him who's outside; Grich ranks eighth at the position in career WAR, 1.6 wins above the standard. Meanwhile, his 46.3 peak WAR ranks 11th, 1.9 wins above the standard. If that seems surprising, consider his run of five top five finishes, plus two more in the top 10, from 1972–81. Even given his two-year offensive dip due to his back injury, his 63.3 WAR from 1972–83 ranks fourth behind only Mike Schmidt (80.8), Morgan (71.7), and Carew (65.1), eventual first-ballot Hall of Famers. Bill James wasn't mincing words.

For as strong as Grich's career and peak standings are individually, together, they're even stronger, as his 58.6 JAWS is seventh among second basemen, 1.7 points above the standard. He's the only above-standard second baseman outside the Hall, the single best available candidate by that metric.

Alas, Grich's candidacy has been in a no-man's-land for 25 years and counting. He hit the BBWAA ballot in 1992, along with Tom Seaver and Tony Perez. Seaver was elected with a record 98.8%, as only five of the 430 voters left his name off. Second-year candidate Rollie Fingers was elected as well, with 81.2%. Future honorees Orlando Cepeda (57.2%) and Perez (50.0%) were the only others to get the support of at least half the electorate. Among other first-year candidates, obvious non–Hall of Famers Vida Blue, George Foster, and Rusty Staub received between 5.0–6.0%, enough to retain eligibility, but Grich, with just 2.6%, did not.

The *Newark Star-Ledger*'s Moss Klein correctly anticipated that Grich would have trouble gaining the attention of voters, fretting that he could slip off without further consideration, yet bypassing him anyway while voting just for Seaver, Fingers, Rose, and Bill Mazeroski. He wrote, "The approach here has always been that only the super elite receive votes in their first year of eligibility. Perez just misses. If he isn't voted in this time, he'll be on this ballot next year. . . . The first year standard applies [to Grich], too. Grich fits the Mazeroski mold as a superb second baseman whose offense was well above average for his position. But he'll be snubbed by most voters."[14] With allies like that, who needs enemies?

Even the *New York Times*'s Murray Chass (!) lamented Grich's falling off the ballot. "One of the best second basemen of his time, Grich had credentials on which an argument could be made for his election. . . . But if a sizable number of voters was waiting to vote for him the second year, they cheated themselves and Grich because he won't appear on the next ballot."[15]

By falling off the ballot, Grich couldn't even be considered by the Veterans Committee until his 15 years of BBWAA eligibility would have expired, in 2006, and since then the slights have continued. The Historical Overview Committee charged with creating the Veterans Committee ballot, which consists not of historians per se but of veteran BBWAA members—the same pool of writers who gave Grich such underwhelming support the first time around—bypassed him for a spot on the 2009 VC ballot, and after the VC was split into three era-based committees, the same thing happened for the 2011 ballot, which did include other one-and-done candidates such as Al Oliver (1991, 4.3%) and Ted Simmons (1994, 3.7%) as well as Staub and Blue. No player was elected that year, with Davey Concepcion the only one to receive at least eight of the committee's 16 votes and executive Pat Gillick the only candidate elected. Grich didn't make it onto the 2014 Expansion Era Committee ballot, though Simmons and another one-and-done, reliever Dan Quisenberry (1996, 3.8%), did. Again, no player was elected, only managers Bobby Cox, Tony La Russa, and Joe Torre.

With the shakeup of that process, Grich's next opening will be on the 2018 Modern Baseball Era Committee ballot, but there's no guarantee that the old-school-oriented writers of the HOC will include him. The similarly mishandled Whitaker and Simmons will also be vying for space, as will Alan Trammell and Jack Morris, both of whom are likely to have the upper hand based on their long runs on the BBWAA ballot.

If there's good news, it's that this fate isn't crushing the man's spirit. "I'm not bitter, I'm not complaining,"[16] Grich told MLB.com Angels beat writer Alden Gonzalez in January 2015. That still doesn't make it right. The Hall of Fame has a distinct lack of Grich.

LOU WHITAKER

"In the ballet that passes as baseball, the double-play twins of Detroit have dipped and twirled and pirouetted in the infield dust. Whitaker, the grasshopper second baseman, glides laterally to collect a grounder as easily as a vendor scoops a sno-cone into a cup. Trammell, the effortless shortstop, backhands a bounder and whips it to Whitaker for the force. The force is with these two guys, not to mention the relay to first."[17]

—MIKE DOWNEY

Lou Whitaker made baseball look easy. No less a writer than Roger Angell marveled over his "ball-bearing smoothness afield and remarkable hand-speed at bat."[18] But to some, the ease with which the game came to the second baseman suggested that he lacked effort, hard work, or passion for the game, and it didn't help that Whitaker wasn't one for self-promotion.

"I just didn't want to talk about baseball," he said in 2015, discussing the reputation for aloofness that he developed during his career. "I knew how well I played and how much I loved playing baseball. I could not do that 162 days a year."[19]

Whitaker let his performance do most of the talking, and for the better part of his 19 seasons in the majors, that performance spoke volumes. A top-of-the-lineup sparkplug and an outstanding defender, he earned All-Star honors five times, won three Gold Gloves, and paired with Alan Trammell to form the longest-running double play combination in history. Analogs to the NBA combination of John Stockton and Karl Malone of the Utah Jazz, forever linked in the public mind, the inseparable pair played an AL-record 1,918 games together and led the Tigers to a championship in 1984, and an AL East title in 1987.

Whitaker retired one year before Trammell did, and thus reached the BBWAA Hall of Fame ballot a year earlier. Shockingly, a player hailed as a potential Hall of Famer during his career received just 2.9% in 2001. Like Bobby Grich before him, not only did that rule Whitaker out from further consideration by the writers, it prevented him from being considered by the Veterans Committee or the Expansion Era Committee during the remaining 14 years that he could have been on the ballot—a window of eligibility that had abruptly slammed shut. Trammell, who became eligible in 2002, wasn't elected by the writers either, but he at least lasted 15 years on the ballot (his case is taken up in Chapter 12). Like Grich, Whitaker faces an uphill battle, because as longtime Tigers beat writer Tom Gage reminded his supporters in 2015, "reconsiderations don't start at the bottom."[20]

The Career

1977–95 Tigers

Player	Career	Peak	JAWS	H	HR	SB	AVG/OBP/SLG	OPS+
Lou Whitaker	74.9	37.8	56.4	2369	244	143	.276/.363/.426	117
Avg HOF 2B	69.3	44.4	56.9					
2B Rank	7th	20th	13th					
(Above HOF)	(14/20)	(8/20)	(10/20)					

Though he was born in Brooklyn in 1957, Whitaker grew up in Martinsville, Virginia, a rural town of about 20,000 people, in a house full of 16 family members across three generations. His mother, Marion Arlene Williams, pregnant with Lou's younger sister, had left Brooklyn and Lou's father behind. "My daddy is a first-class New York pimp,"[21] Whitaker said in 1979, explaining that he never knew Louis Rodman Whitaker Sr. He grew up poor. "When Lou's legs grew crooked, the family couldn't afford orthopedic help," wrote Steve Wulf in a 1983 *Sports Illustrated* profile, "so his uncles twisted and turned them inward every day."[22]

Whitaker's legs straightened out, and he developed prowess on the diamond, impressing scouts with his hands and arm strength while at Martinsville High School, where he played third base and even pitched. On the advice of former All-Star infielder Billy Jurges, then a scout, the Tigers drafted him in the fifth round in 1975. He began his career at the team's Rookie League Bristol affiliate, where he struggled at shortstop and third base, but at A-level Lakeland in 1976, the 19-year-old Whitaker hit .297/.376/.355 and stole 48 bases en route to Florida State League MVP honors.

In the Instructional League that fall, Whitaker met Trammell, the team's 1976 second-round pick, and began a conversion to second base. "Tram and I went out every morning for 30 days in a row," Whitaker recounted. "We took double plays, ground balls to second and short . . . at 10 o'clock in the morning. After that, you played a game at one o'clock."[23] The combination clicked so well that Tigers general manager Jim Campbell, who promised both sport coats at the end of the season, agreed to buy them three-piece suits instead.

The pair roomed together at Double-A Montgomery in 1977. Trammel won Southern League MVP honors, while Whitaker took to his new position and hit .280/.374/.356 with 38 steals. "We went out to eat together every day, we talked baseball every day and we grew together for 19 years,"[24] said Whitaker.

Recalled when Montgomery's season ended, the pair debuted in the nightcap of a September 9 doubleheader against the Red Sox, the first of their 1,918 games together. They joined 1974 first-round pick Lance Parrish, a catcher who had debuted earlier that week; the trio would form the backbone of the Tigers lineup for the next nine years.

Manager Ralph Houk started the rookie double play combo on Opening Day in 1978, but spent the first quarter of the season platooning them with a more experienced, less talented tandem, Steve Dillard and Mark Wagner. By late May, the training wheels were off, and the duo played daily. Whitaker hit .285/.361/.357 for a 101 OPS+ while playing defense that was 10 runs above average en route to 3.8 WAR. He beat out the Brewers' Paul Molitor for AL Rookie of the Year honors, while Trammell tied for fourth. The Tigers, who had gone 74-88 in 1977, and hadn't been above .500 since 1973, won 86 games, the first of 11 straight winning seasons.

Whitaker improved to .286/.395/.378 for a 108 OPS+ in 1979, stealing 20 bases (a mark that would stand as a career high) in 30 attempts, and again played strong defense en route to 4.5 WAR. He struggled the following season, however, as manager Sparky Anderson, who had taken the reins of the Tigers in mid-June 1979, moved him from the number two spot to the leadoff spot to offset the loss of speedster Ron LeFlore to free agency. The experiment was abandoned in early June, but Whitaker couldn't salvage his season after being dropped to the ninth spot. His .233/.331/.283 showing set across-the-board worsts that stood for the remainder of his career, but he rebounded in respectable fashion in the strike-shortened 1981 season (.263/.340/.373).

In his first four full seasons, Whitaker had totaled just 12 home runs, but his power emerged when hitting coach Gates Brown taught him to pull the ball more often. He hit 22 doubles and 15 homers in 1982, both career highs, en route to a .286/.341/.434 showing and 5.4 WAR. Four of his homers came leading off the first inning; he had been overly selective while struggling in that spot in 1980, but took to it the second time around via a more aggressive approach. After the season, he signed a five-year, $3 million extension, giving him the second-highest average annual salary of any second baseman besides Grich ($800,000 per year). He would remain their primary leadoff hitter over that span.

At age 26, Whitaker put together a career year in 1983, hitting .320/.380/.457 for a 133 OPS+ with 12 homers and 17 steals; his 206 hits ranked third in the league, his 40 doubles seventh, his 6.7 WAR fifth. He made his first All-Star team and won his first of three straight Gold Gloves, though his defense, which was four runs above average, was a step down from his +11 annual average from 1978–82.

Though his overall numbers took a step back in 1984 (4.3 WAR, 112 OPS+), Whitaker and the Tigers stormed to a 35-5 start en route to a 104-win season and their first world championship since 1968. While Trammell earned World Series MVP honors against the Padres, Whitaker hit .278/.409/.389 and scored six runs in the five games, three of them in the first inning as the Tigers struck first.

The champagne had barely dried when, 10 days into spring training in 1985, Anderson temporarily broke up his double play combo by moving Whitaker back to third base to accommodate 23-year-old rookie Chris Pittaro, who had spent 1984 in Double-A. Whitaker gave his blessing to the change, and Anderson clucked, "In 10 years, they'll still be talking about how great a move it was."[25] One week later, Whitaker asked to move back to second; while Pittaro got off to a hot start at third base in April, by June he was in the minors, more or less for good.

Though not quite as valuable as Trammell, whose defense at that stage was stronger, Whitaker was remarkably consistent from 1984–87, hitting a combined .275/.350/.432 for a 113 OPS+ while averaging 18 homers, 10 steals, and 4.2 WAR per year, with a high of 4.5 and a low of 3.6. He was elected to start three All-Star Games (1984–86) and made the fourth as a reserve. The 1985 game produced one of the funniest moments of his career. After Whitaker left a bag containing equipment and at least part of his uniform in his car, he had to scramble, borrowing a glove from Cal Ripken, finding an Indians batting helmet, and resorting to a mesh-back adjustable Tigers cap and generic replica jersey from a souvenir stand at the Metrodome. A clubhouse attendant hastily stenciled his number 1 on the back of the ill-fitting jersey, which wound up in the Smithsonian.

In 1987, the Tigers won 98 games and—thanks to an 0-7 skid by the Blue Jays to end the season, the last three losses at the hands of Detroit—another AL East title. Alas, they were steamrolled by the 85-win Twins in the ALCS, losing four games to one. Whitaker went 3-for-17, his solo homer off Bert Blyleven in a Game 2 loss going for naught.

In 1988, the 31-year-old Whitaker was putting together a fine season (.275/.376/.419 for a 127 OPS+, his highest since 1983) when he tore cartilage in his right knee while dancing with his wife at a party in early September. "We were doing a fast dance and I did the splits," he said. "The first time, nothing happened. The second time I went down, I heard it pop."[26] The Tigers, clinging to first place but already skidding in the absence of an injured Trammell, went 13-14 the rest of the way and finished second behind the Red Sox by one game.

It was an embarrassing end to the season, and over the winter he drew criticism for his declining batting averages and the perception of his work ethic. His critics did have a point given that his once adequate performance against left-handers had dipped from .261/.339/.342 for 1977–83 to .224/.297/.315 from 1984–88. But in a March 1989 article in the *Toledo Blade,* Anderson defended Whitaker when asked if he would accomplish more if he had the habits and hustle of Trammell. "Nobody will ever know for sure," said the manager. "Change him and he might not be as good. Everything looks so easy when he does it. He's got the most talent on the club. The most *talent*."[27]

Whitaker chafed at having to wait for a contract extension after the team signed Trammell to a three-year extension that winter; he still had one more year under his current deal. He also took umbrage at the "Sweet Lou" nickname—which teammates had bestowed upon him primarily for his swing, not his demeanor—telling reporters, "Winners don't smile, man. There's a time to have fun, there's a time to be serious. Guys that say I'm distant or aloof, that's a real compliment. They don't need to see me laughing."[28]

Whitaker's 1989 bounceback traded batting average for power; he set career highs of 28 homers and 85 RBI while hitting .251/.361/.462 with 5.3 WAR. In mid-season, he finally signed a three-year, $6 million extension. His season was a bright spot amid dreadful years by Trammell, staff ace Jack Morris, and others that led to the Tigers' worst record (59-103) since 1975. After a solid 1990 performance (107 OPS+, +10 defense, 3.8 WAR), he followed that up with one of his best seasons on both sides of the ball, hitting .279/.391/.489 with 23 homers for a career-best 141 OPS+ and strong glovework (+11 runs) en route to 6.7 WAR, tying his career high, and fourth-best in the AL—strong work for a 34-year-old.

Though his defense would quickly decline, Whitaker would maintain that power even amid dwindling playing time over his final four seasons. Helped by a reduced workload against lefties (accounting for 10–20% of his PA instead of his typical 30–35%), he hit a combined .289/.389/.475 for a 131 OPS+ from 1992–95, averaging 14 homers in 419 plate appearances and reaching milestones that cued talk of Cooperstown. "When discussing possible Hall of Famers, don't forget Tiger second baseman Lou Whitaker," wrote *Sports Illustrated*'s Tim Kurkjian in 1992. "He recently became the only second baseman other than Joe Morgan to play 2,000 games, hit 200 homers and collect 2,000 hits."[29]

"If history is any gauge, Lou Whitaker will be enshrined in the Hall of Fame one day," wrote the AP's Harry Atkins in 1993, as Whitaker approached 1,000 RBI. "I don't think about baseball history," said Whitaker. "I've never been to a library or bought a book on baseball history."[30]

At the end of the 1992 season, Whitaker and Trammell both reached free agency for the first time, but new owner Mike Ilich ensured they remained in Detroit. The Braves and Orioles courted Whitaker, but the Tigers ultimately retained him via a three-year, $10 million deal. By mid-1994, he suggested that he would retire at the end of his contract in 1995.

Though Whitaker was the first Tiger to officially report to spring training upon the settlement of the players' strike, a shoulder strain prevented him from playing until May 12, his 38th birthday. While he hit a robust .293/.372/.518 in 285 PA, he was used sparingly as the team played out the string, starting just eight times apiece at second base and DH after August 12; similarly, Trammell rode the pine frequently, and Anderson looked to the end of the line, either via retirement or firing. In September,

Whitaker and Trammell played their 1,915th game together, breaking the AL record held by George Brett and Frank White, trailing only the Cubs' Ron Santo and Billy Williams (2,015, since broken by Jeff Bagwell and Craig Biggio with 2,029).

With the team closing the season on the road, and with minds not made up about retirement, Trammell asked Tigers management not to hold any special ceremonies to honor the combo for their September 23 Tiger Stadium farewell. Though heartily received by the sparse crowd of 14,083, the team found themselves on the wrong end of a 13–1 blowout by the Orioles. Starter Mike Mussina, who cruised along, instructed catcher Chris Hoiles to tell the pair to look for nothing but fastballs. "I was trying," Mussina said, smiling, "to throw them as skillfully as I could down the middle."[31] Both players made outs, however. After sitting for a week, they made one-inning cameos in Baltimore on the season's final day. Whitaker mulled signing elsewhere, but retired, while Trammell returned for one final year.

The Case

Via excellent health and prolonged productivity during his 19-year career, Whitaker ranks high on several leaderboards specific to second basemen. His 2,308 games at the position rank fourth, behind Eddie Collins (2,650), Joe Morgan (2,527), and relative newcomer Roberto Alomar (2,320). Of the top 15, 11 are in the Hall, with Willie Randolph, (2,152), Frank White (2,151), and Jeff Kent (2,034) the other outsiders.

Meanwhile, among players who spent the majority of their careers at second base, Whitaker's 2,369 hits ranks 13th, more than any of them outside the Hall besides Kent (2,461); when you incorporate walks and hit-by-pitches, Whitaker's 3,588 times on base are tops among that group. He's not quite as high-ranking in rate stats. Using a 7,000-plate-appearance minimum, his .363 on-base percentage ranks 15th, his .426 slugging percentage 17th, and his 117 OPS+ 12th, sixth among those outside the Hall behind the still active Robinson Cano (127), Larry Doyle (126), Grich (125), Kent (123), and Chase Utley (119). His 239 homers while playing second (the strict split, not counting those as DH or pinch-hitting), are seventh, with Kent (351) first.

Still, on the traditional front, Whitaker's résumé feels a bit light. Beyond the Rookie of the Year award, his three Gold Gloves, and five All-Star teams is a lack of black ink and meager postseason numbers (two playoff teams and a .204/.350/.306 line in 61 PA). He scores a modest 92 on the Hall of Fame Monitor, suggesting an uphill battle.

The advanced metrics approximate Whitaker's standing in rate stats: 12th among second basemen in batting runs (209), sixth in baserunning and double play runs (48), 13th in fielding runs (77). It's the combination that's his selling point; his 74.9 WAR ranks seventh, behind six Hall of Famers, a healthy 5.6 WAR above the average enshrined second basemen. Less robust, however, is his 37.8 peak score, which ranks 20th, below 12 of 20 enshrined second-sackers and a substantial 6.7 wins below the standard. While very consistent, with 11 of his 18 full seasons worth between 3.5 and 4.7 WAR—somewhere between an above-average regular and an All-Star—he had just four seasons more valuable than those, and only three that cracked the AL top 10.

Taken together—the point of my system, after all—Whitaker's 56.4 JAWS is a mere half-point below the standard, a negligible amount in this context, and still good for 11th, behind nine Hall of Famers and Grich. He outranks five of the six second basemen to enter Cooperstown since his retirement: Alomar (54.8, 13th), Biggio (53.4, 14th), Joe Gordon (51.4, 16th), Nellie Fox (42.9, 23rd), and Bill Mazeroski (31.0, 50th), and is less than a point behind the sixth, Ryne Sandberg (57.2, ninth). Whitaker may lack Biggio's 3,000 hits, Sandberg's MVP, the defensive reputations of Gordon, Mazeroski, and Fox (all of whom outrank him in fielding runs), or Alomar (who does not), nonetheless, he's a very solid Hall of Fame candidate.

Unfortunately, the BBWAA voters didn't see it that way. Whitaker became eligible on the 2001 ballot, a year that featured one first-ballot lock in 3,000-hit-club member Dave Winfield as well as 10-time All-Star Kirby Puckett (whose career had been cut short by glaucoma), former teammates Kirk Gibson and Lance Parrish, and former AL MVP Don Mattingly. In a record-setting haul of ballots (515) of just middling generosity (6.33 names per ballot), Winfield (84.5%) and Puckett (82.1%) sailed through, while holdovers Gary Carter (64.9%), Jim Rice (57.9%), Bruce Sutter (47.6%), and Goose Gossage (44.3%) gained ground from the previous year en route to their own plaques. While Whitaker outpolled his ex-teammates, his 2.9% wasn't even enough to remain on the ballot.

ESPN's Jayson Stark, whose seven-man ballot included Winfield, Puckett, Carter, Sutter, Gossage, Morris, and Dale Murphy, left Whitaker off, noting, "His career numbers look attractive by second-base standards. But it's hard to remember any period when Whitaker was looked upon as the greatest second baseman of his era. 'Just' a very good player. There's no shame in that."[32] All six of Stark's ESPN's colleagues with a vote—Jim Caple, Peter Gammons, Bob Klapisch, Tim Kurkjian, Sean McAdam, and Phil Rogers—bypassed him as well.

The *Detroit News*'s Lynn Henning, whose coverage of the Tigers extends back to when Whitaker was drafted, said in 2017, "It wasn't that people didn't appreciate him, but if ever I've seen a case where every voter figured, 'Someone else will put him on, I've got other fish to fry,' that was it—a perfect storm. I've never seen anything so utterly flukish in Hall of Fame voting."[33] To Henning, the lack of a boost from television exposure or analytics—two things that would have played in his favor in a later era—hurt him as well.

Whitaker took the rejection in stride, saying, "It hurt my family more than it hurt me. . . . The thing is it had nothing to do with what major-league ballplayers thought of me, and they knew I was a winning ballplayer. I am proud of that."[34]

Whitaker's exclusion cast him into a baseball purgatory, as he was ineligible to be considered by the Veterans Committee or its successors until his 15-year eligibility period expired in 2015. He'll be eligible for consideration on the 2018 Modern Baseball Era Committee ballot, but first he'll have to make it past the Historical Overview Committee charged with creating the ballot, which consists not of historians but of veteran BBWAA members, who of course gave him short shrift in 2001. Given that one-and-done predecessor Grich (2.6% in 1992) hasn't gotten past the HOC and onto a ballot despite a nine-year head start, this doesn't bode well for Whitaker, though it's worth noting the contrast between Grich's high-peak/short-career combo and Whitaker's low-peak/long-career one—382 games and 536 hits separate the two.

Like Tinker, Evers, and Chance in 1946, it would be fitting if Whitaker and Trammell could enter the Hall together, if not in 2018 than '20, '23, or '25, the subsequent years in which Modern Era slates will be considered. Hopefully, the new committee will offer some clear-eyed hindsight on what the BBWAA voters missed about the great double play combo.

THE ROUNDUP

The number before each player name refers to his JAWS ranking *among all players at the position*, not necessarily those in the Hall. Average HOF second baseman: 69.4/44.5/56.9.

The Elite (above standard in career, peak, and JAWS)

1. Rogers Hornsby

Teams:	Cardinals 1915–26, '33 • Giants 1927 • Braves 1928 • Cubs 1929–32 • Browns 1933–37
Stats:	.358/.434/.577 • 175 OPS+ • 2,930 H • 301 HR • 135 SB
Rankings:	12× led OPS+ • 11× led WAR • 7× led AVG • 6× S/S TC • 2× TC All-time: 2nd AVG • 5th OPS+ • 6th OBP • 9th WAR • 10th SLG
Voting/JAWS:	BBWAA 1942 (3rd[†], 78.1%) • 127.0/73.5/100.2

---

† Years receiving votes prior to final year of career not counted.

How dominant was the Rajah? From 1901–46—the pre-integration twentieth century—10 position players combined to produce 29 seasons of at least 10.0 WAR. Babe Ruth produced nine of them, while Hornsby had six (all from 1921–29); no other player produced more than three, and among NL players, only Honus Wagner reached that plateau (twice). The Flying Dutchman holds a slight edge in pre-integration WAR, 131.0–127.0, but Hornsby was undoubtedly the better hitter; though his raw rate stats were inflated by the high-offense 1920s, his OPS+ ranks fifth all-time behind only Ruth, Williams, Bonds, and Gehrig. The seven-time batting champion hit a mind-boggling .402/.474/.690 over a five-year stretch from 1921–25, topping .400 three times while averaging 29 homers. He won the slash stat Triple Crown in each of those years (and 1920) plus traditional Triple Crowns in 1922 and '25. Despite his sizzling rate stats, he fell 70 hits short of 3,000 because a broken ankle and managerial duties limited him to just 274 games from his age-34 season (1930) onward.

2. Eddie Collins

Teams:	A's 1906–14, 1927–30 • White Sox 1915–26
Stats:	.333/.424/.429 • 142 OPS+ • 3,315 H • 47 HR • 741 SB
Rankings:	14× top 5 OBP • 10× top 5 WAR • 10× top 3 SB • 9× top 5 SLG
	All-time: 8th SB • 9th H • 10th WAR • 10th OBP • 10th TOB • 19th BB
Voting/JAWS:	BBWAA 1939 **(4th, 77.7%)** • 123.9/64.2/94.1

Described by various sources as the game's best bunter, best hit-and-run man, smartest player (he graduated from Columbia University), and plenty of other superlatives that you'd gladly take home to Mom, Collins starred for six pennant winners and four champions from 1910–19, most notably as the keystone of Connie Mack's "$100,000 Infield" that won four pennants and three World Series from 1910–14. An on-base machine and an astute observer of pitchers' tendencies, Collins was a constant leaderboard presence, but in the shadow of Ty Cobb and Tris Speaker, he never led in a slash stat and led just once in WAR—yet wound up creating nearly as much value as Hornsby. He did it largely one base at a time, cranking out 2,643 singles, more than anyone besides Cobb (3,053) and Pete Rose (3,215). He wasn't without his flaws: As a clean member of the 1919 White Sox, he offered inconsistent accounts over the years of what he knew about the scandal and when; and as Red Sox VP/GM (1933–47), he signed Hall of Famers Bobby Doerr and Ted Williams during a single scouting trip, but also oversaw Jackie Robinson's sham tryout in 1945.

3. Nap Lajoie

Teams:	Phillies 1896–1900 • A's 1901–02 • Cleveland Bronchos/ Naps 1902–14 • A's 1915–16
Stats:	.338/.380/.466 • 150 OPS+ • 3,243 H • 82 HR • 380 SB
Rankings:	9× top 3 SLG • 8× to 5 OPS+ • 6× led WAR • 4× led AVG All-time: 14th H • 14th AVG
Voting/JAWS:	BBWAA 1937 (2nd, 83.6%) • 107.4/60.3/83.8

You know you're a big deal when they rename the team after you, as the Bronchos (yes, that's how they spelled it) did starting in 1903. Indeed, Lajoie was the nascent AL's dominant player, winning the Triple Crown in 1901, and claiming its first four batting titles. A potential fifth in 1910—involving collusive opponents, Ty Cobb, erroneous record keeping, commissioner Bowie Kuhn, and Pete Rose's chase of the all-time hits record—remains a split decision over a century later. The Browns allowed Lajoie to bunt safely six times and collect eight total hits in a season-ending doubleheader, but AL president Ban Johnson "found" an unrecorded two-hit game for Cobb that restored his lead. Over 70 years later, Pete Palmer identified that found game as a double entry, but Kuhn passed on revising Cobb's hit total due to the media scrutiny produced by Rose's pursuit. MLB's official stats credit Cobb as the batting champ (.385 to .384) but Palmer's data (which underlies Baseball-Reference.com) credits Lajoie (.384 to .383). Beyond that, not only did Lajoie lead the Junior Circuit in WAR in six of its first eight seasons, but when he retired he held the highest total of any position player aside from Wagner. Lajoie was the third player to reach 3,000 hits after Cap Anson and Wagner, and the voting leader in the 1937 class.

4. Joe Morgan

Teams:	Colt .45s/Astros 1963–71, '80 • Reds 1972–79 • Giants 1981–82 • Phillies 1983 • A's 1984
Stats:	.271/.392/.427 • 132 OPS+ • 2,517 H • 268 HR • 689 SB
Rankings:	10× All-Star • 5× GG • 4× led OBP • 4× led WAR All-time: 5th BB • 11th SB • 20th WAR
Voting/JAWS:	BBWAA 1990 (1st, 81.8%) • 100.3/59.2/79.7

The centerpiece of the Big Red Machine's three pennants and two championships from 1972–76, Morgan was one of the very best players of the 1970s. In fact, his 66.9 WAR was the decade's highest, as was his 10.9 WAR in 1975. Morgan had already starred in Houston before arriving in Cincinnati, and remained a valuable player even after leaving, racking up another 15.5 WAR in five seasons, helping the 1980 Astros and '83 "Wheeze Kids" Phillies into the postseason and dealing the 1982 Dodgers a death blow with a game-162-winning homer for the Giants. If there are nits to pick, he hit poorly in the postseason (.182/.323/.348 in 222 PA) and despite rating as 19 runs above average during his run of five straight Gold Gloves (1973–77) finished 48 below average overall. No matter, as his base-running (+80 runs, tied for seventh all-time) more than cancels it out. Such accounting would no doubt exasperate Morgan, whose sabermetric credentials are eclipsed only by his shrill and often incoherent disdain for the entire field of inquiry. Track down Tommy Craggs's *SF Weekly* feature[35] for a reminder of how silly one could get over *Moneyball*.

5. Charlie Gehringer

Teams:	Tigers 1924–42
Stats:	.320/.404/.480 • 124 OPS+ • 2,839 H • 184 HR • 181 SB
Rankings:	9× top 10 WAR • 7× top 10 OPS+ • 6× All-Star • 5× top 5 AVG
Voting/JAWS:	BBWAA 1949 **(5th, run-off)** • 80.6/50.5/65.6

Nicknamed "The Mechanical Man" for both his durability and flat demeanor— "I'm known around baseball as saying very little, and I'm not going to spoil my reputation,"[36] he once said at a civic banquet in his honor—Gehringer helped the Tigers to three pennants and topped 200 hits seven times. Though no slouch in his 20s (27.3 WAR from 1927–32), his 52.5 WAR from his age-30 season ('33) onward ranks 18th among all position players. Not only did he become the oldest player to win a batting title, at age 34 (1937, his MVP-winning year), he set career highs in homers (20) and walks (113) the next year. Having collected 2,731 hits through 1940, a stellar age-37 season (.313/.428/.447) during which he overcame an offseason back injury, he appeared bound for 3,000. Alas, he fell off precipitously in 1941, was limited to pinch-hit duty in '42 before enlisting in the navy, and never played again. He missed his Hall induction due to his own wedding, but in 1953 became the first player appointed to the Veterans Committee—and then the longest serving, holding his post through 1990.

6. Rod Carew

Teams:	Twins 1967–78 • Angels 1979–85
Stats:	.328/.393/.429 • 131 OPS+ • 3,053 H • 92 HR • 353 SB

Rankings:	18× All-Star • 7× led AVG • 7× top 3 OBP • 5× top 5 OPS+ • 3× led WAR
	All-time: 24th H • 24th AVG
Voting/JAWS:	BBWAA 1991 **(1st, 90.5%)** • **81.0/49.7/65.4**

Race aside, Carew wouldn't have been out of place in the dead-ball era, given the combination of slap hitting and speed that he used to win seven batting titles, top .350 four times in a five-year span (1973–77), and win both AL Rookie of the Year and MVP awards. Yet with one exception in either direction, only in those league-leading seasons did he even rank among the league's top 10 in WAR, despite generally providing above-average defense and baserunning, and he only reached double digits in homers twice. As to where he fits in, position-wise, Carew played 1,130 at second base and 1,184 at first; his first two seasons after the switch (1976–77) are the only ones that contribute to his peak score, with 1977 (9.7 WAR, from a career-best .388/.449/.570 line) at the top. Overall, he hit .328/.383/.430/130 OPS+ with -5 fielding runs en route to 42.3 WAR before the move, compared to .328/.402/.429/132 OPS+ with +19 fielding runs for 38.8 WAR after. Positional adjustments and the spread of playing time throw the weight behind putting him at second base.

The Rank and File

8. Frankie Frisch

Teams:	Giants 1919–26 • Cardinals 1927–37
Stats:	.316/.369/.432 • 110 OPS+ • 2,880 H • 105 HR • 419 SB
Rankings:	10× top 3 SB • 8× top 10 WAR
Voting/JAWS:	BBWAA 1947 **(5th,[†] 84.5%)** • **70.4/44.4/57.4**

A protégé of John McGraw who was traded for Hornsby in December 1926, "The Fordham Flash" was an excellent two-way player and an October staple, helping the Giants and Cardinals to four pennants and two championships apiece across a 14-year stretch (1921–34). While not the equal of contemporaries Hornsby, Collins, and Gehringer, the switch-hitting Frisch routinely hit .300 with modest power, backing outstanding glovework (+140 fifth all-time at the position) that placed him among the game's elite. He's fourth in WAR from 1920–29, trailing Ruth and Hornsby by wide margins, and Harry Heilmann by a narrow one. Argu-

[†] Years receiving votes prior to final year of career not counted

ably he belongs on the tier above, as his peak score is 0.1 WAR (one measly, stinkin' run) shy of the standard. Aside from winning the 1934 World Series as a player-manager for the Gashouse Gang Cardinals, he was a less successful skipper, and he did plenty of damage to the Hall via his 1967–72 tenure on the Veterans Committee, as detailed in Chapter 5.

9. Ryne Sandberg

Teams:	Phillies 1981 • Cubs 1982–94 • 1996–97
Stats:	.285/.344/.452 • 114 OPS+ • 2,386 H • 282 HR • 344 SB
Rankings:	10× All-Star • 9× GG • 5× top 5 TB • 4× top 3 WAR
Voting/JAWS:	BBWAA 2005 **(3rd, 76.2%)** • **67.5/46.8/57.2**

A 20th-round draft pick in 1978, Sandberg was stolen from the Phillies in a January 1982 swap of aging shortstops, Larry Bowa for Ivan DeJesus. A shortstop himself at the time, he spent most of his rookie season at third base but flourished upon moving to second for good in 1983, winning the first of nine Gold Gloves thanks to sure hands and good range (though some of his hardware was unsupported by the metrics). A stolen base threat from the outset, he developed good power and soon evolved into one of the NL's top players, winning MVP honors and leading the league in WAR in 1984 while helping the Cubs to their first postseason berth in 39 years. From 1984–92, his 52.6 WAR trailed only Rickey Henderson, Cal Ripken, and Wade Boggs. He walked away in June 1994 at the age of 34 due to family issues, then came back to produce one pretty good season and a mediocre one. Debuting on the BBWAA ballot at 49.2%, he progressed to 75% in two sizable steps. Ron Santo should have been so lucky.

10. Jackie Robinson

Teams:	Dodgers 1947–56
Stats:	.311/.409/.474 • 132 OPS+ • 1,518 H • 137 HR • 197 SB
Rankings:	6× All-Star • 6× top 5 SB • 5× top 3 OBP • 5× top 10 OPS+ • 3× led WAR
Voting/JAWS:	BBWAA 1962 **(1st, 77.5%)** • **61.5/52.1/56.8**

Robinson's statistical impact is dwarfed by his importance as a historical figure, which rivals Babe Ruth for the top spot in the annals of baseball. A decade before the civil rights movement, his arrival forced America to live up to its ideals of equality in ways that continue to resonate. There's not much to nitpick with his stat sheet, either. The color line prevented him from reaching the majors until age 28, and he played just 10 seasons, so his counting stats are modest, but his accomplishments glow even when stripped of historical weight. He excelled at getting on base and added an extra 35 runs on the bases and via double play avoidance, as well as 81 runs afield while playing 748 games at second base, 256 at third, 197 at first, and 150 in left. During a decade in which he helped the Dodgers to six pennants, only Stan Musial (75.5) and Ted Williams (61.6) accrued more WAR, the latter while missing time in the military. Robinson's peak score ranks fifth among second basemen, and his value from age 28 onward ranks 20th among all position players. For him to have excelled to such a degree with so much at stake constitutes the highest-leverage success the game has seen, for it changed not just the outcome of a game but of a country, as imperfect as that performance's aftermath has been.

14. Roberto Alomar

Teams:	Padres 1988–90 • Blue Jays 1991–95 • Orioles 1996–98 • Indians 1999–2001 • Mets 2002–03 • White Sox 2003, '04 • Diamondbacks 2004
Stats:	.300/.371/.443 • 116 OPS+ • 2,724 H • 210 HR • 474 SB
Rankings:	12× All-Star • 10× GG • 6× top 5 SB • 5× top 10 WAR
Voting/JAWS:	BBWAA 2011 **(2nd, 90.0%)** • **66.8/42.8/54.8**

For the better part of his career, Alomar was the gold standard for second basemen, an all-around threat who could hit for average with good plate discipline, outstanding speed and baserunning smarts, highlight-caliber defense, and an excellent postseason résumé. He's sixth in hits among switch-hitters, stole bases at an 80.6% success rate (adding 54 runs via baserunning), and hit a sizzling .313/.381/.448 in seven trips to October, highlighted by back-to-back championships with Toronto in 1992–93. Despite his 10 Gold Gloves from 1991–2001, however, Total Zone pegs him as merely average for that stretch, and -38 runs overall; the views of BP's Fielding Runs Above Average (+6) and Michael Humphreys's Defensive Regression Analysis (+21) jibe slightly better with the public consensus. The combination of a dreadful final three seasons (85 OPS+, -0.1 WAR), and the infamy of the 1996 incident when he spit on umpire John Hirschbeck conspired to leave him eight votes short of first-ballot entry, but he received the highest percentage of the vote of any post-1966 second-year candidate.

15. Craig Biggio

Teams:	Astros 1988–2007
Stats:	.281/.363/.433 • 112 OPS+ • 3,060 H • 291 HR • 414 SB

Rankings:	7× All-Star • 5× top 10 SB • 4× GG • 4× top 10 WAR •
	4× top 10 OBP
	All-time: 2nd HBP • 16th G • 19th TOB • 22nd H
Voting/JAWS:	BBWAA 2015 **(3rd, 82.7%)** • **65.1/41.6/53.4**

The 27th player to reach 3,000 hits, Biggio provided a textbook example of doing more harm than good in pursuit of a milestone. In fact, his -2.1 WAR swan song (-21 runs at the plate, -9 in the field) is the worst of any Hall of Famer, and thanks to dreadful defense he netted just 4.5 WAR over his final six seasons. To be fair, Biggio spent much of his career bouncing around the diamond, catching during his first four seasons, starring at second base for a stellar 11-year run (1992–2002), then making a foray into the outfield to accommodate Jeff Kent, who along with Lance Berkman and briefly Carlos Beltran helped the aging Killer Bs (Biggio and Jeff Bagwell) finally play deep into October. At his best, Biggio paired power with top-of-the-lineup skills that included adding 76 runs via baserunning and double play avoidance. Like his final few years, his journey from retirement to Cooperstown was a slog. PED-linked Rafael Palmeiro aside, he became the first 3,000-hit-club member not to gain first-ballot entry since Paul Waner, who retired before the five-year rule was in place. Biggio received just 68.2% amid the BBWAA's 2013 shutout, then fell two votes short the following year before gaining entry in '15.

16. Joe Gordon

Teams:	Yankees 1938–43, '46 • Indians 1947–50
Stats:	.268/.357/.466 • 120 OPS+ • 1,530 H • 253 HR • 89 SB
Rankings:	9× All-Star • 9× top 10 HR • 7× top 5 WAR
Voting/JAWS:	VC 2009 • **57.1/45.8/51.4**

Though he spent just 11 years in the majors, losing two to the air force and retiring at age 35, "Flash" Gordon ranks second at the position with 150 fielding runs, four behind Bid McPhee and three ahead of Bill Mazeroski. Those numbers support the legend of his acrobatic glovework, which he paired with considerable thump (25 homers per 154 games). The combo placed him among the AL's top five in WAR seven times in eight years of availability (1939–43, '47–48) while he helped his teams to six pennants and five championships; he won AL MVP in '42. After maxing out at 26.3% on the BBWAA ballot, he received 75% from the VC in 1991, but the committee's limit of two selections a year meant that only Tony Lazzeri and Bill Veeck, both with higher percentages, got the nod.

Gordon (who died in 1978) finally gained entry 18 years later, the only player elected amid the 2003–10 reign of the expanded VC, albeit via a small-committee process limited to pre-1943 players. Still, if every VC selection was this good, the Hall would be such a well-oiled machine that complaints wouldn't be necessary.

21. Billy Herman

Teams:	Cubs 1931–41 • Dodgers 1941–43, 1946 • Braves 1946 • Pirates 1947
Stats:	.304/.367/.407 • 112 OPS+ • 2,345 H • 47 HR • 67 SB
Rankings:	10× All-Star • 6× top 5 2B • 5× top 10 AVG • 4× top 10 WAR
Voting/JAWS:	VC 1975 • **54.7/35.5/45.1**

A perennial All-Star who keyed four pennant winners (Cubs 1932, '35, '38 and Dodgers '41), Herman was a hitting machine with gap power. Despite spending most of his career in hitter-friendly parks, he never homered more than eight times in a season, but regularly placed among the hit and doubles leaders. Along with a reputation as a top-notch sign stealer, he was renowned as the best hit-and-run man of his day, though he nonetheless grounded into 191 double plays and piled up so many sac bunts that he ranked either first or second in the league in outs made five times. Service in the navy cost him all of 1944–45, his age-34–35 seasons; he was worth a combined 8.4 WAR in the two seasons on either side, but played just 15 games in 1947 as player-manager of the rebuilding Pirates. Credit him a pair of four-win seasons for his military time and his JAWS would jump to 49.6, marking him still as a subpar selection—though the Hall of Fame Monitor loves him (146)—but a more understandable one.

22. Bobby Doerr

Teams:	Red Sox 1937–44, 1946–51
Stats:	.288/.362/.461 • 115 OPS+ • 2,042 H • 223 HR • 54 SB
Rankings:	9× All-Star • 7× top 10 SLG • 7× top 10 HR • 6× top 10 WAR
Voting/JAWS:	VC 1986 • **51.2/36.4/43.8**

Doerr is inextricably linked to Ted Williams, his teammate and confidant on both the PCL's San Diego Padres and the Red Sox as well as his champion on the VC. The sure-handed second-sacker may have lost more to World War II than either Herman or Gordon, as he was amid his best season (.325/.399/.528/165 OPS+,

5.9 WAR, all career highs) when called up in September 1944; the Red Sox soon exited a four-way race, though they won the pennant when he returned in '46. While Doerr set errorless records at the position, the metrics don't regard him as on par with Gordon (150 to 43 via Total Zone, 188 to 80 via Defensive Regression Analysis). And though he provided robust production for a second baseman, he owed much of it to Fenway Park, where he hit .315/.393/.533 with 145 homers, compared to .261/.327/.389 with 78 homers elsewhere; his 213-point OPS gap is second among players with 7,000 PA. Chronic back problems forced his retirement at age 33. The BBWAA never gave him more than 25%, and the VC bypassed him three straight times before a panel that included first-year committee member Williams elected him.

23. Nellie Fox

Teams:	A's 1947–49 • White Sox 1950–63 • Colt .45s/Astros 1964–65
Stats:	.288/.348/.363 • 93 OPS+ • 2,663 H • 35 HR • 76 SB
Rankings:	12× All-Star • 8× top 10 AVG • 6× top 10 WAR • 3× GG
Voting/JAWS:	VC 1997 • **49.0/36.9/42.9**

Fox, who might never have been photographed without an oversized wad of tobacco in his cheek, was the AL's best second baseman in the 1950s, capping the decade by winning MVP honors for a .306/.380/.389 season with 21 fielding runs and 6.0 WAR (second in the league) for the pennant-winning "Go-Go Sox." A high-average, contact-oriented hitter, he never struck out more than 18 times in a season and set a position record with 798 consecutive games played. Due to his lack of power, the total offensive package was only intermittently better than league average, but his combination of on-base skills and first-rate defense (+120 runs) produced some strong seasons. His 1975 death at age 47 gave his flagging candidacy a push, but he fell two votes short (74.7%) on his final BBWAA ballot in 1985. In 1996, two years after Bill James cited him in *The Politics of Glory* as the best second base candidate outside the Hall, he received 75% from the VC but didn't gain entry; the committee was limited to selecting only one modern-day major leaguer, and he received fewer votes than Jim Bunning. Fox was elected the following year.

24. Tony Lazzeri

Teams:	Yankees 1926–37 • Cubs 1938 • Dodgers 1939 • Giants 1939
Stats:	.292/.380/.467 • 121 OPS+ • 1,840 H • 178 HR • 148 SB

Rankings: 4× top 10 HR • 4× top 10 SLG • 4× top 10 WAR
Voting/JAWS: VC 1991 • **49.9/35.1/42.5**

The Yankees' regular second baseman for nearly the entire Ruth-Gehrig era and the beginning of the Gehrig-DiMaggio one, Lazzeri played on seven pennant winners (including the 1938 Cubs) and five champions; only Frisch, Collins, and Bobby Richardson topped his 30 World Series games at the position. During his heyday, "Poosh 'Em Up Tony" was a favorite of Italian American fans, the bane of reporters' existence (one complained to Red Smith, "Interviewing that guy is like mining coal with a nail file"[37]), and the top rival of Gehringer as the AL's best-hitting second baseman, though Gehringer's defense and longevity gave him much more value. Indeed, Lazzeri only cracked the AL WAR leaderboard four times, and was done as a regular at age 33. He was immortalized in Cooperstown in 1939, sort of: Pete Alexander's plaque mentions "striking out Lazzeri with bases full in final crisis" of the 1926 World Series. Lazzeri himself wasn't elected until 1991, making him the last player from the Hall's most overrepresented period to gain entry—not a great choice, but hardly the worst.

28. Bid McPhee

Teams: Red Stockings (AA)/Reds 1882–99
Stats: .272/.355/.373 • 107 OPS+ • 2,258 H • 53 HR • 568 SB
Rankings: 5× top 10 WAR • 4× top 10 SB • 2× top 10 HR
All-time: 24th SB
Voting/JAWS: VC 2000 • **52.4/29.3/40.8**

A model of stability in an era that lacked it, McPhee served as Cincinnati's regular second baseman across 18 seasons and two leagues; the Red Stockings jumped from the American Association to the NL in 1890, becoming the Reds in the process. Though he didn't wear a glove until 1896, McPhee was a standout defender whose estimated 154 runs above average would stand as the position's all-time mark. He could hit and steal bases as well; even without an official tally of his stolen base total for his first four years, he's 24th all-time, with seven seasons of at least 40 and a high of 95. Among nineteenth-century position players, he's seventh in WAR, but with the exception of the still neglected Jack Glasscock, he took longer to get into the Hall of Fame than any of the top 10:

Player	WAR	Yrs	Elected
Cap Anson	93.9	1871–1897	1939 OTC
Roger Connor	84.1	1880–1897	1976 VC
Dan Brouthers	79.5	1879–1896	1945 OTC
Jack Glasscock	61.9	1879–1895	
Billy Hamilton	60.9	1888–1900	1961 VC
Ed Delahanty	55.0	1888–1900	1945 OTC
Bid McPhee	52.4	1882–1899	2000 VC
Jim O'Rourke	51.3	1872–1893	1945 OTC
Buck Ewing	47.7	1880–1897	1939 OTC
George Davis	46.9	1890–1900	1998 VC

29. Johnny Evers

Teams:	Cubs 1902-13 • Braves 1914-17, '29 • Phillies 1917 • White Sox 1922
Stats:	.270/.356/.334 • 106 OPS+ • 1,659 H • 12 HR • 324 SB
Rankings:	5x top 10 OBP • 5x top 10 WAR • 3x top 10 SB • 2x top 5 OPS+
Voting/JAWS:	OTC 1946 • **47.7/33.3/40.5**

A 125-pound pepper-pot unafraid to mix it up with men who outweighed him by more than 50 pounds, Evers was the heart of five pennant winners and three champions, including not only the powerhouse Cubs of 1906–10 but also the "Miracle Braves" of 1914, the year he won NL MVP honors. Considered one of the smartest players of his day, he was quick to recognize Fred Merkle's failure to touch second base as the Giants scored the apparent winning run during their September 23, 1908, game, resulting in on-field chaos and the ruling of a tie game whose replay the Cubs won. Of the fabled trio of infielders, he has the lowest JAWS, albeit just 0.1 lower than Frank Chance. His ranking here reflects a shortish career; among Hall second baseman, only Lazzeri, Gordon, and Robinson played fewer games than his 1,784. Still, he deserves his reputation as a fielding whiz: his 127 runs above average ranks fifth at the position, and he was a solid 80 runs above average at the plate.

The Basement (the most dubious honorees)

36. Red Schoendienst

Teams:	Cardinals 1945-56, 1961-63 • Giants 1956-57 • Braves 1957-60

Stats:	.289/.337/.387 • 94 OPS+ • 2,449 H • 84 HR • 89 SB
Rankings:	10× All-Star • 5× top 10 AVG • 4× top 10 WAR
Voting/JAWS:	VC 1989 • **42.1/31.8/37.0**

A key player on three pennant winners (1946 Cardinals, 1957–58 Braves) and two champions, Schoendienst was regarded as the NL's best second baseman this side of Jackie Robinson, but during the decade that their careers overlapped, the gap between the two was massive, with Robinson roughly twice as valuable (61.5 to 31.8 in WAR). A steadily above-average fielder who set records for consecutive chances without an error in 1949 and '50, Schoendienst wasn't an asset at the plate unless he was hitting .300; beyond his five seasons of doing so as a regular, his OPS+ ranged from 66 to 98, and his batting runs totals were annually—wait for it—in the red. His case for Cooperstown was helped by a reputation for leadership, including managing the Cardinals' back-to-back pennant winners in 1967–68, though his career winning percentage was just .522. He polled as high as 42.6% via the BBWAA; notably, Stan Musial was on the VC that elected him.

50. Bill Mazeroski

Teams:	Pirates 1956–72
Stats:	.260/.299/.367 • 84 OPS+ • 2,016 H • 138 HR • 27 SB
Rankings:	8× GG • 7× All-Star
Voting/JAWS:	VC 2001 • **36.2/25.7/30.9**

Whether it's the fame from his 1960 World Series–ending homer or his long-term defensive excellence that got him into Cooperstown, Mazeroski simply isn't a convincing choice. Even the metrics that back his elite reputation afield leave his overall value far short of the standards. So fluid while turning a record 1,706 double plays that he earned the nickname "No Touch," Maz was an estimated 148 runs above average defensively (a close second behind McPhee) but his -162 batting runs undercuts that value, lower than every Hall of Famer save Luis Aparicio (-197) and Rabbit Maranville (-228). He cracked the top 10 in WAR just once. Without the homer, he'd be outside of Cooperstown, just like Royals stalwart Frank White, a statistical dead ringer (2,006 hits, eight Gold Gloves, five All-Star appearances, .255/.293 /.383/85 OPS+, 34.7/23.6/29.1 JAWS). Maxing out at 42.3% via the BBWAA, Maz was elected via a VC headed by longtime Pirates GM Joe L. Brown. Ted Williams, who was said to have opposed Mazeroski's election in previous years while championing former teammate Dom DiMaggio, missed the 2001 vote due to open-heart surgery.

Further Consideration (upcoming or overlooked candidates)

11. Chase Utley

Teams:	Phillies 2003–15 • Dodgers 2015–16
Stats:	.276/.361/.472 • 119 OPS+ • 1,777 H • 250 HR • 145 SB
Rankings:	6× All-Star • 5× top 3 WAR • 3× top 10 OBP • 2× top 10 OPS+
Voting/JAWS:	**64.4/49.1/56.7**

One of the best and most underrated players of his time, Utley was more valuable during the Phillies' run of five straight NL East flags (2007–11), two pennants, and a championship than MVP-winning teammates Ryan Howard and Jimmy Rollins. In addition to his power, patience, and baserunning smarts (+44 runs thanks in part to an 87.8% stolen base success rate, tops at the 100-attempt minimum), his glovework has been off the charts. Since the advent of Defensive Runs Saved in 2003, only Adrian Beltre (+297) has outdone his +141 runs. That helped him rank among the NL's top three in WAR annually from 2005–09, with a minimum of 7.2 each year; from 2005–14, only Albert Pujols (67.4 WAR) topped Utley (59.4). His peak score is ninth at the position, but his longevity is in question; he didn't exceed 300 PA until his age-26 season and knee problems limited him to an average of 116 games from 2010–15. If he doesn't reach 2,000 hits, he'll wind up as his generation's Bobby Grich.

12. Robinson Cano

Teams:	Yankees 2005–13 • Mariners 2014–16
Stats:	.307/.355/.498 • 127 OPS+ • 2,210 H • 278 HR • 50 SB
Rankings:	7× All-Star • 6× top 5 WAR • 6× top 10 AVG • 6× top 10 SLG
Voting/JAWS:	**62.4/50.4/56.4**

Even having left the bright lights of the Bronx for the Emerald City, Cano appears well on his way to a bronze plaque. He's already above the peak score at second—the seventh-best, with everyone else but him and Utley from among the top 10 already enshrined. It's not out of the question he pushes his way higher in that category, either. He's got a good chance at 3,000 hits, needing to average just 113 per year until his contract runs out in 2023. The bet here is that he winds up around seventh in JAWS here.

19. Dustin Pedroia

Teams:	Red Sox 2006–16
Stats:	.301/.366/.445 • 115 OPS+ • 1,683 H • 133 HR • 134 SB
Rankings:	4× All-Star • 4× GG • 2008 AL MVP • 2007 AL ROY
Voting/JAWS:	50.7/42.4/46.6

Pedroia's scrappy, hustle-driven style stands in marked contrast to the seeming ease and detachedness of Cano's work in the field and down the first base line, but the preference of aged white ball scribes aside, there's a clear separation that's probably only going to get bigger. Pedroia is the much more valuable fielder (+101 DRS to +25 through 2016), but the erosion of his power suggests that he's past his peak as a hitter. Compare his 53 batting runs from 2012–16 to Cano's 157 in that span and you can see which way the wind blows. Given Pedroia's hardware— including two World Series rings—he'll have the traditional stuff in his favor, but he's unlikely to surpass Cano in career/peak/JAWS, and will have an uphill battle to reach Cooperstown.

20. Jeff Kent

Teams:	Blue Jays 1992 • Mets 1992–96 • Indians 1996 • Giants 1997–2002 • Astros 2003–04 • Dodgers 2005–08
Stats:	.290/.356/.500 • 123 OPS+ • 2,461 H • 377 HR • 94 SB
Rankings:	5× All-Star • 2× top 5 WAR • 2000 NL MVP
Voting/JAWS:	55.2/35.6/45.4

Kent didn't land a regular job until his age-25 season and didn't really settle in until age 29, after being traded three times. Nonetheless, he developed into a middle-of-the-lineup force, setting the record for home runs by a second baseman (351) while helping four different franchises reach the playoffs seven times. Three of those Octobers came with the Giants and Barry Bonds, whom he had a knack for making more sympathetic via his own prickly personality. Despite his penchant for the long ball and for piling up RBI, Kent didn't generate extraordinary value due to a modest 8.4% walk rate, uneven defense (-42 runs, including -53 DRS over his final six seasons), and adjustments for the high-scoring era; he topped 5.0 WAR just three times, and made the top 10 just twice. BBWAA voters have been unmoved thus far, giving him no more than 16.7% through four cycles. Between the second basemen who outrank him here and the strength of other candidates on recent ballots, he's got relatively little beef.

CHAPTER 12

SHORTSTOPS

ALAN TRAMMELL

Trammell didn't have that gun, but his throwing was so fast and so fluid, much like his swing. He got the maximum out of those mechanics that anyone's ever seen out of a top-tier shortstop.[1]

—LYNN HENNING

Once upon a time, shortstops didn't hit. In the 1970s, when Alex Rodriguez, Derek Jeter, and Nomar Garciaparra were still wearing short pants, the idea that a slick-fielding defensive wizard could help his team despite being a total zero with the bat reached its zenith—and the collective offensive production of shortstops reached its nadir. In 1973, when major league teams hit .257/.325/.379 and averaged 4.21 runs per game, shortstops "hit" .236/.292/.301, with only two, the Reds' Davey Concepcion and the Rangers' Toby Harrah, supplying league-average production.

By the early 1980s, things were changing, as the American League produced a trio of talented two-way shortstops who could field their position and pose a substantial threat to pitchers. The Brewers' Robin Yount, who debuted in 1974 at the tender age of 18, evolved into a top-notch hitter and earned MVP honors in 1982 as Milwaukee won the pennant. The Orioles' Cal Ripken kicked off a stretch of 10 straight seasons with at least 20 homers in his official rookie season of 1982— as well as a record-setting consecutive games streak—and the next year, he, too, claimed an MVP award as Baltimore won the World Series.

Debuting between those two, in late 1977, was the Tigers' Alan Trammell. In 1984, he hit .314/.382/.468, won a Gold Glove, and was the MVP of the World

Series. In 1987, he had an even better season while leading the Tigers to the AL East flag, but he was flat-out robbed of an MVP award in a very tight race. Trammell spent 20 years with the Tigers, and while he didn't reach 3,000 hits like Yount (who eventually moved to center field and won another MVP award) or Ripken (who also won a second MVP before moving to third base for his final few years), he did make six All-Star teams and win four Gold Gloves, even while vying for attention with the other two. In fact, he's statistically a dead ringer for another contemporary: longtime Reds star and 2012 Hall of Fame inductee Barry Larkin.

Despite his Hall-caliber numbers, Trammell couldn't buy a vote from the writers, who neglected him to such an extent that he didn't reach 20% until his ninth time around (2010). Only in 2016, his 15th and final year of eligibility, did he exceed the halfway point to 75%, topping out with 40.9%. In doing so, he became the best player to age off the ballot in terms of JAWS, since Ron Santo in 1998, five years before I invented the metric. It took another 13 years for Santo to gain entry, albeit posthumously. We can only hope that Trammell gets his due in more timely fashion.

The Career

Tigers 1977–96

Player	Career	Peak	JAWS	H	HR	SB	AVG/OBP/SLG	OPS+
Alan Trammell	70.4	44.6	57.5	2365	185	236	.285/.352/.415	110
Avg HOF SS	66.7	42.8	54.7					
SS Rank	11th	8th	11th					
(Above HOF)	(14/21)	(15/21)	(13/21)					

Born in Garden Grove, California, in 1958 and raised in San Diego, Trammell was a bigger star in basketball at Kearny High School than in baseball, earning All-City honors and receiving scholarship offers. Baseball scouts were initially unimpressed by his bat, but his arm and hands drew their attention. Hall of Fame catcher Rick Ferrell, then a scout for the Tigers, reported, "He could be first-draft choice but down the line. Will develop into a fine def. SS—Ray Oyler type,"[2] referring to a good-field, no-hit shortstop for the late-'60s Tigers.

Fortunately, Trammell's bat came around, and he was chosen as the second pick of the second round of the 1976 draft, with a $35,000 signing bonus that led him to pass up scholarship offers from Arizona State and UCLA. That was a banner draft for Detroit; while first-round pick Pat Underwood had an undistinguished four-year major league career, fourth-rounder Dan Petry and fifth-rounder Jack Morris eventually anchored their pitching staff, and seventh-rounder

Ozzie Smith, who returned to school instead of signing, is in Cooperstown after being chosen by the Padres the next year.

The teenage Trammell advanced quickly through the minors, spending just 41 games at the Rookie-level Appalachian League, before jumping to Double-A Montgomery. After the season, he and Lou Whitaker, the team's 1975 fifth-round pick, worked intensively in the Instructional League, beginning a partnership that would include an AL (and middle infield) record of 1,918 games played together. The pair spent the 1977 season at Montgomery, where the 19-year-old Trammell earned Southern League MVP honors by hitting .291/.365/.414 with 19 triples but just three homers. The Tigers recalled the duo at season's end, and on September 9, 1977, they made their major league debuts.

Trammell and Whitaker were in the Tigers' Opening Day lineup in 1978, though it took until late May before manager Ralph Houk made them everyday players. Trammell hit .268/.335/.339 for an 89 OPS+ with defense that was six runs above average en route to a solid 2.8 WAR. He tied for fourth in the Rookie of the Year balloting; Whitaker won. After a rough sophomore season, Trammell had his first big year in 1980, the Tigers' first full season under manager Sparky Anderson. The 22-year-old hit .300/.376/.404 for a 113 OPS+, earning All-Star and Gold Glove honors en route to 4.8 WAR. After the season, he signed a seven-year, $2.8 million contract to keep him in Detroit long-term.

While that year provided a preview of what was to come, Trammell at this stage was "so weak you could knock the bat out of his hands,"[3] as Anderson recalled years later. Though he repeated as a deserving (+15 runs) Gold Glove winner in the strike-shortened 1981 season, it wasn't until 1983 that he reached double digits in homers or topped a 100 OPS+ for the second time. In a breakout season, the 25-year-old hit .319/.385/.471 for a 138 OPS+ with 14 homers, 30 steals, and 6.0 WAR; the last of those ranked eighth among AL position players. The Tigers, who had been inching up the standings during his career, went 92-70 for a second-place finish, their best showing since winning the AL East in strike-shortened 1972.

They did even better in 1984, jumping out to a 35-5 start (still the best since 1884), and finishing 104-58. Trammell produced a near–carbon copy of his 1983 breakout offensively (136 OPS+), while his defense improved to 16 runs above average. He made his second All-Star team, won his fourth Gold Glove, and ranked fourth in the AL in WAR (6.6). Red-hot in October, he hit a combined .419/.500/.806 against the Royals and Padres. His 9-for-20 performance in the five-game World Series, including a pair of homers that drove in all four runs in Detroit's Game 4 win, brought him Series MVP honors.

After the season, Trammell went under the knife of Dr. James Andrews to repair torn cartilage in his left knee and clean up his right shoulder. The latter injury had caused considerable discomfort, forcing him to the disabled list for three weeks in July (he didn't play in the All-Star Game) and into DH duty for half of August. "I never had a full day I didn't feel it. But people don't want to hear you making excuses. . . . I was going to play as long as I had to."[4] The knee injury dated to the previous Halloween, when he fell while modeling a Frankenstein costume for his children; surgery to repair the cartilage hadn't taken, requiring a touch-up.

Slowed by recovery as well as a midseason forearm strain, Trammell slumped in 1985, tailing off particularly badly in the second half, but he rebounded in 1986, with 21 homers and 6.3 WAR, sixth in the league. That set the stage for the best season of his career in 1987: .343/.402/.551 for a 155 OPS+ with 28 homers—all highs he'd never surpass—and 21 steals for a 98-win AL East squad that was the class of the AL. Trammell's 8.2 WAR ranked second in the league behind only Wade Boggs's 8.3, for a sub-.500 Red Sox team; alas, he couldn't convert that performance to an MVP award, losing a close vote to Toronto's George Bell, whose 47 homers and 134 RBIs for Toronto yielded just 5.0 WAR. Every bit as disappointing was the Tigers' loss in the ALCS to an 85-win Twins team that had been outscored by their opponents by 20 runs. Trammell went 4-for-20 in the series.

Trammell was very good in 1988 (6.0 WAR and a 138 OPS+ on .311/.373/.464 hitting), but was limited to just 128 games due to injuries, including a bruised left elbow that cost him a role as the starting shortstop for the AL All-Star team. Thus began an all-too-familiar trend as he passed into his 30s; due to injuries, he would top 130 games just once more, in a 146-game, 6.7 WAR season in 1990. As he interspersed good seasons with the bat (1988, '90, '93) with weaker ones, strong defense bolstered his value. Excluding 1992, when a broken right ankle limited him to 29 games, he averaged 4.8 WAR and 122 games from 1988–93.

The Tigers couldn't return to the playoffs during Trammell's tenure in Detroit, plummeting from 88 wins in 1988 to 59 in '89, and breaking .500 just one more time during his career. His 1992 injury opened the door for Travis Fryman, a power-hitting third baseman with a good enough glove to handle shortstop amid Trammell's increasingly frequent absences. When he rebounded to hit .329/.388/.496 in 112 games in 1993, Trammell did so as a utilityman, starting 58 games at short, 27 at third base, and eight more in the outfield, unfamiliar terrain for the 35-year-old. After three more seasons of part-time duty, he retired following the 1996 season at age 38.

The Case

On the traditional merits, Trammell looks like a solid Hall of Fame candidate. His 2,365 hits (14th among players who spent the majority of their careers at shortstop) and 185 homers (16th) may not be in the class of contemporaries Ripken and Yount, but it's worth noting that Trammell spent far more time at the position (2,139 games, 11th all-time) than Yount (1,479). The competition with that pair limited Trammell to six All-Star selections (twice he had to sit out due to injuries) and four Gold Gloves, not to mention just the two postseason appearances, but his 118 points on the Bill James Hall of Fame Monitor translate into having a very good chance of election.

In terms of advanced metrics, Trammell's 132 batting runs is 20th at the position, better than 10 of the 21 Hall of Fame shortstops. To that he added another 25 runs on the bases and 14 for double play avoidance, the combination of which ranks 16th at the position and is better than all but five enshrined shortstops—which is to say that he makes up ground via those secondary offensive contributions. On the defensive side, his total of 77 runs above average (81 above average strictly at shortstop) is good but not great, 44th among shortstops, and ahead of nine Hall of Famers.

Those rankings don't scream "VOTE FOR ME!" separately, but as with Whitaker the whole is more than the sum of the parts; Trammell was the rare two-way shortstop, very good on both sides of the ball. Only nine shortstops (five enshrined) were at least 100 runs above average with the bat and 50 above average with the glove. Hence Trammell's four times in the league's top five in WAR, with two more in the top 10, and the stretch from 1980–90 in which his 59.3 WAR ranked third in the majors behind only Rickey Henderson (80.7) and Boggs (63.1), with Yount (57.6), Ripken (57.5, albeit with just 23 games before 1982), Mike Schmidt (56.4), and Ozzie Smith (55.5) close behind.

Thus Trammell's 70.4 career WAR ranks 11th at the position, and is 3.7 wins above the Hall standard. Among those ahead of him, only the unlikely-to-be-elected Alex Rodriguez (116.8), the forgotten Bill Dahlen (75.2), and 2020 first-ballot lock Derek Jeter (71.8) are outside Cooperstown. No upcoming candidate has even 50 WAR; Miguel Tejada (46.9, eligible in 2019), Jimmy Rollins (46.0, giving his career one last shot), and Omar Vizquel (45.3, eligible in 2018) aren't in the same time zone, let alone the same ballpark.

Trammell's WAR is tied for 13th among all position players outside the Hall, including three active players (Albert Pujols, Adrian Beltre, and Carlos Beltran), three likely first-ballot honorees (Jeter, Chipper Jones, and Jim Thome), and two holdover candidates (Barry Bonds and Larry Walker). His 44.6 peak WAR is eighth among shortstops, 1.8 wins above the standard, and ahead of Larkin (43.1), Smith (42.3), and Jeter (42.2). His JAWS ranks 11th, 2.8 points above the standard, with only A-Rod and Bad Bill (57.7) above him, and 13 of 21 Hall of Famers below.

To say that the BBWAA voters overlooked Trammell's strong résumé would be an understatement. Debuting on the 2002 ballot alongside Smith and Andre

Dawson, he instantly became a forgotten man. Smith breezed into Cooperstown with 91.7% of the vote, while fifth-year candidate Gary Carter drew 72.7%, setting himself up for election the following year. Trammell polled just 15.7%, lower than any post-1966 candidate ever elected by the BBWAA (Duke Snider's 17.0% in 1970 is the low-water mark). His share remained below 20% until 2010; perhaps tellingly, his low-water mark came in 2007 (13.4%) as Ripken and Tony Gwynn sailed in. He reached 36.4% percent in 2012, when Larkin was elected on his third try, but by then Trammell had too much ground to make up, and the ballot grew more crowded. He closed out his eligibility at 40.9% percent in 2016.

What accounts for Trammell's lack of traction? The proximity of so many Hall of Fame peers at the same position—Larkin, Ripken, Smith, and Yount—was probably a factor, as it cost Trammell some accolades, though as noted in my Ted Simmons essay (Chapter 9), five active Hall of Famers at one position is hardly unusual. Every position except third base has had years with at least that many active, and five seasons in the 1930–42 span included six Hall of Fame shortstops spread out over just 16 teams.

Beyond that, Trammell's disastrous stint managing the Tigers from 2003–05, which included a 43-119 season in his first year and sub-.500 records all three seasons, did him no favors, and in a cruel irony neither did the writers' quick dispatch of Whitaker, whose 2.9% in 2001 consigned him to the same no-man's-land as Bobby Grich nine years earlier. In *The Sporting News*, Ken Rosenthal touched on both:

> There seems little dispute that Trammell is one of the top dozen shortstops of all time. But does that make him a Hall of Famer? His career is virtually indistinguishable from that of second baseman Lou Whitaker, his double-play partner with the Tigers. . . . Trammell rarely was the best shortstop in the A.L. Cal Ripken usually was better offensively and Tony Fernandez surpassed him defensively. Trammell was a World Series MVP in 1984, but he was never a league MVP. . . . Also, he never led his league in a major offensive category.[5]

In a follow-up in which he admitted to being "stunned" at Trammell's lack of support, Rosenthal called him "my most difficult exclusion."[6] In 2003, he voted for Trammell, after conceding that his own resistance stemmed from having covered Ripken for the *Baltimore Sun* for 13 years. He maintained his support for Trammell until 2014, when his ballot grew too crowded and the shortstop clearly had no chance via the writers.

To Rosenthal's point, it's true that aside from Trammell's advantage in on-base percentage, his basic offensive numbers—hits, homers, batting average, and slugging percentage—fall short of those of Ripken and Yount, and the same is true with regards to Larkin, aside from Trammell's 25-hit edge. Via advanced metrics, Trammell trails all three in OPS+, with a 110 to Larkin's 116, Yount's 115, and Ripken's 112. Via Total Zone, his 77 fielding runs outdoes Larkin (18) and Yount (-47), trailing only Ripken (181). Additionally, Trammell's offensive numbers trump Smith's across the board, though obviously Oz has the edge defensively via his 239 fielding runs. Trammell trails three of the four in career WAR and is just 0.2 ahead of Larkin; as noted, he's got bigger leads on both Larkin and Smith in terms of peak WAR and has a 0.9 point advantage over Larkin in JAWS.

That Trammell should be outside the Hall when Larkin, the most directly comparable player, is in rates as an injustice. Consider the components that go into WAR:

Player	PA	Batting	Base	DP	Field	Pos	Rep	RAR
Trammell	9376	132	25	14	77	127	323	699
Larkin	9057	200	80	4	18	119	283	703
Difference		-68	-55	+10	+59	+8	+40	-4

Reading across: batting runs, baserunning runs, double play avoidance runs, fielding runs, positional adjustment runs, replacement level runs (based on playing time), and runs above replacement (the total of the six columns). Trammell is at a decided disadvantage when you combine batting and baserunning, the most easily measured and apparent from basic stats; Larkin stole 379 bases at an 83.1% clip, far outstripping Trammell's 236 steals and pedestrian 68.4% success rate. That—and Larkin's 1995 NL MVP award versus Trammell's near-miss in '87—helps to explain why Larkin was more popular with voters, though Trammell regains the ground via defense and playing time, to the point that they're in a dead heat.

With his BBWAA eligibility lapsed, Trammell will have to hope to break through on the Modern Baseball Era Committee ballot starting in 2018 or '20. In that realm, he'll have plenty of historical precedents in terms of those who struggled for BBWAA support, even late in their ballot tenures. For example, Trammell's peak share of the vote is within 10 points of Santo (32.9%) and fellow VC-elected players George Kell (33.2%), Bill Mazeroski (33.5%), Red Schoendienst (36.8%), Phil Rizzuto (38.4%), Richie Asbhurn (41.7%), and Nellie Fox (41.9%)—and he's stronger in JAWS than all but Santo.

If he's going to get his plaque, that will have to do.

THE ROUNDUP

Overall number refers to JAWS ranking *among all players at the position,* not necessarily those in the Hall. Average HOF shortstop: 66.7/42.8/54.8.

The Elite (above standard in career, peak, and JAWS)

1. Honus Wagner

Teams:	Louisville Colonels 1897–99 • Pirates 1900–17
Stats:	.328/.391/.467 • 151 OPS+ • 3,420 H • 101 HR • 723 SB
Rankings:	11× led WAR • 8 led OPS+ • 8× led AVG • 6× led SLG • 5× led SB • 4× led OBP 4× S/S TC
	All-time: 7th WAR • 8th H, 10th SB
Voting/JAWS:	BBWAA 1936 **(1st, 95.1%)** • **131.0/65.4/98.2**

Though the barrel-chested and bowlegged Wagner looked awkward, his speed and athleticism made him the game's most dominant player before Babe Ruth. His run of eight straight league leads in WAR (1902–09) is unmatched, while his 11 leads in the category is tied with the Bambino, Barry Bonds, and Rogers Hornsby for the most all-time, plus he had four other top-four finishes. About the only major category he never led was homers; his career high of 10 placed him second twice. To the extent that we can put faith in Total Zone, his +85 runs is tied for eighth among dead-ball-era shortstops (through 1919)—though he actually didn't settle at the position until 1903, serving stretches in center field, right field, first, and third. In fact, just 68% of his games came at his signature position, though the totality of his contributions towers over the field. At the time he retired, the closest player to him in WAR was Nap Lajoie, more than 23 wins behind him; Ty Cobb stole the top spot in 1923.

3. Cal Ripken

Teams:	Orioles 1981–2001
Stats:	.276/.340/.447 • 112 OPS+ • 3,184 H • 431 HR • 36 SB
Rankings:	19× All-Star • 3× led WAR • 3× top 10 AVG • 3× top 10 SLG • 3× top 10 OPS+ • 2× GG
	All-time: 8th G • 15th H • 15th TB
Voting/JAWS:	BBWAA 2007 **(1st, 98.5%)** • **95.5/56.1/75.8**

Best known for his record-setting streak of 2,632 consecutive games, Ripken did a helluva lot more than show up for work with alarming regularity. He's the only middle infielder among the eight players to reach the dual milestones of 3,000 hits and 400 homers, and third in fielding runs (+181), behind only Mark Belanger (+241) and Ozzie Smith (+239). His MVP seasons were momentous: in 1983, he helped the Orioles win the World Series, while in '91 he posted the highest WAR (11.5) for any infielder since Lou Gehrig in 1927 (11.8). He's one of only five post-integration players with multiple 10-WAR seasons; his two (1984 being the other) are tied with Carl Yastrzemski, behind Bonds and Mickey Mantle (three apiece) and Willie Mays (six). His 98.5% of the vote made him the first position player to top Cobb's 1936 mark of 98.2%, and since then only Ken Griffey Jr. (99.3%) has surpassed him.

4. George Davis

Teams:	Cleveland Spiders 1890–92 • Giants 1893–1901, '03 • White Sox 1902, 1904–09
Stats:	.295/.362/.405 • 121 OPS+ • 2,665 H • 73 HR • 619 SB
Rankings:	7× top 5 in WAR • 5× top 10 SB • 3× top 10 AVG
Voting/JAWS:	VC 1998 • **84.7/44.3/64.5**

Eighty-nine years after his retirement and nearly 58 after his death, the Veterans Committee elected this long-lost great. It's difficult to imagine how Davis, an outfielder and third baseman before moving to shortstop, could have disappeared off the map so completely, for he ranks as the best of his era this side of Wagner. He could do it all: Among shortstops, he's third in both OPS+ and steals, and seventh in fielding runs (+146). Never part of a winning effort in Cleveland or New York—where he was traded straight up for superstar Buck Ewing in 1893—he lost most of 1903 to a protracted battle between the two leagues over player contracts, bouncing back and forth between the Giants and White Sox, but rebounded to set his career high with 7.2 WAR in 1904 and match it in '05. Even at age 35, he was the best player on the 1906 "Hitless Wonder" White Sox who upended the Cubs. He didn't appear on a VC ballot until 1995; his election was the culmination of the efforts not only of Bill James but long-deceased Hall historian Lee Allen and Walt Lipka, the city historian of Davis's native Cohoes, New York.

5. Robin Yount

Teams:	Brewers 1974–93
Stats:	.285/.342/.430 • 115 OPS+ • 3,142 H • 251 HR • 271 SB

Rankings: 6× top 10 WAR • 6× top 10 AVG • 3× All-Star • 3× top 3
                   OPS+ • 3× top 5 SLG • 3× top 10 OBP
                   All-time: 8th H • 15th G
Voting/JAWS: BBWAA 1999 **(1st, 77.5%)** • **77.0/47.2/62.1**

Chosen third in the 1973 draft, Yount played just 64 minor league games before becoming the Brewers' Opening Day shortstop in '74, when he was 18. Hardly an overnight sensation, he hit .257/.294/.335/82 OPS+ with a combined 3.3 WAR in his first three seasons, but the wretched Brewers showed patience, letting slide Yount's brief 1978 threat to ditch baseball for professional golf, a reaction to a potential move to the outfield to accommodate 1977 top pick Paul Molitor. Both Yount's glovework and bat gradually improved, and he broke out in 1980, beginning a sizzling 10-year stretch (.305/365/.485/135 OPS+) where his 55.1 WAR was topped by only Henderson (70.8), Wade Boggs (59.9), and Mike Schmidt (56.4). His 1985 position switch probably cost him two wins a year for half of that stretch, as he was a very good shortstop (+25 runs career) but a lousy centerfielder (-72 runs career). His first-ballot election was a close call for a 3,000-hit man, but not atypical for large classes; the three-man slates of 1972, '84, and '91 all had at least one honoree in the 75–80% range, too.

6. Arky Vaughan

Teams: Pirates 1932–41 • Dodgers 1942–43, 1947–48
Stats: .318/.406/.453 • 136 OPS+ • 2,103 H • 96 HR • 118 SB
Rankings: 11× top 10 WAR • 9× All-Star • 7× top 10 AVG • 4× top 10
                SLG • 3× led OBP
                All-time: 25th OBP
Voting/JAWS: VC 1985 • **72.9/50.6/61.8**

Because of his short career, premature retirement at age 31, and tragic death at 40 in a fishing accident, Vaughan languished outside of Cooperstown for far too long. His stellar hitting and solid glovework (+21 runs career) made him one of the league's two most valuable players via WAR six times during the high-scoring 1933–40 stretch. He never won an MVP award, even when he took the slash stat Triple Crown in 1935 (.385/.491/.607) en route to a career-high 9.2 WAR. Traded to Brooklyn in December 1941, Vaughan played third base until Pee Wee Reese was drafted into the military. Between a clash with manager Leo Durocher over the suspension of pitcher Bobo Newsom for insubordination and the need to tend his California ranch after his brother was drafted, Vaughan retired after 1943, ending a 12-year stretch over which only Mel Ott had been more valuable (75.6 WAR to 70.9). Durocher's 1947 suspension keyed Vaughan's return; he played 129 games over two years. Between that strange coda and his early demise, he slipped through the cracks, voting-wise, peaking at 29.0% in 1968, his final year of eligibility, and needing 17 more years for election.

7. Ernie Banks

Teams:	Cubs 1953–71
Stats:	.274/.330/.500 • 122 OPS+ • 2,583 H • 512 HR • 50 SB
Rankings:	11× All-Star • 7× top 5 HR • 6× top 10 OPS+ • 5× top 5 SLG • 5× top 5 WAR
	All-time: T-23rd HR
Voting/JAWS:	BBWAA 1977 **(1st, 83.8%)** • **67.5/51.9/59.7**

Beyond the infectious enthusiasm that made him one of the game's greatest ambassadors, Banks redefined the caliber of offense possible from a shortstop. His 44 homers in 1955 broke Vern Stephens's previous high of 39, and his five seasons with at least 40 stood as the position's five highest until Alex Rodriguez hit 51 in 2001. Banks followed Stephens as the second shortstop to hit 200 homers, and his 277 at the position (the strict split) trails only Ripken (345, after surpassing him in 1993), Rodriguez (344), and Miguel Tejada (291). As for value, Banks averaged a hefty 7.9 WAR from 1955–60, trailing only Mantle (8.9) and Mays (8.7). Banks played more games at first base (1,259) than shortstop (1,125), though he was far more valuable at short. From 1953–61, he hit for a 138 OPS+ with 54.8 WAR, while from 1962–71 he hit for a 106 OPS+ with 12.8 WAR. Perhaps that slow fade accounts for his fairly tepid first-ballot support, though it's difficult to comprehend one voter in six turning his nose up at a pre-steroid-era 512-homer slugger at any position.

8. Ozzie Smith

Teams:	Padres 1978–81 • Cardinals 1982–96
Stats:	.262/.337/.328 • 87 OPS+ • 2,460 H • 28 HR • 580 SB
Rankings:	15× All-Star • 13× GG • 7× top 10 SB • 6× top 10 WAR • 2× top 10 OBP
Voting/JAWS:	BBWAA 2002 **(1st, 91.7%)** • **76.5/42.3/59.4**

Set the Gold Gloves aside, because voters can find their way into a rut. As best as Total Zone can tell us, nobody produced more defensive value than the Wizard of Oz, not that a highlight reel and a good dose of common sense wouldn't yield the same conclusion. His 43.4 Defensive WAR (fielding runs + positional adjustment) trumps Mark Belanger's 39.4, with third baseman Brooks Robinson (38.8) close behind. Smith's offense improved significantly after being traded following his age-26 season. Spurred by his famous bet with Whitey Herzog—he owed the manager a dollar for every fly ball, and vice versa for every grounder—he posted a .350 OBP as a Cardinal, 20 points above the park-adjusted league average, and offset his lack of power by stealing bases at an 80% clip. In San Diego he produced a 66 OPS+ and was 55 runs below average in batting, baserunning, and double play avoidance, while in St. Louis he was good for a 93 OPS+ and 41 runs above average in the same (+61 in baseruning alone). That's what separates him from the Belangers of the world—that and the somersaults.

9. Luke Appling

Teams:	White Sox 1930–43, 1945–50
Stats:	.310/.399/.398 • 113 OPS+ • 2,749 H • 45 HR • 179 SB
Rankings:	10× top 10 WAR • 9× top 10 OBP • 8× top 10 AVG • 7× All-Star • 6× top 10 SB
Voting/JAWS:	BBWAA 1964 **(12th, run-off)** • **74.5/43.8/59.2**

Notorious for his hypochondria and for wearing pitchers down by fouling off pitches seemingly at will, Appling was a tremendous contact hitter who whiffed in just 5.1% of plate appearances (never more than 41 times in a season) while walking in 12.7%. That plus his singles-hitting prowess regularly placed him on the OBP leaderboard, but the power-starved White Sox—whose hitters produced just five 20-homer seasons during Appling's tenure—batted him fourth, fifth, or sixth in nearly 69% of his plate appearances. The team ranked either last or second to last in scoring 11 times during those 20 years. The record holder for most games played (2,422) without reaching the postseason, he furthered that total while accruing more value from age 39 onward: 19.1—WAR from 1946–49 (ages 39–42)—than any other position player while ranking among the league's top 10 three times.

13. Barry Larkin

Teams:	Reds 1986–2004
Stats:	.295/.371/.444 • 116 OPS+ • 2,340 H • 198 HR • 379 SB
Rankings:	12× All-Star • 7× top 10 WAR • 5× top 10 SB • 4× top 10 AVG • 3× top 10 OBP • 3× GG
Voting/JAWS:	BBWAA 2012 **(3rd, 86.4%)** • **70.2/43.1/56.6**

Elbow, thumb, calf, Achilles, neck, fingers, groin, hernia—you name it, Larkin missed time for it, reaching the 140-game plateau just seven times in 19 seasons, tied with Tony Gwynn for the second-lowest mark among post-1960 Hall of Famers (Willie Stargell's six is lower). It took Larkin until ages 34–35 (1998–99) to string together back-to-back seasons of at least 140 games, though he avoided the disabled list in the strike-shortened 1994 and '95 seasons, claiming MVP honors via a 5.9-WAR season (fourth in the NL) for a division winner in the latter. Even with his absences, he was a leaderboard regular in WAR, leading in 1988. Offensively, his OPS+ ranks seventh among shortstops with at least 7,000 PA, one point ahead of Yount and Jeter. Defensively, his Gold Gloves don't match up well with the metrics; he was two runs below average in those three seasons, 20 above in the rest, though it won't shock you to know that the hardware came in two of his three best offensive seasons.

The Rank and File

14. Bobby Wallace

Teams:	Cleveland Spiders 1894–98 • Cardinals 1899–1901, 1917–18 • Browns 1902–16
Stats:	.268/.332/.358 • 105 OPS+ • 2,309 H • 34 HR • 201 SB
Rankings:	9× top 10 WAR • 2× top 10 SLG
Voting/JAWS:	VC 1953 • **76.3/41.8/59.1***

Total Baseball called Wallace "probably the most obscure"[7] Hall of Famer, and his record 25 seasons played without a World Series appearance may be part of the reason, but he's worth knowing. He started his major league career as a pitcher in a rotation that included Cy Young, throwing 400 innings with a 125 ERA+ en route to 6.2 WAR in his first three seasons (reflected in the career WAR and JAWS above, but not included in calculating position standards). During that time, he dabbled as an outfielder, but his arm strength and fielding prowess led to a switch to third base in 1897, and then shortstop in '99. He's credited with revolutionizing the position thanks to his footwork and ability to throw on the run, and the numbers back his reputation (+133 runs, 14th all-time). His bat lived up to the switch, too. Though not elite, he was 130 runs above average from 1897–1910 (though for his career he was just 67 above average). During that 14-season stretch, he averaged 4.9 WAR per year, including an NL-high 7.7 in 1901.

---

* Pitching WAR included in player's career WAR & JAWS (not used in calculating position standards).

15. Lou Boudreau

Teams:	Indians 1938–50 • Red Sox 1951–52
Stats:	.295/.380/.415 • 120 OPS+ • 1,779 H • 68 HR • 51 SB
Rankings:	8× All-Star • 5× top 5 WAR • 5× top 10 AVG • 3× top 5 OBP
Voting/JAWS:	BBWAA 1970 **(13th, 77.3%)** • **63.0/48.7/55.8**

The list of player-managers who won the World Series while putting up a 10-WAR season starts and stops with Boudreau, who in 1948 hit .355/.453 /.534 with 18 homers, a 165 OPS+, and +20 runs afield en route to 10.4 WAR, the AL MVP award, and the Indians' last championship. It was damn near the ultimate mic drop, and after just one more year of regular duty he chose to focus on managing, playing in just 167 games over his final three seasons, from ages 32–34. Indeed, Boudreau's 7,024 PA is the lowest for any enshrined position player whose career extended past World War II without time in the Negro Leagues or the military; he wasn't drafted into service due to an arthritic right ankle that greatly limited his speed. Nonetheless, he was a hell of a player, brilliant afield (+118 runs) as well as at the plate; his peak score is sixth among shortstops. He likely would have cracked the top 10 in JAWS if not for his managerial career, which began in 1942, his age-24 season, continued through 1950 with the Indians, and went on to include the Red Sox, A's, and Cubs, albeit with diminishing returns.

16. Joe Cronin

Teams:	Pirates 1926–27 • Senators 1928–34 • Red Sox 1935–45
Stats:	.301/.39/.468 • 119 OPS+ • 2,285 H • 170 HR • 87 SB
Rankings:	7× All-Star • 5× top 5 WAR • 5× top 10 OBP
Voting/JAWS:	BBWAA 1956 **(10th, 78.8%)** • **66.4/43.9/55.2**

Like Boudreau, Cronin was a star who took the managerial reins at a young age, and played with decreasing frequency by his mid-30s. Taking over from Walter Johnson after three straight seasons of at least 92 wins, the 26-year-old Cronin led Washington to the AL pennant in 1933, his first year at the helm. His defense was strong in his mid-20s before eroding (+62 through 1934, -37 after), and he had rare power for a shortstop, setting a position record with 24 homers in 1940, following seasons of 18, 17, and 19 in the three years prior. Fenway Park helped that power burst, hosting 58 of Cronin's 94 homers from 1937–41. After batting just 425 times over his final four seasons, he hung up the spikes and led the Red Sox to a pennant in 1946. He managed just one more season, then spent 11 years

(1948–58) as Boston's GM, most notably passing on both Jackie Robinson and Willie Mays while playing a central role in the team's failure to integrate. Not until 1959, after he began his 15-year stint as AL president, did Boston finally field a black player.

17. Pee Wee Reese

Teams:	Dodgers 1940–42, 1946–58
Stats:	.269/.366/.377 • 99 OPS+ • 2,170 H • 126 HR • 232 SB
Rankings:	10× All-Star • 8× top 5 SB • 8× top 10 WAR • 5× top 10 OBP
Voting/JAWS:	VC 1984 • **66.4/41.0/53.6**

For a perennial All-Star who keyed seven pennant winners and played a pivotal role in the fall of the color line, Reese is quite underrated. While Jackie Robinson was by far the most valuable Dodger during his 10-year run (1947–56) in terms of WAR (61.5), Reese (50.0) was a close third behind Duke Snider (53.0), well ahead of Gil Hodges (36.4). He combined a league-average bat—no small matter for a shortstop—with elite baserunning (+43 runs, fourth overall in the 1901–60 span), and an excellent glove (+117 runs, 20th all-time among shortstops) despite spending his age-24–26 seasons in the navy. Given that his service time was bookended by seasons of 5.7 and 6.0 WAR, it's not unthinkable that he lost 15–18 WAR to World War II, which would have pushed him well into the top 10 here. With no Gold Gloves or advanced metrics and only modest Triple Crown stats to guide them, the BBWAA never gave Reese more than 47.9% even while writers complained about the Hall's dearth of shortstops (just 12 prior to his 1978 ballot finale). In one of its best moves, the VC elected him posthaste.

19. Joe Sewell

Teams:	Indians 1920–30 • Yankees 1931–33
Stats:	.312/.391/.413 • 108 OPS+ • 2,226 H • 49 HR • 74 SB
Rankings:	5× top 10 WAR • 2× top 10 AVG • 2× top 10 OBP
Voting/JAWS:	VC 1977 • **53.7/37.3/45.5**

Near the end of his first professional season, the 21-year-old Sewell was saddled with the grim task of replacing Ray Chapman, the victim of a fatal beanball a few weeks earlier. His play helped the Indians stave off the Yankees and White Sox in a tight three-way race, and while he hadn't been rostered before September 1, the Dodgers assented to his participation in the World Series; Cleveland won, though Sewell went just 4-for-23 with six errors. He spent the next decade as a lineup fixture, playing in 1,103 consecutive games from 1922–30, hitting .299 or better in nine straight years and perennially ranking among the leaders in doubles. The toughest player ever to strike out, he whiffed just 114 times in 8,333 PA (1.3%). Though he shifted to third in 1929, his 44.1 WAR is the highest among 1920s shortstops, ahead of Dave Bancroft's 34.9. Sewell maxed out at 8.6% via the BBWAA, but the VC never met a career .312 batting average it could ignore, no matter how light the résumé; George Van Haltren (.316) and Bobby Veach (.310) are the only pre-integration players with 7,000 PA in that vicinity still outside the Hall.

22. Luis Aparicio

Teams:	White Sox 1956–62, 1968–70 • Orioles 1963–67 • Red Sox 1971–73
Stats:	.262/.311/.343 • 82 OPS+ • 2,677 H • 83 HR • 506 SB
Rankings:	10× All-Star • 9× GG • 9× led SB • 2× top 10 WAR
Voting/JAWS:	BBWAA 1984 **(6th, 84.6%)** • **55.8/32.7/44.2**

The game's second star Latin American shortstop, Aparicio followed in the footsteps of fellow Venezuelan Chico Carrasquel, who recommended him to the White Sox, only to be replaced by him in 1956. Aparicio was brilliant as both a defender and baserunner; his +149 fielding runs (seventh at the position) dovetail with his hardware, while his +92 baserunning runs rank fourth all-time. Though he stole bases at an 81% clip while leading the AL annually from 1956–64, he was miscast in the leadoff spot, where his .304 OBP is the lowest of any player with at least 5,000 PA. He topped a 100 OPS+ just once; his -197 batting runs prevented him from attaining a single 6.0 WAR season. With his accolades and a starting role on two pennant winners, he fares much better via the Hall of Fame Monitor (150) than JAWS. His path to election was remarkable: After debuting at just 27.8% in 1979, he crept to 41.9% by '82, then jumped 25.5%—a post-1966 record—to 67.4% in '83; the leap has been ascribed to the BBWAA's inclusion of capsule summaries of players' credentials in the voting packets. He was elected the next year.

24. Joe Tinker

Teams:	Cubs 1902–12, '16 • Reds 1913 • Chicago Chi-Feds/Whales (FL) 1914–15
Stats:	.262/.308/.353 • 96 OPS+ • 1,690 H • 31 HR • 336 SB
Rankings:	6× top 10 WAR • 3× top 10 SB • 2× top 10 SLG
Voting/JAWS:	OTC 1946 • **53.2/33.1/43.2**

The shortstop on four pennant winners and two champions from 1906–10, Tinker has the highest WAR and JAWS of the Cubs' fabled infield combo. Elite defense (+180 fielding runs, fourth at the position) made him remarkably consistent in value; he averaged 4.1 WAR per season from 1902–14, placing as high as second in 1908, with 7.9. He improved significantly as a hitter as he aged, from 85 OPS+ from 1902–07 (ages 21–26) to 101 from 1908–13 (ages 27–32). His long-standing feud with Johnny Evers originated in 1905, when Evers took a cab to the ballpark—for an exhibition!—leaving teammates behind in the hotel lobby. Fisticuffs ensued once Tinker finally arrived, and the two didn't speak for more than 30 years "except in anger,"[8] as Evers once said. Thus when the Cubs appointed Evers player-manager for 1913, Tinker requested a trade and was sent to the Reds, who named him player-manager in his own right. The team went 64-89, and Tinker jumped to the Federal League, where his teams finished second and then first during his two years; he ranked ninth in WAR in 1914 but barely played in '15 due to a muscle tear.

25. Dave Bancroft

Teams:	Phillies 1915–20 • Giants 1920–23, '30 • Braves 1924–27 • Dodgers 1928–29
Stats:	.279/.355/.358 • 98 OPS+ • 2,004 H • 32 HR • 145 SB
Rankings:	6× top 10 WAR • 3× top 10 OBP
Voting/JAWS:	VC 1971 • **48.5/37.2/42.9**

Nicknamed "Beauty" for his cry to opposing hurlers after a good pitch, Bancroft was a vital cog on four pennant winners, including the first in Phillies franchise history (1915) and three in a row (1921–23) in New York. Renowned as a great fielder with the metrics to boot (+93 runs), he was a more or less average hitter, thanks in large part to a keen batting eye; he placed in the top 10 in walks eight times. Across a seven-year stretch (1920–26), his 34.3 WAR ranked third in the league behind Hornsby (63.9) and Frisch (37.6). On the other hand, he hit just .172/.222/.183 in 101 postseason PA, scores just 84 on the Hall Monitor, and broke double digits only in his final two years on the BBWAA ballot (maxing out at 16.2%). Thanks to the Frisch/Terry VC, he was the second of eight ex-Giants voted in from 1970–82, though hardly the worst.

29. Hughie Jennings

Teams:	Louisville Colonels 1891–93 • Baltimore Orioles 1893–99 • Brooklyn Superbas 1899–1900, '03 • Phillies 1901–02 • Tigers 1907, 1909–10, '12, '18

Stats:	.312/.391/.406 • 118 OPS+ • 1,526 H • 18 HR • 359 SB
Rankings:	4× led WAR • 4× top 10 AVG • 4× top 10 OBP • 3× top 10 OPS+ • 3× top 10 SB
Voting/JAWS:	OTC 1945 • **42.3/39.0/40.6**

In *The Politics of Glory*, Bill James called the 1945 election of Jennings the first of "a player who clearly had no damn business being there. . . . [He] wasn't a *dominant* player."[9] When James published that in 1994, no WAR existed, but the current estimate is that Jennings's 38.9 WAR for 1890–99 edges Bill Dahlen (38.6) for tops among shortstops despite the arm injury that forced him to first base in 1898. For the powerhouse 1894–98 Orioles, who won three NL flags, Jennings led the league in WAR the last four of those years, combining ace defense (+71 runs) with a blistering .361/.449/.474/140 OPS+ for that half-decade, thanks in large part to 202 hit-by pitches (he's the all-time leader at 287). While he never led in a slash stat, he's the only shortstop ever to hit .400 (.401 in 1896). Ultimately, his problem isn't a lack of dominance but of substance outside that stretch; he exceeded 82 games just two other times due to major injuries, including three skull fractures, one from a nighttime dive into an empty swimming pool. Mitigating his brief playing career is his early success managing the Tigers to three straight pennants (1907–09) and to a .538 winning percentage through 1920. The Hall has many people with less business owning plaques, including fellow 1945 honorees Hugh Duffy and Roger Bresnahan.

31. Travis Jackson

Teams:	Giants 1922–1936
Stats:	.291/.337/.433 • 102 OPS+ • 1,768 H • 135 HR • 71 SB
Rankings:	6× top 10 WAR • 4× top 10 HR
Voting/JAWS:	VC 1982 • **44.0/35.1/39.5**

Jackson was a key part of four pennant-winning Giants teams, though it's a stretch to call him a constant, as injuries and illnesses limited him to just four seasons with at least 140 games. His superficially impressive offensive numbers were the product of particularly favorable surroundings; he hit 89 of his 135 homers—second-most by a prewar shortstop—at the Polo Grounds but ranked in the top 10 in any slash stat just twice, and grades out as only a slightly above average hitter overall. His strength afield (+139 runs, tied for 12th all-time) helped him rank among the league's top five in WAR four times, but the brevity of his career and his .149/.186/.164 line in 74 World Series PA both detract from his case. He

never got the time of day from the BBWAA, only once cracking 5.0%, but became the eighth ex-Giant in 13 years to benefit from the VC pipeline.

The Basement (the most dubious honorees)

35. Phil Rizzuto

Teams:	Yankees 1941–42, 1946–56
Stats:	.273/.351/.355 • 93 OPS+ • 1,588 H • 38 HR • 149 SB
Rankings:	7× top 5 SB • 5× All-Star • 3× top 10 WAR
Voting/JAWS:	VC 1994 • **40.6/33.7/37.2**

A starter on nine pennant winners and seven champions, Rizzuto was a key player
during the Yankees' long run of success, but a Hall of Famer? That's a stretch. To
be fair, "The Scooter" missed his age 25–27 seasons while in the navy, and had
been worth 10.2 WAR in the two seasons prior; he might have lost 15 WAR and
some peak seasons, which could have pushed him as high as 19th in JAWS. He
was an excellent fielder (+115 runs) whose walks—one-third of which came while
batting eighth, ahem—kept him just 30 runs below average for his career with
the bat, though he rarely ranked among the league WAR leaders save for 6.7 in
his 1950 MVP season, and hit just .246/.355/.295 in 219 World Series PA. Rarely
considered Hall-caliber as his career wound down, he peaked at 38.4% on his final BBWAA ballot in 1976, then became "the center of the loudest Hall of Fame
dispute in the history of Cooperstown"[10] en route to election by a VC panel featuring longtime teammate Yogi Berra as well as crosstown rival Pee Wee Reese.
Holy cow!

37. Rabbit Maranville

Teams:	Braves 1912–20, 1929–33, '35 • Pirates 1921–24 • Cubs 1925 • Dodgers 1926 • Cardinals 1927–28
Stats:	.258/.318/.34 • 82 OPS+ • 2,605 H • 28 HR • 291 SB
Rankings:	5× top 10 WAR • 4× top 10 SB
Voting/JAWS:	BBWAA 1954 **(18th, 82.9%)** • **42.8/30.4/36.6**

A pint-sized (5'5") prankster, Maranville was renowned for his vest-pocket catches,
which involved snagging popups at waist level after watching them fall while his
arms remained by his sides. His glovework must have made quite an impression
to offset his dreadful offense (-228 batting runs and just two seasons topping a
100 OPS+). He placing third in the NL MVP voting in 1913 despite hitting just

.247/.330/.308/83 OPS+ for a 69-82 Braves team, and then second in '14 for the pennant winners despite his .246/.306/.326/85 OPS+ line; via his 26 fielding runs, his 5.0 WAR ranked third in the league that latter year. Indeed, his 130 fielding runs (tied for 16th) helped him to five top 10 WAR finishes, but he was worth just 4.0 WAR from 1925 onward. He missed all or most of three seasons: 1918 due to enlistment in the navy; '27, when he drank his way to the minors; and '34, when he broke his ankle in an exhibition game. He's enshrined thanks to his popularity— yet another reminder that it's the Hall of *Fame*—as the writers elected him after years of solid showings on the ballot.

Further Consideration (upcoming or overlooked candidates)

2. Alex Rodriguez

Teams:	Mariners 1994–2000 • Rangers 2001–03 • Yankees 2004–13, 15–16
Stats:	.295/.380/.550 • 140 OPS+ • 3,115 H • 696 HR • 329 SB
Rankings:	14× All-Star • 6× led WAR • 5× led HR • 4× led SLG
	All-time: 3rd RBI • 4th HR • 6th TB • 12th WAR • 20th H
JAWS:	**117.7/64.2/91.0**

A-Rod's a shortstop by this system on the basis of his 63.5 WAR through 2003, compiled while showing unprecedented power for the position via six straight seasons of at least 40 homers, two with at least 50, and three league leads. By comparison, he accumulated 54.2 WAR and won two of his three MVP awards as a third baseman for the Yankees while leading the league in public cringeworthiness several times. For Hall purposes, it's almost certainly a moot point given his unprecedented full-season suspension in 2014, if not his reported 2003 survey test failure. Yes, MLB got its hands very dirty while digging up dirt, paying for stolen evidence and otherwise violating his due process, but the slugger's recidivism and harebrained legal strategy won him no points. Perhaps the passage of time and the glow of his against-all-odds 2015 rebound—which humanized him as he surpassed the 660-home-run and 3,000-hit milestones—will soften voters' attitudes, but for now, expect the BBWAA electorate to tell him to pound sand come 2022.

10. Bill Dahlen

Teams:	Chicago Colts/Orphans 1891–98 • Brooklyn Superbas/ Dodgers 1899–1903, 10–11 • Giants 1904–07 • Boston Doves/Braves 1908–09

Stats:	.272/.358/.382 • 110 OPS+ • 2,461 H • 84 HR • 548 SB
Rankings:	6× top 5 WAR • 5× top 10 HR • 3× top 10 SLG
Voting/JAWS:	**75.2/40.1/57.7**

Fierce-tempered, fond of drink and horse races—he would intentionally draw ejections and head to the track—"Bad Bill" is the best shortstop outside the Hall according to JAWS, at least until A-Rod is eligible. While renowned for his glove-work and his heady, aggressive baserunning, he could hit, too; his 42-game hitting streak in 1894 set a briefly held NL record, and his 84 homers were the third most by a pre-1920 shortstop. While his 975 errors are second among shortstops, they're the product of great range and primitive equipment; his +139 fielding runs ranks 13th at the position. A key part of four pennant winners (Brooklyn in 1899–1900, New York in '04–05), his acquisition was considered "the most successful deal I ever made"[11] according to John McGraw. Hallwise, he slipped through the cracks prior to the sabermetric revival. While he fell short on the 2009 VC ballot and '13 and '16 Pre-Integration ones, he received as many as 10 of 16 votes in 2013, the year after SABR named him their "Overlooked 19th Century Baseball Legend."

12. Derek Jeter

Teams:	Yankees 1995–2014
Stats:	.310/.377/.440 • 115 OPS+ • 3,465 H • 260 HR • 358 SB
Rankings:	14× All-Star • 7× top 5 AVG • 6× top 10 OBP • 5× GG • 4× top 10 WAR
	All-time: 6th H • 10th PA • 11th R
Voting/JAWS:	**71.8/42.2/57.0**

Seemingly engineered to withstand the spotlight's glare, Jeter spent two decades in Yankee pinstripes pulling off the remarkable feat of simultaneously exuding charisma and remaining completely enigmatic, able to evade virtually every controversy that surrounded the franchise. A starter for 16 playoff teams, seven pennant winners, and five champions, he ranks among the position's best hitters, collecting more hits than any other infielder, and ranking third in batting runs among shortstops (353) behind only Wagner (639) and Vaughan (363). Defensively, his strong arm, sure hands, and low error totals helped him pass the eye tests of casual fans, broadcasters, and even the opposing managers who bestowed those Gold Gloves. However, his range was limited—he moved to his left about as well as Dick Cheney—and his -246 fielding runs is more than double the total of the next-closest shortstop; he was at least 10 runs below average in three Gold

Glove seasons. Still, "Captain Clutch" was unflappable in the big moments, hitting .304/.374/.465 with 20 homers in the postseason. Expect him to pull in at least 97% in 2020.

18. Jack Glasscock

Teams:	Cleveland Blues 1879–84 • Cincinnati Outlaw Reds (UA) 1884 • St. Louis Maroons 1885–86 • Indianapolis Hoosiers 1887–89 • Giants 1890–91 • St. Louis Browns (Cardinals) 1892–93 • Pirates 1893–94 • Louisville Colonels 1895 • Washington Senators 1895
Stats:	.290/.337/.374 • 112 OPS+ • 2,041 H • 27 HR • 372 SB
Rankings:	6× top 5 WAR • 4× top 10 SLG • 4× top 10 OPS+ • 3× top 10 AVG • 3× top 10 OBP
Voting/JAWS:	**61.9/41.0/51.4**

"Pebbly Jack"—nicknamed for his habit of removing stones from his passway—played while the rules were still taking shape, and didn't use a glove until 1890. Even so, many consider Glasscock the best nineteenth-century shortstop, and the metrics support the notion. His 61.9 WAR ranks fourth among all players through 1900, behind Cap Anson (93.9), Roger Connor (84.1), and Dan Brouthers (79.5). Considering the conditions, he was quite the fielder; his +149 runs ranks sixth at the position, and he's credited with being the first infielder to signal to a catcher which middle infielder would cover second on an attempted steal. He led the NL in WAR and hits twice, including in 1890, when he hit .336/.395/.439/147 OPS+ en route to a batting title in a circuit weakened by Players League defections. So why isn't he enshrined? He never played on a championship team and was regarded as somewhat colorless, his name aside. He's impressively close to the WAR standards given that NL schedules were less than 100 games prior to 1884. SABR's 2013 "Overlooked 19th Century Baseball Legend" figures to have a shot on a future Early Baseball Era Committee ballot.

42. Omar Vizquel

Teams:	Mariners 1989–93 • Indians 1994–2004 • Giants 2005–08 • Rangers 2009 • White Sox 2010–11 • Blue Jays 2012
Stats:	.272/.336/.352 • 82 OPS+ • 2,877 H • 80 HR • 404 SB
Rankings:	11× GG • 6× top 10 SB • 3× All-Star
Voting/JAWS:	**45.3/26.6/36.0**

The combination of the switch-hitting Vizquel's light bat, collection of Gold Gloves, and ubiquity on highlight shows have some people convinced that he's the second coming of Ozzie Smith and thus a lock for Cooperstown. From here, even given his role as a key player during the Indians' late-1990s run, I'm not convinced. Via Total Zone and Defensive Runs Saved, Vizquel's +128 runs ranks a very respectable 18th among shortstops, albeit 110 runs behind Smith; his range factors were just 0.1 play per nine above league average, whereas Smith's were 0.44 above. While Vizquel collected a ton of singles and even got within sight of 3,000 hits, he played in a much higher-scoring context than Smith; Omar's -244 batting runs and +8 runs on baserunning and double plays are no match for Ozzie (-117 batting runs, +102 baserunning and double plays). Thus Vizquel's just 29th in WAR among shortstops; only once did he crack his league's top 10, and he's even worse off in peak (60th) and JAWS. Expect a battle that echoes the Jack Morris fight come 2018.

CHAPTER 13

THIRD BASEMEN

CASE STUDY: DICK ALLEN

> Dick Allen forced Philadelphia baseball and its fans to come to terms with
> the racism that existed in this city in the '60s and '70s. He may not have
> done it with the self-discipline or tact of Jackie Robinson, but he exempli-
> fied the emerging independence of major league baseball players as well as
> growing black consciousness.[1]
>
> —WILLIAM KASHATUS

At first glance, Dick Allen might be viewed as the Gary Sheffield or Albert Belle of his day, a heavy hitter seemingly engaged in a constant
battle with the world around him, generating controversy at every stop
of his 15-year career. It's unfair and reductive to lump Allen in with those two
players, however, for they all faced different obstacles and bore different scars from
the wounds they suffered early in their careers.

In Allen's case, those wounds predated his 1963 arrival in the majors with a
team that was far behind the integration curve, and a city that was in no better
shape. In Philadelphia and beyond, he was a polarizing presence, covered by a media contingent so unable or unwilling to relate to him that writers often refused
to call him by the name of his choosing: Dick Allen, not Richie.

Even while earning All-Star honors seven times and winning both NL Rookie of
the Year and AL Most Valuable Player awards, Allen rebelled against his surroundings and presented himself in a way that often reinforced negative impressions while
overshadowing his tremendous talent. Had he not missed so much time due to injuries, absenteeism, and alcohol, he'd almost certainly have the counting stats for Coo-

perstown. While past generations of voters wrote him off for those shortcomings, more recent reseach has yielded a better understanding of the context for his behavior—and shown that for all of the negativity that colored the coverage of him, he was respected and even beloved by many a teammate and manager.

Allen struggled for support during his 1983–97 run on the BBWAA ballot, never reaching 20%, and he similarly lagged in the voting of the expanded Veterans Committee from 2003–09. Thanks in part to a grassroots campaign, he received a fresh look from the 2015 Golden Era Committee and fell just one vote short of election. Alas, the reshuffling of the Era Committees means that he won't get another look until the 2021 Golden Days panel, making it difficult to build upon that momentum.

The Career

Phillies 1963–69, 1975–76 • Cardinals 1970 • Dodgers 1971 • White Sox 1972–74 • A's 1977

Player	Career	Peak	JAWS	H	HR	SB	AVG/OBP/SLG	OPS+
Dick Allen	58.7	45.9	52.3	1848	351	133	.292/.378/.534	156
Avg HOF 3B	67.4	42.7	55.0					
3B Rank	17th	11th	17th					
(Above HOF)	(5/13)	(6/13)	(5/13)					

Allen was born in 1942 in Wampum, Pennsylvania, a small town 30 miles northwest of Pittsburgh, the second-youngest of eight children born to Era Allen, a domestic employee, and Coy Allen, a traveling truck driver and sanitation worker. One of just five black students in a class of 146, he starred not only as the shortstop of the Wampum High School baseball team but as the captain and point guard of the basketball team, the latter despite standing just 5'11", 187 pounds. In 1958, he played alongside his brothers Hank (b. 1940) and Ron (b. 1943), all three of whom would earn All-State honors on the court and later play Major League Baseball.

Phillies scout Jack Ogden, a former pitcher whose major league career spanned 1918–32, courted all three Allen brothers, and endeared himself to Era by agreeing to sign the trio—Hank and Dick in 1960, Ron in 1964. Dick's $70,000 bonus was the largest ever paid to a black ballplayer at the time. Ogden would later say, "Dick Allen was my best find. I scouted 90,000 players in my lifetime and Allen was the greatest I ever saw. It's too bad he had so many difficulties."[2]

Nineteen-year-old Hank and 18-year-old Dick were both assigned to Elmira of the New York-Penn League, where the latter made a whopping 48 errors in 85 games at shortstop, though his bat showed more promise. His offense improved even more as he passed through Magic Valley (Utah) of the Pioneer League and Williamsport of the Eastern League in 1961 and '62, shifting to second base and then the outfield, hitting .329/.409/.548 with 20 homers and 109 RBI at the latter stop.

The Phillies had spent most of the previous four and a half decades as embarrassments, with 20 last-place finishes and just six seasons above .500 from 1918–62. In 1947, they treated Jackie Robinson as poorly as any NL team, with general manager Herb Pennock (now a Hall of Fame pitcher) threatening a boycott if Robinson played in Philadelphia and manager Ben Chapman viciously taunting the integration pioneer once he did. Though the team captured its first pennant in 35 years in 1950 and remained contenders for the next few seasons, they were the last NL team to integrate, in 1957. With the Dodgers, Giants, and Braves having gotten the jump much earlier, the Phillies' stance cost them dearly. They finished at .500 twice from 1954–61, but never above, and ran dead last for four straight years before climbing to 81-80 in '62 under second-year manager Gene Mauch.

Invited to spring training in 1963, Allen hit nine home runs, but with the Phillies' outfield set between Wes Covington, Tony Gonzalez, and Johnny Callison, the team sent him to its Triple-A affiliate, the Little Rock–based Arkansas Travelers. Just six years earlier, Little Rock had been the site of an ugly scene when Governor Orval Faubus called in the Arkansas National Guard in order to prevent the court-ordered desegregation of Little Rock High School. The Phillies gave Allen no idea what to expect in becoming the first black professional baseball player in the state; the *Arkansas Gazette* and *Arkansas Democrat* both told their reporters not to mention that fact to avoid stirring things up.

Racial tensions ran particularly high the night that Allen debuted, with Faubus himself throwing out the first pitch and picketers carrying signs with slogans such as "Don't Negro-ize baseball" and "Nigger go home."[3] Similar signs had greeted him at the Little Rock airport. Allen was so rattled that the first ball hit to him in left field flew way over his head. He recovered to hit two doubles, including one amid the winning rally, but on his car after the game, he was greeted with a note: "DON'T COME BACK AGAIN NIGGER."[4] After receiving death threats and telling the Phillies he was quitting, he was rebuked by older brother Coy as well as his mother for pleading to come home. He developed a resolve to stick it out, vowing, "If I'm going to die, why not die doing what God gave me a gift to do? I'll die right there in that batter's box without any fear."[5]

Fortunately it didn't come to that, though Allen received countless threats throughout the season. He lived with a black family in the black section of the segregated town, was often stopped by local police for no apparent reason, and couldn't be served in restaurants unless accompanied by a white teammate. Manager Frank Lucchesi, who respected his ability, couldn't relate to his circumstances, and Allen had few friends on the team. Nonetheless, he hit .289/.341/.550 while leading the league with 33 homers and 97 RBI and being voted team MVP by fans, even while enduring epithets on a regular basis. Called up to Philadelphia at season's end, he went 7-for-24 in a 10-game trial, mostly in left field.

The following spring Mauch decided to squeeze the righty-swinging Allen into the predominantly left-handed lineup at third base, a position he had never played regularly. "He can play third good enough to get by," said Mauch. "He has good reactions and good hands and third isn't as demanding a spot as short or second where he began his career."[6] For unclear reasons, the Phillies insisted upon calling him "Richie," a name he detested but which appeared on all of the team's rosters, scorecards, and promotional material. In September, just before the Phillies' infamous collapse, Allen complained, "[Richie] makes me sound like I'm ten years old. I'm 22. . . . Anyone who knows me well calls me Dick. I don't know why as soon as I put on a uniform it's Richie."[7]

By any name, Allen put up a season for the ages, batting .318/.382/.557 with 201 hits, 13 triples, and 29 homers in 162 games, enough to make him the runaway NL Rookie of the Year. His 162 OPS+ and 8.8 WAR both ranked third in the league, and the latter ranks third among all rookie position players, topped only by Shoeless Joe Jackson (9.2 in 1911) and Mike Trout (10.8 in 2012). Allen's performance nearly carried the Phillies to a pennant; they led by 6½ games with just 12 to play, but a 10-game losing streak spelled their doom. Lest anyone think Allen was at fault, he batted .341/.434/.618 in September and October, going 17-for-41 during their 10-game slide.

That rookie season began a six-year run over which Allen hit .300/.380/.555 for a 164 OPS+ and an average of 30 homers per year. He led the NL in slugging percentage in '66 (.632), in on-base percentage in '67 (.404), and in OPS+ in both years (181 and 174, respectively). He ranked among the league's top 10 in homers five times in that span, including second in both '66 (40) and '68 (33), and made three straight All-Star teams. The Phillies bounced him around the diamond on a nearly annual basis; he spent significant time in left field in '66 and '68, and at first base in '69.

As good as he was, Allen couldn't singlehandedly push the Phillies over the top, though they finished above .500 in 1965, '66, and '67. And he did not have an easy time of it. Those outstanding numbers glossed over no shortage of controversies, starting with a July 3, 1965, pregame altercation with reserve outfielder Frank Thomas—triggered by taunting from Callison—that escalated with Thomas calling Allen "Richie X" and "another Muhammad Clay, always running your mouth off,"[8] Allen punching Thomas in the jaw, and Thomas countering with his bat to Allen's left shoulder. Allen had previously experienced difficulties with Thomas, who "would pretend to offer his hand in a soul shake to a young black player. . . . When the player would offer his hand in return, Thomas would grab his thumb and bend it back. To him, it was a big joke."[9]

Though Thomas homered as a pinch-hitter in the game following the altercation—after which Allen shook his hand, considering the matter settled—the 36-year-old was placed on waivers immediately afterward, over Allen's protestations. Mauch, happy to jettison an aging, disruptive player, threatened to fine Allen $2,500 and any other Phillie $1,500 if they discussed the incident with the press. Thus, only the departed Thomas aired his side, claiming that the Phillies acted unfairly in punishing one player but not the other and that Allen "can dish it out but can't take it."[10] The manager later regretted his course of action, saying, "The way it was handled brought the town down on Richie's head. . . . I should have shipped [Thomas] sooner."[11]

"That was unfortunate as the press and the fans heard just Thomas's side, and they did not take kindly to a young black guy popping a white veteran,"[12] wrote sabermetrician Craig Wright in 1995. In a city that had been torn by race riots less than a year before, fans hung banners in support of Thomas and sent Allen hate mail, called him "darkie" and "monkey" from the stands, and threw bottles, bolts, and coins at him in the outfield to the point that he took to wearing a helmet in the field. The press labeled him a troublemaker. Amid the pressure and abuse Allen turned to alcohol: "Instead of going straight to the ballpark," he recalled later, "I started making regular stops at watering holes along the way."[13] Mauch fined him regularly, but tried to protect him from the press.

Even without the bottle, Allen found trouble, and his critics assumed the worst with regards to his conduct. On August 24, 1967, while trying to push his stalled car up a driveway, he put his right hand through a headlight, severing tendons and nerves and requiring a five-hour operation that ended his season 40 games early. Unsubstantiated rumors spread that he had been stabbed in a bar fight or jumped out a window after being caught with a teammate's wife. The injury cost Allen some sensation in two of his fingers; he struggled with throwing during the rest of his career, especially in cold weather, and never spent a full season at third base again.

Though Allen negotiated a salary of $85,000 for 1968—the highest for a fourth-year player in the game at that point—he wanted out of Philadelphia. With free agency not yet an option, he embarked upon a series of minor transgressions in hopes of triggering a trade. He left spring training without permission, claiming to have gone to see a doctor in Philadelphia about his hand. He showed up for games late and, in late May, drunk. The team suspended him for two weeks, covering by saying he had a groin injury. When he returned, Allen declared "a sit-down strike" and refused to play until he could give his side of the story.

Behind closed doors, Allen agreed to a truce, telling owner Bob Carpenter he was ready to play. An incensed Mauch gave the owner a "me or him" ultimatum, but was fired on June 15, when the team was 27-27. He took the high road on the way out. "I'm not going to knock Richie Allen. . . . That son-of-a-gun gave me many a thrill. There was nothing personal in my handling of Allen."[14] Still, the press hung the blame for Mauch's firing on Allen, and while he went on a hot streak under new manager Bob Skinner, the team finished 76-86.

In the winter of 1968–69, the Phillies tried to move Allen to the Mets or Indians, but their asking price was too high. Soon Allen was up to his old tricks, missing flights and even games. He wanted out, blamed the press for turning fans against him, and spoke openly about the part he felt race played in the matter:

> I get along great with my teammates. But you fellas have created an atmosphere where people who have never met me, hate me. You can knock me and say I'm a no good black so and so and I can still be your friend. But if you don't ask me about something and take someone else's word for it and write it as fact, then I got to cut you loose. Sometimes I get so disgusted. I really do love to play the game, but the writers take all the fun out of it.[15]

Soon Allen's teammates tore into him for his lackadaisical approach, which only led the slugger to rebel further. He missed a doubleheader against the Mets in favor of a horse race, and was suspended indefinitely—26 days, eventually, costing him $11,700 in salary—returning only after ownership agreed to trade him at the end of the season. The controversy led Phillies fans to abstain from voting him into the All-Star Game or onto the franchise's all-time team as part of baseball's centennial celebration.

After a drawn-out battle over Allen's use of a storage area as a private dressing room, Skinner resigned, and Allen was again scapegoated. A *Sporting News* editorial took a stand against him: "If ever a young man needed some counseling and guidance, that man is Richie Allen. The Phillies slugger has $1,000,000 worth of talent and 10¢ worth of ability to understand what his role is with a team that has 24 other players besides himself. Unless a firm hand is taken with Allen, he'll go through more managers than Bluebeard does wives."[16]

Going nowhere given their pitching, the Phillies finished 63-99. Allen took advantage of interim manager George Myatt's refusal to stir up further trouble, and began scratching out words in the dirt around first base, such as "OCT. 2" (the final date of the season), "BOO" (the fans obliged), "NO," and "WHY?" (in response to commissioner Bowie Kuhn's order to stop doing that). On October 7, five days after the end of the season, he was traded to the Cardinals in a seven-player blockbuster, with Tim McCarver and Curt Flood heading the other direction. Flood—who would later describe Philadelphia as "America's northernmost Southern city"[17]—refused to report, setting off a challenge to the Reserve Clause that would go all the way to the U.S. Supreme Court (Flood lost but the challenge paved the way for free agency).

Allen was overjoyed at the deal. "You don't know how good it feels to get out of Philadelphia," he said. "They treat you like cattle."[18]

The Cardinals had won back-to-back pennants in 1967–68, but slipped to fourth place in the new NL East in 1969. Allen hit well (.279/.377/.560 with 34 homers in 122 games), but a hamstring injury limited him to five of the final 44 games. Come October 5, 1970, he was traded to the Dodgers for two young players. While he avoided trouble in St. Louis, the Cardinals wanted to emphasize defense, not Allen's forte; today's metrics estimate that he was 14 runs below average splitting time at first and third. He delivered 5.4 WAR in his lone season in L.A. while again bouncing around the diamond, but chafed at what he felt were distracting public relations commitments. The Dodgers went 89-73, finishing one game back in the NL West.

For the third offseason in a row, Allen was traded, this time to the White Sox for two players, including pitcher Tommy John. Playing for manager Chuck Tanner, a native of New Castle, Pennsylvania (not far from Wampum), and again letting the media know that he preferred to be called Dick instead of Richie (a request still routinely ignored), Allen settled in at first base and hit .308/.420/.603 with a 199 OPS+, 37 homers, and 113 RBI. All of those numbers except his batting average led the league, while his 8.6 WAR, his best since his rookie campaign, ranked third. The White Sox, who had not finished above .500 since 1967, went 87-67, finishing 5½ games out, and Allen was the runaway AL MVP, receiving 21 of 24 first-place votes. His appearance on the June 12, 1972, *Sports Illustrated* produced an indelible image. With a lit cigarette between his lips, mustache and muttonchop sideburns nearly intersecting, he looks like a lost funk bassist wearing the White Sox's red pinstriped uniform. What's more, he's juggling three baseballs next to an on-the-nose caption: "Season of Surprises: Dick Allen Juggles His Image."

After signing a three-year, $675,000 deal, believed to be the largest in the game at the time, Allen was similarly effective in both 1973 and '74 despite injuries that limited him to just 200 games. On June 28, 1973, he collided at first base while stretching for a throw, suffering a hairline fracture of his left fibula. He returned five weeks later, limped while going 3-for-4 in his return, and was shut down for the season after two pinch-hitting appearances. Some accused him of malingering, but as White Sox general manager Roland Hemond later told Craig Wright, "The leg wasn't healed. The doctor knew it, but Dick wanted to try. . . . His teammates appreciated the effort, but some people in the press may not have understood. He seemed indestructible to them."[19]

Allen hit .301/.375/.563 in 1974, making his seventh All-Star team and leading the league in both slugging percentage and homers (32) in just 128 games. Alas, a mid-August shoulder injury sapped both his power and his will to play. On September 13, he showed up at Comiskey Park, took batting and infield practice, then gave an emotional speech to his teammates and announced his retirement at age 32, with a year and $225,000 still to go on his contract. "This is hard for me to say," he told them. "I've never been happier anywhere than here."[20]

Hemond and Tanner talked Allen out of officially filing retirement paperwork, which would have prevented him from returning until six weeks into 1975. On the off chance that he might play, the Braves acquired his rights for a player to be named later in December. Meanwhile, Phillies broadcaster Richie Ashburn lobbied the organization to reacquire him. Now playing in Veterans Stadium rather than Connie Mack Stadium, which had been situated in a racially divided neighborhood, the Phillies were a different team. Laden with young talents Mike Schmidt (who grew up idolizing Allen), Greg Luzinski, Dave Cash, Larry Bowa, and Bob Boone, they were managed by Danny Ozark, who had coached the Dodgers during Allen's 1971 stay.

Allen remained at home until the Phillies negotiated a four-player trade on May 7. He debuted on May 14, receiving a standing ovation from the Veterans Stadium crowd of 30,908. "You don't know what it means to me," he told reporters. "It's a different situation altogether."[21] The fans could heal only so much; Allen hit just .233/.327/.385 with 12 homers in 119 games.

In 1976, Ozark and Allen clashed over the quality of the latter's defense, and he found himself benched. Shoulder woes and a 39-game absence due to dizziness following a jarring collision at first base further cut into his time but he still hit .268/.346/.480 with 15 homers in 339 PA. The Phillies won 101 games and their first NL East flag. In his only postseason appearance, Allen went 2-for-9 with three walks, but made a key error in Game 2 of the NLCS as the Phillies were swept by the Reds.

Informed that he would not be re-signed, Allen caught on with the A's, who had been decimated by the first winter of free agency. Though productive early in the season, he not only cooled off but refused to DH; unbeknownst to manager Jack McKeon, owner Charlie Finley had written a clause into Allen's contract excusing him from DH duty. Eventually shoulder problems, a slump, and another unexcused absence led to his release. While Tanner tried to talk him into joining the Pirates— whom he was then managing—in 1979, when Allen was 37, he never played again.

The Case

Allen spent more time at first base (807 games) than third (652) or left field (256), but for JAWS purposes, he's a third baseman; five of his top six WAR totals came in seasons where he played more third than anywhere else. His was a short career by Hall of Fame standards, in part due to his injuries and other absences, and in part to his early retirement. His totals of games played (1,749) and hits (1,848) present a problem in this context. Only one Hall of Famer from the post-1960 expansion era played in fewer than 2,000 games (Kirby Puckett, 1,783) and none had fewer than 2,000 hits. All of which underscores the uphill battle Allen has to enshrinement, at least with regards to traditional counting stats.

Allen's total of 351 homers is less impressive for its volume than its context. In the 16-season span from 1961–76, a low-scoring period demarcated by the first and third waves of expansion, Allen hit 346 homers, more than all but Harmon Killebrew (489), Willie McCovey (439), and Norm Cash (355). From 1964–74, the 11-season heart of his career, he led his league twice, ranked second twice, and had four other top 10 finishes.

The rate stats further testify to Allen's dominance. In that same 11-year stretch, he had 20 top 10 finishes in a slash stat, leading in OBP twice and in slugging three times. He led in OPS+ three times and was twice runner-up, with five more finishes in the top 10, meaning that in each of the 10 years in which he qualified for the batting title he was one of the league's 10 most potent hitters.

Career-wise, among players with at least 7,000 PA, Allen's 156 OPS+ is tied for 15th all-time with Frank Thomas (the White Sox slugger, not the Phillies assailant) and Willie Mays—both of whom had much longer careers, but that's the point of the cutoff. Convert that potency to batting runs and Allen's 435 above average ranks 52nd, a tad less impressive but still on par with Hall of Famers Joe Morgan, Wade Boggs, Ken Griffey Jr., Willie Stargell, and George Brett, all of whom needed at least 1,712 more plate appearances to approximate Allen's total.

Combine all that with his seven All-Star appearances and his Rookie of the Year and MVP awards, and Allen scores a 99 on the Hall of Fame Monitor, in the general vicinity of a "likely" Hall of Famer. That score is held down by his minimal postseason résumé and his defensive shortcomings. He was nothing close to a Gold Glove candidate, but then, given the Phillies' desperate rush to convert him to third base, what should anyone have expected?

Via Total Zone, Allen's total of 110 runs below average at all positions ranks as the 11th-worst in history. He was 45 runs below average at third (nine per 1,200 innings); 40 below average at first (seven per 1,200 innings), and 24 below average in leftfield (13 per 1,200 innings). That's nearly DH-caliber, but of course the DH didn't exist in those days, and Allen was none too keen on the idea once it did. Yet even while costing his team roughly nine runs per year with his glove, Allen's bat carried the weight and more. He ranked among the league's top 10 in WAR six times, thrice in the top five. For that 1964–74 span, only Hall of Famers Hank Aaron, Carl Yastrzemski, Ron Santo, and Brooks Robinson topped Allen's 58.3 WAR.

Measured against third basemen, Allen's 58.7 career WAR ranks 17th, 8.8 wins below the standard; among Hall of Famers, he's ahead of only the three bottom-tier guys (George Kell, Pie Traynor, and Fred Lindstrom) and two with their roots in the

nineteenth century, Deacon White and Jimmy Collins. His 45.8 WAR peak ranks
11th, 3.1 wins above the standard, however, and, ahead of the aforementioned plus
Molitor, not to mention popular defense-first candidates such as Scott Rolen and
Graig Nettles. Overall, his 52.3 JAWS ranks 17th, 2.7 points below the standard.
Considering Allen as a first baseman doesn't change a whole lot. At that position
he'd rank 11th in peak (3.4 above the standard) and 17th in JAWS, 1.9 points below
the standard but ahead of 10 enshrined first basemen, including another slugger
who bounced around the diamond in an effort to hide his glove, Killebrew.

Any way you slice it, Allen's a bit short on the JAWS front, so choosing to vote
for him means focusing on that considerable peak while giving him the benefit of
the doubt on the factors that shortened his career. From here, the litany is sizable
enough to justify that. Allen did nothing to deserve the racism and hatred he
battled in Little Rock and Philadelphia, or the condescension of the lily-white
media that refused to even call him by his correct name. To underplay the extent
to which those forces shaped his conduct and his public persona thereafter is to
hold him to an impossibly high standard; not everyone can be Jackie Robinson
or Ernie Banks. The distortions that influenced the negative views of him—
including Bill James's crushing dismissal ("[Allen] did more to keep his teams from
winning than anybody else who ever played major league baseball. And if that's a
Hall of Famer, I'm a lug nut"[22]) in *The Politics of Glory*—were damaging. To give
them the upper hand is to reject honest inquiry into his career.

Sabermetrician Don Malcolm called that passage "the absolute nadir of Bill
James' career, a summary statement so blatantly biased that his long-time friend
and associate Craig Wright felt compelled to write an essay refuting Bill's perspective. . . . Everyone knows that Dick Allen was a great hitter; there's just all that
other baggage that they're afraid to open."[22] Having opened it, well, it's not pretty,
but it's also abundantly clear that it wasn't all Allen's baggage to begin with.
Wright's work, which featured interviews with all but one of Allen's big league
managers (the late Dodgers skipper Walter Alston) as well as several teammates,
refutes the notion that Allen was a divisive clubhouse presence or a particular
problem for his managers aside from his early-career tardiness (and his extreme
behavior in 1969). Even Skinner and Ozark, the two managers portrayed as the
most openly critical of him, said that Allen wasn't the problem with their teams
and that they'd have him back again if given the chance.

Perhaps not surprisingly given his tumultuous career and shortage in the counting stats, Allen never fared well in front of BBWAA voters. He received just 3.7%
in his 1983 debut (when venerable scribes such as Jack Lang and Charley Feeney
patronizingly resurrected "Richie Allen" in their *Sporting News* coverage), enough
to bump him off the ballot. Via a 1985 compromise between the writers and the
Hall over some rejiggering of the Five Percent Rule, 150 such candidates were

reviewed by the BBWAA Screening Committee, with 11 getting "one more chance" including Allen, Ken Boyer, Flood, and Ron Santo. Allen received 7.1%, more than all of the others save for Boyer (17.2%) and Santo (13.4%), enough at least to keep his name in circulation. He lingered on the ballot through 1997, topping out at 18.9% in '96.

After aging off the writers' ballot, Allen fell under the purview of the enlarged Veterans Committee, where he maxed out at 16.0% in 2003, the first of four tries. He wasn't included on the 2012 Expansion Era Committee ballot, via which Santo was posthumously elected, but was on in 2015. Thanks to the outreach campaign led by Mark Carfagno, a former Phillies grounds crew member, his candidacy drew widespread attention. On a committee that included former teammate Jim Bunning (the Phillies' ace during Allen's first stint), Pat Gillick (then-president of the Phillies), and Hemond (GM of the White Sox during his stay there), Allen received 11 of 16 votes—tied with Tony Oliva for the highest among the 10 candidates, but one vote short of election nonetheless. It was a bittersweet result. Gillick did attempt to reassure the public that Allen's candidacy was viewed with a fresh eye. "If anybody had any concern about any press that was associated with Dick, that was not a concern."[24]

The good news is that Allen finally received a fair hearing on the merits of his skill rather than the chorus of his detractors. The bad news is that since he's been classified for inclusion on the Golden Days Era Committee (for players whose greatest impact was between 1950–69) instead of the Modern Baseball one (1970–87), his candidacy won't be reviewed again until the 2021 ballot, rather than 2018 and/or '20. He had more value in the earlier period (35.2 WAR to 23.5) but more games in the latter (883 to 866), not to mention more All-Star appearances (four to three) and his MVP award. It's an understandable decision but a tough break for a man who will be 78 when the voters next convene, and he'll hardly be without competition, as Minnie Minoso, Tony Oliva, and Gil Hodges, all of whom have received substantial support in a similar context, figure to be on that ballot as well. Here's hoping Allen's candidacy can maintain its momentum until then.

CASE STUDY: EDGAR MARTINEZ

I've faced a lot of Hall of Fame hitters, and my gosh, Edgar is the best hitter that I ever saw. . . . You know how you love something and you carry it around with you? When I got to Seattle, Edgar was walking around with a bat all the time. . . . I'd look at the top of his locker and he would have his bats lined up and his own scale to weigh the bats. Who does that?[25]

—RANDY JOHNSON

All Edgar Martinez did was hit—the statement is almost completely true in both the literal and figurative senses. Even after adjusting for his high-scoring surroundings, Martinez could flat-out rake. A high-average, high-on-base percentage hitting machine with plenty of power, he put up numbers that place him among the top 30 or 40 hitters of all-time even after adjusting for the high-offense era.

Martinez played a key role in putting the Seattle Mariners on the map as an AL West powerhouse, emerging as a folk hero to a fan base that watched Ken Griffey Jr., Randy Johnson, and Alex Rodriguez lead the franchise's charge to relevancy, then force their way out of town over contract issues. But while Griffey and Rodriguez were two-way stars at key up-the-middle positions, Martinez spent the bulk of his career as a designated hitter, and all he did in that capacity was put a claim on being the best one in baseball history.

More than 40 years after it was introduced—in perhaps the most significant rule change since the AL adopted the foul strike rule in 1903—the DH continues to rankle purists who would rather watch pitchers risk injury as they flail away with ineptitude. Not until 2014 was the first player ever to spend a majority of his career as a DH inducted into the Hall of Fame, namely Frank Thomas, who made 57% of his plate appearances in that capacity. Thomas's election came a full decade after Paul Molitor provided the Hall with its first player to spend the plurality of his career (44%) as a DH after bouncing all around the infield. By comparison, Martinez took 72% of his plate appearances as a DH, while David Ortiz took 88%.

In reviewing candidates who spent a significant chunk of their careers at DH, the precedent I've set—starting with Molitor in 2004, before the system was even called JAWS—is to compare them with respect both to the position where they spent the most time and to all Hall position players. Both Molitor and Thomas, who had milestones that made their enshrinement near-automatic (3,000 hits for the former, 500 homers for the latter), exceed the JAWS standards at their positions (third base and first base) and relative to all position players despite incurring WAR's substantial built-in penalty for not playing the field. Other DH candidates with superficially impressive counting stats, such as Harold Baines, Jose Canseco, and Chili Davis, did not.

Martinez, who ranks fourth in games by a DH at 1,403, but who also played 564 games at third base and another 28 at first base, is above the standards for Hall third basemen, Hall corner infielders, and Hall position players despite not playing at least 100 major league games in a season until age 27. A two-time batting champion and seven-time All-Star, he put up eye-opening numbers even in an era full of them, and created enough value even while riding the pine between trips to the plate to score well via advanced metrics—better than many of his era's more celebrated position players. He's well qualified for Cooperstown, and after a slow start to his candidacy, strong showings on both the 2016 and '17 ballots have put him within range of his bronze plaque, albeit with just two years of eligibility remaining.

The Career

Mariners 1987–2004

Player	Career	Peak	JAWS	H	HR	SB	AVG/OBP/SLG	OPS+
Edgar Martinez	68.3	43.6	56.0	2247	309	49	.312/.418/.515	147
Avg HOF Hitter	67.1	42.2	54.7					
Avg HOF CI	66.8	42.7	54.8					
Avg HOF 3B	67.5	42.8	55.2					
3B Rank (Above HOF)	11th (6/13)	13th (6/13)	11th (6/13)					

Though born in New York City in 1963, Martinez was raised by his maternal grandparents in the Maguayo neighborhood of Dorado, Puerto Rico, when his parents divorced shortly after he was born. Three houses away, cousin Carmelo Martinez, a major leaguer from 1983–91, grew up as well. Martinez's parents remarried when Edgar was 11, but he chose to remain with his grandparents. By then he'd caught the baseball bug, drawn to the game by the heroics of Puerto Rican icon Roberto Clemente. He honed his swing with a broomstick, obliterating bottle caps, rocks, and droplets of water as they fell from the roof.

In 1982, a nearly 20-year-old Martinez was making $4 an hour on an assembly line at a pharmaceutical plant, taking classes at American University in San Juan, and playing semipro ball on the weekends when Mariners scout Marty Martinez (no relation) signed him for a bonus of just $4,000. Old by prospect standards, he hit just .173/.304/.202 in 126 plate appearances for the Mariners' Northwest League affiliate in 1983, but he quickly improved, though he didn't really break out until his age-24 season in 1987, when he hit .329/.434/.473 at Triple-A Calgary.

Blocked at third base by Jim Presley, a one-tool player whose eight major league seasons and 135 homers amounted to 0.2 WAR, Martinez had to settle for cups of coffee from the Mariners in 1987 and '88. He opened the 1989 season as the starting third baseman, but struggled mightily and was briefly sent back down. Not until 1990 did he stick around for good. Having reworked his swing to incorporate a high leg kick to boost his bat speed and pull the ball with greater frequency, he hit .302/.397/.433 for a 133 OPS+ and 5.5 WAR (seventh in the league) thanks to Total Zone's hefty estimate of his hot corner defense at 13 runs above average. A year later, Martinez hit .307/.405/.452—the first of 11 seasons with an OBP above .400—and helped the Mariners crack .500 for the first time in franchise history. Again he was above average defensively (+6 runs) en route to 6.1 WAR, eighth in the league.

In 1992, Martinez won his first AL batting title, hitting .343/.404/.544 with 18 homers and a league-leading 46 doubles; his 6.5 WAR tied for fifth in the league, behind only Kirby Puckett, Thomas, Roberto Alomar, and Kenny Lofton. Alas, his season ended about three weeks early due to impingement and a bone spur in his right shoulder, requiring surgery. His injury troubles were just beginning, as hamstring and wrist injuries—as well as the players' strike—limited him to 131 games over the next two seasons.

Though still a more than serviceable third baseman (seven runs above average in 1994, 19 above for his career), Martinez's string of injuries led the Mariners to relieve him of regular defensive responsibilities; they needed his bat far more than his glove. Over the remaining decade of his career, he would play just 34 more games in the field, never making more than seven starts in a single season, usually interleague road games.

The decision paid immediate dividends, as Martinez hit .356/.479/.628 in 1995, winning his second batting title and leading the league in on-base percentage, OPS+ (185), and doubles (52), and setting new career highs in homers (29) and WAR (7.0, second in the league), the last despite playing just seven games in the field. He helped the Mariners to their first playoff berth in franchise history, then turned into a one-man wrecking crew in the Division Series against the Yankees, batting .571/.667/1.000 with four three-hit efforts, reaching base safely 18 times in five games. He's still the co-holder of the record for most hits in a Division Series, with 12, while his 21 total bases rank fifth. He drove in seven runs in Game 4, with a third-inning three-run shot helping to trim a 5–0 deficit and an eighth-inning grand slam breaking a 6–6 tie in what wound up an 11–8 victory, but the signature hit of his career came in the 11th inning of the decisive Game 5, bringing home both the tying and winning runs in the form of Joey Cora and Ken Griffey Jr. "The Double" is on the short list of hits that have taken on a life of their own; it's got its own Wikipedia page, like Babe Ruth's "Called Shot" or Bobby Thomson's "The Shot Heard 'Round the World." The euphoria of that moment helped generate the groundswell of support that secured the Mariners a new taxpayer-funded stadium within a week of the series ending. In 2004, the city of Seattle renamed one of the streets leading to Safeco Field "Edgar Martinez Drive."

That 1995 season began a seven-year stretch in which Martinez hit a combined .329/.446/.574 while averaging 42 doubles, 28 homers, 107 walks, and 5.8 WAR per year (40.6 total). He led the AL in on-base percentage again in 1998 (.429) and '99 (.447) after finishing second with even higher figures in '96 (.464, behind Mark McGwire's .467) and '97 (.4558 to Thomas's .4561), and placed third in OPS+ three straight times (1996–'98) before falling to fifth or sixth in the next three seasons. During that span, he was the second-best hitter in baseball, at least based on the batting component of WAR; his 380 runs above average trailed only Barry Bonds's 443.

Defensive value is built into WAR in two ways: by estimating a player's relative value (runs above or below average via Total Zone or, from 2003 onward, Defensive Runs Saved); and with positional adjustments that change over time to account for skill required to play the position, based largely on the distribution of balls in play. In the Baseball-Reference.com version of WAR, a full season at third base in the twenty-first century has a value of +2 runs, which is to say that showing up for work and filling that spot without burning down the stadium is worth two extra runs beyond average. By comparison, a full season at DH has a value of -15 runs, so it takes an extra 17 runs per year for an average fielder at the hot corner to offset such a move with his bat.

In other words, the "But he was a DH, not a complete player!" sentiment is baked into the valuations, and even while being docked 13 or 14 runs per year due to his time at DH (he played just 33 games at third and first in that span), Martinez tied with Sammy Sosa as the majors' fifth-most-valuable position player from 1995–2001, behind Bonds (56.7), Rodriguez (46.6), Jeff Bagwell (44.8), and Griffey (41.0). The Griffey comparison is particularly startling: Martinez's teammate won an MVP award and four Gold Gloves during that stretch and led the AL in homers for three years in a row (twice with 56)—*and he was more valuable than Martinez by an annual margin of roughly half a run.*

Remarkably, Edgar maintained his keen batting eye and high level of production despite a serious vision abnormality. While in the minors, optometrist Dr. Douglas Nikaitani diagnosed him with strabismus, which caused his right eye (his nondominant one, and the one further from the pitcher) to drift out of alignment, costing him depth perception and an ability to pick up velocity changes. In 1999, his problems became particularly acute, as he struggled to pick up the ball as it left the pitcher's hand, and learned to duck his head and tuck in his shoulder to protect his head and hands in case he lost complete sight of the pitch. A stint on the disabled list loomed, with retirement a possibility. He returned to Dr. Nikaitani, who fired tennis balls at Martinez, forcing him to focus on aligning his eyes, and developed an exercise regimen for him to enhance his depth perception. "This is my theory: Edgar has lasted this long because he had the discipline to really work on his eyes so that they're not a weak link,"[26] said Nikaitani in 2001.

Vision problems or no, opponents marveled at Martinez's patient, disciplined approach, and his tenacity at the plate. Said free-swinging Rangers slugger Juan Gonzalez to *Sports Illustrated* in 1996, "Edgar never swings at bad pitches. He has great peace of mind at the plate."[27] Said Pedro Martinez (no relation) on the occasion of his own election in 2015, when asked about the toughest hitter he ever faced:

The toughest guy I faced . . . was Edgar Martinez. He had to make me throw at least 13 fastballs above 95 [each time we faced]. I was hard-breathing after that. Edgar was a guy that had the ability to foul off pitches, and it pissed me off because I couldn't get the guy out. [28]

The Mariners reached the playoffs three more times in that 1995–2001 period, including their record-tying 116-win '01 campaign after Johnson, Griffey, and Rodriguez had all departed via free agency or trade. Even in the last of those years, his age-38 season, Martinez was hardly window dressing, hitting .306/.423/.543 with 40 doubles, 23 homers, a 160 OPS+ (fifth in the league), and 4.8 WAR. He played three more seasons, hitting well in 2002 (despite missing two months due to surgery to repair a ruptured tendon in his left knee) and 2003 (despite gutting out a broken toe over the final two-plus weeks) but slipping in 2004 before retiring. In a ceremony following Martinez's final game on October 3, 2004, commissioner Bud Selig announced that the annual Outstanding Designated Hitter Award, which he had won five times, would be renamed in his honor.

The Case

Martinez isn't the first Hall of Fame candidate to benefit from spending his twilight years as a designated hitter; Molitor reached the 3,000-hit plateau and Cooperstown largely via the role, and likewise for Thomas and the 500-homer benchmark. George Brett's 3,000th hit and the 500th home runs of Reggie Jackson, Eddie Murray, and Jim Thome all came when they were serving as DH, with 101 of Jackson's 573 dingers, 92 of Murray's 504, and 205 of Thome's 612 (including number 600, too) coming in that capacity. Nonetheless, Martinez's case is an interesting test for the voters. He played so few games in the field not only because he didn't establish himself until a relatively advanced age but because the risk/reward payoff became so imbalanced once he emerged as an elite hitter, though it's likely the Mariners could have stuck him at first base—a much easier position than third, requiring less mobility—had they so desired.

Because he didn't play regularly until his age-27 season, Martinez's raw counting stats (2,247 hits, 309 homers) don't jump off the page without additional context. His 2,181 hits from his age-27 season onward ranks 30th all-time, better than all but 22 of the 148 enshrined position players, including 3,000-hit-club members Cal Ripken (2,100), George Brett (2,072), Rickey Henderson (2,033), and Roberto Clemente (1,938). Likewise, Martinez's 307 homers from that point onward rank 44th, exceeded only by 21 Hall of Famers. From a rate stat standpoint, his 149 OPS+ from 27 onward is tied for 13th among batters with at least 7,000 PA, with Bonds and Thome the only ones from among the top 15 not already enshrined. From a value standpoint, only 20 players produced more than his 67.6 WAR from 27 onward; of those 20, only Bonds is outside the gates.

In terms of his work as a DH, Martinez ranks third in both hits (1,607, behind Ortiz and Harold Baines) and homers (243, behind Ortiz and Thomas). His .314 batting average and .428 on-base percentage are both unsurpassed among DHs with at least 2,000 PA; the latter is 34 points better than runner-up Thomas. Meanwhile, his .532 slugging percentage as a DH trails only Ortiz's .559. While Baseball-Reference.com doesn't do OPS+ for splits, Martinez has the edge on Ortiz in career OPS+, 147 to 141, not to mention a roughly 13-win edge in terms of WAR (68.3 to 55.4) in 1,417 fewer career plate appearances. Prorated, Martinez produced 5.1 WAR per 650 plate appearances compared to Ortiz's 3.6 WAR—a 43% advantage for Edgar even before career length is considered. Even with WAR's DH penalty of roughly 1.5 wins per year for the last decade of his career, he ranked among the AL's top 10 in WAR seven times; by comparison, Ortiz did so three times.

If you can't quite wrap your head around that, consider that Martinez played in an era of increased specialization, particularly regarding bullpen roles. Teams concerned with the limitations of a pitcher's stamina, health, and/or repertoire often convert starters to relievers, who rarely produce enough value within their smaller roles to merit consideration for the Hall. Mariano Rivera is the best example; he pitched through his age-43 season, one inning at a time, all the way to the all-time saves record while relying almost completely on his cut fastball. More than likely he never would have approached a Hall of Fame level had he remained a starter. Martinez was the Mariano Rivera of DHs, so outstanding within his limited role that he produced enough value to transcend it.

(By the way, Martinez owned Rivera, hitting him at a .579/.652/1.053 clip in a modest sample of 23 PA. The great reliever told Charlie Rose in 2013: "The only guy that I didn't want to face, when a tough situation comes, was Edgar Martínez. . . . It didn't matter how I threw the ball. I couldn't get him out. Oh, my god, he had more than my number. He had my breakfast, lunch and dinner."[29])

Having said all of that, Martinez's case doesn't have to rest entirely on his credentials as a DH, as he spent only 72% of his career there. The other 28%, during which he played the field, isn't window dressing; he won the first of his two batting titles and made one of his seven All-Star appearances and three of his seven top 10 finishes in WAR as a third baseman, not to mention two of his nine top 10 finishes in OPS+. He wasn't forced into DHing due to an iron glove or a disinterest in defense. The scouting reports on him in the Hall of Fame's Diamond Mines database, which date from the 1988–91 period, describe his defense as "solid" or "adequate." As noted before, the metrics suggest he was a slightly above average third baseman, 18 runs above average for his career and five per 1,200 innings, bolstering his overall value.

Still, the bat is what people will remember him for, and it was a special one. Compared among hitters of all ages and positions with at least 7,000 PA, Martinez's 147 OPS+ is in a virtual tie with Thome, Mike Schmidt, Willie Stargell, and Willie McCovey for 30th place, while his .418 OBP ranks 14th. Counting-stat-wise, Martinez's 532 batting runs rank 34th.

Even given all of that time at DH, which creates a penalty of roughly 1.7 WAR per year relative to his time at third base, Martinez created enough value as a hitter to surpass the career, peak, and JAWS standards among Hall of Fame third basemen by about one win apiece. He's 11th in career WAR and JAWS among that set, 13th in peak. The margin by which he clears the bar is another half a win higher when you expand the comparison to enshrined corner infielders (first and third base) or all hitters (with catchers given a boost to put them on the same scale as the other positions). That's a solid, well-qualified Hall of Famer.

It's taken a long time for voters to come around to that conclusion, but at this writing there's hope that the tide may have turned. Martinez debuted on the ballot in 2010 with a respectable 36.2%—higher than the debuts of 11 players elected by the writers since 1966—but failed to gain ground, sinking as low as 25.2% in 2014 and then losing five years of eligibility to the Hall's rule change. Just when it appeared he was doomed to slip off the ballot, however, he finally caught some breaks. Between a vigorous outreach campaign by the Mariners, his return to the team as its hitting coach, testimonials from recent honorees such as Johnson, Griffey, and Pedro Martinez, the attention paid to the end of Ortiz's career, and the growing acceptance of advanced stats in Hall debates—with my own work on Edgar specifically cited by voters—he gained a hefty 31.6% in 2016 and '17, rocketing him all the way to 58.6%.

With two years of eligibility remaining, Martinez is now slightly ahead of where 2017 honoree Tim Raines was in 2015 (55.0%). While his election isn't a foregone conclusion, particularly given the upcoming crowd on the ballot (Chipper Jones, Jim Thome, Scott Rolen, Andruw Jones, and Omar Vizquel in 2018 alone), his crossing of the 50% threshold bodes well. Like Griffey racing home from first base on The Double, it could make for a fittingly thrilling finish.

THE ROUNDUP

The number before each player name refers to his JAWS ranking *among all players at the position*, not necessarily those in the Hall. Average HOF third baseman: 67.5/42.8/55.2.

The Elite (above standard in career, peak, and JAWS)

1. Mike Schmidt

Teams:	Phillies 1972–89
Stats:	.267/.38/.527 • 147 OPS+ • 2,234 H • 548 HR • 174 SB
Rankings:	12× All-Star • 11× GG • 8× led HR • 6× led OPS+ • 5× led SLG • 4× led WAR • 3× led OBP
	All-time: 16th HR • 19th WAR • T-30th OPS+
Voting/JAWS:	BBWAA 1995 **(1st, 96.5%)** • 106.5/58.5/82.5

Thanks to his outstanding combination of power, patience (1,507 walks), and defense (+129 runs, ninth all-time at the position), Schmidt not only has a claim as the game's greatest third baseman, but as its most valuable player during the 1961–92 span, i.e., through the first three waves of expansion. That carefully manicured strip of history excludes the opening salvos of Willie Mays, Mickey Mantle, and Hank Aaron—Joe Morgan is the only other player to reach 100 WAR in that span—but it testifies to Schmidt's dominance of the traditional and advanced leaderboards of his time. Only Babe Ruth led his league in homers more often, only seven players led in OPS+ more often, and only seven players had more top three finishes in WAR than his seven. On that note, even if you lopped Schmidt's three best seasons off both his career and his peak, his 79.2/52.5/65.9 line would edge Chipper Jones for fourth at the position in JAWS. For all of the voters' issues with honoring the third baseman, Schmidt's percentage ranked fourth in history when he was elected, behind Tom Seaver, Ty Cobb, and Aaron, and today it's still 11th.

2. Eddie Mathews

Teams:	Braves 1952–66 • Astros 1967 • Tigers 1967–68
Stats:	.271/.376/.509 • 143 OPS+ • 2,315 H • 512 HR • 68 SB
Rankings:	9× All-Star • 9× top 5 HR • 8× top 5 WAR • 8× top 10 SLG • 7× top 5 OBP
	All-time: T-22nd HR
Voting/JAWS:	BBWAA 1978 **(5th, 79.4%)** • 96.4/54.4/75.4

Mathews was such a home run prodigy that after he bashed an NL-high 47 as a 21-year-old in 1953, many went on record to suggest that he could break Ruth's single-season mark. He never did, of course, though he ranked in the NL's top five in homers in each of his first nine seasons while teaming with Hank Aaron to help the Braves to two pennants and a world championship. When he retired, he was second in NL homer history behind Mays and sixth all-time. Capable of the occasional .290–.300 average, a frequent presence on the OBP and SLG leaderboards, and a more than adequate glove man (+33 runs career, with two double-digit seasons) despite an early reputation as less than that, he was more valuable than all but Mays (92.8 WAR) and Mantle (85.1) during his 1953–63 run, outdoing Aaron, 79.4 to 73.5 thanks in part to his two-year head start. As noted in Chapter 4, despite his credentials, he was the first modern 500-homer slugger not to gain first-ballot entry, needing five years to reach 75%.

3. Wade Boggs

Teams:	Red Sox 1982–92 • Yankees 1993–97 • Devil Rays 1998–99
Stats:	.328/.415/.443 • 131 OPS+ • 3,010 H • 118 HR • 24 SB
Rankings:	12× All-Star • 7× top 5 WAR • 6× led OBP • 5× led AVG • 5× top 5 OPS+ • 2× GG
	All-time: 17th OBP • 24th AVG • 27th H • 29th WAR
Voting/JAWS:	BBWAA 2005 **(1st, 91.9%)** • **91.1/56.2/73.6**

A poultry-fueled hitting machine whose moonlight avocations included knuckleballing mop-up reliever and celebratory equestrian, Boggs won five batting titles in his first six full seasons, all with averages of at least .357; among postwar players, only Tony Gwynn had more times above .350 (six). Yet Boggs is somewhat underrated, because he was more than just those batting averages. He led the AL in times on base in eight straight seasons (1983–90), and in OBP six times. His total of four seasons with at least 200 hits and 100 walks trails only Lou Gehrig's seven, with Ruth the only other player to do so more than twice. He quite reasonably could have won even more Gold Gloves given his defensive prowess (+95 runs) and multiple MVP awards given that he led the AL in WAR each year from 1986–88, bookended by even higher totals that ranked second; alas, he never finished above fourth in the voting. Blame his reaching double digits in homers just twice, and never driving in 100 runs. He eventually got his due, thanks to the 1996 World Series win and his 3,000th hit.

4. George Brett

Teams:	Royals 1973–93
Stats:	.305/.369/.487 • 135 OPS+ • 3,154 H • 317 HR • 201 SB

Rankings:	13× All-Star • 7× top 10 OBP • 6× top 5 OPS+ • 5× top 3 WAR • 3× led AVG • 3× led SLG
	All-time: 16th H • 18th TB
Voting/JAWS:	BBWAA 1999 **(1st, 98.2%)** • **88.4/53.2/70.8**

Though he was a three-time batting champion—once with a .390 average, the AL's highest since Ted Williams's .406 in 1941—Brett didn't dominate the leaderboards to quite the extent that Schmidt (chosen one pick behind him in the second round of the 1971 draft) or Boggs did. He was more of a fixture in the postseason, helping the Royals to seven division titles in a 10-year span, and hitting .337/.397/.627 with 10 homers in 184 PA once he got there, for the fourth-highest OPS among players with at least 150 PA; unlike two of the three above him (Carlos Beltran and Albert Pujols), he didn't have the benefit of the third tier of playoffs. One can only wonder how high his hit total might have been had he stayed healthy. The *ESPN Baseball Encylopedia* lists him with 251 days on the disabled list spread over seven seasons, which seems low given that from 1977–93, he played in only 2,243 out of the team's 2,694 games, missing 451. Project his hit rate over two more 150-game seasons and that's 3,503 hits, sixth all-time, bearing down on Tris Speaker (3,514), with perhaps another 10.0 WAR, enough to push him ahead of Mathews here. He was that good.

7. Ron Santo

Teams:	Cubs 1960–73 • White Sox 1974
Stats:	.277/.362/.464 • 125 OPS+ • 2,254 H • 342 HR • 35 SB
Rankings:	9× All-Star • 7× top 10 OBP • 7× top 10 HR • 5× top 10 SLG • 5× GG • 5× top 5 WAR • 4× top 10 OPS+
Voting/JAWS:	GEC 2012 • **70.4/53.8/62.1**

Consider this horse flogged. See Chapter 4.

8. Brooks Robinson

Teams:	Orioles 1955–77
Stats:	.267/.322/.401 • 104 OPS+ • 2,848 H • 268 HR • 28 SB
Rankings:	16× GG • 15× All-Star • 9× top 10 WAR • 4× top 10 AVG
Voting/JAWS:	BBWAA 1983 **(1st, 92.0%)** • **78.4/45.8/62.1**

Ambidexterity and supernaturally quick reflexes helped "The Human Vacuum Cleaner" rate as one of the most valuable defenders in history, and his exposure via four World Series—including 1970, when he won MVP honors and got into the Reds' heads—etched him into the national consciousness. "If I dropped this paper plate, he'd pick it up on one hop and throw me out at first,"[30] said Cincinnati manager Sparky Anderson. Robinson's 293 fielding runs are tops at any position, though once you account for the positional adjustments for third base and short-stop, both Ozzie Smith (43.4 defensive WAR) and longtime Orioles teammate Mark Belanger (39.4) outdo his 38.4 dWAR. Though he stuck around long enough to approach 3,000 hits, and might have gotten there with a slightly less precipitous decline, Robinson was really only an above-average offensive force from 1960–71, with a 114 OPS+ during that span, just one season of 100 or better outside of it, and some Belanger-like ones near the end. Still, he led the AL in WAR twice (1962 and '64, his MVP year), was runner-up twice, and was an easy first-ballot choice.

The Rank and File

9. Paul Molitor

Teams:	Brewers 1978–92 • Blue Jays 1993–95 • Twins 1996–98
Stats:	.306/.369/.448 • 122 OPS+ • 3,319 H • 234 HR • 504 SB
Rankings:	11× top 10 AVG • 6× top 10 OBP • 7× All-Star • 4× top 10 WAR • 4× top 10 OPS+
	All-time: 10th H • 20th TOB
Voting/JAWS:	BBWAA 2004 **(1st, 85.2%)** • 75.4/39.6/57.5

Molitor played more games as a designated hitter (1,171) than at any other position, but accumulated more value as a third baseman (where he played 791 games), so that's how he's classified for JAWS purposes. Chosen with the third pick of the 1977 draft at a time when the Brewers weren't sure of Robin Yount's commitment to base-ball, he spent most of his early years at the keystone, with a brief foray into center field before moving to the hot corner. No matter the position, he struggled to stay healthy, missing at least 50 games in six of his first 13 seasons even while averaging 3.8 WAR in 118 games per year during that span. Finally, the Brewers got wise and parked him at DH on a regular basis in 1991, and over the remainder of his career he averaged 143 games, 181 hits, and 3.2 WAR while remaining similarly produc-tive offensively (121 OPS+ before, 123 after). That durability helped him push well past 3,000 hits, and while his peak score is suppressed by his absences and his DH duty, he nonetheless clears the third base bar with plenty of room to spare.

13. Home Run Baker

Teams:	A's 1908–14 • Yankees 1916–19, 1921–22
Stats:	.307/.363/.442 • 135 OPS+ • 1,838 H • 96 HR • 235 SB
Rankings:	9× top 10 WAR • 7× top 10 SLG • 6× top 10 AVG • 6× top 10 OPS+ • 4× led HR
Voting/JAWS:	VC 1955 • **62.8/46.8/54.8**

A plausible candidate to be the Hall's first third baseman, Frank Baker helped the A's to four pennants and three championships from 1910–14, with a pair of key round-trippers in the '11 World Series endowing him with a nickname that endures over a century later. He led the AL in homers every year from 1911–14 with dead-ball-era-appropriate totals ranging from nine to 12. While famed for his offense, the bowlegged and awkward-looking third baseman's fielding drew mixed reviews, but Total Zone views him as solidly above-average defensively (+35 runs). Even while losing all of 1915 to a salary dispute with Connie Mack and 1920 in the aftermath of his wife's death, leaving him with young children to care for, he rates as significantly more valuable than the two third basemen who preceded him into Cooperstown, Jimmy Collins (1945) and Pie Traynor ('48). See Chapter 4.

20. Jimmy Collins

Teams:	Louisville Colonels 1895 • Boston Beaneaters/Braves 1895–1900 • Boston Americans 1901–07 • A's 1907–08
Stats:	.294/.343/.409 • 113 OPS+ • 1,999 H • 65 HR • 194 SB
Rankings:	7× top 10 HR • 6× top 10 WAR • 5× top 10 SLG • 3× top 10 OBP • 3× top 10 AVG
Voting/JAWS:	OTC 1945 • **53.2/38.4/45.8**

For decades, the agile and cerebral Collins was considered the yardstick by which third basemen were measured. He had revolutionized the position in an 1895 game against the powerhouse Orioles, when he was summoned from center field after the regular third baseman had made four errors on bunts, he moved closer to the plate, on the edge of the grass, and successfully threw out four bunters in a row, including John McGraw and Willie Keeler. Returned to the Beaneaters (who had loaned him to Louisville), he attained stardom in Boston more for his defense (+121 runs for his career, tops among prewar third basemen) than his offense, though the latter greatly improved upon moving to the upstart AL. As player-manager, he led the Americans to back-to-back pennants in 1903 (with a victory over the Pirates in the first World Series) and '04 (when there was no World Series). Alas, he died two years before he was elected. See Chapter 4.

36. Deacon White

Teams:	Cleveland Forest Citys (NA), 1871–72 • Boston Red Stockings (NA) 1873–75 • Chicago White Stockings 1876 • Boston Red Stockings 1877 • Reds 1878–80 • Buffalo Bisons 1881–85, '90 • Detroit Wolverines 1886–88 • Pittsburgh Alleghenys 1889
Stats:	.312/.346/.393 • 127 OPS+ • 2,067 H • 24 HR • 70 SB
Rankings:	8× top 10 AVG • 8× top 10 OBP • 7× top 10 WAR • 6 top 10 OPS+ • 5× top 10 SLG
Voting/JAWS:	PIEC 2013 • **45.5/26.0/35.7**

Hailed as the "Most Admirable Superstar of the 1870s" by Bill James, who noted that he "picked up his nickname from the strange habit of going to church,"[31] White was renowned for his integrity and gentlemanly nature if not his scientific acumen; he actually believed that the earth is flat. His career dates to the inception of professional baseball: He took the first plate appearance, collected the first hit, and made the first catch in National Association history in 1871. Amid the mess of the professional game's first decade, with its underhanded or sidearm pitching, near-annual fluctuations in ball/strike payoff combos, barehand fielding, and shorter schedules, he ranked among the game's top hitters, fifth in OPS+ (150) from 1871–80, with batting titles in 1875 and '77. Mostly a catcher during the first half of his career (b.c.p.: before chest protectors), he tired of taking his lumps and settled at third, where he played 827 of his 1,560 games. While he suffers relative to the Hall standards due to shortened schedules, his career WAR ranks 11th among nineteenth-century position players. Considered as early as 1936, he was the lone player recognized by the short-lived Pre-Integration Era Committee.

The Basement (the most dubious honorees)

48. George Kell

Teams:	Philadelphia A's 1943–46 • Tigers 1947–52 • Red Sox 1952–54 • White Sox 1954–56 • Orioles 1956–57
Stats:	.306/.367/.414 • 112 OPS+ • 2,054 H • 78 HR • 51 SB

Rankings:	10× All-Star • 7× top 5 AVG • 4× top 10 OBP • 3× top 10 WAR
Voting/JAWS:	VC 1983 • **37.4/27.8/32.6**

A skilled contact hitter who struck out more than 23 times in a season just twice, Kell finished above .300 in eight straight seasons and won the 1949 AL batting title, but most of his value is tied up in those superficially snazzy batting averages. He didn't walk a great deal or hit for much power, with double-digit homers just once, and two top 10 finishes in OPS+. Even with a decent glove (+15 runs), he did so in WAR just three times, never posting a single season of 5.0 WAR. In career and peak value, he's very similar to Bill Madlock (38.0/28.3/33.1), the only four-time batting champion outside the Hall, though Madlock's iron glove (−107 fielding runs) cut into the impact of his more valuable bat. Kell never received more than 36.8% from the BBWAA, but was elected by the VC in his first year of eligibility. Notably, former Tigers teammate Birdie Tebbetts was on the committee, as was Tigers legend Charlie Gehringer, the team's general manager from 1951–53. Hmmm.

58. Pie Traynor

Teams:	Pirates 1920–35, 1937
Stats:	.320/.362/.435 • 107 OPS+ • 2,416 H • 58 HR • 158 SB
Rankings:	6× top 10 AVG • 4× top 10 SB • 2× All-Star
Voting/JAWS:	BBWAA 1948 **(7th, 76.9%)** • **36.2/25.7/31.0**

The first third baseman elected by the BBWAA, Traynor was at the vanguard of a wave of players from the 1920s and '30s whose gaudy offensive stats were far less valuable than they appeared, He drove in 100 or more runs seven times, and hit .317 or better in eight seasons; while he was between .337 and .366 every year from 1927–30, he never finished above fifth in the batting race, and only once cracked a top 10 in another slash stat. In fact, his 107 OPS+ is the second-lowest of any post-nineteenth-century player with a .310 average or above, ahead of only teammate Lloyd Waner. Defensively, he was lauded for his quick hands and arm, but his throws often pulled first basemen off the bag; he led the league in throwing errors three times from 1930–33 (the first years for which we have error type breakdowns). Total Zone *really* doesn't like him (-32 runs), but even if that sign were reversed, he'd be vastly overrated relative to WAR, because that offense (+93 runs) wasn't special enough. See Chapter 4.

69. Freddie Lindstrom

Teams:	Giants 1924–32 • Pirates 1933–34 • Cubs 1935 • Dodgers 1936
Stats:	.311/.351/.449 • 110 OPS+ • 1,747 H • 103 HR • 84 SB
Rankings:	3× top 10 AVG • 3× top 10 WAR • 2× top 10 SB
Voting/JAWS:	VC 1976 • **28.3/26.2/27.3**

Short career, empty batting averages from a high-offense era, and an election where cronyism probably played a part—Lindstrom represents the Veterans Committee at its worst. Pressed into duty as an 18-year-old on the pennant-winning Giants, he was the goat of the 1924 World Series, victimized by a couple of bad-hop groundballs in Game 7. He overcame that to spend nine years as a regular, hitting as high as .358 in 1928 (when he led the league with 231 hits) and .379 in '30, while being hailed for his defense as well, though he rarely dented the leaderboard. A broken leg in 1931 led the team to realize they could live without him, particularly amid hurt feelings over being bypassed to succeed McGraw as Giants manager. Traded to the Pirates, he was forced to move to the outfield due to Traynor's presence, and had just one good year out of his final four while bouncing around. His 1,719 hits through his age-29 season ranked sixth at the time (17th now), behind five future Hall of Famers, but he collected just 28 more, and it took a VC featuring Bill Terry (who did succeed McGraw) to elect him.

Further Consideration (upcoming or overlooked candidates)

5. Adrian Beltre

Teams:	Dodgers 1998–2004 • Mariners 2005–2009 • Red Sox 2010 • Rangers 2011–2016
Stats:	.286/.338/.480 • 116 OPS+ • 2,942 H • 445 HR • 119 SB
Rankings:	9× top 10 WAR • 5× top 5 AVG • 5× top 10 SLG • 5× top 10 OPS+ • 5× GG • 4× top 10 HR
Voting/JAWS:	**90.2/49.7/69.9**

A regular upon reaching the majors at age 19, Beltre spent his first 12 seasons in pitcher-friendly parks that suppressed his offensive stats, and because he failed to replicate his massive 2004 walk year (.334/.388/.629 with 48 homers and 9.5 WAR), was viewed as an underachiever. Though his defensive numbers in that span were eye-opening—four seasons with at least +19 DRS—his 105 OPS+ was nothing special, and he had only two other seasons worth at least 4.0 WAR.

Moving into hitter-friendly environments, he raised his game, becoming a perennial 30-homer slugger, checking off milestones, and receiving broader acclaim. He posted a 133 OPS+ from 2010–16, with his age-31–36 seasons all worth at least 5.6 WAR; five of them count toward his peak. Signed through 2018, he should surpass 3,000 hits and approach 500 homers, which will punch his ticket even without considering the impact of his tremendous glovework, which at +224 runs is second at the position behind Robinson. Yowzah.

6. Chipper Jones

Teams:	Braves 1993, 1995–2012
Stats:	.303/.401/.529 • 141 OPS+ • 2,726 H • 468 HR • 150 SB
Rankings:	8× All-Star • 7× top 10 OBP • 6× top 10 OPS+• 5× top 10 AVG • 5× top 10 SLG • 5× top 10 WAR
Voting/JAWS:	**85.0/46.6/65.8**

It took until 2016—51 years after the inception of the amateur draft—for the first overall number one pick, Ken Griffey Jr., to be elected to the Hall. Jones, chosen first three years after Griffey in 1990, will be the second. The offensive cornerstone of the Braves' 1995–2005 run of playoff-bound teams, he was an eight-time All-Star who added an MVP award (1999) and a batting title (2008, at age 36) to his mantel—and speaking of Mantle, Jones ranks third among switch-hitters in homers, fifth in hits, and second in WAR behind the Mick himself. He ranked among the league's top 10 in WAR "only" five times because defense was never his strong suit (-23 runs), but he was basically average after a mid-career foray to left field, justifying his resistance to switching to first base as he aged. Thanks to a spotless reputation on the PED front, he'll have no trouble joining Greg Maddux, Tom Glavine, John Smoltz, and Bobby Cox in 2018.

10. Scott Rolen

Teams:	Phillies 1996–2002 • Cardinals 2002–07 • Blue Jays 2008–09 • Reds 2009-12
Stats:	.281/.364/.490 • 122 OPS+ • 2,077 H • 316 HR • 118 SB
Rankings:	8× GG • 7× All-Star • 4× top 10 WAR
Voting/JAWS:	**70.0/43.5/56.8**

The defensive metrics don't always jibe with the hardware, but Rolen ranks third at the hot corner in fielding runs (+175) to go with his Gold Gloves, and he was more than solid offensively, if not much of a leaderboard presence. The 1997 NL

Rookie of the Year, he placed as high as fourth in the MVP voting, and helped his teams to five playoff appearances, two pennants, and a championship. What he couldn't do—aside from get the respect he deserved in Philadelphia, particularly from manager Larry Bowa and senior advisor Dallas Green while being stuck on terrible teams—was stay healthy. His left shoulder was the primary culprit, requiring three surgeries from 2005–12, costing him at least 245 games on the disabled list, with additional time lost to a concussion and lower back woes during his final years. Thus he had six seasons of fewer than 120 games, three with fewer than 100, and was done at age 37. Even with the missed time, he clears the standards across the board, but may well become the position's Bobby Grich, held back by his good-not-great career totals and the perpetual undervaluing of his best assets.

12. Graig Nettles

Teams:	Twins 1967–69 • Indians 1970–72 • Yankees 1973–83 • Padres 1984–86 • Braves 1987 • Expos 1988
Stats:	.248/.329/.421 • 110 OPS+ • 2,225 H • 390 HR • 32 SB
Rankings:	6× All-Star • 6× top 10 WAR • 5× top 10 HR • 2× GG
Voting/JAWS:	**68.0/42.3/55.1**

A dazzling defender (+140 runs, seventh), Nettles had the misfortune to play in the shadow of Brooks Robinson, so he was shut out from the Gold Gloves until 1977 and won only twice. His acrobatic play in the 1978 World Series—and particularly in the series-turning Game 3, where he made diving stop after diving stop with men on base—still haunts this writer and exemplifies this criminally underrated player's virtues. The starting third baseman on five pennant winners, Nettles rarely hit for average but powered his way to the AL lead in homers in 1976, with five top 10 finishes; his total of 206 from 1971–78 ranks sixth. His 46.5 WAR for that same period ranked third behind only Joe Morgan and Rod Carew; twice he led the league (1971 and '76), but he never placed higher than fifth in the MVP voting due to his modest batting averages. Debuting at 8.3% in 1994, he went downhill from there, and has yet to sniff a committee ballot. Though he's within a few runs either way of all three standards, he's fated to remain in the shadows for a while.

14. Ken Boyer

Teams:	Cardinals 1955–65 • Mets 1966–67 • White Sox 1967–68 • Dodgers 1968–69
Stats:	.287/.349/.462 • 116 OPS+ • 2,143 H • 282 HR • 105 SB

Rankings: 7× All-Star • 7× top 10 WAR • 5× GG • 5× top 10 AVG • 5× top 10 OBP • 4× top 10 SLG • 4 top 10 HR

Voting/JAWS: **62.8/46.3/54.5**

One of three brothers who spent time in the majors, Boyer preceded Ron Santo as the NL's top third baseman, and ranks an impressive ninth in peak, 3.6 wins above the standard. A perennial All-Star who averaged 25 homers, a 124 OPS+, and 6.1 WAR from 1956–64, he capped that with an MVP award in '64, when he hit 24 homers, drove in an NL-best 119, runs and hit .295/.365/.489 for a team that edged Dick Allen's Phillies for the NL pennant. Even so, his 6.1 WAR was well behind Allen's 8.8. Traded to the Mets at age 34, he had just one more solid season as a regular before bouncing around as a part-timer. A better fielder than Santo according to the metrics (+73 runs to +27), if not as good a hitter (116 OPS+ to 125), he got similarly little love from BBWAA voters, temporarily getting bumped by the Five Percent Rule and maxing out at 25.5%; thus far, he's 0-for-5 in front of the small committees. Given the quality of his peak, the volume of his other honors, and the shortage of enshrined third basemen, he'd be a solid choice.

15. Buddy Bell

Teams: Indians 1972–78 • Rangers 1979–85, 1989 • Reds 1985–88 • Astros 1988

Stats: .279/.341/.406 • 109 OPS+ • 2,514 H • 201 HR • 55 SB

Rankings: 6× GG • 5× All-Star • 5× top 10 WAR

Voting/JAWS: **66.1/40.4/53.2**

Chosen here over the higher-peak Sal Bando (61.4/44.3/52.9 but just 1,790 hits), Bell was the middle man in a three-generation dynasty of major leaguers, a promising enough all-around player as a 20-year-old to nudge the 27-year-old Nettles out of Cleveland. It's fair to wonder which one would be more famous had the younger player been traded to the Yankees; as it was, Nettles made more All-Star appearances (six to five) but Bell won more Gold Gloves (six to two), taking over the AL residency long occupied by Robinson, and climbing to fourth in fielding runs (+174). Between Cleveland and three other stops, he never reached the postseason or garnered much fame, received just 1.7% in his ballot debut and hasn't had a sniff from a small committee. He's very close to the standards on all three fronts, but the foundation of his case rests on defense, and the line for third basemen to get into Cooperstown starts in Oneonta, so don't wait up.

CHAPTER 14

LEFTFIELDERS

TIM RAINES

Right now he's the best player in the National League. Mike Schmidt is a tremendous player and so are Dale Murphy and Andre Dawson, but Rock . . . can beat you in more ways than any other player in the league. He can beat you with his glove, his speed and his hitting from either side of the plate. And he has the perfect disposition for a great player—he has fun.[1]

—PETE ROSE

Tim Raines spent much of his 23-year career playing second fiddle. Bursting upon the National League scene in 1981, he set a modern rookie record for stolen bases with 71, but lost out in the NL Rookie of the Year voting to Fernando Valenzuela, whose Dodgers beat Raines's Expos in their only postseason appearance. Raines had to yield to Andre Dawson, first as an Expos teammate occupying center field while Raines played left, then as a slugging rival who snatched away the NL MVP award in what might have been the speedy switch-hitter's best season.

It was Raines's fate to be cast as number two among the rankings of leadoff hitters, the best this side of contemporary Rickey Henderson, who set all-time records for stolen bases, walks, runs scored, and third-person references. Raines didn't play in a World Series until 1996, after injuries reduced him to a supporting role, and he could only watch while Tony Gwynn, a superstar of comparable value but far more glitzy accomplishments, waltzed into the Hall of Fame on the first ballot in 2007, the year before he became eligible.

Where Gwynn collected 3,000 hits, won eight batting titles, and spent his entire career with one team, Raines fell 395 hits shy of the milestone due to injuries and illnesses that took a chunk out of the second half of his career. Which isn't to say that he didn't accomplish plenty. His seven All-Star appearances, four stolen base titles, two championship rings, and a batting title are more than most players bring home, and for a considerable stretch in the mid-1980s he had a claim as the NL's top player. Taking his career as a whole, he's the greatest percentage base stealer of all time, and as of 2017 he's added another title: Hall of Famer.

Unlike the other lengthy profiles in Part II, the Raines one already has its happy outcome. Benefiting from a similar combination of advanced-stat reckoning and grassroots outreach that propelled Bert Blyleven into Cooperstown after a slow start to his candidacy (see Chapter 6), Raines was elected in his final year of eligibility. His story is worth review.

The Career

Expos 1979–90, 2001 • White Sox 1991–95 • Yankees 1996–98 • A's 1999 • Orioles 2001 • Marlins 2002

Player	Career	Peak	JAWS	H	HR	SB	AVG/OBP/SLG	OPS+
Tim Raines	69.1	42.2	55.6	2605	170	808	.294/.385/.425	123
Avg HOF LF	65.2	41.5	53.3					
LF Rank	8th	10th	8th					
(Above HOF)	(15/19)	(12/19)	(14/19)					

Raines was born and raised in Sanford, Florida, where he was the fifth of seven children, two of whom, Levi and Ned, played professional baseball ahead of their more famous brother in the second half of the 1970s. Tim starred in football and track as well as baseball at Seminole High School. On the gridiron, he averaged 10.5 yards a carry and scored 18 touchdowns as a senior tailback. On the track, running only on days where he had no baseball games, he set school records in the 100-yard dash (9.7 seconds), 330-yard hurdles (41 seconds), and long jump (23'2").

Though he received over 100 college football scholarship offers including Florida, Raines realized that his 5'8" height limited his upside. He signed with the Expos, who drafted him as a shortstop in the fifth round in 1977, but quickly moved him to second base, the same position as his similarly compact-but-sturdy idol, Joe Morgan. He learned to switch-hit in the minors. After spending the 1979 season at Double-A Memphis, Raines received a September call-up from the Expos, appearing in six games as a pinch-runner and stealing two bases without making a plate appearance. He was called up three separate times in 1980, going

1-for-20 at the plate but 5-for-5 on the bases; meanwhile, he earned The Sporting News Minor League Player of the Year honors for hitting .354/.439/.501 with 77 steals in 90 attempts at Triple-A Denver.

Satisfied with light-hitting Rodney Scott at second base, the Expos opted to shift Raines to left field to replace the departed Ron LeFlore, who had swiped an NL-high 97 bases in 1980. Dawson was the center field incumbent, the team's top star, and a reigning Gold Glove winner, but the 21-year-old Raines quickly emerged as a star in his own right, running his multiyear streak of successful stolen bases to 27 before being caught for the first time. Stopwatch-toting first base coach Steve Boros, who had worked with speedster Willie Wilson in Kansas City and would later manage Henderson, helped Raines work on timing pitchers' deliveries to get optimal jumps.

In that strike-torn season, Raines hit .304/.391/.438, stealing a league-leading 71 bases in 82 attempts—all in just 88 games, as a broken bone in his right hand limited him to sporadic pinch-running duty from mid-September through the first round of the playoffs. If not for the injury and the strike, he likely would have become the fourth player since 1901 to steal at least 100 bases in a season, as Henderson had done the year before, and might have toppled Lou Brock's single-season record of 118 steals before Henderson shattered it with 130 in 1982.

The Expos made the 1981 playoffs by winning the post-strike leg of the NL East race. After they defeated the first-half champion Phillies in a five-game Division Series, Raines returned in time for the NLCS against the Dodgers. Though he collected three hits (two off Valenzuela) and drove in a run in the Expos' Game 2 win, the Dodgers prevailed on the strength of Rick Monday's two-out, ninth-inning home run in Game 5, a shot forever known among Expos fans as Blue Monday. Raines earned All-Star honors and finished with 3.5 WAR, good for eighth in the NL, but the BBWAA chose Valenzuela as its NL Rookie of the Year.

Though Raines again led the league in steals in 1982 with 78, his performance (.277/.353/.369, 2.8 WAR) was a mild disappointment, with a few games missed for reasons that went unexplained, at least publicly. In September, a bombshell dropped: Raines admitted that he had "used drugs"[2] earlier in the season but had stopped in May and was seeing a doctor at the insistence of the team. At season's end, he entered a rehab program, and upon completing a 30-day program, said, "I was playing with a handicap. I was playing on instincts. . . . A lot of times I got no sleep. A lot of times I couldn't even see the ball."[3] He revealed that he had spent $40,000 on cocaine over the course of nine months.

Raines's drug woes came in the context of being 22 years old and living in the majors' most notorious party city at a time when cocaine was rampant throughout the game. In 1985, he was one of over a dozen current or former players called to testify in the so-called "Pittsburgh drug trials" centered around dealer Curtis

Strong. Raines's testimony included the now infamous revelation that he had taken up sliding headfirst to avoid breaking the vials of coke (not crack) in his back pocket; he would do lines in the bathroom between innings. Thankfully, by all accounts, he successfully kicked his habit. He turned to Dawson as a role model and mentor, discussed his misadventures openly, and reached out to other players who found trouble with cocaine as well.

Free of his burden, Raines broke out in 1983, beginning a five-year stretch during which he hit a combined .318/.406/.467, averaging 114 runs scored, 11 homers, 71 steals, a 142 OPS+, and 6.4 WAR, never falling below 5.5. He led the NL in steals in '83 (a career-high 90) and '84 (75) while ranking third or fourth among NL position players in WAR in four of those five years, and seventh in the other. For the period as a whole, only Wade Boggs, Henderson, and Cal Ripken—all AL players and future Hall of Famers—were more valuable. The NL players immediately below him were Mike Schmidt, Gwynn, Dale Murphy, Ozzie Smith, and Gary Carter: four future Hall of Famers plus a two-time MVP (Murphy). By the end of that run, Bill James hailed Raines as the second-best player in baseball after Boggs.

In 1986, Raines led the NL in both batting (.334) and on-base percentage (.413). Just 27 by the end of the season, he reached free agency that winter, but suspiciously received nothing but low-ball contract offers along the lines of a one-year, $1.1 million deal from the Padres. Baseball was in the midst of its collusion era, in which commissioner Peter Ueberroth and team owners conspired to hold down free agent prices. In 1990, they would be forced to pay $280 million in damages to the MLB Players Association as a result. By the rules in place at the time, Raines was allowed to return to the Expos, but ineligible to play until May.

As soon as he was permitted to negotiate, Raines signed a three-year, $5 million deal with the Expos, up slightly from their pre-deadline offer of $4.8 million. After just one day of extended spring training, he stepped into the lineup on May 2, turning a Saturday afternoon NBC *Game of the Week* against the Mets at Shea Stadium into the greatest comeback special since Elvis Presley's. In the first inning, he hit a first-pitch triple off David Cone. In the third, he walked and stole second, kindling a two-run rally. In the ninth, he sparked a game-tying, two-run rally by beating out a routine grounder to shortstop, his third hit of the day. In the 10th, he smashed a grand slam off Jesse Orosco, providing the margin of victory in Montreal's 11–7 win and finishing with a beefy 5-3-4-4 box score line. After the game, he joked, "I had forgotten how to throw the high five. It had been so long. They're now using forearms instead of hands."[4]

For an encore, Raines led off with a homer the next day, a 2–0 win, and hit a go-ahead home run in the seventh inning against the Braves in his fourth game back. At the All-Star Game on July 14, he provided a late-inning tour de force, going 3-for-3 with a stolen base after entering the game in the bottom of the sixth, capped by a game-winning two-run triple in the 13th inning en route to MVP honors.

Raines set career bests for on-base and slugging percentages in 1987, hitting .330/.429/.526 with a career-high 18 homers as well as 50 steals. Despite missing a month, he led the league in runs scored with 123 and ranked fourth in WAR with 6.7, behind Gwynn (a career-high 8.5), Eric Davis (7.9, on a 37-homer, 50-steal season in just 129 games), and Murphy (7.7 in his final great season). Alas, the MVP award went to Dawson, whose 4.0 WAR ranked 18th; a victim of collusion himself, the Hawk hit 49 homers and drove in 137 runs after signing with the Cubs, who wrote "$500,000" on the blank check he offered, less than half of what he had made in Montreal the year before. Raines's seventh-place finish was part of a long-standing pattern of neglect by the BBWAA voters. Despite receiving MVP votes in seven separate seasons, he never placed above fifth.

After that 1983–87 peak, injuries cut into Raines's playing time, starting with a nagging left shoulder injury that limited him to 109 games in 1988, requiring season-ending surgery in early September. In December 1990, on the heels of his least productive season since 1982, he was traded to the White Sox in a five-player deal centered around outfielder Ivan Calderon. Raines spent five years on the South Side, the most valuable of which was his 1992 campaign (6.3 WAR, good for eighth in the league). He actually hit better in 1993 (.306/.401/.480 with 16 homers) than in 1992 (.294/.380/.405 with seven homers) while helping the Sox win the AL West, but missed six weeks due to torn ligaments in his right thumb. Between injuries and the 1994–95 strike, he averaged just 130 games for Chicago, though through his age-35 season, he collected 2,295 hits, enough to suggest he had a shot at 3,000.

It wasn't to be. In December 1995, the 36-year-old Raines was dealt to the Yankees, who eased him into a platoon role that was further reduced by hamstring woes. He caught fire in September 1996, clubbing seven home runs and slugging .595 while helping the Yanks win the AL East and then the World Series; his two-out walk in the 10th inning of Game 4 turned into the decisive run via Boggs's bases-loaded walk. In three years in New York, he hit a combined .299/.395/.429 while averaging 81 games a year; he was part of their 1998 championship as well. Moving to Oakland in 1999, he struggled mightily before being diagnosed with lupus, a chronic autoimmune disease in which the immune system attacks normal tissue. He missed the final two months of the season while being subject to radiation and medication.

Though still with the bug to play, Raines was cut from both the Yankees and the U.S. Olympic team in 2000. In 2001, he returned to the Expos in a bench role, then was traded to the Orioles in late September so as to get a chance to play with son Tim Raines Jr.—the second father-son duo to play in the same lineup, after Ken Griffey Sr. and Jr. Raines finally hung up his spikes after spending 2002 with the Marlins.

The Case

Between the two player strikes and collusion, Raines lost nearly a full season to labor issues, one key reason (along with the injuries) why he fell short of 3,000 hits. Still, coupled with his keen batting eye and outstanding plate discipline, he reached base 3,977 times, good for 47th all-time. More impressively, he finished his career with 808 stolen bases, fifth all-time, and an 84.7% success rate, tops among those with at least 400 stolen base attempts (note that caught stealing data is sporadic before 1951) and well ahead of Henderson's 80.8%.

Even so, Raines came up somewhat short in the things that tend to draw Hall of Fame voters' attention, in part because aside from his four stolen base titles, he didn't lead his league in key categories very often, didn't take home major awards, or play for many postseason teams. His Hall of Fame Monitor score of 90 is short of the "likely" mark of 100, in the vicinity of other ill-fated candidates such as Willie Randolph (92), Lou Whitaker (92), Kenny Lofton (91), and Thurman Munson (90), of whom only the last stayed on the ballot for longer than a year.

The advanced stats made a much stronger case for Raines, who ranks eighth in both career WAR and JAWS among all leftfielders, exceeding the standard for Hall of Famers by 4.0 WAR and 2.3 points, respectively. Meanwhile, he's 10th in peak WAR, 0.7 above the standard. Of the seven leftfielders above him in JAWS, five (Ted Williams, Henderson, Carl Yastrzemski, Ed Delahanty, and Al Simmons) are enshrined, with Barry Bonds and the banned Pete Rose the exceptions. Perhaps coincidentally, Raines's number eight ranking coincides with the 2001 one from *The New Bill James Historical Baseball Abstract*, though in James's system, it's Williams, Stan Musial (classified as a rightfielder in JAWS), Bonds, Henderson, Yaz, Shoeless Joe Jackson, and Simmons ahead of him.

Raines is often slighted because he doesn't measure up to Henderson, his direct contemporary, a 2009 Hall of Fame inductee who has been widely hailed as the best leadoff hitter of all time, and who produced 60% more value over the course of his career while rewriting the record books. Over the span of Henderson's career, which ran from 1979–2003, the only outfielders who outproduced Raines were Rickey, Bonds (143.9), and Griffey (78.5). Next on the list is Gwynn, whose career spanned from 1982–2001, and whose career, peak, and JAWS numbers (68.1/41.1/54.9) Raines beats across the board.

Gwynn, who ranks 14th in JAWS among rightfielders, 3.2 points below the standard, gets the glory because of his 3,141 hits, five 200-hit seasons, and eight batting titles. Raines won only one batting title, and never reached 200 hits due to his ability to generate so many walks. Even so, he holds up quite well in a direct comparison:

Player	AVG/OBP/SLG (OPS+)	ISO	HR	SB	TOB	TB	BG
Gwynn	.338/.388/.459 (132)	.121	135	319	3955	4259	5267
Raines	.294/.385/.425 (123)	.131	170	838	3977	3771	5805

TOB is times on base (H + BB + HBP), while BG is bases gained, the numerator of Tom Boswell's briefly chic mid-'80s Total Average stat (TB + BB + HBP + SB - CS), presented here to show that Raines's edge on the basepaths helped to make up for Gwynn's ability to crank out hits. The point is better served via the more comprehensive WAR component valuations:

Player	Batting	Base	DP	Field	Pos	Rep	RAR
Gwynn	403	23	6	6	-85	325	678
Raines	291	115	8	-7	-86	350	670

Reading across: batting runs, baserunning runs, double play avoidance runs, fielding runs, positional adjustment runs, replacement level runs (based on playing time), and runs above replacement (the total of the six columns).

Either way, the conclusion is the same: Gwynn and Raines were two fantastic ballplayers, one disproportionately heralded in his time thanks to his extreme success by the traditional measures of batting average and hits, the other underappreciated despite a broader skill set that was better appreciated via advanced statistics. The point wasn't that Raines was a hair more valuable on both career and peak measures, it was that the two were equivalent, with no reason why one should languish outside the Hall while the other was in.

Yet Raines languished. Debuting on the 2008 ballot, he received just 24.3%, less than one-third of what he would need for election. Was it the cocaine problem from his past? No voter came forward to say so, and given that in 2004 Paul Molitor, who had his own dalliances with the drug, was elected, it takes some imagination to think that the writers would use such a double standard given that Raines was able to overcome his problem.

After dipping even lower in the voting in 2009, Raines gradually moved in the right direction, aided in part by the growing acceptance of sabermetrics within Hall of Fame debates. He reached 37.5% in 2011, and then 52.2% in 2013, a mark that strongly suggested eventual enshrinement. Alas, when the 2014 first-ballot trio of Tom Glavine, Greg Maddux, and Frank Thomas arrived, Raines's share slipped back down to 46.1%, and to add insult to injury, immediately after their induction the Hall unilaterally introduced a rule truncating the eligibility of all candidates save for Lee Smith, Alan Trammell, and Don Mattingly (heading into their 13th, 14th, and 15th years on the ballot, respectively) from 15 years to 10. If this was a grandfather clause, it was the one in which grandpa was sent to that crooked home the Simpson family saw on *60 Minutes*. Instead of having just passed the midpoint of what appeared to be a slow, Blyleven-esque climb to the 75% consensus, Raines had three turns left.

As the Raines gospel spread over the Internet and television (primarily via MLB Network and in particular Brian Kenny's *MLB Now* show), an increasing number of voters came to appreciate not only his credentials, but the urgency of his situation. With voters setting records for names per ballot (8.41) and 10-slot use (51%), Raines rebounded to 55.0% in 2015, as holdover Craig Biggio and first-timers Randy Johnson, Pedro Martinez, and John Smoltz were elected. Still needing a final 20-point push over two election cycles, his momentum didn't stop; he jumped to 69.8% in 2016, missing by just 23 votes. With an assist from Montreal-born writer Jonah Keri—the author of *Up, Up, & Away*, a history of the Expos, and a contributor to *Sports Illustrated* and CBS.com—who conducted a targeted outreach to voters reminiscent of Rich Lederer's campaign for Blyleven, Raines reached 86.0% in his final turn on the ballot, the highest share for any last-call honoree.

Raines finally received the recognition he deserved for his tremendous career, and his advocates chalked up a victory in rescuing his candidacy from oblivion. Of the 84 players elected by the writers since 1966, only five fared worse in their ballot debuts: Duke Snider (17.0%), Blyelven (17.5%), Don Drysdale (21.0%), Billy Williams (23.4%), and Bruce Sutter (23.9%). Together, Raines and his fans expanded the realm of what's possible regarding the Hall of Fame in the twenty-first century. In the wake of the announcement of his election, he issued a statement via Twitter, thanking his teammates and his fans, and setting aside a few words for the unique path he took to Cooperstown: "I would like to thank everyone in the media who advocated for my [H]all of [F]ame candidacy. I can't tell you how much it means to me that this honor was so important to you as well."[5]

At the Hall of Fame press conference the next day at the St. Regis Hotel in New York, the 57-year-old Raines beamed as he was introduced. Watching him, it was difficult not to think of the late Ron Santo and other Hall of Famers who never got to bask in the limelight. "This is my tenth year, my last year of eligibility, and the writers finally got it right,"[6] he joked. Amen.

CASE STUDY: MINNIE MINOSO

He played with reckless abandon aimed always at achieving nothing short of total victory; his was flair with a clear work ethic. He stole bases with a game on the line, harassed pitchers with daring base-running ploys, took extra bases and made impossible wall-crashes catches.[7]

—PETER BJARKMAN

In May 2014, the Hall of Fame unveiled "The New Face of Baseball: Osvaldo Salas's American Baseball Photographs 1950–1958," exhibiting the work of a Cuban-born photojournalist who documented the influx of Latin and African American players into the majors in the wake of Jackie Robinson's debut. Prominently featured near photos of icons Ernie Banks and Willie Mays is a shot of Orestes "Minnie" Minoso, recognized as "the first Afro-Latino big leaguer and the first black player to don a Chicago White Sox uniform."[8] Nearby is an inscription, set high on the wall:

Orestes Minoso was the Jackie Robinson for all Latinos; the first star who opened doors for all Latin American players. He was everybody's hero. I wanted to be Minoso. Clemente wanted to be Minoso.[9]—Orlando Cepeda

Cepeda's words are from an interview with the Puerto Rico–born Hall of Fame slugger that plays in the museum's "¡Viva Baseball!" exhibit, in which Minoso, "The Cuban Comet," is prominently featured. While Minoso's work as a pioneer is thus acknowledged in the Hall, he's been deprived of the ultimate honor of induction despite his run as one of the American League's top players, one of the institution's most glaring injustices.

Some history is in order. Before Robinson broke the color barrier in 1947, dozens of players from Latin America played their part in bending it—53 from 1902-46, according to historian Adrian Burgos Jr.[10] While darker-skinned Latinos who came stateside had no hope of crossing the color line, a smattering of lighter-skinned ones were signed by major league teams, starting with Cuban-born Esteban "Steve" Bellan, who played with the Troy Haymakers and New York Mutuals of the National Association from 1871–73. In 1910, the Reds signed Cubans Rafael Almeida and Armando Marsans, with team president and owner Gerry Herrmann convincing the Cincinnati press that the pair were "two of the purest bars of Castille soap that ever floated to these shores."[11] Others followed in their wake, including Reds pitcher Dolf Luque in the early 1920s, the first Cuban to attain stardom. Mel Almada became the first Mexican major leaguer in 1933, Alex Carrasquel the first from Venezuela in 1939, and Hiram Birthorn the first Puerto Rican player in 1942.

Still, the majors were off limits to dark-skinned Latinos before Robinson arrived. Indians owner Bill Veeck, the maverick who integrated the AL by signing Larry Doby less than three months after Robinson's debut, signed Minoso out of the Negro Leagues after the 1948 season, though he didn't get a chance to establish himself in the majors until 1951. Once he did, he became one of the game's top all-around players, a dynamo with speed, an excellent batting eye, considerable pop, and no shortage of flair. From 1951–64, he earned All-Star honors seven times, won three Gold Gloves, and drew MVP consideration. Not only did he have to endure discriminatory practices and racial slights similar to what the first wave of black American players encountered, he faced a language barrier and a foreign culture as well. Opponents hit him with pitches and spewed venomous slurs at him. One team released a black cat onto the field in front of him, calling it "Minnie." Segregated restaurants and hotels prevented him from dining and staying with his teammates. Amid such trying circumstances, Minoso not only avoided intimidation and retaliation—taking great pains not to play into the stereotype of the hot-blooded Latino—but thrived.

After that 1951–1964 run, Minoso played and managed in the Mexican League, then returned to the Veeck-owned White Sox, first as a coach, and then in both 1976 and 1980 as a late-season DH/pinch-hitter. Those stints, which carried into his 50s, made him the second major leaguer to play in parts of five decades (1940s through '80s) and elevated his status as one of the game's great ambassadors. Alas, they might have cost him Hall of Fame votes, because the gimmickry may have obscured the greatness of his prime, and the writers most familiar with Minoso may have missed the full opportunity to vote for him. The Hall's own rules, which have prevented voters from considering the totality of his accomplishments on both sides of the color line, have cost him as well. Less than three months after falling short via the 2015 Golden Era Committee balloting, Minoso passed away, well into his 90s. That his exact age is something of a mystery figures into our story.

The Career

Indians 1949 • 1951, 1958–59 • White Sox 1951–57, 1960–61, '64, '76, '80 • Cardinals 1962 • Senators 1963

Player	Career	Peak	JAWS	H	HR	SB	AVG/OBP/SLG	OPS+
Minnie Minoso	50.2	39.8	45.0	1,963	186	205	.298/.389/.459	130
Avg HOF LF	65.2	41.5	53.3					
LF Rank	25th	13th	22nd					
(Above HOF)	(5/20)	(11/20)	(6/20)					

Minoso's most basic biographic details are confusing. The son of Carlos Arrieta and Cecilia Armas was born in El Perico, Cuba, a town near Havana, on November 29 sometime between 1922 and 1925. In his 1994 memoir, *Just Call Me Minnie*, Minoso claimed, "I was 19 years old when I arrived in the United States in 1945, but my papers said I was 22. I told a white lie . . . to obtain a visa, so I could qualify for service in the Cuban army. My true date of birth is the 29th of November, 1925."[12]

On this matter, however, he must be regarded as an unreliable narrator. His official Web site uses the 1922 birthdate, while his 1946 Cuban passport shows 1923. Upon news of his passing, the White Sox claimed he was 90 years old, which would put 1924 as his birth year. Baseball-Reference.com uses 1925. That's hitting for the cycle—call it The Four Ages of Minnie.

More clearly, the hero of The Four Ages of Minnie was baptized as Saturnino Orestes Arrieta Armas, but became known as Minoso because his mother had four children from a previous marriage by that name. "Minnie," as the story goes, came from a misunderstanding involving a dentist named Dr. Robinson calling for his female receptionist, Minnie. Upon becoming a U.S. citizen sometime in the 1980s, he legally changed his name to Orestes Minoso.

Growing up, Minoso worked in the sugarcane fields like his father, and learned baseball while playing in the sandlots with older half-brother Francisco Minoso. Modeling his game after Cuban star Martin Dihigo (elected to the Hall of Fame in 1977), he played every position at one time or another, including catcher and pitcher. In 1943, he began playing semipro ball for $2 per game for Ambrosia Candy, and worked his way up the sport's ladder, moving on to cigar manufacturer Partegas's team, the Marianao winter Cuban League team (where he won Rookie of the Year honors in 1945 while making $200 per month), and then the New York Cubans of the Negro National League, who offered him $300 per month. The aforementioned Carrasquel was the one who signed him.

Encouraged by the Dodgers' signing of Robinson in October 1945—heralding the upcoming challenge to MLB's long-standing color barrier—Minoso came to the United States. Playing primarily at third base, he starred for the Cubans from 1946–48, helping them win the NNL pennant in 1947 and starting for the East team in the All-Star Game. Acting on a tip from Harlem Globetrotters owner Abe Saperstein, whose players sometimes suited up for Negro League teams to earn extra money, Veeck purchased Minoso's contractual rights from Cubans owner Alex Pompez for $15,000 after Minoso helped them win the Negro League World Series in 1948. Sent to the Indians' Dayton affiliate to finish the season, Minoso set the Central League ablaze, going 21-for-40 with nine extra-base hits in 11 games.

That wasn't enough to crack the lineup of the Indians, who had won the World Series in 1948 with a lineup that featured All-Star Ken Keltner at third base as well as Doby and hot-hitting Dale Mitchell in the outfield. In addition to Doby, the Indians' roster also included Satchel Paige, another former Negro Leaguer. Adding another, at a time when three-quarters of AL teams had yet to integrate, may have seemed like a bridge too far. Thus Minoso spent most of 1949 and '50 pulverizing Pacific Coast League pitching for the San Diego Padres, the Indians' highest-level affiliate. He did play nine games for the big club in '49, debuting on April 19 and becoming just the eighth black player in modern major league history.

Minoso went 3-for-20 during his brief stay in Cleveland and was lost in the shuffle after Veeck sold the team in November 1949 to raise cash to settle his divorce. Minoso spent 1950 in San Diego, and while he broke camp with the Indians to start '51, he was limited to pinch-hitting and backing up starting first baseman Luke Easter, another former Negro Leagues star. On April 30, a day after Minoso went 5-for-8 with a pair of doubles while starting at first for both games of a doubleheader, he was dealt to the White Sox as part of a three-team, seven-player trade that also included the Philadelphia A's. The newly liberated Cuban Comet announced his presence in Chicago the next day by clouting a two-run homer off the Yankees' Vic Raschi as part of a 2-for-4 day. His debut made the White Sox the sixth team to integrate, following the Dodgers, Indians, Browns, Giants, and Braves.

Minoso split time between third base and both outfield corners for the Sox in 1951, hitting a sizzling .326/.422/.500 with 10 homers and a 151 OPS+ while leading the league in triples (14), steals (31), and hit-by-pitches (16), finishing second in batting average and fourth in WAR (5.5). Sox fans took to him to such a degree that September 23 of that season became Minnie Minoso Day, when the rookie was showered with gifts, including a television and a Packard. Thanks to Minoso's performance and the maturations of double play combo Nellie Fox and Chico Carrasquel (nephew of Alex) as well as staff ace Billy Pierce, the White Sox snapped a streak of seven straight losing seasons, improving from 60-94 in 1950 to 81-73.

For his stellar season, Minoso placed second in the AL Rookie of the Year voting behind the Yankees' Gil McDougald, and fourth in the AL MVP vote behind three of McDougald's New York teammates, including the winner, Yogi Berra. Many around the game, including venerable *New York World-Telegram and Sun* scribe Dan Daniel and White Sox general manager Frank Lane, suggested that the Yankees' pennant weighed too heavily in determining the Rookie of the Year. *The Sporting News* gave its own AL Rookie of the Year award to Minoso, based upon a poll of 227 BBWAA writers instead of just the three per city from the BBWAA vote.

Award or no, Minoso's stellar season began an 11-year stretch over which he hit .305/.395/.471 (134 OPS+) while averaging 16 homers, 18 steals, and 4.7 WAR per year. He was a constant presence on AL leaderboards topping the circuit in steals and triples three times apiece, and in total bases once. He ranked among the top 10 in on-base percentage nine times (five times in the top five), in batting average and OPS+ eight times apiece, and in slugging percentage six times. His OBP received an extra boost via his tendency to crowd the plate and get hit by pitches; he led the league a record 10 times in that painful category, and more than a half-century after the end of his days as a regular, his 192 times taking one for the team still ranks ninth all-time.

Those hit-by-pitches carried a cost. In 1955, three years before the AL began requiring batting helmets, a pitch from the Yankees' Bob Grim fractured Minoso's skull, sidelining him for 15 games. "I been hit in head eight times. But I rather die than stop playing. Is best game in the world,"[13] Minoso told the *New York World-Telegram and Sun's* Lou Miller, who like many other scribes of the era insisted upon quoting Minoso in broken English. "My first year in big league in 1951 one team—I no tell who—always call me names. They say, 'We hit you in head, you black——.' I think they try make me afraid."[14]

Given all of the times he was drilled, remarkably the 1955 season was the only one in that 1951–61 span in which Minoso played fewer than 146 games, and the schedule didn't expand from 154 games to 162 until the final year of that stretch. Nearly 60 years after that incident, in the final interview of his life, Minoso illuminated the connection between his propensity for being plunked and a larger philosophy of life:

> What was I doing wrong in the game, that they'd purposefully want to hit me? They didn't do it because I'm nice-looking, and I didn't do it to get the record. I crowded the plate, because if you only have to look middle-outside, you can kill a pitcher, and if it's outside it's a ball.
>
> My father and my mother taught me there was a way to pay somebody back, if they tried to break your arm or break your face: Pay them back on the field with a smile on your face. I used to keep my teeth clean all the time, just to make sure that's how I gave it back to them.[15]

Minoso earned All-Star honors seven times, starting for the AL in 1954, '59 (the first of two games), and '60 (both games), and he won three Gold Gloves after the award was introduced in 1957. He finished fourth in the AL MVP voting four times, and ranked among the top 10 in WAR six times, with his 8.2 WAR leading the league in 1954. His 52.1 WAR over the 1951–61 span ranked eighth in the majors, and second in the slow-to-integrate AL behind only Mickey Mantle. Only Fox and Richie Ashburn collected more hits than Minoso's 1,861 in that span, while only Ashburn and Mantle topped his 2,806 times on base.

Minoso helped the White Sox to seven straight winning seasons from 1951–57, but despite winning as many as 94 games, the team climbed no higher than second place. In December 1957, he was traded back to the Indians in a four-player deal that sent future Hall of Famer Early Wynn to Chicago. Taking over the mantle of staff ace, Wynn would win the 1959 AL Cy Young Award while helping the "Go-Go Sox"—by this time owned by Veeck—to their first pennant since their infamous 1919 one, though they lost to the Dodgers in the World Series.

The Sox reacquired Minoso via a seven-player deal in December 1959, with Veeck granting him an honorary AL championship ring for his role in helping return the club to prominence via the Wynn trade. Again the Cuban Comet made a splash in his first game with Chicago, hitting a pair of homers (including a grand slam) against the Kansas City A's on Opening Day, thus setting off fireworks on Comiskey Park's new $350,000 "exploding" scoreboard. Believed to be 37 years old at the time, Minoso hit a fairly typical .311/.374/.481 with 20 homers, 17 steals, and his final All-Star berth.

After his performance slipped a bit in 1961, Minoso was traded to the Cardinals in November. Though slated to join an outfield that included Curt Flood and Stan Musial, he was limited to 39 games and a meager .196/.271/.278 showing due to a pulled rib cage muscle, then fractures of his skull (again) and right wrist suffered when he crashed into a concrete wall in Busch Stadium. Cardinals trainer Doc Bauman told reporters, "His skull was cracked in five places. It was like hitting a coconut with a hammer."[16] A day after being activated, Minoso was hit in the right eye by an errant warm-up throw.

Just after the season, the Cardinals traded for All-Star outfielder George Altman, and the following spring Minoso was sold to the Senators, who were bound for 106 losses. He struggled to a .229/.315/.317 performance in a reserve role, then returned to the White Sox in 1964, but made just 38 plate appearances, mainly as a pinch-hitter, before drawing his release. Commissioner Ford Frick blocked Chicago's attempt to restore him to the active roster in September, on the grounds that the team had violated the intent of the rules by sending Minoso to the PCL and then repurchasing him six weeks later.

Still a drawing card in Latin America, and able to play baseball at a reasonably competitive level, Minoso spent the 1965–74 period in the Mexican League and its minor leagues, generally serving as player-manager. When Veeck repurchased the White Sox in 1976, he hired Minoso as a coach. Introducing some levity into their 97-loss season, the Sox activated him in September of that year, and Minoso went 1-for-8 in three games as a designated hitter. His September 12 single off the Angels' Sid Monge led to a 1977 Topps baseball card celebrating him as the oldest player to hit safely, just short of his 54th birthday, breaking the record of 53-year-old Nick Altrock. That distinction was based on the 1922 birthdate; using the '25 date, he's merely the fourth-oldest to get a hit. Minoso remained as a coach through the 1978 season and reappeared with the team in '80, Veeck's final season of ownership. Though he was hitless in two pinch-hitting appearances, he joined Altrock as the only other player to appear in the majors in five different decades.

Commissioner Fay Vincent quashed the White Sox attempt to reprise that role in 1990, calling it "a publicity stunt that would hurt baseball's integrity" for a 68-year-old player (as Minoso was believed to be) to appear in a major league game, and thus not "in the best interests of baseball."[17] The independent Northern League's St. Paul Saints, who did not have to answer to Vincent—and who were partly owned by Mike Veeck, a chip off the old block—signed Minoso to make a cameo in June 1993. In late September that year, after the White Sox had clinched the AL West, acting commissioner Bud Selig and AL president Bobby Brown overturned Vincent's ruling, clearing the way for another big league cameo, but when the players union immediately denounced the plan as "ridiculous"[18] due to his age, the idea was quashed. Minoso did suit up once more for the Saints in 2003, giving him professional appearances in seven decades.

The Case

On the surface, Minoso's traditional stats—particularly his 1,963 hits, 186 homers, and 205 steals—don't cry out for enshrinement, nor do his WAR-based numbers. Among leftfielders, he's 25th in career WAR, 15 wins below the standard at the position and ahead of just five out of 20 Hall of Famers (Ralph Kiner, Jim Rice, Heinie Manush, Lou Brock, and Chick Hafey). His peak WAR makes a stronger case, as he ranks 13th, 1.7 wins below the standard, but still ahead of 11 out of the 19 enshrined, including Joe Medwick, Willie Stargell, and Jesse Burkett. Minoso's 45.0 JAWS ranks 22nd at the position, above just six of the 20.

The big question is how much of Minoso's major league career is missing due to circumstances beyond his control, namely baseball's color line and his age when it was broken, given the uncertainty surrounding his birthdate. The 1922 date that was assumed to be correct during his career places him at 28 years old—the same age as the rookie Robinson—when he got his first shot at full-time play in 1951 while the '25 date would make him 25. Given his performances against PCL pitching (.297/.371/.483 in 1949, and .339/.405/.539 in '50) it seems clear that Minoso was deprived of at least two big league seasons, and he may have lost as many as five, given his star-caliber play in the Negro Leagues as early as 1946, when he reportedly hit .309; he was an All-Star in his other two Negro League seasons. Recall that Minoso put up 5.5 WAR in in his first full season and that the seventh-best season within that aforementioned peak score was worth 4.0 WAR; it seems entirely possible that he could have improved upon that with an earlier arrival, to say nothing of boosting his total value.

Alas, the long coda to Minoso's major league career caused his Hall of Fame candidacy to slip through the cracks in a variety of ways, but not before one of the stranger clerical errors in the modern history of the voting. Though he had been out of the majors for just three years instead of the necessary five, Minoso was mistakenly included on the 1968 ballot. As forgettable as his '63 and '64 seasons may have been, they did count. Minoso didn't get any votes in '68, but when he was listed again the following year, he received six stray votes.

Minoso did not appear on the 1970 ballot, the one on which he would have debuted under current rules. Because the Mexican League, in which he was playing at the time, was (and is) considered part of organized baseball, he was still considered an active player by a rule that was only in place for a few years. That same rule delayed consideration of Hall of Famers Warren Spahn and Robin Roberts (see Chapter 17). At that point, Hall voters of any stripe had not yet begun to consider players on the basis of Negro League accomplishments; the Committee on Negro League Veterans that elected Satchel Paige wasn't established until 1971.

Minoso's 1976 and '80 returns to the majors both reset his eligibility clock, so that he didn't reappear on the writers' ballot until '86, more than two decades removed from his time as a regular. By that point, many if not most of the voters were more familiar with his token appearances than his brilliant prime, to say nothing of the conditions under which he broke in. He never drew more than 21.1% before his BBWAA eligibility lapsed in 1999. The Veterans Committee, which radically expanded to include all living Hall of Famers and Spink and Frick Award winners (for writers and broadcasters) in 2001, gave Minoso just 16 out of 81 votes in 2003, his first year of consideration. He fared even worse on the 2005, '07, and '09 ballots, none of which elected a single player whose major league career began after 1943.

Minoso was also bypassed by the Special Committee on the Negro Leagues, which in 2006 elected 17 players to the Hall from a panel of 39 finalists, following half a decade of extensive research into the history of the Negro Leagues and its predecessors. Neither Minoso nor Negro Leagues star and manager (and major league scout) Buck O'Neill, the only two candidates still alive at the time, were among the 17. As historian and committee member Adrian Burgos Jr. wrote, the committee could not consider Minoso's accomplishments in the major leagues in this context, a rule he termed "arcane." He added: "The end result is that a player who ranks as one of the definitive stars of baseball's integration era has repeatedly fallen short of election."[19]

Indeed, the Hall's insistence upon pigeonholing honorees has worked against Minoso, since candidates are elected either as Negro Leaguers or major leaguers, players or managers/executives. While Paige, Monte Irvin, and Willard Brown played in the majors, they didn't have the requisite 10 years in the MLB to be considered in that context, so they were elected as Negro Leaguers. Robinson and Doby, on the other hand, had the 10 years, but while the former was elected at the first opportunity in 1962, the latter was slighted until 1998, 51 years after he made history, 39 years after the end of his career, and just five years before his death. Doby, who began playing in the Negro Leagues in 1942, five years before his MLB debut, had a comparable on-field impact to Minoso:

Player	PA	AVG/OBP/SLG	OPS+	Field	dWAR	Career	Peak	JAWS
Doby	6,299	.283/.386/.490	136	22	-0.1	49.5	39.6	44.6
Minoso	7,712	.298/.389/.459	130	26	-5.7	50.2	39.8	45.0

The VC recognized Doby's historical importance, albeit belatedly, while placing his short-career numbers in the context both of his peers and the obstacles that he faced. They ought to have been able to do the same for Minoso, particularly in light of testimonials such as those of Cepeda, Cuban-born Hall of Famer Tony Perez, and more recent Cuban defectors such as the White Sox's Jose Abreu and Alexi Ramirez, for whom Minoso's success in the majors set an example. "Without Minnie, without his courage to leave Cuba for the major leagues, without his willingness to accept taunts and slights, none of us would be major leaguers,"[20] said Ramirez in 2015.

The VC was overhauled in favor of the three era-based committees in time for the 2012 slate. Minoso received nine out of 16 votes from the Golden Era Committee that year—a better result than from the expanded VC, at least—while Ron Santo was posthumously elected. Minoso came up for election again on the 2015 ballot and received eight out of 16 votes; nobody from among the 10 candidates was elected. At the press conference to announce the results, voter Steve Hirdt said the committee's disappointment over the failure to elect anyone "is mitigated to some degree by the fact that there will be another day for the candidates,"[21] a load of hogwash that not only stood as a bitter reminder of Santo's fate, but foreshadowed Minoso's. "Don't tell me that maybe I'll get in after I pass away," Minoso said in his final interview. "I don't want it to happen after I pass. I want it while I'm here, because I want to enjoy it."[22]

Unfortunately, Minoso's death on March 1, 2015, means that, at best, the Hall will write another chapter in its cruel history of belatedly bestowing baseball immortality on all-too-mortal candidates. His candidacy won't be considered again until the 2021 Golden Days Era Committee. Given not only his statistical accomplishments but his cultural importance, his omission will continue to stand out like a sore thumb. He belongs in Cooperstown alongside Robinson, Doby, Clemente, Banks, and the other pioneers and icons who changed the face of baseball.

THE ROUNDUP

The number before each player name refers to his JAWS ranking *among all players at the position*, not necessarily those in the Hall. Average HOF leftfielder: 65.2/41.5/53.3.

The Elite (above standard in career, peak, and JAWS)

2. Ted Williams

Teams:	Red Sox 1939–42, 1946–60
Stats:	.344/.482/.634 • 190 OPS+ • 2,654 H • 521 HR • 24 SB
Rankings:	17× All-Star • 6× led AVG • 6× led WAR • 5× S/S TC
	All-time: 1st OBP • 2nd SLG • 2nd OPS+ • 4th BB • 6th
	AVG • 11th WAR • 18th HR
Voting/JAWS:	BBWAA 1966 **(1st, 93.4%)** • **123.1/69.2/96.2**

Is "The Greatest Hitter Who Ever Lived" an accurate honorific? Teddy Ballgame's got a case, even while trailing Babe Ruth by 56 points in slugging percentage and 16 in OPS+. His military service (1943–45 and all but 43 games in 1952–53) cost him 3,000-hit and 600-homer milestones, and probably the lead in batting runs, where his 1,069 trails only Ruth (1,335) and Barry Bonds (1,128); at his career rate, he'd have needed another 573 games to surpass the Bambino. He might have challenged both in WAR (Ruth 163.1, Bonds 162.4) as well, considering that he *averaged* 10.5 in the two years on either side of his World War II stint. Beyond his greatness, Williams had an outsized impact on the Hall via his 1966 induction speech, which called for the inclusion of Satchel Paige and Josh Gibson "as symbols of the great Negro players who are not here only because they weren't given the chance."[23] Paige was elected by the Committee on Negro League Veterans in 1971, Gibson in '72. Williams's 1986–2001 tenure on the VC was a mixed bag, though the elections of Larry Doby and George Davis rank as two of its best choices.

3. Rickey Henderson

Teams:	A's 1979–84, 89–93, 94–95, '98 • Yankees 1985–89 • Blue Jays 1993 • Padres 1996–97, 2001 • Angels 1997 • Mets 1999–2000 • Mariners 2000 • Red Sox 2002 • Dodgers 2003
Stats:	.279/.401/.419 • 127 OPS+ • 3,055 H • 297 HR • 1,406 SB
Rankings:	12× led SB • 10× All-Star • 9× top 3 OBP

All-time: 1st SB • 1st Runs • 1st CS • 2nd BB • 4th TOB •
14th WAR
Voting/JAWS: BBWAA 2009 **(1st, 94.8%)** • **110.8/57.4/84.1**

"If you could split him in two, you'd have two Hall of Famers . . . the greatest power/speed combination of all time (except maybe Barry Bonds)." [24]

—Bill James

Henderson's single-season and all-time stolen base records are his top calling card, but his dazzling speed and derring-do on the basepaths—worth a record 145 runs on its own (you were expecting Bengie Molina?)—shouldn't obscure how complete a ballplayer he was. Reaching base more times (5,304) than all but Pete Rose, Bonds, and Ty Cobb, he was a constant on the OBP leaderboard, with 16 top 10 finishes, and scored a record 2,295 runs. Via his considerable pop, he hit a record 81 career leadoff home runs, and fell just short of 300 total. With excellent range (if not a great arm), he added another 65 runs defensively. Add it all up and he's 14th all-time in WAR, and yes, there are 63 MLB position players in Cooperstown with 55.4 WAR or less. The Half-Hendersons, we'll call 'em . . .

4. Carl Yastrzemski

Teams: Red Sox 1961–83
Stats: .285/.379/.462 • 130 OPS+ • 3,419 H • 452 HR • 168 SB
Rankings: 18× All-Star • 7× GG • 5× led OBP • 4× led OPS+ • 3× led
                    SLG • 3× led AVG • 3× led WAR • 1967 AL Triple Crown
                    All-time: 2nd G • 5th TOB • 6th BB • 9th H • 9th TB
Voting/JAWS: BBWAA 1989 **(1st, 94.6%)** • **96.1/55.4/75.8**

The Splendid Splinter's successor sometimes gets lost in his shadow, but Yaz deserves his own spotlight. Remarkably durable, he played in more games than anyone but Rose, and among post-nineteenth-century players is tied for second with Dave Winfield for the most batting-title-qualified seasons with an OPS+ of at least 100, at 19 (Cobb had 21). Particularly dominant from 1967–70, he led the AL in a slash stat eight times, and in OPS+ and WAR three times apiece. His 12.4 WAR in 1967, his Triple Crown season, is tops among position players besides Ruth, and his 10.5 WAR follow-up makes him one of just five post-Ruth players with back-to-back 10-win seasons—along with Williams (1941–42), Mickey Mantle (1956–57), Willie Mays (1962–65) (!), and Bonds (2001–02). Stellar defensive metrics (+134 runs in left field, second only to Bonds's 179, with +48 at first base as well) bolster both his claim on those Gold Gloves and his WAR. His final four years were window dressing, but as just the fourth hitter to reach the twin plateaus of 3,000 hits and 400 homers behind Stan Musial, Mays, and Hank Aaron, he earned a bit of slack.

6. Ed Delahanty

Teams: Philadelphia Quakers/Phillies 1888–89, 1891–1901 •
                 Cleveland Infants (PL) 1890 • Senators 1902–03

Stats: .346/.411/.505 • 152 OPS+ • 2,597 H • 101 HR • 455 SB

Rankings: 9× top 5 WAR • 5× led SLG • 4× led OPS+ • 2× led OBP •
                 2× led AVG

Voting/JAWS: OTC 1945 • **69.5/48.5/59.0**

The oldest and best of five major league brothers, Delahanty is most famous for dying at age 35 by falling off a bridge into Niagara Falls. Despondent over the voiding of a lucrative three-year deal with the Giants, he went on a months-long drinking binge that culminated with his being kicked off a train on the Canadian side of the Falls for brandishing a razor, and soon afterward either slipped or jumped off the bridge. He was perhaps the game's best player from 1893 until his death, posting videogame numbers half a century before the word "video" was invented. He hit .400 or better three times, led in a slash stat category nine times, and in 1902 hit .376/.453/.590 to win the slash stat Triple Crown—or did he? Napoleon Lajoie was believed to have hit .368 that year, but more than 90 years later researchers discovered Lajoie was missing four hits; his revised .378 is tops via the qualification standard of the day (appearance in 60% of a team's games). From 1893–1902, Delahanty ranked fourth in WAR, finishing outside the top 10 in WAR just once, and leading in the bookend years. Even so, amid the illness of his wife, mounting gambling debts, and his nullified 1903 contract, the bottle was figuratively and literally his downfall.

7. Al Simmons

Teams: A's 1924–32, 1940–41, '44 • White Sox 1933–35 • Tigers
                 1936 • Senators 1937–38 • Braves 1939 • Reds 1939 • Red
                 Sox 1943

Stats: .334/.380/.535 • 133 OPS+ • 2,927 H • 307 HR • 88 SB

Rankings: 10× top 10 OPS+ • 8× top 5 AVG • 8× top 5 SLG • 7× top
                 10 WAR • 5× top 10 OBP • 3× All-Star

Voting/JAWS: BBWAA 1953 **(7th, 75.4%)** • **68.7/45.7/57.2**

A staple of three pennant-winning A's teams from 1929–31, "Bucketfoot Al"—after his unorthodox batting stance—was the fastest player to 1,500, 2,000, and 2,500 hits in terms of games played. Simmons put up lofty slash stats when offense was at its twentieth-century peak, winning batting titles in 1930 (.381) and '31 (.390), and topping .350 six times in a seven-year span during which the nonpitcher league average was .299. With his considerable pop, he ran off eight straight years (1925–32) in the league's top five in slugging percentage. After hitting a combined .354/.398/.574/146 OPS+ through 1934 (his age-32 season), he tailed off, managing merely a 100 OPS+ while changing teams seven times. Though it had no bearing on his enshrinement, falling short of 3,000 hits bothered him: "When I think of the days I goofed off, the times I played sick or something and took myself out of the lineup because the game didn't mean anything, I could cut my throat."[25]

9. Goose Goslin

Teams:	Senators 1921–30, '33, '38 • Browns 1930–32 • Tigers 1934–37
Stats:	.316/.387/.500 • 128 OPS+ • 2,735 H • 248 HR • 176 SB
Rankings:	9× top 10 HR • 8× top 10 SLG • 7× top 10 OPS+
Voting/JAWS:	VC 1968 • **66.1/43.3/54.7**

A mainstay of five AL champions—three in Washington, two in Detroit—Goslin was an outstanding all-around player, the fifth most valuable outfielder during the 1920–45 period behind Ruth, Mel Ott, Paul Waner, and Simmons. Much of his power was camouflaged by Washington's cavernous Griffith Stadium, the worst home run park of its era for a lefty. As a Senator, he hit 31 homers there, as opposed to 96 on the road. He had speed and a good enough arm to play right field, though with Washington, the presence of Sam Rice prevented that; even so, Goslin was 50 runs above average, mostly in left. From 1924–28, he ranked third in the AL in WAR four times, and only Ruth (49.2) and Rogers Hornsby (45.6) topped his 32.4 WAR in that span. While he never polled above 13% via the BBWAA, he's among the VC's best selections; among twentieth-century position players inducted via that route, only Ron Santo, Johnny Mize, Arky Vaughan, and Frank Baker score higher in JAWS.

The Rank and File

11. Billy Williams

Teams:	Cubs 1959–74 • A's 1975–76
Stats:	.290/.361/.492 • 133 OPS+ • 2,711 H • 426 HR • 90 SB

Rankings:	6× All-Star, 6× top 10 OPS+ • 5× top 5 HR • 4× top 10 WAR • 3× led TB
Voting/JAWS:	BBWAA 1987 **(6th, 85.7%)** • **63.5/41.3/52.4**

Younger than Ernie Banks by seven years and older than Santo by two, Williams was the last of the trio to establish himself in Chicago. A quiet, understated thumper, he ranked among the league's top 10 in total bases every year from 1962–72, leading three times, winning a batting title, and setting an NL record with 1,117 consecutive games, no small task in the broad daylight of Wrigley Field. The Friendly Confines boosted his stats (.309/.378/.539 with 231 homers there, .274/.348/.452 with 195 homers elsewhere), but his peak was fairly diffuse, with four seasons of 6+ WAR spread between 1963 (age 25) and 1972 (age 34). He remained an above-average hitter through 1975, when he became the 16th player to reach 400 homers and finally tasted the postseason. He debuted with just 23.4% in 1982, behind 11 future Hall of Famers, but within two years he was at 50.1%, his profile boosted by Steve Garvey's 1983 breaking of his iron man record.

12. Fred Clarke

Teams:	Louisville Colonels 1894–99 • Pirates 1901–11, 1913–15
Stats:	.312/.386/.429 • 133 OPS+ • 2,678 H • 67 HR • 509 SB
Rankings:	8× top 10 WAR • 8× top 10 OBP • 7× top 10 SLG • 7× top 10 AVG • 5× top 5 OPS+
Voting/JAWS:	VC 1945 • **67.8/36.1/52.0**

The best leftfielder of the dead-ball era after Delahanty, Clarke spent his career in the shadow of teammate Honus Wagner, though in serving as the Colonels' and Pirates' player-manager from mid-1897 through 1915—most of the Flying Dutchman's career—he was a prime beneficiary as well. As a hitter, Clarke spent 15 seasons (1897–1911) peppering NL slash stat leaderboards with a pair of runner-up finishes in batting races (one to Wagner in '03); both times he led in OPS+. Taking advantage of the speed that helped him to 220 triples (seventh all-time) and over 500 steals, he was a spectacular defender, known for playing deep and then coming in to make diving catches (as innovations go, he also patented flip-down sunglasses). His 91 fielding runs ranks fourth at the position, helping to push his WAR to within two wins of Delahanty for the lead among pre-1920 left-fielders. Throw in his success as a manager (1,602-1,181, .576), winning four pennants and the 1909 World Series, and he's a no-doubter, one of the most worthy entrants in the 1945 VC parade.

13. Jesse Burkett

Teams: Giants 1890 • Spiders 1891–98 • St. Louis Perfectos/
               Cardinals 1899–1901 • Browns 1902–04 • Red Sox 1905
Stats: .338/.415/.446 • 140 OPS+ • 2,850 H • 75 HR • 389 SB •
               17 SB
Rankings: 8x top 10 WAR • 7x top 5 AVG • 6x top 2 H
Voting/JAWS: VC 1946 • **62.9/37.2/50.0**

Known as "The Crab" for his ill temper toward fans, opponents, writers, and um-pires—he was the first player ejected from both ends of a doubleheader—the di-minutive (5′8″, 155 pounds) Burkett excelled at both bunting and fouling off pitches during the era before fouls counted as strikes. From 1893–1902, he won three batting titles, twice with averages above .400, with 16 top five finishes in slash stats and a combined .369/.445/.483 line; he averaged 206 hits in that span, and set a single-season record with 240 in 1896 (Cobb broke it in 1911). Though still effective at age 36, Burkett chose to purchase a franchise in the New England League after the 1905 season, and continued playing (and managing) in the minors past his 50th birthday. With another year or two in the majors in-stead, he'd have followed Cap Anson as the second player to reach 3,000 hits. Elected in 1946, he remained surly, remarking, "It took them a long time and I thought they weren't going to because everybody had forgotten me."[26]

15. Willie Stargell

Teams: Pirates 1962–82
Stats: .282/.360/.529 • 147 OPS+ • 2,232 H • 475 HR • 17 SB
Rankings: 7x All-Star • 6x top 5 SLG • 6x top 5 OPS+ • 5x top 5 HR
               • 3x top 10 WAR
               All-time: 30th HR • T-30th OPS+
Voting/JAWS: BBWAA 1988 **(1st, 82.4%)** • **57.5/38.0/47.7**

A tape-measure king, Stargell at one point held the distance record for home runs in nearly half of NL parks—some of which marked the spot, an awesome tribute to a visiting player. For all of that as well as his magnetic personality, particularly as the elder statesman of the 1979 champs (and a childhood favorite of this author), the reality is that he was somewhat overrated. True, he led the NL in homers and OPS+ twice apiece, was a key member of two championship teams, and was tied for 14th in homers when he retired. He was also lousy enough in both left field (-22 runs) and first base (-44 runs) to be near-DH caliber; his -19.7 defensive WAR (fielding runs + position adjustment) ranks as the 15th worst all-time, limiting his overall value. He was worth just 8.5 WAR from 1976 onward, including 2.5 in his '79 co-MVP season. Strong Octobers (MVP in both the NLCS and World Series in 1979, .278/.359/.511 in 153 postseason PA) help to explain his first-ballot election.

16. Joe Medwick

Teams:	Cardinals 1932–40, 1947–48 • Dodger 1940–43, '46 • Giants 1943–45 • Braves 1945
Stats:	.324/.362/.505 • 134 OPS+ • 2,471 H • 205 HR • 42 SB
Rankings:	10× All-Star • 7× top 5 AVG • 7× top 5 SLG • 6× top 10 WAR
Voting/JAWS:	BBWAA 1968 **(9th†, 84.8%)** • **55.6/39.7/47.6**

A "prize chip-on-the-shoulder muscleman"[27] for the Gashouse Gang–era Cardinals, Medwick was a much reviled brawler but a perennial All-Star. He ranked fifth in WAR for the 1933–44 span, helped St. Louis to a championship in '34 (even while being pelted with garbage by Tigers fans after a hard slide in the World Series), and won the MVP and the NL's last Triple Crown in '37, his only time leading in batting average, homers, or WAR. Traded to the Dodgers in June 1940, he sustained a severe beaning by ex-teammate Bob Bowman in his second post-trade game against St. Louis. Though commonly cited as a turning point for his career, the theory holds little water statistically—he missed three of the next four games, but hit much better over the remainder of the season than before, and his 1941 OPS+ and WAR are on par with his 1938–39 numbers. His "20-year slump"[28] from retirement to election owed to a frosty relationship with writers and his own overt campaigning; elected in his final year of eligibility, he died just seven years later at age 63.

17. Zack Wheat

Teams:	Superbas/Robins/Dodgers 1909–26 • A's 1927
Stats:	.317/.367/.450 • 129 OPS+ • 2,884 H • 132 HR • 205 SB
Rankings:	11× top 10 SLG • 11× top 10 HR • 7× top 5 AVG • 6× top 10 WAR • 5× top 5 OPS+
Voting/JAWS:	VC 1959 • **60.2/34.7/47.4**

The son of a Cherokee mother, Wheat set still standing franchise records for games and hits in 17 full seasons as a staple of Brooklyn lineups and NL leaderboards; he

---

† Years receiving votes prior to final year of career not counted.

was the big bat on the Robins' 1916 and '20 pennant winners. Though just the third batting champ in NL history to go homerless (in 1918), he was renowned as a slugger, refusing to choke up, swinging for the fences and weathering criticism for not bunting. Seven of his top 10 finishes in homers came via single-digit totals, but he reached double digits four times from 1921–25. His stylish play—"What Lajoie was to infielders, Zach [sic] Wheat is to outfielders, the finest mechanical craftsman of them all,"[29] wrote *Baseball Magazine* in 1917—added considerable defensive value (+54 runs) to his potent bat. Among pre-expansion-era leftfielders, only Simmons accumulated more hits, so the impulse to enshrine Wheat is understandable, though in retrospect half a dozen were more valuable. For the "Clerical Follies" file: The VC elected Wheat in 1957, then realized he was a year short of eligibility, and waited until convening two years later to officially give him the nod.

19. Ralph Kiner

Teams: Pirates 1946–53 • Cubs 1953–54 • Indians 1955

Stats: .279/.398/.548 • 149 OPS+ • 1,451 H • 369 HR • 22 SB

Rankings: 7× led HR • 6× All-Star • 6× top 5 SLG • 5× top 5 OPS+ • 4× top 5 WAR • 3× led BB

Voting/JAWS: BBWAA 1975 **(13th, 75.4%)** • **49.3/43.6/46.5**

When I designed JAWS, my focus on the peak component had everything to do with attempting to account for the election of players such as Kiner, Hank Greenberg, and Sandy Koufax, who dominated for stretches within shorter careers. After spending more than 2½ seasons as a navy pilot, Kiner led the NL in homers in each of his first seven campaigns, including a 54-homer year that ranked as the NL high between 1931–97. Fearsome enough to draw 98 or more walks in seven straight seasons, he had a combined 13 top ten finishes in OBP and SLG, with three leads in OPS+. Though a nagging back injury forced his retirement at age 32, he hit 80 more homers than any other player during his decade in the majors, and was more valuable than all but Musial, Williams, Jackie Robinson, and Pee Wee Reese. His peak score ranks eighth among leftfielders, but his road to Cooperstown took the full 20 years after retirement, and would have been derailed had the Five Percent Rule existed back then.

23. Joe Kelley

Teams: Boston Beaneaters/Doves 1891, 1908 • Pittsburgh Pirates 1892 • Baltimore Orioles (NL) 1892–98 • Brooklyn Superbas 1899–1901 • Baltimore Orioles (AL) 1902 • Reds 1902–06

Stats:	.317/.402/.451 • 134 OPS+ • 2,220 H • 65 HR • 443 SB
Rankings:	9× top 10 3B • 7× top 10 OBP • 7× top 10 SLG • 6× top 10 OPS+
	All-time: 9th 3B
Voting/JAWS:	VC 1971 • **50.6/36.2/43.4**

Alongside John McGraw, Willie Keeler, and Hughie Jennings, Kelley was the "Kingpin of the Orioles" during their mid-1890s heyday, part of three straight pennant winners there as well as two more in Brooklyn. A handsome devil, he kept a small mirror and comb in his back pocket to remain well groomed for female admirers in Kelleyville, the left field bleachers of Baltimore's Union Park, and kept extra baseballs in the outfield grass for when his speed and powerful arm weren't enough. Via his combination of speed and pop, he placed among the league's top 10 in triples nine times, and in a slash stat 17 times. Peeved by Oriole president Ned Hanlon's decision to move the team's nucleus to Brooklyn and then frustrated by a return to Baltimore with the fledgling AL, he moved to Cincinnati as player-manager as his skills declined, but couldn't push the team any higher than third. He's fifth in WAR among pre-1920 leftfielders, well behind Burkett and Clarke even with a nearly equivalent peak, yet still among the better choices of the Frisch VC—if there is such a thing.

28. Jim Rice

Teams:	Red Sox 1974–89
Stats:	.298/.352/.502 • 128 OPS+ • 2,452 H • 382 HR
Rankings:	8× All-Star • 5× top 3 SLG • 5× top 10 OPS+ • 3× led HR
Voting/JAWS:	BBWAA 2009 **(15th, 76.4%)** • **47.4/36.2/41.8**

En route to election in his final year of eligibility, Rice became a focal point in the war over old-school and new-school stats. His proponents cited the way his power numbers dominated his era, the respect he drew for his performances, and the fear he elicited in opposing players. They have points on the first two counts; from 1976–83, Rice had five top two finishes in slugging percentage, led four times in total bases and three times in homers, and placed in the top five in MVP balloting six times. Most of that is captured in his 147 Hall of Fame Monitor score. He did a ton of things that typical Hall of Famers do.

Regarding the fear factor, there's a lot of hot air in circulation. Rice may have intimidated the writers who covered him; Howard Bryant's *Shut Out: A Story of Race and Baseball in Boston* goes into great and painful detail, unraveling the slugger's tumultuous relationship with the media and the complex dynamics in play regarding his team and his city. At least some of the late momentum his candidacy picked up may have related to guilty consciences over his treatment, but a raw deal from the media does not cover for a flimsy statistical case. Opposing pitchers didn't pitch around Rice they way they did around Bonds or Pujols; he's tied for 195th in intentional walks (a stat uncounted before 1955) and has the 20th-lowest walk rate among the 141 players with 300 homers. Once you adjust for Fenway Park, his OPS+ showings aren't impressive, and he loses an MLB-high 42 runs for his tendency to ground into double plays. Aside from his league-leading 7.5 in WAR in 1978, he had just three other top 10 finishes, and ranks 27th among leftfielders in peak WAR, 29th in career WAR. If he's the standard, the Hall needs a wing to accommodate everyone who outranks him.

32. Heinie Manush

Teams: Tigers 1923–27 • Browns 1928–30 • Senators 1930–35 • Red Sox 1936 • Dodgers 1937–38 • Pirates 1938–39
Stats: .330/.377/.479 • 121 OPS+ • 2,524 H • 110 HR • 113 SB
Rankings: 6× top 5 AVG • 5× top 10 SLG • 5× OPS+ • 3× top 10 WAR
Voting/JAWS: VC 1964 • **45.8/34.7/40.2**

An acolyte of Cobb's with a noteworthy temper of his own—he's the rare player to be ejected from a World Series game—Manush peppered the AL leaderboards with high batting averages during the 1920s and '30s, winning a batting title in 1926. While he cranked out plenty of doubles and triples, the high-offense context lessens the impact of his contributions; he had four top five finishes in MVP voting, but just one in WAR. He's just 31st in WAR among position players from 1920–1945 (the start of the live-ball era to the end of the war), and never broke single digits in six BBWAA elections, yet the VC elected him the first time he was eligible, with a case that's less than half as interesting as the two players below him here.

36. Lou Brock

Teams: Cubs 1961–64 • Cardinals 1964–79
Stats: .293/.343/.410 • 109 OPS+ • 3,023 H • 149 HR • 938 SB
Rankings: 6× led SB • 6× All-Star • 5× top 10 AVG
All-time: 2nd SB • 25th H
Voting/JAWS: BBWAA 1985 **(1st, 79.7%)** • **45.2/32.0/38.6**

Cerebral and forward-thinking enough to film pitchers' windups and pickoff motions via 8mm camera as early as late 1964, Brock owned both the single-season and all-time stolen base records when he retired, and stood as the winning side of one of the more lopsided trades in history (Ernie Broglio gave the Cubs -1.5 WAR in exchange). Nonetheless, he ranks last in WAR among the 30 players with 3,000 hits, 18.6 WAR behind Dave Winfield, and second to last among enshrined left-fielders. His 75.3% success rate diluted the impact of his steals, so his total of 78 baserunning runs (which also count for advancement on hits and outs) ranks just 12th, well behind Henderson's 145. That's still a boost, but it's offset by a 6.8% walk rate, a modest OBP, and -51 fielding runs. Thus this viscerally exciting player ranked in the league's top 10 in WAR just twice, and had just three five-win seasons. His .391/.424/.655 line in 92 World Series PA—in victory in 1964 and '67, in defeat in '68—enhances his case, as do the since shattered records, but he's not a model Hall of Famer.

39. Jim O'Rourke

Teams:	Middlestown Mansfields (NA) 1872 • Boston Red Stockings (NA) 1873–75 • Boston Red Stockings (NL) 1876–78, '80 • Providence Grays 1879 • Buffalo Bisons 1881–84 • Giants 1885–89, 1891–92, 1904 • Giants (PL) 1890 • Senators 1893
Stats:	.310/.352/.422 • 134 OPS+ • 2,639 • 62 HR • 229 SB
Rankings:	12× top 10 AVG • 11× top 10 OPS+ • 6× top 10 WAR • 3× led HR
Voting/JAWS:	VC 1945 • **51.3/24.2/37.8**

An educated, well-spoken gentleman from baseball's bare-knuckle days, "Orator Jim" habitually recited Hamlet's soliloquy to his teammates before every game, and midway through his career earned a law degree from Yale. The heart of his career spanned 22 seasons, from the second year of the National Association through the inception of the National League (he collected its first hit) to the inaugural year of 60'6" pitching in 1893. After that, he undertook forays into umpiring and minor league organization—the latter while playing upward of 90 games a year into his late 50s. In his heyday, he was a leaderboard regular who dabbled at every position, with 231 games behind the plate, 404 in the infield, and six on the mound. Though a key part of champion teams (1877–78 in Boston, 1879 in Providence, 1888–89 in New York), he was hardly dominant, leading the league in batting average once, OBP twice, and homers three times. Even with his longevity, he ranks just eighth in nineteenth-century WAR, though he's second in hits. He was elected more for his fame than his greatness.

The Basement (the most dubious honorees)

59. Chick Hafey

Teams:	Cardinals 1924–31 • Reds 1932–35, '37
Stats:	.317/.372/.526 • 133 OPS+ • 1,466 H • 164 HR • 70 SB
Rankings:	5× top-5 SLG • 5× top-10 OPS+
Voting/JAWS:	VC 1971 • **30.1/27.1/28.6**

Hafey was among the first products of Branch Rickey's farm system, but repeated beanings cut into his playing time and caused severe sinus and vision problems. Not only did he become one of the first prominent position players to wear glasses (albeit not until 1929)—and the first player depicted on his plaque with them—his vision was so variable that he rotated among three pairs with different prescriptions. He missed part of 1932, and all but 104 games after 1934 (his age-31 season) due to health woes. Despite the obstacles he overcame, he's an all-time clunker among Hall of Famers due to his short playing career and era-inflated stats. Hafey had fewer plate appearances (5,115) than any elected major league position player save for Roy Campanella and Frank Chance, both constrained in part by time as catchers (not to mention the color line and the nineteenth century, respectively). Despite gaudy slash stats, only once did he rank among the league's top 10 in WAR, and he's miles off the standards. A teammate of Frisch's from 1927–31, he was among the many appalling selections during the Fordham Flash's VC tenure.

Further Consideration (upcoming or overlooked candidates)

1. Barry Bonds

Teams:	Pirates 1986–92 • Giants 1993–2007
Stats:	.298/.444/.607 • 182 OPS+ • 2,935 H • 762 HR • 514 SB
Rankings:	14× All-Star • 11× led WAR • 10× led OBP • 9× led OPS+ • 8 Gold Glove • 7× led SLG • 7× MVP • 2× led HR
	All-time: 1st HR • 1st BB • 2nd WAR • 3rd OPS+ • 3rd R • 4th TB • 5th RBI
JAWS:	**162.4/72.7/117.6**

Bonds has a claim as the greatest position player of all time, given that Ruth played before integration, that neither he nor Williams were much on the bases or afield, and that Mays didn't dominate opposing pitchers to the same extent. Blending speed, power, and surgical precision with regard to the strike zone, Bonds outdid them all, setting the single-season and all-time home run records, reaching base more often than any player this side of Rose and winning a record seven MVP awards. His claim remains in dispute, however, because of his connections to PEDs, which—thanks to the BALCO show trial, which cost more than $50 million of taxpayer money and in his case produced one conviction that was eventually overturned—turned his late career and surpassing of records and milestones into a joyless slog. If you want to play the "He was a Hall of Famer before he touched the stuff" game, considering only what he did through 1998, his 411 homers, 1,917 hits, 445 steals, and .290/.411/.556 hitting produced a 99.6/62.4/81.0 JAWS line, which would rank third here. As his PED allegations date to the pre-testing era, I'm for his election, warts and all; his rise to 53.8% in 2017 suggests he'll get there before his eligibility expires on the 2022 ballot.

5. Pete Rose

Teams:	Reds 1963–78, 1984–86 • Phillies 1979–83 • Expos 1984
Stats:	.303/.375/.409 • 118 OPS+ • 4,256 H • 160 HR • 198 SB
Rankings:	17× All-Star • 8× top 5 OBP • 6× top 10 WAR • 3× led AVG
	All-time: 1st H • 1st G • 1st TOB
Voting/JAWS:	**79.1/44.7/61.9**

Statistically, there's no debate that the Hit King—a vastly entertaining player who brought a hair-on-fire intensity to the game—is worthy of enshrinement given his records for hits (4,256), times on base (5,929), and more. Rose won the NL Rookie of the Year and MVP awards and three batting titles, tied an NL record with a 44-game hitting streak in 1978, helped his teams to six pennants and three championships and started All-Star games at a record five different positions (first, second, and third base, and both left field and right field). Though he played more games at first base (939) than in left field (673), he accrued more value as an outfielder than as an infielder, and then more value in left than the other two outfield spots. Three of his best five seasons in terms of WAR came as a leftfielder, including his MVP-winning 1973 (a career-best 8.2 WAR).

Alas, his lifetime ban for gambling, and the Hall's 1991 rule preventing ineligible players from being considered, likely means that he'll never get his plaque. Nor should he. He broke The One Rule, the prohibition against gambling posted in every clubhouse since Judge Landis kicked the Black Sox to the curb. Forget his claim that he only bet on his teams to win; any manager can marshal his resources to treat those games as do-or-die by emptying bullpens and avoiding resting regulars, or conversely signal to gamblers that he doesn't expect to win by not betting during the starts of certain pitchers, as Rose was said to do. He withheld the truth about his gambling for a decade and a half before cashing in with *My Prison Without Bars* in 2004, and continued to lie about not gambling as a player until evidence to the contrary surfaced in '15. Charlie Hustle indeed.

10. Manny Ramirez

Teams:	Indians 1993–2000 • Red Sox 2001–08 • Dodgers 2008–10 • White Sox 2010 • Rays 2011
Stats:	.312/.411/.585 • 154 OPS+ • 2,574 H • 555 HR • 38 SB
Rankings:	12× All-Star • 10× top 5 SLG • 7× top 5 OBP • 7× top 3 OPS+
	All-time: 7th SLG • 15th HR • 18th OBP • 22nd OPS+
Voting/JAWS:	69.2/39.9/54.6

A savant in the batter's box, an idiot just about everywhere else—sometimes amusingly, sometimes much less so. After adjusting for Fenway Park, Ramirez was arguably the third-best hitter of the post-1992 expansion era behind Bonds (199 OPS+) and Pujols (162), with significant playing time advantages over Miguel Cabrera (155) and Frank Thomas (152). Alas, there's more to life than just the lumber, and beyond Manny-Being-Manny's often comical liabilities afoot (-49 runs including both baserunning and double plays) and afield (-129 runs, fourth worst among all outfielders) lay ugly off-field altercations with Boston's traveling secretary (in 2008, keying his trade to the Dodgers) and his own wife (in '11). That's not even counting his two PED suspensions: 50 games in 2010 and 100 in '11, the latter effectively a career-ender. Those will probably block him from Cooperstown, though a sizable bloc of performance-only voters gave him 23.8% in his 2017 ballot debut.

14. Sherry Magee

Teams:	Phillies 1904–14 • Braves 1915–17 • Reds 1917–19
Stats:	.291/.364/.427 • 137 OPS+ • 2,167 H • 83 HR • 441 SB
Rankings:	7× top 10 WAR • 7× top 10 HR • 7× top 5 SLG • 6× top 5 SB
Voting/JAWS:	59.0/38.5/48.7

A burly, hot-headed Irishman, Magee stands among the best players from the first decade of the twentieth century, a legitimate five-tool star who debuted before his 20th birthday. From 1905–10, he ranked among the top five in slugging percentage four times (leading twice) and in steals every year; for that span, he ranked fourth in WAR behind only Wagner, Lajoie, and Cobb. He won the slash stat Triple Crown in that last season via a .331/.445/.507 performance that he never approached again; a year later, he was suspended for 36 games for assaulting an umpire. His December 1914 trade from Philadelphia to Boston meant not only missing out on the Phillies' first pennant but arriving too late for the "Miracle" Braves one. Magee never topped 1.0% among BBWAA voters and didn't make a VC ballot until 2008; he deserves a closer look, as he's fourth in WAR among unenshrined pre-1950 players behind Bill Dahlen, the ineligible Shoeless Joe Jackson, and Jack Glasscock.

CHAPTER 15

CENTERFIELDERS

ANDRUW JONES

No other player has been so burdened by two plate appearances in the infancy of his career. In the cathedral of Yankee Stadium, a 19-year-old Jones homered in his first two World Series at bats without bothering to genuflect. As Smoltz expresses it, from that point everyone expected this wunderkind from Curaçao 'to be Mickey Mantle. Or better.' Directions to Cooperstown? Play 15 years and hang a left.[1]

—Michael Farber

I t happened so quickly. Freshly anointed the game's top prospect by *Baseball America* in the spring of 1996, the soon-to-be-19-year-old Andruw Jones was sent to play for the Durham Bulls, the Braves' High-A affiliate. By mid-August, he had been promoted three times, having blazed through the Carolina League, the Double-A Southern League, and the Triple-A International League and debuted for the defending world champion Braves. By October 20, with just 31 regular season games under his belt, he was a household name, not only the youngest player ever to homer in a World Series game —breaking Mantle's record—but doing so twice at Yankee Stadium.

Jones was no flash in the pan. The Braves didn't win the 1996 World Series, and he didn't win the 1997 NL Rookie of the Year award, but along with Chipper Jones (no relation) and the big three of Greg Maddux, Tom Glavine, and John Smoltz, he became a pillar of a franchise that was amid a remarkable stretch of 14 NL East titles from 1991–2005 (all but the 1994 strike season). From 1998–2007,

Jones won 10 straight Gold Gloves, more than any centerfielder except Willie Mays.

By the end of 2006, Jones had tallied 342 homers and 1,556 hits. He looked bound for a berth in Cooperstown, but after a subpar finale in Atlanta and a departure for Los Angeles via free agency, he fell apart so completely that the Dodgers bought out his contract. He spent the next four years with three different teams before heading to Japan at age 35, and while he hoped for a return to the majors, he couldn't find a deal to his liking after either the 2014 or 2015 seasons. He retired before his 39th birthday, and thanks to his rapid descent, risks being overlooked by Hall of Fame voters.

The Career

Braves 1996–2007 • Dodgers 2008 • Rangers 2009 • White Sox 2010 • Yankees 2011–12

Player	Career	Peak	JAWS	H	HR	SB	AVG/OBP/SLG	OPS+
Andruw Jones	62.8	46.4	54.6	1933	434	152	.254/.337/.486	111
Avg HOF CF	71.1	44.5	57.8					
CF Rank	13th	9th	10th					
(Above HOF)	(10/19)	(12/19)	(12/19)					

Jones was born in 1977 in Willemstad, Curaçao, the capital city of roughly 150,000 of the Dutch-Caribbean island, which lies about 35 miles north of the coast of Venezuela. Father Henry Jones was a catcher for Curaçao's national team in the 1970s, good enough to play professionally—except that the island wasn't scouted by major league teams at that time, and attending a major league tryout ended a player's amateur status. Henry gave Andruw his first glove at three and his first bat at four, and the kid remained years ahead of the curve at every stage. He went to Japan with a traveling team at 11, one year before Hensley Meulens became the first Curaçao-born major leaguer with the Yankees in 1989, and at 15 played against Juvenile League teams featuring kids 16–18 years old. At a tournament in Puerto Rico, Braves scout Giovanni Viceisza, who had been scouring the Netherlands Antilles for Atlanta for five years, recognized Jones's five-tool talent and summoned longtime Braves director of scouting Paul Snyder, who advised the team to sign him once he turned 16. They paid a $46,000 bonus.

Still shy of his 17th birthday, Jones struggled in the spring training complex-based Gulf Coast League in 1994, but he fared better upon being moved up to the Appalachian League. His raw numbers at the two stops (.290/.368/.412 with three homers and 21 steals in 63 games) were respectable; that he held his own in leagues where the average player was two or three years older was far more important. Just shy of his 18th birthday, Jones was ranked 21st on *Baseball America*'s top prospect list in the spring of 1995, second on the Braves behind Chipper Jones. His performance that year with Macon in the South Atlantic League (.277/.372/.512 with 25 homers in 139 games) earned him *Baseball America* Minor League Player of the Year honors, and the overall number one prospect ranking heading into the 1996 season. Before his promotion to the Braves, Jones hit a combined .339/.421/.652 with 34 homers in 66 games at High-A Durham, 38 at Double-A Greenville, and 12 at Triple-A Richmond.

"Andruw was beyond his years, baseball maturity-wise," Snyder told *Baseball America* in 2006. "The biggest problem was that we couldn't find any level that he didn't dominate. . . . Very seldom do you get a guy like this to come through so quickly."[2]

The Braves owned a seven-game cushion when they recalled Jones from Richmond on August 14. They'd lost regular rightfielder David Justice to a season-ending dislocated shoulder back in May, and wanted to test the teenager before the August 31 deadline to set their postseason roster. Jones went 1-for-5 in his debut against the Phillies on August 15, striking out twice against Curt Schilling but collecting a ninth-inning single off Toby Borland. The next night, facing the Pirates, he homered off Denny Neagle, one of five he'd hit in 31 games. He started 17 games in right field, and five in center. "Some scouts say he's on a par with Atlanta's Gold Glove centerfielder, Marquis Grissom,"[3] noted *Sports Illustrated*'s Tim Kurkjian, less than two weeks after he arrived.

In the postseason, Braves manager Bobby Cox initially used Jones as a defensive replacement for lumbering leftfielder Ryan Klesko. He didn't start until Game 3 of the NLCS against the Cardinals, and didn't collect his first hits until Game 7, via a two-out RBI single in the first inning, then a two-run homer in the sixth in a 15–0 rout. Then came his big night in the World Series opener, with a two-run homer off Andy Pettitte, and a three-run homer off Brian Boehringer in a 12–1 rout. Jones hit .400/.500/.750 while starting all six games, though the Braves lost.

Jones repeated as *Baseball America*'s Minor League Player of the Year (the second player to do so since the publication's 1981 inception) and number one prospect (the first since they began ranking them in 1991). Even so, the Braves didn't immediately clear him a path to a full-time job. Toward the end of spring training, they traded Grissom and Justice to the Indians for Kenny Lofton, and dealt Jermaine Dye, who had played 96 games with the Braves as a rookie in 1996, to the Royals for Michael Tucker. Klesko, Lofton, and Tucker were the regulars, with Jones either coming off the bench in late innings or starting against lefties while

Tucker sat. He did spend six weeks in center field when hamstring and groin injuries sidelined Lofton. For the year, he played in 153 games but started just 96 (55 in right, 41 in center), hitting a modest .231/.329/.416 with 18 homers. Still, his defense—valued at +28 runs via Total Zone—turned enough heads that he finished fifth in the NL Rookie of the Year voting, well behind winner Scott Rolen but ahead of Vlad Guerrero.

Lofton returned to the Indians as a free agent after the 1997 season, opening center field for the 21-year-old Jones. He hit .271/.321/.515 with 31 homers, 27 steals, +35 defense (!), and 7.4 WAR, tops on the team and fifth in the league, 0.1 WAR behind Mark McGwire, and a full win ahead of Sammy Sosa in the year of the great home run chase. Jones's first Gold Glove kicked off his 10-year streak.

Continuing to provide outstanding defense along with power and speed, Jones ranked second in the NL in WAR in both 1999 (7.1) and 2000 (a career-best 8.2), and made his first All-Star team in the latter year with a .303/.366/.541 line with 36 homers and 21 steals. The Braves, who had been ousted in the NLCS in both 1997 and '98, returned to face the Yankees in the 1999 World Series, but Jones could muster no magic, going 1-for-13 as Atlanta was swept.

Following that big 2000 season, Jones (and agent Scott Boras) won a record $8.2 million salary via arbitration the following spring. After a slightly off 2001 (.251/.312/.461 with 4.9 WAR), the 24-year-old ballhawk, who was one year away from free agency, agreed to a six-year, $75 million extension. Said Boras at the time, "We've had managers and coaches say that Andruw Jones is the best center fielder they've seen since Willie Mays. It's a visual understanding. Andruw's routes to balls are excellent. His first step is excellent. His ability to come in and go back is excellent. He can catch the ball running at many different angles."[4]

Jones wasn't immune to off years such as 2001 and '04 (.261/.345/.488 with just +8 defense and 3.2 WAR) but even so, his power and glovework guaranteed a substantial baseline of value every year from 1998–2006; he made five All-Star teams during that stretch, homering in the 2003 and '05 games. Adjusting to a wider stance in which his head stayed lower and moved less, he broke out to lead the NL in both homers (51) and RBIs (128) in 2005 while ranking fourth with 6.7 WAR and finishing a close second in the NL MVP voting behind Albert Pujols, then followed that up with a 41-homer, 5.6 WAR season in 2006. From 1998–2006, he hit a combined .270/.347/.513 for a 118 OPS+ while averaging 35 homers, 21 fielding runs, and 6.1 WAR, trailing only Alex Rodriguez (7.8 WAR) and Barry Bonds (7.5 WAR) in that span.

Read that again: For a nine-year period, only A-Rod and Bonds were more valuable. If that seems like hyperbole, consider the extent to which the Braves' trio of Hall of Fame pitchers, Maddux, Glavine, and Smoltz, prevented runs and brought home Cy Young Awards despite Smoltz being the trio's only true strike-out pitcher. Those pitchers needed defensive support, and year in and year out, no defender played a bigger part.

"Andruw was always moving before the ball was even hit," said Matt Kemp, briefly Jones's teammate on the Dodgers but before that, a centerfielder he studied. "He would read the pitch, anticipate where the ball was going to be hit and already be moving to that spot."[5]

Jones's shallow positioning, quick first step, and uncanny knack for the right routes made for fewer spectacular dives than, say, Jim Edmonds, but those skills translated to defense that was an estimated 192 runs above average during that nine-year span, 58 runs better than any other player in baseball (Darin Erstad was second). Including the entirety of his Braves' run—which by the end had seen Maddux and Glavine both depart—Jones was 239 runs above average in the field, miles ahead of outfielder Brian Jordan (56) and shortstop Rafael Furcal (52).

Note that I've cut the 2007 season from the consideration of Jones's heyday. After clouting 92 homers in 2005–06, his final year before free agency was a disappointment, as he hit just .222/.311/.413 for an 87 OPS+, with 26 homers. Though still 19 runs above average afield, his 3.0 WAR was lower than even his rookie season. He was far from full health, battling soreness in both knees as well as a hyperextended left elbow suffered on May 27, but refused to lean on those as explanations. "I'm not going to make excuses about the injuries that I had," Jones said in September. "I just didn't play on a high level."[6]

Jones left the Braves after 2007, his age-30 season, and signed a two-year, $36.2 million deal with the Dodgers, whose general manager, Ned Colletti, cited the elbow injury as an explanation for the outfielder's struggles. Boras told the media that Jones had reviewed video suggesting his stance was too wide by four inches, costing him balance.

The deal with the Dodgers began unraveling when Jones showed up to camp out of shape, overweight by 15 to 25 pounds according to various reports. His batting average slipped below .200 in the season's fifth game, and stayed there. In late May, he went on the disabled list for the first time in his career, losing six weeks to surgery to repair a torn meniscus and remove a cyst in his right knee, the all-important back knee in his batting stance, which lessened his ability to drive the ball. Inflammation and tendinitis further limited him to just one game after August 9, sandwiched around two more DL stints. With his strikeout rate spiking from 21% in 2007 to 31% in that abysmal campaign, he finished at .158/.256/.249 with just three home runs and an astounding -1.6 WAR in 75 games.

Worse than Jones's performance was the perception that he didn't care, not that his showing up out of shape could have created any other impression. Caustic *Los Angeles Times* columnist T. J. Simers called him "the Tubbo,"[7] in print on multiple occasions. In one column, Jones continued to answer variants of "I don't care," in response to a barrage of unflattering questions, including whether he was bothered by the boos from Dodgers fans. "Don't you care that the fans in Dodger Stadium have turned on you?" asked Simers.

"No," said Jones. "That's their problem. . . . You play for the team, you don't play for the fans. The fans never played the game. They don't know."[8]

Such comments only exacerbated the situation as Jones spiraled downward. But as badly as his season played out for him, the Dodgers won the NL West and advanced to the NLCS before falling to the Phillies. The disappointment of the Jones signing was replaced by the mania caused by the July 31 trade for Manny Ramirez, who hit .396/.489/.743 in 53 games.

After failing to find any takers for Jones in trade, the Dodgers negotiated a rare contract buyout, releasing him while spreading the remaining $22.1 million on his deal over six years; they wound up putting some of the savings toward retaining Ramirez. Soon afterward, the Rangers signed Jones to a minimum-salary deal on the basis of a January 26 workout via which he was said to have lost 25 pounds. In part-time duty, primarily against lefties, he hit .214/.323/.459 with 17 homers in 82 games, though he battled hamstring woes.

Jones spent three more seasons in the majors tacking a similar course as a part-timer, one with the White Sox and then two with the Yankees. He hit 19 homers and was worth 1.9 WAR in 2010, his year in Chicago, though his performance with the bat was actually better in his first year in New York (.247/.356/.495 with 13 homers in 222 PA); for as potent as he was, his contributions were limited by pain in his left knee that eventually required offseason surgery. In December 2012, following a disappointing second season in pinstripes, he signed a one-year, $3.5 million deal with the Tohoku Rakuten Golden Eagles of the Japanese Pacific League. Less than two weeks later, on Christmas Day, he was arrested in his Duluth, Georgia home in connection with a domestic dispute. According to the police report, after consuming several drinks he allegedly assaulted his wife, Nicole, putting his hands around her neck and threatening to kill her. He was charged with battery, and a week later Nicole filed for divorce. In a sad irony, the *Washington Post* article reporting his arrest included the note that the Joneses had been major supporters of Jaden's Ladder, a group that helps victims of domestic violence.

The divorce was soon canceled, as the couple attempted to reconcile. Jones pled guilty, paid a fine, and received probation that allowed him to leave the U.S. to continue his career. In Japan he hit a combined .232/.392/.441 with 50 homers in 2013 and '14. He explored a return to the majors in early 2015, but reports of interest from multiple teams failed to produce a guaranteed contract. In early 2016, he officially retired.

The Case

From a traditional standpoint, Jones's biggest obstacle to election isn't his abrupt decline and departure from the majors itself—more on which below—but its impact on his career hit total, since he fell 67 hits short of 2,000. For whatever reason, BBWAA and committee voters have rejected every post-1960 expansion candidate who fell short of that mark, some very swiftly and some much less so. Bobby Grich, Jim Edmonds, Robin Ventura, and Jimmy Wynn went one-and-done on the BBWAA ballot and never got another shot from the VC. Dick Allen and Minnie Minoso never got 50% of the vote from the writers and have failed to break through on the committees despite multiple chances. Those players all had excellent careers and accumulated at least 50 WAR. Someday, one such player will break through, but will it be Jones?

He's got a few things working against him beyond just the hit total, including his lifetime .254 batting average. Only three players in the Hall are below .260: shortstop Rabbit Maranville (.258), first baseman Harmon Killebrew (.256), and catcher Ray Schalk (.253). Maranville and Schalk played key defensive positions and had strong defensive reputations that predate the Gold Glove era but are at least partially upheld by the metrics, though the former ranks dead last in JAWS among enshrined shortstops, the latter second to last among enshrined catchers. Killebrew punched his ticket to Cooperstown with 573 home runs and ranks 12th among the 19 enshrined first basemen, below the standards in all three categories. Jones has stronger defensive metrics in his favor than any of that trio, and at a key position to boot, not to mention 434 homers, but still, the paucity of Hall of Famers in the .250s doesn't bode well for him.

What's more, though his ample power and patience boosted the impact of that low batting average, Jones hails from a high-offense era. His 111 OPS+, from a .254/.337/.486 line, is unexceptional, lower than 16 of the 19 enshrined centerfielders, matching that of Richie Ashburn, with only Max Carey (108) and Lloyd Waner (99) lower. It's lower than 51 of the 73 enshrined up-the-middle players (catchers, second basemen, shortstops, and centerfielders).

Even the 10 Gold Gloves aren't as big a help as one would expect. While all five 12-time winners are in (Brooks Robinson, Ozzie Smith, Ivan Rodriguez, Willie Mays, and Roberto Clemente), the two 11-time winners (Keith Hernandez and Omar Vizquel) aren't; the former fell off the ballot without ever reaching 11.0%, the latter, eligible in 2018 but 18.8 points below the JAWS standard, will be the subject of polarizing debate.

As a member of the Braves' dynasty, Jones saw plenty of postseason action. His .273/.363/.433 line with 10 homers in 279 PA is not a particularly strong showing, however, and it doesn't help that the Braves went 2-8 in series in which he posted an OPS of .575 or above.

His Hall of Fame Monitor score of 109, which recognizes his big home run seasons and his reaching the 400 level for his career, his regular play at key defensive positions on playoff-bound teams, the Gold Gloves, and so on, leaves him somewhere between "a good possibility" at 100 and "a virtual cinch" at 130. Among his contemporaries, players such as Jimmy Rollins (121), Magglio Ordonez (114), Nomar Garciaparra and Michael Young (112), Matt Holliday (111), Carlos Delgado (110), Edgar Renteria (109), and Jason Giambi (108) show that the distance between those two levels is where Hall of Fame dreams go to die.

Jones's candidacy does have points in its favor on both traditional and advanced fronts, and on both sides of the ball. First, the homers. While only 27 of the 50 players with at least 425 homers are in the Hall, 10 others were either active in 2016 or have yet to hit the ballot (Chipper and Jim Thome will join Andruw on the 2018 docket), and eight more were connected to PEDs. None of the remaining four (Delgado, Vlad Guerrero, Dave Kingman, Fred McGriff) played a key defensive position, as Jones did. In fact, only three up-the-middle players (Mays, Ken Griffey Jr., and Mantle) top his 434 homers. Meanwhile, Jones's total of 236 fielding runs not only leads all centerfielders, but all outfielders, 51 runs ahead of second-ranked Mays.

As for his WAR-based numbers, the strongest point in Jones's favor is his 46.4 peak WAR, which ranks ninth, 1.8 wins above the standard and second among those outside the Hall besides Mike Trout (!). Jones's 62.8 career WAR isn't quite as robust, ranking 13th at the position, below 10 of the 19 enshrinees and 8.4 wins below the standard. His 54.6 JAWS is 3.5 points below the standard, but still good for 11th all-time, behind seven enshrinees plus Carlos Beltran (57.3) and Lofton (55.7), whose profile would be in this book if he weren't ineligible until 2023 (he went one-and-done on the 2013 ballot).

On the subject of Jones's fade, through his age-29 season he ranks 24th among position players in WAR (57.9), 40th in hits (1,556), tied for seventh in homers (342), and fourth in Gold Gloves (nine, trailing only Rodriguez, Griffey, and Johnny Bench with 10). Remove the Hall of Famers and those not yet eligible from the equation and Jones's through-age-29 home run total is tops (Bonds is 10th at 259), while his WAR is second:

Rk	Player	Through 29	30 onward	Above Peak	Above JAWS
1	Barry Bonds	66.2	96.2	Y	Y
2	Andruw Jones	57.9	4.9	Y	N
3	Cesar Cedeno	49.2	3.5	N	N
4	Shoeless Joe Jackson	48.0	14.3	Y	N
5	Sherry Magee	47.8	11.2	N	N
6	Vada Pinson	47.7	6.4	N	N
7	Jim Fregosi	45.9	2.8	N	N
8	Scott Rolen	45.8	24.2	Y	Y
9	Alan Trammell	45.7	24.7	Y	Y
10	Buddy Bell	43.9	22.2	N	N
11	Bobby Bonds	43.0	14.7	N	N
12	Dick Allen	42.9	15.8	Y	N
13	Nomar Garciaparra	41.2	3.0	Y	N
14	Bobby Grich	40.8	30.1	Y	Y
15	Chuck Knoblauch	40.6	4.0	N	N

What a list. As you can see, some of these players acquitted themselves reasonably well after 30, while others flamed out in spectacular fashion. Jones's drop-off—a gap of 53.0 WAR between the two halves of his career—is the steepest of the bunch. He's still one of the eight who exceed the peak standard at their positions, but not one of the four who exceed the career standard.

I suspect Jones's quick fade may spell his doom in front of voters. The year with the Dodgers—from his showing up out of shape to his comments regarding fans to his unorthodox buyout—gives ammunition to anyone looking for reasons not to vote for him that have nothing to do with numbers. Likewise for the ugly domestic violence allegation, particularly as the issue has become front and center with the game's new policy, introduced late in the 2015 season.

The writers gave rude treatment of Lofton (ninth in JAWS but just 3.2% in 2013) and Jim Edmonds (14th in JAWS, 2.5% in 2016) even without such factors. While Jones may have enjoyed a higher profile than that pair thanks to the 10 straight Gold Gloves on the perennial playoff participant, much of the credit for the Braves' run has already been apportioned to the trio of enshrined hurlers and Chipper Jones, a lock for first-ballot entry in 2018. For as fitting as it would be for the two Joneses to go in side by side as did Maddux and Glavine in 2014, the odds of that happening are long indeed.

THE ROUNDUP

The number before each player name refers to his JAWS ranking *among all players at the position*, not necessarily those in the Hall. Average HOF centerfielder: 71.2/44.6/57.9.

The Elite (above standard in career, peak, and JAWS)

1. Willie Mays

Teams:	Giants 1951–52, 1954–72 • Mets 1972–73
Stats:	.302/.384/.557 • 156 OPS+ • 3,283 H • 660 HR • 338 SB
Rankings:	20× All-Star • 12× GG • 10× led WAR • 5× led SLG • 5× led OPS+ • 4× led HR • 4× led SB
	All-time: 3rd WAR • 5th HR • 9th G • 12th H • 17th SLG • 17th OPS+
Voting/JAWS:	BBWAA 1979 **(1st, 94.7%)** • **156.2/73.7/115.0**

The numbers are as impressive as the legend; Mays was every bit as good as you've been told, his case as the greatest all-around player supported by advanced stats. He's third all-time in position player WAR behind only Babe Ruth and Barry Bonds, with far greater shares of his value coming from defense (+185 runs, second among centerfielders) and baserunning/double play avoidance (+69 runs) than the other two. To be fair, his advantage over Bonds in those secondary runs is just 29, but then again, losing most of his 1952 season and all of '53 (ages 21 and 22) to military service kept those remarkable numbers from climbing even higher, no small consideration given his 41-homer, 10.6 WAR, batting-title- and MVP-winning '54. That began a 13-year run of dominance during which he *averaged* 9.5 WAR, topping 10.0 six times; the entirety of civilization has combined for 14 10-WAR seasons in 51 seasons since. While it's tough to imagine how the BBWAA came up with 23 clowns who left Mays off their ballots in 1979, to that point, only three candidates, all Class of 1936 inductees (Ty Cobb, Ruth, and Honus Wagner), had received higher shares of the vote.

2. Ty Cobb

Teams:	Tigers 1905–26 • A's 1927–28
Stats:	.366/.433/.512 • 168 OPS+ • 4,189 H • 117 HR • 897 SB

Rankings: 12x led OPS+ • 11x led AVG • 8x led SLG • 7x led OBP • 6x led SB • 5x led WAR • 4x S/S TC
All-time: 1st AVG • 2nd H • 3rd TOB • 4th WAR • 5th G • 5th TB • 7th OBP

Voting/JAWS: BBWAA 1936 **(1st, 98.2%)** • **151.0/69.0/110.0**

The Georgia Peach's reputation as a toxic monstrosity is undergoing a reevaluation thanks to Charles Leerhsen's acclaimed myth-busting 2015 book, *A Terrible Beauty*, which argues that much (though not all) of what we think we know about his character—particularly his bigotry and rage both on and off the field—is the product of gross distortions, many by biographer Al Stump. Statistically, Cobb's run of dominance is jaw-dropping: 11 AL batting titles and 10 OPS+ leads in a 13-year span (1907–19, not including the disputed 1910 title), with four slash stat Triple Crowns to go with his traditional one (1909); for that span he hit .377/.441/.527 en route to a 189 OPS+. And then there's his precociousness: His 1909–11 league leads in WAR, totaling 31.0, came in his age-22–24 seasons; it took more than a century for someone, namely Mike Trout, to eclipse him through that age (48.5 to 46.7). Cobb still holds the age-based leads for 25 though 32, meaning that Trout will have to maintain a blistering pace. Beyond his outpacing Ruth's 95.2% in the original balloting, what stands out regarding Cobb and the Hall is an unexpected magnanimity. When he took up the causes of former teammates/nemeses Sam Crawford and Harry Heilemann, or pitchers Kid Nichols and Eppa Rixey, either with a well-placed quote to reporters or a letter to the Veterans Committee, they soon gained entry.

3. Tris Speaker

Teams: Red Sox 1907–15 • Indians 1916–26 • Senators 1927 • A's 1928

Stats: .345/.428/.500 • 157 OPS+ • 3,514 H • 117 HR • 436 SB

Rankings: 15x top 5 WAR • 15 top 5 OPS+ • 15x top 5 OBP • 13x top 5 AVG • 12x top 5 SLG
All-time: 4th AVG • 5th H • 6th WAR • 8th OBP • 8th TOB • 14th OPS+ • 16th TB

Voting/JAWS: BBWAA 1937 **(2nd, 82.1%)** • **133.7/62.1/97.9**

Often overshadowed by Cobb—with whom he shared both position and league—"The Grey Eagle" led the AL in batting average and OPS+ only in 1916, when he took the slash stat Triple Crown (.386/.470/.502 with 186 OPS+), though he was perennially among the AL's elite. The speedy, strong-armed Speaker revolutionized center field play with his shallow positioning, surrendering a few extra-base hits to prevent a whole lot more singles. The metrics support the impact of this: His +92 fielding runs is tops at the position through the pre-integration era, while Cobb rates as merely average, an advantage that enabled Speaker to lead the AL in WAR three times. He also had more October success than the Georgia Peach, batting .306/.398/.458 in 83 PA over three World Series (1912, '15, '20), all on the winning side; by contrast, Cobb hit .262/.314/.354 in 71 PA in losing causes in 1907, '08, and '09. It's not enough to push Speaker past Cobb, but up through 1928, when both players ended their careers, they ranked 1–2 in WAR for players of any position.

4. Mickey Mantle

Teams:	Yankees 1951–68
Stats:	.298/.421/.557 • 172 OPS+ • 2,415 H • 536 HR • 153 SB
Rankings:	16× All-Star • 12× top 5 OBP • 11× top 3 SLG • 6× led WAR • 6× top 5 AVG • 4× led HR
	All-time: 6th OPS+ • 12th OBP • 16th SLG • 17th HR
Voting/JAWS:	BBWAA 1974 **(1st, 88.2%)** • **109.7/64.7/87.2**

We lack numbers for how many times "The Mick" blew off curfew, to say nothing of how many homers he'd have hit on a pair of good knees. But we do know that he ranks third among centerfielders in peak score, in part because he owns two of the top four seasons at the position, with 11.3 WAR in 1957 (tied for first, via .365/.512/.665, 34 HR, 146 BB) and 11.2 in his Triple Crown '56 (tied for third, via .353/.464/.705, 52 HR, 130 RBI); those are two of his three MVP seasons. His third-best season was not his 1962 MVP campaign but '61, which featured a career-high 54 homers and 10.5 WAR, The tally among the top dozen seasons for centerfielders is five for Mays, three for Mantle, and two apiece for Cobb and Trout. Relative to his era, of course, Mantle dominated, all while helping the Yankees to 12 pennants and seven titles and launching a World Series–record 18 homers. If there's a knock against his play, it's his defense (-41 runs), but for a slugger with his offensive résumé, that's like complaining that you can't see enough of the Mona Lisa's teeth.

5. Ken Griffey Jr.

Teams:	Mariners 1989–99, 2009–10 • Reds 2000–08 • White Sox 2008
Stats:	.284/.370/.538 • 136 OPS+ • 2,781 H • 630 HR • 184 SB

Rankings:	13× All-Star • 10× GG • 9× top 10 OPS+ • 5× top 2 WAR • 4× led HR
	All-time: 6th HR • 13th TB
Voting/JAWS:	BBWAA 2016 **(1st, 99.3%)** • 83.6/53.9/68.8

Debating whether Griffey's smile or swing shone brighter is like comparing Mantle versus Mays. The Kid's bloodlines made him a familiar name before he'd shown off either that beaming grin or that picturesque swing in the majors, and he soon became a human highlight film, clouting home runs (twice reaching 56 in a season) and stealing them. Though his 438 homers through his age-30 season surpassed anyone before him, a never-ending series of injuries made his thirties a slog. By the time he reached 600 homers in 2008, Sammy Sosa had beaten him to that milestone, and Bonds had blown past him to top Hank Aaron's record. We can lament what might have been, but the combination of his traditional accomplishments and his PED-free reputation helped him to the highest voting percentage ever; just three of 440 writers left him off. Fifty-one years after the draft began, not only did he become the first overall number one pick elected, he was the first such pick to receive more than 6.1%.

6. Joe DiMaggio

Teams:	Yankees 1936–42, C.1946–51
Stats:	.325/.398/.579 • 155 OPS+ • 2,214 H • 361 HR • 30 SB
Rankings:	13× All-Star • 10× top 5 SLG • 8× top 5 WAR • 4× top 5 AVG
	All-time: T-19th OPS+ • T-27th AVG
Voting/JAWS:	BBWAA 1955 **(3rd†, 88.8%)** • 78.1/51.0/64.5

"There is a trend toward baseball analytics now and the more you apply them, the more you chip away at the DiMaggio myth. . . . In 1969 he was voted baseball's greatest living player. Today we would find that hilarious, considering that Ted Williams and Willie Mays were alive at the time."[9]

—JOHN THORN

The Yankee Clipper's numbers don't quite match the legend, in part because he played just 13 seasons, losing three prime years (ages 28–30), around 500 hits, 60 homers, and anywhere from 15–20 WAR to World War II. Matched up against

† Years receiving votes prior to final year of career not counted.

Williams, DiMaggio won "only" two batting titles, led the league in homers twice and in OPS+ just once, but his elite offense and exceptional defense (+49 runs) at a key position placed him in the top 10 in WAR every year but his final one—eight times in the top five. He did it for 10 pennant winners; the Yankees went 9-1 in those World Series, even though Joltin' Joe hit just .271/.338/.422 in 220 PA. As a Hall candidate, DiMaggio was the last player grandfathered in before the five-year waiting period rule took effect. He began receiving significant support (44.3%) in 1953, a year before the rule went into effect, and climbed to 69.4% and then 88.8%. He's one of just five players elected inside the five-year period (not including the special elections of Lou Gehrig and Roberto Clemente), alongside Ruth, Rogers Hornsby, Carl Hubbell, and Mel Ott.

7. Duke Snider

Teams:	Dodgers 1947–62 • Mets 1963 • Giants 1964
Stats:	.295/.380/.540 • 140 OPS+ • 2,116 H • 407 HR • 99 SB
Rankings:	9× top 10 HR • 8× All-Star • 7× top 10 WAR • 7× top 10 OPS+ • 5× top 5 SLG • 4× top 5 AVG • 4× top 3 OBP
Voting/JAWS:	BBWAA 1980 **(11th, 86.5%)** • **66.5/50.0/58.2**

Though Mantle and Mays ultimately eclipsed him, "The Duke of Flatbush" had a four-year head start in establishing supremacy among New York's renowned triumvirate. Aided by the bandbox of Ebbets Field (297′ to right field, 344′ to right-center), he mashed at least 40 homers annually from 1953–57; 117 of those 207 homers came at home. Indeed, he hit .313/.396/.603 with 175 home runs overall at Ebbets, compared to .286/.371/.505 everywhere else, including cavernous Los Angeles Coliseum (300′ to right, but 380′ to right-center). His defense suffered with the move, too; he was +30 runs through 1957 (his age-30 season) and -35 over the next four seasons (-22 in all). Outstanding in October (.286/.351/.594 with 11 homers—fourth behind Mantle, Ruth, and Berra—in 149 PA), he's the only player with two four-homer World Series (1952 and '55). Yet Snider struggled to get elected, debuting with just 17.0% and inching only to 41.0% by his seventh try before his candidacy gained momentum. After he fell 16 votes short in 1979, a boost from a magnanimous Mays helped him to the highest share of any candidate in his fifth year or later.

The Rank and File

11. Richie Ashburn

Teams:	Phillies 1948–59 • Cubs 1960–61 • Mets 1962
Stats:	.308/.396/.382 • 111 OPS+ • 2,574 H • 29 HR • 234 SB

| **Rankings:** | 7× top 10 WAR • 7× top 5 OPB • 6× top 5 SB • 5× All-Star • 4× top 2 AVG |
| **Voting/JAWS:** | VC 1995 • **63.6/44.3/53.9** |

A two-time batting champion and an outstanding table-setter, Ashburn was among the "Whiz Kids" who injected life into the moribund Philadelphia franchise, helping them to their first pennant in 35 years in 1950. An excellent fielder in his heyday (+112 runs through 1958, but -36 thereafter), he covered plenty of ground and led the league in baserunner kills four times, using positioning and guile to compensate for a lack of arm strength. But between his lack of power, the presence of both Snider and Mays in the same league, and his retirement after a strong age-35 season as a Met (.306/.424/.393) in favor of broadcasting, recognition was hard to come by. He never finished higher than seventh in MVP voting, and maxed out at 41.7% on the BBWAA ballot. After missing VC election by two votes in 1990, he was frozen out by a short-lived (1991–93) "60% Rule" for candidates whose careers began after 1946. The rule was overturned thanks to a grassroots effort (see Chapter 6), and two years later Ashburn was elected so he was inducted alongside fellow Phillie Mike Schmidt. Unfortunately, a heart attack killed him just two years after that.

12. Andre Dawson

Teams:	Expos 1976–86 • Cubs 1987–92 • Red Sox 1993–94 • Marlins 1995–96
Stats:	.279/.323/.482 • 119 OPS+ • 2,774 H • 438 HR • 314 SB
Rankings:	9× top 10 HR • 8× All-Star • 8× GG • 8× top 10 SLG • 5× top 5 AVG • 4× top 5 WAR
Voting/JAWS:	BBWAA 2010 **(9th, 77.9%)** • **64.5/42.5/53.5**

With a rare five-tool mix, the Hawk averaged 22 homers, 25 steals, +9 defense, and 4.8 WAR in 10 full seasons in Montreal, twice finishing second in the NL MVP voting. Unfortunately, the toll of Olympic Stadium's artificial turf on his knees forced a move to right field in 1984. As a Cub, he was simply a lesser player, averaging 29 homers, 10 steals, and 3.1 WAR, a decline masked by the Friendly Confines; he hit .332/.373/.668 there in 1987, .246/.288/.480 elsewhere. Even on a last-place team, his league-leading 49 homers and 137 RBI—and the blank-check contract narrative amid the owners' collusion, which resulted in a paltry $500,000 salary—carried the day in the MVP voting, but his 4.0 WAR tied for just 18th.

An allergy toward walks (4.1% unintentional) hampered his value throughout his career; he never cracked the WAR top 10 outside of 1980–83. He spent his final four seasons *subtracting* 2.3 WAR while adding 230 hits and 39 homers. That he ranked among the top 10 centerfielders in JAWS before Griffey, Beltran, Lofton, and Jones surpassed him does justify his election, though its slow pace following a 45.3% debut was puzzling.

13. Billy Hamilton

Teams:	Kansas City Cowboys (AA) 1888–89 • Phillies 1890–95 • Boston Beaneaters 1896–1901
Stats:	.344/.455/.432 • 141 OPS+ • 2,164 H • 40 HR • 914 SB
Rankings:	10× top 10 WAR • 5× led OBP • 5× led SB
	All-time: 3rd OBP • 3rd SB
Voting/JAWS:	VC 1961 • **63.3/42.6/53.0**

Dear Sir:

In the November 16 issue of your paper you made reference to Billy Hamilton, of the old Philadelphia and Boston NL clubs of the 1890s as one of the prolific base stealers of the 19th century. I'll have you know sir that I was and will be the greatest stealer of all times. I did stole [sic] over 100 bases on many years and if they ever re-count the record I will get my just reward.

Very Truly,

Sliding Billy Hamilton[10]

Unlike his twenty-first-century namesake, who has speed but little else, the nineteenth-century Billy Hamilton was a 5′6″ sparkplug, the first great leadoff man in the game's history and a pioneer in the arts of drag bunting and base stealing. From 1889–98, while NL teams averaged six runs per game, Hamilton averaged 144 runs scored in 124 games per season thanks in part to an OBP that ranks third all-time; he topped a .400 OBP every year except his rookie one. He won two batting titles, topping .400 once (albeit only after a posthumous review of the stats; it's .399 on his plaque). Meanwhile, he swiped at least 100 bases four times, though from 1886–97 the rules counted any extra bases advanced beyond a hit (e.g., going from first to third on a single) as a steal. While credited with over 900 (937 via his plaque, 912 via MLB, 914 via B-Ref), he wasn't recognized as the record holder; Cobb was, with 892—a sore point, as Hamilton's 1937 letter to *The Sporting News* suggests. Nonetheless, his overwhelming credentials were enough for election by the VC in 1961 despite a dearth of surrounding lore.

21. Larry Doby

Teams:	Indians 1947–55, '58 • White Sox 1956–57, '59 • Tigers 1959
Stats:	.283/.386/.490 • 136 OPS+ • 1,515 H • 253 HR • 47 SB
Rankings:	8× top 10 WAR • 8× top 10 OPS+ • 8× top 10 SLG • 7× All-Star • 6× top 10 AVG • 4× top 3 HR
Voting/JAWS:	VC 1998 • **49.5/39.6/44.6**

Signed by Bill Veeck after spending parts of six seasons with the Negro National League's Newark Eagles, Doby broke the AL's color barrier just 11 weeks after Jackie Robinson's arrival, yet never received anything close to an equitable level of acclaim as a pioneer. Granted, he made just 33 PA in 1947, but with the help of Speaker—by then an Indians coach—Doby converted from second base to center field the following spring and was off to the races, hitting .301/.384/.490/134 OPS+ with 4.6 WAR for a 97-win world champion. He developed into one of the AL's heaviest hitters and from 1948–56 ranked fifth in WAR among a top 10 where every player wound up in Cooperstown. After helping the Indians to another pennant in 1954, he bounced around and battled back and rotator cuff injuries. Done at 35, he later worked as an interim manager (the second black manager in MLB history) and executive, but his modest career totals led the BBWAA to spurn him with less than 5.0% in both 1966 and '67. It took another 31 years for the VC to elect him, just five years before he passed. Unfuckingbelievable.

23. Kirby Puckett

Teams:	Twins 1984–95
Stats:	.318/.360/.477 • 124 OPS+ • 2,304 H • 207 HR • 134 SB
Rankings:	10× All-Star • 6× GG • 5× top 5 AVG • 3× top 10 WAR • 3× top 10 SLG • 3× top 10 OPS+
Voting/JAWS:	BBWAA 2001 **(1st, 82.1%)** • **50.9/37.5/44.2**

Glaucoma shortened the career of this beloved, iconic two-time champion, whose election to the Hall at age 41 made sense on an emotional level in the moment and became even more poignant when he died five years later due to complications from a stroke. Objectively, his case is shakier. Puckett's accolades produced a beefy Hall of Fame Monitor score of 160, but beyond his shiny batting averages he never cracked the league's top 10 in OBP, and did so only three times in SLG and OPS+. His defensive reputation is overstated according to the metrics; he was

11 runs below average in his six Gold Glove seasons, −14 for his career. While he led the AL in WAR in 1992 and was runner-up in '88, only one other time did he place among the top 10. His postseason line (.309/.361/.536 in 109 PA) is outstanding, but now that we know he wasn't such a nice guy—via ugly allegations of violence from both his wife and his mistress as well as charges of sexual assault and false imprisonment filed by a third woman—the rush to coronation seems particularly premature.

26. Max Carey

Teams:	Pirates 1910–26 • Dodgers 1926–29
Stats:	.285/.361/.386 • 108 OPS+ • 2,665 H • 70 HR • 738 SB
Rankings:	10× led SB • 7× top 10 WAR • 6× top 10 OBP
	All-time: 9th SB
Voting/JAWS:	VC 1961 • **54.2/32.9/43.6**

In 1958, a three-man panel convened by *The Sporting News* named this switch-hitting speedster—who at the time held the NL record for stolen bases—"the outstanding base bandit of all time" ahead of Cobb on the basis of his knack for studying pitchers and for rarely getting nabbed (though his caught stealing totals are incomplete). Built like a greyhound, Carey led the league in steals 10 times (second only to Rickey Henderson's 12) and swiped 51 in 53 attempts in 1922, when he hit .329/.408/.459/122 OPS+ en route to 5.1 WAR, matching his career high. Alas, his brand of offense produced less value than perceived, with his modest power limiting him to just one 10th-place finish in OPS+. Nicknamed "Scoops" for his low-to-the-ground snags, he does rank second among prewar centerfielders with 86 fielding runs. Though short on the WAR fronts, his outstanding 1925 World Series (.458/552/.625 including four hits off Walter Johnson—whose tipoff of the curveball he could read—in Game 7) and the flash of his steals makes the VC's choosing him easy to understand, particularly given his surge to 51.1% as his BBWAA ballot tenure ended.

28. Earl Averill

Teams:	Indians 1929–39 • Tigers 1939–40 • Braves 1941
Stats:	.318/.395/.534 • 133 OPS+ • 2,019 H • 238 HR
Rankings:	8× top-10 SLG • 7× top 10 HR • 6× All-Star • 5× top 10 OPS+ • 5× top 10 WAR
Voting/JAWS:	VC 1975 • **48.0/37.3/42.7**

"The Earl of Snohomish" (Washington) debuted five weeks shy of his 27th birthday, having played semipro ball while working in saw mills and spending three years with the PCL's San Francisco Seals. The 5'7½" Averill emerged as Cleveland's first great power hitter thanks to League Park's favorable layout (290' to right field, 319' to right-center) and an approach so pull-happy that teams shifted against him years before the Indians did so against Ted Williams. Averill averaged 22 homers, a 137 OPS+, and 4.8 WAR during 10 full seasons in Cleveland; traded to Detroit in mid-1939, he had little left due to the lingering effects of a back injury. While it's tantalizing to reimagine his career with an earlier debut, BBWAA voters virtually ignored him in seven turns on the ballot. Upon election by the VC, a sour Averill revealed, "Had I been elected after my death, I had made arrangements that my name never be placed in the Hall of Fame. My disagreements [sic] with how the Hall of Fame elections are held, and who is elected, is not based on bitterness that I had to wait 34 years . . . it is based on the fact that statistics alone are not enough to gain a player admittance."[11]

37. Earle Combs

Teams: Yankees 1924–35
Stats: .325/.397/.462 • 125 OPS+ • 1,866 H • 58 HR • 98 SB
Rankings: 5x top 10 OBP • 3x top 10 AVG • 3x top 10 WAR
Voting/JAWS: VC 1970 • **42.5/34.3/38.4**

A gentlemanly teetotaler and sportswriter favorite who could be found reading his Bible at night after games—in marked contrast to his more hedonistic teammates—Combs may have charmed his way into Cooperstown. The fourth-most-valuable position player on the Yankees during his 12-year career (behind Ruth, Gehrig, and Tony Lazzeri), he was an excellent leadoff hitter whose era-inflated .465 SLG is tops among those with 5,000 PA from that spot, while his .399 OBP is in a virtual tie with Ashburn for third. Despite a notoriously poor arm, he was an adequate centerfielder (+6 runs), but collisions resulting in a 1934 skull fracture, a '35 collarbone fracture, and a '36 date with destiny in the form of a kid named DiMaggio ushered him offstage at age 36. He maxed out at 16.0% in front of BBWAA voters, but the VC rode to his rescue. Combs may have given the game away upon election when he said, "I thought the Hall of Fame was for superstars, not just average players like me."[12]

38. Edd Roush

Teams:	White Sox 1913 • Indianapolis Hoosiers (FL) 1914 • Newark Pepper (FL) 1915 • Giants 1916, 1927–29 • Reds 1916–26, 1931
Stats:	.323/.369/.446 • 126 OPS+ • 2,376 H • 68 HR • 268 SB
Rankings:	7x top 5 AVG • 7x top 10 SLG • 5x top 10 WAR
Voting/JAWS:	VC 1962 • **45.2/31.5/38.3**

Roush was known for his fiery temper as well as for wielding a 48-ounce war club with which he placed hits to all fields, shifting his feet mid-pitch to help guide them. It worked well enough for him to win two batting titles and reel off 10 straight years with an average of .321 or better from 1917–26; he finished among the league's top 10 in OBP and SLG a combined 13 times in that span. Roush is the only Hall of Famer who established himself in the short-lived Federal League rather than passing through in late career, as Chief Bender, Three-Finger Brown, Eddie Plank, and Joe Tinker did. Though considered by many to be the NL's best defensive outfielder during the dead-ball era thanks to his knack for getting to the ball with his back turned, the metrics view him as basically average. Barely noticed by the BBWAA initially—he received votes as early as 1936 but didn't reach 20% until '54—he climbed to 54.3% by '60, then gained entry through the VC two years later.

43. Hack Wilson

Teams:	Giants 1923–25 • Cubs 1926–31 • Dodgers 1932–33 • Phillies 1934
Stats:	.307/.395/.545 • 144 OPS+ • 1,461 H • 244 HR • 52 SB
Rankings:	6x top 10 SLG • 5x top 5 WAR • 5x top 10 OBP • 4x led HR
Voting/JAWS:	VC 1979 • **38.8/35.8/37.3**

The barrel-chested Wilson, who stood 5'6" but weighed 190 pounds, led the NL in homers four times from 1926–30, setting NL records with 56 homers and 190 RBI (since revised to 191) in that last season; the former has been surpassed, the latter endures. Of course, offense was at its twentieth-century apex at that point, but even with dreadful defense (-10 runs), Wilson's 7.4 WAR ranked second in the league. While his 29.9 WAR for the five-year span ranked behind only Ruth, Gehrig, Hornsby, and Al Simmons, that's almost all there is to his career; he produced just 8.9 WAR in his seven other seasons, just two of which were any good. Alas, he wore out his welcome in Chicago due to alcoholism—"Gin was his tonic," it was said—and a penchant for brawling, was out of the majors by the end of 1934, and died penniless at age 48; NL president Ford Frick wired $350 to cover the funeral expenses. Wilson climbed as high as 38.3% on the BBWAA ballot, but support quickly waned. The VC's election was inevitable given the committee's long-standing bias toward shiny numbers from the 1925–35 era.

46. Hugh Duffy

Teams:	Chicago White Stockings 1888–89 • Chicago Pirates (PL) 1890 • Boston Reds (AA) 1891 • Boston Beaneaters 1892–1900 • Milwaukee Brewers 1901 • Phillies 1904–06
Stats:	.326/.386/.451 • 123 OPS+ • 2,293 H • 106 HR • 574 SB
Rankings:	4× top 10 AVG • 4× top 10 SB • 3× top 3 WAR
Voting/JAWS:	OTC 1945 • **43.0/30.8/36.9**

Mistaken for a batboy by Cap Anson when he reported to the White Stockings, the 5'7" Duffy soon emerged as one of the game's top hitters, placing among the top three in hits across three different leagues from 1890–94 and setting a still standing record for batting average in '94, though while it's .438 on his Hall of Fame plaque, it's now believed to be .440. Pesky statistical revisionists have also obscured his other noteworthy accomplishments, including his 1893 Triple Crown (.363-18-145); researchers have since discovered that Sam Thompson outdid him with 147 ribbies. Duffy did play on five league champions, but for all of his hits and high batting averages—above .300 every year from 1889–97—his impact on leaderboards was limited to a few seasons. He had his last good one at age 31 and is just 21st among nineteenth-century position players in WAR and 26th in OPS+ (5,000 PA minimum). Despite the bulk of his career predating the twentieth century, he received votes in five BBWAA cycles before being elected by the OTC in 1945.

The Basement (the most dubious honorees)

116. Lloyd Waner

Teams:	Pirates 1927–41, 1944–45 • Braves 1941 • Reds 1941 • Phillies 1942 • Dodgers 1944
Stats:	.316/.353/.393 • 99 OPS+ • 2,459 H • 27 HR • 67 SB
Rankings:	6× top 10 AVG
Voting/JAWS:	VC 1967 • **24.1/20.3/22.2**

Via JAWS, literally over 100 centerfielders are better suited for Cooperstown than Lloyd Waner, who was elected thanks to his famous name and hot start back when shiny batting averages were a dime a dozen. "Little Poison" rapped out 223 hits and hit .355/.396/.410 as a rookie in 1927, while older brother Paul, "Big Poison," won the first of three batting titles; the two helped the Pirates to the pennant. But despite racking up 200 hits in four of his first five seasons, the younger Waner wasn't half the ballplayer that his sibling was. Though he excelled at making contact, he had very little power, a 5% walk rate, and just one batting average finish higher than eighth, not to mention just one top 10 finish in OBP and, none in OPS+ or WAR. Using Win Shares, Bill James suggested he was worthy of eight Gold Gloves, but his strong defensive reputation shows up neither in fielding runs (+17) nor Defensive Regression Analysis (-9). Justifiably, the BBWAA never gave him more than 23.4%, but a year after he was mistakenly included on the writers' ballot due to sloppy clerical work (his 20-year window having elapsed), he was elected by the VC. Yeesh.

Further Consideration (upcoming or overlooked candidates)

8. Carlos Beltran

Teams:	Royals 1998–2004 • Astros 2004 • Mets 2005–11 • Giants 2011 • Cardinals 2012–13 • Yankees 2014–16 • Rangers 2016
Stats:	.281/.354/.492 • 121 OPS+ • 2,617 H • 421 HR • 312 SB
Rankings:	9× All-Star • 5× top 10 WAR • 5× top 10 SB • 3× GG • 3× top 10 HR
Voting/JAWS:	**68.4/44.3/56.4**

Despite knee woes that cost him roughly a full season in 2009–10—part of a stay in Queens for which he received a disproportionate share of the blame for the Mets' shortfalls—Beltran offered the game's best power-speed combination in the first decade of the new millennium. Though he had only one 30-30 season (a 38-homer, 42-steal monster split between the Royals and Astros), he reached each plateau four times; his seven 20-20 seasons are the most of any other player since 1992 except Bobby Abreu. What's more, he stole at an 86.4% clip, tops among players with more than 150 steals, was an excellent fielder before the knee trouble (+71 runs through 2008, -33 thereafter), and was rivaled only by David Ortiz as the Wild Card era's best postseason position player, with a .323/.432/.646 line and 16 homers (eight of them in 2004) in 235 PA. A 2016 bounceback after two injury-marked seasons not only pushed him past the 400-homer and 2,500-hit plateaus but earned him another one-year deal to further make his case.

9. Kenny Lofton

Teams:	Astros 1991 • Indians 1992–96, '98–2001, '07 • Braves 1997 • White Sox 2002 • Giants 2002 • Pirates 2003 • Cubs 2003 • Yankees 2004 • Phillies 2005 • Dodgers 2006 • Rangers 2007
Stats:	.299/.372/.423 • 107 OPS+ • 2,428 H • 130 HR • 622 SB
Rankings:	6× All-Star • 5× led SB • 5× top 10 WAR • 4× GG • 3× top 10 AVG • 3× top 10 OBP
	All-time: 15th SB
Voting/JAWS:	**68.2/43.3/55.7**

Given Tim Raines's election, the next leadoff hitter worthy of a Cooperstown push from statheads is Lofton. Unfortunately, there's no rush, as his 3.2% on the overloaded 2013 slate means he won't be eligible until 2023, when his 10-year window is up. Atop power-laden Indians lineups, the electrifying Lofton rode his combination of table-setting and defensive skills to the majors' fourth-highest WAR from 1992–99 (47.4), trailing only Bonds (62.3), Griffey (55.0), and Jeff Bagwell (51.9); he led his league once and ranked among the top five two other times. His +108 runs defensively rank eighth at the position, while his +102 runs in baserunning and double play avoidance is tied for ninth since 1951; of the eight players above him, only Henderson, Joe Morgan, and Raines had higher OBPs. Alas, his stealing more bases than anybody since 1990 (at a 79.5% clip) got lost amid all the homers, and the nomadic second half of his career couldn't have helped his case in front of voters, even if he did make 11 postseasons in a 13-year span with six different franchises (plus his two return stints in Cleveland).

14. Jim Edmonds

Teams:	Angels 1993–99 • Cardinals 2000–07 • Padres 2008 • Cubs 2008 • Brewers 2010 • Reds 2010
Stats:	.284/.376/.527 • 132 OPS+ • 1,949 H • 393 HR • 67 SB
Rankings:	8× GG • 5 top 10 WAR 4× All-Star • 4× top 10 HR • 3× top 5 OPS+
Voting/JAWS:	**60.3/42.5/51.4**

One of his era's most viscerally exciting players on both sides of the ball— "the highlight man,"[13] Johnny Damon called him—Edmonds was as capable of spectacular catches and towering home runs as Griffey, who allegedly once called ESPN to complain about how frequently clips of his division rival's spectacular plays made *SportsCenter*. A key player on eight playoff teams, Edmonds's signature intensity nonetheless forced him into several stays on the disabled list due to repeated sacrifices of his body in pursuit of fly balls. Those absences—including sitting out the entire 2009 season—prevented him from reaching 400 homers and 2,000 hits, the bright-line test for post-1960 Hall candidates, so he went one-and-done with just 2.5% of the vote in 2016. A future Today's Game Era Committee could be swayed in his direction if they watch enough video.

17. Jim Wynn

Teams:	Astros 1963–73 • Dodgers 1974–75 • Braves 1976 • Yankees 1977 • Brewers 1977
Stats:	.250/.366/.436 • 129 OPS+ • 1,665 H • 291 HR • 225 SB
Rankings:	6x top 10 OPS+ • 5x top 10 WAR • 4x top 10 SLG • 4x top 10 OBP • 3x All-Star
JAWS:	**55.6/43.2/49.4**

"The Toy Cannon" was a 5'10" sparkplug with power, outstanding control of the strike zone, and good defense, a player whom Bill James compared to early-career teammate Joe Morgan while ranking Wynn 10th all-time among centerfielders in *The New Bill James Historical Abstract*. Wynn spent his first 13 years in tough pitcher's parks, and went underappreciated because of his low batting averages and high walk totals. He did reach 20 homers eight times, 30 homers three times, and 100 walks six times; in 1969, he had more walks (148) than hits (133) to go with 33 homers en route to a .269/.436/.507/166 OPS+/7.1 WAR line. Alas, shoulder woes cut his career short after wrecking his age -34–35 seasons, leaving his career totals light, and he was shut out entirely on the BBWAA ballot in 1983, yet another player whose broad skill set was ignored by voters. Even with shaky defense (-28 runs), he's 13th in peak and 17th in career WAR at the position. Where's Frankie Frisch when you need him?

26. Dale Murphy

Teams:	Braves 1976–90 • Phillies 1990–92 • Rockies 1993
Stats:	.265/.346/.469 • 121 OPS+ • 2,111 H • 398 HR • 161 SB
Rankings:	7x All-Star • 7x top 5 HR • 6x GG • 5x top 5 SLG • 5x top 10 OBP • 4x top 5 OPS+
JAWS:	**46.2/41.0/43.6**

Murphy's career didn't take off until the Braves moved him from behind the plate, and then from first base to center field. Once it did, he enjoyed a stellar eight-year run (1980–87, ages 24–31), averaging 33 homers, 5.3 WAR, and a 140 OPS+ and two home run titles and two MVP awards (1982 and '83). Alas, his career declined precipitously after 1987, in part due to knee troubles; he was worth just 4.8 WAR from C.88–93 while hitting for a 96 OPS+, and wound up light in the counting stats. His peak score is nearly Hall caliber, but he had almost no value outside of it, and while a base of support among BBWAA voters kept him on the ballot for the full 15 years, only in his second year did he reach 20% of the vote. Transport his career to the 1920s or '30s and he'd easily be in, a better player than Combs or Wilson, but times change.

27. Bernie Williams

Teams:	Yankees 1991–2006
Stats:	.297/.381/.477 • 125 OPS+ • 2,336 H • 287 HR • 147 SB
Rankings:	5× All-Star • 5× top 10 OBP • 4× GG • 4× top 5 AVG
Voting/JAWS:	**49.4/37.5/43.5**

As the Yankees emerged from a barren stretch of 13 seasons (1982–94) without a trip to the playoffs, their young switch-hitting centerfielder stood as a symbol for the franchise's resurgence. Allowed to develop instead of being traded for a veteran, Williams emerged as a core player during the team's run of six pennants and four championships from 1996–2003, won a batting title, and enjoyed some big postseason moments, hitting 22 homers to go with a .275/.371/.480 line in 545 PA—credentials tailor-made to waltz into Cooperstown had they occurred 70 years earlier. Alas, Williams was never as good defensively as the hardware suggested; once his speed faded, he could no longer outrun his mistakes, and he got old quickly, spending his age -34–37 seasons around replacement level. His total of -139 fielding runs is the worst for any outfielder, let alone a centerfielder. For the high-offense era, his career totals didn't stand out on the ballot, and after debuting at 9.6% in 2012, he fell off the following year.

CHAPTER 16

RIGHTFIELDERS

CASE STUDY: LARRY WALKER

When it comes to all-around play—hitting for power and average, fielding, throwing and baserunning—Walker may be peerless. "He's better than one of the best," Atlanta Braves manager Bobby Cox once said. "He is the best."[1]

—RICHARD HOFFER

Like so many Canadians, Larry Walker grew up preferring hockey to baseball. Born and raised near Vancouver, British Columbia, he idolized four-time Stanley Cup winning goalie Billy Smith of the New York Islanders, and like older brother Carey—not to be confused with older brothers Barry and Gary, the other offspring of father Larry and mother Mary (you can't make this up)—dreamed of NHL stardom. The men of the family played fast-pitch softball together, but young Larry's high school team didn't even field a baseball team. Only when his hockey dreams died did he turn his full focus toward the diamond.

Despite not being drafted, Walker not only developed into an outstanding all-around player, he did it with the Montreal Expos, becoming the only Canadian-born All-Star and Gold Glove winner in franchise history and arguably the best ballplayer ever produced by the country. Sadly, he spent less time with the team than the elite outfielders in whose footsteps he followed, Andre Dawson and Tim Raines. After starring on Montreal's legendary 1994 squad, which carried the majors' best record into the players' strike but never got to test its mettle in the postseason, he was among those Expos deemed too expensive to keep. Via free agency, he took up residence with the Rockies and put up eye-popping numbers at high altitude—numbers that hold up well even once they're brought back to earth.

Throughout his 17-year career, Walker excelled at every phase of the game. As a hitter, he won three batting titles and led his league in on-base and slugging percentages twice. As a baserunner, he stole at a 75% clip for his career, and became just the 18th player to join the 30-homer–30-steal club. As a rightfielder, he combined great range with a strong arm (at least early in his career), establishing himself as one of the best ever to play the position. Had he done it all for longer, there's little question he'd already have a plaque in Cooperstown, but injuries cut into his playing time, suppressing his career totals.

Walker's relatively short career, high peak, and time spent in an extreme offensive environment put the JAWS system to the test. Via his excellence at so many facets of the game, he compares favorably to the average Hall of Fame rightfielder and to contemporary candidates Vlad Guerrero and Gary Sheffield, even after adjusting for his advantageous surroundings. The electorate hasn't absorbed that message, however. In seven years on the ballot, he's received tepid support, peaking at 22.9% of the vote in 2012, his second year on the ballot; his 21.9% in 2017 marked his highest share since.

The Career

Expos 1989–94 • Rockies 1995–2004 • Cardinals 2004–05

Player	Career	Peak	JAWS	H	HR	SB	AVG/OBP/SLG	OPS+
Larry Walker	72.6	44.6	58.6	2160	383	230	.313/.400/.565	141
Avg HOF RF	73.2	43.0	58.1					
RF Rank	11th	11th	10th					
(Above HOF)	(14/24)	(15/24)	(15/24)					

Walker was born in Maple Ridge, 20 miles outside Vancouver, in 1966. Like brother Carey, who was drafted by the Montreal Canadiens, he aspired to be an NHL goalie, and honed his skills by blocking the shots of friend and future Hockey Hall of Famer Cam Neely. Baseball was secondary, something he'd play for 10–15 games a year, until he was cut from a pair of Junior A hockey teams, but while playing for the Canadian team at the 1984 World Youth Championships in Saskatchewan, he caught the eye of Expos scouting director Jim Fanning; his impressive home run with a wooden bat stood out among so many aluminum-swinging players.

Particularly willing to take a chance on a Canadian kid, the Expos signed Walker in November 1984 via a $1,500 bonus—paltry but not inappropriate given the rawness of his game. As he described his background to Jonah Keri for his 2014 history of the Expos, *Up, Up, & Away*, "My approach to hitting was, 'Guy throws the ball, I try to hit it. If I hit it, I run.' But the hard part was hitting something with a wrinkle in it. I had never seen a forkball before. Sliders and curves killed me."[2]

What saved Walker was his outstanding athleticism, freakish hand-eye coordination, and mental approach, traits that stood out to his first minor league manager, Ken Brett (older brother of Hall of Famer George Brett), who oversaw him in Utica in 1986. "He was just so tough,"[3] recalled Brett in 1993 of the 18-year-old, who hit just .223 with two homers in 62 games. Mastery of the rules was another matter; Walker once cut across the diamond from third to first after a hit-and-run resulted in a fly-out, failing to stop and retouch second. "He was as fast a learner as I've ever seen. He never made the same mistake twice,"[4] said third base coach Gene Glynn.

A stint in the Florida Instructional League in the fall of 1986 helped Walker advance his game by leaps and bounds; the following season, he hit a combined 33 homers at two A-ball stops, then another 26 to go with a .287/.383/.534 line at Double-A Jacksonville in 1987. Anticipating the arrival of a Canadian star, reporters followed his progress through the minors, but a cartilage tear in his right knee while playing winter ball in Mexico cost him all of 1988 due to reconstructive surgery; even in 2005, the knee still bothered him. His play in 1989 at Triple-A Indianapolis earned him a promotion to the Expos in mid-August. Though he singled and had three walks in his August 16 debut, he reached base just nine more times in his other 19 games, finishing in a 1-for-22 slump.

Walker claimed the starting right field job the following spring, joining an outfield featuring Raines and Marquis Grissom. Despite a low batting average, his .241/.326/.434 line with a 112 OPS+, 19 homers, and 21 steals was good for 3.4 WAR. He soon emerged as a potent all-around threat, hitting a combined .293/.366/.501 for a 134 OPS+ over the next four seasons while averaging 20 homers and 19 steals. Adding defense that was 10 runs above average per year thanks to his sure hands and strong arm, he was worth 4.5 WAR per year even while averaging just 130 games due to DL stints (in 1991 and '93) and the strike.

Walker's 1992 season was his most valuable in Monteral; he hit .301/.353/.506 with 23 homers, 5.5 WAR, and his first All-Star and Gold Glove honors. He was en route to a similarly fine season in 1994 despite suffering a torn rotator cuff in his right shoulder, which affected his throwing and forced him to first base. Before moving from right field, he made one of the season's most memorable gaffes during an April 24 Sunday night game on ESPN. He handed a foul ball caught off the bat of Mike Piazza to a child in the stands, forgetting that there were only two outs; the two-base error became moot after Pedro Martinez yielded a homer on the next pitch. The Expos lost that night, but the team was a major league best 74-40 (.649) when the players struck on August 11, with Walker batting .322/.394/.587, running eighth in both batting average and slugging percentage.

The strike canceled the entire postseason and deprived the Expos not only of their second postseason appearance in franchise history but of the financial windfall that comes with making the playoffs. With general manager Kevin Malone under strict orders to cut payroll, the Expos didn't even offer Walker arbitration, and traded Grissom, staff ace Ken Hill, and closer John Wetteland once the strike ended. When it did, the 28-year-old Walker signed a four-year, $22.5 million deal with the Rockies.

Stepping into the most favorable hitting environment of the post–World War II era, Walker hit .306/.381/.607 with 36 homers, but in a 5.4-run-per-game environment, his OPS+ actually fell by 20 points relative to the league, from 151 to 131. Still, he helped the Rockies, a third-year expansion team, win the NL Wild Card, though they were ousted by the Braves in the Division Series. A broken collarbone cost him more than two months in 1996, but upon returning to full strength in '97, he hit a sizzling .366/.452/.720 for a 178 OPS+, leading the league in on-base and slugging percentages as well as homers (49). He missed the rare slash stat Triple Crown by just six points, as Tony Gwynn won the batting title, but his 409 total bases were the majors' most since Stan Musial's 429 in 1948. He also swiped 33 bases in 41 attempts, making him the 18th player in the 30-30 club to that point; his home run total remains the highest of the 38 players to accomplish the feat through 2016.

Adding 10 extra runs via defense and another nine via baserunning and double play avoidance, Walker totaled an NL-best 9.8 WAR—remember, that's adjusted for the scoring environment. In the 20 seasons since, only Barry Bonds (three times), Mike Trout (twice), Sammy Sosa, Alex Rodriguez, and Bryce Harper have topped that mark. Walker won the NL MVP award going away, receiving 22 of 28 first-place votes.

The 1997 season also produced another indelible highlight, and a reminder of Walker's reputation as a cut-up. At the All-Star Game in Cleveland, he faced Mariners ace (and former Expos teammate) Randy Johnson, whom he had conspicuously dodged during a recent roadtrip, taking an off day against the fierce southpaw; a fan carrying a "WHERE'S WALKER?" sign gained national attention. Johnson sailed his first pitch high over Walker's head as Walker flinched. Reprising John Kruk's similar approach in the 1993 All-Star Game, he turned his batting helmet backward, tried not to crack up, and took the next pitch as a righty before returning to the left-handed batter's box and working a walk, as fans and members of both teams laughed. "It was the funniest thing I've ever seen,"[5] said All-Star teammate Piazza.

Note that Walker didn't habitually dodge lefties; he took 30% of his plate appearances against them in his career, comparable to Ken Griffey Jr. (31%) and Wade Boggs (29%) if not Gwynn (34%)—the last three lefty-swingers elected, all from an era of increased bullpen specialization. Walker hardly struggled against Johnson (.393/.485/.571 in 33 PA) or the southpaw he faced most frequently, Hall of Famer Tom Glavine (.301/.370/.506 in 92 PA). Among post-1960-expansion-era lefties with at least 2,000 PA against same-side pitching, his .903 OPS (on .306/.385/.518 hitting) is second only to Bonds's .986, albeit with a push from Coors Field.

After falling short in 1997, Walker claimed batting titles in both 1998 (.363/.445/.630/158 OPS+) and '99 (.379/.458/.710/164 OPS+). In the latter year, he became the first player since 1980 to win the slash stat Triple Crown—leads in all three categories—and the first of a new wave of players to do it during the game's high-offense years. Unfortunately, trips to the DL for elbow and rib cage injuries limited him to 257 games and a combined 10.8 WAR for those two seasons. Worse, he missed nearly half of 2000—the first season of a six-year, $75 million extension signed the previous spring—due to a right elbow stress fracture and cleanup surgery.

Clear of the disabled list in 2001, Walker hit .350/.449/.662 (160 OPS+), winning his third and final batting title and adding 38 homers and 7.8 WAR, both the second-highest of his career and the latter the fourth-highest in the league. He played two more relatively full seasons in Colorado, but spent the first 2½ months of 2004 sidelined by a groin strain. After playing 38 games, he was traded to St. Louis in August. Lest anyone think his power was simply a function of high altitude, he bashed 11 homers—including two grand slams within a five-game span—in just 44 games while hitting .280/.393/.560, then added six more homers, two in each postseason round, while hitting .293/.379/.707 and helping the 105-win Cardinals to the World Series, where the Red Sox swept them to claim their first championship since 1918.

While Walker hit a very respectable .289/.384/.502 in 2005, he was limited to 100 games due to a herniated disc in his neck, and began hinting at retirement in June. Though the Cardinals likely would have exercised his $15 million option for 2006, he retired after the team was ousted from the postseason. His Cardinals teammates lauded his career, with manager Tony La Russa speaking in particularly glowing terms: "Most people know the kind of player that he has been his whole career. . . . I think he probably would be in the top three of just about every category: baserunning, defense, handling the bat."[6]

The Case

Undeniably, Walker's key counting stats (2,160 hits, 383 home runs) are low for the hitter-friendly era, even without considering the advantages that came with spending time in Coors Field, more on which momentarily. Due to injuries and the strike, he played more than 143 games just once, and averaged just 123 games a year, excluding his September 1988 call-up. Of the 24 Hall of Fame rightfielders, only seven played fewer games; four began their careers in the nineteenth century, while the last of those who didn't, Chuck Klein, retired in 1944. Likewise only six enshrined rightfielders had fewer hits than Walker, including the same nineteenth-century quartet and Klein.

More on Klein in a moment, but first Coors Field, where Walker took 31% of his total plate appearances (2,501) and posted videogame numbers: .381/.462/.710 with 154 homers compared to .282/.372/.501 elsewhere, still very respectable. In other words, his performance at Coors added 28 points of OBP and 64 points of SLG en route to a lifetime batting line of .313/.400/.565.

Looking at it a different way, Walker owns the third-largest gap between his home OPS (including his time with the Expos and Cardinals as well as the Rockies) and his road OPS among players with at least 7,000 PA:

Player	Years	Home OPS	Road OPS	Diff
Chuck Klein*	1928–1944	1.027	.813	.214
Bobby Doerr *	1937–1951	.929	.716	.213
Larry Walker	1989–2005	1.068	.865	.203
Cy Williams	1913–1930	.936	.736	.200
Todd Helton	1997–2013	1.048	.855	.193
Earl Averill*	1929–1941	1.009	.846	.163
Ron Santo*	1960–1975	.905	.747	.158
Wade Boggs*	1982–1999	.934	.781	.153
Jimmie Foxx *	1925–1945	1.116	.966	.150
Kirby Puckett*	1984–1995	.909	.761	.148

* Hall of Famer

Coors Field isn't the only venue that's contributed to hitters enjoying historically large home-field advantages. Both Klein and Williams (whose splits from his 28-game 1912 rookie season aren't available) spent the majority of their careers calling the Phillies' Baker Bowl—where the right field foul pole was 272 to 280 feet away—home, while Boggs, Doerr, and Foxx took advantage of Fenway Park's short foul lines and inviting Green Monster in left field. Most of that list is Hall of Famers or those I'm arguing should be; even after adjusting for their environmental advantages via more all-encompassing stats such as OPS+ and WAR, they compare favorably to those enshrined.

Again using that 7,000 PA cutoff, Walker's 141 OPS+ is in a virtual tie with Hall of Famer Sliding Billy Hamilton and likely honorees Chipper Jones and David Ortiz for 43rd all-time. That's certainly Cooperstown caliber, just ahead of Duke Snider (140), Reggie Jackson (139), Klein (137), Griffey (136), and more. The problem is that some of those players accumulated thousands more plate appearances than Walker, but moving from a rate stat to a counting stat, batting runs—which measures a player relative to the average hitter in his league—upholds his elite standing. Walker's total of 420 ranks 62nd, slightly ahead of four players with 3,000 hits (Dave Winfield, Eddie Murray, Tony Gwynn, and Rod Carew), the first two with over 400 homers, the last two with a combined 15 batting titles. In other words, he created as much value with his bat as players routinely lauded for major milestones.

Batting runs is included within WAR, and so are all of the other things that Walker did—and did well. He was 40 runs above average in baserunning and another 10 in double play avoidance. That extra 50 runs—roughly five wins—ranks 53rd among players in the post-1960 expansion period (chosen for its completeness of data in these departments), sandwiched between Alex Rodriguez and Bonds, and within 10 runs of five players who stole at least twice as many bases as Walker's 230, namely Cesar Cedeno, Roberto Alomar, Bonds, Omar Moreno, and Delino DeShields. Those players all had more apparent speed than Walker, but scouts saw above-average baserunning potential in him as early as 1984, and two scouting reports from the 1993–94 period in the Hall of Fame's Diamond Mines database graded him as a 6 ("plus") in both speed and baserunning.

Defensively, via Total Zone and (from 2003 onward) Defensive Runs Saved, Walker was 94 runs above average for his career, thanks to his arm (which did decline as his injuries mounted), range, and instincts. That ranks eighth all-time behind Roberto Clemente (205 runs), Jesse Barfield, Brian Jordan, Al Kaline, Jason Heyward, Ichiro Suzuki, and Hank Aaron.

By adding value at every turn, Walker finished with 72.6 career WAR, 11th-best among rightfielders, 0.6 below the standard but better than 14 of the 24 enshrined rightfielders. His 44.6 peak WAR ranks 11th as well, 1.6 above the standard and ahead of 15 of the 24 enshrinees. His 58.6 JAWS is 10th, 0.6 above the standard. Via career WAR and JAWS, he's the best rightfielder outside the Hall, with the banned-for-life Shoeless Joe Jackson the only one with a higher peak score (52.5). Here it's worth noting that Walker also outdoes both ballot-mates Gary Sheffield and Vlad Guerrero—both with flashier traditional stats but far less value beyond their bats—on all three fronts as well. Looking into their WAR components:

Player	PA	Rbat	Rbase	Rdp	Rfield	Rpos	WAR
Walker	8,030	420	40	10	94	-75	72.6
Guerrero	9,059	429	-3	-17	7	-114	59.3
Sheffield	10,947	561	-1	11	-195	-84	60.3

Sheffield, with a considerable advantage in playing time, produced more value with the bat but was legendarily awful with the glove (second-worst all-time according to Total Zone + Defensive Runs Saved), albeit while playing tougher positions in the infield early in his career. Guerrero, a better fielder, still loses value for DHing in 508 games (Sheffield did so in 302, the NL-only Walker in just 27). Walker also has a huge advantage over both players in baserunning and double play avoidance. The all-around strength of his case is why he's profiled at length here, while those two are confined to my annual SI.com series and briefs below.

Walker also fares well when the weight of his traditional accomplishments is measured. He made only five All-Star teams, which is toward the lower end among modern Hall of Famers, but his seven Gold Gloves aren't out of line with the fielding metrics, and his three batting titles, while helped by his ballpark, at least show that he wasn't winning by fluke. His Hall of Fame Monitor score of 148 is in the "virtual cinch" territory. To be fair, that metric wasn't designed with Coors Field or the sustained scoring levels of the 1993–2009 period in mind, which is a big reason why JAWS came into being: I wanted a tool that could adjust accordingly.

His accomplishments should still be enough for Cooperstown, but whether due to the distortions of Coors Field, his modest career length, or the crowd on the ballot, actual BBWAA voters can't seem to get on board the Walker bandwagon. He debuted at 20.3% in 2011, peaked the next year at 22.9%, but sank to about half that level amid the 2014–15 crowd. Even with 21.9% in 2017, his best showing in four years, he's in no-man's-land when it comes to voting history. Since 1966, the lowest percentage any candidate has received in year seven while still being elected by the BBWAA is Bert Blyleven (35.4%), who needed 14 years to gain entry, time that Walker doesn't have given an eligibility window that's been truncated to 10 years.

Like Alan Trammell and others whose résumés have similarly failed to impress voters in a timely fashion, Walker appears destined to join the growing parade of qualified candidates who will have to call upon the Today's Game Era Committee to set things right. Assuming the rules stay the same, the earliest that would happen will be in 2022. He can only hope the traffic thins out before his arrival.

THE ROUNDUP

The number before each player name refers to his JAWS ranking *among all players at the position*, not necessarily those in the Hall. Average HOF rightfielder: 73.2/43.0/58.1.

The Elite (above standard in career, peak, and JAWS)

1. Babe Ruth

Teams:	Red Sox 1914–19 • Yankees 1920–34 • Braves 1935
Stats:	.342/.474/.69 • 206 OPS+ • 2,873 H • 714 HR • 123 SB
Rankings:	13x led SLG • 12x led OPS+ • 12x led HR • 11x led WAR • 10x led OBP
	All-time: 1st WAR • 1st OPS+ • 1st SLG • 2nd OBP • 3rd HR • 6th TB • 8th AVG
Voting/JAWS:	BBWAA 1936 **(1st, 95.1%)** • 189.1/84.7/134.2*

By swinging for the fences, both literally and figuratively, the Sultan of Swat revolutionized baseball, offering a thrilling alternative to the one-run-at-a-time approach and popularizing the game both domestically and abroad. A man of excesses, he became "the most colorful and most lovable figure any sport has known."[7] Not surprisingly, the Bambino is the heavyweight champ of advanced stats, too. His narrow edge over Barry Bonds in position player WAR (163.1 to 162.4) doesn't count his 20.6 pitching WAR, a run that includes his second-place finish in 1916 (8.7, plus an AL-best 1.75 ERA); those numbers are included in his career and JAWS above but not in the position calculations. As a hitter, he either holds or shares the record for the most league leads in homers, slugging percentage, OPS+, and WAR. The early resistance to the home run as somehow impure led Ty Cobb to outpoll Ruth in the Hall's inaugural election (98.2% to 95.1%), but by 1950 the slugger had the upper hand in an Associated Press poll of sportswriters and sportscasters to determine the greatest player of all time.[8]

2. Hank Aaron

Teams:	Braves 1954–74 • Brewers 1975–76
Stats:	.305/.374/.555 • 155 OPS+ • 3,771 H • 755 HR • 240 SB
Rankings:	21x All-Star • 8x led TB • 4x led HR • 4x led SLG • 3x led OPS+

---

* Pitching WAR included in player's career WAR & JAWS (not used in calculating position standards).

All-time: 1st TB • 1st RBI • 2nd HR • 3rd H • 5th WAR • 18th SLG • 20th OPS+

Voting/JAWS: BBWAA 1982 **(1st, 97.8%)** • **142.6/60.1/101.3**

Though he didn't dominate leagues or capture the public's imagination as Ruth or even Willie Mays did, Hammerin' Hank forged a remarkably consistent career, one that allowed him to overtake the Bambino on the all-time home run list in 1974— amid death threats from racists—and to set as-yet-unsurpassed records for total bases (6,856) and RBIs (2,297) while collecting more hits than anyone besides Cobb and Pete Rose. Aaron regularly led various offensive categories, but only led once in WAR; in four of his seven years as runner-up and three of his five in third place he trailed the Say Hey Kid. As for consistency, his 17 consecutive seasons (1955–71) with at least 5.0 WAR are a record, while his 18 consecutive (1955–72) of at least a 125 OPS+ while qualifying for the batting title trail only Cobb (22). On the home run front, Aaron's 245 homers from his age-35 season onward outdistances everyone but Bonds (317), aided by Atlanta-Fulton County Stadium's MLB-high 1,057-foot elevation, hence "The Launching Pad." While it appears ridiculous that nine BBWAA voters out of 415 left Aaron off their ballots, his voting share was still the highest since Cobb in 1936, outdistancing even Mays (94.7% in '79).

3. Stan Musial

Teams: Cardinals 1941–44, 1946–63
Stats: .331/.417/.559 • 159 OPS+ • 3,630 H • 475 HR • 78 SB
Rankings: 20× All-Star • 7× led AVG • 6× led OBP • 6× led SLG • 6× led OPS+ • 4× led WAR • 2× slash-stat TC
                  All-time: 2nd TB • 4th H • 8th WAR • 11th OPS+ • 15th SLG
Voting/JAWS: BBWAA 1969 **(1st, 93.2%)** • **128.1/64.2/96.2**

A 1940 injury to his left shoulder while diving for a ball closed off his future as a pitcher, but it all worked out for Stan the Man. With a corkscrew stance that looked "like a kid peeking around the corner to see if the cops were coming,"[9] Musial peppered NL leaderboards for two decades while leading the Cardinals to four pennants and three championships, and taking home three MVP awards. When he retired, he trailed only Cobb in hits, and even today he's second in total bases (6,134), the rare player to best Ruth in a power-based category. He's eighth in position player WAR, but his classification is the thorny question. While he played more games at first base (1,016) than any other single position, his total in the outfield (1,890) trumps that. He played 929 in left field, 785 in right, and 331 in center, often switching during games, and migrating to harder positions from year to year—from first base in 1947 to right field in '48, from left field in '51 to center in '52, and so on. Ultimately, he's here because he compiled 45.5 WAR in seasons while primarily playing right field, compared to 38.8 as a leftfielder and 35.3 as a first baseman.

4. Mel Ott

Teams:	Giants 1926–47
Stats:	.304/.414/.533 • 155 OPS+ • 2,876 H • 511 HR • 89 SB
Rankings:	12× All-Star • 6× led HR • 5× led WAR • 5× led OPS+ • 4× led SLG
	All-time: 16th WAR • 24th HR
Voting/JAWS:	BBWAA 1951 **(3rd, 87.2%)** • **107.8/52.8/80.3**

Both prodigy and prodigious home run hitter, Ott signed with the Giants before his 17th birthday. Rather than farm him out, manager John McGraw kept him around to be tutored on the game's finer points by future Hall of Famers Ross Youngs (his predecessor in right field) and then-coach Roger Bresnahan, though he was forbidden from fraternizing with the team's hardened veterans. He became a regular in 1928 (after Youngs's death from Bright's disease) and hit 18 homers with a 139 OPS+ as a 19-year-old, then 42 homers with a 165 OPS+ at age 20. Some of his power owed to the Polo Grounds' unique shape (480' to center, 279' to left field, and 258' to right, most inviting for a lefty slugger); he hit 323 homers there, compared to 188 elsewhere, though his overall rate stats weren't all that different (.297/.422/.558 at home, .311/.408/.510 elsewhere). He retired as the NL's all-time home run leader, third overall behind Ruth and Jimmie Foxx. He's one of just five players to gain induction before the now standard five-year waiting period, along with Ruth, Hornsby, longtime teammate Carl Hubbell, and Joe DiMaggio.

5. Frank Robinson

Teams:	Reds 1956–65 • Orioles 1966–71 • Dodgers 1972 • Angels 1973–74 • Indians 1974–76
Stats:	.294/.389/.537 • 154 OPS+ • 2,943 H • 586 HR • 204 SB
Rankings:	12× All-Star • 7× top 5 WAR • 4× led SLG • 4× led OPS+
	All-time: 9th HR • 12th TB • 18th WAR • 23rd OPS+
Voting/JAWS:	BBWAA 1982 **(1st, 89.2%)** • **107.2/52.9/80.0**

"Frank Robinson always went into second like a guy jumping through a skylight with a drawn Luger."[10]

—JIM MURRAY

Robinson's acceptance of the Indians' managerial job following the 1974 season—making him the game's first black manager—cost him shots at both 3,000 hits and 600 home runs, but as a 12-time All-Star, two-time world champion, and the only player to win MVP in both leagues, his career was more than complete, if often overshadowed by Mays and Aaron. Robinson set a rookie record for homers (38) that stood until 1987, and bashed 324 homers in his decade with the Reds, but upon being dismissed as "not a young 30"[11] by owner Bill DeWitt, carried his talent and red-hot intensity to the AL, where he immediately hit a career-high 49 homers, won the Triple Crown, and led the Orioles to their first championship. Though he never replicated his playing success in the dugout, Robinson broke barriers as the first black manager in each league, and turned around moribund squads in San Francisco, Baltimore, and Montreal before working in MLB's front office in a variety of high-profile capacities, often as the game's most prominent black executive.

6. Roberto Clemente

Teams:	Pirates 1955–72
Stats:	.317/.359/.475 • 130 OPS+ • 3,000 H • 240 HR • 83 SB
Rankings:	12× All-Star • 12× GG • 10× top 10 OPS+ • 5× top 5 WAR •
	4× led AVG
	All-time: 26th WAR
Voting/JAWS:	BBWAA 1973 (special election) • 94.5/54.3/74.4

Clemente's legend as a pioneering Latin American star, and later as a martyr who died while helping to distribute humanitarian aid, sometimes obscures his on-field accomplishments. Topping out at 29 homers, he wasn't a power hitter like Aaron, Mays, or Robinson, but his four batting titles exceeded that trio's combined total, and his peripheral skills placed him in the top 10 in OPS+ 10 times. His powerful, accurate right arm remains the gold standard; beyond the Gold Gloves, his 253 assists and 205 runs above average are both tops among rightfielders. Throw in a .362/.383/.534 line in 60 PA for two World Series winners, and you'd have a Hall of Famer even if he hadn't reached 3,000 hits. As for his trailblazing, Clemente battled not only racism but also a language barrier and a condescending press that quoted him in broken English with phonetic spelling and accused him of hypochondria. He used his fame as a platform to speak out against discrimination and to further his charitable efforts in Puerto Rico and elsewhere in the region. In response to his tragic death, the Hall allowed the BBWAA to waive the standard five-year waiting period; his election in March 1973 made him Cooperstown's first Latin American–born player.

7. Al Kaline

Teams:	Tigers 1953–74
Stats:	.297/.376/.480 • 134 OPS+ • 3,007 H • 399 HR • 137 SB
Rankings:	15× All-Star • 10× GG • 9× top 10 OPS+ • 8× top 5 WAR • 7× top 5 AVG • 7× top 5 OBP • 5× top 5 SLG
	All-time: 28th H • 28th WAR
Voting/JAWS:	BBWAA 1980 **(1st, 88.3%)** • **92.5/48.8/70.7**

A bonus baby who debuted at 18, Kaline became the youngest batting champion ever at 20, hitting .340/.421/.546 in 1955; his OBP, SLG, 162 OPS+, and 8.2 WAR ranked second only to Mickey Mantle, who edged him in the MVP race. The sky must have seemed the limit, but only once in Kaline's remaining 20 seasons did he exceed that WAR or OPS+. He was great nonetheless thanks in part to outstanding defense (+155 runs, second only to Clemente). Lord only knows what numbers Kaline might have compiled if not for the osteomyelitis that required the removal of diseased bone in his left foot when he was eight—he learned to run on the side of his foot—and that bothered him throughout his career. He averaged 125 games a year from 1962 onward amid myriad injuries, but remained generally productive, and hit .379/.400/.655 in the 1968 World Series. He reached 3,000 hits in the penultimate week of his career, but went homerless in his final 12 games to remain stuck just short of the milestone 400, not that his credentials needed further burnishing.

8. Reggie Jackson

Teams:	Kansas City/Oakland A's 1967–75, '87 • Orioles 1976 • Yankees 1977–81 • Angels 1982–86
Stats:	.262/.356/.49 • 139 OPS+ • 2,584 H • 563 HR • 228 SB
Rankings:	14× All-Star • 8× top 10 WAR • 4× led HR • 4× led OPS+ • 3× led SLG
	All-time: 13th HR • 27th TB
Voting/JAWS:	BBWAA 1993 **(1st, 93.6%)** • **73.8/46.8/60.3**

Reggie Jackson was a hot dog, with extra mustard: "I represent both the underdog and the overdog in our society."[12] No other player so enjoyed being the center of attention, either at the plate or in front of a microphone: "I'm the straw that stirs the drink." [13] None had such a knack for rising to the occasion with a dramatic home run or a well-timed quip: "I guess I underestimated the magnitude of me." [14] Best known for his postseason prowess, "Mr. October" won five championships while hitting .357/.457/.755 with 10 homers in 116 World Series PA; his 18 postseason homers are tied for the pre–Wild Card–era record. Regular-season-wise, from 1968–76, only Joe Morgan and Johnny Bench topped Jackson's 54.1 WAR, but once he hit the Big Apple, DHing, indifferent defense (-70 runs from 1977 on, compared to +47 prior), and platooning cut into his value—in the lineup, if not on the marquee. His all-time record in strikeouts (2,597) wasn't as big a deal as advertised, for it prevented him from hitting into double plays (he's +10 runs in that department). For all of his controversies, he sailed into Cooperstown.

9. Harry Heilmann

Teams:	Tigers 1914, '16–29 • Reds 1930, '32
Stats:	.342/.410/.520 • 148 OPS+ • 2,660 H • 183 HR • 113 SB
Rankings:	12× top 10 OPS+ • 12× top 10 SLG • 7× top 5 OBP • 5× top 3 WAR • 4× led AVG
Voting/JAWS:	BBWAA 1952 **(11th, 86.8%)** • 72.1/47.1/59.6

As a teenager, Heilman was groomed to replace the legendary "Wahoo" Sam Crawford as Detroit's rightfielder, but his career didn't take off until after detours to the Pacific Coast League (1915) and the navy (half of 1918). Once it did, "Slug" (for his notorious lack of speed) won four batting titles with averages of .393 or higher, edging out fellow future Hall of Famers: Cobb in 1921 (.394 to .389), Ruth in '23 (.403 to .393), Tris Speaker in '25 (.393 to .389), Al Simmons in '27 (.398 to .392); in the last two, he came from behind on the season's final day. Upon retirement, Heilmann became the first ex-player-turned-play-by-play broadcaster, doing so with great acclaim for Detroit's WXYZ for 17 years (1934–50). He died of lung cancer on July 9, 1951, at age 56—rotten timing, as Cobb, at times his mentor and rival while managing him, had spearheaded an effort to call a special election on his behalf at the All-Star Game the next day in Detroit; Heilmann had received 67.7% the previous winter. It didn't happen, but he was elected posthumously in 1952.

The Rank and File

11. Paul Waner

Teams:	Pirates 1926–40 • Dodgers 1941, '43–44 • Braves 1941–42 • Yankees 1944–45
Stats:	.333/.404/.473 • 134 OPS+ • 3,152 H • 113 HR • 104 SB
Rankings:	9× top 10 WAR • 8× top 10 OPS+ • 7× top 5 OBP • 7× top 10 SLG • 4× All-Star • 3× led AVG All-Time: 10th 3B • 17th H
Voting/JAWS:	BBWAA 1952 **(5th, 83.3%)** • **72.8/42.2/57.5**

Though his "Big Poison" nickname stemmed from a Brooklynese pronunciation of "person"—and was somewhat inaccurate given his modest size (5' 8½", 155 lbs)—rather than from his penchant for the sauce, Waner was as renowned for his drinking as for his hitting. "It was said that he had the sharpest bloodshot eyes in baseball,"[15] recalled contemporary Billy Werber. Joined by brother Lloyd, who would play alongside him for 14 years, he led the Pirates to the 1927 pennant, winning NL MVP honors and the first of three batting titles with a .380/.437/.549 season. Waner didn't hit many homers, but racked up eight 200-hit seasons, generally with OBPs well above .400. Cavernous Forbes Field made him a triples machine; his 191 rank 10th all-time. Released at age 38 by the Pirates in December 1940, when he had 2,868 hits, he reached 3,000 with the Braves in '42, the seventh player to do so (the only one between 1925 and '58). Due to a backlog of worthy candidates, he needed five election cycles to gain entry.

12. Sam Crawford

Teams:	Reds 1899–1902 • Tigers 1903–17
Stats:	.309/.362/.452 • 144 OPS+ • 2,961 H • 97 HR • 367 SB
Rankings:	11× top 5 SLG • 10× top 10 WAR • 9 top 5 OPS+. 7× top 5 AVG All-time: 1st 3B
Voting/JAWS:	VC 1957 • **75.1/39.7/57.4**

Nicknamed for his Nebraska hometown, "Wahoo" Sam Crawford was the dead-ball era's prototypical slugger, less for knocking the ball over fences than for hitting it deep into cavernous outfields. He's the all-time leader in triples (309) and second to Jesse Burkett in inside-the-park homers (51). Crawford helped the Tigers to three straight pennants (1907–09) but hit just .243/.264/.357 in 72 World Series PA. Though he collected 2,851 hits through 1915, his age-35 season, and declared reaching 3,000 to be his "chief ambition,"[16] he was supplanted by Heilmann in 1916, and released after the '17 season. He spent four years with the PCL's Los Angeles Angels, never returning to the majors despite flickers of interest. In the Hall's early years, he was largely ignored by the BBWAA, failing to reach 5% through 1945. Mending fences with Cobb—who resented having been hazed by Crawford as a teen in 1905–06—at Heilmann's funeral helped get the ball rolling; Crawford was considered by the VC in 1953 and '55 before gaining entry in '57.

14. Tony Gwynn

Teams:	Padres 1982–2001
Stats:	.338/.388/.459 • 132 OPS+ • 3,141 H • 135 HR • 319 SB
Rankings:	15× All-Star • 8× led AVG • 6× top 5 OBP • 5× GG • 4× top 5 WAR
	All-time: 16th AVG • 19th H
Voting/JAWS:	BBWAA 2007 **(1st, 97.6%)** • 68.8/41.1/54.9

An outstanding pure hitter, Gwynn batted above .300 in every season but his rookie year, though he fell short of qualifying for the batting title four times due to injuries and aging. Despite his accomplishments and accolades—summarized by his 279 Hall of Fame Monitor points (17th all-time)—he's shy of all three WAR standards, mainly due to his modest secondary contributions. Even with 13 top five finishes in batting average, he ranked among the top five in OBP just six times due to his 7.7% walk rate, and among the top 10 in SLG just twice. He wasn't a particularly productive base stealer (71.8%), though he did add 23 runs on the basepaths and another six on avoiding double plays. Defensively, while he was 76 runs above average through 1992, he was 70 below thereafter. The slide, which coincided with his weight gain—he described himself as having "a body by Betty Crocker"[17]—offset his mid-career offensive resurgence, so his last five-win season came in 1991. That's not to say he shouldn't be enshrined, but his voting share, the eighth highest ever, overstates his case.

19. Dave Winfield

Teams:	Padres 1973–80 • Yankees 1981–88, '90 • Angels 1990–91 • Blue Jays 1992 • Twins 1993–94 • Indians 1995
Stats:	.283/.353/.475 • 130 OPS+ • 3,110 H • 465 HR • 223 SB

Rankings: 12× All-Star • 7× GG • 7× top 10 OPS+7× top 10 SLG • 4×
top 10 AVG • 3× top 10 WAR
All-time: 20th H • 14th TB

Voting/JAWS: BBWAA 2001 **(1st, 84.5%)** • **63.8/37.7/50.8**

Drafted by the NBA's Atlanta Hawks, the ABA's Utah Stars, and the NFL's Minnesota Vikings, the 6′6″ Winfield went directly to the majors after being chosen with the fourth pick in 1973, the rare right move for the hapless Padres, who briefly contemplated moving him to shortstop in '74. Though graceful and powerful, with a fair bit of speed, Winfield had a hard time living up to expectations, particularly during his 10-year deal with the Yankees; George Steinbrenner's second suspension resulted from paying $40,000 to known gambler Howard Spira to dig up dirt on him. While Winfield's offensive credentials aren't in question, Total Zone abhors his defense, a surprise given his Gold Gloves and reputation. His -91 runs is the third worst of any rightfielder, and the alternative systems, Defensive Regression Analysis (-77) and Fielding Runs Above Average (-51) take dim views, too. His WAR is the third lowest among the 30 players with at least 3,000 hits. More charitably, Winfield was a compiler in the best sense; reaching those milestones and shedding Steinbrenner's "Mr. May" tag (for his 1-for-22 1981 World Series) with the Series-clinching hit in 1992 had to be gratifying.

24. Elmer Flick

Teams: Phillies 1898–1901 • A's 1902 • Cleveland Bronchos/Naps
1902–10

Stats: .313/.389/.445 • 149 OPS+ • 1,752 H • 48 HR • 330 SB

Rankings: 7× top 10 AVG • 6× top 5 OBP • 6× top 5 SLG • 6× top 5
OPS+ • 6× top 5 WAR

Voting/JAWS: VC 1963 • **53.2/41.3/47.2**

A fleet-footed, turn-of-the-century power hitter, Flick is best known for having been the target of a trade inquiry from the Tigers, who in the spring of 1907 offered the 20-year-old Ty Cobb to Cleveland straight up given the strife he was causing among teammates. The Naps, who valued Flick's agreeable nature, passed. Flick was 31 at the time, heading into the final year of a 10-year run during which he averaged 5.2 WAR with a 152 OPS+. Unfortunately, a mysterious gastrointestinal illness soon sapped his strength, limiting him to 99 games and comparatively meager production over his age-32–34 seasons, followed by a couple years in the American Association. Cobb's 1961 death revived stories of the abortive trade and thus interest in the forgotten Flick, who was elected by the VC two years later at age 87, making him the oldest living inductee in the institution's history. So surprised was he that he thought the call from ex-teammate and VC member Branch Rickey was a joke.

25. Willie Keeler

Teams:	Giants 1892–93, 1910 • Brooklyn Grooms/Superbas 1893, '99–1902 • Orioles 1894–98 • New York Highlanders 1903–09
Stats:	.341/.388/.415 • 127 OPS+ • 2,932 H • 33 HR • 495 SB
Rankings:	9× top 5 AVG • 8× top 10 OBP • 6× top 10 WAR All-time: 11th AVG
Voting/JAWS:	BBWAA 1939 **(4th, 75.5%)** • 54.0/36.2/45.1

Standing 5'4", 140 pounds and swinging a 30-inch bat, "Wee Willie" Keeler was known for his plan of attack: "Hit 'em where they ain't." He did, collecting at least 200 hits every year from 1894–1901. Though he played with all three New York teams (two before they acquired their modern-day nicknames), the little lefty is primarily identified with the original Orioles, whom he helped win three pennants (1894–96) with batting averages in the .370s; he then raised his game and led the NL with marks of .424 (1897) and .385 ('98). Though lacking in power, he had the speed to beat out infield hits and turn doubles into triples, not to mention the savvy to perfect the "Baltimore chop." Among pre-1920 position players, he's 22nd in WAR, second among rightfielders behind Crawford. With one more year of playing regularly, he likely would have been the second player to 3,000 hits after Cap Anson, but he collected just three hits as a player-coach under Mc-Graw in 1910. The lore surrounding him was deep enough that he was elected in 1939, though, sadly, he had passed on 16 years earlier.

26. Enos Slaughter

Teams:	Cardinals 1938–42, 1946–53 • Yankees 1954–55, '56–59 • A's 1955–56 • Braves 1959
Stats:	.300/.382/.453 • 124 OPS+ • 2,383 H • 169 HR • 71 SB
Rankings:	10× All-Star • 8× top 10 AVG • 6× top 10 OPS+ • 5× top 10 WAR
Voting/JAWS:	VC 1985 • **55.1/35.1/45.1**

The intense, hard-nosed Slaughter etched himself in the national consciousness with his "Mad Dash" from first base to score the winning run in Game 7 of the 1946 World Series and again in '47, when he spiked Jackie Robinson's ankle while running out a groundball, an incident believed by many (including Robinson) to be intentional. When combined with persistent rumors of his involvement in the Cardinals' planned boycott of Robinson, he spent decades refuting allegations of racism. What's beyond dispute is that Slaughter was a 10-time All-Star who lost three prime years (ages 27–29)—and perhaps 15 WAR and 8 JAWS—to World War II, but barely missed a beat, helping St. Louis to championships in 1942 and '46. After the Cardinals decided he was too old, he helped the Yankees to a trio of pennants as a part-timer. He hit .291/.406/.468 in 96 World Series PA, including .350/.440/.500 in 1956, at age 40. After topping out at 68.8% in his 1979 BBWAA finale, he was elected by the VC six years later. Negro Leagues star, Hall of Famer, and committee member Monte Irvin championed Slaughter's skill and character, saying "Old Eno's all right. He plays in my golf tournament every year."[18]

29. Sam Rice

Teams: Senators 1915–33 • Indians 1934
Stats: .322/.374/.427 • 112 OPS+ • 2,987 H • 34 HR • 351 SB
Rankings: 8× top 10 AVG • 8× top 5 SB • 3× top 10 WAR
                    All-time: 14th 3B
Voting/JAWS: VC 1963 • **52.8/30.8/41.8**

Few baseball controversies have taken on such life as that over whether Rice actually caught the ball for the final out of Game 3 of the 1925 World Series while tumbling into Griffith Stadium's temporary stands to preserve a 4–3 win (though the Senators fell in seven games). Two years after election, Rice sent a sealed letter to Hall president Paul Kerr to be opened after his death, which occurred in 1974; its wording ("At no time did I lose possession of the ball")[19] has been endlessly parsed, as has his lifelong refrain ("The umpire said I did")[20]. An undersized (5'9", 150 pounds) pitcher when he reached the majors at 25, Rice converted to the outfield amid shoulder woes. He reached Cooperstown on the strength of 13 qualifying seasons with a batting average of .300 or above, albeit mostly from a high-offense era and without great patience or power; he rarely dented the leaderboards. Griffith Stadium's unfriendliness to lefty power limited his home runs, though he did collect 184 triples. While his retirement 13 hits short of 3,000 is said to illustrate his era's incognizance of milestones, note that near-miss predecessor Sam Crawford was focused on the goal two decades earlier.

30. Harry Hooper

Teams: Red Sox 1909–20 • White Sox 1921–25
Stats: .281/.368/.387 • 114 OPS+ • 2,466 H • 75 HR • 375 SB
Rankings: 8× top 10 SB • 4× top 10 OPS+ • 3× top 10 OBP • 3× top 10 WAR
Voting/JAWS: VC 1971 • **53.1/30.0/41.5**

Hooper's offensive numbers and low peak (58th among rightfielders) hardly scream Hall-worthy, but praise from McGraw and former teammates Ruth, Speaker, and Smokey Joe Wood (the last in *The Glory of Their Times*), plus an outsized reputation for clutch play led to his election after the BBWAA had ignored him. Along with Speaker and Duffy Lewis, Hooper was part of the "Golden Outfield" that anchored the Red Sox from 1910–15, a span during which they won two championships; they added two more before Hooper's trade to the White Sox in '21. He hit .293/.375/.435 in 108 PA in his four Series, with a key defensive play in the decisive Game 8 in 1912 and two homers in the '15 clincher. The defensive metrics back his sterling reputation, as his 77 fielding runs are 20 more than any other prewar rightfielder. Though his batting averages often dipped below .260, he was an effective leadoff hitter thanks to walks and steals. He was the best of VC member Waite Hoyt's four ex-teammates elected during Hoyt's 1971–76 run, but that's not saying much.

32. Kiki Cuyler

Teams: Pirates 1921–27 • Cubs 1928–35 • Reds 1935–37 • Dodgers 1938
Stats: .321/.386/.474 • 125 OPS+ • 2,299 H • 128 HR • 328 SB
Rankings: 6× top 10 WAR • 5× top 5 AVG • 5× top 5 OBP • 4× led SB
Voting/JAWS: VC 1968 • **46.7/34.9/40.8**

A sensation in his first three full seasons, Culyer hit a combined .343/.402/.532 for a 140 OPS+ from 1924–26, and helped the Pirates to a championship in '25, during which he placed second in both WAR and the MVP voting. Speedy, strong-armed, and wielding a potent bat, he was considered one of the NL's top all-around players around that period, not to mention the top practitioner of the stolen base before it went out of fashion for three decades, leading the NL four times in five years (1926–30). The emergence of the Waner brothers and a feud with rookie manager Donie Bush over batting second instead of third sent Cuyler to the bench by the time of the Bucs' 1927 pennant, and to Chicago after that. He helped the Cubs to pennants in 1929 and '32, but by the latter year (his age-33 season), he was already in decline. Amid injuries and inconsistencies, he averaged just 110 games and 1.6 WAR per year over his final seven seasons. He peaked at 33.8% in 1958, eight years after his death, and gained entry via the VC a decade later.

33. Chuck Klein

Teams:	Phillies 1928–33, '36–39, '40–44 • Cubs 1934–36 • Pirates 1939
Stats:	.320/.379/.543 • 137 OPS+ • 2,076 H • 300 HR • 79 SB
Rankings:	8x top 10 OPS+ • 5x top 10 WAR • 5x top 2 SLG • 4x led HR
Voting/JAWS:	VC 1980 • **43.6/36.7/40.2**

It's not entirely fair to say that Klein was a product of his home park, but no hitter with at least 7,000 PA owns a wider split between home and road OPS than his .215. Klein hit .354/.410/.618 at home, compared to .286/.346/.466 on the road. Given the added advantage of playing in a high-offense era, the lefty swinger hit like turn-of-the-millennium Bonds (.395/.448/.705 in 2,600 PA) at the Baker Bowl, a bandbox that was 281' down the right field line and 300' to right-center, albeit with a 60' wall-and-screen barrier, 23' higher than the Green Monster. The same cozy confines that caused impoverished Phillies pitching staffs to surrender upward of 1,000 runs in some seasons helped Klein to four NL homer titles from 1929–33, capped by both the Triple Crown and the slash stat version of same in '33. Outside of that run, his other 12 seasons were only worth a combined 13.1 WAR. It's no crime to take advantage of one's park, and it's not like he wasn't a potent hitter for a decade (149 OPS+ from 1928–37), but even so, he's sixth in WAR among rightfielders from 1920–45, and not a particularly inspiring choice by the VC.

36. Sam Thompson

Teams:	Detroit Wolverines 1885–88 • Quakers/Phillies 1889–98 • Tigers 1906
Stats:	.331/.384/.505 • 147 OPS+ • 1,988 H • 126 HR • 232 SB
Rankings:	10x top 10 HR • 8x top 10 SLG • 8x top 10 AVG • 6x top 10 WAR • 4x top 5 OPS+
Voting/JAWS:	VC 1974 • **44.3/33.2/38.7**

At 6'2", Big Sam Thompson was one of the nineteenth century's tallest players—outsized enough to split his undersized pants while running out a double in his 1885 debut—and top sluggers, out-homered only by Roger Connor; nobody touched Thompson's record 166 RBI in 1887 until Babe Ruth broke it in 1921. Thompson packed a lot into a career that was effectively 12 years and change due to a late start at age 25, and to injuries and illnesses. In Philadelphia he became the first lefty to hit 20 homers in a season (1889), and shared the outfield with fellow Hall of Famers Billy Hamilton and Ed Delahanty (1891–95). All three hit over .400 in 1894, led by Thompson's .415—this despite losing six weeks to an amputated left pinky fingertip, as the digit had been pulverized by batted balls. Despite his short career, Thompson ranks first in WAR among nineteenth-century rightfielders, and 15th among position players. An eight-time VC candidate from 1953–64, his election was aided by a SABR finding that his rate of 0.926 RBI per game ranks first in MLB history.

42. King Kelly

Teams:	Reds 1878–79 • Chicago White Stockings 1880–86 • Boston Beaneaters 1887–89, '91–92 • Boston Reds (PL) 1890 • Boston Reds (AA) 1891 • Cincinnati Kelly's Killers (AA) 1891 • Giants 1893
Stats:	.308/.368/.438 • 139 OPS+ • 1,813 H • 69 HR • 368 SB
Rankings:	10× top 10 OBP • 8× top 10 AVG • 6× top 10 WAR • 6× top 10 OPS+ • 6× top 10 HR • 5× top 10 SB
Voting/JAWS:	OTC 1945 • **44.3/31.1/37.7**

Baseball's first matinee idol, its first subject of a hit song ("Slide, Kelly Slide"), and an as-told-to autobiography, Kelly was also an early casualty, a hard drinker who spent every penny he earned and didn't live to see his 37th birthday. He rose to prominence while helping the Cap Anson–led White Stockings to five pennants in seven years, was sold to Boston for a record $10,000, entered the league-jumping phase of his career as his skills and conditioning were in decline, and died of pneumonia in 1894, a year after leaving baseball for vaudeville. Kelly played all around the diamond, including 583 games at catcher. His cumulative numbers are depressed by short seasons, but his 4.5 WAR per 650 PA ranks 20th among rightfielders. Beyond the numbers, he's credited with inventing the hook slide, and of popularizing tactics ranging from the smart (the squeeze play, leading off of a base to get a better jump, intentionally fouling off a string of pitches to fatigue the pitcher) to the illegal (skipping bases when umpires weren't looking, entering the field of play as a coach to impersonate a baserunner, keeping an extra ball in his pocket). His combination of superior play, innovation, and fame make him one of the more sensible choices of the 10-man 1945 OTC slate.

The Basement (the most dubious honorees)

67. Ross Youngs

Teams:	Giants 1917–26
Stats:	.322/.399/.441 • 130 OPS+ • 1,491 H • 42 HR • 153 SB
Rankings:	7× top 10 OBP • 6× top 10 AVG • 4× top 10 WAR
Voting/JAWS:	VC 1972 • **32.2/30.3/31.2**

Had he not been a McGraw favorite for a Giants team that featured Frankie Frisch and Bill Terry, Youngs's premature death at age 30 due to the kidney disorder Bright's disease almost certainly would have kept him outside of Cooperstown. He played just the minimum of 10 seasons, the first of which featured only seven games, the last 95 due to the ailment that killed him a year later; his health was so poor that during his final season, McGraw hired a nurse to travel with the team. Youngs helped the Giants to four straight pennants (1921–24) and two championships, and his 17.0 WAR in that four-year run is in a dead heat with Dave Bancroft for second on the team behind Frisch's 25.8. Still, only one of those seasons—and only two on his entire ledger—was worth at least 4.0 WAR. It's not enough, and as tragic as his premature death was, the cabal that elected him did the institution a disservice by lowering the bar.

130. Tommy McCarthy

Teams:	Boston Reds (UA) 1884 • Boston Beaneaters 1885, '92–95 • Philadelphia Quakers 1886–87 • St. Louis Browns (AA) 1888–91 • Brooklyn Bridegrooms 1896
Stats:	.292/.364/.375 • 102 OPS+ • 1,493 H • 44 HR • 468 SB
Rankings:	3× top 10 AVG • 3× top 10 SB
Voting/JAWS:	OTC 1946 • **16.1/18.9/17.5**

Statistically, nobody elected to the Hall as a major league player is less qualified than McCarthy, whose 16.1 career WAR is 8.0 behind Lloyd Waner for the lowest total in Cooperstown. In his prime (1888–96), McCarthy hit a thin .301/.377/.389 for a 107 OPS+ with 452 steals. He had his moments, driving in at least 90 runs three times and finishing fifth in the NL in 1894 with a career-high 13 homers, but his résumé is brief and underwhelming. During his run with the 1892 and '93 pennant-winning Beaneaters, he and teammate Hugh Duffy—a pair of small (5'7", 170 pounds in McCarthy's case), fleet-footed, and crafty outfielders with high baseball IQs—became known as the "Heavenly Twins." That baseball IQ was his ticket to Cooperstown, for McCarthy popularized a few innovations: the hit-and-run play, the fake bunt, and the outfield trap (intentional drop) for the purposes of fooling baserunners. He was also an early adopter of sunglasses in the outfield, and an expert at sign stealing. Whatever recognition he received from the Hall should have been as a pioneer, not as a player, but the VC didn't distinguish him within the infamous 11-man class of 1946.

Further Consideration (upcoming or overlooked candidates)

13. Shoeless Joe Jackson

Teams:	A's 1908–09 • Indians 1910–15 • White Sox 1915–20
Stats:	.356/.423/.517 • 170 OPS+ • 1,772 H • 54 HR • 202 SB
Rankings:	9× top 5 OPS+ • 9× top 5 SLG • 8× top 10 WAR • 7× top 5 AVG • 7× top 5 OBP
Voting/JAWS:	62.3/52.5/57.4

Shoeless Joe had Hall of Fame talent. While he never beat out Cobb for a batting title, his 170 OPS+ from 1911–20 trails only the Georgia Peach's 185, and he's fourth in WAR for that span. He was one of eight "Black Sox" banned by Judge Landis for throwing the 1919 World Series, though Jackson's level of complicity has been debated for nearly a century, with his supporters arguing for his posthumous reinstatement to give him a chance for election by a committee to be named later. Jackson led the Sox in hits (12) and RBIs (six) while batting .375/.394/.563 in that Series. But while he may not have actively done his worst, his grand jury testimony makes clear his awareness of the fix ("We went ahead and threw the second game . . .")[21] and his acceptance of $5,000 from gamblers (out of a promised $20,000). He later told conflicting versions of his story and publicly recanted his confessions, but the rest is just commentary, as the great baseball scholar Rabbi Hillel would have said. Multiple commissioners have declined reinstatement requests from his supporters, so his candidacy is purely hypothetical.

15. Dwight Evans

Teams:	Red Sox 1972–90 • Orioles 1991
Stats:	.272/.370/.470 • 127 OPS+ • 2,446 H • 385 HR • 78 SB

Rankings:	8× GG • 6× top 10 OBP • 5× top 10 HR • 4× top 5 OPS+ • 4× top 10 SLG • 3× All-Star
Voting/JAWS:	66.9/37.1/52.0

An underappreciated cornerstone of Boston's 1970s and '80s contenders, "Dewey" reached the majors two years ahead of outfield-mates Fred Lynn and Jim Rice, and outlasted both while helping the team to four division titles and two pennants. A dependable slugger with a keen batting eye, he had 11 seasons of at least 20 homers (including a league lead-tying 22 in 1981), and six with at least 90 walks, three of which led the league. In the field, his excellent range and cannon arm helped him win eight Gold Gloves; he's 12th among rightfielders in fielding runs (+71). His defensive value peaked early (+104 runs through age 29), while his offense peaked late (+274 batting runs for ages 29–37), so he cracked the league's top 10 in WAR just twice; while he's 14th among rightfielders in career WAR, he's just 27th in peak, and he lasted only three years on the ballot.

16. Ichiro Suzuki

Teams:	Mariners 2001–12 • Yankees 2012–14 • Marlins 2015–16
Stats:	.313/.356/.405 • 108 OPS+ • 3,030 H • 114 HR • 508 SB
Rankings:	10× All-Star • 10× GG • 9× top 10 AVG • 6× top 10 WAR
Voting/JAWS:	59.9/43.6/51.8

Arriving stateside when offense was near its peak, Japan's greatest baseball export delighted MLB fans by revitalizing a slash-and-run style that had fallen out of vogue. As a 27-year-old, he won the AL Rookie of the Year and MVP honors plus the first of two batting titles in 2001, that while kicking off 10-year streaks of Gold Gloves, All-Star appearances, and 200-hit seasons; his 55.0 WAR over that decade trailed only Albert Pujols and Alex Rodriguez. Though only intermittently valuable thereafter, he reached 3,000 hits stateside and collected more than 4,300 total including his time in Nippon Professional Baseball—less a matter of surpassing Cobb or Rose than a testament to his niche as a player beloved by two baseball cultures. Despite his late start, he's fifth among modern players in baserunning and DP runs (118) behind Rickey Henderson (148), Willie Wilson (145), Johnny Damon (126), and Tim Raines (123), and sixth among rightfielders in fielding runs (119). Even without matching the value of the top sluggers to whom he provided great contrast, that's a Hall of Famer. He'll be a first-ballot choice, regardless of the advanced metrics.

17. Reggie Smith

Teams:	Red Sox 1966–73 • Cardinals 1974–76 • Dodgers 1976–81 • Giants 1982
Stats:	.287/.366/.489 • 137 OPS+ • 2,020 H • 314 HR • 137 SB
Rankings:	8× top 10 SLG • 7× All-Star • 5× top ten OPS+ • 5× top 10 HR • 4× top 10 WAR
Voting/JAWS:	64.5/38.6/51.6

"The Other Reggie" was the antithesis of his contemporary namesake in terms of self-promotion, a quietly efficient star whose bat and arm helped power three pennant winners, the "Impossible Dream" Red Sox in 1967 and the '77–78 Dodgers. His biggest year was 1977, when he led in OPS+ (168), ranked fourth in WAR (6.1) and sixth in homers (32) as one of the first quartet of 30-homer teammates in history. Though he had big World Series in losing causes in 1967 and '77, his overall October résumé (.234/.303/.449) was hardly Jacksonesque, and his meager total of just 307 games after '78 due to injuries doomed his Hall chances; he received just 0.7% in 1988. He's here as a personal favorite who outdistances a handful of VC-elected rightfielders by a country mile.

18. Sammy Sosa

Teams:	Rangers 1989, 2007 • White Sox 1989–91 • Cubs 1992–2004 • Orioles 2005
Stats:	.273/.344/.534 • 128 OPS+ • 2,408 H • 609 HR • 234 SB
Rankings:	7× All-Star • 7× top 10 SLG • 6× top 2 HR • 5× top 10 OPS+ • 3× top 10 WAR All-time: 8th HR
Voting/JAWS:	58.4/43.7/51.0

Slammin' Sammy topped 61 homers three times from 1998–2001, captivating the baseball world with his friendly rivalry with Mark McGwire—whom he outdid for the '98 NL MVP award—and his flamboyant displays of celebration. He homered more times over a five- or 10-year stretch than any player in history and became just the fifth player to reach 600 homers. To an even greater degree than Big Mac, he fell from grace once MLB cracked down on PEDs, with a disproportionate level of ire directed at him for not speaking English during the 2005 congressional hearing. In 2009 the *New York Times* reported that he failed the supposedly anonymous '03 survey test—where's Rob Manfred to stand up for him?—but his Hall case isn't very strong via advanced stats. As a free swinger, he walked a lot only at his peak, and placed among the league's top 10 in WAR just three times, with his positive defensive numbers heavily skewed toward his pre-stardom period (+107 runs through 1997, -22 after). His peak is above the standard, but he's 15 wins short on the career front. BBWAA voters have shown little compassion, with support that fell into the single digits after his first year.

20. Bobby Abreu

Teams:	Astros 1996–97 • Phillies 1998–2006 • Yankees 2006–08 • Angels 2009–12 • Dodgers 2012 • Mets 2014
Stats:	.291/.395/.475 • 128 OPS+ • 2,470 H • 288 HR • 400 SB
Rankings:	8× top 10 OBP • 7× top 10 SB • 5× top 10 WAR
Voting/JAWS:	59.9/41.5/50.7

The criminally underappreciated Abreu made just two All-Star teams despite a 12-year run (1998–2009) during which he hit .301/.406/.497. He combined power and speed with an expert batting eye, with eight 100-walk seasons, two with 30 homers and 30 steals, and seven 20-20 seasons, the last the best mark this side of Bobby and Barry Bonds (10 apiece). Selected by the Devil Rays in the 1997 expansion draft and then flipped to the Phillies for forgotten shortstop Kevin Stocker in one of the '90s great heists, he was exceptionally valuable for the first half of his career thanks to good-to-great defense, worth between 5.2 and 6.5 WAR annually from 1998–2004; that seven-year stretch is actually his peak score. His decline as a defender, which included a noticeable fear of contact with walls, eroded his value in his 30s, and by the time he reached the Yankees, he'd have been better off DHing. His voting share will hardly reflect how close he is to Hall-worthy.

21. Vladimir Guerrero

Teams:	Expos 1996–2003 • Angels 2004–09 • Rangers 2010 • Orioles 2011
Stats:	.318/.379/.553 • 140 OPS+ • 2,590 H • 449 HR • 181 SB
Rankings:	9× All-Star • 9× top 10 SLG • 8× top 10 HR • 7× top 5 AVG • 10× top 10 OBP • 4× top 10 WAR
Voting/JAWS:	59.3/41.1/50.2

Whether collecting hits off ankle-high pitches in the left-handed batter's box or airmailing a cutoff man to gun down a runner, Guerrero played with impressive, spectacular abandon, and retained the raw edges of his game for most of his career. An outstanding contact hitter who whiffed more than 80 times in a season just twice, his maintenance of a high batting average despite his free-swinging ways is the eighth wonder of the world. As an Expo he had outstanding speed to go with his power, with 30-30 seasons in 2001 and '02 but Back and leg injuries trimmed the dimensions of his game once he got to Anaheim, though a scorching September 2004 secured him an MVP award. Subpar range and 508 games at DH put a dent in his WAR, knocking him below all three right field standards. Even without the JAWS imprimatur, every eligible player who hit at least .317 in 7,000 PA is enshrined, and after receiving 71.7% in his 2017 ballot debut, he won't wait long.

23. Gary Sheffield

Teams:	Brewers 1988–91 • Padres 1992–93 • Marlins 1993–98 • Dodgers 1998–2001 • Braves 2002–03 • Yankees 2004–06 • Tigers 2007–08 • Mets 2009
Stats:	.292/.393/.514 • 140 OPS+ • 2,689 H • 509 HR • 253 SB
Rankings:	10× top 10 OBP • 9× All-Star • 9× top 10 OPS+ • 7× top 10 HR • 5× top 10 SLG • 4× top 10 WAR All-time: 25th HR
JAWS:	60.3/37.9/49.1

It was Festivus every day for Sheffield, who was always willing to air his grievances, and spent the better part of 22 seasons enveloped in controversy, perpetually agitating for his next contract. The Brewers made him pee in a cup because he was Dwight Gooden's nephew, accused him of "indifferent fielding," and attempted to demote him while he had a broken foot, leading to an infamous (but idle) threat to make intentional errors. The Padres and Marlins dealt him amid fire sales, the latter after he helped win a championship. He was involved in BALCO, perhaps unwittingly (he testified to not knowing the cream he was rubbing on his surgical scars was loaded). Wherever he went, the owner of the game's most intimidating bat waggle/scowl combo was a devastatingly effective hitter, 28th in batting runs (561) and tied for 48th in OPS+. Unfortunately, he was also a terrible defender whose -195 fielding runs out-stanks every player except Derek Jeter, though neither Defensive Regression Analysis (-109 runs) nor Fielding Runs Above Average (-95 runs) see him as quite an outlier. The defense suppresses his WAR, leaving him well off the standards. Whether it's that, BALCO, or his perceived bad attitude, voters aren't biting; his 13.3% in 2017 was his highest in three tries.

31. Tony Oliva

Teams:	Twins 1962–76
Stats:	.304/.353/.476 • 131 OPS+ • 1,917 H • 220 HR • 86 SB
Rankings:	8× All-Star • 7× top 10 SLG • 6× top 10 OBP • 6× top 10 OPS+ • 4× top 5 WAR • 3× led AVG
JAWS:	43.0/38.6/40.8

With batting titles in each of his first two full seasons (1964 and '65) and All-Star honors in each of his first eight, Oliva appeared to be Cooperstown-bound, hitting a combined .313/.360/.507 for a 140 OPS+ while averaging 22 homers and 5.3 WAR. He won AL Rookie of the Year honors while leading with 217 hits and 374 total bases, then helped the Twins win the pennant and finished second to teammate Zoilo Versalles in the MVP voting. Alas, an endless series of knee injuries requiring surgery as early as 1966 diminished his effectiveness and cut into his playing time. Despite winning another batting title in 1971, he needed another surgery, played in just 10 games in '72, and was never the same, netting 0.6 WAR from 1973–76 while batting a combined .277/.331/.391 primarily as a DH. He maxed out at 47.3% on the BBWAA ballot, polled between 56–59% in three expanded VC votes, then fell just one vote short on the 2015 Golden Era Committee ballot, suggesting that he could someday gain entry. If so, he could bring down the "Rule of 2,000 Hits" as could Dick Allen, a stronger candidate who fell one vote short on the same ballot.

CHAPTER 17

STARTING PITCHERS

CURT SCHILLING

Back in the 1990s, Phillies general manager Ed Wade said, "Schilling is a horse every fifth day and a horse's ass the other four."[1]

—Jon Heyman

Curt Schilling was at his best when the spotlight shone the brightest—at least on the field. A top starter on four pennant winners and three champions, the burly 6'4" righty built a strong claim as the best postseason pitcher of his generation. His case for Cooperstown is backed by a track record of regular season dominance as well, founded in pinpoint command of his mid-90s fastball and a devastating splitter. He's one of just 16 pitchers to strike out more than 3,000 hitters, and owner of the highest strikeout-to-walk ratio in modern major league history.

Though he was runner-up three times, Schilling never won a Cy Young Award, and he finished with "only" 216 regular season wins. Given the BBWAA's recent voting history, that's a problem, as only three starting pitchers with fewer than 300 wins have been elected since 1992. That said, the first-ballot entries of Pedro Martinez and John Smoltz suggest that the tide may be shifting away from using wins as a Hall yardstick (see Chapter 6).

A late bloomer, Schilling didn't cement a spot in a rotation until midway through his age-25 season, after being traded three times. He spent much of his peak pitching in the shadows of even more famous teammates. During the 1993 postseason, Phillies manager Jim Fregosi gave him the nickname "Red Light Curt" for his desire to be the center of attention when the cameras were rolling; for better and worse, that desire eventually extended beyond the mound. He used his platform to raise money for research into amyotrophic lateral sclerosis (Lou Gehrig's disease) and, after a bout of oral cancer, recorded public service announcements on the dangers of smokeless tobacco. In 1996, *USA Today* named him "Baseball's Most Caring Athlete." But he also generated no end of controversy while expounding about politics, performance-enhancing drugs, pitch-tracking systems, and his postseason legend, cultivating feuds with high-profile members of the media in the process. In 2006, he made *GQ*'s "Ten Most Hated Athletes" list.

Schilling has become even more polarizing since retiring, thanks to his inflammatory rhetoric on social media. Normally, that wouldn't be germane to the Hall of Fame discussion, but his praise for a tweet promoting the lynching of journalists—yes, really—during the tense 2016 presidential campaign brought his momentum to a screeching halt. Having slowly climbed from 38.8% in 2013 to 52.3% in '16, he plummeted to 45.0% in '17. Whether explicitly or implicitly citing the character clause, several previous supporters left him off their ballots even when they had space to spare. While he'll benefit from a lack of 300-win pitchers to cut the line during his five remaining years of eligibility, his capacity for self-sabotage has placed his candidacy in a uniquely precarious position.

The Career

Orioles 1988–90 • Astros 1991 • Phillies 1992–2000 • Diamondbacks 2000–03 • Red Sox 2004–07

Pitcher	Career	Peak	JAWS	W-L	SO	ERA	ERA+
Curt Schilling	79.9	49.0	64.5	216-146	3,116	3.46	127
Avg. HOF SP	73.4	50.2	61.8				
SP Rank	26th	48th	27th				
(Above HOF)	(39/62)	(29/62)	(37/62)				

Born in Anchorage, Alaska, in 1966, the son of a career army man, Schilling was part of a family that bounced around the U.S. before settling in Phoenix, Arizona. Though he impressed scouts at a tryout camp held by the Reds after his junior year at Shadow Mountain High School, he didn't make the varsity squad until his senior year, and went undrafted out of school.

Instead, Schilling enrolled at Yavapai Junior College in Arizona, pitched in the Junior College World Series, and was chosen by the Red Sox in the second round of the now bygone January draft in 1986. He signed for a $20,000 bonus and put himself on the prospect map in 1987, leading the A-level South Atlantic League with 189 strikeouts in 184 innings as a 20-year-old. He held his own upon advancing to Double-A in 1988, but on July 29 he was traded to the Orioles in a deadline deal for starter Mike Boddicker. He was rocked for a 9.82 ERA in four major league starts that September.

After spending most of 1989 and the first half of '90 at Triple-A Rochester, he secured a role in Baltimore's bullpen upon being recalled in late June. While he posted a 2.54 ERA in 46 innings, he didn't exactly impress Orioles manager Frank Robinson upon arrival, as Schilling recounted in a 1998 *Sports Illustrated* profile: "I walk in, I got the earring and half my head shaved, a blue streak dyed in it. [Robinson] says, 'Sit down,' and then just cocks his head and stares at me for a while. Finally, he says, 'What's wrong with you, son?' "[2]

Schilling lost the earring and the blue streak, but his immaturity persisted. Summoned from the bullpen in a September game, he admitted to not having paid attention to the opposing lineup. "The 'Who's Up?' story spread through the organization until it became synonymous with his name. Million-dollar arm. Ten-cent head,"[3] wrote Thomas Boswell of the *Washington Post*. In January 1991, the Orioles sent Schilling, outfielder Steve Finley, and pitcher Pete Harnisch to the Astros for first baseman Glenn Davis, a deal still reviled in Baltimore—less for the future stardom of those departing than for Davis's flop in Baltimore.

After making 56 relief appearances with a 3.81 ERA for Houston in 1991, Schilling was traded to Philadelphia for Jason Grimsley the following spring. The Phillies initially viewed the 25-year-old as a future closer, but in mid-May gave him another shot at starting, and he made the most of it, tossing 10 complete games, including four shutouts, in 26 starts. He finished 14-11 in 226⅓ innings, with both his 2.35 ERA and 5.9 WAR ranking fourth in the league.

Though his ERA ballooned to 4.02 (99 ERA+) in 1993, Schilling's first season as a full-time starter, he helped the Phillies win their first division title in a decade. He allowed there earned runs and struck out 19 in two eight-inning NLCS no-decisions aganist the Braves, earning MVP honors. Pummeled in the World Series opener against the Blue Jays, he rebounded to throw a 147-pitch, five-hit shutout in Game 5 to stave off elimination, but back in Toronto, Joe Carter's Game 6 walkoff homer gave the Jays their second straight championship.

The combination of the 1994–95 players' strike and a trio of surgeries—for a bone spur in his elbow, torn cartilage in his left knee, and, most seriously, a torn labrum and frayed rotator cuff—limited Schilling to just 56 starts from 1994–96, though he returned from his shoulder surgery with improved velocity. He whiffed 182 batters in 183⅓ innings in 1996, reaching double digits in seven of his final 11 starts, and led the league with eight complete games in just 26 starts. Both his 3.19 ERA (134 ERA+) and his 4.9 WAR cracked the league's top 10.

The Phillies were three years into a string of six straight losing seasons, but Schilling opted to sign a below-market three-year, $15.45 million extension in

April 1997. While the hapless team lost 94 games, he went 17-11 with a 2.97 ERA (143 ERA+) in 254⅓ innings. Via steady improvements in his mental preparation and physical conditioning that helped his fastball reach 97 mph when needed, he notched 319 strikeouts, the majors' highest total since Nolan Ryan's 341 in 1977, and a record for an NL righty. "A remarkable blend of power and pinpoint control,"[4] marveled Yankees pitcher David Cone after Schilling's 16-strikeout, zero-walk September 1 start against New York. Schilling made his first All-Star team and finished fourth both in WAR (6.3) and in the Cy Young voting, losing out to the Expos' Pedro Martinez.

Schilling's NL-high 300 strikeouts in 1998 made him the first pitcher to reach that plateau in back-to-back seasons since J. R. Richard in 1978 and '79; he also led in innings (268⅔) and complete games (15, still the highest total since 1992) and again ranked fourth in WAR (6.2). While a strong first half earned him the All-Star Game start in 1999, the mileage caught up: He made just three starts after July 23 due to shoulder inflammation, underwent offseason surgery to tighten his shoulder capsule, and didn't return until April 30, 2000. With the Phillies bound for 97 losses, he agreed to waive his no-trade clause and on July 26 was dealt to the Diamondbacks for a four-player package.

Paired with lefty Randy Johnson to form the league's strongest one-two punch, the 34-year-old Schilling settled into his new surroundings in 2001 with his best season: career highs in wins (22), WAR (8.8) plus an NL-best 7.5 strikeout-to-walk ratio (293 punch-outs against 37 walks) in 256⅔ innings. He would have won the Cy Young had Johnson not struck out 372 and won 21 games himself. Schilling placed second in the vote.

More importantly, the Diamondbacks won the NL West, and Schilling sparkled in the postseason, throwing three complete game victories in the first two rounds against the Cardinals and Braves, striking out 30 while allowing just two runs. In the World Series against a Yankees team seeking its fourth straight championship, he yielded one run in seven innings in a winning effort in Game 1, and duplicated that performance on three days' rest in Game 4, but Diamondbacks closer Byun-Hyung Kim allowed game-tying and game-winning homers.

With the series stretching to Game 7, Schilling again took the ball on three days' rest. He pitched one-hit shutout ball for the first six innings, but surrendered five hits and two runs in the seventh and eighth before departing, trailing 2–1. Johnson came on in relief, and Arizona rallied for two runs in the bottom of the ninth inning against Mariano Rivera to win a championship in just their fourth season of existence. Schilling shared Series MVP honors with Johnson and finished the postseason 4-0 with a 1.12 ERA, setting records for innings (48⅓, broken by Madison Bumgarner in 2014) and strikeouts (56) while walking just six.

Schilling was nearly as outstanding in 2002, 23 wins and 316 strikeouts with a 9.6 strikeout-to-walk ratio, the second of five times he'd lead his league from 2001–06. "He's Picasso with a machine gun," marveled Blue Jays pitcher Dan Plesac. "The command of his fastball, to all four quadrants of the plate, [is] like no power pitcher in years."[5] Schilling's 23 wins, 8.7 WAR, and Cy Young vote total took a backseat only to Johnson.

After a 2003 season abbreviated by an appendectomy and two fractured metacarpals, Schilling waived his no-trade clause for a trade to the Red Sox, fresh off their agonizing ALCS loss to the Yankees via Aaron Boone's walkoff homer. As part of the trade Schilling signed a three-year, $37.5 million extension with a $13 million vesting option contingent on the Red Sox winning the World Series, something that hadn't happened since 1918; the clause actually ran afoul of MLB's contract rules.

As he'd done with Johnson in Arizona, Schilling paired with Martinez as Boston's co-ace, and at age 37 put up another All-Star season, with 21 wins, a 3.26 ERA (148 ERA+ in hitter-friendly Fenway Park), and 203 strikeouts. Hampered by a torn tendon sheath in his right ankle during the postseason, he was chased by the Yankees after just three innings in the ALCS opener. The injury appeared to be a moot point once New York built a 3–0 series lead, but when the Sox clawed their way back, Schilling took the ball for Game 6 in the Bronx. The day before the start, doctors performed an experimental procedure—first tried on a cadaver—to secure the tendon using three stitches. TV shots that night captured blood seeping through Schilling's sock, but the stitches held long enough for him to pitch seven innings, allowing one run, as the Sox forced a Game 7 that they would win handily. He added six innings of one-run ball against the Cardinals in Game 2 of the World Series, en route to Boston's first world championship in 86 years.

Despite offseason surgery, Schilling's ankle troubled him well into 2005. Splitting his time between starting and closing, something he'd done regularly only in early 1991, he was cuffed for a 5.69 ERA in just 93⅓ innings, but he rebounded in 2006 to throw 204 innings with a 3.97 ERA (120 ERA+) with a stellar 6.5 strikeout-to-walk ratio. He was solid through the first two months of '07, but his age-40 season unraveled after he fell one out shy of no-hitting the A's on June 7, and lost six weeks to shoulder inflammation. Mustering some semblance of his old form down the stretch and in the postseason, he tossed seven shutout innings in the Division Series clincher against the Angels, rebounded from an ALCS Game 2 pounding from the Indians to yield two runs over seven innings in Game 6, and wobbled through 5⅓ innings in a Game 2 World Series victory over the Rockies, part of another Sox sweep.

He never pitched a competitive game again. Though he signed an incentive-laden one-year, $8 million deal to return to Boston for 2008, further shoulder problems that winter led to a public battle with the team over his treatment. Schilling didn't undergo surgery to repair his biceps tendon and labrum until June, and couldn't rehab in time to rejoin the team. The following spring, he announced his retirement.

The Case

Schilling's 216 wins is a lower total than all but 16 of the 62 starting pitchers in the Hall of Fame, only three of whom (Sandy Koufax, Don Drysdale, and Smoltz) pitched during the post-1960 expansion era. The BBWAA voters have taken a long time to accept the idea that pitcher wins aren't the ideal measure of success in an era where offensive, defensive, and bullpen support are major factors in the compilation of those precious Ws. After electing Fergie Jenkins in 1991, it took 20 years—until Bert Blyleven in 2011—for another starter with fewer than 300 wins to be elected by the writers. It remains to be seen whether a majority of voters has detached themselves from old-school win totals.

Schilling was the first among a wave of non-300 win pitchers to hit the ballot, followed by Mike Mussina (270 wins) in 2014 and Martinez (219) and Smoltz (213) in '15. Pitching in the highest-scoring era since the 1930s, those men more than held their own against lineups much deeper than those their predecessors faced, working deep into counts to rack up high strikeout totals before yielding to increasingly specialized bullpens. The shape of their accomplishments may be different from the even larger cohort of pitchers from the 1960s and '70s who helped set that 300-or-bust standard, but the recent aces belong in Cooperstown just the same. The elections of Martinez and Smoltz should eventually open the door for Schilling and Mussina.

Schilling's merits go far beyond his win total. He was the turn-of-the-millennium equivalent of Bob Gibson in the postseason, going 11-2 with a 2.23 ERA in 19 starts and 133⅓ innings, helping his teams to four pennants and three championships. In the World Series alone, he was 4-1 with a 2.06 ERA in seven starts totaling 48 innings. In five starts in which his team faced elimination, he had a 1.37 ERA; his teams won all five. Other pitchers racked up more postseason appearances and wins, but no starter from the expansion era with at least 100 postseason innings had as low an ERA. Among expansion-era pitchers with at least 40 World Series innings, only Koufax (0.94) and Gibson (1.89) have lower ERAs, albeit in the lower-scoring 1960s, making Schilling's accomplishments all the more impressive.

Turning back to the regular season, Schilling's 3,116 strikeouts ranks 15th all time, while his 8.6 strikeouts per nine ranks third among pitchers with at least 3,000 innings, behind only Johnson and Ryan, and just ahead of Roger Clemens.

While it's true that, besides Ryan, those pitchers pitched in an era where strikeout rates were on the rise, Schilling was consistently among the elite, with eight top five finishes in strikeout totals and seven in strikeout rates. He's one of four expansion-era pitchers with at least three 300 K seasons, along with Johnson, Ryan, and Koufax.

What's more, Schilling's impeccable control allowed him to lead the league in strikeout-to-walk ratio five times and place in the top five another four times. His 4.4 career ratio is the highest of any post-nineteenth-century pitcher. He's among the elite in run prevention as well: Though he never led in ERA, he had four finishes among the league's top five, and nine in the top 10. Among pitchers with at least 3,000 innings, his 127 ERA+ is in a virtual tie for 15th all-time with Hall of Famers Gibson, Tom Seaver, and Stan Coveleski, plus Kevin Brown. Among his contemporaries with 3,000 innings, only Clemens, Johnson, and Greg Maddux were stingier relative to their leagues.

Despite never winning a Cy Young, Schilling's frequent placement on the leaderboards in key categories and his postseason exploits give him 171 points on the Bill James Hall of Fame Monitor, well beyond the 130 mark that indicates "a virtual cinch" for election. Every post-nineteenth-century starter within 20 points of him in either direction—including Bob Feller, Smoltz, and four 300-game winners—is enshrined.

In terms of advanced metrics, Schilling's ability to miss bats and prevent runs enabled him to finish in his league's top five in WAR eight times and to rack up nine seasons of at least 5.0 WAR; among his contemporaries, only Clemens (14), Johnson (11), Maddux (11), and Mussina (nine) had as many or more. Schilling's 80.7 career WAR ranks 26th all-time, six wins above the standard for Hall of Fame starters. His peak score of 49.0 WAR is 1.3 wins below the standard, but his overall JAWS is 2.4 above it, good for 27th all-time and ahead of five 300-game winners (Tom Glavine, Ryan, Don Sutton, Early Wynn, and Mickey Welch) as well as 33 other enshrined starters. That's a no-doubt Hall of Fame pitcher.

BBWAA voters have not yet been convinced, though when he debuted on the 2013 ballot alongside the bumper crop of other newcomers (Craig Biggio, Barry Bonds, Clemens, Mike Piazza, and Sammy Sosa), it was easy to get lost. His 38.8% that year suggested eventual election, but hardly guaranteed it. He dropped nearly nine points the following year, overshadowed by the presence of Maddux and Glavine, but regained that ground in 2015 alongside Johnson and Martinez, and in 2016 passed the all-important 50% threshold, climbing to 52.3%. With six years of eligibility remaining, he appeared to be on his way to eventual election.

To that point, Schilling's candidacy had withstood numerous controversies, including but not limited to:

- His long-standing public feuds with high-profile writers such as ESPN's Pedro Gomez, *Newsday*'s Jon Heyman, and the *Boston Globe*'s Dan Shaughnessy.

- The demise of his videogame company, 38 Studios, which received a $75 million loan from the Rhode Island Economic Development Corporation to relocate from Massachusetts but went bankrupt and laid off its staff of 379 without notice, violating federal law. The state of Rhode Island filed suit and recouped just $16.9 million in two partial settlements.

- A fall 2015 suspension from his job as an ESPN analyst for posting a Twitter meme that compared Muslim extremists to German Nazis.

- His January 2015 claim (later repeated) that his conservative political views were costing him votes.

That last claim was belied by back-to-back double-digit gains on the 2015 and '16 ballots. Despite his surge, Schilling continued to run afoul of ESPN until being fired in April 2016 for "unacceptable" conduct stemming from his posting of an offensive Facebook meme about transgender bathroom laws, and his publicly commenting on the 2016 presidential election. While nobody should be wild about an employer suppressing his public expression, employment in such a high-profile job within the Disney empire doesn't come without certain expectations and conditions that Schilling repeatedly chose to violate, bringing a great volume of negative attention to the company.

His firing didn't stop that. On Twitter, days before the 2016 presidential election, Schilling praised a photo showing a pro–Donald Trump T-shirt that advocated lynching; "So much awesome here,"[6] he said of a shirt that read, "Rope. Tree. Journalist. Some assembly required." While Schilling later claimed his comments were "sarcasm," by that point several BBWAA voters including past presidents Susan Slusser and Jose de Jesus Ortiz as well as Heyman and Shaughnessy proclaimed that they were withdrawing their support of his candidacy, at least for 2017, citing the same character clause that many voters use to justify not voting for players connected to PED use. In those voters' eyes, Schilling had moved beyond expressing political beliefs to condoning violence. Wrote Ortiz, "Proposing lynching pretty much sinks his chance on my ballot on character clause."[7] Wrote Shaughnessy, "[Schilling] has transitioned from a mere nuisance to an actual menace to society."[8]

Via Ryan Thibodaux's ballot tracker, which collects the published votes of every voter willing to share (which 70.8% did in 2017, either before or after the election), Schilling was dropped from the ballots of 35 voters who had supported him the previous year, including both Heyman and Shaughnessy, who in December 2013 had written, "I consider a vote for Schill a demonstration that BBWAA members do not use the ballot to settle scores. Sometimes I think I vote for him because I can't stand him."[9] While 18 returning voters and 12 out of 15 new voters added him to their 2017 ballots, presumably on the strength of his statistical credentials rather than his offensive rhetoric, he was the only one of 34 candidates to lose significant ground relative to 2016.

For his part, Schilling has refused to temper his views for the benefit of his candidacy. Just before the 2016 voting results were announced, he told Boston radio station WEEI, "I'm not going to change who I am to make people think differently of me. . . . If my mouth keeps me out of the Hall of Fame, then it's a flawed process."[10] He made similar comments before the 2017 announcement, calling the voters "some of the worst human beings I've ever known . . . scumbags all across," and adding, "I promise you if I had said 'lynch Trump,' I'd be getting in with about 90 percent."[11]

To these eyes, Schilling's lynching tweet went beyond the pale as far as public discourse is concerned, in that it moved from his personally held beliefs (however noxious) to a condoning of violence, and his claim of "sarcasm" doesn't wash given his failure to apologize or repudiate the post. But while I can't blame anyone for thinking less of the man given his conduct, it's a mistake to connect it to the "integrity, sportsmanship, character" portion of the Hall's voting instructions. His comments had no bearing on his playing career, and I don't believe that the character clause is worthy of increased investment by voters for reasons outlined in Chapter 8.

It remains to be seen whether the damage Schilling has inflicted upon his candidacy is permanent or if voters were simply sending him a little "chin music" with the intent of knocking him down temporarily rather than ruling him out. While he could regain the lost ground, he may find further ways to alienate voters, particularly given his latest job hosting an online radio show on Breitbart (a far-right Web site that the Southern Poverty Law Center has called a "white ethno-nationalist propaganda mill"[12]) or his plans to run for Elizabeth Warren's Massachusetts Senate seat in 2018.

I wouldn't invite Schilling into my own home, and I wouldn't encourage anyone to view him as a role model, but in my view, nothing in his career leaves a doubt that he belongs in Cooperstown. He ranks among the all-time greats via his run prevention skill, his dominance in the game's most elemental battle of balls and strikes, and his repeated ability to rise to the occasion when the on-field stakes were highest. If that's not a Hall of Famer, I don't know what is.

MIKE MUSSINA

> You try to give kids a Mike Mussina wind-up, so they never get hurt, they throw the ball over the plate, everybody likes them and they like what they're doing.[13]
>
> —JIM PALMER

Had the order of the two stops of Mike Mussina's career been reversed, with its perennial All-Star/Cy Young contender peak in the Bronx, and his up-and-down years in Baltimore, there's a strong possibility that he'd be in the Hall of Fame already, the final accolade in a career that included at least one Cy Young and a championship ring won during the early years of the Yankees' dynasty under Joe Torre. It's tantalizing to imagine such an alternate timeline where the cerebral righty's talent, consistency, and durability garnered greater appreciation and respect via a prime spent on the game's biggest stage, checking off the marquee accomplishments that otherwise eluded him due to a bit of bad luck or bad timing.

Alas, "Moose" never won a Cy Young Award, in part because a teammate practically stole one out of his hands thanks to superior run support. His teams never won a World Series despite his occasional brilliance in October, because even the best relievers sometimes falter, to say nothing of what happens to the rest. Still, he strung together an exceptional 18-year career spent entirely in the crucible of the American League East. Despite its high-offense ballparks and high-pressure atmosphere, he projected an air of detached intensity on the mound, at home in its solitude, left to his own devices. "You're pitching on feel, you're out there on your own," he said in 2007. "There's no coach, there's no video. When something's going wrong or it doesn't feel right, you have to be able to solve the problem right there."[14]

Mussina usually did. His expansive arsenal starred a 93 mph fastball and a signature knuckle-curve, but at times contained six or seven distinct pitches. Via his mixing and matching, he not only missed bats with regularity, he had pinpoint control. Though he never led the league in either strikeouts or ERA, he ranked in the league's top five six times in the former category, seven in the latter. He earned All-Star honors five times, and received Cy Young votes in eight separate seasons across a 10-year span, at one point finishing in the top five four times in five years.

Unlike 2014 and '15 Hall of Fame honorees Greg Maddux, Tom Glavine, and Randy Johnson, Mussina didn't reach 300 wins in his career, but despite a late-career dip from which he recovered in memorable fashion, his résumé is strong enough for Cooperstown. He delivered tremendous value, and holds up well in comparison to the more decorated contemporaries who have overshadowed him.

After a sluggish start to his run candidacy, he posted significant gains in 2016 and '17 that pushed his share of the vote to 51.8%, suggesting he's on the right track to a berth in Cooperstown.

The Career

Orioles 1991–2000 • Yankees 2001–2008

Pitcher	Career	Peak	JAWS	W -L	SO	ERA	ERA+
Mike Mussina	83.0	44.5	63.8	270-153	2,813	3.68	123
Avg. HOF SP	73.4	50.2	61.8				
SP Rank	23rd	65th	28th				
(Above HOF)	(41/62)	(24/62)	(38/62)				

The son of an attorney and a head nurse, Mussina was born in 1968 in Williamsport, Pennsylvania, and grew up in nearby Montoursvile, a tiny town of less than 5,000. By age 12, he threw so hard that his father had to stop playing catch with him. At Montoursville High School, he earned varsity letters for playing guard on the basketball team and wide receiver and kicker on the football team in addition to baseball. As a senior, he won two games kicking last-second field goals, drawing the interest of Penn State University.

Pitching was the young Mussina's forte, though, and the solitude of the mound suited his intensity and natural reserve. A strong student as well, he nearly earned valedictorian honors, but according to legend may have tanked a test in order to avoid speaking at graduation. Despite being considered one of the country's top prep prospects, he accepted a baseball scholarship to Stanford, and helped the Cardinals win the College World Series as a freshman in 1988. He earned his economics degree in 3½ years, capped by a provocatively titled senior thesis: "The Economics of Signing out of High School as Opposed to College."

The Orioles drafted Mussina with the 20th overall pick in 1990, and signed him for a $225,000 bonus. He beat a quick path to the majors. After seven starts at Double-A Hagerstown and two at Triple-A Rochester, he was ranked 19th on *Baseball America*'s Top 100 Prospects list the following spring. He made 19 more starts at Rochester before debuting for the Orioles on August 4, 1991. Though stuck on a club bound for 95 losses, he posted a 2.87 ERA in his 12-start trial, roughly half the ugly 5.55 mark of the other Baltimore starters combined.

That 95-loss season marked the Orioles' fifth sub-.500 finish out of six, but Mussina helped put the franchise back on the road back to respectability. Already remarkably polished, he assumed the mantle of staff ace, a role that 1989 overall number one pick Ben McDonald couldn't fulfill. The O's improved to 89 wins in

1992, as the 23-year-old Mussina tossed 241 innings of 2.54 ERA ball while going 18-5, making the All-Star team and placing fourth in the Cy Young voting. His ERA ranked third in the league, his walk rate (1.8 per nine) and WAR (8.2) second, the latter trailing only Roger Clemens's 8.8. Not surprisingly, his heavy workload carried a cost; shoulder soreness limited him to 167⅔ innings and a 4.46 ERA the following year.

Mussina restored his claim as one of the league's top starters in the strike-shortened seasons, with top four finishes in ERA (3.04 in 1994, 3.29 in '95) and WAR (5.4 and 6.1, respectively). He also led the AL in wins (19) and walk rate (2.0 per nine) for the only times in his career in the latter year, but placed a distant fifth in the Cy Young balloting, well behind the deserving Johnson (18-2, 2.48 ERA, 8.6 WAR). The Orioles challenged for the new Wild Card spot before the strike hit, going 63-49, but they slipped to 71-73 the following year.

In a 1994 *Sports Illustrated* profile, Tom Verducci described Mussina inventing a cut fastball on the fly to escape a jam, quoting battery-mate Chris Hoiles. "Well, I guess if you're going to use that pitch, we ought to have a sign for it." Verducci continued:

> What's most impressive is that from 60 feet, six inches, Mussina can dot the *i* in his autograph with any one of six pitches. He has three fastballs (a cutter, a sinker and a riser), two curveballs (a slow curve and the knuckle curve) and an astonishingly deceptive changeup that is his best pitch. The rest of the pitching population is usually content to throw all changeups on the outer third of the plate. But Mussina is so adept at spotting his changeup that Hoiles often gives a location sign when calling for the pitch, a rare practice.[15]

In 1996, under new manager Davey Johnson, a star-studded cast featuring future Hall of Famers Roberto Alomar, Eddie Murray, and Cal Ripken, plus Brady Anderson, Rafael Palmeiro, and more came together to win 88 games and the AL Wild Card. Aided by an offense that cranked out 5.82 runs per game, Mussina overcame his own gaudy 4.81 ERA (still a 103 ERA+) and again notched 19 wins, with 204 whiffs, good for fourth in the league and the first of four times he'd reach the 200 plateau. In his first postseason, he wasn't particularly effective, allowing a combined nine runs in 13⅔ innings against the Indians in the Division Series and the Yankees in the ALCS; a three-run Cecil Fielder homer in the eighth inning of the latter start undid an otherwise impressive outing.

In May 1997, Mussina signed a below-market three-year, $21.5 million contract extension, covering 1998–2000. He returned to form that year via a 3.20 ERA (sixth in the league) and 218 strikeouts (fourth) in 224⅔ innings while the

Orioles stormed to 98 wins and their first AL East title since 1983. He was brilliant in the playoffs, posting a 1.24 ERA with 41 strikeouts in 29 innings over four starts. Facing the Mariners in the Division Series, he outdueled the Big Unit in Games 1 and 4, administering the coup de grâce with a combined two-hitter in the latter. In his coverage for *SI*, Verducci wrote approvingly of Mussina's pitching style ("he morphs the best qualities of a power pitcher and a finesse pitcher"[16]) but harped on his repeated failure to win 20 games without acknowledging factors such as the four times in 1996 that Baltimore's bullpen surrendered leads he'd turned over, or the paltry run support he received down the stretch in '97 while collecting wins in just two of his final nine turns.

Mussina's brilliance in the ALCS against the Indians went for naught. He whiffed an LCS-record 15 batters while allowing just three hits and one run in Game 3, but the Orioles lost 2–1 in 12 innings via Marquis Grissom's steal of home. Similarly in Game 6, his eight innings of one-hit shutout ball were forgotten when Tony Fernandez hit a pennant-clinching 11th-inning home run off Armando Benitez.

Despite the loss, the Orioles' future looked bright, but a feud with owner Peter Angelos led Johnson to resign the same day he won AL Manager of the Year. The O's wouldn't finish above .500 again until 2012. Mussina played out the string as Baltimore collapsed into 70-something-win ignominy, averaging 216 innings with a 3.60 ERA (129 ERA+), 5.0 WAR, and his typically stellar 4.0 strikeout-to-walk ratio from 1998–2000. He finished second in the Cy Young voting in 1999, the best showing of his career, but Martinez (23-4, 2.07 ERA, 243 ERA+) deservedly won unanimously.

As the Orioles rebuilt, Angelos's glacial approach to Mussina's pending free agency led the pitcher to opt for a six-year, $88.5 million deal from the three-time-defending champion Yankees. "There have been only a couple years in my career when I knew we were going to win," he said of his time in Baltimore upon signing. "That's what I look forward to experiencing again."[17] The new deal made Mussina the game's fifth-highest-paid player.

Mussina and the Yankees did their share of winning in 2001. In his pinstriped debut on April 5, he tossed 7⅔ shutout innings against the Royals, winning a 1–0 squeaker. On May 1, he threw a three-hit, 10-K complete game shutout against the Twins. On September 2 at Fenway Park—matched up against David Cone, whom he replaced in the Yankees' rotation—he came within one strike of completing a perfect game, allowing a two-out, two-strike single to Carl Everett before closing out a 1–0 win "with the losing pitcher more or less in triumph and the winner in near-despair,"[18] as Roger Angell recounted for *The New Yorker*.

Mussina finished 2001 ranked second in the AL in ERA (3.15), strikeouts (214), and strikeout-to-walk ratio (5.1), with the last two career highs, while his

7.1 WAR led the AL for the only time in his career. Alas, he placed fifth in the Cy Young race, robbed by teammate Clemens, who had an inferior season save for the W's (20-3, 3.51 ERA, 5.6 WAR), which rested on his offensive support: Clemens's 5.7 runs per game ranked fourth in the league, while Mussina, who went 17-11, got just 4.2 runs per game, the fifth-lowest rate.

Mussina again came up big in October, helping the 95-win Yankees claim their fourth straight pennant. With the team down two games to none in the Division Series against the A's, he delivered seven shutout innings in Game 3, aided by Derek Jeter's legendary flip play on an errant relay throw to nab Jeremy Giambi at the plate in the 1–0 nail-biter. After a solid six-inning, two-run start in Game 2 of the ALCS against the Mariners, he was chased after three innings by the Diamondbacks in the World Series opener, but rebounded to whiff 10 in eight strong innings in Game 5, which the Yankees won in the 12th. The Yankees ultimately came within one inning of their fourth straight title—and Mussina's first—but Mariano Rivera unraveled in the ninth inning of Game 7. So it goes.

After a so-so 2002, Mussina helped the Yankees back to the World Series in 2003. He ranked eighth in ERA (3.40) and fifth in WAR (6.6) for the 101-win AL East champs, though his October had its ups and downs, as he wound up on the short end in his first three starts, two of them strong ones. In Game 7 of the ALCS against the Red Sox, after Clemens fell behind 4–0 and failed to retire any of the three batters he faced in the fourth inning, Torre summoned Mussina for the first relief appearance of his professional career. He was nails: With runners on the corners, he whiffed Jason Varitek on three pitches, then induced Johnny Damon to ground into a double play to escape the jam. His three scoreless innings made him an unsung hero in the Yankees' 11-inning win.

Mussina started Game 3 of the World Series against the Marlins, battling Josh Beckett to a 1–1 draw through seven innings despite a 39-minute rain delay in the fifth. The Yankees took the lead in the eighth and broke the game open in the ninth, giving them a 2–1 series lead. Lined up for Game 7, he never got the call, as New York lost each of the next three games.

Things started going downhill for Mussina in 2004, his age-35 season, as he lost six weeks to elbow tightness. From 2004–07, he averaged just 173 innings a year due to injuries, never topping 200. His 4.36 ERA over that span was still good for a 102 ERA+, but that owed to one exceptional season (2006, 3.51 ERA, 129 ERA+, 5.0 WAR) offsetting three mediocre ones; for the stretch, he averaged 2.9 WAR, productive but hardly exceptional.

Not ready to part ways, the Yankees reworked Mussina's $17 million option for 2007 into a two-year $23 million deal that started on a down note, as back and leg woes led to a career-worst 5.15 ERA, not to mention a brief exile to the bullpen. Even so, Mussina salvaged some dignity with a stretch of 13⅔ scoreless innings upon returning, and the next year defied both his age (39) and a rocky first month to deliver his best performance since 2003. Making a league-high 34 starts, he tossed 200⅓ innings en route to a 3.37 ERA (sixth) and 5.2 WAR (seventh). While the Yankees missed the playoffs for the first time since the strike, Mussina finally reached 20 wins by allowing just one run over his final 17 innings across three starts. The last came in Fenway Park, the site of his crushing near-perfecto, as the opener of a doubleheader on the final day of the season. With six shutout innings against the Wild Card–winning Red Sox, he claimed the mile-stone victory that had long eluded him, becoming the oldest to reach that plateau for the first time.

That win was the 270th of his career. Realizing that a pursuit of 300 might mean a three-year slog, and feeling the strong pull of Montoursville, he instead retired, virtually unprecedented for a 20-game winner. Of the three pitchers who won at least 20 games in their final seasons, two (Eddie Cicotte and Lefty Wil-iams) were banned after the 1920 season for their involvement in the Black Sox scandal; the third was Sandy Koufax, forced into retirement at the end of 1966 due to elbow problems. Though Mussina had millions of reasons to stay, in the form of dollars on his next contract, he walked away, following the old showbiz adage: Always leave 'em wanting more.

The Case

Wins are not the be-all and end-all of pitcher achievement, and 270 is not 300, but still it's worth noting: Mussina ranks 33rd all-time, above 34 Hall of Famer starters including Jim Palmer (268), Bob Feller (266), Bob Gibson (251), Martinez (219), and Smoltz (213), the last two representing twice as many starting pitchers with fewer than 300 wins who were elected by the BBWAA from 1992–2014. Moving beyond the deathless discussion of wins, Mussina's all-time standing in other areas is even more impressive. His 2,813 strikeouts ranks 19th all-time, while among pitchers with at least 3,000 innings, his 7.1 strikeouts per nine is ninth, and his 3.58 strikeout-to-walk ratio is second behind only Schilling.

Run-prevention-wise, Mussina's 3.68 ERA is higher than any Hall starter save for Red Ruffing (3.80), which in the eyes of voters might represent a bigger prob-lem for him than his win total, particularly in the wake of the tooth-and-nail battle over Jack Morris (3.90), but context is everything. Mussina spent 18 years in the AL East, an environment generally more favorable to hitters than pitchers, and he did so in a high-scoring era. He stood out among his peers, with seven top-five finishes in ERA, plus another four in the top 10. His 123 ERA+ is tied with Cicotte and Juan Marichal for 23rd all time at the 3,000-inning level, ahead of 32 Hall of Fame starters, including 12 with 300 wins.

As for the postseason, Mussina may not have won a ring, but his 3.42 ERA in 139⅔ innings is no small feat; it's 0.26 lower than his regular season ERA, against a higher caliber of competition. Aided by the expansion of the playoffs to three tiers, his 145 postseason strikeouts ranks fourth all-time, while his 9.3 strikeouts per nine is second among the 24 pitchers with at least 100 postseason innings (Johnson is first at 9.8). Sadly, Mussina's teams only won nine of his 23 postseason starts, because they supported him with just 3.1 runs per game; only four times (!) did they give him more than four runs. He had a few dud starts (three of less than five innings) among them, but one can't pin his teams' failure to win a championship solely on him. In five elimination-game appearances, two of them out of the bullpen, he posted a 2.49 ERA in 25⅓ innings, though his teams won just twice.

As for the advanced metrics, Mussina stands tall thanks to his combination of run prevention and strikeouts (for which he doesn't have to share credit—and thus value—with his fielders). His 83.0 career WAR ranks 23rd, ahead of 41 of the 62 enshrined starting pitchers; it's second among pitchers outside the Hall behind Clemens, and 14th among post–World War II pitchers. He's 1.6 WAR above 2014 honoree Glavine, who has an almost identical career/peak/JAWS line, and 9.1 above the average for enshrined starters. Mussina's peak WAR of 44.5 doesn't stack up as well; it's 65th all-time, topping only 22 enshrined starters, 5.8 wins below the standard. Even so, his 63.8 JAWS is 1.7 points above the standard, 28th all-time, one spot below Schilling (64.5), two above Glavine (62.9), three above Nolan Ryan (62.6), and ahead of 38 enshrined starters in all. That's more than good enough for Cooperstown.

Even so, Mussina struggled when he reached the ballot. Matched up against the five 2014 and '15 first-year candidates (Maddux, Glavine, Johnson, Martinez, and Smoltz) who won at least one Cy Young Award, and three of whom won at least 300 games, he received a disappointing 20.3% in his debut and then 24.6% in his second year, lower than all but two post-1966 candidates who were eventually elected, Duke Snider (24.7%) and Bert Blyleven (14.1%). Fortunately, he gained 18.4% in 2016, more than any holdover on the ballot, and backed that with another substantial jump to 51.8% in 2017. That 50% threshold is key; excluding current candidates, only Gil Hodges, Jack Morris, and Lee Smith have gotten such support without getting elected; the last two took 11 and 10 years to get there, respectively.

With no starting pitchers with even borderline credentials reaching the ballot until 2019, when Roy Halladay and Andy Pettitte become eligible, Mussina and

Schilling have a couple years to share the ballot spotlight alongside Clemens, whose connection to performance-enhancing drug allegations has put him in a different limbo. Like Blyleven, a high-strikeout pitcher from an earlier era whose dominance over hitters and excellence in run prevention was initially overshadowed by his lack of Cy Young hardware, the numbers and the facts are on Mussina's side. Soon enough, they'll carry the day.

THE ROUNDUP

The number before each player name refers to his JAWS ranking *among all players at the position*, not necessarily those in the Hall. Average HOF starting pitcher: 73.9/50.3/62.1.

The Elite (above standard in career, peak, and JAWS)

1. Walter Johnson RHP

Teams:	Senators 1907–27
Stats:	417-279 • 2.17 ERA • 147 ERA+ • 5,914.1 IP • 3,509 K
Rankings:	12× led K • 8× led WAR • 6× led W • 5× led ERA • 3× TC
	All-time: 1st SHO • 2nd W • 2nd ERA+ • 4th ERA • 3rd IP
	• 5th CG • 9th K
Voting/JAWS:	BBWAA 1936 **(1st, 83.6%)** • **165.6/89.5/127.5**

Blessed with the best fastball of his day, delivered sidearm, the Big Train tops the pitching list here because he missed bats like nobody else of his time, not even Cy Young. In 1910, Johnson became just the second post-1893 pitcher to strike out 300 in a season and led his league for the first of 12 times. He took over the all-time lead from Young in 1921 and held it until '83, when Steve Carlton surpassed him. Particularly in the context of the dead-ball era, when so many balls were put into play, those whiffs gave him tremendous value; he surpassed 10.0 WAR seven times (tied with Young for tops) and set a still standing post-1893 single-season record with 14.6 in 1913. He won the Triple Crown three times (1913, '18, and '24) and the MVP twice ('13, '24), led the Senators to back-to-back pennants in 1924–25, and, oh, he could hit, too—.235/.274/.342 with 24 homers, adding another 13.3 WAR. Small wonder he was among the inaugural five.

2. Cy Young RHP

Teams:	Cleveland Spiders 1890–98 • St. Louis Perfectos/Cardinals 1899–1900 • Boston Americans/Red Sox 1901–08 • Indians 1909–11 • Braves 1911
Stats:	511-316 • 2.63 ERA • 138 ERA+ • 7,356 IP • 2,803 K
Rankings:	12× top 5 ERA • 10× top 5 K • 6× led WAR • 5× led W All-time: 1st IP • 1st W • 1st GS • 1st CG • 6th ERA+ • 15th ERA • 20th K
Voting/JAWS:	BBWAA 1937 **(2nd, 76.1%)** • **168.5/79.3/123.9**

Remarkably, Young—whose nickname was short for "Cyclone," either in testament to his fastball's speed or to the fences it destroyed—wasn't among the Class of 1936 because the BBWAA and Old-Timers Committee weren't sure to which century his career belonged; it took a year to iron that out. Young's career began when the pitching distance was just 50 feet, but unlike many top hurlers from that early era, he survived the transition to the modern distance. Despite a blazing fastball, he whiffed just 3.4 per nine for his career, but had exceptional control for his day, turning in the league's lowest walk rate 14 times and rarely allowing homers (0.2 per nine career). A true workhorse, he topped 400 innings five times in his first six full seasons, and 300 innings in 15 straight years (1891–1905); via that volume, he led in WAR six times, with seven other top three finishes. His record totals of wins, losses, starts (815), complete games (749), innings, hits allowed (7,092), and batters faced (29,565) aren't likely to be broken.

4. Kid Nichols RHP

Teams:	Boston Beaneaters 1890–1901 • Cardinals 1904–05 • Phillies 1905–06
Stats:	361-208 • 2.96 ERA • 140 ERA+ • 5,067.1 IP • 1881 K
Rankings:	8× top 5 ERA+ • 6× top 5 ERA • 4× led WAR • 3× led W All-time: 4th ERA+ • 4th CG • 7th W • 11th IP • 26th GS
Voting/JAWS:	OTC 1949 • **116.4/75.1/95.8**

Boyish-looking and just 135 pounds when his professional career started, Charles "Kid" Nichols debuted a few months before Young and essentially equaled that legend's performance over the first 12 years of their careers. Through 1901, Young went 319-180 with a 2.93 ERA and 110.2 WAR in 4,415 innings, while Nichols went 329-183 with a 3.00 ERA and 108.5 WAR in 4,549 innings. While Young's Spiders went nowhere, Nichols was the staff ace for five pennant winners. He ranked among the top three in WAR eight times, and had a total of five seasons worth at least 10.0 WAR. With his performance declining, he spent 1902 and '03 (his age-32–33 seasons) as the player-manager-co-owner for the Kansas City Blue Stockings of the Western League before returning to the majors as player-manager of the Cardinals, for whom he summoned one strong season. Overshadowed by the remarkably durable Young, he received scant support from the BBWAA or OTC until a 1948 plug from Ty Cobb was picked up by the Associated Press. He was elected the following year.

5. Pete Alexander RHP

Teams:	Phillies 1911–17, '30 • Cubs 1918–26 • Cardinals 1926–29
Stats:	373-208 • 2.56 ERA • 135 ERA+ • 5,190 IP • 2,198 K
Rankings:	6x led WAR • 6x led W • 6x led K • 4x led ERA • 4x TC All-Time: 3rd W • 8th ERA+ • 10th IP • 11th ERA • 22nd GS
Voting/JAWS:	BBWAA 1938 **(3rd, 80.9%)** • 120.0/69.6/94.8

Named for a sitting president (Grover Cleveland) and portrayed on film by a future one (Ronald Reagan), Alexander was the NL's dominant pitcher at the tail end of the dead-ball era. From 1915–20, he won five ERA titles and four Triple Crowns while posting a combined a 1.64 ERA (174 ERA+). Concerned about the possibility of losing their ace to the military, the Phillies traded Alexander to the Cubs in December 1917. He made just three starts before heading off to combat in France, suffered injuries to both ears, and came home suffering from shell shock and epilepsy, which exacerbated his preexisting problems with alcohol. He rebounded with two of his strongest seasons in 1919 and '20, thereafter reinventing himself as a finesse pitcher who helped the Cardinals to a pair of pennants and the 1926 championship. The '26 World Series produced the rare moment memorialized on a Hall plaque; in the "final crisis at Yankee Stadium," he struck out Tony Lazzeri with the base loaded in the sixth inning, allegedly while either still drunk or at least hungover, and finished the game for the save.

6. Tom Seaver RHP

Teams:	Mets 1967–77, '83 • Reds 1977–82 • White Sox 1984–86 • Red Sox 1986
Stats:	311-205 • 2.86 ERA • 127 ERA+ • 4,783 IP • 3,640 K
Rankings:	12x All-Star • 11x top 5 WAR • 9x top 3 K • 3x led ERA • 3x led ERA+

All-time: 6th K • 7th SHO • 18th W • 19th IP

Voting/JAWS: BBWAA 1992 **(1st, 98.8%)** • 110.5/59.5/85.0

A three-time Cy Young winner who helped the Amazin' Mets win the 1969 World Series and the '73 NL pennant, "Tom Terrific" ranks as the best postwar pitcher this side of Roger Clemens. Only three other pitchers with at least 4,000 innings since World War II have as good or better an ERA+ than Seaver's 127, and only Clemens tops him in WAR. The progenitor of the "drop-and-drive" motion, with the dirty right knee and multiple variants of his fastball, curve, and changeup, he was exceptional at missing bats; more than 30 years after retirement, he's still sixth all-time in strikeouts. He led a Triple Crown category 10 times and compiled a record 18 seasons with an ERA+ of at least 100 while qualifying for the title, including his final one. That wire-to-wire consistency helped him garner 98.82% of the vote in 1992, a record that stood until 2016. Via Jeff Idelson (at the time the Hall veep of communications), of the five voters who omitted Seaver, three submitted blank ballots in protest of the Pete Rose ineligibility decision, a fourth overlooked him while recovering from open-heart surgery, and a fifth said he didn't vote for first-time candidates.

7. Christy Mathewson RHP

Teams: Giants 1900–16 • Reds 1916

Stats: 373-188 • 2.13 ERA • 135 ERA+ • 4,788.2 IP • 2,507 K

Rankings: 9× led K/BB • 7× led BB • 5× led WAR • 5× led ERA • 5× led K • 4× led W • 2× TC

All-time: 2nd ERA • 3rd W • 3rd SHO • T-7th ERA+ • 14th CG • 18th IP

Voting/JAWS: BBWAA 1936 **(1st, 90.7%)** • 101.7/66.5/84.1

Standing 6'1" at a time when such height was an anomaly—hence the "Big Six" nickname—Mathewson was the best pitcher of the first decade of the dead-ball era, and one of the game's first superstars thanks to the combination of his mound expertise, good looks, college education (Bucknell University), and gallant demeanor. Via impeccable control of his fastball/fadeaway (screwball) combo, he dominated NL leaderboards while helping the powerhouse Giants to four pennants and one championship; in the 1905 World Series, he delivered 27 shutout innings against the A's. His career went into rapid decline in 1914, and in mid-'16 John McGraw engineered a trade to Cincinnati so that Mathewson could manage. He did so for just one full season before leaving for France, commissioned as a captain in the army's Chemical Warfare Division. Exposed to mustard gas while training, he battled health problems, most notably tuberculosis, which limited his future baseball endeavors and led to his death at age 45 in 1925, 11 years before being voted into the inaugural Hall of Fame class.

8. Lefty Grove LHP

Teams:	A's 1925–33 • Red Sox 1934–41
Stats:	300-141 • 3.06 ERA • 148 ERA+ • 3,940.2 IP • 2,266 K
Rankings:	9× led ERA • 9× led ERA+ • 8× led WAR • 8× led K/BB • 7× led K • 2× TC
	All-time: 1st ERA+
Voting/JAWS:	BBWAA 1947 **(3rd†, 76.4%)** • **103.6/63.6/83.6**

Despite spending his age-20–24 seasons dominating the International League as a Baltimore Oriole instead of pitching in the majors, Grove stands as the top southpaw in WAR and the top pitcher of either hand in ERA+ at the 3,000-inning cutoff. Grove led the AL in strikeouts in each of his first seven seasons; the A's won pennants in the last three of those, with championships in 1929 and '30. He led the AL in ERA a record nine times between 1926 and '39, the last four after reinventing himself as a "curve and control" pitcher at age 35, in the wake of a sore arm that wrecked his first season in Boston. He was the 12th pitcher to reach 300 wins, and the only one between Pete Alexander in 1924 and Warren Spahn in '61. Though he received support as early as 1936, Grove was elected in '47, but the really crazy thing is that he received six votes (2.2%) in 1960, 13 years *after* election—votes likely intended for Lefty Gomez, who received 19.0% that year.

9. Randy Johnson LHP

Teams:	Expos 1988–89 • Mariners 1989–98 • Astros 1998 • Diamondbacks 1999–2004, '07–08 • Yankees 2005–06 • Giants 2009
Stats:	303-166 • 3.29 ERA • 135 ERA+ • 4,135.1 IP • 4,875 K
Rankings:	10× All-Star • 9× led K • 9× led K/9 • 8× top 3 K/BB • 6× led WAR • 4× led ERA
	All-time: 1st K/9 • 2nd K • T-7th ERA+ • 21st GS
Voting/JAWS:	BBWAA 2015 **(1st, 97.3%)** • **102.1/62.0/82.0**

† Years receiving votes prior to final year of career not counted.

Standing 6'10", with a get-off-my-property scowl, a wingspan approximating a Boeing 747, and a three-quarters release point that left batters almost no time to distinguish between a sizzling fastball that could touch 100 and a slider that some consider the game's greatest, Johnson dealt in intimidation like no one of his day. Difficulty getting those long levers in sync prevented him from establishing himself as an elite pitcher until age 29, but he pitched past his 46th birthday, tossed two no-hitters (including a perfect game) and whiffed more batters than anyone but Nolan Ryan; if not for significant back injuries in 1996 and 2007, plus a knee injury in 2003, he'd have blazed past 5,000 K. His six 300-strikeout seasons is one fewer than all other pitchers since his 1988 debut *combined*; he had four straight from 1999–2002, when he tied Greg Maddux's record of four straight Cy Youngs. He left an impression on voters; among pitchers, only Seaver and Ryan received higher percentages.

10. Greg Maddux RHP

Teams:	Cubs 1986–92, '04–06 • Braves 1993–2003 • Dodgers 2006, '08 • Padres 2007–08
Stats:	355-227 • 3.16 ERA • 132 ERA+ • 5,008.1 IP • 3,371 K
Rankings:	14× led W • 11× top 5 WAR • 9× led BB/9 • 8× top 3 ERA • 8× All-Star • 5×led IP • 5× led ERA+
	All-time: 4th GS • 8th W • 10th K • 12th ERA+ • 13th IP
Voting/JAWS:	BBWAA 2014 **(1st, 97.2%)** • **106.9/56.3/81.6**

Winner of four straight Cy Youngs (1992–95) and ace of the Braves dynasty that made 10 straight postseasons (1993, '95–2003), Maddux succeeded without high velocity, generally throwing in the mid-to-high 80s in his prime. Rob Neyer dubbed him "the smartest pitcher who ever lived"[19] for his exceptional command of a wide array of pitches, ability to avoid hard contact, and a cerebral approach founded in an understanding of effective velocity—the combination of speed and location. Durable enough to reach 190 innings 21 times (tied with Don Sutton for the all-time lead), Maddux was regularly in the top five of most key categories, and often number one; he led in starts eight times, ERA four times, and WAR three times. He's tops among postwar righties in wins despite a lack of run support (96 SUP+), a problem that extended into the postseason; he went 2-3 with a 2.09 ERA in five World Series starts, and 11-14, 3.27 ERA in 198 IP overall.

11. John Clarkson RHP

Teams:	Worcester Ruby Legs 1882 • Chicago White Stockings 1884–87 • Boston Beaneaters 1888–92 • Cleveland Spiders 1892–94

Stats:	328-178 • 2.81 ERA • 133 ERA+ • 4,536.1 IP • 1,978 K
Rankings:	6× top 5 W • 6× top 5 WAR • 5× top 5 ERA • 5× top 3 K •
	4× led IP
	All-time: T-10th ERA+ • 12th W • 20th ERA
Voting/JAWS:	VC 1963 • **84.0/74.9/79.4**

Clarkson owns the highest JAWS ranking among a quintet of enshrined nineteenth-century hurlers—Pud Galvin, Tim Keefe, Old Hoss Radbourn, and Mickey Welch are the others—who made their bones prior to 1893, when the pitching distance was set at 60′6″. During that time, the rules were particularly in flux regarding the distance, type of delivery, ability of the batter to request a high or low pitch, number of balls required for a walk, and equipment. The era's pitchers carried workloads now unthinkable, routinely throwing 400 innings or even 600 in a season, accompanied by astronomical totals of starts, complete games, wins, and WAR. Their numbers, and those with comparable numbers who aren't enshrined, should be taken with a grain of salt. Standards-wise, the quintet doesn't move the needle much; without them, the JAWS standard falls from 62.1 to 61.3.

The modestly sized (5′10″, 155 pounds) Clarkson was a control artist who relied upon a sinker, curve, and changeup, and focused on preventing hard contact. He often used the glare of a huge, shiny belt buckle to distract batters until the umpire inevitably ordered it removed. From 1885–89, he averaged 543 innings, 59 complete games, and 42 wins per year, leading the NL in wins, strikeouts, and WAR three times apiece, with a high of 16.7 in '89. The staff ace of the 1885 and '86 White Stockings pennant winners, he was sold to the Beaneaters for $10,000, reuniting with Chicago catcher King Kelly to become part of the "$20,000 battery" and helping them to the 1891 pennant. In Cleveland he became the fifth pitcher to reach 300 wins, and showed a young Young how to improve his curveball and control. Excessive drinking curtailed his career and, accompanied by other psychological problems, led to his death at age 47 in 1909. The research of Hall historian Lee Allen was key to his election.

12. Tim Keefe RHP

Teams:	Troy Trojans 1880–82 • New York Metropolitans (AA)
	1883–84 • Giants 1885–89, '91 • Giants (PL) 1890 •
	Phillies 1891–93
Stats:	342-225 • 2.63 ERA • 126 ERA+ • 5,049.2 IP • 2,564 K

Rankings:	7× top 3 W • 6× top 3 K • 6× top 5 WAR • 3× led ERA • TC
	All-time: 12th IP • 23rd GS • 28th K
Voting/JAWS:	VC 1964 • **86.6/66.5/76.6**

Keefe left his mark all over nineteenth-century baseball, setting records, compiling the highest WAR (87.7) of any pitcher prior to the distance change, serving as a labor leader and the model pitcher for "Casey at the Bat." Keefe used the entirety of the pitcher's box to take multiple hops and steps before delivery, using a variety of angles, arm heights (including submarine style), and speeds. His early mastery of the changeup helped him set single-season and career strikeout records; he held the latter from 1888–1908. Bouncing between teams and leagues, he fought for every dollar and became one of the sport's earliest holdouts in 1882. His monster 1883 season featured 41 wins, 68 starts (all complete games), 619 innings, and 19.7 WAR, a record surpassed by Galvin a year later. He helped the Metropolitans to the 1884 pennant, and the Giants to back-to-back pennants in '88 and '89 despite holdouts in both years; his 19 straight wins in '88 still stands as the record. While in the Players League he became the second 300-win pitcher, but struggled upon returning to the NL, and lasted just one season at the new distance. Considered in all eight VC elections from 1953–64, he gained entry alongside brother-in-law Monte Ward.

13. Warren Spahn LHP

Teams:	Braves 1942, '46–64 • Mets 1965 • Giants 1965
Stats:	363-245 • 3.09 ERA • 119 ERA+ • 5,243.2 IP • 2,583 K
Rankings:	14× All-Star • 12× top 5 WAR • 9× led CG • 8× led W • 4× led IP • 4× led K • 3× led ERA
	All-time: 6th W • 8th IP • 14th GS • 21st CG • 26th K
Voting/JAWS:	BBWAA 1973 **(1st, 83.2%)** • **100.2/51.7/75.9**

Spahn didn't notch his first win until age 25, after three-plus seasons in the army. As a combat engineer he saw action in the Battle of the Bulge and became the most decorated soldier among ballplayers, earning a Bronze Star, a Purple Heart, a battlefield promotion, and a Presidential Citation. Despite that late start, his 363 victories are still tops all-time among lefties, not to mention post–World War II pitchers of either hand. Incredibly durable, he reeled off 17 straight years (1947–63) with at least 245 innings; his heyday encompassed the Braves' only three pennant winners between 1915–1990. He won the 1957 Cy Young and placing second three times, all before the award was split into leagues; twice he topped the NL in votes, so it's fair to assume he'd have won a couple more. Though his final year in the majors was 1965, his age-44 season, he was ineligible for election until 1973 due to cameos while coaching in the Mexican League in '66 and managing in the PCL in '67, a rule that soon fell by the wayside.

14. Bob Gibson RHP

Teams:	Cardinals 1959–75
Stats:	251-174 • 2.91 ERA • 127 ERA+ • 3,884.1 IP • 3,117 K
Rankings:	10x top 5 K • 8x All-Star • 7x top 5 ERA • 7x top 5 WAR
	All-time: 13th SHO • 14th K • T-15th ERA+
Voting/JAWS:	BBWAA 1981 **(1st, 84.0%)** • 89.9/61.6/75.8

With his trademark scowl, violent delivery, and willingness to pitch inside, Gibson dealt in intimidation, and took pride in "mess[ing] with a batter's head without letting him into mine."[20] He enjoyed a 13-year run (1961–73) as one of the game's most dominant pitchers, though in a league that also featured the primes of Sandy Koufax, Juan Marichal, and the ageless Spahn, he didn't top the NL leaderboard often. While he had 23 top five finishes in Triple Crown categories, he led each just once apiece, with the strikeout and ERA leads in 1968, when he set a modern record with a 1.12 ERA and won NL MVP and the first of two Cy Youngs. He led the NL in WAR each year from '68–70, topping 10.0 twice. The MVP of the 1964 and '67 World Series—the only two-time winner this side of Koufax—he went 7-2 with a 1.89 ERA, 92 strikeouts, and eight complete games in nine Series starts. Though short of 300 wins, he was the first NL pitcher to 3,000 strikeouts, retiring with the second-highest mark behind Walter Johnson, and breezing into Cooperstown.

15. Phil Niekro RHP

Teams:	Braves 1964–83, '87 • Yankees 1984–85 • Indians 1986–87 • Blue Jays 1987
Stats:	318-274 • 3.35 ERA • 115 ERA+ • 5,404 IP • 3,342 K
Rankings:	6x top 5 WAR • 6x top 5 K • 5x All-Star • 5x top 5 W • 4x led IP • 4x top 10 ERA
	All-time: 4th IP • 5th GS • 11th K
Voting/JAWS:	BBWAA 1997 **(5th, 80.3%)** • 96.6/54.5/75.6

He didn't start regularly until he was 28, never won a Cy Young or pitched in a World Series, and racked up a ton of losses on mediocre teams. Nonetheless,

Niekro's durability and longevity made him the game's greatest knuckleballer. Not only did he throw more innings than all but Young, Walter Johnson, and Galvin, he had 19 seasons of at least 200 innings (all above average, ERA+-wise, save for three in the 96–99 range) and four of at least 300. He aged exceptionally well. His 65.7 WAR from age 35 onward is tops by nearly five wins; that stretch featured his six top five finishes, including a league-leading 10.0 WAR in 1978 (age 39, a record) and another league lead in '79. He was an All-Star on merit at age 45 (4.6 WAR in 1984), a 300-game winner at 46, and still a league-average innings eater through age 47. The perception that he was "merely" a compiler delayed his enshrinement during a span in which miserly voters slighted Ted Simmons, Ron Santo, Dick Allen, or Minnie Minoso and let fellow 300-game winner Don Sutton languish for five ballots as well.

16. Bert Blyleven RHP

Teams:	Twins 1970–76, 1985–88 • Rangers 1976–77 • Pirates 1978–80 • Indians 1981–85 • Angels 1989–90, '92
Stats:	287-250 • 3.31 ERA • 118 ERA+ • 4,970 IP • 3,701 K
Rankings:	13× top 5 K • 9× top 5 WAR • 7× top 5 ERA • 6× top 5 IP • 3× led SHO • 2× All-Star
	All-time: 5th K • 9th SHO • 11th GS • 14th IP
Voting/JAWS:	BBWAA 2011 **(14th, 79.7%)** • **95.3/50.7/73.0**

See Chapter 6.

17. Steve Carlton LHP

Teams:	Cardinals 1965–71 • Phillies 1972–86 • Giants 1986 • White Sox 1986 • Indians 1987 • Twins 1987–88
Stats:	329-244 • 3.22 ERA • 115 ERA+ • 5,217.2 IP • 4,136 K
Rankings:	10× All-Star • 5× led IP • 5× led K • 5× top 5 ERA • 4× led W • 3× led WAR • TC
	All-time: 4th K • 6th GS • 9th IP • 11th W • 14th SHO
Voting/JAWS:	BBWAA 1994 **(1st, 95.6%)** • **90.4/54.3/72.4**

The first four-time Cy Young winner and first lefty to notch 4,000 strikeouts was an odd duck. Behind his deadly slider was an unorthodox training regimen founded in martial arts, one that included exercises such as twisting his hand deep into a vat of rice, and an approach that borrowed from Eastern philosophy and reduced the game to its most minimal component: getting the ball to the catcher.

In 1972, he not only won the pitching Triple Crown (27-10, 1.97 ERA, 310 K) while toiling for a 59-97 team, his 12.1 WAR that year is tied with Alexander (1920) and Dwight Gooden ('85) for the highest mark since 1914; he also had a 10.2 WAR season in 1980. He finished among the top five in strikeouts 12 times, and at points during the 1983–84 seasons held the all-time record before being left in the dust by Nolan Ryan. He overstayed his welcome with a dreadful late-career slog, -3.2 WAR for five teams from 1986–88, but neither that nor his infamous unwillingness to speak to the media slowed his election.

18. Old Hoss Radbourn RHP

Teams:	Providence Grays 1880–85 • Boston Beaneaters 1886–89 • Boston Reds (PL) 1890 • Reds 1891
Stats:	309-194 • 2.68 ERA • 119 ERA+ • 4,527.1 IP • 1,830 K
Rankings:	5× top 3 WAR • 5× top 5 ERA • 5× top 5 W • 3× top 3 K • TC
	All-time: 8th CG • 19th W • 26th IP
Voting/JAWS:	OTC 1939 • **76.0/68.1/72.1**

Attacking from a variety of arm angles while controlling a wide array of pitches, Radbourn posted jaw-dropping numbers in the pre–60'6" era. He earned his nickname not on the basis of size (5'9", 168 pounds) but his ability to handle huge workloads: an average of 412 innings, with a combined 1,311 in 1883–84 while successively setting single-season wins records with 48 (in 68 starts) and 59 (in 73 starts, all complete games). Accompanied by a 1.38 ERA and 441 strikeouts, he became the second pitcher to win a Triple Crown in 1884. He produced 19.1 WAR that year—the third-highest single-season total—while accounting for 65% of the NL champion Grays' innings. He volunteered to pitch every remaining game after a feud led co-ace Charlie Sweeney to jump the team amid a pennant race and went 35-4-1 while starting 41 of Providence's final 51 games. Radbourn retired at 36, but his post-career life was short, as he lost his left eye and suffered facial disfigurement and some speech loss in a hunting accident, with alcohol and possible brain damage due to syphilis taking their toll as well; he died at 42. Unlike his fellow pre-1893 aces, he quickly received his due from Hall voters.

20. Gaylord Perry RHP

Teams:	Giants 1962–71 • Indians 1972–75 • Rangers 1975–77, '80 • Padres 1978–79 • Yankees 1980 • Braves 1981 • Mariners 1982–83 • Royals 1983
Stats:	314-265 • 3.11 ERA • 117 ERA+ • 5,350 IP • 3,534 K

Rankings:	11× top 10 WAR • 11× top 10 ERA • 10× top 5 IP • 7× top 5 K • 5× All-Star • 3× led W
	All-time: 6th IP • 8th K • 9th GS • 16th SHO • 17th W
Voting/JAWS:	BBWAA 1991 **(3rd, 77.2%)** • **91.0/52.8/71.9**

The spitball was formally outlawed after the 1920 season, with 17 pitchers grand-fathered. In nearly a century since, nobody flouted the ban more brazenly nor more successfully than Perry, who titled his 1974 confessional *Me and the Spitter*. Thanks to lax enforcement of the rules and a fair bit of reverse psychology via an elaborate series of pre-pitch feints and a quality sinker/slider combo, he became the first player to win Cy Young awards in each league, the third to 3,000 strikeouts (after Walter Johnson and Gibson), and the 15th to 300 wins. The belief that he was loading the ball up drove opposing managers crazy; Ralph Houk swiped his cap, Billy Martin brought a bloodhound to sniff balls, and Dick Williams ordered him strip-searched, to no avail. A workhorse who ranked among the top five in innings annually from 1967–75, he had five top five finishes in WAR in that span, including league-leading seasons of 11.0 in 1972 and 8.6 in '74. Though ranked 11th in wins and third in strikeouts when he retired, he had to wait his turn behind Johnny Bench and Carl Yastrzemski in 1989 and then Jim Palmer and Joe Morgan in '90.

21. Pedro Martinez RHP

Teams:	Dodgers 1992–93 • Expos 1994–97 • Red Sox 1998–2004 • Mets 2005–08 • Phillies 2009
Stats:	219-100 • 2.93 ERA • 154 ERA+ • 2,827.1 IP • 3,154 K
Rankings:	10× top 3 H/9 • 9× top 3 K • 8× All-Star • 8× top 5 WAR • 5× led ERA
	All-time: 13th K
Voting/JAWS:	BBWAA 2015 **(1st, 91.1%)** • **84.0/58.2/71.1**

Inning for inning and inch for inch, the 5'11", 170-pound Martinez has a case as the best pitcher in history. Pairing a mid-90s fastball with a changeup that some consider the best ever—both thrown with the same confounding arm action—he dominated hitters en route to three Cy Youngs and three WAR leads apiece. His two best seasons, 1999 (9.7 WAR, 243 ERA+) and 2000 (11.7 WAR, 291 ERA+), came at the height of the highest-scoring era since the mid-1930s, and in one of the least-pitcher-friendly ballparks. Though he qualified for the ERA title just 11 times, he had a top five strikeout rate in each, and a top three hit rate in 10 of them. At the 2,500-inning cutoff, his 10.0 strikeouts per nine was the highest among righties, and his ERA+ is the highest of all time, as is his 5.9 WAR per 200 innings; Clemens (5.7), Walter Johnson (5.6), Grove (5.3), and Johan Santana (5.1) round out the top five in that category. As part of the 2015 bumper crop of inductees, Martinez and John Smoltz became just the second and third BBWAA-elected starters since 1992 with fewer than 300 wins.

22. Robin Roberts RHP

Teams:	Phillies 1948–61 • Orioles 1962–65 • Astros 1965–66 • Cubs 1966
Stats:	286-245 • 3.41 ERA • 113 ERA+ • 4,688.2 IP • 2,357 K
Rankings:	7× All-Star • 7× top 5 ERA • 6× led GS • 6× top 5 K • 5× led IP • 5× led WAR • 5× led K/BB • 4× led W • 4× led BB/9
	All-time: 20th GS • 21st IP • 29th SHO
Voting/JAWS:	BBWAA 1976 **(4th, 86.9%)** • **86.0/54.8/70.4**

Durability and pinpoint control were the hallmarks of Roberts's career, helping him lead the "Whiz Kid" Phillies to the 1950 NL pennant as a 23-year-old and kicking off a seven-year stretch of All-Star appearances and leaderboard dominance—including WAR leads from 1950–54. Blessed with uncanny control, Roberts walked just 1.7 per nine, the lowest career rate among post-dead-ball hurlers with at least 3,000 innings. That was critical to Roberts's survival; as his elite fastball declined, he became homer-prone enough to serve up a since-broken record of 505. After a stretch of mediocrity from 1956–61, he enjoyed a resurgence as a finesse pitcher in Baltimore. Had he been surrounded by better teams during the second half of his Philly stint, he might have won 300. His eligibility delayed by a year due to a minor league stint, he reached the ballot in 1973 alongside Spahn and Whitey Ford, and needed four years to get in.

23. Eddie Plank LHP

Teams:	A's 1901–14 • St. Louis Terriers (FL) 1915 • Browns 1916–17
Stats:	326-194 • 2.35 ERA • 122 ERA+ • 4,495.2 IP • 2,246 K
Rankings:	13× top 10 K/BB • 8× top 5 W • 8× top 5 WAR • 8× top 10 ERA • 6× top 5 K
	All-time: 5th SHO • 6th ERA • 13th W • 26th ERA+
Voting/JAWS:	OTC 1946 • **89.9/50.5/70.2**

A staple of four pennant winners and two champions for Connie Mack's A's, Gettysburg Eddie—that's where he hailed from, and where he gave battlefield tours, post-retirement—has a claim as the top southpaw in history prior to Lefty Grove. Readjusting his cap, shirt, and pants before staring in for the sign—and if it was late in the game, talking to the ball—his pre-pitch routine drove hitters, fielders, fans, and deadline-minded writers crazy. His delivery was no more conventional, as he stepped sideways toward first base while throwing across his body, attacking the batter from an angle with a crossfire motion he called a "slant ball." Somehow he maintained control while fooling hitters. While he never led in a Triple Crown category or WAR, he was so consistently among the top handful that only Young, Johnson, and Mathewson compiled more WAR in the 1893–1919 period. He had hard luck in the postseason (2-5, 1.32 ERA); in his six starts, all complete games, his teams totaled six runs and were shut out four times. He was the 1946 OTC's strongest selection, but alas, he'd been dead of a stroke for 20 years.

24. Fergie Jenkins RHP

Teams:	Phillies 1965–66 • Cubs 1966–73, 1982–83 • Rangers 1974–75, '78–81 • Red Sox 1976–77
Stats:	284-226 • 3.34 ERA • 115 ERA+ • 4,500.2 IP • 3,192 K
Rankings:	8x top 5 K • 8x top 10 WAR • 7x top 3 W • 5x led BB/9 • 5x led K/BB • 3x All-Star
	All-time: 12th K • 23rd GS • 27th IP • 29th W
Voting/JAWS:	BBWAA 1991 **(3rd, 75.4%)** • 84.9/51.8/68.3

Though overshadowed by a cohort of 300-win pitchers, Jenkins belongs among his era's elite. From 1967–74, he averaged 304 innings with a 123 ERA+ while reaching the 20-win plateau seven times, helping to make both the Cubs and Rangers respectable, winning a Cy Young (with four other top three finishes) yet never reaching the postseason. Like Roberts, outstanding control helped offset his gopher problem: He led the league in homers allowed seven times. Up against prime Carlton and Seaver in the NL, and Ryan in the AL, he led in strikeouts just once, but in 1982 became the seventh pitcher to reach 3,000. His election was slowed less by his 1980 drug arrest (in which his suspension by an overzealous Bowie Kuhn was overturned, and his conviction ultimately wiped out) than by becoming eligible alongside Bench, Yastrzemski, and Perry in 1989. His election made him the Hall's first (and to date only) Canadian-born player, but the joy was short-lived due to the death of his wife four days after the announcement, via complications following a car accident.

25. Amos Rusie RHP

Teams:	Indianapolis Hoosiers (NL) 1889 • Giants 1890–95, '97–98 • Reds 1901
Stats:	246-174 • 3.07 ERA • 129 ERA+ • 3,778.2 IP • 1,950 K
Rankings:	6× top 3 IP • 6× top 5 W • 5× led K • 5× top 5 ERA • 5× top five WAR • TC
Voting/JAWS:	VC 1977 • **69.3/66.8/68.0**

Control-challenged both on and off the field, the physically imposing (6′1″, 200 pounds) "Hoosier Thunderbolt" was considered the fastest pitcher of the 1890s and the reason for the '93 distance change. Allegedly discovered at 17 throwing balls through a wooden fence at the Indiana state fair, he later spurred Giants catcher Dick Buckley to insert a sheet of lead and a sponge into his glove to absorb the impact of his heater. The Ryanesque Rusie had four seasons pairing walk and strikeout leads, and averaged a staggering 503 innings from 1890–94, on either side of the change. In 1894, he won the NL Pitching Triple Crown and posted a career-high 14.3 WAR. He lost his big fastball due to an arm injury, sat out two seasons due to marital problems, and lasted just three games in his 1901 comeback with the Reds, who had traded a 20-year-old Mathewson for him. The cameo did give Rusie the 10-year minimum for a Hall career; the VC got around to him in 1977, thanks largely to the efforts of SABR, which via Bill Madden (!) had recently "overwhelmingly ranked Rusie first among those deserving of enshrinement"[21] based on their statistical research.

26. Pud Galvin RHP

Teams:	St Louis Brown Stockings (NA) 1875 • Buffalo Bisons (NL) 1879–85 • Pittsburgh Alleghenys (AA) 1885–89, (NL) 1891–82 • Pittsburgh Burghers (PL) 1890 • St. Louis Browns 1892
Stats:	365-310 • 2.85 ERA • 107 ERA+ • 6,003.1 IP • 1,807 K
Rankings:	10× top 10 W • 9× top 10 WAR • 7× top 5 IP • 6× top 10 K • 5× top 5 ERA All-time: 2nd IP • 5th W • 10th GS • 11th SHO
Voting/JAWS:	VC 1965 • **73.7/62.1/67.9**

Only Young threw more innings than Galvin, whose nickname stemmed either from his pudgy build (5′8″, 190 pounds) or his ability to turn batters into pudding with his fastball. A charismatic fan favorite who was unequaled in picking off baserunners, Galvin only fleetingly had a case as the league's best pitcher, but he was quite the workhorse. He threw more than 600 innings twice, with another season of 593 and six more above 400, all before the distance change. The workloads added up: His 20.5 WAR in 1884 (72 starts, 636⅓ innings, 1.99 ERA) is a single-season record, though one of just four times he ranked among the league's top five. He threw two no-hitters, not counting the first recorded perfect game in an 1876 nonleague tournament in Ionia, Michigan, and in 1888 became the first pitcher to 300 wins, not that anybody recognized the milestone's significance. His early death from chronic gastritis at age 45 in 1902 caused him to fade from the consciousness of fans and historians, but the research of Lee Allen led to his election.

The Rank and File

29. Ed Walsh RHP

Teams:	White Sox 1904–16 • Braves 1917
Stats:	195-126 • 1.82 ERA • 145 ERA+ • 2,964.1 IP • 1,736 K
Rankings:	6× top 3 WAR • 6× top 3 K • 5× top 3 ERA • 4× led IP • 3× led K/BB
	All-time: 11th SHO
Voting/JAWS:	OTC 1946 • **65.5/61.9/63.7**

The dead-ball era's foremost spitballer—"sometimes nine out of ten balls I throw are of that style,"[22] he said in 1912—Walsh piled up some of the twentieth century's heaviest workloads, which shortened his career considerably. Even so, he owns the lowest ERA and fourth-highest ERA+ at the 2,500-inning level behind Martinez (154), Grove (148), and Walter Johnson (147). Walsh began spitballing in 1906, the year his "Hitless Wonder" White Sox upset the crosstown Cubs in the World Series, kicking off a seven-year run during which he averaged 24 wins, 361 innings, a 1.71 ERA (155 ERA+), and 8.6 WAR. After winning the first of two ERA titles with a 1.60 ERA in 422⅓ innings in 1907, he threw 464 innings—a post-nineteenth-century record—the next year, with a 1.42 ERA and 40 wins. Arm troubles limited him to just 190⅔ innings from 1913–17. He began receiving support on the writers' ballot in 1936, climbed to 55.5% in 1945, and was part of the OTC's "unanimously elected" group of 11 the next year.

30. Tom Glavine LHP

Teams:	Braves 1987–2002, '08 • Mets 2003–07
Stats:	305-203 • 3.54 ERA • 118 ERA+ • 4,413.1 IP • 2,607 K

Rankings:	10× All Star • 7× top 5 IP • 5× led W • 5× top five WAR • 5× top 5 ERA
	All-time: 12th GS • 21st W • 25th K • 30th IP
Voting/JAWS:	BBWAA 2014 **(1st, 91.9%)** • 81.4/44.3/62.9

The epitome of the crafty lefty, Glavine relied on modest stuff—primarily a mid-to-high-80s fastball/changeup combo—masterfully sequenced and perfectly placed on the outside edge of the plate. His uncanny ability to expand the strike zone put hitters in unfavorable counts, helping him avoid hard contact. Though his raw rate stats (5.3 strikeouts and 3.1 walks per nine) didn't jump off the stat sheet, that recipe worked well enough for him to help his teams to 12 playoff appearances and five pennants. His five 20-win seasons are more than any DH-era pitcher except Clemens. Underlying that was exceptional durability, as he topped 200 innings 14 times and 180 innings 19 times, avoiding the disabled list until his final season. It added up, making him the 22nd pitcher to 300 wins, and thanks to the Braves' perennial postseason runs, he's all over the October leaderboards, ranking second in playoff starts (35) and innings (218⅓), third in wins (14), and first in losses (16) despite a 3.30 ERA, 0.24 lower than his regular season mark. A slam-dunk choice, he entered alongside longtime teammate Maddux and manager Bobby Cox.

31. Nolan Ryan RHP

Teams:	Mets 1966, '68–71 • Angels 1972–79 • Astros 1980–88 • Rangers 1989–93
Stats:	324-292 • 3.19 ERA • 112 ERA+ • 5,386 IP • 5,714 K
Rankings:	11× led K • 9× top 10 WAR • 8× All-Star • 8× top 10 W • 8× top 10 ERA
	All-time: 1st K • 1st BB • 5th IP • 14th W
Voting/JAWS:	BBWAA 1999 **(1st, 98.79%)** • 81.8/43.3/62.6

Electrifying but polarizing, Ryan is the most overpowering pitcher of all time based on his record low-hit rate (6.6 per nine) and strikeout rate relative to the league (78% above average), not to mention his records for strikeouts (5,714), walks (2,795), no-hitters (seven), and seasons pitched (27). He was a freak show early in his career, when astronomical walk rates and mediocre won-loss records offset his first four no-hitters and his strikeout and velocity records (383 whiffs in 1973, and a pitch that registered 100.9 mph 10 feet from the plate in 1974, suggesting a release velocity 6–8 mph higher). As he harnessed both his fastball and a high-80s curve, respect for his talent grew, particularly as he dominated in his 40s while pushing his records out of reach. Beyond the strikeouts and walks, he won ERA titles in 1981 and '87, the latter, accompanied by a league-high 270 strikeouts, might have won him a Cy Young had bad offensive support not left him 8-16. While he's below the peak standard, his 22.6 WAR from age 40 onward helps him outdistance the career mark. His 98.79%, just shy of Seaver's 1992 mark, overstates his case, but he deserves his plaque.

36. Mickey Welch RHP

Teams:	Troy Trojans 1880–82 • New York Gothams/Giants 1883–92
Stats:	307-210 • 2.71 ERA • 113 ERA+ • 4,802 IP • 1,850 K
Rankings:	9× top 10 W • 9× top 10 K • 6× top five WAR • 6× top 5 IP All-time: 17th IP • 20th W • 30th GS
Voting/JAWS:	VC 1973 • **63.1/54.5/58.8**

Prone to penning odes to his favorite beverage, beer—"Pure elixir of malt and hops, beats all the drugs and all the drops"[23] was one—"Smiling Mickey" was among the best and hardest-worked pre-1893 hurlers. In fact, a clause in his contract prohibited managers from starting him more often than every other day. Just 5'8", 160 pounds, he was a proponent of brains over brawn, more reliant upon his changeup and an assortment of curves than his fastball. Though he never led in a Triple Crown category, six times he ranked among the top five in WAR, including 12.1 in 1884 (fourth, while going 39-21, 2.50 ERA) and 10.5 in '85 (second, while going 44-11, 1.66 ERA). In 1886, he paired with Troy/New York teammate Tim Keefe to start 44 games in a row; the dynamic duo pitched the Giants to pennants and postseason series wins over the American Association champions in both 1888 and '89. Keefe beat Welch to the 300-win milestone by eight weeks—the pair were second and third behind Galvin—and to Cooperstown by nine years.

37. Jim Palmer RHP

Teams:	Orioles 1965–67, '69–84
Stats:	268-152 • 2.86 ERA • 125 ERA+ • 3,948 IP • 2,212 K
Rankings:	10× top 5 ERA • 8× All-Star • 8× top 5 W • 8× top 10 WAR • 4× led IP All-time: 16th SHO • T-21st ERA+ • T-23rd ERA
Voting/JAWS:	BBWAA 1990 **(1st, 92.6%)** • **69.4/48/58.7**

An eight-time 20-game winner, six-time pennant winner, and the first AL pitcher to win three Cy Youngs, Palmer stood apart from the 300-win cohort—and not just because he was handsome enough to model underwear, neurotic enough to be labeled a hypochondriac, or narcissistic enough to be considered a prima donna. Though initially a hard thrower who specialized in the high fastball, he was far less strikeout-oriented than Seaver, Carlton, Perry, and Ryan. He never finished higher than fourth in the league in whiffs, but with two all-time great defenders, Brooks Robinson and Mark Belanger, on the left side of the infield, he didn't need to; his .251 BABIP is the second-lowest among expansion era pitchers with at least 2,500 innings, trailing only Catfish Hunter (.246). Remarkably, in an era before sports medicine could reliably repair pitchers, he overcame a torn rotator cuff that limited him to nine starts in 1967 and cost him all of '68. Though he dealt with further arm injuries once he recovered, he led the AL in innings four times. Shoulder and back woes that sidelined him in 1983 ended his shot at 300 wins, but he sailed into Cooperstown.

40. Bob Feller RHP

Teams:	Indians 1936–41, '45–56
Stats:	266-162 • 3.25 ERA • 122 ERA+ • 3,827 IP • 2,581 K
Rankings:	8× All-Star • 7× led K • 7× top 5 WAR • 6× led W • 6× top 5 ERA • 5× led IP
	All-time: T-26th ERA+ • 27th K
Voting/JAWS:	BBWAA 1962 **(1st, 93.8%)** • 63.6/51.8/57.7

"Rapid Robert" was the fastest pitcher of his day, with his fastball estimated at 104 mph (a 1940 test pitting against a Harley-Davidson) and then 107.9 (a '46 test using two photoelectric cells). That gas, accompanied by a devilish curve and later a slider, helped Feller lead the league in strikeouts seven times, and yet he was durable enough to lead in innings five times and WAR three times. How much higher might he have rated if not for his nearly four full seasons lost to military service? With a pitcher that's especially difficult to answer, given that his heavy workloads might have broken him down sooner; Feller led in innings in three straight years before becoming the first American professional athlete to enlist. As it was, his last 200-inning season was at age 32 (1951) and he threw just 281 innings from ages 35–37. He produced 27.2 WAR in 1939–41, but just 17.1 from 1946–48. A conservative estimate that he would have produced 24 WAR from 1942–1945 would have pushed him above Jenkins via an 85.6/53.4/69.5 line, and likely to 300 wins if not Walter Johnson's strikeout record of 3,509. The numbers were plenty for Cooperstown as it was.

41. Hal Newhouser LHP

Teams:	Tigers 1939–53 • Indians 1954–55
Stats:	207-150 • 3.06 ERA • 130 ERA+ • 2,993 IP • 1,796 K
Rankings:	7× All-Star • 7× top 3 K • 6× top 5 WAR • 6× top 3 IP • 4× led W
Voting/JAWS:	VC 1992 • **63.0/52.4/57.7**

Newhouser was classified as 4-F due to a heart murmur just before being inducted into the army in late July 1942. To that point, he was a 21-year-old phenom with a big fastball/curve combo, a first-time All-Star amid a breakout season. Instead of the service, he repeated as an All-Star in 1943, then earned back-to-back AL MVP honors in '44 and '45 on the strength of monster seasons (29-9, 2.22 ERA, 8.0 WAR; then 25-9, 1.81 ERA, 11.2 WAR), the latter accompanied by two World Series wins as the Tigers won a championship. The absence of so many stars due to military service devalues those seasons somewhat, but Newhouser remained an excellent pitcher once the war ended, ranking first or second in WAR annually from 1946–48, and fourth in '49. All of that makes for a Hall-caliber peak and a wide WAR lead over any other 1941–50 pitcher. Arm trouble limited him to just 321 innings and 5.7 WAR from his age-30 season (1951) onward; he was done before his 34th birthday. His 42.8% in 1975 nearly doubled his previous BBWAA support, so it's not surprising he needed 17 more years to get elected.

43. Juan Marichal RHP

Teams:	Giants 1960–73 • Red Sox 1974 • Dodgers 1975
Stats:	243-142 • 2.89 ERA • 123 ERA+ • 3,507 IP • 2,303 K
Rankings:	9× All-Star • 9× top 5 K/BB • 6× top 5 W • 6× top 10 K • 5× top 5 ERA • 4× led BB/9
Voting/JAWS:	BBWAA 1983 **(3rd, 83.7%)** • **63.1/51.9/57.5**

The majors' fifth Dominican-born player, and the only one enshrined until Martinez in 2015, Marichal spent his Hall-caliber peak pitching in the shadows of Koufax and Gibson, so he never won a Cy Young Award. His two best shots collided with history. In 1965 (22-13, 2.13 ERA, 240 K), Koufax accompanied the single-season strikeout record (382) with snazzier superficial stats (26-8, 2.04 ERA). While Marichal had the edge in both ERA+ (169 to 160) and WAR (10.3 to 8.1), the voting was unanimous for Koufax; Marichal's attack of John Roseboro with a bat—an incident that the catcher played a role in instigating, and forgave after the mayhem—was still fresh in memory. Meanwhile, Marichal's 1968 (26-9,

2.43 ERA) was no match for Gibson's 1.12 ERA. Despite an extreme leg kick and an assortment of pitches, including a screwball, delivered from a variety of arm angles, Marichal had exceptional control, with nine top fives in strikeout-to-walk ratio. Eligible in 1981, he got lost behind Gibson, and then Hank Aaron and Frank Robinson in 1982; after missing by just seven votes that year, he got in the next.

44. Carl Hubbell LHP

Teams:	Giants 1928–43
Stats:	253-154 • 2.98 ERA • 130 ERA+ • 3,590.1 IP • 1,677 K
Rankings:	10× top 10 WAR • 9× All-Star • 8× top 5 K • 7× top 3 ERA
	All-time: 13th ERA+
Voting/JAWS:	BBWAA 1947 **(3rd, 87.0%)** • **67.5/47.3/57.4**

Famously reliant upon his screwball—which dove down and away to righties, and which eventually disfigured him to the point that his palm faced outward—Hubbell was the NL's best pitcher in the high-scoring 1930s. His signature pitch delayed his debut; the Tigers, who purchased him in 1926, forbade it out of concern for his arm and let him languish in the minors, but the Giants, who bought the 25-year-old righty in mid-1928, had no qualms. By 1929, he ranked among the NL's top 10 in ERA, wins and strikeouts. From 1933–37, he posted five straight 20-win seasons during which he won three ERA titles and helped the Giants to three pennants; he was a World Series hero in '33, and NL MVP in both '33 and '36. In 1934, he provided the All-Star Game's first signature moment, striking out Babe Ruth, Lou Gehrig, Jimmie Foxx, Al Simmons, and Joe Cronin in succession, and in 1936–37 reeled off a record 24-game winning streak. Effective through 1941, he began receiving Hall support in 1945, and became the third of just five players elected within five years of retiring.

47. Vic Willis RHP

Teams:	Boston Beaneaters 1898–1905 • Pirates 1906–09 • Cardinals 1910
Stats:	249-205 • 2.63 ERA • 117 ERA+ • 3,996 IP • 1,651 K
Rankings:	6× top 5 W • 5× top 5 WAR • 5× top 10 ERA • 4× top 5 K
	All-time: 19th SHO • 19th CG
Voting/JAWS:	VC 1995 • **63.5/49.6/56.5**

Over the span of his 13 seasons, only Young and Mathewson were more valuable than the "The Delaware Peach," who predated "The Georgia Peach." An imposing

6'2", 185-pounder known for a big, sweeping curve, he burst upon the scene in 1898 (25-13, 2.84 ERA, 311 IP), helping Boston to its second straight pennant, then bettered that (27-8, with NL-bests of 2.50 ERA and 10.5 WAR, plus a no-hitter) in '99. As the Beaneaters slipped into decrepitude, Willis resisted overtures from the nascent AL; from 1900–05, he averaged 320 innings—including 410 in '02, via 45 complete games in 46 turns—while going a combined 99-126, with a modern record 29 losses in '05. A trade to Pittsburgh gave him a new lease on life, as he went 89-46 there; though his loss to the Cubs on the final day of 1908 eliminated Pittsburgh and forced Chicago to replay the "Merkle's Boner" game, the Pirates reached the World Series in '09. A near-constant in VC elections from 1957–95, Willis actually exceeded 75% in '86, but the better-supported Bobby Doerr and Ernie Lombardi fulfilled the committee's two-man limit. It took nine more years for Willis's election.

48. Ted Lyons RHP

Teams:	White Sox 1923–42, '46
Stats:	260-230 • 3.67 ERA • 118 ERA+ • 4,161 IP • 1,073 K
Rankings:	10× top 10 ERA • 9× top 10 WAR • 4× top 5 W • 4× led BB/9
Voting/JAWS:	BBWAA 1955 (8th†, 86.5%) • 71.5/40.9/56.2

A 5'11", 200-pound strongman who regularly arm-wrestled Lou Gehrig, "Sunday Teddy" is best remembered for his career's third act, as an aging knuckleballer pitching the front end of weekly doubleheaders. The young Lyons was a master of changing speeds who won 20 games three times with second-division White Sox squads from 1925–30. Robbed of his "sailing fastball" (cutter) by a 1931 arm injury, he evolved into a junkballer who featured the knuckler. In 1935, Sox manager Jimmy Dykes began giving the 34-year-old six days between starts more often than not. He went 98-69 with a 3.47 ERA (131 ERA+) while averaging 22 starts, 17 complete games, and 3.5 WAR over the next eight seasons. At 41 in 1942, he went 14-6 with a league-best 2.10 ERA while completing all 20 starts, then spent three years with the marines, and was named manager in May 1946 after briefly reprising the role. With a better team and no war, he might have won 300. As it is, his career WAR ranks 31st all-time and approaches the standard for starters, though his peak was significantly shy.

49. Don Drysdale RHP

Teams:	Dodgers 1956–69
Stats:	209-166 • 2.95 ERA • 121 ERA+ • 3,432 IP • 2,486 K

---

† Years receiving votes prior to final year of career not counted.

Rankings:	9× top 10 ERA • 9× top 5 IP • 8× All-Star • 7× top 5 K • 6× top 10 W • 5× top 3 WAR
	All-time: 21st SHO • T-28th ERA+
Voting/JAWS:	BBWAA 1984 (10th, 78.4%) • 67.1/44.7/55.9

Dealing mid-90s heat with exceptional control, yet unafraid to knock a plate-crowding hitter on his ass, the 6'5", 190-pound "Big D" was one of the most imposing pitchers of his time. Maturing ahead of Koufax—whom he outranks here thanks to 48% more career innings—he led the NL in WAR at age 20 in 1957, led in strikeouts while helping the Dodgers to a championship in '59, and snuck in a Cy Young award in '62 while going 25-9 and winning his third strikeout title. Koufax soon eclipsed Drysdale, who remained a tough frontline pitcher and a vital part of three more pennant winners and two champions. He added 5.9 WAR with his bat, thanks largely to 29 career homers. A torn rotator cuff led to retirement in late 1969, less than a year removed from his record-setting 58-inning scoreless streak and just past his 33rd birthday. No doubt his modest won-loss record—hurt by losing 44 games while allowing two runs or less (that's 0-44, 1.65 ERA, 322⅔ IP)—slowed his entry to Cooperstown. Though he broke 50% in his third year of eligibility, he needed seven more years.

50. Red Ruffing RHP

Teams:	Red Sox 1924–30 • Yankees 1930–42, '45–46 • White Sox 1947
Stats:	273-225 • 3.80 ERA • 109 ERA+ • 4,344 IP • 1,987 K
Rankings:	8× top 5 K • 8× top 10 ERA • 6× All-Star • 6× top 5 W • 5× top 10 WAR
Voting/JAWS:	BBWAA 1967 (15th, run-off) • 70.4/41.3/55.8

The owner of the Hall's highest ERA is far from its worst pitcher. Beyond hailing from a high-scoring era (his ERA+ is tied for eighth-worst), Ruffing is the career leader in offensive WAR among pitchers, with 15.0 based on his .269/.306/.389 line with 36 homers. The dreadful Red Sox even considered shifting him to the outfield, but his left foot, missing four toes via a coal mining accident at age 15, made that impractical. A palooka for a perennial Sox cellar dweller, Ruffing went 39-96 with a 4.61 ERA (92 ERA+) from 1924–30. Sold to the Yankees in mid-1930, he was suddenly surrounded by a stronger team; manager Bob Shawkey retooled his delivery, and he developed early expertise with the slider. The pinstriped Ruffing went 231-124 with a 3.47 ERA (119 ERA+), helping the Yankees to six championships by going 7-2 with a 2.63 ERA in 10 World Series starts. His 2½ years training soldiers in physical fitness and a 1946 broken kneecap cost him a shot at 300 wins. He was elected in his 20th and final year of eligibility—via a runoff, the last time that procedure was used—after receiving 72.6% in the regular balloting.

53. Joe McGinnity RHP

Teams:	Orioles (NL) 1899 • Brooklyn Superbas 1900 • Orioles (AL) 1901–02 • Giants 1902–08
Stats:	246-142 • 2.66 ERA • 120 ERA+ • 3,441.1 IP • 1,068 K
Rankings:	5x led W • 5x top 5 WAR • 5x top 10 ERA • 4x led IPs • 4x top 10 K
Voting/JAWS:	OTC 1946 • **57.7/52.4/55.1**

"Iron Man" earned one of the sport's great nicknames by working in his in-laws' iron foundry during the offseason; pitching both ends of five doubleheaders (he swept three); averaging 362 innings for his first nine seasons; and pitching professionally until age 54, tallying 231 minor league wins to go with his 246 major league Ws. McGinnity claimed never to have suffered a sore arm, attributing it to varying his delivery between overhand (for his fastball) and sidearm or underhanded for "Old Sal," his curve. He didn't reach the majors until age 28, but placed among the top six in innings annually from 1899–1907, and in the top seven in ERA five times, leading with a 1.61 mark in 1904 while going 35-8 in 408 innings for the pennant-winning Giants. In 1905 he began to fade to a merely above-average pitcher, but didn't allow an earned run in 17 World Series innings as the Giants beat the A's. His last contribution, during the 1908 pennant race, went for naught: In the Merkle game he recovered the ball from the apparent game-winning hit and threw it out of the Polo Grounds to prevent second base from being tagged.

54. Stan Coveleski RHP

Teams:	A's 1912 • Indians 1916–24 • Senators 1925–27 • Yankees '28
Stats:	215-142 • 2.89 ERA • 127 ERA+ • 3,082 IP • 981 K
Rankings:	9x top 10 ERA • 7x top 5 WAR • 5x top 5 W • 3x top 5 K All-time T-15th ERA+ • T-26th ERA
Voting/JAWS:	VC 1969 • **60.2/49.9/55.0**

The youngest and most successful of four brothers who escaped the Pennsylvania coal mines to play professionally, Coveleski was nicknamed "The Big Pole," though he stood just 5'11", 166 pounds. A spitballer known for deceiving batters by going to his mouth before every pitch, he often went several innings between wet ones. He had several strong seasons for contending Indians teams, including the 1920 champions, for whom he went 24-12 with a 2.61 ERA (154 ERA+) and a league-high 133 strikeouts; he then won three World Series games against Brooklyn, allowing just two runs in 27 innings—all in a year in which both his wife and teammate Ray Chapman died. At 35, he went 20-5 with a league-best 2.84 ERA while helping the Senators to their second straight pennant. In a career that was effectively 11 seasons and change, he had five top five finishes in ERA (he also led in '23) and seven in WAR. Largely ignored by the BBWAA, he benefited greatly from being featured in *The Glory of Their Times* in 1966, was elected by the VC three years later at age 78, and lived another 15 years.

56. Dazzy Vance RHP

Teams:	Pirates 1915 • Yankees 1915, '18 • Dodgers 1922–32, '35 • Cardinals 1933, '34 • Reds 1934
Stats:	197-140 • 3.24 ERA • 125 ERA+ • 2,966.2 IP • 2,045 K
Rankings:	7× led K • 4× led WAR • 3× led ERA • 4× top 5 W
Voting/JAWS:	BBWAA 1955 (16th, 81.7%) • 59.9/49.2/54.6

Relative to his league, Vance struck out batters at a higher rate than Ryan, Clemens, Martinez—any of 'em, though he didn't establish himself in the majors until age 31 due to arm trouble. On the strength of a blazing fastball/sharp overhand curve combo, thrown "with a sweep that would shame a windmill,"[24] he led the NL in strikeouts seven straight years (1922–28), including 262 in '24, the highest total by any NL pitcher not named Mathewson in the 1901–60 span. He won the NL MVP and the pitching Triple Crown that year with a 28-6 record and a 2.16 ERA and 262 strikeouts. As for WAR, he led four times, including 10.5 in 1924 and 10.0 in '28. Even with Vance's late start, only Grove and Hubbell eclipsed his 63.0 WAR from 1920–41. Vance started receiving support on the writers' ballot as of 1936, but didn't crack 50% until 1953. He was elected two years later as part of a rare four-player class that included Lyons, Joe DiMaggio, and Gabby Hartnett.

57. Jim Bunning RHP

Teams:	Tigers 1955–63 • Phillies 1964–67, 1970–71 • Pirates 1968–69 • Dodgers 1969
Stats:	224-184 • 3.27 ERA • 115 ERA+ • 3,760.1 IP • 2,855 K

Rankings: 11× top 5 K • 8× top 10 WAR • 7× All-Star • 6× top 5 ERA
• 6× top 5 W
All-time: 17th K

Voting/JAWS: VC 1996 • **59.4/48.9/54.2**

Because the Tigers tried to get him to abandon his sidearm/three-quarters delivery—which produced a violent follow-through in which his glove often brushed the ground—in favor of an overhand one, Bunning didn't stick until age 25, but he led the AL with 20 wins in 1957, his first full season. For much of his career, however, his most valuable seasons were camouflaged by mediocre won-loss records. He led his leagues in WAR and strikeouts in both 1960 (11-14, 2.79 ERA, 201 K, 6.7 WAR) and '67 (17-15, 2.29 ERA, 253 K, 7.8 WAR). The first pitcher to throw no-hitters in both leagues and the third to 100 wins in each league, he trailed only Walter Johnson in strikeouts when he retired. He rode a roller coaster to Cooperstown, receiving 38.1% in his 1977 debut, climbing to 74.2% in '88—only to crash back to 63.3% in '89 and get lost in the shuffle before being rescued by the VC. He fared better in politics, at least if you like yours on the far right (me, no), representing Kentucky with 12 years apiece in the House (1987–99) and Senate (1999–2011).

58. John Smoltz RHP

Teams: Braves 1988–99, 2001–08 • Red Sox 2009 • Cardinals
2009

Stats: 213-155 • 3.33 ERA • 125 ERA+ • 3,473 IP • 3,084 K

Rankings: 8× All-Star • 8× top 10 WAR • 8× top 10 ERA • 7× top 3 K
• 7× top 5 IP • 3× top 5 Sv
All-time: 16th K • T-21st ERA+

Voting/JAWS: BBWAA 2015 **(1st, 82.9%)** • **69.5/38.8/54.2**

With an outstanding fastball/slider combo that he eventually augmented with a splitter, Smoltz was the most strikeout-oriented of the trio that fueled the Braves' epic playoff run. He didn't light up the leaderboards in the same manner as Glavine or Maddux save for the K department, but he earned a reputation as a big-game pitcher thanks to stellar postseason work (15-4, 2.67 ERA, 199 K in 209 IP), and snagged a Cy Young with a big 1996 season in which he led in wins (24) and strikeouts (276) while ranking second in WAR (7.3) and fourth in ERA (2.94). Tommy John surgery and a 3½-year detour as a top-flight closer—during which he notched 154 saves, and after which he enjoyed three strong seasons as a starter—cost him a shot at 250+ wins, but made him a unique case for Hall voters. He's a quasi-Eckersley for his success in both roles, the first TJ survivor to be enshrined, and, until Mike Piazza's election, was the lowest-drafted player (22nd round) in Cooperstown.

59. Rube Waddell LHP

Teams:	Louisville Colonels 1897, '99 • Pirates 1900–01 • Cubs 1901 • A's 1902–07 • Browns 1908–10
Stats:	193-143 • 2.16 ERA • 135 ERA+ • 2,961.1 IP • 2,316 K
Rankings:	6× led K • 5× top 3 WAR • 5× top 5 W • 4× top 3 ERA All-time: 19th SHO
Voting/JAWS:	OTC 1946 • **58.6/49.6/54.1**

The nascent AL's top pitcher and drawing card, Waddell had better control of his blazing fastball/hard curve combo than of himself. From his fascination with fire trucks to his inability to handle money to his penchant for wearing out managers' patience, his eccentricities are legendary. Both in his day and a half-century removed from it, facets of his man/child nature and emotional immaturity were viewed with humor and described as "colorful." From a twenty-first-century standpoint, it's more apparent that he was dealing with mental illness or developmental disability, as well as alcoholism. Beyond the antics, the talent was legendary. After passing through Louisville, Pittsburgh (for whom he had the NL's lowest ERA in 1900), Chicago, and various semipro and minor league teams, he was purchased by the A's, with Connie Mack sending Pinkertons to escort him from California. Over the season's final 87 games, he went 24-7 with a 2.05 ERA and a league-high 210 strikeouts, his first of six straight AL leads; his 349 in 1904 stood as the AL record until 1973. During that six-season span he posted MLB-bests in WAR (46.5) and ERA (1.97). He won the pitchers Triple Crown in 1905 (27-10, 1.48 ERA, 287 K), but a September shoulder injury (allegedly sustained in a scuffle with a teammate over a straw hat) knocked him out of the World Series. Released in mid-1910, he continued in the minors, but contracted pneumonia and then tuberculosis, dying in 1914 at age 37. Though he reached 65.3% on the 1939 BBWAA ballot, it took the OTC to elect him.

NR. Monte Ward RHP/SS

Teams:	Providence Grays 1878–82 • New York Gothams/Giants 1883–89, '93–94 • Brooklyn Ward's Wonders (PL) 1890 • Brooklyn Bridegrooms (NL) 1891–92
Stats:	164-103 • 2.10 ERA • 119 ERA+ • 2,469.2 IP • 920 K

	.275/.314/.341 • 92 OPS+ • 2,107 H • 26 HR • 540 SB
Rankings:	7× top 10 WAR • 5× top 10 W • 4× top 3 ERA • 4× top 10 K • 4× top 5 SB
Voting/JAWS:	VC 1964 • **64.0/41.3/52.7**

Pitcher, infielder, manager, pioneering labor leader, executive—John Montgomery Ward left his stamp all over nineteenth-century baseball. Though inducted as a player, for JAWS purposes he's neither fish nor fowl; the only player to reach both the 2,000-hit and 100-win milestones isn't included in any standards, though the above line, which aggregates both his pitching and position-playing contributions, wouldn't be out of place at pitcher or shortstop. As an 18-year-old rookie hurler, Ward led the NL with a 1.51 ERA (147 ERA+) in 1878, and with 47 wins and 239 strikeouts as in '79 while helping the Grays to the NL pennant. He piled up ungodly innings totals—587 in 1879 and 595 in 1880—though by 1881 he was spending more time as an outfielder or shortstop than in the box. The trend continued after he was acquired by the Gothams, but an injury to his right arm while sliding in 1884 ended his pitching career. He became a full-time shortstop in 1885, the same year he graduated from Columbia Law School and founded the Brotherhood of Professional Baseball Players, the sport's first players' union. As a position player, Ward was a better fielder and baserunner than hitter; he had an OPS+ above 100 in only five of 17 seasons. In 1890, he left the Giants to found the co-operative Players League, taking the Brotherhood—which included most of the NL's best players—with him. The league lasted only one year, however, and after returning to the NL he retired at age 35 to focus on his legal practice. No doubt because he ruffled so many feathers, it took nearly 40 years after his death for enshrinement.

61. Red Faber RHP

Teams:	White Sox 1914–33
Stats:	254-213 • 3.15 ERA • 119 ERA+ • 4,086.2 IP • 1,471 K
Rankings:	7× top 10 ERA • 4× top 5 W • 4× top 5 IP • 4× top 5 K • 3× top 10 WAR
Voting/JAWS:	VC 1964 • **64.8/40.6/52.7**

A Charles Comiskey favorite who spent his entire career with the White Sox, the spitballing Faber won three games in their 1917 World Series triumph but missed the 1919 debacle due to injury and illness. He learned the spitter after suffering an arm injury in a distance-throwing competition at minor league Minneapolis in 1911, and emerged as a solid starter for Chicago at age 25 in mid-1914. He won 24 games in 1915 (second in the AL), and ranked among the top five in ERA and top 10 in wins in 1916 and '17. He lost about a season's worth of playing time in 1918–19 via a stint in the navy, a bout of influenza, and injuries, but returned to form in 1920, before the Black Sox scandal broke, leading the AL in ERA, complete games, and WAR in '21 and '22 (11.3 and 9.6 of the latter, respectively). Thereafter, he was a good-not-great pitcher on a reduced workload; he didn't top 4.0 WAR after 1922. He only broke 20% twice in a BBWAA ballot run from 1937–62, but was quickly elected by the VC.

69. Don Sutton RHP

Teams:	Dodgers 1966–80, '88 • Astros 1981–82 • Brewers 1982–84 • A's 1985 • Angels 1985–'87
Stats:	324-256 • 3.26 ERA • 108 ERA+ • 5,282.1 IP • 3,574 K
Rankings:	14× top 10 K • 10× top 10 IP • 8× top 10 W • 4× All-Star • 4× top 10 WAR
	All-time: 3rd GS • 7th IP • 7th K • 10th SHO • 14th W
Voting/JAWS:	BBWAA 1998 **(5th, 81.6%)** • **67.4/34.0/50.7**

Sutton never won a Cy Young, led his league in ERA just once despite spending virtually his entire career in pitcher-friendly parks, and never led in strikeouts, though when he retired he ranked fourth all-time. He never won a World Series despite pitching in four, and has the lowest peak score of the 24 300-game winners. Overshadowed by Seaver, Carlton, et al., he was the ultimate compiler, riding his durability—he started more games than anybody besides Young and Ryan, and didn't miss a turn until his final season—and adaptability into Cooperstown. Breaking in behind Koufax and Drysdale, he whiffed 209 batters in 225⅔ innings as a rookie, and never stopped missing bats. As he aged, he understood the changing dynamics that made him a free agent ("I'm the most loyal player money can buy"[25]), a six-inning pitcher, and a dabbler in the art of ball doctoring; he joked about doing commercials for Black & Decker. Park adjustment takes a heavy toll on Sutton's valuations; he topped 5.0 WAR just three times, and while he's 39th in career WAR, he's 169th in peak, which helps explain his five-year wait for enshrinement.

71. Early Wynn RHP

Teams:	Senators 1939, 1941–44, 1946–48 • Indians 1949-57, '63 • White Sox 1958–62
Stats:	300-244 • 3.54 ERA • 107 ERA+ • 4,564 IP • 2,334 K

Rankings:	8× top 5 W • 7× All-Star • 5× top 5 ERA • 4× top 3 WAR
	All-time: 19th GS • 21st SHO • 22nd IP • 23rd W
Voting/JAWS:	BBWAA 1972 **(4th, 76.0%)** • **61.3/38.6/50.0**

The analogy only goes so far, but Wynn's something of a cross between Sutton and Ruffing: more compiler than superstar, and much better at his second stop (164-102, 119 ERA+ and six of his seven peak seasons) than his first (72-87, 92 ERA+ and just 7.4 WAR)—with a boost from his bat (9.7 WAR) offsetting his high ERA. Wynn didn't have much more than a good fastball until arriving in Cleveland, where pitching coach Mel Harder taught him both curve and slider; from 1950–56, he had six top 10 finishes in WAR, including two firsts and two seconds. Traded to Chicago in a deal that sent Minnie Minoso back to Cleveland, he won the Cy Young for the pennant-winning "Go-Go Sox" in 1959—the oldest winner to that point at age 39, though runner-up Sam Jones bested him in ERA, innings, strikeouts, and WAR (5.7 to 2.8). After finishing an ugly 1962 season with 299 wins, he was cut in the spring and took until June to find a new home, finally returning to Cleveland at age 43 to reach the milestone. His 27.9% debut in 1969 is the modern low for a 300-win pitcher; he needed four years for election.

77. Three-Finger Brown RHP

Teams:	Cardinals 1903 • Cubs 1904–12, '16 • Reds 1913 • St. Louis Terriers (FL) 1914 • Brooklyn Tip-Tops (FL) 1914 • Chicago Whales 1915
Stats:	239-130 • 2.06 ERA • 139 ERA+ • 3,172.1 IP • 1,375 K
Rankings:	8× top 5 ERA • 6× top 5 BB/9 • 5× top 5 W • 5× top 5 WAR
	All-time: 1st ERA • 5th ERA+ • 14th SHO
Voting/JAWS:	OTC 1949 • **56.4/41.4/48.9**

Two childhood accidents—an index finger reduced to a stump by a feed cutter, and then a fall that broke his remaining fingers, paralyzing his pinky and permanently bending his middle finger—gave Mordecai Peter Centennial Brown a gnarled right hand, an unenviable nickname, and an overhand curve that Ty Cobb called "the most deceiving, the most devastating pitch I ever faced."[26] Also possessing a good fastball and the ability to throw sidearm, the late-blooming Brown didn't reach the Cubs until age 27, after a solid rookie season for the cellar-dwelling Cardinals, who dealt him for 1902 NL ERA leader Jack Taylor. The ace of four pennant winners, Brown challenged Mathewson as the NL's best pitcher. His 1.04 ERA in 1906 is still the modern record, and his 2.06 career mark is the lowest among pitchers with 3,000 innings. He never led in WAR, but was in the top five every year from 1906–1910; for that span, his 34.2 WAR trailed only Walsh (39.5) and Mathewson (37.7). His numbers are more Hall-worthy than those of Tinker, Evers, or Chance. Modestly supported on BBWAA ballots from 1936–46, he wasn't elected until 1949, 15 months after passing away.

87. Sandy Koufax LHP

Teams:	Dodgers 1955–66
Stats:	165-87 • 2.76 ERA • 131 ERA+ • 2,324.1 IP • 2,396 K
Rankings:	6x All-Star • 5x led ERA • 5x top 5 WAR • 4x led K • 3x TC
Voting/JAWS:	BBWAA 1972 **(1st, 86.9%)** • **49.0/46.1/47.5**

Given his black ink, four no-hitters, three Cy Youngs (before the award was split by league), and a 0.95 ERA in seven World Series starts, Koufax's rank among the bottom quartile of enshrined starters via JAWS may rankle some. Many of the aforementioned achievements aren't captured by WAR, however, and neither is the miracle of a wiry Jewish lefty from Brooklyn perfecting his mechanics to the point of owning as nasty a fastball/curve combo as anybody ever saw. Still, Koufax had just five seasons of at least 200 innings, threw fewer innings than all but one enshrined starter (Dizzy Dean), and retired before his 31st birthday due to his arthritic elbow. His league-leading ERAs owed a debt to the most run-suppressing park of a low-offense era; he posted a 1.37 ERA at Dodger Stadium, 3.38 everywhere else. Boiled down to WAR, Koufax has two incredible seasons (10.7 in 1963 and 10.3 in '66), two outstanding ones (8.1 in '65 and 7.4 in '64, despite missing the final six weeks due to an elbow injury), and a third that might have been (4.4 WAR in '62, when he won his first ERA title but threw just 9⅔ innings after July 12 due to a blood clot in his left index finger). It's not that he wasn't great, or Hall-worthy; if you needed one pitcher to win one game, prime Koufax would get strong consideration.

90. Burleigh Grimes RHP

Teams:	Pirates 1916-17, '28-29, '34 • Dodgers 1918-26 • Giants 1927 • Braves 1930 • Cardinals 1930-31, '33-34 • Cubs 1932-33 • Yankees 1934
Stats:	270-212 • 3.53 ERA • 108 ERA+ • 4,180 IP • 1,512 K

Rankings:	8x top 5 K • 7x top 5 W • 6x top 10 ERA • 6x top 5 IP •
	5x top 5 WAR
Voting/JAWS:	VC 1964 • **53.0/40.9/47.0**

Burly "Ol' Stubblebeard" was the last of the legal spitballers, though the wet one—wetter than most, to the point that it annoyed fielders—was just one weapon in an arsenal alongside a live fastball and a good curve. Grimes emerged as one of the NL's top pitchers in 1918, with top five rankings in wins, strikeouts, ERA, and WAR. Two years later he was the ace of a pennant-winning squad, ranking third in ERA and wins (2.22 and 23, respectively), and second in strikeouts (131) and WAR (6.8). While he frequented the leaderboards, he had three seasons with an ERA+ of 86 or worse during what should have been his prime, owing at least in part to lousy defensive support. His luck improved after leaving Brooklyn; from 1927–31, he posted a 126 ERA+, averaged 3.9 WAR, and helped the Cardinals to back-to-back pennants. All told, he pitched in four World Series for three teams, but aside from his win total, longevity, and the distinction of being the last of his breed, he's not tremendously Hall-worthy. The VC elected him (along with fellow spitballer Faber) as part of a sextet in '64, his first year under their purview.

96. Whitey Ford LHP

Teams:	Yankees 1950, '52–67
Stats:	236-106 • 2.75 ERA • 133 ERA+ • 3,170.1 IP • 1,956 K
Rankings:	11x top 10 K • 8x All-Star • 8x top 10 WAR • 7x top 5 ERA
	• 5x top 5 W • 4x top 5 IP
	All-time: 10th ERA+ • 19th ERA
Voting/JAWS:	BBWAA 1974 **(2nd, 77.8%)** • **57.3/34.7/46.0**

A rotation staple of 11 pennant winners and six champions, "The Chairman of the Board" still owns World Series records for wins (10), starts (22), innings (146), and strikeouts (94), accompanied by a 2.71 ERA. Neither that October résumé nor his record .690 winning percentage (thanks to run support 15% above average) is included in WAR. His ranking lags here mainly due to workload, including two full seasons missed due to military service (though he remained stateside), a late-career circulatory problem, and selective usage. Under Casey Stengel, who managed him through 1960, Ford made 40% more starts against the AL's top two non-Yankees teams than its bottom two, according to researcher Jason Brannon. As a result, only once under Stengel did Ford make more than 30 starts or throw more than 225⅔ innings. In his first five years under successor

Ralph Houk, Ford averaged 37 starts and 260 innings, and reached the 20-win plateau for the only two times in his career, including a 25-win Cy Young campaign in 1961. He finished with fewer innings than all but 13 enshrined starters (not counting Ward), but like Koufax, the focus on longevity without accounting for the postseason does him few favors.

109. Eppa Rixey LHP

Teams:	Phillies 1912–17, '19–20 • Reds 1921–33
Stats:	266-251 • 3.15 ERA • 115 ERA+ • 4,494.2 IP • 1,350 K
Rankings:	10× top 10 IP • 9× top 10 WAR • 7× top 10 W • 5× top 5 ERA • 5× top 10 K
Voting/JAWS:	VC 1963 • **55.4/33.4/44.4**

A towering 6′5″ finesse pitcher whose success bridged dead- and live-ball eras, Rixey was the NL's all-time leader in wins among southpaws until Spahn surpassed him in 1959. He rode a roller coaster during his Philadelphia tenure, helping the team to its 1915 pennant as a spot starter and going 22-10 with a 1.85 ERA in '16, but leading the league in losses twice and struggling to regain form after spending '18 in the army's Chemical Warfare Division, putting his master's degree in chemistry to use. He fared better in Cincinnati, winning 20 games three times including an NL-high 25 in 1922, posting respectable sub-3.00 ERAs as offensive levels rose and retaining his effectiveness into his early forties. Due to his low strikeout rate and erratic early years, he topped 5.0 WAR just three times; his peak score ranks just 179th, lower than all but two Hall of Famers. He peaked at 52.8% in 1960—just months after Cobb endorsed him—but slipped to 30.6% in 1962, his final year of eligibility. The VC elected him the following year, one month before he died of a heart attack at age 71.

114. Dizzy Dean RHP

Teams:	Cardinals 1930, '32–37 • Cubs 1938–41 • Browns 1947
Stats:	150–83 • 3.02 ERA • 131 ERA+ • 1,967.1 IP • 1,163 K
Rankings:	6× top 3 WAR • 5× top 5 W • 5× top 3 IP • 4× All-Star • 4× led K • 3× top 5 ERA
Voting/JAWS:	BBWAA 1953 **(9th, 75.2%)** • **44.9/42.8/43.9**

Dean parlayed a second-grade education, a gregarious public persona, and a killer fastball/curve/changeup combo into folk hero status during the Depression. In 1934, he led the "Gashouse Gang" Cardinals to a championship while winning

30 games—still the only NL pitcher to do so since 1917—and MVP honors, not to mention two more wins in the World Series against Detroit. His run as an elite pitcher lasted only 5½ seasons, bookended by Branch Rickey farming him out due to impertinence in 1931, and shoulder problems stemming from an altered delivery after a line drive off the bat of Earl Averill in the '37 All-Star Game broke his left big toe. But from 1932–36 Dean averaged 24 wins, 306 innings, a 3.04 ERA (130 ERA+), and 6.7 WAR. Traded to the Cubs for three players and $185,000 in April 1938, he helped them to a pennant, but never pitched 100 innings in a season again. Eleven enshrined starters pitched fewer than 3,000 innings, but only Dean is short of 2,000; three of his 12 seasons consisted of a single appearance. Nonetheless, BBWAA voters supported him with over 50% five times before electing him.

115. Bob Lemon RHP

Teams:	Indians 1941–42 • 1946–58
Stats:	207-128 • 3.23 ERA • 119 ERA+ • 2,850 IP • 1,277 K
Rankings:	8× top 3 W • 7× All-Star • 6× top 10 WAR • 5× top 5 ERA • 4× led IP • 4× top 3 K
Voting/JAWS:	BBWAA 1976 **(12th, 78.6%)** • 48.8/39.0/43.9

A vital cog in Cleveland's legendary 1948 and '54 rotations, Lemon debuted as a position player, making token appearances at third base (1941–42) and center field ('46) sandwiched around three years in the navy. Spiraling downward in a slump, he converted to the mound *on the fly at the major league level* in mid-May 1946, armed with only a sinker and a knuckleball until pitching coach Mel Harder taught him a curve and slider; the latter became his money pitch. In 1948, Lemon's first full season starting, he led in innings (293⅔), complete games (20), and shutouts (10), ranked third in ERA (2.82) and WAR (4.8), and made the first of seven straight All-Star teams, then went 2-0, 1.65 ERA in the World Series. From 1948–56, he led in wins three times, with seven 20-win seasons; offensive support 14% above league average didn't hurt. Though he couldn't hit enough to play every day, he added 11.3 career WAR on .232/.288/.386 hitting with 37 homers. Even with that, his late start and early retirement due to elbow woes make for a colorful but less-than-convincing Hall case. First eligible in 1964, he was elected just before returning to the limelight as a manager.

122. Waite Hoyt RHP

Teams:	Giants 1918, '32 • Red Sox 1919–20 • Yankees 1921–30 • Tigers 1930–31 • A's 1931 • Dodgers 1932, '37–38 • Pirates 1933–37
Stats:	237-182 • 3.59 • 112 ERA+ • 3,762.1 IP • 1,206 K
Rankings:	7x top 10 W • 5x top 10 IP • 4x top 5 ERA • 4x top 10 WAR
Voting/JAWS:	VC 1969 • **51.8/34.0/42.9**

Though "Schoolboy" Hoyt—later "The Merry Mortician" for his moonlighting as a funeral home director—was signed by the Giants at 15 and broke in with the Red Sox at 19, he made his mark as a Yankee, acquired in one of cash-strapped Boston owner Harry Frazee's many sell-offs. Hoyt pitched in six World Series for New York from 1921–28 (plus a seventh for the A's in '31), winning three championships while going 6-4 with a 1.83 ERA in 83⅔ innings, including 27 innings without an earned run in '21. A hard thrower but hardly a high-strikeout pitcher, he rarely approached his October dominance during the regular season. Only in 1927 did he lead in a Triple Crown category (first in wins with 22) or crack the top five in WAR (third with 5.7). Thus his peak score is tied for the fourth-lowest among enshrined starters. He got little traction on the writers' ballot, but helped by a 24-year run as a popular broadcaster with the Reds, he was elected by the Frisch-driven VC in 1969, then joined that bunch and partook in the election of four former teammates (see Chapter 5).

128. Chief Bender RHP

Teams:	A's 1903–14 • Baltimore Terrapins (FL) 1915 • Phillies 1916–17 • White Sox 1925
Stats:	212-127 • 2.46 ERA • 112 ERA+ • 3,017 IP • 1,711 K
Rankings:	7x top 10 ERA • 6x top 10 K • 5x top 10 WAR • 5x top 10 W • 5x top 5 BB/9
Voting/JAWS:	VC 1953 • **49.5/35.0/42.3**

Though he never reached the heights of teammates Plank or Waddell, Charles Albert Bender developed an outsized reputation as Connie Mack's "money pitcher" for five pennant-winning A's teams. The son of a German father and Chippewa mother did it while forced to contend with the stereotypes that came with being the AL's first Native American player, from the nickname "Chief" to war-whoop jeers to caricatures of him wielding a tomahawk to newspaper headlines that had him "scalping" opponents or worse. Bender answered the slights with strong, focused performances, armed with a well-spotted fastball, a sharp proto-slider, and a submarine fadeaway. He emerged as a consistently exceptional pitcher in 1907, beginning a five-year run with a 1.83 ERA (142 ERA+). Prone to injuries and battling alcoholism later in his career, he topped 30 starts and 250 innings only as a rookie, and often worked in relief; in 1913, he went 21-10 in 21 starts and 27 relief appearances, with a league-high 13 saves (retroactively counted). Though his numbers are subpar relative to Hall of Fame starters, he arguably earned his election with the half-century he put into the game despite his mistreatment, as well as his World Series prowess (6-4, 2.44 ERA, 85 IP, 9 CG). Sadly, he died between election—the first Native American so honored—and induction.

139. Addie Joss RHP

Teams:	Cleveland Bronchos/Naps 1902–10
Stats:	160–97 • 1.89 ERA • 142 ERA+ • 2,327 IP • 920 K
Rankings:	7× top 10 WAR • 7× top 5 BB/9 • 6× top 5 ERA • 5× top 10 W
Voting/JAWS:	VC 1978 • 43.7/38.4/41.1

Tubercular meningitis killed Joss, one of the top pitchers of the nascent AL, at age 31. With just nine seasons under his belt, he was ineligible for the Hall until October 1977, when the board of directors voted to waive the 10-year minimum requirement for players whose career was cut short by injury or death. That set the stage for Joss's election 67 years after his death; the waiver has otherwise never been used. Known for a corkscrew delivery in which he turned his back to the hitter, kicked his leg high, and delivered sidearm—"out of his hip pocket"[27]—with exceptional control, the rangy 6'3" Joss led the AL in ERA in 1904 (1.59) and '07 (1.16), and ranked among the top seven every year but 1910. He twice posted the league's lowest walk rate, and owns the lowest WHIP (0.968) of any pitcher with at least 1,000 innings. Via WAR, he ranked among the top 10 annually from 1903–09; his 45.9 WAR is seventh for the 1901–10 span. He was the first player to no-hit the same team twice, doing so against the White Sox in 1908 (a perfect game) and '10.

141. Jack Chesbro RHP

Teams:	Pirates 1899–1902 • Highlanders 1903–09 • Red Sox 1909
Stats:	198–132 • 2.68 ERA • 111 ERA+ • 2,896.2 IP • 1,265 K

Rankings:	6× top 10 WAR • 5× top 5 W • 5× top 10 K • 5× top 10 IP • 4× top 10 ERA
Voting/JAWS:	OTC 1946 • 41.4/40.3/40.9

Though he led the NL with 28 wins in 1902 on the strength of his fastball, Chesbro's adoption of the spitball—learned while barnstorming after the '03 season—as his primary weapon in '04 led to a season for the ages; he set still standing modern records of 41 wins (against 12 losses), 51 starts, and 48 complete games while throwing an astonishing 454⅔ innings en route to 10.2 WAR. Without that season—which ended with Boston scoring the pennant-clinching run on his two-out, ninth-inning wild pitch—"Happy Jack" likely wouldn't be enshrined given his short career and otherwise modest accomplishments. He didn't debut until age 25, and was mediocre before breaking out in 1901 (21-10, 2.38 ERA, 138 ERA+). Though Highlanders manager Clark Griffith and catcher Jim McGuire both disliked the spitter, they agreed to let Chesbro throw it after he started 4-3; he reeled off 14 wins in a row. Between the heavy workload and the change in his delivery from overhand to three-quarters, he developed a sore arm, and both his effectiveness and conditioning waned after 1905. He was the worst of the half-dozen pitchers in the OTC's 1946 group.

145. Herb Pennock LHP

Teams:	A's 1912–15 • Red Sox 1915–17, '19–22, '34 • Yankees 1924–33
Stats:	241-162 • 3.60 ERA • 106 ERA+ • 3,571.2 IP • 1,227 K
Rankings:	7× top 5 BB/9 • 6× top 10 W • 5× top 10 ERA • 4× top 5 WAR
Voting/JAWS:	BBWAA 1948 (8th, 77.7%) • 44.9/35.9/40.4

Another Ruth-era Yankee who arrived via cash-strapped Red Sox owner Frazee, Pennock got his start at the tail end of another dynasty. He debuted as a teenager, and pitched well as a swing man for the 1914 AL pennant-winning A's, but Connie Mack, who never fully committed to him, waived him in 1915, "the biggest blunder of my managing career."[28] Still, not until he returned from a 1918 navy hitch did Pennock start full-time, and only upon joining the Yankees did he find consistent success. From 1923–28, he averaged 19 wins, 248 innings, a 3.03 ERA (132 ERA+), and 5.3 WAR while helping New York to three pennants and two championships. He never led a Triple Crown category, won 20 games only twice, and whiffed 100 in a season only once. Even with a sterling World Series line

(5-0, 3 Sv, 1.95 ERA in 55⅓ innings), that's a thin portfolio for Cooperstown; he's Jamie Moyer with better teammates. The writers elected Pennock in 1948, four weeks after he died of a stroke at age 53; *The Sporting News* editorial hailed him as "an eminently fair and square shooter"[29] but in 1976, longtime Dodgers traveling secretary Harold Parrott's *The Lords of Baseball* revealed Pennock's threat to have the Phillies (of whom he was GM) boycott Jackie Robinson's Philadelphia debut in May 1947. Fifty years after his death, the revelation quashed a statue of Pennock in his hometown of Kennett Square, Pennsylvania.

The Basement (the most dubious honorees)

165. Catfish Hunter RHP

Teams:	A's 1965–74 • Yankees 1975–79
Stats:	224-166 • 3.26 ERA • 104 ERA+ • 3,449.1 IP • 2,012 K
Rankings:	8× All-Star • 7× top 10 W • 7× top 10 K • 6× top 10 BB/9 • 4× top 10 WAR • 3× top 3 ERA
Voting/JAWS:	BBWAA 1987 **(3rd, 76.3%)** • **41.4/35.1/38.2**

Though he didn't come close to winning 300 games due to chronic arm troubles and diabetes, which ended his career at age 33, Hunter was as famous as any of his cohorts thanks to his colorful nickname and role as a key starter for six AL pennant winners and five champions from 1972–78. After helping the A's to their third straight championship in 1974 via a Cy Young–winning season (25-12 with a league-best 2.49 ERA), he became the first modern free agent when owner Charlie O. Finley breached his contract by failing to make an annuity payment. Signed to a record $3.35 million deal by George Steinbrenner, he went 23-14 with a 2.58 ERA in 1975, then helped the team reel off three straight pennants even as his own performance eroded; he was worth just 2.3 WAR from 1976–78. Beyond his early decline, his low ranking here owes to lackluster run prevention outside his peak. Through 1970, his ERA+ was just 94, during his five big 20-win years it ticked up to 127 (Seaver's lifetime mark), and over his final four years it was just 91. Though elected with little trouble, he'd likely face a Jack Morris–like fight today.

179. Lefty Gomez LHP

Teams:	Yankees 1930–42 • Senators 1943
Stats:	189-102 • 3.34 ERA • 125 ERA+ • 2,503 IP • 1,468 K
Rankings:	7× All-Star • 7× top 5 K • 6× top 5 ERA • 5× top 10 WAR
Voting/JAWS:	VC 1972 • **38.4/35.6/37.0**

A mainstay on six championship winners, Vernon Louis Gomez was a favorite among writers thanks to his self-deprecating wit and screwball antics that earned him a multitude of nicknames including "El Goofo" and "The Gay Caballero" (after his skill as a horseman). A hard-throwing southpaw who excelled during the high-scoring 1930s, aided by some of the best offensive support of any Hall of Famer (16% above average), Gomez won the pitcher Triple Crown both in 1934 (26-5, 2.33 ERA, 158 K) and '37 (21-11, 2.33 ERA, 194 K), with ERA+ of 176 and 193, respectively. He was a perennial All-Star Game fixture (1933–39), and was stellar in the World Series for the Yankees' 1932 and '36–39 champs (6-0, 2.86 ERA, 50⅓ IP). That's a lot to pack into a short career; injuries turned Gomez into a replacement-level pitcher over his final four seasons (ages 31–34), and his draft board classified him 4-F in 1942 due to torn muscles in his shoulder, back, and side. BBWAA voters gave him a maximum of 46.1% during his 1945–62 ballot run. The Frisch/Terry VC, which featured ex-teammate Hoyt, elected him.

259. Rube Marquard LHP

Teams: Giants 1908–15 • Dodgers/Robins 1915–20 • Reds 1921 • Braves 1922–'25

Stats: 201-177 • 3.08 ERA • 103 ERA+ • 3,306.2 IP • 1,593 K

Rankings: 5× top 10 W • 4× top 5 K • 4× top 10 ERA • 4× top 10 WAR

Voting/JAWS: VC 1971 • **31.9/29.0/30.5**

Gangly 6'3" Richard William Marquard's striking resemblance to Waddell yielded his first nickname. Sold to the Giants for an unprecedented sum, he subsequently became the "$11,000 Peach" and then the "$11,000 Lemon" for his subpar debut in the heat of the 1908 pennant race. By 1911, he had matured into a strong complement to Mathewson, going 24-7 with a 2.50 ERA (133 ERA+) and a league-high 237 strikeouts, then following up with a similarly strong season including an NL-high 26 wins. Through his age-26 season, he was 82-46, with a 2.66 ERA (118 ERA+), but it was mostly downhill from there; over the next 12 years, he went 119-131 with a 3.28 ERA (97 ERA+), with replacement-level seasons interspersed among average ones. After a trade to Brooklyn, he helped the Robins win pennants in 1916 and '20, the former with a 13-6 record and 1.58 ERA (second in the league) as a swing man. He barely registered with BBWAA voters during his 1936–55 ballot run, but after being featured as the lead chapter in *The Glory of Their Times*, the Frisch/Terry VC turned cartwheels at the thought of electing a former Giant, even one who wasn't actually a teammate.

303. Jesse Haines RHP

Teams:	Reds 1918 • Cardinals 1920–37
Stats:	210-158 • 3.64 ERA • 109 ERA+ • 3,208.2 IP • 891 K
Rankings:	4x top 10 W • 4x top 10 K • 3x top 10 ERA • 3x top 10 WAR
Voting/JAWS:	VC 1970 • **32.6/21.9/27.3**

The bottom of the barrel among enshrined starters, "Pop" Haines spent all but his major league debut as a Cardinal, pitching for five pennant winners, three as a rotation regular. A three-time 20-game winner, he didn't stick in the majors until age 26 but nonetheless had fortunate timing: His biggest year, a 24-10, 2.72 ERA (148 ERA+) showing with a career-high 5.5 WAR, came in 1927, Frankie Frisch's first year with the team. His second-biggest year (20-8, 4.6 WAR) followed in 1928 and culminated in a pennant for the Cards, creating an impression that Frisch apparently never forgot despite it being Haines's last year as a 200-inning starter. Haines never led in a Triple Crown category, and had just three years topping 3.0 WAR. Nonetheless, he rode Frisch's Veterans Committee Express to Cooperstown. Even allowing for his strong World Series showings (3-1, 1.67 ERA, with a five-hit shutout in 1926 and a four-hit, one-run complete game in '30), there's no earthly reason why a pitcher with the 422nd-highest peak score (tied with Mark Mulder) and the 303rd-best JAWS (tied with Mike Hampton) should be enshrined.

Further Consideration (upcoming or overlooked candidates)

3. Roger Clemens RHP

Teams:	Red Sox 1984–96 • Blue Jays 1997–98 • Yankees 1999–2003, '07 • Astros 2004–06
Stats:	354-184 • 3.12 ERA • 143 ERA+ • 4,916.2 IP • 4,672 K
Rankings:	11x All-Star • 7x led WAR • 7x led ERA • 5x led K • 4x led W
	All-time: 3rd K • 3rd ERA+ • 7th GS • 9th W • 16th IP • 26th SHO
JAWS:	**140.3/66.3/103.3**

Given the timing of his career—post-integration, in a high-scoring era—and his sheer dominance, "The Rocket" has a claim as the greatest pitcher of all time, albeit one clouded by allegations of PED usage during the pre-testing era, as detailed in the Mitchell Report, in his ensuing Congressional hearing, and in subsequent trials for perjury and obstruction of Congress. Though found not guilty on six counts in 2012, his reputation won't soon recover. An imposing power pitcher whose splitter became his key pitch in the 2000s, his numbers and longevity are remarkable. He spread his seven ERA leads across 20 seasons (1986–2005), and his seven WAR leads and Cy Youngs across slightly staggered 19-season ranges as well. He ranked among the league's top five in strikeouts 16 times and in WAR 13 times, helped his team to the postseason 12 times and to the World Series six times (he went 3-0 with a 2.37 ERA in 49⅓ innings there, though his 3.75 postseason ERA wasn't as strong). Like Barry Bonds, the voters are split on whether to recognize him, but his jump to 54.1% in 2017, his fifth year of eligibility, portends eventual enshrinement.

34. Tony Mullane RHP

Teams:	Detroit Wolverines (NL) 1881 • Louisville Eclipse (AA) 1882 • St. Louis Browns (AA) 1883 • Toledo Blue Stockings (AA) 1884 • Cincinnati Red Stockings (AA) 1886–89 • Reds 1890–93 • Orioles 1893–94 • Spiders 1894
Stats:	284-220 • 3.05 ERA • 117 ERA+ • 4,531.1 IP • 1,803 K
Rankings:	8× top 10 IP • 7× top 10 WAR • 7× top 10 ERA • 5× top 5 W
JAWS:	67.8/50.6/59.2

Jim McCormick, Tommy Bond, Charlie Buffinton, Bob Carruthers, and Mullane all rank among the top 38 in JAWS due to their nineteenth-century exploits, which largely came before the distance change; none of them pitched past 1894, and they all remain outside the Hall. Mullane, born in Cork, Ireland, in 1859, is the only one of that group who pitched more than 11 seasons and perhaps the most interesting of them, for on at least a few occasions he pitched lefty to a batter instead of righty. Known as "The Apollo of the Box," he was a handsome devil who won 30 games in five straight seasons (1882–84, '86–87) interrupted by a year-long ban for frequent team jumping. He's the all-time wins and WAR leader for the short-lived American Association (202 and 42.0, respectively), but he never led the league in a Triple Crown category, and never pitched for a pennant winner save for the Orioles at the end of his career. Oh, and there's this: When Toledo employed black catcher Fleet Walker in 1884, before baseball's "gentleman's agreement" to uphold the color line had been implemented, Mullane refused to take pitch signals from him, at times deliberately crossing him up. So to hell with him.

39. Wes Ferrell RHP

Teams:	Indians 1927–33 • Red Sox 1934–37 • Senators 1937–38 • Yankees 1938–39 • Dodgers 1940 • Braves 1941
Stats:	193-128 • 4.04 ERA • 116 ERA+ • 2,623 IP • 985 K
Rankings:	7× top 10 ERA • 6× top 5 WAR • 6× top 5 W • 6× top 5 IP • 2× All-Star
JAWS:	61.6/55.0/58.3

The younger brother of Hall of Fame catcher Rick Ferrell is the sibling more qualified for enshrinement. In his heyday, Wes was regarded as the equal of Grove, and while his career stats are far short of Lefty's numbers, researcher Dick Thompson showed that he faced much tougher competition. From 1929–36, Grove was the only AL hurler who outdid Ferrell's 49.2 pitching WAR—and Ferrell added 10.6 offensive WAR in that span as well; he was an outstanding hitter who batted .280/.351/.446/100 OPS+ with 38 career homers, 10 more than his brother. In 1935, by far his best season, Ferrell finished second in the AL MVP vote via an 11.0-WAR showing, having pitched 322⅓ innings wih a 134 ERA+ and 25 wins, plus a .347/.427/.533 line with seven homers. After leading in complete games and innings annually from 1935–37, his career went downhill due to arm troubles and a volatile temperament; he posted a 6.07 ERA with -1.0 WAR from 1938 (his age-30 season) onward. Including his offense, his peak score ranks 24th all-time, nearly five wins above the standard for pitchers. The BBWAA ignored him and he's disappeared on VC/EC ballots, but he's hardly a bad candidate.

42. Roy Halladay RHP

Teams:	Blue Jays 1998–2009 • Phillies 2010-13
Stats:	203-105 • 3.38 • 131 ERA+ • 2,749.1 IP • 2,117 K
Rankings:	8× All-Star • 7× top 5 ERA • 6× top 5 W • 6× top 3 BB/9 • 4× led WAR • 4× led IP
JAWS:	64.6/50.6/57.6

The fifth pitcher to win Cy Youngs in both leagues and the second to throw a postseason no-hitter (plus a regular season perfect game), "Doc" Halladay packed a lot into a 16-year career that's nonetheless short of 3,000 innings. A highly regarded prospect, he slogged through a 10.64 ERA in 2000, a season that led to a demotion to High-A and a mechanical overhaul; but from 2002–11 he was the game's most valuable pitcher, with 62.4 WAR (12.3 more than second-ranked Johan Santana). A sinkerballer who generated a ton of grounders, then boosted his strikeout rate with a late-career addition of a splitter, he topped 220 innings in eight of those seasons, finishing in the top four in WAR each time, and in the top three in Cy Young voting five times. A 2005 broken fibula derailed a Cy bid, and myriad shoulder problems diminished his effectiveness and forced his retirement at 36. Though short in career WAR, he's above the peak standard; come 2019, he'll likely draw strong enough consideration to wind up with a plaque.

46. Kevin Brown RHP

Teams: Rangers 1986, '88–94 • Orioles 1995 • Marlins 1996–97 • Padres 1998 • Dodgers 1999–2003 • Yankees 2004–05

Stats: 211-144 • 3.28 ERA • 127 ERA+ • 3,256.1 IP • 2,379 K

Rankings: 6× All-Star • 6× top 5 ERA • 5× top 3 WAR • 4× top 5 K • 4× top 5 W
All-time: T-15th ERA+

JAWS: 68.3/45.4/56.9

A wiry, ornery sinkerballer, Brown was the best pitcher in baseball this side of Martinez from 1996–2000, accumulating 36.9 WAR to Pedro's 41.6. During that span he served as the ace of the 1997 champion Marlins and the '98 NL pennant-winning Padres, led in ERA and WAR twice apiece, had two top three finishes in the Cy Young voting, and became baseball's first $100 million man via a seven-year, $105 million contract with the Dodgers. Outside of that concentrated peak, he had his moments, but the contract—signed in 1998 when he was 34—painted a target on his back, and neither the deal nor the pitcher aged well. After two strong seasons in L.A., he made only 96 starts over the next five due to back and elbow woes. His 32-start 2003 All-Star season facilitated a trade to the Yankees, but he made just 22 starts in 2004 due to further back troubles, broke his non-pitching hand punching a clubhouse wall, and gained further infamy with a dreadful ALCS performance against Boston. Though his JAWS outranks 29 enshrined starters, he was virtually ignored by BBWAA voters, receiving 2.1% in 2011, owing at least in part to his appearance in the Mitchell Report.

51. Luis Tiant RHP

Teams: Indians 1964–69 • Twins 1970 • Red Sox 1971–78 • Yankees 1979–80 • Pirates 1981 • Angels 1982

Stats: 229-172 • 3.30 ERA • 114 ERA+ • 3,486.1 IP • 2,416 K

Rankings:	8× top 10 WAR • 5× top 10 W • 5× top 10 K • 4× top 10 ERA • 3× All-Star All-time: 21st SHO
Voting/JAWS:	**66.7/44.6/55.6**

The Cuban-born son of legendary Negro Leagues pitcher Luis Tiant Sr., Tiant was as colorful a character as the island produced, known for his Fu Manchu mustache and ubiquitous stogies—which he would even take into the shower—as well as his assortment of unique deliveries. He rose to prominence with the Indians, leading the AL in ERA (1.60) and WAR (8.4) in 1968 while going 21-9, but 31-win Denny McLain was the unanimous Cy Young pick. After bouncing around while battling injuries, he resurfaced in Boston, won an ERA title in 1972, notched 20 wins three times, and turned in a Herculean effort in Game 4 of the 1975 World Series, "delivering 163 pitches in 100 ways,"[30] as *Sports Illustrated*'s Roy Blount Jr. described it. Though he measures up better to That Seventies Group than lower-peaking compilers Tommy John (62.0/34.7/48.4) or Jim Kaat (51.4/38.4/44.9), he's still short on all three fronts, and one has to give him substantial credit for cultural ambassadorship to justify a vote for enshrinement; the BBWAA gave him 30.9% in his debut, but never above 20% thereafter.

65. Clayton Kershaw LHP

Teams:	Dodgers 2008–16
Stats:	126–60 • 2.37 ERA • 159 ERA+ • 1,765 IP • 1,918 K
Rankings:	6× All-Star • 6× top 5 WAR • 4× led ERA • 3× led K
JAWS:	**54.4/48.7/51.5**

At 29 years old, just nine years into his career, Kershaw has already reeled off a run of dominance to rival another Dodgers lefty whose name starts with K—at least save for the postseason, where his 4-7, 4.55 ERA record contains more lows than highs. At this writing, it's not yet clear whether he's peaked, but while amid the most dominant season since Pedro Martinez c. 2000, he missed over two months with a herniated disc and still finished second in WAR. No three-time Cy Young winner is outside the Hall save for Clemens; let us hope that Kershaw rebounds strongly enough to avoid becoming a test case.

73. CC Sabathia LHP

Teams:	Indians 2001–08 • Brewers 2008 • Yankees 2009–16
Stats:	223-141 • 3.70 ERA • 117 ERA+ • 3,168.1 IP • 2,726 K

Rankings:	10× top 10 K • 9× top 10 W • 8× top 10 ERA • 6× All-Star •
	6× top 10 WAR
JAWS:	**58.7/40.4/49.5**

Through 2012 the gentle giant was on a Hall of Fame course, winning 191 games with a 125 ERA+, 2,214 strikeouts, and 54.1 WAR while helping his teams to seven postseason appearances. Since then, the mileage on his arm and the stress on his legs from bearing the impact of a 6′6″, 300-pound behemoth throwing 100+ pitches every five days has caught up to him, and he's struggled to stay effective and available. A knee brace and acknowledgment of a drinking problem helped him to a modest rebound in 2016, but he's got a ways to go. His best bet for Cooperstown is getting to 3,000 strikeouts, in the neighborhood of 250 wins.

88. Andy Pettitte LHP

Teams:	Yankees 1995–2003, 2007–10, '12–13 • Astros 2004–06
Stats:	256-153 • 3.85 ERA • 117 ERA+ • 3,316 IP • 2,448 K
Rankings:	5× top 5 W • 4× top 10 K • 3× All-Star • 3× top 10 WAR •
	3× top 10 ERA
JAWS:	**60.8/34.1/47.4**

Pettite's win total and lengthy postseason résumé (he has all-time leads with 19 wins, 44 starts, and 276⅔ innings, with a 3.81 ERA) for eight pennant winners and five champions are his best argument for enshrinement. More plow horse than thoroughbred, he was a durable innings eater who received excellent run support (110 SUP+) while rarely dominating or placing high on leaderboards. His ERA would be the highest of anyone enshrined, though in its proper context, it's roughly on par with Blyleven, Glavine, and Perry; he's no Jack Morris. His appearance in the Mitchell Report, for taking HGH while recuperating from an elbow injury—as good an excuse as any, frankly, if you believe him—will burden an already fringy candidacy when he becomes eligible in 2019.

CHAPTER 18

RELIEF PITCHERS

MARIANO RIVERA

You always see guys who want to . . . look mean and have people think that they're a little off or a little crazy and they don't have command of their hundred-mile-an-hour fastball, they try to use that intimidation to beat guys. The thing about Mariano is he didn't have to use any of those weapons. . . . He went out there cool, calm and collected for all these years and dominated at that position without having to use that as an edge.[1]

—Bronson Arroyo

Nobody closed the door like Mariano Rivera. The wiry, unflappable Panamanian not only set the all-time record for saves (652), he prevented runs at a greater clip relative to his league than any other pitcher—and he was even better in October. During Rivera's 19-year-career, the Yankees missed the playoffs just twice, and for all of his regular season dominance, he raised his game when the stakes were the highest, helping the Yankees to five championships. He was the last man standing on the mound an unprecedented four times, securing the final out of the 1998, '99, 2000, and '09 World Series.

Rivera did it all while relying almost exclusively on one pitch, a cut fastball discovered almost by accident in 1997, his first year as closer. Even when batters knew what was coming—and at speeds as high as 98 mph in his younger days, it was coming fast—they could rarely predict its sideways movement well enough to make hard contact. If they connected at all, they often broke their bats. Teammates and opponents marveled at the success of the pitch, while writers placed it in the pantheon of great signature offerings, alongside Nolan Ryan's fastball, Roger

Clemens's splitter, Sandy Koufax's curve, Steve Carlton's slider, Pedro Martinez's changeup, and Hoyt Wilhelm's knuckleball.

Debates have long raged over how to value relievers and how to determine their fitness for the Hall of Fame, no small task given that just five of them are enshrined, as much for their role in shifting the paradigm for closers as for the numbers they racked up. Rivera, so great for so long, shuts down those debates like they're opponents trailing by three runs in the ninth inning of a postseason clincher. He's so far ahead of the rest of the field on so many levels that one can argue he's the lone reliever outside the Hall worthy of entry. When he gains eligibility in 2019, he'll likely join Dennis Eckersley (2004) as the only relievers elected on the first ballot. While Trevor Hoffman—whose all-time saves record Rivera broke in 2011—may be enshrined by then, it could be a long time before another reliever joins that esteemed group.

The Career

Yankees 1995–2013

Pitcher	Career	Peak	JAWS	W	L	S	ERA	ERA+
Mariano Rivera	57.1	28.9	43.0	82	60	652	2.21	205
Avg HOF RP	40.6	28.2	34.4					
RP Rank	2nd	3rd	2nd					
(Above HOF)	(4/5)	(3/5)	(4/5)					

Born in Panama City, Panama, in 1969, Rivera was raised 25 miles west of the capital in Puerto Caimito, a fishing village of around 17,000. His first love was soccer, but he played baseball on the beach with makeshift equipment such as tennis balls, milk cartons, and tree branches. At 16, he dropped out of high school to work on his father's commercial fishing boat, but the death of his uncle, Miguel Rivera, from an accident at sea in which the young Rivera was also injured intensified his desire to find a life outside of fishing. Baseball became his way out.

As a scrawny, 155-pound amateur shortstop Rivera caught the eye of Royals scout Herb Raybourn at the national 18-to-25 tournament in La Chorrera in 1988. A year later, after Raybourn had become the Yankees' director of Latin American operations, he saw Rivera pitch in the tournament, and fell in love with the 20-year-old's athleticism and the movement of his pitches despite his pedestrian 85-to-87 mph velocity. He signed Rivera for a $2,000 bonus in February 1990.

Rivera dominated the Gulf Coast League that year, capping his first professional season with a seven-inning no-hitter in his final start to claim the ERA title with a 0.17 mark, but surgery to fix nerve damage in his elbow in 1992 slowed his upward progress. After rocketing from High-A to Triple-A in 1994, he returned to the last stop, Columbus (Ohio) of the International League, to start the 1995 season as a 25-year-old with an 88–90 mph fastball, and decent secondary pitches—a fringe prospect. Recalled for his debut on May 23 against the Angels, he didn't escape the fourth inning, and was demoted after compiling a 10.20 ERA in four starts. Later that month, his fastball suddenly skyrocketed into the 95–96 range according to organizational reports, and Yankees general manager Gene Michael cut off trade talks with the Tigers—who showed interest in Rivera as part of a return for David Wells—once a Detroit scout confirmed the velocity.

When the Yankees brought Rivera back on July 4, he struck out 11 over eight shutout innings against the White Sox, but couldn't replicate that success. Moving to the bullpen after September 5, he showed manager Buck Showalter enough to make the Yankees' postseason roster, but it took desperation to call upon the rookie with the 5.51 ERA. Entering in the 12th inning of Division Series Game 2 against the Mariners, Rivera earned the win with 3⅓ shutout innings and five strikeouts. He made two other scoreless appearances, though the Yankees lost the series in five games.

Rivera clearly had a big league future, but again the Yankees nearly dealt him in March 1996, this time to acquire shortstop Felix Fermin from Seattle. Starter Tony Fernandez had been lost for the season in March due to a fractured right elbow, and the team was concerned that 21-year-old Derek Jeter, their 1992 first-round pick, wasn't quite ready. Their resistance to temptation was rewarded; Jeter won AL Rookie of the Year honors, and Rivera fared well, too. Under new manager Joe Torre, he broke camp with the team and by late April graduated to a setup role, often pitching two- or three-inning stints in front of closer John Wetteland. He sparkled in the role (2.09 ERA, 107⅔ innings, 130 strikeouts); his 5.0 WAR hasn't been surpassed by a reliever since. The Yankees won 92 games and the AL East, and Rivera allowed just one run in 14⅓ postseason innings, including two scoreless frames in Game 6 of the World Series against Atlanta, protecting a one-run lead to help seal the Yankees' first championship since 1978.

When Wetteland, the World Series MVP, left via free agency, Rivera inherited the closer role. He blew three of his first six save chances, but Torre reassured him: "Joe told me that, 'As long as you are here, you'll be the closer.' That's exactly what I needed to hear."[2]

Two months later in Detroit, Rivera annoyed teammate Ramiro Mendoza while playing catch, as the closer's throws kept veering to his right. "[Mendoza] thought I was making the ball move," he said later. "From that moment, I told [pitching coach] Mel [Stottlemyre], I have no control over this."[3]

Using the same grip, Rivera worked with Stottlemyre on the serendipitous discovery, a cut fastball, in the bullpen. The offering's late break—away from right-handed batters, and in on lefties—made it a weapon. Rivera saved all three games in Detroit, and the rest is history. "A gift from God" he called the pitch. As beat writer Buster Olney described it:

> Most pitchers release the fastball with their fingers draped over the top of the ball, essentially aimed straight at the catcher. But Rivera throws his cutter with the index and middle fingers of his right hand tilted slightly inward—as if he is pointing at eleven on the face of the clock, rather than twelve o'clock. That means that while the ball is flying toward the hitter, it actually is rotating sideways, spinning backward. . . . It is like a car skidding across ice, the front veering to the side, the whole thing fishtailing."[4]

Rivera finished his inaugural year as closer with a 1.88 ERA in 71⅔ innings, with 43 saves in 52 opportunities, not to mention his first All-Star appearance. The Yankees won the AL Wild Card, and while he converted his first save chance in Game 1 of the Division Series against the Indians, he faltered in Game 4, serving up an eighth-inning, game-tying homer to Sandy Alomar Jr. via a high fastball (not a cutter); they lost that contest and Game 5. Rivera remained stoic in defeat, buttressed by both his religious faith and confidence in his own ability. "You can't let them get to you," he said of the hitters who would beat him. "You have to be the same, no matter what."[5] Remarkably, Rivera would allow just one more postseason home run in his career, a span totaling 119⅓ innings.

That 1997 season began a remarkable 15-year run over which Rivera posted a 2.01 ERA (223 ERA+) and 8.1 strikeouts per nine while averaging 69 innings, 40 saves, and 3.2 WAR. He made 12 All-Star teams in that span, and three top three finishes in the AL Cy Young voting. Only 11 pitchers—all starters—topped his 48.6 WAR during that stretch, 10 of whom doubled Rivera's total of 1,036⅔ innings.

Rivera gained higher visibility that year for another reason: For the 50th anniversary of Jackie Robinson's debut, Major League Baseball retired his uniform number 42 league-wide, grandfathering the 14 players who already wore it, including Rivera. He would outlast them all, growing into the responsibility that came with the jersey number. "He carried himself with dignity and grace, and that made carrying the number a tribute to Jack,"[6] said Rachel Robinson, Jackie's widow, in 2013.

Bouncing back from the Alomar home run in 1998, Rivera didn't allow his first run until his 11th appearance, on May 14, and didn't allow his second until a month later, by which point the Yankees had opened up a 10-game lead in the AL East. They would set a modern record with 114 wins, winning the AL East by

22 games and going 11-2 in the postseason, capped by a sweep of the Padres in the World Series. Rivera saved 36 games in 41 chances with a 1.91 ERA, threw 13⅓ scoreless postseason innings, and secured the Yankees' 24th championship by retiring Mark Sweeney on a weak groundball.

In 1999, inspired by the Padres' use of AC/DC's "Hells Bells" to cue Hoffman's entrance, the Yankee Stadium scoreboard staff began using Metallica's rousing "Enter Sandman" to accompany Rivera's entrances. Backed by that soundtrack, Rivera led the AL with 45 saves, posted a 1.83 ERA, finished third in the Cy Young vote, and sent the Braves off to never-never land to seal the Yankees' 25th championship. He slipped to a 2.85 ERA with 36 saves in 2000, but capped the team's 26th championship by closing out the Mets at Shea Stadium.

After leading the league again with 50 saves in 2001, not to mention eye-opening strikeout and walk rates (9.3 and 1.3 per nine, respectively), Rivera was poised to nail down the team's 27th championship when all hell broke loose. Protecting a 2–1 lead against the Diamondbacks in Game 7 of the World Series in Arizona, he made a throwing error while trying to get the forceout at second and surrendered three hits, including a game-tying double by light-hitting Tony Womack and a broken-bat bloop single by Luis Gonzalez, bringing home the series-winning run.

Where that high-profile defeat might have wrecked the confidence of other closers, the resilient Rivera continued to excel. After injuries sent him to the disabled list three times in 2002, he set a new career best with a 1.66 ERA in 2003 and produced an indelible highlight in Game 7 of the ALCS against the Red Sox. The Yankees had just rallied for three runs against a flagging Pedro Martinez in the bottom of the eighth inning, tying the score at 5–5. Rivera kept Boston at bay for three innings before Aaron Boone hit his 11th-inning walkoff homer off Tim Wakefield. The sight of the exhausted closer rushing to the mound to kneel, kiss the ground, and thank God as Boone circled the bases produced the most famous photo of his career. Though he pitched two scoreless appearances in the World Series, Torre's resistance to calling upon him in the extra innings of Game 4 against the upstart Marlins proved the team's undoing, as the erratic Jeff Weaver allowed a walkoff homer to Alex Gonzalez in the 12th.

Following a career-high and AL-best 53 saves in 2004, Rivera had rough luck in the ALCS rematch against Boston. Called upon to protect a 4–3 lead in the eighth inning of Game 4—the potential clincher, as the Yankees had built up a three-games-to-none lead—he shut Boston down in the eighth, but allowed the tying run in the ninth, keyed by pinch-runner Dave Roberts's stolen base; the Red Sox stayed alive via David Ortiz's 12th-inning homer. Less than 24 hours later, Rivera blew another save after entering another 4–3 game in the eighth, with Roberts scoring the tying run via Jason Varitek's sacrifice fly, and Ortiz singling in the winning run in the 14th. The Sox won the next two games and swept the World Series, their first championship since 1918.

Thanks to a few stunning early exits, it took until 2009 for the Yankees to return to the World Series, with free agents CC Sabathia, A. J. Burnett, and Mark Teixeira joining the "Core Four" of homegrown stars—Andy Pettitte, Jorge Posada, Jeter, and Rivera—remaining from the 1998–2001 run. The closers of seven of the eight postseason teams each blew at least one save. Rivera, the only closer who did not, was the last man standing when Philadelphia's Shane Victorino grounded out to end Game 6, giving the Yankees their elusive 27th championship.

Though he turned 40 less than a month after that World Series, Rivera continued to roll along. As stifling as ever, he posted ERAs below 2.00 annually from 2008–11, with fewer than 10 walks in the two bookend seasons. On September 19, 2011, with his 602nd save, he surpassed Hoffman for the record. His run of dominance was interrupted on May 3, 2012, when he tore his right ACL while shagging fly balls in Kansas City, a season-ending—and, for a 42-year-old, career-threatening—injury. Even with his contract expiring, Rivera didn't want to depart on that note. After arduously rehabbing, he returned for 2013, pitched like a man in his prime (2.11 ERA, 44 saves, 6.0 K/BB) and earned his 13th All-Star berth as well as the AL Comeback Player of the Year award.

Teams around the majors paid tribute to Rivera via a retirement tour, showering him with gifts, and Rivera returned the favor, spending hours meeting with specially selected groups of fans in the 17 cities he passed through—grieving families, children battling cancer, wounded warriors, survivors of some trauma or another. Rivera inspired those people, and in turn, he drew inspiration from them. The end came on September 26, 2013, when manager Joe Girardi deputized Jeter and Pettitte to go the mound to pull Rivera from his final appearance, a mop-up effort for a team that had just been mathematically eliminated from playoff contention. The waterworks flowed before the all-time saves leader doffed his cap and departed to an extended standing ovation.

The Case

Whether judged on traditional or advanced stats, Rivera's merits for a plaque in Cooperstown are clear. Beyond the saves record, the All-Star appearances, and the five World Series rings, three things stand out: his ERA relative to the league, his total of long saves, and his postseason record.

Rivera's 2.21 ERA is not itself a record. Even at the 1,000-inning threshold, he ranks 13th, behind a dozen pitchers who spent most or all of their careers in the 1870s or the dead-ball era, when scoring rates were low; of that group, only Walter Johnson pitched past 1920. Adjusting for park and league scoring environment, however, Rivera's 205 ERA+ is tops by a wide margin—he allowed fewer than half the number of runs a league-average pitcher would have allowed over the same number of innings—with Clayton Kershaw second at 159 and ERA leader Ed Walsh 10th at 146.

As the job of relief ace has evolved from that of a multi-inning fireman who might enter games with runners on base before the ninth inning to that of the specialist who ideally pitches only the ninth, and only in save situations, Rivera's ability to work overtime stands out. For 119 of his 652 saves, he pitched more than one full inning, entering in the eighth, usually with runners on base. The total of long saves ranks "only" 11th (Rollie Fingers is first at 201), but of the 10 pitchers above him, only former all-time saves leader Lee Smith's career overlapped with Rivera's, and he last pitched in 1997; he's fourth in long saves at 169. Of the pitchers from the post-1992 expansion era, Wetteland is second with 70, while Hoffman is tied for fifth with 55, and the active leader, Jonathan Papelbon, is 14th with 37. Nobody is catching Rivera.

Torre and Girardi called upon Rivera for long saves with even greater frequency in October. Of his 42 postseason saves, 31 were of at least four outs; Rich Gossage (seven) is second overall, while Jason Motte (five) is second in the Wild Card era. Seven of Rivera's long saves came in series clinchers, including the 1998 and '99 World Series, but those performances are merely part of a larger, more jaw-dropping body of work: In 141 postseason innings—the equivalent of two seasons—he compiled a 0.70 ERA while allowing just two homers and 21 walks (1.3 per nine), with 110 strikeouts (7.0 per nine). Nobody with more than 26 innings has a lower postseason ERA. No pitcher has more postseason appearances (96); Rivera's former setup men Jeff Nelson and Mike Stanton are a distant second and third with 55 and 53, respectively, while Brad Lidge is second in saves with 18. Granted, Rivera's high totals are a function of the expanded Wild Card–era playoff format, but they are impressive nonetheless.

While it might seem obvious enough that Rivera has earned his plaque, it's worth a refresher course regarding the limited number of relievers in the Hall. Through the 2017 election cycle, just five have been elected, starting with Wilhelm in 1985. The ones who have joined him since—Fingers (1992), Eckersley (2004), Bruce Sutter ('06), and Gossage ('08)—roughly reflect the aforementioned evolution of the role, and aren't there merely for their save totals. Of that quintet, only Wilhelm and Fingers have held the all-time record for saves, which didn't even become an official stat until 1969, a decade after being invented by sportswriter Jerome Holtzman.

As with RBIs, the stat was not only tracked prior to it becoming official, but researchers have since pored over ancient box scores to tabulate saves all the way back to 1871, so we know that Wilhelm held the all-time lead from 1964–80, when Fingers surpassed his 228 saves. Fingers, whose résumé was burnished by Cy Young and MVP hardware, not to mention a strong postseason track record, retired in 1985 and was elected in the same year that Jeff Reardon surpassed his 341 saves. Reardon's record of 357 saves lasted less than a year; he sank without a trace upon reaching the ballot in 2000. Smith surpassed him in 1993 and retired in 1997 with 478 saves, a mark that held until 2006. Where it once appeared as though Smith might be elected—particularly after he reached 50.6% in 2012—his support receded before he aged off the ballot in 2017, the same year that Hoffman, who broke his record, fell five votes short of election. Neither Sutter nor Eckersley held the all-time saves record, but both dominated as the closer role was redefined; the former became lights out when largely confined to save situations, and likewise for the latter in ninth-inning save situations.

For statheads, the shift toward WAR illustrated that as the closer's job has evolved to occupy a smaller footprint of innings, only a small handful of them approach the values of even above-average starters in a given season. The Baseball-Reference.com version of WAR that's used in JAWS does contain an adjustment for leverage—the quantitatively greater impact on winning and losing that a reliever has at the end of the ballgame than a starter does earlier—but it also measures relievers against a higher replacement level than starters, since they tend to allow fewer runs per nine innings. Seasons worth 3.0 WAR are uncommon for relievers. Rivera's 11 such seasons are as many as the second-ranked Gossage (six) and third-ranked Foulke (five) put together.

Even so, Rivera's 57.1 career WAR would rank only 77th all-time if measured against starting pitchers, between Orel Hershiser and dead-ball-era Hall of Famer Three-Finger Brown. Hoffman, who had only 51 fewer saves than Rivera, was almost exactly half as valuable; his 28.4 WAR would rank 312th among starters, in the general vicinity of Jarrod Washburn and Jack McDowell—nobody you'd put in Cooperstown. Likewise for Wagner, who finished with 28.1 WAR, and like Hoffman, who debuted on the 2016 ballot. The peak scores of Rivera (28.9), Hoffman (19.6), and Wagner (19.9) would stack up even less impressively if measured against starters, with Rivera tied for 251st, a hair below the lowest Hall of Fame starter, Rube Marquard, and the other two even lower.

Relative to other relievers, which is to say pitchers who spent more than half their careers in the bullpen, Rivera's WAR trails only Eckersley (63.0), though the dirty little secret is that the bulk of the latter's WAR—and all of his peak score (38.1)—was compiled during his early years as a starter. Rivera's 43.0 JAWS trails Eckersley's 50.5, but even if you include Eckersley as part of the standard, only that pair, Wilhelm and Gossage are above the bar, with Gossage the only other pitcher whose peak score (32.0) surpasses Rivera's. Smith (25.4 JAWS), Hoffman, and Wagner (24.0 each) are well below the JAWS standard of 34.4, and they'd be below the modified standard of 30.4 if Eckersley is excluded from the set.

WAR and JAWS may not be the ideal solution for valuing relievers' Hall-worthiness. With the debate over the extent to which leverage and its cousin, Win Expectancy, should be incorporated into reliever valuation I've continually sought alternative ways to gauge reliever fitness for the Hall. At the very least, Win Probability Added (WPA) is worth a look, but even while offering different answers with regards to some relievers, Rivera is still king of the hill.

WPA is a context-sensitive measure that accounts for the incremental increase (or decrease) in chances of winning produced in each plate appearance given the inning, score, and base-out situation. It rewards degree of difficulty, something that the save itself does not. A pitcher throwing a 1-2-3 ninth inning in a one-run game adds 0.16 WPA (a value that rises with scoring levels), while the same performance in a three-run game in the same scoring environment adds just 0.03 WPA. Relievers' single-season WPA scales similarly to single-season WAR, in that a season above 3.0 is rare. Rivera (56.6 WPA) is miles ahead of the second-ranked Hoffman (34.1), who fares better in this light than via WAR. Gossage (32.5), Wilhelm (31.1), and the still active Joe Nathan (30.9) round out the top five, with Eckersley (30.8) sixth, Wagner and Papelbon (29.0) tied for seventh; Sutter (24th at 18.2) and Fingers (26th at 16.2) are both far behind. The five enshrined relievers average 25.8 WPA, worth remembering when we turn our attention to the relievers who may follow in Rivera's wake—or in Hoffman's case, will precede it.

When Rivera reaches the ballot, his records and postseason accomplishments will carry the day, with the near-universal regard for his character making it a near-certainty that he'll not only join Eckersley as the second reliever ever elected on the first ballot, he'll surpass Eck (83.2%) and Gossage (85.8%) for the highest share of the vote by a reliever. Even 95% wouldn't seem out of line for a man with a solid claim as the greatest closer of all time.

THE ROUNDUP

The number before each player name refers to his JAWS ranking *among all players at the position*, not necessarily those in the Hall. Average HOF relief pitcher: 40.6/28.2/34.4 3.

The Elite (above standard in career, peak, and JAWS)

1. Dennis Eckersley RHP

Teams:	Indians 1975–77 • Red Sox 1978–84, '98 • Cubs 1984–86 • A's 1987–95 • Cardinals 1996–97
Stats:	197-171 • 390 Sv • 3.50 ERA • 116 ERA+ • 3,285.2 IP • 2,401 K
Rankings:	8× top 5 Sv • 7× top 10 WAR • 6× All-Star All-time: 5th G • 6th Sv
Voting/JAWS:	BBWAA 2004 (1st, 83.2%) • 63.0/38.1/50.5

With his violent sidearm/three-quarters delivery that belied pinpoint control, Eckersley spent his first 12 seasons as an occasionally dominant starter, tossing a no-hitter, making two All-Star teams, and receiving Cy Young votes in 1978 and '79. Struggles with alcohol—exacerbated by the Cubs' daytime schedule, leaving his nights free—abetted his decline, but after rehab following the 1986 season, he emerged as the A's closer the next summer. From 1988–92, he averaged 72 innings, 44 saves (leading the AL twice), 9.5 K/9, 10.0 K/BB, 1.90 ERA, and 2.5 WAR while Oakland won four division titles, three pennants, and the 1989 World Series. While viewed as a paradigm shifter, 35% of those saves were longer. When he retired, he ranked first in appearances (1,071) and third in saves, not to mention first in postseason saves (15, though the one that got away—Kirk Gibson's homer—looms large). He confounds JAWS, as his peak years were all as a starter; his 1992 AL Cy Young/ MVP combo looks less flattering given his modest 2.9 WAR. Excluding him from calculations for comparative purposes yields standards of 35.0/25.7/30.4. BBWAA voters had no qualms about making him the first reliever elected on the first ballot.

4. Rich Gossage RHP

Teams:	White Sox 1972–76 • Pirates 1977 • Yankees 1978–83, '89 • Padres 1984–87 • Cubs 1988 • Giants 1989 • Rangers 1991 • A's 1992–93 • Mariners 1994
Stats:	124-107 • 310 Sv • 3.01 ERA • 126 ERA+ • 1,809.1 IP • 1,502 K
Rankings:	9× All-Star • 8× top 5 Sv • 3× top 10 WAR
Voting/JAWS:	BBWAA 2008 (9th, 85.8%) • 42.0/32.0/37.0

The intimidating Gossage was a standard-setting reliever for a decade (1975–85, minus a year-long experiment as a starter), blowing away hitters with 100 mph heat while helping his teams to three pennants. Gossage first emerged as a force in 1975 under White Sox pitching coach Johnny Sain, who helped him add a changeup and slider; the loose Goose set a single-season WAR record for relievers (8.2, second in the AL) while throwing 141⅔ innings with a 1.84 ERA, 8.3 K/9, and a league-high 26 saves. After a mediocre season in the rotation, he returned to relief dominance in Pittsburgh, prompting George Steinbrenner to sign him to a six-year, $2.75 million deal despite the presence of reigning Cy Young winner Sparky Lyle. With his big-money imprimatur, Gossage usurped Lyle's role and was brilliant, posting a 2.10 ERA (183 ERA+) while averaging 86 innings, 25 saves, and 3.1 WAR in six years in the Bronx despite not only the 1981 strike but also a sprained thumb suffered in a 1979 clubhouse scuffle. His heavy workload, postseason exposure (31⅓ innings, 2.87 ERA, eight saves), and number four ranking in saves (now 23rd) earmarked him as Hall-worthy, but Eckersley and Bruce Sutter both cut him in line.

The Rank and File

3. Hoyt Wilhelm RHP

Teams:	Giants 1952–56 • Cardinals 1957 • Indians 1957–58 • Orioles 1958–62 • White Sox 1963–68 • Angels 1969 • Braves 1969–70, '71 • Cubs 1970 • Dodgers 1971–72
Stats:	143-122 • 228 Sv • 2.52 ERA • 147 ERA+ • 2,254.1 IP • 1,610 K
Rankings:	8× top 5 Sv • 5× All-Star • 3× top 10 WAR • 2× led ERA All-Time: 6th G
Voting/JAWS:	BBWAA 1985 **(8th, 83.8%)** • 47.3/26.9/37.1

The greatest knuckleballer didn't debut in the majors until he was nearly 30, thanks in part to a three-year hitch in the army that included a Purple Heart for taking shrapnel in the Battle of the Bulge. The rookie Wilhelm instantly emerged as a top reliever, leading the NL in games (71) and ERA (2.43) with 11 saves and 2.7 WAR in 159⅓ innings. Over his first 14 seasons (through 1965, his age-42 year), he delivered a 144 ERA+ while averaging 2.6 WAR and topping 100 innings 11 times. He almost certainly could have thrived as a starter given his 2.68 ERA in 52 turns from 1958–61; in 1959, his only year with over a dozen starts, he led the AL in ERA (2.19) in 226 innings while ranking second in WAR (7.6). From 1966–70, Wilhelm dialed down to 85 innings per year, with a 2.04 ERA (168 ERA+) and 2.3 WAR per year; only his final two seasons were throwaways. Though he never led his league in saves, he held the all-time lead from 1964–80, and in games pitched from 1968–98 (1,070). He debuted with 41.7%, but despite topping 50% two years later, his march to Cooperstown was drawn out.

17. Bruce Sutter RHP

Teams:	Cubs 1976–80 • Cardinals 1981–84 • Braves 1985–86, '88
Stats:	68-71 • 300 Sv • 2.83 ERA • 136 ERA+ • 1,042 IP • 861 K
Rankings:	6× All-Star • 5× led Sv • 3× top 5 WAR
Voting/JAWS:	BBWAA 2006 **(13th, 76.9%)** • **24.6/24.6/24.6**

While recovering from elbow surgery in 1973, the 20-year-old Sutter learned the split-fingered fastball from minor league instructor Fred Martin. He rode the pitch to the majors, becoming the first successful practitioner of what would later be dubbed "The Pitch of the '80s."[7] By 1977, he was lights out, saving 31 games in 107 innings with a 1.34 ERA, 10.8 K/9, 6.5 WAR (his first of three top five finishes). In '79, prompted by his ace reliever's late-season declines, Cubs manager Herman Franks began limiting his usage mainly to save situations. Sutter tied the NL record with 37 and won the Cy Young via a 2.22 ERA/101-IP/4.9 WAR season. Traded to the Cardinals in December 1980, he was instrumental for the '82 champs, and in '84 saved an NL record 45 games with a 1.45 ERA in a career-high 122⅔ innings. Shoulder woes turned a new contract with Atlanta into a disaster; he was done at 35. His lack of longevity limits his WAR, and his ballot tenure was as long as his career, but between the splitter and being the first fire-man used in a particularly save-focused manner, innovation offset his throwing fewer innings than any other Hall of Fame pitcher.

26. Rollie Fingers RHP

Teams:	A's 1968–76 • Padres 1977–80 • Brewers 1981–82, 1984–85
Stats:	114-118 • 341 Sv • 2.90 ERA • 120 ERA+ • 1,701.1 IP • 1,299 K
Rankings:	11× top 5 Sv • 7× All-Star
Voting/JAWS:	BBWAA 1992 **(2nd, 81.2%)** • **26.1/19.2/22.7**

A distinctive handlebar mustache, a key role on three straight world champions, and the first Cy Young/MVP sweep for a reliever helped Fingers become the second fireman enshrined. In Oakland, Fingers ranked among the top five in saves in six straight seasons (1971–76) while averaging 66 appearances and 125 innings (but just 2.0 WAR) per year and posting a 1.35 ERA in 33⅓ World Series innings with six saves and the 1974 series MVP award. The heavy workloads continued after free agency carried him to San Diego. He led the NL in saves three times and dominated in strike-shortened '81 (78 IP, 1.04 ERA, and 4.2 WAR, fourth in the league) while helping Milwaukee to its first postseason berth, running away with the Cy and edging Rickey Henderson in a very close MVP vote. Though he became the first pitcher to reach 300 saves, in 1982, an elbow injury sidelined him for October. Between the accolades, the postseason, and his 1980–91 ownership of the saves record, his election was inevitable, though it didn't set a tremendously high bar, value-wise.

Further Consideration (upcoming or overlooked candidates)

14. Lee Smith

Teams:	Cubs 1980–87 • Red Sox 1988–90 • Cardinals 1990–1993 • Yankees 1993 • Orioles 1994 • Angels 1995–96 • Reds 1996 • Expos 1997
Stats:	71–92 • 478 Sv • 3.03 ERA • 132 ERA+ • 1,289.1 IP • 1,251 K
Rankings:	11x top 5 saves • 7x All-Star
	All-Time: 3rd Sv • 12th G
JAWS:	**29.6/21.1/25.4**

The physically intimidating (6'5", 220 pounds) Smith arrived during Sutter's final season in Chicago, though he didn't take over closer duties until mid-1982. Over the next 13 years, while his workload diminished from 100-plus innings to fewer than 50, he struck out more than a batter per inning and dominated the saves category, leading his league four times, ranking second four times, and among the top five three others. He set an NL record with 47 saves in 1991 while finishing second in the Cy Young voting, and two years later claimed the all-time saves lead, which he held until 2006. Given his postseason struggles (8.10 ERA in 5⅓ innings in 1984 and '88), those saves are the bulk of his case for Cooperstown. It looked sufficient for a while; he debuted at 42.3% in 2003 and meandered to 50.6% in 2012, but couldn't push any further. He doesn't fare well in term of WAR or WPA (21.3, 14th all-time), but it seems likely the Today's Game Era Committee will eventually smile upon him.

18. Joe Nathan

Teams:	Giants 1999–2000, '02–03, '16 • Twins 2004–09, '11 • Rangers 2012–13 • Tigers 2014–15 • Cubs 2016 •

Stats:	64-34 • 377 Sv • 2.87 ERA • 151 ERA+ • 923.1 IP • 976 K
Rankings:	7× top 5 Sv • 6× All-Star
JAWS:	**26.8/21.8/24.3**

From 2004–09, Nathan helped the Twins to three playoff appearances while serving as the best reliever this side of Rivera, posting a 1.87 ERA and 18.4 WAR in 418⅔ innings to Mo's 1.90 and 21.9 WAR in 440⅓ innings. His first of two Tommy John surgeries ended that run, and while he had good seasons with Texas and Detroit afterward, he had dreadful ones as well, and his 8.10 ERA in 10 postseason innings doesn't exactly elevate him above a handful of fine relievers whose runs of dominance didn't last.

20. Billy Wagner

Teams:	Astros 1995–2003 • Phillies 2004–05 • Mets 2006–09 • Red Sox 2009 • Braves 2010
Stats:	47-40 • 422 Sv • 2.31 ERA • 187 ERA+ • 903 IP • 1,196 K
Rankings:	10× top 10 Sv • 7× All-Star
	All-time: 6th Sv
JAWS:	**28.1/19.9/24.0**

"Billy the Kid" was the ultimate underdog. Undersized (5'10"), from a broken home and an impoverished background, he channeled his frustrations into throwing incredibly hard—with his left hand, despite being a natural righty, for he broke his right arm twice as a child. Thanks to outstanding lower body strength and extraordinary range of motion, Wagner reached 100 mph with consistency, complementing his heat with a hard slider that helped him compile the highest strikeout rate (11.9 per nine) and lowest opponent batting average (.187) of any pitcher with at least 800 innings, and to dominate hitters to the very end of his career. Tommy John surgery at 36 and retirement at 38 left him with fewer innings than even Sutter. Low career totals, less black ink than most star closers, and a JAWS far below the standard suggest he's another also-ran, but those rate stats and his 29.0 WPA (sixth all-time, 3.2 wins above the average enshrined reliever) shouldn't be dismissed. His 10.5% in his 2016 ballot debut doesn't bode well, though.

21. Trevor Hoffman

Teams:	Marlins 1993 • Padres 1993–2008 • Brewers 2009–10
Stats:	61-75 • 601 Sv • 2.87 ERA • 141 ERA+ • 1,089.1 IP • 1,133 K

Rankings:	9× top 3 Sv • 7× All-Star
	All-time: 2nd Sv • 11th G
JAWS:	28.4/19.6/24.0

Like Wilhelm, Sutter, and Rivera, Hoffman rode a signature pitch—a changeup, thrown with the same arm action and spin as his fastball—to the Cooperstown doorstep, that after converting from shortstop in the minors. Though far from the prototype of the smoke-throwing closer, Hoffman whiffed more than a batter per inning nine times and tied Rivera, Fingers, Smith, and Johnny Murphy for the most top three finishes in saves (nine). He was plenty resilient, too, overcoming two rotator cuff surgeries and arthritic degeneration in his clavicle, the last of which cost him most of 2003. He rebounded to break Smith's saves record in 2006 and become the first pitcher to 500 and 600 saves. WAR and JAWS don't make a good case for him, but his 34.1 WPA is second all-time, 8.3 wins above the average enshrined reliever. That's enough of an advanced-stat rationale to accept his inevitable enshrinement given his 67.3% debut in 2016 and then his 74.0% (five votes short) in '17.

29. Francisco Rodriguez

Teams:	Angels 2002–08 • Mets 2009–11 • Brewers 2011–13, '14–15
	• Orioles 2014 • Tigers 2016
Stats:	50-48 • 430 Sv • 2.73 ERA • 154 ERA+ • 950.2 IP • 1,119 K
Rankings:	7× top 5 Sv • 6× All-Star
	All-time: 4th Sv • 22nd G
JAWS:	25.4/17.9/21.6

"K-Rod" burst upon the major league scene as an October surprise, throwing 18⅔ postseason innings during the Angels' 2002 title run after just 5⅔ regular season innings. He didn't take over closer duties until 2005, but once he did, he led the AL in saves three times, setting a single-season record with 62 in 2008. A far less productive stretch followed, punctuated by his assault on his girlfriend's father in New York and a domestic violence arrest in Milwaukee, but he put his career back on track with his second run with the Brewers, becoming the fourth pitcher to reach 400 saves. A year younger than Jonathan Papelbon (24.0/19.8/21.9, 368 saves), he's got far more upward momentum entering 2017. Surpassing 500 saves and 1,000 appearances could be his ticket to Cooperstown, though his rate stats will never touch Wagner's.

CHAPTER 19

SLOUCHING TOWARD COOPERSTOWN

I t was the second week of February 2016, days before pitchers and catchers reported to spring training—the deadest spot on the baseball calendar. Snow blanketed Cooperstown, and the thermometer promised to dip below zero every day. I had taken leave of my day job and my pregnant wife in Brooklyn to schlep upstate and scour the Hall of Fame's research library for some crucial herbs and spices to flavor this book.

I found so much more. At that time of year, the town is all but shuttered and tourist-free, the Hall so deserted that staff can outnumber visitors. Beyond the hours I spent digging through folders in the library, I walked through its three floors of exhibits—which I hadn't visited in over a decade—unencumbered, alternately awed and amused, full of reverence or marveling at absurdity. In some corners, audio looped endlessly for the entertainment of the ghosts, but in the gallery I enjoyed silent, solitary stretches with the 312 plaques.

I had the run of the place, but I wasn't entirely alone. Hall president Jeff Idelson dropped by the library for a chat. Senior curator Tom Shieber and researcher Bill Francis took me behind the scenes for a tour of the library and the museum's treasures—newspapers, ledgers, books, caps, uniforms, photographs, and oh so many bats. Jeff Katz, the mayor of Cooperstown and a fellow Thomas Dunne Books author (*Split Season: 1981*) took me for burgers at a local brewpub. Those unforgettable four days renewed my appreciation for the Hall as both a resource and a destination, reminding me that the institution is so much more than the sum of its glaring imperfections and overheated annual debates.

During that frigid week in February, the ground floor of the Hall still contained a colorful display celebrating the careers of the quartet of 2015 newcomers: Craig Biggio, Randy Johnson, Pedro Martinez, and John Smoltz. As the weather warmed, those would give way to a similar display dedicated to the 2016 honorees, Ken Griffey Jr. and Mike Piazza.

To these eyes, it already felt as though change was in the air. In the voting results announced just a month previous, Griffey had received 99.3%—437 of 440 ballots—breaking Tom Seaver's 24-year-old record. None of the three schmucks who held out had revealed their names, but the days of voters hiding in the shadows were numbered. Over 70% of them had voluntarily published their ballots via Ryan Thibodaux's online ballot tracker, either before or after the election results were revealed. With an increased appetite for transparency, the BBWAA would vote in December to publish every single ballot beginning with the 2018 cycle. The move may lead to the Hall's first unanimous selection; who wants to be known as The Guy Who Voted Against Derek Jeter?

If Griffey's result heralded an end to an infuriatingly silly tradition of non-unanimity, as well as a pressure toward voter conformity, Piazza's election brought a mixed blessing as well. It was a defeat for the backne police, who were content to accuse players of performance-enhancing-drug wrongdoing without hard evidence, and the first acknowledgment from the voters that an imperfect reckoning with the unclean era from which he hailed was overdue.

Eleven and a half months later, the 2017 elections of seventh-year candidate Jeff Bagwell and first-year candidate Ivan Rodriguez (both similarly suspected of PED use, albeit without any hard evidence) underscored the Piazza result. Piazza, the best-hitting catcher of all time, had waited four years to gain entry, but with Rodriguez—perhaps the best defensive catcher of all time—the electorate collectively said, "Cut the bullshit. Elect him and move on." Likewise for Bagwell, whose long-overdue entry also struck a blow for analytics. Ranked just 28th in hits and 14th in homers among players who spent at least half their careers as first basemen, his combination of offense, baserunning, and defense—much of it done against the backdrop of the run-suppressing Astrodome—marked him as the game's sixth-best first baseman according to WAR and JAWS, and second among those since World War II.

The bigger blow struck for analytics, of course, was the election of Tim Raines in his 10th and final year of eligibility. For far too long, the speedster had taken a backseat—to Fernando Valenzuela among 1981 NL rookies, to Andre Dawson in Montreal, to Rickey Henderson among leadoff hitters, to Tony Gwynn among corner outfielders elected in the late 2000s, and to all too many candidates whom voters squeezed onto their ballots at his expense.

For 10 long years, on the pages of Baseball Prospectus and SI.com, I drew the comparison between Gwynn, he of the 3,141 hits, eight batting titles, and 97.6% share of the vote in 2007, and Raines, with "only" 2,605 hits and one batting title, showing that the latter's advantages in power and walks plus his 808 steals with an 84.7% success rate put him on the same level—slightly ahead, even—by whatever version of WAR was in vogue that year, and among the top 10 leftfielders of all time.

Yet a year after Gwynn received the seventh-highest voting share of all time, Raines debuted with just 24.3%. Particularly with his eligibility window trimmed from 15 years to 10 by the Hall's rule change, it took a combination of analytics and grassroots support to jump-start his candidacy. After he dipped to 46.1% in 2014 and then lost those five years, the voters treated his case with urgency. Raines gained 39.9% over the next three years, finally reaching 86.0%.

Watching the 57-year-old Raines beam at the Hall of Fame press conference at New York's St. Regis Hotel the day after the results were announced—"The writers finally got it right,"[1] he joked—it was difficult not to think of the late Ron Santo, and all the other Hall of Famers who never got to bask in the limelight after being elected, or to recall Minnie Minoso's plea in his final interview ("I don't want it to happen after I pass. I want it while I'm here, because I want to enjoy it").[2]

Bagwell, Raines, and Rodriguez brought the total number of candidates elected from 2014–17 to 12, a surge not seen since 1936–39, the Hall's big bang. We're a long way from the shutout of 2013, which triggered fretting over the institution's future and, at least within the BBWAA, talk of rule changes. With the Hall ever-reluctant to take a chance on tinkering (sorry) with its time-honored format, it's clear that an evolving electorate is the force driving the change.

Some of that is the Hall's doing, via the 2015 rule they put forth while side-stepping the BBWAA's effort to expand the ballot to 12 slots. The board voted to strip the vote from honorary BBWAA members who had previously been qualified to vote but were more than 10 years removed from actively covering the game—a practice that made for some strange optics when a writer who had moved on to covering football, golf, or ice skating chimed in with an odd ballot. According to BBWAA secretary-treasurer Jack O'Connell, the move purged 90 voters, roughly 14% of the initial pool of 650, but in terms of actual votes received, the total dropped by 20%, from 549 in 2015 to 440 in '16, and 442 in '17. (Note that not everyone with the privilege to vote actually exercises it—some eligible voters don't participate out of protest, forgetfulness, or failure to follow procedure; others, such as those from the *Los Angeles Times*, *New York Times*, and *Washington Post*, are forbidden to vote by their employers, on the principle that reporters shouldn't be making the news.) Via O'Connell, after shutouts in 1958 and '60, the Hall had similarly stripped 175 honorary members of the vote.

With two elections since the culling, it's too early to draw firm conclusions about its effect, but what we have seen thus far is significant upward movement from two groups of players: top candidates with some link—even a tenuous one—to PEDs (Bagwell, Piazza, Rodriguez, Barry Bonds, and Roger Clemens) and analytically favored candidates who lack the round-numbered milestones that tend to accelerate election (Raines, Bagwell, Edgar Martinez, Mike Mussina, and, before he alienated some voters via his social media rants, Curt Schilling). Bonds, Clemens, Martinez, and Mussina all crossed the 50% threshold for the first time in 2017, with the latter duo more than doubling their shares of the vote relative to 2015. The inference is that the purged older writers tended toward a more hard-line stance regarding PED use and were less fluent in analytics, therefore less likely to be swayed by WAR, JAWS, and so on. What's more, those older writers were less inclined to publish their ballots, so the "public versus private" split in Thibodaux's ballot tracker mirrors those trends. In 2017, Bonds, Clemens, Mussina, and Schilling had an average drop-off of 20% between their public and private support levels, with Martinez and Rodriguez around 12%, and Raines and Bagwell around 7%.

We'll need more time to assess how those trends will play out, though it's worth noting that the pace of JAWS-approved candidates hitting the ballot in the next five years will slow down:

2018: Chipper Jones, Jim Thome, Scott Rolen, Andruw Jones, Omar
    Vizquel, Johnny Damon, Johan Santana
2019: Mariano Rivera, Roy Halladay, **Todd Helton,** Andy Pettitte
2020: Derek Jeter, Bobby Abreu, Jason Giambi, Paul Konerko, Cliff Lee
2021: Tim Hudson, Torii Hunter, Mark Buehrle
2022: Alex Rodriguez, David Ortiz, Mark Teixeira, Prince Fielder

Martinez (58.6%) is the high-vote-getter from among the aforementioned quartet of 2017 holdovers, but he and others are too far from 75% to be elected in 2018, particularly with another top-heavy ballot featuring likely first-year honorees Thome and Chipper Jones, plus holdovers Trevor Hoffman (74.0% in 2017) and Vlad Guerrero (71.7%). In danger of being lost amid the second four-man class in four years—after just two in the previous 77 years—are Rolen and Andruw Jones, analytical favorites who are also well decorated with Gold Gloves but short on traditional counting stats due to early exits from the majors. They may wind up getting treated like Bobby Grich and Kenny Lofton, knocked into oblivion in their first chance, or simply lingering on the ballot underappreciated, like Alan Trammell and Larry Walker. On the other hand, the arrival of Vizquel, who scores poorly in WAR and JAWS—below every enshrined shortstop in the latter—threatens to reignite the debate over old-school eye test vs. new-school stats. Meanwhile, the elections of Bonds and Clemens, both halfway through their candidacies, appear inevitable despite their pre-testing-era PED links. There's no uniformity to the effect, though: Sammy Sosa, who's on the same schedule, polled just 8.6% in 2017, with Gary Sheffield (13.3%) not faring much better. Neither was suspended even once, yet twice-suspended Manny Ramirez outdid them at 23.8%.

We'll need even longer to see the impact of the second big electorate-based rule change from 2015: the BBWAA's decision to extend membership to MLB.com writers, after years of resistance unrelated to Hall of Fame voting. The short version is that MLB.com writers don't need the guaranteed access protections of the BBWAA, since it's their employer who controls access in the first place. (Here it's worth noting that anything I say about the BBWAA in this context merely reflects my views and interpretations and should not be taken to reflect the official position of the organization.) A by-product of this is that their welcoming to the fold could stabilize the size of the organization at a time when traditional newspaper coverage is dwindling and older writers are being pushed into retirement or unemployment—definitely not a good thing, regardless of the effect on Hall of Fame voting.

While MLB.com writers who previously put in 10 years at BBWAA-affiliated publications have continued to vote in Hall elections, those joining the BBWAA for the first time will still need to put in their 10 years to get their ballots; they're not being credited retroactively. Writers with fewer than 10 years at a BBWAA-affiliated publication can now keep their service streaks intact while moving to MLB.com.

The lack of retroactive crediting is worth bearing in mind while contemplating the expansion of the electorate as a means of voting reform. Common sense dictates that the BBWAA isn't likely to petition the Hall to dilute its own authority by adding other voices to the process; it would ultimately be the Hall's call to add other voices in the mix, such as broadcasters (or at least the Frick Award–winning ones). A case could certainly be made to add non-BBWAA writers of certain stature to the pool, such as Roger Angell (the only non-BBWAA member to win the Spink Award), Bill James, John Thorn, Pete Palmer, Rob Neyer (who lost his BBWAA membership with a job change), Brian Kenny, and others whose work has demonstrated a command of baseball history and made a significant contribution to our knowledge of the game. You could even fantasize about some handful of super-literate members of the Society for American Baseball Research—hardly a monolithic organization of stat geeks, despite James hijacking its acronym to coin the term sabermetrics circa 1980—gaining the right to vote after demonstrating their fluency in baseball history. However, 100 or 50 or even 25 new voices from such groups is probably too radical a notion for the Hall to consider. Even if the BBWAA were to do an end-around the Hall by granting those people some tiered level of membership within its group (i.e., less than full press box and clubhouse access), it's extremely unlikely that those newcomers would be allowed to bypass the 10-year membership rule before voting. Buddy, they don't even let *me* vote on the Hall of Fame yet.

On that note, the next few years will see the first wave of the analytically inclined Internet-based writers get the vote. It was only in 2007 that the BBWAA added Internet-based writers, the first group of whom were mostly newspaper veterans who had already put in their 10 years before moving to online outlets. Two Baseball Prospectus alumni now working for ESPN, Christina Kahrl and Keith Law, will get ballots for the 2019 cycle; mine, initially granted through BP, will follow for 2021. Over the next several years, another trickle from BP and Fan-Graphs will get the vote as well. The analytical community has already had an indirect effect on the electorate, both for the Hall and for the annual awards, and it's begun to have a direct effect on the latter, for which no 10-year waiting period applies; Law, Kahrl, and FanGraphs' David Cameron are among those who've already voted for Cy Youngs and other awards.

The evolution of the voting body parallels the evolution of our understanding of what makes a Hall of Famer. For decades, the lack of television meant that the writers were the only ones who saw players on a daily basis. While their authority may not have been unquestioned, their knowledge was far more comprehensive than that of the average fan. Today, that isn't necessarily the case, at least as it pertains to the action on the field (the writers' access of course gives them a great leg-up on behind-the-scenes detail). Fans aren't as dependent upon reporters to tell them which players are tearing up the league, or who the best third baseman is. They can view all 30 teams, isolate highlight clips, and analyze the game from micro- and macro-perspectives using sophisticated advanced stats.

Ultimately, everyone who cares now has access to tools to help make up their own minds about who belongs in Cooperstown. They—*we*, really, as my ballots are still virtual ones—can then share their choices with the world via the Internet, which can make for quite the cacophony. The process is less a democracy than a republic, or at least the expectation of one, with bystanders hoping that their voices will be heard by voters. The evidence suggests that they have been.

The Hall of Fame processes, for as clunky as they may be, will continue to draw outsized attention and generate great passion. The BBWAA ballot will likely continue to act as a bottleneck, but the backlog means that the slate will remain packed with compelling candidates for the foreseeable future, and the debates over who belongs will never end.

TABLE OF ABBREVIATIONS

ABBREVIATION	STATISTIC
1B	single
2B	double
3B	triple
AVG	batting average
BABIP	batting average on balls in play
BB/9	bases on balls per nine innings
BB%	bases on balls per plate appearance
CG	complete game
CS	caught stealing
DRA	Defensive Regression Analysis
DRS	Defensive Runs Saved
ERA	earned run average
ERA+	Adjusted ERA
FIP	Fielding Independent Pitching
GG	Gold Glove
H	hits
HBP	hit-by-pitch
HR	home runs
HR/9	home runs per nine innings
HR%	home runs per plate appearance
ISO	isolated power
JAWS	Jaffe WAR Score
K	strikeouts
K/%	strikeouts per plate appearance
K/9	strikeouts per nine innings
L	losses
OBP	on-base percentage
OPS	On-base Plus Slugging
OPS+	Adjusted OPS
PA	plate appearances
RA9	runs allowed per nine innings
RBI	runs batted in

ABBREVIATION	LEAGUE
RF	Range Factor
S/S TC	slash stat triple crown
SB	stolen bases
SHO	shutouts
SLG	slugging percentage
SUP+	adjusted run support
Sv	saves
TC	Triple Crown
TOB	times on base
TZ	Total Zone
UZR	Ultimate Zone Rating
W	wins
WAR	Wins Above Replacement
WARP	Wins Above Replacement Player

ABBREVIATION	LEAGUE
AA	American Association
AL	American League
FL	Federal League
UA	Union Association
NA	National Association
NL	National League
PL	Players League

ACKNOWLEDGMENTS

The Cooperstown Casebook was a decade in the making, sort of. Its seed was planted in Philadelphia over several drinks at Rouge and some long-forgotten hotel bar during the *Baseball Prospectus 2007* book tour by colleagues Steven Goldman and Christina Kahrl. Soon afterward came my first attempt at a proposal, not to mention a title spiced up by BP colleague Derek Jacquess enduring suggestion for a subtitle. Various endeavors, including the introduction of my Prospectus Hit and Run column—a regular outlet for my Hall of Fame musings, among other things—pushed the project to the back burner, and likewise for a second stab in 2010 that was diverted by Steve inviting me to join him at the Pinstriped Bible.

Long story short, when Thomas Dunne Books editor Rob Kirkpatrick reached out in January 2014 to ask if I was interested in meeting to discuss a book project, I actually had one up my sleeve. With some guidance from Eric Nelson at the Susan Rabiner Literary Agency, my proposal came together and a deal was completed. Alas, both Rob and Eric changed jobs and departed the project while I was in the early stages of writing, but they have my deep gratitude for their roles making *The Cooperstown Casebook* a reality.

Likewise for Emily Angell at Thomas Dunne and Sydelle Kramer at Susan Rabiner, who both came on in long relief and saw the project through. Emily did her best to keep this book from becoming longer than the *Oxford English Dictionary* while Sydelle navigated the contractual waters as real-life events—my engagement and wedding to Emma Span, her pregnancy and the birth of our daughter Robin—stretched out my writing and editing process to the point that the book felt like it might take a second decade to realize. At Thomas Dunne, Lisa Bonvissuto's late-inning work was a boon as well.

I owe dozens of other people thanks for their help and support for the completion of this book and/or in carving out the career that made it possible. At the risk of leaving anyone out, here goes.

From the diaspora of Baseball Prospectus, where JAWS was born and raised, Steve (who gave an early draft of some chapters herein a measure of tough love) and Christina as well as Will Carroll, Clay Davenport, Mike Fast, Kevin Goldstein, Joe Hamrahi, Gary Huckabay, Derek Jacques, Rany Jazayerli, Jonah Keri, Ben Lindberg, Max Marchi, Rob McQuown, Sam Miller, Marc Normandin, Jason Parks, Dave Pease, John Perrotto, Dayn Perry, Joe Sheehan, Nate Silver, Keith Woolner, and Colin Wyers.

At *Sports Illustrated*, special thanks to editor Ted Keith, who first gave JAWS a spotlight on SI.com in 2009 via a content-sharing agreement with BP, and brought me in-house in 2012. He encouraged me to do as much with JAWS as my achy fingers could accommodate and gave me the breathing room I needed to ensure that this book happened. Ted and Jon Tayler whipped the SI versions of several profiles here into shape the first time around, while Cliff Corcoran offered key insights and daily support as well. Bobby Clay and Stefanie Kaufman facilitated the use of those profiles in this book. Steven Cannella and Chris Stone gave JAWS its first exposure in the magazine. Albert Chen, Paul Fichtenbaum, Stefanie Gordon, Maggie Gray, Stephanie Haberman, Ryan Hunt, Joe Lemire, Ben Reiter, DT Slouffman, and the staff of SI Now and the SI legal department have my thanks as well.

Special thanks to MLB Network's Brian Kenny and his staff at *Clubhouse Confidential* and *MLB Now*, who put me and my Hall of Fame work in the television spotlight on a regular basis, increasing my audience exponentially. Thanks to Jon Heyman, Ken Rosenthal, Joel Sherman, and Tom Verducci, who have served as frequent on-air sparring partners. As heavyweight reporters, their daily work informs much of the contemporary portion of this book, and as debaters, they've kept me on my toes in honing many a Hall of Fame argument.

Special thanks to WNYW Fox 5's Duke Castiglione and ESPN's Keith Olbermann for having me on their TV shows multiple times as well. On the radio side, special thanks to El Paso's Steve Kaplowitz and Toledo's Norm Wamer for years worth of weekly radio spots. St. Louis' Kevin Wheeler and San Francisco's Ted Ramey have been particularly engaging when it comes to discussing my Hall of Fame stuff as well.

Special thanks as well to Baseball-Reference.com founder Sean Forman, who gave JAWS a prominent place on the best Web site ever created, making my metric far more accessible than it had ever been. Hans Van Slooten has been especially helpful in maintaining its presence there. I am indebted to the sabermetric work of Tom Tango, Sean Smith, John Dewan and Baseball Info Solutions, and

Mitchel Lichtman for what they have put into various versions of WAR. Of course, I am also indebted to the pioneering sabermetric work of Bill James, John Thorn, and Pete Palmer, which continues to inform and inspire me.

Special thanks to Peter Gammons for putting in the good word for my work over the years and for writing the foreword. In a book about the Hall of Fame, it is a wonderful thing to have a Spink Award winner batting leadoff.

Baseball Writers Association of America presidents LaVelle E. Neal III, Jose de Jesus Ortiz, Susan Slusser, and Derrick Goold helped me and my Hall expertise find a place within the organization, no small thing for someone who had spent more than a decade critiquing its voting, not always in polite terms. Secretary/treasurer Jack O'Connell answered numerous questions about the annual election cycles and provided some key historical perspective on the voting process. Within the BBWAA, my thanks to the Hall voters who have cited JAWS and my work as helpful to their voting process including Peter Abraham, Jerry Crasnick, Ken Davidoff, Ryan Fagan, Lynn Henning, Richard Justice, Tim Kawakami, Bernie Miklasz, Mark Newman, Joe Posnanski, C. Trent Rosecrans, Mike Silverman, and Jayson Stark.

At the Hall of Fame, president Jeff Idelson, researcher Bill Francis, and senior curator Tom Shieber showed me great hospitality during my 2016 visit. Brad Horn, Craig Muder, and Jon Shestakofsky fielded many a query from me over the years. Reference librarian Cassidy Lent of the Hall's Giamatti Research Center was particularly patient and helpful in guiding me through the library's resources. Also, if you are going to write a book about the Hall of Fame, it is a very good idea to become friends with the mayor of Cooperstown, Jeff Katz. He has been a tremendous ally throughout this project.

Likewise for Ryan Thibodaux, operator of the Hall of Fame Ballot Tracker and someone who sweats out the annual election cycle as I do. The ballot-tracking efforts of Darren Viola and Leonora Unser-Schutz deserve tips of the cap as well.

Alex Belth and Brett Trainor each provided some crucial pep talks along the way. Also on the honor roll for reasons professional, personal, or somewhere in between: Ken Arneson, Mike Axisa, Michael Baumann, Lana Berry, Carl Bialik, Jeff Blair, Eric Boland, Corey Brock, Craig Calcaterra, David Cameron, Marc Carig, Jason Collette, David Cone, Tommy Craggs, Jack Curry, Adam Darowski, Neil deMause, Chris Dial, Dan Epstein, Jeff Erickson, Mark Feinsand, Mike Ferrin, Diane Firstman, Alyson Footer, Jason Fry, Vince Gennaro, Mike Gianella, Michael Gluckstadt, Jay Gordon, Stacey Gotsulias, Allison Hagen, Holly Hollenbeck, Shaun Johnson, Ben Kabak, Micah Karg, King Kaufman, Kevin Kennedy, Tyler Kepner, Molly Knight, Matthew Kory, Mark Lamster, Keith Law, Matthew Leach, Will Leitch, Zachary Levine, Megan Marshall, Anna McDonald, Sean McNally, Chris McShane, Howard Megdal, Matt Meyers,

Scott Miller, Craig Minami, Kate Morrison, Thyrll Nelson, Zack Newman, Rob Neyer, Dan Okrent, Jeff Passan, Travis Petersen, Mike Petriello, Jacob Pomrenke, T. J. Quinn, Glen Radecki, Marly Riverda, Liz Roscher, Caryn Rose, David Roth, Amanda Rykoff, Richard Sandomir, Mark Simon, Ryan Spaeder, Jesse Spector, Alex Speier, Eric Stephen, Dan Szymborski, Bruce Taylor, John Thorn, Wendy Thurm, Jon Weisman, and Graham Womack.

Special thanks to my daily support group at the virtual water cooler: Issa Clubb, Adam Gravois, Eric Hoffsten, Larry Benzie, David Hurst, Ben Semel, and Greg Tucker.

None of this would have been possible without the love and support of my family: parents Richard and Helene Jaffe; brother Bryan Jaffe, sister-in-law Jennifer Lewis, and their daughter Amalie; and my in-laws, Paula Span, Jon Katz, and Maria Wulf. Love also to "the Edgar Martinez wing" of the Jaffe family, which is survived by aunt Kim Jaffe and cousins Allan Jaffe and Lisa Jaffe; uncle Harold Jaffe, "The Mayor of Safeco Field," who passed away in January 2017, was never far from my mind as I revised the manuscript to cover the most recent election cycle.

Last and best of all, extra special thanks to Emma Span, who filled in the gaps on this project in countless ways, but most of all with her love, and to Robin Span Jaffe. You both put a smile on my face every day.

NOTES

ABBREVIATIONS
AP: Associated Press
HOF: National Baseball Hall of Fame and Museum
LAT: *Los Angeles Times*
NYT: *New York Times*
SABR: Society for American Baseball Research
SI: *Sports Illustrated*
TSN: *The Sporting News*
UPI: United Press International

1. The Ins and Outs of the Hall of Fame
1 "Mission," HOF, http://baseballhall.org/support/mission.

2. Stat School
1 Bill James, *The Bill James Baseball Abstract 1982* (New York: Ballantine, 1982), p. 25.
2 Branch Rickey, "Goodby [*sic*] to Some Old Baseball Ideas," *Life*, August 2, 1954, p. 83.

3. Swimming with *JAWS*
1 Baseball Writers Association of America, *2017 BBWAA Hall of Fame ballot.*
2 Ibid.

4. How Voters Put Third Base in a Corner
1 "Character, Sportsmanship, Integrity Long Included in Formal Rules for Election," HOF, archived
   at   http://web.archive.org/web/20130208134705/http://baseballhall.org/character-sportsmanship
   -integrity.
2 Ken Smith, *Baseball's Hall of Fame*, 11th ed. (New York: Tempo Books, 1981), p. 56.
3 "Character, Sportsmanship, Integrity Long Included in Formal Rules for Election," HOF.
4 Franklin Pierce Adams, "Baseball's Sad Lexicon," *New York Evening Mail*, July 12, 1910.
5 Jacob C. Morse, "Boston Briefs," *The Sporting Life*, June 21, 1902, p. 3.
6 "Daguerreotypes: James J. (Jimmy Collins)," *TSN*, July 27, 1933, p. 2.

7 "About Time Jimmy Collins Made Hall of Fame," *TSN*, January 21, 1943, p. 4.

8 Bob Broeg, *Superstars of Baseball* (South Bend: Diamond Communications, 1994), p. 473.

9 James Forr and David Proctor, *Pie Traynor: A Baseball Biography* (Jefferson, NC: McFarland, 2010), p. 58.

10 Red Smith, "Pie Traynor Still Soft-Spoken in Opinions of Modern Baseball," *Lincoln Star*, September 5, 1971, p. 27.

11 Donald Honig, *Baseball When the Grass Was Real* (New York: Berkley, 1974), p. 129.

12 Clifton Blue Parker, *Big and Little Poison* (Jefferson, NC: McFarland, 2003), p. 163.

13 F. C. Lane, "Who Is the Greatest Third Baseman and Why?," *Baseball Magazine*, August 1913, p. 36.

14 Hugh S. Fullerton, "Fullerton's First Comparison Shows McInnis Leading Merkle," *NYT*, September 27, 1913, p. 10.

15 Jack Hand, "Baker and Schalk Latest Hall Additions," *Bakersfield Californian*, February 1, 1955, p. 21.

16 "Snider Edges Mathews in Slugging," *Corpus Christi Caller-Times*, January 5, 1954, p. 12.

17 AP, "Spahn Discloses Knee Injury 'Made Me Pitch Better,'" *Tucson Daily Citizen*, January 8, 1954, p. 16.

18 Ron Santo with Randy Minkoff, *Ron Santo: For the Love of Ivy* (Chicago: Bonus Books, 1993), p. 147.

19 Moss Klein, "Patient Approach Is Best for Chisox," *TSN*, January 22, 1990, p. 47.

20 Moss Klein, "Remembering Billy: Excitement Personified," *TSN*, January 8, 1990, p. 39.

21 Moss Klein, "A Vote for Carew, Fingers and Maz," *TSN*, January 7, 1991, p. 36.

22 Moss Klein, "Seaver Aces Key Hall Test: He Belongs," *TSN*, January 22, 1992, p. 23.

23 Ibid.

24 Mike Downey, "Induction Requires Deduction," *LAT*, January 13, 1993, http://articles.latimes.com/1993-01-13/sports/sp-1249_1_ballot.

25 Jerome Holtzman, "Santo's Numbers Hall of Fame Sized," *Chicago Tribune*, December 1, 1988, http://www.chicagotribune.com/sports/baseball/cubs/cs-881201cubsholtzmansanto-story.html.

26 Susan Kubian, "About the Hall of Fame," *Chicago Tribune*, November 8, 1992, http://articles.chicagotribune.com/1992-11-08/features/9204110129_1_ballot-five-years-jerome-holtzman-ron-santo.

27 Santo with Minkoff, *Ron Santo*, p. 94.

28 Jerome Holtzman, "'Incident' Doesn't Haunt Former Cub," *Chicago Tribune*, November 24, 1992, http://articles.chicagotribune.com/1992-11-24/sports/9204170367_1_cubs-ron-santo-jimmy-qualls.

29 Ibid.

30 Rich Cohen, "Where Are They Now: Catching Up with Cubs Legend Ernie Banks," *SI*, July 7, 2014, p. 49.

31 Phil Rogers, "Remembering Ron Santo," *Chicago Tribune*, December 3, 2010, archived at http://web.archive.org/web/20101206065053/http://www.chicagobreakingsports.com/2010/12/rogers-remembering-santo.html.

32 Ibid.

33 Paul Sullivan, "Ron Santo Dead at 70," *Chicago Tribune*, December 3, 2010, http://www.chicagotribune.com/sports/baseball/cubs/ct-spt-1204-ron-santo-dead-chicago-cu20101203-story.html.

34 Ibid.

35 Barry M. Bloom, "Cub Legend Santo Elected to Hall of Fame," MLB.com, December 5, 2011, http://m.mlb.com/news/article/26060702.

36 Ibid.

5. The Hall of Cronyism

1 Jim Murray, "Baseball Hall of Fame Has No Order," *LAT*, January 24, 1978, p. 9.

2 National Baseball Hall of Fame Library, "Veterans Committee" folder.

3 Bill James, *The Politics of Glory* (New York: Macmillan, 1994), p. 44.

4 "Spink Resigns Shrine Post, Stresses Need of Electing Old-Time All-Stars," *TSN*, August 5, 1959, p. 6.

5 Joe King, "Old-Timers Ask Careful Study of Shrine Balloting," *TSN*, August 19, 1959, p. 1.

6 "Hall of Fame Bosses Pull Boner," *TSN*, July 6, 1960, p. 10.

7 Leonard Koppett, *The Man in the Dugout* (New York: Crown, 1993), p. 185.

8 James, *The Politics of Glory*, p. 162.

9 Zev Chafets, *Cooperstown Confidential* (New York: Bloomsbury USA, 2009), p. 42.

10 Jack Lang, "Seven Seniors Enter Hall Via Vet Group Vote," *TSN*, February 13, 1971, p. 30.

11 Bob Burnes, "Does Vet Panel Vote Pals into Shrine?," *TSN*, February 17, 1973, p. 39.

12 Jack Brummell, "Baseball's Hall of Shame," *San Antonio Express*, January 12, 1975, p. 121.

13 Jim Murray, "Hall of Fame—Baseball's Eye of the Needle," *LAT*, January 21, 1977, p. 51.

14 C. C. Johnson Spink, "Hall of Fame Hassle," *TSN*, January 22, 1977, p. 12.

15 James, *The Politics of Glory*, p. 166.

16 Ibid., p. 168.

17 James Vail, *The Road to Cooperstown: A Critical History of Baseball's Hall of Fame Selection Process* (Jefferson, NC: McFarland, 2001), p. 107.

18 Jack Lang, "Treaty by Hall Voters," *TSN*, February 17, 1973, p. 39.

19 AP, "Hall of Fame Revamps Voting," *The Augusta Chronicle*, August 7, 2001, http://chronicle.augusta.com/stories/2001/08/07/bas_317322.shtml#.V1mC55MrIUE.

20 Jay Jaffe, "Pre-Integration Era Vote Again Shows Flaws in Hall of Fame's Process," SI.com, December 7, 2015, http://www.si.com/mlb/2015/12/07/hall-of-fame-veterans-committee-pre-integration-era-vote.

6. Blyleven, Morris, and the War on *WAR*

1 Bill Madden, "Stingy Yankees Are Making Life Difficult for GM Brian Cashman," New York *Daily News*, December 22, 2012, http://www.nydailynews.com/sports/baseball/yankees/madden-stingy-yanks-life-difficult-brian-article-1.1226001.

2 Jack Ellison, "Dutch Boy Cleaning Up on Hill," *TSN*, December 6, 1969, p. 62.

3 Herschel Nissenson, "New York Yankees Defeat White Sox," AP in *Corbin Times*, June 7, 1970, p. 2.

4 Randy Galloway, "New Ranger Bert Does U-Turn on Hill," *TSN*, July 10, 1976, p. 15.

5 Joseph Durso, "Injuries, Squabbles Part of Pirates' Family," *NYT*, June 1, 1980, p. S5.

6 Charley Feeney, "Blyleven Walks Out, Wants Trade," *Pittsburgh Post-Gazette*, May 1, 1980, p. 9.

7 Dayn Perry, "Synergy 101," Baseball Prospectus, August 28, 2003, http://www.baseballprospectus.com/article.php?articleid=2250.

8 Michael Lewis, *Moneyball* (New York: W. W. Norton, 2004), p. 291.

9 Ibid., p. 287.

10 Tyler Kepner, "Use of Statistics Helps Greinke to A.L. Cy Young," *NYT*, November 19, 2009, p. B16.

11 Mitch Albom, "Miguel Cabrera's Award a Win for Fans, Defeat for Stats Geeks," *Detroit Free Press*, November 16, 2012, archived at https://web.archive.org/web/20121121022645/http://www .freep.com/article/20121116/COL01/311160108/Miggy-s-award-a-win-for-fans-defeat-for-stats -geeks.

12 Thom Loverro, Twitter, November 15, 2012, https://twitter.com/thomloverro/status/2692290 29998075905.

13 Tommy Craggs, "The Basement Tapes: A Compendium of Sportswriters' Hacky Jokes About Bloggers," Deadspin, November 20, 2009, http://deadspin.com/5408682/the-basement-tapes-a -compendium-of-sportswriters-hacky-jokes-about-bloggers.

14 Greg Spira, "Pitching to the Score," *Baseball Prospectus 1997* (California: Ravenlock Media, 1997), republished at http://www.baseballprospectus.com/article.php?articleid=15750.

15 Joe Sheehan, "The Jack Morris Project," Baseball Prospectus, April 24, 2003, http://www .baseballprospectus.com/article.php?articleid=1815.

16 Joe Posnanski, "More More Morris," The Joe Posnanski Blog, April 25, 2013, http://joeposnanski .com/more-more-morris/.

17 Bob Klapisch, "The Case for Bert Blyleven: A Late Convert Joins the Flock," *Baseball Analysts*, December 17, 2005, http://baseballanalysts.com/archives/2005/12/the_case_for_be.php.

18 Rich Lederer, "A Larger Step for Blyleven," *Baseball Analysts*, December 28, 2006, http:// baseballanalysts.com/archives/2006/12/a_larger_step_f_1.php.

19 Klapisch, "The Case for Bert Blyleven: A Late Convert Joins the Flock."

20 Leonard Koppett, "Hall Voting Is Personal Matter," *TSN*, December 26, 1981, p. 7.

21 David Shaw, "Literacy Finds a Home in Sports Pages," *LAT*, February 7, 1975, p. 3.

22 Rich Lederer, "400 down and 5 to Go . . . ," *Baseball Analysts*, January 7, 2010, http://baseball analysts.com/archives/2010/01/400_down_5_to_g.php.

23 Rich Lederer, "Hey Man, Your Comments Don't Hold Water," *Baseball Analysts*, January 13, 2009, http://baseballanalysts.com/archives/2009/01/hey_man_your_co.php.

24 Jon Heyman, "Why I Didn't Cast a Hall of Fame Vote for Bert Blyleven, Again," SI.com, December 20, 2010, archived at https://web.archive.org/web/20101223063620/http://sportsillustrated .cnn.com/2010/writers/jon_heyman/12/20/hall.blyleven/index.html.

25 Murray Chass, "As Season Approaches, Some Topics Should Be Off Limits," *NYT*, February 27, 2007, p. D5.

26 Ibid.

27 Murray Chass, "The Vote Baseball Writers Don't Need," Murray Chass on Baseball, January 3, 2013, http://www.murraychass.com/?p=5663.

28 Murray Chass, "Anti-Morris Mob in Action," Murray Chass on Baseball, November 10, 2013, http://www.murraychass.com/?p=6823.

29 Dan Shaughnessy, "Casting His Votes for the Hall of Fame," *Boston Globe*, December 29, 2013, http://www.bostonglobe.com/sports/2013/12/29/time-cast-his-votes-for-baseball-hall-fame /ojPVH3NSylmZg1vJAGW6fJ/story.html.

30 Tim Cowlishaw, "Cowlishaw's Five on Friday: How I Voted for This Year's Baseball Hall of Fame," *Dallas Morning News*, December 23, 2011, http://sportsday.dallasnews.com/texas-rangers/sportsdaydfw /2011/12/23/cowlishaw-s-five-on-friday-how-i-voted-for-this-years-baseball-hall-of-fame.

31 Chass, "Anti-Morris Mob in Action."

7. Booms, Busts, Bottlenecks, and Ballot Reform

1 Chafets, *Cooperstown Confidential*, p. 194.

2 Red Smith, "Who Was M. G. Bulkeley," *NYT*, March 17, 1980, p. 35.

3 Barry M. Bloom, "No One Elected to Baseball Hall of Fame," MLB.com, Dec 8, 2014, http://m.mlb.com/news/article/103480656/no-one-elected-to-baseball-hall-of-fame.

4 Derrick Goold, "A Modest Proposal to Improve Hall of Fame Voting," *St. Louis Post-Dispatch*, December 8, 2014, accessed February 26, 2017, http://www.stltoday.com/sports/baseball/professional/birdland/goold-a-modest-proposal-to-improve-hall-of-fame-voting/article_06c25835-6086-5ce7-b195-09e503bcf8db.html.

5 Jayson Stark, "Baseball Hall of Fame Retains 10-Player Limit," ESPN.com, November 10, 2015, http://espn.go.com/mlb/story/_/id/14101470/baseball-hall-fame-retains-10-player-limit-voters-bbwaa-proposal.

6 Anthony McCarron, "Baseball Hall of Fame Cuts the Number of Years Players Are Eligible to Stay on Ballot from 15 to 10," New York *Daily News*, July 26, 2014, http://www.nydailynews.com/sports/baseball/baseball-hall-fame-cuts-eligibility-ten-years-article-1.1881144.

7 Ibid.

8. This Is Your Ballot on Drugs

1 Robert Smith, "A Different Kind of Performance Enhancer," NPR.com, March 31, 2006, http://www.npr.org/templates/story/story.php?storyId=5314753.

2 Jack Curry, "Museum of Artifacts, Tainted or Not," *NYT*, April 4, 2007, p. D5.

3 Ken Rosenthal, "Saying No to 'Roids in HOF, for Now," Fox Sports, December 27, 2012, http://www.foxsports.com/mlb/story/hall-of-fame-steroid-debate-difficult-decision-not-voting-them-in-yet-barry-bonds-roger-clemens-jeff-bagwell-122712.

4 "BBWAA Election Rules," HOF, http://baseballhall.org/hall-famers/rules-election/bbwaa.

5 Joe Posnanski, "The Hall of Fame Recap," SI.com, January 5, 2011, archived at https://web.archive.org/web/20120307221846/http://joeposnanski.si.com/2011/01/05/the-hall-of-fame-recap/.

6 Ibid.

7 Ibid.

8 Ronald Blum and Ben Walker, "McGwire Likely to Fall Far Short in Hall Vote," AP in *San Diego Union Tribune*, November 27, 2006, archived at http://web.archive.org/web/20160106183533/http://legacy.utsandiego.com/sports/baseball/20061127-1545-bbo-halloffame-mcgwire.html.

9 Ann Killion, "Why McGwire Won't Get My Hall Vote," *San Jose Mercury News,* December 19, 2006, http://www.mercurynews.com/ci_4867263.

10 John Shea, "McGwire for Hall of Fame? It's a No Vote This Time," *San Francisco Chronicle*, January 7, 2007, http://www.sfgate.com/sports/article/McGwire-for-Hall-of-Fame-It-s-a-no-vote-this-time-2658546.php.

11 Tim Brown, "Pandora's Boxes," *LAT*, July 31, 2006, http://articles.latimes.com/2006/jul/31/sports/sp-baseball31/2.

12 Henry McLemore, "Diz and Frisch Mac's Men," McNaught Syndicate, Inc. in *Abilene Reporter-News*, December 3, 1945, p. 12.

13 Frank Eck, "Harry Heilmann," AP in *The Evening Independent* (Massillon, OH), February 14, 1948, p. 8.

14 Arthur Daley, "No Electioneering Near the Polls," *TSN*, February 18, 1948, p. 13.

15 Walter L. Johns, "Sport Sputterings," *The Morning Herald* (Hagerstown, MD), January 25, 1950, p. 11.

16 Frank Eck, "Lopez, Boudreau Both Rate in Cooperstown Balloting," AP in *The Robesonian* (Lumberton, NC), January 10, 1958, p. 8.

17 Jimmy Cannon, "Making a Pitch for Koufax," *Pottstown Mercury*, January 3, 1972, p. 28.

18 Bill Moeller, "Bill's Board," *The Journal News* (Hamilton, OH), December 20, 1972, p. 20.

19 Dick Young, "Young Ideas," *TSN*, January 17, 1976, p. 12.

20 Red Smith, "The Minting of Immortals," *NYT*, December 28, 1979, p. A24.

21 Ira Berkow, "The Thumb in Baseball's Hall of Fame," *NYT*, February 4, 1991, http://www.ny times.com/1991/02/04/sports/the-thumb-in-baseball-s-hall-of-fame.html.

22 Dan Daniel, "Restrictions on Hall of Fame Voting Rapped," *TSN*, January 15, 1947, p. 12.

23 Smith, "The Minting of Immortals."

24 Will Grimsley, "Hall of Fame a Popularity Prize," AP in *Sedalia Democrat*, January 20, 1978, p. 9.

25 William C. Rhoden, "Keep the Vote Between the Lines," *TSN*, January 31, 1994, p. 7.

26 Fred Lieb, *Baseball As I Have Known It* (Lincoln: University of Nebraska Press, 1977), pp. 57–58.

27 Shaun Assael, Peter Keating, Buster Olney, Amy K. Nelson, and Tom Farrey, "Who Knew?," *ESPN The Magazine*, November 9, 2005, http://www.espn.com/espn/eticket/story?page=steroids& num=4.

28 Ron Kroichick, "House a 'Failed Experiment' with Steroids," *San Francisco Chronicle*, May 3, 2005, http://www.sfgate.com/sports/kroichick/article/House-a-failed-experiment-with-ste-roids-2637503.php.

29 Tom Verducci with reporting by Don Yaeger, George Dohrmann, Luis Fernando Llosa, and Lester Munson, "Totally Juiced," *SI*, June 3, 2002, pp. 36–48.

30 George J. Mitchell, "Report to the Commissioner of Baseball of an Independent Investigation into the Illegal Use of Steroids and Other Performance Enhancing Substances by Players in Major League Baseball," December 13, 2007, pp. 307–11.

31 Maury Brown, "MLB's Billion Dollar TV Deals, Free Agency, and Why Robinson Cano's Deal with the Mariners Isn't 'Crazy,'" Forbes.com, January 7, 2014, http://www.forbes.com/sites /maurybrown/2014/01/07/mlbs-billion-dollar-tv-deals-free-agency-and-why-robinson-canos-deal -with-the-mariners-isnt-crazy.

32 Dan Shaughnessy, "The Persecution of McGwire Is a Crime," *Boston Globe*, August 26, 1998, ar-chived at https://www.highbeam.com/doc/1P2-8500821.html.

33 Susan Slusser, Twitter, December 4, 2017, https://twitter.com/susanslusser/status/80556 1827434168320.

34 David Waldstein, "Shunned Stars of Steroid Era Are on Deck for Cooperstown," *NYT*, January 2, 2017, p. A1.

9. Catchers

1 Roger Angell, "One Hard Way to Make a Living," in *Late Innings* (New York: Ballantine, 1982), p. 350.

2 Stew Thornley, "The Demise of the Reserve Clause: The Players' Path to Freedom," *Baseball Re-search Journal* (Cleveland: SABR, 2007, Vol. 35), pp. 115–23.

3 Uniform Player Contract, Paragraph 10 (a), as quoted in Brad Snyder, *A Well-Paid Slave* (New York: Viking Penguin, 2006), p. 317.

4 Ron Fimrite, "He's Some Piece of Work," *SI*, June 5, 1978, p. 39.

5 Whitey Herzog and Jonathan Pitts, *You're Missin' a Great Game* (New York: Simon & Schuster, 1999), pp. 82–83.

6 Bill James, *The Bill James Baseball Abstract 1983* (New York: Ballantine, 1983), p. 150.

7 Bob Broeg, "Simba Simmons Deserves Hall of Fame Look," *St. Louis Post-Dispatch*, February 7, 1994, p. 15.

8 Rick Hummel, "Commish's Classics: Ted Simmons," *St. Louis Post-Dispatch* video, May 19, 2015,

http://video.stltoday.com/Commishs-Classics-Ted-Simmons-29111792?vcid=29111792 &freewheel=91130&sitesection=stltoday.

9 Derrick Goold, "Why Isn't Simba in the Hall?," *St. Louis Post-Dispatch*, January 3, 2017, http://www.stltoday.com/sports/why-isn-t-simba-in-the-hall/article_11578a62-fc56-5f4e-b5b2 -1e96f596eadc.html.

10 Kelly Whiteside, "A Piazza with Everything," *SI*, July 5, 1993, p. 15.

11 National Baseball Hall of Fame Library, "Veterans Committee" folder.

12 Bill James, *The Politics of Glory*, p. 41.

10. First Basemen

1 Tom Verducci, "Boston's Bambino," *Sports Illustrated David Ortiz Special Retirement Tribute*, October 2016, p. 11.

2 Jackie MacMullan, "Sweet Dreams for Ortiz," *Boston Globe*, October 23, 2004, http://archive .boston.com/sports/baseball/redsox/articles/2004/10/23/sweet_dreams_for_ortiz?pg=full.

3 Tom Verducci, "Who's Your Papi?," *SI*, June 19, 2006, p. 46.

4 Ibid.

5 David Ortiz, "Just a Kid from Santo Domingo," The Players' Tribune, September 23, 2015, http://www.theplayerstribune.com/david-ortiz-pedro-martinez-red-sox-dominican-republic/.

6 Adam Kilgore, "David Ortiz's Origin Story with the Boston Red Sox," *Washington Post*, November 18, 2015, https://www.washingtonpost.com/news/sports/wp/2015/11/18/how-david-ortiz -became-a-star-and-an-icon-for-the-boston-red-sox/.

7 Bob Hohler, "Steroid Scandal Hits Home," *Boston Globe,* July 31, 2009, http://www.boston.com /sports/baseball/redsox/articles/2009/07/31/ortiz_confirms_he_tested_positive_in_2003/.

8 Barry M. Bloom, "In Response, Ortiz Denies Using Steroids," MLB.com, August 8, 2009, http://m.mlb.com/news/article/6316054/.

9 Barry Petchesky, "Every Viewer Complaint About Big Papi's Post-Bombing Swear Word," Deadspin.com, July 4, 2013, http://deadspin.com/heres-every-viewer-complaint-about-big-papis-post -bom-661072193.

10 Julius Genachowski, Twitter, April 20, 2013, https://twitter.com/FCC/statuses/3257144121430 13888.

11 Thomas Boswell, "Boston Red Sox Star David Ortiz Playing His Way to Cooperstown in the World Series," *Washington Post*, October 29, 2013, https://www.washingtonpost.com/sports /nationals/boston-red-sox-star-david-ortiz-playing-his-way-to-cooperstown-in-the-world-series /2013/10/29/3421b8ca-40e3-11e3-a624-41d661b0bb78_story.html.

12 Ken Davidoff, "David Ortiz Can Join Babe Ruth with 3 Red Sox Titles," *New York Post*, October 23, 2013, http://nypost.com/2013/10/23/david-ortiz-can-join-babe-ruth-with-3-red-sox-titles/.

13 Ibid.

14 Christian Red and Teri Thompson, "Big Papi's Big Loophole," New York *Daily News*, August 3, 2009, http://www.nydailynews.com/sports/baseball/big-papi-big-loophole-red-sox-slugger-david -ortiz-blame-test-supplement-article-1.394551.

15 Ibid.

16 Bloom, "In Response, Ortiz Denies Using Steroids."

17 Bob Nightengale, "Manfred Questions David Ortiz's Positive Drug Test, Urges Leniency by Hall Voters," *USA Today*, October 2, 2016, http://www.usatoday.com/story/sports/mlb/2016/10/02/rob -manfred-david-ortiz-drug-test-hall-of-fame/91442256/.

18 Gene Collier, "Willie Stargell: Numbers Couldn't Measure the Man," *Pittsburgh Post-Gazette*, April 10, 2001, http://old.post-gazette.com/obituaries/20010410stargell2.asp.

19 Bill Jenkinson, "The Real Jimmie Foxx," *The National Pastime: From Swampdoodle to South Philly* (Arizona: SABR, 2013), p. 73.

20 Bill James, *The New Bill James Historical Baseball Abstract* (New York: Free Press, 2001), p. 441.

11. Second Basemen

 1 Ron Luciano and David Fisher, *The Fall of the Roman Umpire* (New York: Bantam, 1986), p. 186.

 2 James, *The Bill James Baseball Abstract 1982,* p. 134.

 3 James, *The Bill James Baseball Abstract 1983,* p. 161.

 4 Joe Jares, "The Back Is Back, Better than Ever," *SI*, July 16, 1979, p. 53.

 5 Phil Jackman, "O's Have Real Hardnose in Infielder Bobby Grich," *TSN*, February 5, 1972, p. 36.

 6 Ibid.

 7 Al Weber, "Grich? It's Another Word for Great, Red Wings Say," *TSN*, July 12, 1971, p. 57.

 8 Dick Miller, "Star-Kissed Angels Rejoice with Grich," *TSN*, December 11, 1976, p. 49.

 9 John Helyar, *Lords of the Realm* (New York: Villard, 1994), p. 207.

10 Jares, "The Back Is Back, Better than Ever," p. 50.

11 AP, "Everything on the Line in Game 7," *Kerrville Times*, October 15, 1986, p. 17.

12 AP, "Grich Says He's Going to Retire," *San Bernardino County Sun*, October 16, 1986, p. C5.

13 Mike Klingaman, "Catching Up with . . . Former Orioles Second Baseman Bobby Grich," *Baltimore Sun*, July 11, 2015, http://www.baltimoresun.com/sports/orioles/bs-sp-catching-up-grich -20150710-story.html.

14 Klein, "Seaver Aces Key Hall Test: He Belongs."

15 Murray Chass, "Bidding in the Dark Amid the Free Agent Market," *NYT*, January 12, 1992, http://www.nytimes.com/1992/01/12/sports/baseball-bidding-in-the-dark-amid-the-free-agent -market.html?pagewanted=2

16 Alden Gonzalez, "After Missing Out on Hall, Grich Finds Supporters," MLB.com, January 6, 2015, http://m.mlb.com/news/article/105686208/after-missing-out-on-hall-of-fame-bobby-grich -finds-supporters.

17 Mike Downey, "Detroit's Double Play Twins Have Fans Roaring in Approval," Knight Ridder Newspapers, in *Boca Raton News,* August 30, 1983, p. 1D.

18 Roger Angell, "Tiger Tiger," in *Season Ticket* (New York: Ballantine, 1989), p. 145.

19 Terry Foster, "Whitaker Shows Sweet Side at Negro Leagues Luncheon," *Detroit News*, April 24, 2015, http://www.detroitnews.com/story/sports/mlb/tigers/2015/04/24/foster-whitaker-shows-sweet -side-luncheon/26333775/.

20 Tom Gage, "Lou Whitaker Part of One-and-Done Fame," Fox Sports Detroit, April 24, 2015, http://stg1.foxsports.com/detroit/story/gage-lou-whitaker-part-of-one-and-done-fame-042415.

21 Jim Hawkins, "Forget 'Junior'—It's Sweet Lou Forever," *Detroit Free Press*, January 24, 1979, p. 14.

22 Steve Wulf, "Short to Second to None," *SI*, September 12, 1983, p. 31.

23 Jared Purcell, "Lou Whitaker Accepts Award from Tigers, Says He 'Loved' Detroit," mlive.com, April 24, 2015, http://www.mlive.com/tigers/index.ssf/2015/04/lou_whitaker_accepts_award_fro .html.

24 Ibid.

25 Andy Cohen, "Tiger's Prospect for Second Title Starts at Third," *South Florida Sun-Sentinel*, March 31, 1985, http://articles.sun-sentinel.com/1985-03-31/sports/8501120479_1_anderson-chris -pittaro-lou-whitaker.

26 AP, "Injury Sidelines Whitaker," *NYT*, September 5, 1988, http://www.nytimes.com/1988/09/05 /sports/injury-sidelines-whitaker.html.

27 John Gugger, "Whitaker Enters New Year Under Old Cloud of Doubt," *Toledo Blade*, March 26, 1989, p. B2.

28 AP, "It's No Longer 'Sweet Lou,'" *The Argus-Press*, March 18, 1989, p. 13.

29 Tim Kurkjian, "Baseball," *SI*, August 24, 1992, p. 60.

30 Harry Atkins, "Sweet Lou on Hall: No Sweat," AP in *Battle Creek Enquirer*, August 3, 1993, p. 9.

31 Buster Olney, "Mussina Grooves Send-off to Tigers Pair Whitaker, Trammell Aided in Last At-Bat," *Baltimore Sun*, September 22, 1995, http://articles.baltimoresun.com/1995-09-22/sports /1995265118_1_whitaker-trammell-tigers.

32 Jayson Stark, "My Hall of Fame Ballot," ESPN.com, January 15, 2001, https://espn.go.com/classic /s/2001/0115/1016923.html.

33 Lynn Henning, interview with author, January 14, 2017.

34 "Lou Whitaker Quotes," *Baseball Almanac*, http://www.baseball-almanac.com/quotes/lou_whitaker _quotes.shtml.

35 Tommy Craggs, "Say-It-Ain't-So Joe," *SF Weekly*, July 6, 2005, http://archives.sfweekly.com /sanfrancisco/say-it-aint-so-joe/Content?oid=2156768.

36 Detroit News, *They Earned Their Stripes: The Detroit Tigers All-Time Team* (Sports Publishing LLC, 2000), p. 63.

37 Red Smith, "A Man Who Knew the Crowds," *On Baseball* (Chicago: Ivan R. Dee, 2000), p. 17.

12. Shortstops

1 Lynn Henning, interview with author, January 14, 2017.

2 Wulf, "Short to Second to None," p. 34.

3 Harry Atkins, "Trammell, Whitaker: So Alike on Baseball Fields, So Different off It," AP in *Ludington Daily News*, March 24, 1987, p. 7.

4 Tom Gage, "Trammell Is Recovering Smoothly," *TSN*, January 17, 1985, p. 40.

5 Ken Rosenthal, "Hawk Could Fly, but Tram Is Stalled," *TSN*, January 7, 2002, p. 57.

6 Ken Rosenthal, "The Imperfect Science of the Perfect Ballot," *TSN*, January 6, 2003, p. 52.

7 David Pietrusza, Matthew Silverman, Michael Gershman, and Mikhail Horowitz, "The Top 100 Players," in *Total Baseball*, 7th ed. (Kingston, NY: Total Sports Publishing, 2001), p. 148.

8 Dave Anderson, "Sports of The Times; In Scorebook, the Double Play Reaches 100," *NYT*, September 15, 2002, http://www.nytimes.com/2002/09/15/sports/sports-of-the-times-in-scorebook -the-double-play-reaches-100.html.

9 James, *The Politics of Glory*, p. 42.

10 James, *The New Bill James Historical Abstract*, p. 604.

11 John J. McGraw, *My Thirty Years in Baseball* (Lincoln: University of Nebraska Press, 1995), p. 136.

13. Third Basemen

1 William Kashatus, "Allen Forced Philadelphians to Confront Racism Head-on," *Philadelphia Inquirer*, April 2, 1996, p. 11.

2 Bill Weiss and Marshall Wright, "Top 100 Teams: 1922 Baltimore Orioles," MiLB.com, 2001, http://www.milb.com/milb/history/top100.jsp?idx=15.

3 Bob Razer, "Dick Allen," *The Encyclopedia of Arkansas*, March 29, 2016, http://www .encyclopediaofarkansas.net/encyclopedia/entry-detail.aspx?entryID=646.

4 Dick Allen and Tim Whitaker, *Crash: The Life and Times of Dick Allen* (New York: Ticknor & Fields, 1989), p. 14.

5 William C. Rhoden, "Weighing the Complexity of a Hall Candidate, and His Times," *NYT*, December 7, 2014, http://www.nytimes.com/2014/12/07/sports/baseball/weighing-the-complexity-of-a-hall-candidate-and-his-times.html.

6 Allen Lewis, "Phils May Transplant Speedy Gardener Allen at Hot Corner," *TSN*, October 26, 1963, p. 18.

7 George Kiseda, "Candidates Run a Hard Campaign," *Philadelphia Evening Bulletin*, September 14, 1964, p. 39.

8 Allen and Whitaker, *Crash*, p. 6.

9 Ibid., p. 4

10 Allen Lewis, "Thomas Regrets Fight, Calls Waiver Unfair," *Philadelphia Inquirer*, July 5, 1965, p. 20.

11 Bill Conlin, "Richie Allen Is Beautiful, He Don't Give a Damn for Nobody," *Jock*, January 1970, archived at http://thestacks.deadspin.com/for-one-great-ballplayer-philadelphia-was-a-perpetual-1498843343.

12 Craig R. Wright, "Dick Allen: Another View," *Baseball Research Journal* (Cleveland: SABR, 1995, Vol. 24), republished with permission at http://www.whitesoxinteractive.com/rwas/index.php?category=11&id=2065.

13 Allen and Whitaker, *Crash*, pp. 71–72.

14 AP, "Ex-Phils Boss Mauch 'Not Bitter,'" *Arizona Republic*, June 20, 1968, p. 42.

15 AP, "Richie Allen Is Not All Peck's Bad Boy," *NYT*, May 18, 1969, p. 2S.

16 "Who's in Charge Around Here?," *TSN*, August 23, 1969, p. 14.

17 Snyder, *A Well-Paid Slave,* p. 13.

18 Conlin, "Richie Allen Is Beautiful, He Don't Give a Damn for Nobody."

19 Wright, "Dick Allen: Another View."

20 AP, "Dick Allen Announces Retirement," *Lakeland Ledger*, September, 16, 1974, p. 2B.

21 Frank Dolson, "The Boos Turn to Cheers for Richie Allen," *Philadelphia Inquirer*, May 15, 1975, p. 35.

22 James, *The Politics of Glory*, p. 325.

23 Don Malcolm, "The Man on the Outside Looking In," Baseball Think Factory, March 21, 2002, http://www.baseballthinkfactory.org/primate_studies/discussion/malcolm_2002-03-21_0.

24 Mike Sielski, "Dick Allen Comes Up One Vote Short of Hall of Fame," *Philadelphia Inquirer*, December 9, 2014, http://articles.philly.com/2014-12-10/news/56884535_1_dick-allen-mark-frog-carfagno-connie-mack-stadium.

25 Jerry Crasnick, "Randy Johnson: Vote Edgar Martinez," ESPN.com, January 7, 2015, http://www.espn.com/mlb/story/_/id/12132849/randy-johnson-endorses-former-seattle-mariners-teammate-edgar-martinez-baseball-hall-fame.

26 Ken Rosenthal, "Martinez Keeps the Hits Coming Despite Eye Disorder," *TSN*, May 7, 2001, p. 13.

27 Kelli Anderson, "Lethal Weapon," *SI*, March 12, 1996, p. 50.

28 Jason Mastrodonato, "Designated Hitter Edgar Martinez the Guy Pedro Martinez 'Hated Facing the Most,'" Masslive.com, January 7, 2015, http://www.masslive.com/redsox/index.ssf/2015/01/designated_hitter_edgar_martin.html.

29 Mariano Rivera interview on *Charlie Rose*, October 16, 2013, https://charlierose.com/videos/17148.

30 AP, "'Human Vacuum Cleaner' Sweeping Up Redlegs," *Naples Daily News*, October 14, 1970, p. 13.

31 James, *The New Bill James Historical Abstract*, p. 25.

14. Leftfielders

1 Ron Fimrite, "Don't Knock the Rock," *SI*, June 25, 1984, p. 49.

2 UPI, "Raines Admits to Drug Use," *Press-Republican*, September 17, 1982, p. 16.

3 UPI, "Raines Admits He Spent $40,000 on a Cocaine Habit in Nine Months," *Baltimore Afro-American*, December 14, 1982, p. 14.

4 Steve Wulf, "More Bang for More Bucks," *SI*, May 11, 1987, p. 33.

5 Tim Raines, Twitter, January 18, 2017, https://twitter.com/TimRaines30/status/8218558965 65321730.

6 Bill Francis, "Class of 2017 Overwhelmed by Honor," HOF, January 19, 2017, http://baseballhall .org/hof/class-of-2017-overwhelmed-by-honor.

7 Peter Bjarkman, *Baseball with a Latin Beat* (Jefferson, NC: McFarland, 1994), p. 210.

8 "The New Face of Baseball: Osvaldo Salas's American Baseball Photographs, 1950–1958," exhibit at HOF, 2014.

9 Orlando Cepeda interview, "¡Viva Baseball!" exhibit at HOF, 2009.

10 Adrian Burgos, "What Chris Rock got wrong: Black Latinos and race in baseball," *TSN*, May 10, 2015, http://www.sportingnews.com/mlb/news/african-americans-baseball-chris-rock-latinos /1spqgzamfumih1eprzkmlfpki7.

11 Harold Seymour, *Baseball: The Golden Age* (New York: Oxford University Press, 1971), p. 85.

12 Minnie Minoso and Herb Fagan, *Just Call Me Minnie: My Six Decades in Baseball* (Urbana, IL: Sagamore Publishing, 1994), p. 5.

13 Lou Miller, "'I Not Afraid,' Says Minnie, Back after 50th Plunking," *Cleveland Press*, July 15, 1955.

14 Ibid.

15 Christina Kahrl, "If Jackie Could Make It, I Could Too," ESPN.com, March 1 2015, http://espn .go.com/mlb/story/_/page/blackhistoryMLBminoso/white-sox-great-minnie-minoso-integration -fan-appreciation-cuba-hof-slight.

16 Mickey Herskowitz, "It Has Been Some Kind of a Year for Cardinals' Minnie Minoso," *Houston Post*, July 23, 1962.

17 Bob Greene, "Vincent Forgets What Baseball Is For," *Chicago Tribune*, September 26, 1990, http:// articles.chicagotribune.com/1990-09-26/features/9003200495_1_minnie-minoso-national -pastime-interests.

18 AP, "Minoso Is a Late Scratch," *LAT*, September 30, 1993, http://articles.latimes.com/1993-09-30 /sports/sp-40546_1_white-sox.

19 Adrian Burgos Jr., "Minnie Minoso Was Victim of Unfair Hall of Fame Election Rules," *TSN*, March 1, 2015, http://www.sportingnews.com/mlb-news/4637193-minnie-minoso-dead-dies-hall -of-fame-obituary-white-sox-indians-election.

20 Cash Kruth, "Minoso Eulogized by Family, Friends at Funeral," MLB.com, March 7th, 2015, http://m.mlb.com/news/article/111657722/minnie-minoso-eulogized-by-family-friends-at -funeral/.

21 Jay Jaffe, "Golden Era Vote Shutout Is Disappointing Result for Hall of Fame," SI.com, December 8, 2014, http://www.si.com/mlb/2014/12/08/golden-era-vote-hall-of-fame-shutout.

22 Kahrl, "'If Jackie Could Make It, I Could Too.'"

23 Ted Williams, Hall of Fame induction speech, July 25, 1966.

24 James, *The New Bill James Historical Abstract*, p. 654.

25 Red Smith, "The Duke of Milwaukee," *Ogden Standard-Examiner*, June 2, 1956, p. 4.

26 UPI, "Old Time Slugger, Burkett Dies at 84," *Detroit Free Press*, May 28, 1953, p. 28.

27 Arthur Daley, "Sports of the Times," *NYT*, January 13, 1964, p. 31.

28 UPI, "Joe Medwick Finally Makes Hall of Fame," *The Dispatch*, January 24, 1968, p. 14.

29 "Zach Wheat, Most Graceful of Outfielders," *Baseball Magazine,* January 1917, p. 49. [author un-credited]

15. Centerfielders

1 Michael Farber, "Joltin' Jones," *SI*, July 11, 2005, p. 71.
2 Shar Zarea, "25 for 25: Andruw Jones," *Baseball America*, July 17, 2006, http://www.baseball america.com/majors/25-for-25-andruw-jones-omar-linares-joe-mauer-mark-mcgwire-peter-o -malley-1959/.
3 Tim Kurkjian, "Keeping Up with the Joneses," *SI*, August 26, 1996, p. 120.
4 Ken Rosenthal, "Defensive Stats Need to Be Improved," *TSN*, December 3, 2001, p. 43.
5 Lindsay Berra, "Pure Gold: Best Outfielders Need More than Speed," MLB.com, July 22, 2013, http://m.mlb.com/news/article/54054402/.
6 Mark Bowman, "Jones Not Making Excuses," MLB.com, September 18, 2007, http://m.mlb.com /news/article/2216310.
7 T. J. Simers, "Dodgers' Jones Won't Even Swing at a Fat Pitch," *LAT*, April 13, 2008, http://articles .latimes.com/2008/apr/13/sports/sp-simers13.
8 T. J. Simers, "Dodgers Didn't Receive Care Package with Jones," *LAT*, May 11, 2008, http://articles .latimes.com/2008/may/11/sports/sp-simers11.
9 John Harper, "Yankees Great Joe DiMaggio Was Overrated, Says MLB Historian," New York *Daily News*, November 25, 2014, http://www.nydailynews.com/sports/baseball/yankees/harper -mlb-historian-joe-dimaggio-overrated-article-1.2022747.
10 National Baseball Hall of Fame Library, "Billy Hamilton" folder.
11 AP, "Hall Gets an Earful," *Wilmington News-Journal*, August 19, 1975, p. 12.
12 Tony Kornheiser, "Combs of Yanks Dies at 77; Led Off 'Murderers' Row,'" *NYT*, July 22, 1976, p. 34.
13 Tom Yantz, "Attention Grabber," *Hartford Courant*, October 23, 2004, http://articles.courant.com /2004-10-23/sports/0410230404_1_edmonds-pujols-and-rolen-albert-pujols.

16. Rightfielders

1 Richard Hoffer, "Handy Man," *SI*, June 11, 2001, p. 103.
2 Jonah Keri, *Up, Up, & Away* (Toronto: Random House Canada, 2014), p. 254.
3 Leigh Montville, "The Accidental Ballplayer," *SI,* April 5, 1993, p. 85.
4 Gerry Callahan, "See It, Hit It," *SI,* July 14, 1997, p. 42.
5 Chris Baker, "Johnson's Wild Toss Amuses Walker," *LAT,* July 9, 1997, http://articles.latimes.com /1997/jul/09/sports/sp-11026.
6 John Schlegel, "Walker Says Goodbye to Baseball," MLB.com, October 19, 2005, http://m.mlb .com/news/article/1255119/.
7 Lieb, *Baseball As I Have Known It*, p. 151.
8 AP, "Babe Ruth Voted Baseball's Greatest Player; Cobb Second," *Chicago Tribune*, February 5, 1950, http://archives.chicagotribune.com/1950/02/05/page/47/article/the-babe-a-mighty-slugger -and-baseballs-greatest-player-of-century.
9 Bob Broeg, "The Mystery of Stan Musial," *Saturday Evening Post*, August 28, 1954, p. 52.
10 Jim Murray, "Frank's Style," *LAT*, May 10, 1974, p. 171.
11 AP, "DeWitt Statement Irks Frank Robinson," *The Post-Crescent*, April 4, 1966, p. 15.
12 Stan Hochman, "Reggie Jackson an Underdog and Overdog," *Philadelphia Daily News*, October 17, 1977, p. 71.
13 Robert Ward, "Reggie Jackson in No-Man's Land," *Sport Magazine*, June 1977, p. 94.

14 David Remnick, "Reggie at Sunset," *Esquire*, June 1987, p. 136.

15 Bill Werber and C. Paul Rogers III, *Memories of a Ballplayer* (Cleveland: SABR, 2001), p. 131.

16 Sam Crawford, "My Three Thousandth Hit," *Baseball Magazine*, August 1917, p. 420.

17 AP, "Gwynn, San Diego Fit Each Other," *Lubbock Avalanche-Journal*, October 21, 1998, http://lubbockonline.com/stories/102198/LS0223.shtml.

18 Bob Broeg, "Country Denies Trying to Hurt Robinson," *St. Louis Post-Dispatch*, October 14, 1994.

19 Sam Rice, Letter to Paul S. Kerr, July 26, 1965, reprinted in "Sam Rice's Letter Says He Caught Ball in 1925," UPI in Berkshire Eagle, November 6, 1974, p. 33.

20 Francis Stann, "Rice Still Silent on 'Catch' in '25 Series", *TSN*, October 17, 1964, p. 13.

21 Ira Berkow, "The Signed Confession of Shoeless Joe," *NYT*, June 24, 1989.

17. Starting Pitchers

1 Jon Heyman, "Schilling's Tune: Me, Me, Me," *Newsday*, October 24, 2004, p. B4.

2 Gerry Callahan, "Fast and in Your Face," *SI*, February 2, 1998, p. 81.

3 Thomas Boswell, "One Team's Scraps, Another's Just Deserts," *Washington Post*, October 17, 1993, archived at https://www.highbeam.com/doc/1P2-970159.html.

4 Jason Diamos, "Schilling Shows the Yankees How It's Done," *NYT*, September 2, 1997, http://www.nytimes.com/1997/09/02/sports/schilling-shows-the-yankees-how-it-s-done.html.

5 Jayson Stark, "The Pitches That Scare Major Leaguers," ESPN.com, May 17, 2002, http://static.espn.go.com/mlb/columns/stark_jayson/1382666.html.

6 Kevin Slane, "Curt Schilling Thinks Shirt Threatening to Lynch Journalists Is 'Awesome,'" Boston.com, November 8, 2016, https://www.boston.com/news/politics/2016/11/08/curt-schilling-thinks-shirt-threatening-to-lynch-journalists-is-awesome.

7 Jose de Jesus Ortiz, Twitter, November 7, 2016, https://twitter.com/OrtizKicks/status/795782102361001984.

8 Dan Shaughnessy, "Bud Selig Could Be Bound for the Hall of Fame," *Boston Globe*, November 30, 2016, https://www.bostonglobe.com/sports/redsox/2016/11/29/bud-selig-could-bound-for-hall-fame/ZURUsmtmRq2MRfbdiGY5WL/story.html.

9 Dan Shaughnessy, "Casting His Votes for the Hall of Fame," *Boston Globe*, December 29, 2013, https://www.bostonglobe.com/sports/2013/12/29/time-cast-his-votes-for-baseball-hall-fame/ojPVH3NSylmZg1vJAGW6fJ/story.html.

10 Rob Bradford, "Bradfo Show: Curt Schilling Talks Hall of Fame Candidacy, World of Baseball," WEEI.com, January 5, 2016, http://media.weei.com/a/112316493/bradfo-show-curt-schilling-talks-hall-of-fame-candidacy-world-of-baseball.htm.

11 Curt Schilling, "I'd Be in Hall of Fame Already . . . If I Was Anti-Trump," TMZ Sports, January 2, 2017, http://www.tmz.com/2017/01/02/curt-schilling-hof-trump/.

12 Southern Poverty Law Center, Twitter, November 13, 2016, https://twitter.com/splcenter/status/797937732530110464.

13 Tyler Kepner, "An Appreciation of Mike Mussina," *NYT*, November 19, 2008, http://bats.blogs.nytimes.com/2008/11/19/an-appreciation-of-mike-mussina/?_r=0.

14 Ibid.

15 Tom Verducci, "The M&M Boys: Plain and Peanut," *SI*, July 18, 1994, p. 21.

16 Tom Verducci, "Mike Mussina," *SI*, October 13, 1997, p. 45.

17 Joe Strauss, "Yankees Get Mussina: 6 Years, $88.5 million," *Baltimore Sun*, December 1, 2000, http://articles.baltimoresun.com/2000-12-01/news/0012010026_1_mussina-orioles-roger-clemens.

18 Roger Angell, "Legend of the Fens," *The New Yorker,* September 24, 2001, p. 46.

19 Rob Neyer, "Atlanta Braves: 1999 in Review," ESPN.com, April 20, 2000, http://static.espn.go .com/mlb/s/hotstove/atl.html.

20 Bob Gibson and Lonnie Wheeler, *Stranger to the Game: The Autobiography of Bob Gibson* (New York: Penguin, 1994), pp. 166–67.

21 Bill Madden, "The Sports Collector," *TSN,* March 5, 1977, p. 46.

22 Ed Walsh, "The Spit Ball," *Baseball Magazine,* February 1912, p. 84.

23 Bill Lamb, "Mickey Welch: SABR Bio," http://sabr.org/bioproj/person/62fde0bd.

24 Irving Vaughan, *Chicago Tribune,* August 24, 1924, in John C. Skipper, *Dazzy Vance: A Biography* (Jefferson, NC: McFarland, 2007), p. 56.

25 Thomas Boswell, "Injustice Corrected," *Washington Post* (syndicated), January 11, 1998, http://articles .latimes.com/1998/jan/11/sports/sp-7346.

26 "Mordecai Brown," HOF, http://baseballhall.org/hof/brown-mordecai.

27 Bob Broeg, "Gloss Was the Word for Joss," *TSN,* March 4, 1978, p. 20.

28 Dan Daniel, "Pennock Poetry in Motion," *TSN,* February 11, 1948, p. 3.

29 "Pennock Set a Pattern for Youth," *TSN,* February 11, 1948, p. 11.

30 Roy Blount Jr., "The Greatest Game I Ever Saw: October 21, 1975," *SI,* July 19, 1993, p. 39.

18. Relief Pitchers

1 ESPNNewYork.com Staff, "Testi-Mo-nials: Mariano Rivera, Archrival," ESPN.com, September 21, 2013, http://www.espn.com/blog/new-york/yankees/post/_/id/64691/testi-mo-nials -mariano-rivera-archrival.

2 Mel Antonen, "Yanks' Rivera Continues to Learn," *USA Today,* October 9, 2006, http://usato-day30.usatoday.com/sports/soac/2006-10-09-rivera_x.htm.

3 Scott Miller, "Mariano Rivera: Birth of Cut Fastball Was 'Gift from God' (Part 4 of 5)," *CBS Sports,* July 14, 2013, http://www.cbssports.com/mlb/writer/scott-miller/22758002/mariano-rivera -birth-of-the-cutter-was-gift-from-god-part-4-of-5.

4 Buster Olney, "The Confidence Man," *New York,* May 21, 2005, http://nymag.com/nymetro/news /sports/features/9375/.

5 Ibid.

6 Ian O'Connor, "Jackie's Widow: Mo Worthy of No. 42," ESPN.com, March 6, 2013, http://www .espn.com/new-york/mlb/story/_/id/9028898/jackie-robinson-widow-rachel-proud-new-york -yankees-mariano-rivera.

7 Ron Fimrite, "The Pitch of the '80s," *SI,* June 9, 1986, p. 67.

19. Slouching Toward Cooperstown

1 Francis, "Class of 2017 Overwhelmed by Honor."

2 Kahrl,"If Jackie Could Make It, I Could Too."

SUGGESTED FURTHER READING

Lee Allen, *Cooperstown Corner: Columns from The Sporting News, 1962–1969* (Cleveland: SABR, 1990).

Thomas Boswell, *How Life Imitates the World Series* (New York: Penguin, 1983).

Thomas Boswell, *Why Time Begins on Opening Day* (New York: Penguin, 1985).

Howard Bryant, *Juicing the Game* (New York: Viking, 2005).

Howard Bryant, *Shut Out: A Story of Race and Baseball in Boston* (Boston: Beacon Press, 2002).

Jim Bouton, *Ball Four* (Cleveland: World, 1970).

Jim Brosnan, *The Long Season* (Chicago: Ivan R. Dee, 2002).

Dennis Corcoran, *Induction Day at Cooperstown* (Jefferson, NC: McFarland, 2011).

Paul Dickson, *The Dickson Baseball Dictionary,* 3rd ed. (New York: W. W. Norton, 2009).

Steven Goldman, ed., *Extra Innings: More Baseball Between the Numbers from the Team at Baseball Prospectus* (New York: Basic Books, 2012).

Bill James and Rob Neyer, *The Neyer/James Guide to Pitchers* (New York: Fireside, 2004).

David Jones, ed., *Deadball Stars of the American League* (Dulles, VA: Potomac Books, 2006).

F. C. Lane, *Batting* (Cleveland: SABR, 2001)

Ernest J. Lanigan, *Baseball Cyclopedia* (Jefferson, NC: McFarland, 2005).

Ben Lindbergh, ed. *The Best of Baseball Prospectus, 1996–2011,* Vols. 1 & 2 (Prospectus Entertainment Ventures, 2011).

George L. Moreland, *Balldom: The Britannica of Baseball Reprint* (St. Louis: Horton, 1989).

Peter Morris, *A Game of Inches: The Stories Behind the Innovations That Shaped Baseball, Revised and Expanded* (Chicago: Ivan R. Dee, 2010).

Daniel Okrent, *Nine Innings: The Anatomy of Baseball as Seen Through the Playing of a Single Game* (New York: McGraw-Hill, 1985).

Daniel Okrent and Harris Lewine, eds., *The Ultimate Baseball Book* (Boston: Houghton Mifflin, 1981).

Pete Palmer and Gary Gillette, eds., *The 2005 ESPN Baseball Encyclopedia* (New York: Sterling, 2005).

Harold Parrott, *The Lords of Baseball* (New York: Praeger, 1976).

Lawrence S. Ritter, *The Glory of Their Times, New Enlarged Edition* (New York: William Morrow, 1984).

SABR Baseball Biography Project, http://sabr.org/bio.

Tom Simon, ed., *Deadball Stars of the National League* (Dulles, VA: Potomac Books, 2004).

James K. Skipper Jr., *Baseball Nicknames: A Dictionary of Origins and Meanings* (Jefferson, NC: McFarland, 1992).

Sports Illustrated Vault, http://SI.com/vault.

John Thorn and Pete Palmer, *The Hidden Game of Baseball: A Revolutionary Approach to Baseball and Its Statistics* (New York: Doubleday, 1984).

INDEX